Distinguished African American Scientists of the 20th Century

James H. Kessler, J. S. Kidd, Renée A. Kidd, Katherine A. Morin

with Sigrid Berge, portrait artist, and
Alyce Neukirk, computer graphics artist

ORYX PRESS
1996

© 1996 by The Oryx Press
4041 North Central at Indian School Road
Phoenix, Arizona 85012-3397

Published simultaneously in Canada
Printed and Bound in the United States of America

♾ The paper used in this publication meets the minimum requirements of
American National Standard for Information Science—Permanence of Paper
for Printed Library Materials, ANSI Z39.48, 1984.

Library of Congress Cataloging-in-Publication Data
Kessler, James H.
    Distinguished African American scientists of the twentieth century
    by James H. Kessler, J.S. Kidd, Renée A. Kidd, and Katherine A. Morin
        p. cm.
    Includes bibliographical references and index.
    ISBN 0-89774-955-3 (cloth : alk. paper)
1. Scientists—United States—Biography. 2. Afro-American
scientists—Biography. I. Kessler, James H. II. J. S. Kidd
A. III. Title.
Q141.K455 1995
509.2'273—dc20
[B]   95-16582
                                                            CIP

This book is for all the boys:
Aubry, Nick, Matt, and Dan.

Table of Contents

Preface

The 100 scientists represented by the biographical sketches in this book were identified by several different methods. In some cases, they were nominated by their peers. In other cases, their full-length biographies were available in the general literature. In still other cases, they were made visible and noteworthy by their appearance in such sources as *Blacks in Science and Medicine,* compiled by Vivian O. Sammons; the *Dictionary of American Negro Biography,* edited by Rayford Logan and Michael Winston; *The Black 100* by Columbus Salley, *Black Women in American History,* edited by Jessie Smith; and *American Men and Women of Science,* the standard biographical reference work covering scientists and engineering and biomedical research specialists.

In our judgment, many of the entries in the standard reference works and in other biographical sources are too short to be useful to students. In particular, most such entries do not adequately capture the true texture of the individual's life and almost never describe any of the formative experiences of the subjects. One of our goals is to provide students with expanded and more well-rounded presentations. We have attempted to reveal some of the drama in the lives of our subjects and show some of the real costs and benefits associated with the pursuit of a career in scientific research. In addition, these biographical sketches convey several kinds of generally useful information: aspects of

the general social history of our country, a bit of the institutional structure of higher education, some sense of the procedural steps involved in claiming professional status as a scientist, and some of the actual scientific content of our subject's own research projects.

The set of scientists included in our sample is not necessarily representative of any sociological category. For example, initially we searched out people who had completed or nearly completed their careers. We believed that such lives would contain a richer stock of information, and more personal insights into the characteristics of a career in research, than would the lives of those earlier in their careers. Later in our collection efforts, however, we realized that so much had changed during the twentieth century that we needed to include younger scientists to illustrate more accurately the conditions that prevail today, as well as to show what a scientific career in the upcoming century might entail.

Our oldest subject is the venerable George Washington Carver, who was born, it is thought, in early 1861. Our youngest subject, Dr. Mae Jemison, was born late in 1956. Eighty-seven of the subjects are still living. The mix includes four mathematicians, thirteen physicists, thirty-one chemists, thirty biologists, two geologists, seven engineers, eleven physicians and two anthropologists. Twenty of the total are women. The number of geologists is low because there are still very few African Americans in that specialty. It should also be noted that the engineers and medical doctors were included because of their accomplishments as researchers rather than as practitioners of their professions. The two anthropologists might be considered social scientists rather than physical scientists, but their work cuts across such boundaries.

It should be emphasized that there are many additional distinguished—even outstanding—African American scientists and engineers who have not been included for a variety of mundane reasons. Specifically, some who were invited to participate were simply too deeply engaged in their research and other work to spend the rather significant time required to prepare the information upon which the biographies were constructed. We feel, however, that our set of biographies represents a good cross-section of distinguished African American participation in scientific professions.

When available, a photograph of the profiled scientist was included with his or her entry. In some cases, however, photographs were unavailable and illustrations have been used.

In addition, it should be noted that in preparing this volume, we served mainly as scribes and compilers. The true authors are the people who lived the lives and understood the struggles. In fact, when possible, the biographies were reviewed by the subjects themselves.

The reader will notice that overcoming obstacles is the underlying theme tying together these 100 stories of African American scientists. Anyone who seeks to become a scientist, engineer, or research physician must be able to handle adversity and resist the depressing effects that can come from what, at times, seems like an endless struggle just to get to the bottom of the ladder. When the ordinary tribulations of research are com-

pounded by minority status, the path to success can be steeper still. All the people who succeed in reaching such career goals must be talented—with high aptitudes for their chosen careers. They must also be persistent. Persistence is, perhaps, the more important trait. When reading these life stories, therefore, one comes finally to an inescapable position of considered respect for those who achieved what they set out to achieve.

Acknowledgments

We thank Golda Haines for her help in getting the project off the ground by preparing a large batch of solicitation letters in the 1992–93 time frame. In addition, very helpful research support and aid was provided by Dr. Arthuree Wright of the Freedmen's Library at Howard University, by the staff at the Moorland-Spingarn Research Center on the Howard campus, by Gabrielle Morris at the Regional Oral History Office, Bancroft Library, University of California at Berkeley, and by the staff at the Martin Luther King Memorial Library in the District of Columbia. We also thank the staff of the Schomburg Center for Research in Black Culture at the New York Public Library and the scholarly workers at the Anacostia Museum in the District of Columbia.

The faculty and staff of the College of Library and Information Services at the University of Maryland, College Park, also deserve gratitude. In particular, Drs. Claude Walston, Anne MacLeod, Ann Prentice, and Diane Barlow gave both formal administrative and informal moral support to the project.

Our illustrator, Sigrid Berge, did an outstanding job of capturing the quality of her subjects in her composite portraits. These illustrations and most of the various forms of photographic materials were scanned into the computer and artfully processed by Alyce Neukirk.

In addition to interviews and personal papers provided by the subjects, many different source documents were used to compile the information on each scientist. Periodicals such as *Jet* and *Ebony* were rich sources, and *Black Enterprise* and *Sage* also were useful. Book sources that were particularly valuable include:

Berry, Leonidas. *I Wouldn't Take Nothin' for My Journey.* Chicago: Johnson Publishing Co., 1981.

Carwell, Hattie. *Blacks in Science: Astrophysicists to Zoologist.* Oakland, CA: Carwell, 1988.

Donovan, Richard X. *Black Scientists of America.* Portland, OR: National Book Co., 1990.

Hayden, Robert. *Seven African-American Scientists.* New York: Twenty-First Century Books, 1992.

Lightfoot, Sarah Lawrence. *Balm in Gilead.* Reading, MA: Addison-Wesley. 1989.

Mahone-Lonesome, Robyn. *Charles R. Drew.* New York: Chelsea House, 1990.

Manning, Kenneth. *Black Apollo of Science: The Life of Ernest Everett Just.* New York: Oxford, 1983.

Naden, Corrine J., ed. *Black Americans of Achievement.* New York: Chelsea House, 1994.

Neyland, James. *George Washington Carver.* New York: Holloway House, 1992.

General reference resources included:

Cloyd, Iris, ed. *Who's Who Among Black Americans (1990–91).* Detroit: Gale, 1994.

Hawkins, Walter L. *African American Biographies.* Jefferson, NC: McFarland & Co., 1994.

Hine, Darlene C., Elsa B. Brown, and Rosalyn Terborg-Penn, eds. *Black Women in America: An Historical Encyclopedia.* Brooklyn, NY: Carlson Publishing, 1993.

LaBlanc, Michael. *Contemporary Black Biography.* Detroit: Gale, 1994.

Ploski, Harry, and James Williams, eds. *The Negro Almanac.* Bronxville, NY: Bellwether Publisher, 1989.

Profiles

Benjamin H. Alexander

Born: October 18, 1921, in Roberta, Georgia

Status: Chief Executive Officer, Drew Dawn Enterprises, Inc., Silver Spring, Maryland

Education:

Bachelor of Arts degree, University of Cincinnati, Cincinnati, Ohio, 1943

Master of Science degree, Bradley University, Peoria, Illinois, 1950

Doctor of Philosophy degree, Georgetown University, Washington, D.C., 1957

Research Area: Organic Chemistry

Early Years

Benjamin Alexander's grandparents on his father's side were slaves on a plantation near the city of Macon, Georgia. This was cotton-growing country, but peaches were also cultivated there. Benjamin's grandfather worked on the plantation where the Elberta Peach was developed. The Elberta is an unusual peach with a seed that is easy to separate from the fruit, and so it is called a freestone peach. It travels better than the yellow-cling peach, which has a seed or pit that has to be cut out with a knife. The new breed of peach could be picked in Georgia and sent north to be sold in New York City for a large profit.

Benjamin's mother's parents also had a talent for growing plants. His maternal grandfather was born after the Civil War. Starting on rented land, he grew corn, sweet potatoes, pecans, and peanuts. When he sold these crops, he saved almost every penny. He used the money to buy his own farm land. He soon became one of the largest landowners in the central Georgia region.

His oldest daughter, Annie, was Benjamin's mother. She met Manoah Bush Alexander at a church gathering, and they were married in 1914 against the wishes of Annie's father.

Bush Alexander wanted to prove himself to his father-in-law. He rented large tracts of land to grow cotton. He was very successful until 1919, when an insect called the cotton boll weevil invaded central Georgia and destroyed crop after crop. By 1923, Bush Alexander had lost all his money. He decided to move to Cincinnati, Ohio, where he found a job in an iron foundry. Meanwhile, Ben's mother stayed in Georgia with her six children. They lived with her father for a year before the family was reunited in Ohio.

Even though he had found a good job, Bush, Benjamin's father, was upset by what he had lost in Georgia, and he began to drink heavily. Benjamin's mother, Annie, did not approve. Finally, in 1927, after many warnings, she divorced him. She rented her own apartment and went to work. She took a job as a cleaning woman in a local hospital and tried to raise her six children on an income of only $16 a week. It was difficult, but she did it. She even built up a savings account at a local bank.

Meanwhile, Benjamin sold newspapers on street corners in downtown Cincinnati. He saved money too, but he also got into his share of trouble. When he was eleven, he had to learn to box because of trouble with the leader of a local street gang. The next year, he almost lost his left eye in a Fourth-of-July accident with fireworks. His mother convinced the doctors to try to save the eye. Although they were successful, Ben never regained normal eyesight. Even with a contact lens, the sight in his left eye was impaired.

He took up boxing as a sport in high school. Ezzard Charles, who later became world heavyweight champion, was a member of his high school boxing team. Benjamin Alexander, however, was no champion. He soon dropped boxing and tried out for the track team. He made the team but was not a top runner.

Ben attended Woodward High School, which was located in the southeast section of Cincinnati. It enrolled young people of all races from the low-income families who lived in that district. Few of its graduates went on to college, but those who did usually were well prepared and received good grades when they got there. Benjamin Alexander liked high school. He took both vocational and college preparatory courses. He enjoyed his studies so much and worked so hard that he was able to graduate at age sixteen.

Higher Education

Benjamin Alexander used the money he had saved from various jobs to get started in college. His costs were low because he was able to live at home while attending the University of Cincinnati. Since he was younger than most college students, he did not participate in many social activities during his first year. Mainly, he studied and worked at the university's cafeteria as a dishwasher. The few dates he had were with girlfriends who were still in high school.

In his second year of college, Alexander was assigned a new academic advisor who was a teacher in the chemistry department. Although Alexander had encountered some faculty members with racist attitudes, he also found many White students and faculty who stood up for racial justice, even back in the late 1930s. For example, the members of the chemistry department generally did not tolerate racial prejudice. Four of the seventeen second-year chemistry majors were African Americans, and this led Alexander to think about the possibility of a career in chemistry.

Most science majors did not participate in sports at college because their laboratory work took up too much time. Nevertheless, Benjamin Alexander pursued his athletic interests. Even though he was often late for practice, he made the track team as a distance runner. The team members included Willard (Willie) Stargill, who later became a famous baseball player for the Pittsburgh

Pirates, as well as an inductee of the Baseball Hall of Fame in 1987.

Before Alexander began his third year of college, he was elected to be the African American representative to the student senate. This position allowed him to meet another senate representative, Mary Ellen Spurlock, whom he would later marry.

World War II broke out during Alexander's college years. His science studies kept him from being drafted, and he was able to land a part-time job in a local defense plant, which paid four times more than he had been making at the university cafeteria. However, in early 1942, Alexander's older brother James was drafted. James operated two successful business ventures: a restaurant near the Cincinnati railroad station and an illegal gambling casino across the street. James convinced Bush, his father, to take over the restaurant, and reluctantly, Alexander agreed to take over the casino. Even though Alexander had to learn how to defend himself against sore losers and rival casino owners, he made good money and learned how to manage tough people.

Because of all his activities, Benjamin Alexander had to cut back on his university courses, which stretched his college program for one additional year. By doing so, he could stay in Cincinnati until his brother returned from his military service. He could also take some extra chemistry courses that helped him in his professional work later.

Alexander took a job with the Cincinnati Chemical Works after graduation, even though he suspected he would soon be drafted. At the Chemical Works he helped manufacture the powerful insecticide DDT. But for Benjamin Alexander, this was boring work.

In 1944 he took the Civil Service Examination for chemists, and the following year he was invited to join the Northern Regional Research Laboratory of the U.S. Department of Agriculture, which is located in Peoria, Illinois. Soon after he began his new job, he was involved in his own independent research. He enjoyed his work very much, but it was suddenly interrupted when he received notification that he had been drafted. He was ordered to report to Fort Lewis in Washington State on January 12, 1946. After completing basic training there, Benjamin Alexander was sent to Japan. The war was over, but there was still much work for the U.S. Army to do. Unfortunately, racial discrimination was a big problem in the army. African Americans were given the worst jobs; Benjamin Alexander was assigned to a laundry battalion in Kobe, Japan. Nevertheless, he tried to make the best of a poor situation. He read and studied, and he started a base newspaper. He even organized a sports program. Soon Alexander was promoted to corporal and then to sergeant. He was asked to teach science at the school for officer's children in Kobe. He also found good use for his boxing skills before he was finally released from military service in May of 1947, at which time Alexander entered the U.S. Army Reserve. He retired from the U.S. Army Reserve in 1967 with the rank of major.

Because of his veteran's status and good record at research work, he knew he would be welcomed back at the Agriculture Department's laboratory in Peoria. He also knew that he could now make real plans for his future. His main goal was to begin his graduate studies, and he decided to enroll at Bradley University in Peoria so that he could continue his government job.

When Benjamin Alexander returned to the United States, he found a happy surprise waiting for him. He had thought that his former fellow student senator, Mary Ellen Spurlock, was already married, but she had remained single. Mary Ellen wrote Alexander a letter when she found out he was coming home from Japan. They met as soon as he arrived in Cincinnati. After a brief conversation, he proposed marriage and she accepted. They were married in March of 1948. In the meantime, he went back to work as a chemist and started his graduate studies.

When the young couple settled in Peoria after their wedding, Mary Ellen soon became unhappy. African Americans made up only a small portion of the population of Peoria, and of those, only a small group were college educated. Mary Ellen did not enjoy having such a small circle of friends. There were also disagreements over religion, which resulted in Mary Ellen and Benjamin joining different churches. Benjamin also became involved in the Civil Rights movement. When Mary Ellen was pregnant with their first child, she hoped Benjamin would give more of his time to family matters.

Although his home life was sometimes difficult, Benjamin enjoyed success at work. He and his supervisor, Dr. Charles Mehltretter, were working on a special project to make a particular medicinal compound. This compound came from a certain plant species and was very costly to extract. Alexander and Mehltretter thought they could make it less expensively, even though other chemists thought it could not be done. In 1950, they succeeded, and the price dropped from $400 to $40 an ounce. A report of their research was presented at a 1951 meeting of the American Chemical Society. Alexander was already becoming a famous researcher, even though he had only a master's degree.

Mary Ellen had given birth to a son, Drew, in December of 1948. She saw that Alexander was successful in his work, and she did not think he should go back to graduate school. Benjamin Alexander, however, wanted very much to begin work on his Ph.D. He knew that Howard University in Washington, D.C.

was planning to begin a doctoral program in chemistry and he applied for admission.

Mary Ellen thought she was being abandoned. She took her son and went back to her parents' house in Cincinnati. The couple were divorced a year later.

Alexander continued his research, even though he was very upset. During this time, he worked with one of his university professors, and they discovered the correct structure of a particularly complicated molecule. This discovery was widely applauded by other chemists.

Benjamin Alexander eventually arranged to be transferred from Peoria to the Agriculture Department's research center at Beltsville, Maryland. There he would be close to Washington, D.C., and could work while attending evening classes at Howard University. Unfortunately, Howard University did not accept him into its program

One of his fellow workers at the Beltsville center suggested he apply to the doctoral program at Georgetown University, a Catholic institution in Washington, D.C. Both race and religion stood in the way of his admission to Georgetown; however, faculty members there had heard of the research Alexander had done in Peoria. They made a special plea for his acceptance, and he was admitted in the fall of 1954. Three years later, when Benjamin Alexander was almost ready to receive his doctoral degree, he and his wife reunited. Family and friends were very happy when the couple remarried in December, 1957, and a year later, their daughter Dawn was born.

Career Highlights

After finishing his studies, Dr. Alexander continued his research at Beltsville. There he worked on chemicals to control insects.

In particular, he developed compounds that could attract certain insects, while also developing compounds that repelled other insects. The attracting compounds were used to lure insects into traps. The repellant compounds could be applied to the skin when boating or camping in areas infested by mosquitos or biting flies. Dr. Alexander received a U.S. patent for a compound that attracted melon flies. He holds three other U.S. patents on compounds used as insecticides.

In 1962, Dr. Alexander was invited to join the staff at Walter Reed Hospital. He was offered the job of Chief Research Chemist in the Department of Immunology.

While working on ways to protect soldiers from nerve gas, Dr. Alexander and two colleagues were accidentally exposed to a poisonous chemical. All three were close to death, and Dr. Alexander lost most of his white blood cells—the cells that help the body fight infections. The medical doctors who treated Dr. Alexander forbade him from ever doing laboratory research again. Even though he loved research and had produced thirty-five published reports from his research projects, he knew his career had to take a new direction. He decided to shift his focus from laboratory research to science administration.

In the meantime, Dr. Alexander had become active in the local educational system as a member of the parent-teacher association at the school his son attended. In 1966, Dr. Alexander was appointed to the Board of Education for the District of Columbia.

To help make the transfer from research to management, Dr. Alexander took one year of training at the National Institutes of Health. Such training is provided only to individuals of proven scientific ability and integrity. When he finished the training in the Grants Associates Program, he became a staff member at the National Center for Health Services Research and Development, which is part of the U.S. government. His main job was to plan and direct programs that would bring minority people into health care careers. In 1971, he was promoted, and his responsibilities expanded to include minority recruitment for health science research careers.

After serving the U.S. government as soldier, scientist, and research program manager for thirty years, Dr. Alexander's life suddenly changed direction. In 1974, he was asked to become the president of Chicago State University in Chicago, Illinois, even though he had no experience in managing an institution of higher education. His experience with such organizations was limited to what he had learned as a member of the Board of Education in the District of Columbia, where he had fought problems of poverty and neglect.

Chicago State University had similar problems, as well as more complicated and challenging ones. Some students were receiving good grades for work not done; some teachers were spending more time on outside jobs than on teaching; people in the neighborhood were renting and using university buildings for purposes unrelated to education; the university was under warning about its accreditation; and its graduates were regularly failing the National Teacher Education examination.

Dr. Alexander's goal was to raise academic standards and to dismiss faculty and staff members who were cheating on the job. Hundreds of students were put on academic probation. The staff people who were asked to leave fought back with political actions. Some of the university trustees even reminded Dr. Alexander that his contract only lasted for one year.

In spite of these difficulties, Dr. Alexander prevailed. His success in putting the university back on the right path was symbolized when President Gerald Ford gave the commencement speech at the school's graduation ceremonies in 1975. Dr. Alexander remained as the university's president until 1982. In that year he was awarded a plaque for outstanding leadership by the Student Government Association.

The next challenge to be faced by Dr. Alexander was the presidency of the University of the District of Columbia. The problems there were even more difficult than at Chicago. Six of the fifteen trustees were opposed to hiring Dr. Alexander in the first place, while the remainder hoped Dr. Alexander would do for the University of the District of Columbia what he had done for Chicago State University. After he took the new job, he placed over 1,000 students on probation in the fall of 1982. Over 3,000 were put on probation in the second semester, but this medicine was too strong. The trustees took away Dr. Alexander's power to hire and fire employees, and he had to resign, since his position had become meaningless.

For a time, Dr. Alexander went back to work for the U.S. government, where he was put in charge of one of the many programs that give loans and grants to college students. Meanwhile, his daughter, Dawn Alexander, had started a research consulting firm in 1984. Dr. Alexander provided support for this venture and some managerial assistance. Just when the new company began to succeed, young Ms. Alexander was invited by Yale University to work on a graduate degree. She needed someone to take over and manage the business while she completed her advanced studies. Dr. Alexander resigned his government job and stepped in to manage the family firm, Drew Dawn Enterprises, Inc., which he has done ever since.

Lloyd E. Alexander

Born: August 17, 1902, in Catawba, Virginia

Status: Retired, Professor of Biology, Kentucky State College, Louisville, Kentucky, 1972

Education:

Bachelor of Science degree, University of Michigan, Ann Arbor, Michigan, 1927

Master of Science degree, University of Michigan, 1928

Doctor of Philosophy degree, University of Rochester, Rochester, New York, 1936

Research Area: Embryology

Early Years

Lloyd Alexander was born in a log cabin in the Appalachian Mountains of Virginia, where he developed a love of nature. His home, one of the few small farms scattered among the hills, was surrounded by wilderness. Lloyd roamed these hills and learned about wild plants and animals by direct experience, as he observed these creatures in their natural condition. He saw them develop through all the different stages in their lives and became curious about how each plant and animal grew. He was especially fascinated by the life cycle of the caterpillar, which changed from a wormlike creature into the dormant chrysalis and then into a beautiful butterfly.

Lloyd also saw nature as a source of sustenance. He came from a large family, the youngest of 12 brothers and sisters. His parents had many mouths to feed, and Lloyd helped by gathering wild fruits and berries for his family's table. He also sold such produce in the little town of Catawba, and the few coins that he earned from these sales gave Lloyd a sense of independence.

Tragedy struck Lloyd when he was only 14 years old. His parents passed away, leaving him with his brother's family in Landgraff, West Virginia. Soon, he began attending Kimball High School, even though the school was a five-mile walk to and from his home. The principal at the school, Nathaniel Wiley, quickly realized that Lloyd was a dedicated student. He knew that his small, rural high school could not give the studious young man the education he deserved. Mr. Wiley wrote letters to his friends around the state asking them to suggest a better school for Lloyd. They suggested Bluefield Institute in Bluefield, West Virginia, a boarding school founded specifically to prepare young African American students for college.

Lloyd had to work at the school to pay for his tuition and living costs. He also had to take part-time jobs in the town. In spite of the time that Lloyd spent on this outside work, he earned good grades. He loved school and soon discovered that he enjoyed his science courses, especially biology, the most.

Lloyd graduated from Bluefield Institute as an honor student. He was the first member of his family to receive a high school diploma.

Higher Education

Lloyd Alexander's teachers at Bluefield Institute thought he should apply for college, and he was soon accepted at the University of Michigan in Ann Arbor, Michigan. Since Alexander had very little money, he stayed in Bluefield so that he could earn enough to meet his college expenses. In the fall of 1923, he boarded the train for his new school in Ann Arbor.

He finished his undergraduate program at the University of Michigan in 1927. In his senior year, he was elected to Phi Sigma, an honorary fraternity, in recognition of his outstanding work in biology. Because of his excellent record, he was able to continue at Michigan as a graduate student and finished his master's degree in just one year.

Alexander wanted to continue his studies, but he knew he would have to work for a while before beginning on his doctoral program. His first professional job was teaching general science and biology courses at a high school in Loudon, West Virginia. After two years in Loudon, Alexander was invited to be an instructor in biology at Fisk University in Nashville, Tennessee.

Lloyd Alexander was at Fisk for only one year when, in 1931, the General Education Board gave him a fellowship to continue his graduate studies. The General Education Board, a branch of the Rockefeller Foundation, had been supporting education for African Americans for many years. In the 1930s, the foundation set out to improve biological research in the United States. The fellowship enabled Alexander to begin his doctoral studies at the University of Chicago in September, 1931.

Lloyd Alexander's academic advisor at the University of Chicago was Professor B. H. Willier, a world famous embryologist. He was an expert on how creatures grow during their first stages of life. Alexander began to specialize in this area of study and became a member of the Willier research team. Alexander and the other team members were especially interested in studying how chicken embryos develop before hatching from eggs. To do so, the biologists removed the tissue that contained the tiny embryo and studied this tissue under a microscope.

Lloyd Alexander was particularly interested in the way the eye is formed. Understanding how the eye develops helps explain the stages in the growth of the brain. In a tiny animal, a stalk pushes out from the early brain and forms a round, cup-shaped knob at its end. Soon the lens of the embryonic eye begins to form in the open part of the cup. This development can be seen under a microscope.

Lloyd Alexander decided to observe what happens when cells from different parts of the chicken embryo were placed in the embryonic eye. He developed a way to transfer groups of cells to this immature organ. His surgical procedure was so expert that the tiny chicks were kept alive and Alexander could observe what happened when the chicks continued to grow.

The cells taken from other parts of the chick embryo are transformed into eye cells when they are introduced into the forming eye early in the process of embryonic development. This powerful effect on the identity of the embryonic cells is called "induction" by embryologists.

The Willier research team moved to the University of Rochester in Rochester, New York, in 1933, and Lloyd Alexander transferred his doctoral studies there. In 1934, Lloyd met and married Evelyn Baker, a young woman from Hopkinsville, Kentucky. They had two sons before she died at an early age.

He continued his work with chicken embryos and this was the main topic for his dissertation. The high quality of this research led to his election to Sigma Xi, an honorary scientific society. With the continued support from the General Education Board, he was able to complete his studies and graduated from Rochester in 1936.

Career Highlights

Dr. Alexander was a teacher at Fisk University all during his doctoral studies. The university administrators, pleased that one of their faculty members was being trained at such fine institutions, allowed him to travel to Chicago or to Rochester whenever necessary.

Dr. Alexander taught at Fisk University a total of 19 years. He trained many people who became successful scientists and medical doctors. During World War II, he spent one year at Meharry Medical College, an institution famous for training Black doctors. During the war, there was a shortage of doctors, and the faculty members at Meharry were asked to accelerate the training program. There was also a shortage of teachers at the medical school, and Dr. Alexander was happy to concentrate his attention on training additional faculty for Meharry.

Because of his heavy teaching load, Dr. Alexander did most of his own research during the summer months. Many of the summers were spent at Woods Hole Marine Biological Laboratory on Cape Cod in Massachusetts. Famous scientists from all over the United States and abroad came to Wood's Hole, year after year. At Woods Hole, scientists could do research for hours without interruptions, exchange ideas at meals and, after work, argue new, controversial theories.

Later, Dr. Alexander spent summers at the University of Chicago and the University of Wisconsin. These summer activities were often sponsored by the Rockefeller Foundation as part of their continuing program to improve biological research in the United States.

In 1949, Dr. Alexander became chairman of the biology department at Kentucky State College in Louisville, Kentucky. He held that position for 23 years, before his retirement in 1972.

Dr. Alexander married a second time in 1952. His new wife was a teacher in the public school system in Louisville. They had a son who became the chairman of the history department at Norfolk State University in Virginia, and a daughter who became a high school history teacher in Newark, New Jersey.

During Dr. Alexander's time at Kentucky State College, he worked on several science education programs for use in the United States and abroad. In recognition of his efforts abroad, Kentucky State was presented with a collection of 900 butterflies by Farouk I, then King of Egypt. Dr. Alexander used this collection as a teaching tool to illustrate principles of evolution and biological classification and demonstrate biological adaptations such as disguise and camouflage. He was able to demonstrate that some nonpoisonous butterflies, which are a good food for birds, had evolved to look like poisonous species. Their disguise keeps the birds away and the butterflies alive.

In 1975, three years after his retirement, Kentucky State College held its first special ceremony in recognition of Dr. Alexander's achievements. Lloyd E. Alexander Day has become an annual celebration. The day's main event is the presentation of research projects by students from the biology department. Because of this special day of recognition, Dr. Alexander's legacy of excellence in biological research will continue to inspire young men and women.

Leonidas Berry

Born: July 20, 1902, in Woodsdale, North Carolina

Status: Retired, Private Medical Practice, 1975

Education:

Bachelor of Science degree, Wilberforce University, Wilberforce, Ohio, 1924

Doctor of Medicine degree, University of Chicago, Chicago, Illinois, 1925

Master of Science degree, Rush Medical School, Chicago, Illinois, 1929

Research Area: Gastrointestinal System

Early Years

Leonidas Berry's father, Llewellyn Berry, was the son of a former slave who had run away from his master to join the Union Army during the Civil War. Llewellyn was fascinated by his father's stories about the times of slavery and became interested in the history of his people and their religious practices. Years later, he passed these interests on to his son, Leonidas.

Llewellyn's parents worked very hard to send him to Kitrell Institute, a college in North Carolina. Fortunately, a scholarship from the local conference of the African Methodist Episcopal Church helped them pay for their son's education. Llewellyn studied religion diligently at Kitrell and became recognized as a good preacher. While at college, he met a young woman named Beulah Harris who was studying to become a teacher. Llewellyn and Beulah were married in Roxboro, North Carolina, in 1900. On July 20, 1902, Beulah gave birth to their first child, Leonidas. Leonidas soon had a younger brother, Richard, and a younger sister named Erma. Tragically, Erma died at six months after she developed whooping cough and pneumonia. Beulah and Llewellyn later had three more children.

Leonidas received his elementary education in a one-room school house in Chapel Hill, North Carolina. He enjoyed school and also liked sports. He played baseball with his friends almost every day, even though they only had one ball, one bat, and one glove.

When Leonidas was 12 years old, the family moved to Norfolk, Virginia. Because this was during World War I, and Norfolk was already one of the country's largest naval bases, there were sailors everywhere—and soldiers, too, from nearby army camps. These young people were only a few years older than Leonidas, and when he saw some of the young African American men in officer's uniforms, he was proud and enthusiastic. He saw them as having adventurous lives and learning interesting and important things.

Leonidas, too, wanted to learn. He was interested in history, politics, and other countries. He studied hard at school, read all about the war to keep up with the news, and sold newspapers every afternoon. Through these activities, Leonidas tried to broaden his horizons.

Leonidas had a number of jobs after school. He shined shoes for sailors at a barber shop and delivered packages for a gift shop. He also worked at the shipyard hauling gravel to make cement, and he worked at a drugstore. Several African American doctors and dentists had their offices on the floor above the drugstore, and Leonidas enjoyed listening to them discuss their interests when they came in to make a purchase. Sometimes they would talk about famous black doctors like Daniel Hale Williams. Dr. Williams was the surgeon who performed the first successful heart operation in the early 1890s. Leonidas loved hearing these stories and began to dream about going to medical school some day.

Even though Leonidas was very busy with his studying, his reading, and his work, he had time to become a leader at Booker T. Washington High School in Norfolk. He was on the debating team and served as president of his class. His high school did not have many science courses, but Leonidas was still convinced that he could become a doctor. After graduating from high school, he went to Wilberforce University, an all-Black school in Ohio.

Higher Education

Leonidas Berry did well at Wilberforce. In his senior year, he was selected as a student instructor in zoology, the scientific study of animals. In 1924, Berry graduated from Wilberforce and applied to the University of Chicago Medical School, one of the best in the country. He was accepted on the condition that, at the end of his first year, he would be able to pass examinations in chemistry and physics. He did so well on those exams that he was officially accepted into the medical school.

During his time at medical school, Berry studied patients at a private clinic set up by

Dr. Ulysses Daily. Dr. Dailey was an African American surgeon who had worked with Dr. Daniel H. Williams at Provident Hospital in Chicago. Berry worked with Dr. Dailey for two years. Berry then did his internship in Washington, D.C., at Freedmen's Hospital, which was affiliated with Howard University. As an intern, Berry was able to practice being a doctor while under the supervision of a more experienced physician. Near the end of his internship, Berry passed the national test to become certified as a doctor. He scored near the very top in the section covering physiology.

Career Highlights

After finishing his internship and certification procedures, Dr. Berry took a job at Provident Hospital in Chicago. During this time, Dr. Rudolph Schindler, an expert in a type of medicine called gastroenterology, came from Germany to practice at another hospital in Chicago. Gastroenterology is the study of the stomach and the other organs in the digestive system. Dr. Schindler had invented the gastroscope, a special piece of equipment which allowed a doctor to look into a patient's stomach. It had long flexible tubes and a little electric light and lens at the end of the tube. Dr. Berry asked Dr. Schindler if he (Dr. Berry) could work with the gastroscope at Provident Hospital once a week. Dr. Schindler agreed. This was the beginning of an important part of Dr. Berry's career.

Dr. Schindler taught Dr. Berry how to use the gastroscope, and under Dr. Schindler's supervision, Dr. Berry soon used it on over 100 patients. Dr. Berry then purchased his own gastroscope. Using this instrument, he continued to treat many patients who had stomach diseases and other digestive problems. In a few years, Dr. Berry had examined more patients with the gastroscope than any other doctor in the country. He had also written more scientific papers on this technique than anyone except Dr. Schindler, himself. Dr. Berry reported some of his research at the American Medical Association (AMA) convention in 1941. It was the first presentation ever given by an African American doctor at an AMA convention.

Based on his experience with the gastroscope, Dr. Berry helped invent a medical device called the gastrobiopsy-scope. It allowed a doctor to see into a patient's stomach and also permitted him or her to take a little sample of stomach tissue for examination. This new feature made the device much more valuable than the gastroscope. By allowing the doctors to test a sample of stomach tissue, it helped them determine whether a stomach problem was caused by an ulcer or by something else, including cancer.

Dr. Berry worked diligently to become a leader in the field of digestive diseases, but racial prejudice often stood in his way. Black doctors could not get jobs working in hospitals with White patients. Medical associations like the Gastroenterological Society and the American Medical Association would not admit Dr. Berry or other qualified African American doctors.

During the first years of World War II, treatment of African American soldiers and sailors took place in segregated facilities. Dr. Berry resented this procedure. He was determined to fight for equal opportunities for Black doctors, Black patients, and, indeed, for all Black people. After much struggle, Dr. Berry was appointed to the Cook County Hospital in Chicago. Only two other African American doctors had ever been allowed to practice medicine there. In 1947, Dr. Berry became an instructor at the Cook County Graduate School of Medicine and continued to teach there for 25 years.

Dr. Berry wanted to give each of his patients the best care possible. He also wanted to reach out to his community. He joined the

Health Committee set up by the mayor of Chicago and served as the chairman for five years. He then became president of the Cook County Physicians Association. He started a program to treat drug addiction in teenagers. He continued to study the stomach problems of alcoholics. Dr. Berry also got married during this busy time. Two years later, he and his wife, Ophelia, had a baby daughter they named Judy.

In 1954, the same year Dr. Berry spoke at an international conference on stomach diseases in Paris, the United States Supreme Court banned forced segregation in public schools. This allowed Dr. Berry to increase his efforts to improve the opportunities of young African Americans. He worked in Chicago to recruit African American young adults into careers in the medical professions. All of his hard work was rewarded in 1965 by the National Medical Association, an organization started by Black doctors not admitted to the AMA, when they elected Dr. Berry as their president.

Soon Dr. Berry's work became even more famous. President Lyndon B. Johnson appointed him as a national advisor on the problems of heart disease, cancer, and strokes. He also traveled to Kenya, Uganda, Nigeria, and other African countries to study health problems and to demonstrate the use of the gastroscope.

He continued to fight racial prejudice, too. He started a group of 32 African American doctors, nurses, and technicians called "The Flying Black Medics" to help Black people in Cairo, Illinois. Dr. Berry had heard that these people were being refused medical care—because of their race—in the town's only hospital. Dr. Berry brought in the Flying Black Medics and hospital equipment to Cairo. He set up a clinic in a church basement and treated all people who needed care.

Later in his career, Dr. Berry received a grant of $175,000 to do research on cancers of the stomach and esophagus. He worked with a new piece of equipment similar to the gastroscope but more advanced. It is called the fiberoptic endoscope. This device could detect cancers that could not be seen on X rays. After he completed the research, Dr. Berry was the main author of a major textbook about the use of the new device. The University of Chicago awarded Dr. Berry the Alumni Public Service Award in 1966 and the Alumni Professional Achievement Award in 1978 for his work on the endoscope.

Dr. Leonidas Berry has spent his entire career helping people with digestive problems. He has also done much to make sure that everyone receives proper medical attention regardless of race. He has set a wonderful example for many young men and women, including his daughter, Judy. She continues her father's distinguished tradition of medical service as a psychiatrist in New York City.

David Harold Blackwell

Born: April 24, 1919, in Centralia, Illinois

Status: Professor Emeritus, Unversity of California at Berkeley

Education:

Bachelor of Arts degree, University of Illinois, Champaign-Urbana, Illinois, 1938

Master of Arts degree, University of Illinois, 1939

Doctor of Philosophy degree, University of Illinois, 1941

Research Area: Mathematical Statistics

Early Years

When David Blackwell was growing up in Centralia, Illinois, there were very few African American families in the community. In his sixth grade class of 45 pupils, only three others were African Americans. He continued his education in the only high school in Centralia that enrolled both Black and White students. The other two schools enrolled either all Black or all White students. David was aware that racial discrimination was a problem, but at the time, he was not particularly bothered about it.

Although his parents had very little schooling, his grandfather had been a teacher in Ohio and in Tennessee. He died when David was still very young, but he left a large collection of books to David's family. David read many of these books, and from one on algebra he developed his first ideas about mathematics. David was also influenced by his uncle who lived nearby. This uncle enjoyed mathematical tricks and was able to add three columns of numbers in one step.

David's parents expected him to follow in his grandfather's footsteps and become a teacher. David expected this for himself as well. His prime ambition was to teach grade school. He did not think about the subjects he might teach until after he had entered high school, when he discovered he particularly liked geometry. He saw geometry problems as puzzles that often had interesting solutions. If the right answer was found, something that was mysterious changed into something that was simple.

When one of his high school teachers, Mr. Huck, formed a mathematics club, David joined. Mr. Huck would give the club members problems to solve that were not in the books. These were problems made up by adult mathematicians. If a student could solve one of these special problems, the teacher would write down the steps to the solution, then put this solution into the form of a short article and send it to a magazine called *School Science and Mathematics*. The magazine usually would publish the short article using the student's name. David had three such articles published while he was still in school. He was very proud to see his name in print in a real mathematician's magazine.

Higher Education

David Blackwell finished high school in 1935 when he was just sixteen years old. His good grades allowed him to enter the University of Illinois in Champaign-Urbana in the fall of that same year.

At first his parents borrowed the money to pay his tuition costs and expenses. When Blackwell found out about the loans, he told his father that he could pay his own way. Consequently, he worked as a waiter and a dishwasher in local restaurants during his second year in college. Later, he took a job in a university laboratory where insects were studied. The laboratory director had a small grant from the U.S. Department of Agriculture to study the insects that destroyed crops. Blackwell cleaned the cases where the dead insects were mounted and did other odd jobs. He was paid with money from the research grant.

While most students need four years to get their degrees, Blackwell was able to finish in only three. He skipped some courses by passing examinations, and he also took courses in the summer so he could finish his degree more quickly.

After he graduated, Blackwell was given a scholarship to begin his graduate studies. He still thought he would teach grade school as his grandfather had done, but after he started to work on a master's degree, he began to think that perhaps he could teach at the high school level.

David Blackwell's father had a friend on the school board in a small town in southern Illinois. This friend had promised to give Blackwell a teaching job when he finished college. However, Blackwell delayed taking the education courses he needed for certification. His college teachers encouraged him to take more and more advanced course work in mathematics instead He finished his master's degree in one year. He then enrolled immediately in the doctoral program in mathematics at the University of Illinois. He completed his Ph.D. studies in only two years. During this time, the university gave Blackwell a fellowship that provided money for tuition costs and living expenses.

His primary professor during his graduate studies was Joseph Doob. Professor Doob directed Blackwell's research and encouraged him to study a part of pure mathematics called probability theory. Probability theory covers problems such as the outcome of coin tossing. In that game, the probability of having the coin come up heads is 50 percent or 0.5. One question a gambler might ask is what happens when you flip the coin many times and the coin comes up heads ten times in a row. Is it more probable that tails will come up on the next toss? The answer is no. The probability stays the same. The coin has no memory, so the odds on heads or tails stay the same, no matter how long a run of either heads or tails lasts.

In some situations, however, probabilities do change. For example, in a basketball league, all the teams are supposed to be nearly evenly matched. But perhaps one team wins its first five games. Does that change the probability that it will win the sixth game? The answer is yes. Because the team has won five games, it is reasonable to believe that it has a real advantage. Perhaps the players on the team are better than they were expected to be. If this is so, then they have a better than 50-50 chance of winning the next game.

These are the kinds of questions Blackwell studied. When he finished his doctoral research in 1941, both he and Professor Doob were invited to Princeton University in Princeton, New Jersey, where Dr. Blackwell was made the Rosenwald Fellow at the Institute for Advanced Study. It was a very good time to be at the Institute for Advanced Study. Albert Einstein, a permanent fellow of the institute, and other world-famous physicists and mathematicians gathered there. Blackwell, therefore, was able to discuss his research with senior mathematicians. One such scientist was John Von Neumann, who had just come to the United States from Europe.

Career Highlights

Dr. Blackwell still wanted to be a teacher. He was now qualified to teach at the college-level, and he began looking for a job while he was at Princeton. He applied only to colleges that had a strong link to the African American community, because he believed racial discrimination would prevent him from being hired at a mostly White institution. He sent out 105 letters—one to each Black college that existed at that time—and took the first job he was offered. It was at Southern University in Baton Rouge, Louisiana, where he stayed for just one year. He then went to Clark College in Atlanta, Georgia, and again stayed for just one year. Finally, in 1944, he received an offer from Howard University in Washington, D.C. Although Howard was a top Black institution at that time, the mathematics faculty was still quite small. There were only three other mathematics teachers in the department when Dr. Blackwell arrived on the campus. He stayed at Howard for ten years.

During his first year at Howard University, Dr. Blackwell wanted to continue to learn about new ideas. He attended the meetings of the local chapter of the American Statistical Association. At one of the evening meetings, he listened to a lecture by Dr. Abraham Girshick. At the time, Dr. Girshick was already a famous mathematician working for the government at the Department of Agriculture. Dr. Blackwell thought he caught a mistake in one of the ideas that Girshick used in his lecture, and he wrote Girshick a letter describing it. It turned out, however, that it was David Blackwell who had made the mistake. Dr. Girshick was not upset by having his work questioned by a newcomer to the field. He called Dr. Blackwell and they met for lunch. They became great friends, and a few years later they formed a team to write a book on statistical theory which was published in 1954. It was Blackwell's meeting with Girshick that turned him from general mathematics to statistics.

In 1950, Dr. Blackwell took a leave of absence from Howard University for one year, which he spent at the RAND Corporation in Santa Monica, California. RAND is a famous institution that hires very smart civilians to work on hard technical problems. At that time, RAND's total budget was supported by the U.S. Air Force. While at the RAND Corporation, Dr. Blackwell discussed one of his projects with Dr. James Savage. Dr. Savage was working on ideas about how to make good decisions. He saw that someone faced with a decision should try to obtain as much

information as possible. He knew, however, that most decisions have deadlines; therefore, a person faced with a decision cannot collect information forever. Savage wanted to find out if there were ways to know when a decision-maker had enough information to make a good decision. Did each new piece of information help? What was the best way to put new information together with older information? These were hard questions. To get useful answers, Dr. Savage needed to think in ways that were different from the ways most statisticians had thought before. Strangely enough, the origin of these "new" ways of thinking was over 200 years old. Thomas Bayes, an Englishman who died in 1761, had developed a form of algebra that shows how each piece of new information brings a decision-maker a bit closer to the truth, and how each new piece makes a smaller contribution than the piece before it. Dr. Blackwell became very interested in the problems in the mathematics of decision making. Such problems became the main part of his further studies. In fact, he wrote a book in 1970 about these kinds of problems and the new ways of thinking about them.

In the meantime, he continued to teach at Howard University until 1954, when he was asked to join the faculty at the University of California at Berkeley. Dr. Blackwell had been interviewed for a similar job years before, but race had been a barrier. By 1954, however, race was not so important. Many officials of prominent colleges and universities had come to see the advantages of a more diverse faculty and had begun to seek Black faculty members in an active way. Dr. Blackwell was pleased by this opportunity because the University of California at Berkeley is rated among the top 10 or 12 institutions of its kind in the United States.

At about the time Dr. Blackwell arrived in California, the mathematics department was divided into two segments, and a new Department of Statistics was formed. Dr. Blackwell thought this was a good idea, because he felt that people cooperate with each other better in small group arrangements.

Coincidentally, he began to study the mathematics of cooperation and competition at this time. For example, he tried to use numbers to describe one of the oldest and deadliest forms of competition, the duel with single-shot pistols. The problem for the duelist is when to shoot. If s/he shoots first and hits, the duel is over and s/he has won. If s/he shoots first and misses, s/he will probably be killed. What is the best strategy? It would depend on how likely one is to hit the opponent with one shot. The mathematics soon become quite complicated even in this simple situation.

Dr. Blackwell worked on many other puzzles as well. His reputation grew, and in 1965, he was the first African American mathematician to be made a member of the National Academy of Sciences, which is a great honor.

Dr. Blackwell accepted more and more responsibilities as a leader in his profession. He served as chairperson of his department at the University of California and was elected president of the Institute of Mathematical Statistics in 1955. He also was elected president of the Bernouli Society and served as vice president of several other major professional organizations. He has been honored here in the United States, in Europe, and elsewhere in the world, and he won the Von Neumann Theory Prize in 1979. In spite of this recognition for his inventive ideas, his favorite work has always been teaching. After he retired, he looked forward to spending more time with his eight children and many grandchildren. Nevertheless, he continued to teach a few courses at Berkeley every year.

Fitzgerald B. Bramwell

Born: May 16, 1945, in Brooklyn, New York

Status: Vice President for Research and Graduate Studies, University of Kentucky, Lexington, Kentucky

Education:

Bachelor of Arts degree, Columbia University, New York, New York, 1966

Master of Science degree, University of Michigan, Ann Arbor, Michigan, 1967

Doctor of Philosophy degree, University of Michigan, 1970

Research Area: Chemistry

Early Years

Fitzgerald (Jerry) Bramwell and his older brother grew up in the Bedford-Stuyvesant section of Brooklyn, New York. Their mother, one of the first female African American school principals in New York City, graduated from New York's Hunter College and earned her master's degree at Atlanta University under Dr. W.E.B. Du Bois. Their father graduated in 1934 with a degree in chemical engineering from Cooper Union

College in New York City. Few African Americans had engineering degrees at that time.

After graduating and finding a job, Jerry's father helped pay for the education of his six brothers and sisters—each of whom went on to important professional positions. One became a federal judge, another a deputy commissioner for the city of New York, and a third, an executive in the Transit Authority. One of Jerry's aunts became an international fashion designer, and his mother's relatives were health care professionals. All the relatives served as positive role models for Jerry and his brother—who earned a doctoral degree in molecular biophysics from Pennsylvania State University and now heads an information technology company.

Jerry attended integrated elementary and middle schools in New York City. At times, Jerry was the only African American in his classes and some of his classmates made no secret of their belief in the academic inferiority of African Americans. Indeed, it pleased Jerry to prove them wrong by his outstanding school performance. Furthermore, he realized that his family was composed of unusually high achievers. This fact bolstered his self respect.

When Jerry was 13, his family pooled their resources and sent him to Phillips Academy in Andover, Massachusetts, a top ranked college preparatory institution. One day shortly after his arrival, he was standing outside one of the buildings boasting about his academic skills. He was interrupted when an instructor—whose quiz he had just failed—asked him when he intended to stop talking and start studying. After this embarrassing incident, Jerry became serious about his education. He gained his teachers' respect, and they encouraged his ambition to become a research chemist.

Higher Education

Jerry Bramwell entered Columbia University in upper Manhattan in the fall of 1962. Once again, he found himself to be one of the few African American students in the school and the only one majoring in chemistry. However, Bramwell did not feel isolated and became friends with many of his fellow students.

During this turbulent period in our history, there were both political and social tensions on college campuses. Many students were trying different lifestyles and using mind-altering and recreational drugs. Race relations were extremely difficult and the Black Muslim movement, whose headquarters were near Columbia, was gathering momentum. Its leader, Malcolm X, was arguing against the nonviolent approach to racial justice promoted by Dr. Martin Luther King, Jr. The "Freedom Riders"—volunteers who helped with voter registration drives in the South—were becoming more important. In addition, other activist organizations such as the Black Panther Party and the Students for a Democratic Society were busy building support among college students.

The war in Viet Nam was also becoming a factor in the lives of the students. Many students and faculty thought that the Viet Nam conflict was a mistake and wanted no part in it. The antiwar protests that took place in the late 1960s were particularly prominent in student life at Columbia University.

This unrest was a distraction for many students, and some dropped out of college. It took substantial mental discipline to keep focused on such difficult topics as chemistry. Fortunately, Bramwell worked under the supervision of several outstanding faculty members such as Dr. Martin Karplus, a world-famous theoretician; Dr. Harry Gray, a young but highly productive researcher in inorganic chemistry; and Dr. John Applequist, a gifted biochemist. Bramwell was kept so busy that there was little time for nonacademic activities, even eating. His meals were mainly pick-up snacks—soft drinks, peanut butter and jam sandwiches, and fortunately, some vitamin pills. Because of his diligence, Bramwell graduated from Columbia in 1966, after only three and one-half years. That spring, he received a scholarship that allowed him to spend three months doing advanced study at the Royal Dutch Shell Corporation laboratories at Delft in the Netherlands.

Jerry Bramwell knew that he must attend graduate school to become a research chemist. At Professor Gray's suggestion, he applied for admission to the graduate chemistry program at the University of Michigan in Ann Arbor and was awarded a research assistantship. He was fortunate that two distinguished faculty members, Dr. Thomas Dunn and Dr. Julien Gendell, acted as his advisors. Dr. Gendell supervised Bramwell's laboratory work, helped design his initial research projects, and coauthored his first two published reports.

Bramwell's research was focused on how beams of laser light quickly change the structure and reactivity of certain complicated carbon-based compounds. In order to study these changes, Bramwell slowed down the process by cooling the material to a few degrees above absolute zero (minus 273 degrees Celsius). In order to detect the slowed-down but still submicroscopic reaction, he used electron spin resonance, which revealed the greatly enlarged reaction on a screen. Bramwell was especially interested in corranulene, a carbon-based compound that is particularly sensi-

tive to the effects of light. He completed his thesis and was awarded his master's degree from Michigan in 1967.

Bramwell's doctoral studies—in the same area as his master's thesis research—were guided by Dr. Dunn, then head of the chemistry department. Bramwell finished the requirements for his degree and graduated in 1970 from the University of Michigan.

Career Highlights

Dr. Bramwell's first job after graduating was with the ESSO Research and Engineering Company in Linden, New Jersey. He worked in the Corporate Research Laboratories on the electrical properties of petroleum products. He soon realized that industrial research was not to his liking. The following year, he accepted a faculty appointment at Brooklyn College, a part of the City University of New York (CUNY).

Within one year of his arrival at Brooklyn College, Dr. Bramwell was appointed to the doctoral faculty of the City University of New York. He now directed his own graduate students and begin to educate the next generation of research chemists. In 1988, he achieved the rank of full professor and, in 1989, served as acting dean for research and graduate studies. The following year, he was confirmed as dean by the university administrators.

During these years, Dr. Bramwell continued his research on the properties of highly reactive molecules that are formed by the action of light waves on carbon-based compounds. He also worked on projects with colleagues from the Bell Laboratories in Murray Hill, New Jersey. One such project was the development of carbon-based superconductors, materials that when cooled to very low temperatures can conduct electricity with little or no resistance.

From 1980 onward much of Dr. Bramwell's research was focused on the development of new carbon-based molecules to which atoms of tin have been attached, known as organo-tins. These materials have the useful property of being effective fungicides and potential destroyers of organisms that cause Dutch Elm disease. Many of Dr. Bramwell's students have used these materials as the basis for their thesis and dissertation research projects.

Teaching at Brooklyn College permitted Dr. Bramwell to develop methods of teaching young people the rudiments of general chemistry. Collaborating with faculty and students, he developed new laboratory manuals that encouraged students to work with scientific equipment and materials.

Dr. Bramwell and his colleagues also developed a more detailed laboratory manual and an instructor's guide that were published in 1978 and revised in 1990. In addition, Dr. Bramwell has published articles for chemistry students and teachers in the *Journal of Chemical Education.*

Throughout his career, Dr. Bramwell has sought to develop new methods of science education for all levels of instruction. He has been a key participant in CHEMCOM, the precollege program of the American Chemical Society. Dr. Bramwell believes that by providing positive experiences in science, more minority students will decide to enter the field. This situation will benefit society, the scientific community, and, of course, the young people themselves.

In July 1995, Dr. Bramwell became the vice president for research and graduate studies at the University of Kentucky in Lexington. There, he will continue to provide science opportunities for all students.

Scurlock Studio

Herman R. Branson

Born: August 14, 1914, in Pocahontas, Virginia

Status: Retired, President, Lincoln University, Lincoln University, Pennsylvania, 1985

Education:

Bachelor of Science degree, Virginia State University, Petersburg, Virginia, 1936

Doctor of Philosophy degree, University of Cincinnati, Cincinnati, Ohio, 1939

Research Area: Biophysics

Early Years

As a young child, Herman Branson's main inspiration was his mother. She read to her children almost every day and encouraged them to read for themselves. After one or the other had finished several paragraphs, she would ask them questions about what they had learned. The questions made the children think about the material, and they discovered that not everything they read was the truth.

Herman's father was a coal miner. Mr. Branson was not well educated, but some of his relatives had been pioneers in the field of medicine. Herman's great uncle was Dr. Charles H. Carroll, an early African American graduate of the medical school at the University of Pittsburgh. There were also relatives in medical careers on his mother's side of the family. The professional success of these family members showed Herman that he, too, could excel if he worked hard.

The boy attended a segregated grade school in the mining town of Pocahontas, Virginia. In those days, many well educated African Americans taught in small towns, like Pocahontas, because as Black teachers they had few choices of employment. Therefore, the training Herman received in his grade school years prepared him extremely well for all his further education.

Herman enrolled in Dunbar High School in the District of Columbia in 1928, and, again, he was fortunate to have good teachers. His science and mathematics teachers were particularly helpful. Herman graduated at the top of his high school class in 1932.

Higher Education

Herman Branson first attended the University of Pittsburgh where his father's uncle had been successful. He did not feel comfortable there, however. After his second year, he transferred to Virginia State University in Petersburg, Virginia. Not only did he feel more at home in the state of his birth, but the tuition and living costs were much lower. He graduated in 1936 with high honors.

His excellent work won him admission to the graduate program in physics at the University of Cincinnati in Ohio. While there, he received good financial support from several university fellowships. He received a Special Fellowship in physics his first year. In his second year, he received a Laws Fellowship donated by the Laws family. In his third

year, in addition to the continuing Laws Fellowship, Branson received an Alpha Phi Alpha Fellowship. Alpha Phi Alpha is a fraternity that supports excellent science students. With the help of these fellowships, he was able to finish his doctoral studies in just three years, graduating in 1939.

Career Highlights

Dr. Herman Branson's first major research project was in biophysics. At the time, this area of science was in its infancy. Before the 1930s, most research in biology was descriptive. The main emphasis was placed on identifying living creatures and showing how each fit into the overall pattern of life, as well as describing the stages a creature went through as it grew and developed.

Then, in the 1930s, biologists began to seek other information. They wanted to know what would happen if the conditions of life for a particular creature were changed. They also sought to understand many other things, such as whether an animal would grow faster or slower if it ate different food, and whether a plant would thrive better if it got more sunlight. Such questions became more popular because physicists were able to provide biologists with new research tools, such as X rays. Physicists had discovered how to generate X rays in their laboratories, which allowed researchers to study the effect of X rays on biological creatures.

While Branson was still a student, he studied the effect of X rays on small worms. He was particularly interested in trying to control the amount of X rays beamed onto the worms. He had to devise a method to measure the strength of the X rays and to determine how much of the radiation was absorbed by the worms. The new focus in biology forced Branson to analyze the animal in new and different ways. It was important to discover, for example, which chemicals made up the body of the worm, if these chemicals were spread evenly through the body, and if some of the worms organs had more of a particular chemical than others. His successful research on the worms placed Dr. Branson in the center of the field of biophysics.

His first job after completing his doctoral research was teaching at Dillard University, a medium-sized coeducational institution in New Orleans, Louisiana. Dillard was established by the merger of two smaller institutions in 1930. It had a predominantly African American faculty and student body and still does. Here, Dr. Branson taught not only physics but also mathematics and chemistry. He had to work long hours, but he enjoyed being with his students.

After two years, he was invited to join the faculty at Howard University in Washington, D.C. There, he had fewer duties and began to follow-up on his original research. He became particularly interested in how the body uses raw materials such as phosphorus. When food is digested, phosphorus compounds enter the blood stream, and these compounds go to all parts of the body. They are used to build proteins and to make DNA and RNA (deoxyribonucleic acid and ribonucleic acid)—the spiral molecules that control the genetic make-up of every living thing.

Dr. Branson wanted to know how quickly phosphorus was used by the body. He first developed a theory about the chemical stages phosphorus goes through before it can be used by the cells. He wrote his theory in mathematical language to explain how much phosphorus was used in each of these stages.

Because of his previous research with X rays, Dr. Branson knew about atomic radiation. He saw that he could test his theory by using radioactive phosphorus in a living animal. The radioactive phosphorus acts as a tracer, and he kept track of the amounts of phosphorus in each organ of the body over a period of time.

His work was so successful that in 1948, he was invited to describe the results of his research at a conference on biophysics. This conference was held every summer at the Cold Spring Harbor Laboratories on Long Island, New York. It was there that the field of biophysics had been founded in 1933.

Dr. Branson continued to study how raw materials were used by the body, and he encouraged his many students to do research on this problem. He and his students were given money for the research by the Office of Naval Research and also by the Atomic Energy Commission (now part of the U.S. Department of Energy).

Dr. Branson did not limit himself to this type of research, however. He also studied the physical structures of proteins. As early as 1948, he was working in a cross-country collaboration with Professor Linus Pauling, who would later win a Nobel Prize for showing how atoms link together to form molecules. Pauling was working then on the most complicated molecules in the world, trying to describe the exact structure of proteins. At the time, most scientists believed that DNA and RNA were proteins, and finding the structure of DNA was one of Pauling's goals.

Only crude measurements of the spacing of atoms in a molecule could be made at the time. Using this limited information, scientists could only guess about the exact structure of protein molecules, which contained hundreds of atoms. Determining the structure of DNA, therefore, would prove to be a very difficult problem.

Dr. Branson took the crude measurements and made careful calculations. He decided that in the most basic molecules there was a definite pattern. The molecule hemoglobin was particularly interesting. Hemoglobin is the container that carries oxygen from the lungs to other parts of the body, and is the molecule that gives blood its red color.

In 1950, Branson discovered a spiral structural pattern in hemoglobin, which helped lead the way to unlocking the secret behind the structure of DNA. The researchers who successfully described DNA were greatly assisted by Branson's discovery of spiral proteins.

Dr. Branson's work with hemoglobin also led him to more research on the red blood cells of humans. In particular, he became interested in the problem of sickle-cell anemia, a hereditary disease which is found most often in people of African heritage. Dr. Branson's research helped reveal why these oddly shaped blood cells could not carry as much oxygen as the body needed. Because of these studies, he was elected to the Institute of Medicine, a branch of the National Academy of Sciences, in 1975. Dr. Branson did not just limit himself to work in the laboratory. He served as the chairperson of the Department of Physics at Howard University for 27 years. In 1968, he became the president of Central State University in Wilberforce, Ohio, and in 1970, he was asked to serve as president of Lincoln University in the town of Lincoln University, Pennsylvania, a position he held until his retirement in 1985. Dr. Branson was not only an excellent scientist but also a good administrator, as evidenced by the nomination for the National Medal of Science made on his behalf by the students and faculty of Lincoln University in 1980.

Dr. Branson's influence was not limited to the United States. He began his professional travels in 1951, when he was sponsored by the Office of Naval Research, and he made visits to England, France, and Germany. In Germany, he consulted with other research scientists at the Max Planck Institute for Biophysics in Frankfort and the Max Planck Institute for Physics in Hamburg. He traveled overseas again in 1962 and 1963. On these journeys, sponsored by the National Science Foundation, he was asked to teach his techniques to researchers at the University of Hamburg in Germany and at the French Atomic Energy Commission in Saclay, France. From late 1966 to early 1967, and again from late 1970 to early 1971, he was a consultant on science education to the government of India. In 1985, he became a member of the Council of the National University of Lesotho in Africa. Dr. Branson also served as a trustee of the Massachusetts Institute of Technology from 1979 to 1984 and of the Carver Research Foundation at Tuskegee University in Alabama since 1960. After resigning these trusteeships in early 1992, he returned to Howard University as the director of their Precollege Science and Mathematics Research Program.

Dr. Branson has been acclaimed by many educators. He has been awarded honorary doctoral degrees by eight U.S. universities, including such prestigious institutions as Brandeis University and Drexel University. During his productive career, Dr. Branson has been a scientific pioneer and an educator of international stature.

Randolph W. Bromery

Born: January 18, 1926, in Cumberland, Maryland

Status: President, Springfield College, Springfield, Massachusetts

Education:

Bachelor of Science degree, Howard University, Washington, D.C., 1956

Master of Science degree, American University, Washington, D.C., 1962

Doctor of Philosophy degree, Johns Hopkins University, Baltimore, Maryland, 1968

Research Area: Geology

Early Years

Randolph William "Bill" Bromery grew up in the town of Cumberland, Maryland, a few miles south of the Mason-Dixon Line, the border that symbolically divided the North from the South.

Bill lived in a small house with his grandmother and grandfather, his mother and father, and his sister and two brothers. Bill's father worked at a local hotel as the dining room supervisor and was also an accomplished jazz musician. Bill's grandfather was one of the elite Pullman Porters, a job that kept him away from home much of the time. Bill's grandmother worked as a hairdresser for many of the wealthier women in Cumberland. She and her daughter, Bill's mother, also operated a part-time catering service from their home.

In the early 1930s, the Great Depression caused many businesses and industries to fail, and 30 percent of the nation's workers were left unemployed. The hotel where Bill's father worked was in financial difficulty and had to close its dining room. Mr. Bromery was forced to take low-paying janitorial jobs to support his family. Fortunately, he was able to add to his income by playing the trumpet in a local jazz quintet.

Bill attended the segregated Frederick Street School in Cumberland. In order to preserve segregation, African American students from neighboring West Virginia were bused to the Frederick Street School because this was the closest Black school.

Since the schools for Black students were poorly funded, there were many deficiencies in the curriculum. The instructional program for male students at Bill's school was limited to Industrial Arts, and graduates of such programs were rarely considered to be ready for higher education. However, Bill's parents and his grandmother were determined to see their children go on to college. Therefore, his grandmother arranged for them to be tutored by a mathematics teacher after school.

The lack of funding caused other unfair policies to be made by the school administration, as well. Because of a shortage of classroom space, the school board dropped the entire eighth grade from the Frederick Street School's program. For several years, students went from seventh grade directly into ninth grade. Then, in 1941, the school was reorganized, and the high school was separated from the lower school and given a new name—George Washington Carver High School. Along with sixteen other students, Randolph W. Bromery was a member of the first graduating class in June of 1942.

Bill's family was unable to pay his college tuition, so he went to work after graduation. Because of the advanced machine shop training he had received in an after school program funded by President Roosevelt's National Youth Administration, Bill, who now preferred to be called Randolph, was able to find work as an apprentice tool and die maker in one of the big factories in Detroit, Michigan.

By this time, the United States was deeply involved in World War II, and Randolph Bromery had enlisted in the Army Air Corps.

He was called up at the end of the summer of 1943. After basic military training in Virginia and Mississippi, he was sent to the pilot training facility in Tuskegee, Alabama, where he qualified as a pilot of high performance fighter aircraft. He then joined the 99th Air Squadron and was stationed in southern Italy. The pilots in this squadron flew fighter escorts for the bombers that attacked industrial targets in Austria, northern Italy, and southern Germany. The Tuskegee Airmen of the 99th flew over 300 missions without losing a single bomber to enemy action. It was a proud, frightening, and exciting time for Randolph Bromery.

Higher Education

After completing his military duties in 1945, Randolph Bromery wanted to go to college. He knew that his benefits as a war veteran would cover most of his college expenses, so he applied to the University of Michigan in Ann Arbor. His application to the university was turned down because of his limited high school background. He wanted to specialize in mathematics, but of course, his high school records did not show the tutoring he had received. Therefore, the university officials were skeptical of his ability. When Randolph Bromery explained the situation to the admission officials in Ann Arbor, they agreed to a compromise arrangement. If Bromery successfully completed a correspondence course in mathematics offered by the University of Utah and passed the performance test, he would be admitted as a matriculated undergraduate student. Bromery did outstanding work in the course and was admitted to the university.

In the summer of 1946, after one year at Michigan, Randolph Bromery was informed that his mother had become seriously ill, so in order to be closer to home, he transferred to Howard University in Washington, D.C. He enrolled in their summer program and

continued at Howard even when his mother's illness seemed to improve.

It was an exciting time for the mathematics department at Howard University. The faculty included Professor Albert F. Cox, the first African American to earn a doctorate in mathematics; David Blackwell (see p. 12), the noted statistician, and Professor Alain Locke, a well known professor of logic.

Sadly, Randolph's mother did not recover from her illness and died at the age of 43 in the spring of 1947. By this time, Randolph Bromery was well established at Howard University and did not return to the University of Michigan.

In the spring of 1948, Bromery thought he had enough credits to graduate from Howard, but discovered that he had been given wrong information by his faculty advisor and needed more credits in physical education to meet Howard's graduation requirements. This situation seemed ridiculous to Randolph and his bride, Cecile Trescott Bromery, who had also completed her degree, especially since he had earned 46 credits in mathematics—14 more than were required for a major.

Bromery was so upset that he left Howard University without his degree. Instead of taking the time and money required to earn the four missing credits in physical education, he began to look for professional employment in the Washington, D.C., area. After some unpleasant racist dealings with the Naval Research Laboratory, he chanced upon an employment advertisement from the U.S. Geological Survey. He discovered that the organization was seeking mathematicians and physicists. Bromery was pleasantly surprised by the welcoming atmosphere at the Geological Survey's offices. After the personnel administrator found out about Bromery's background, education, and military experience, she suggested that he apply for a position in a newly formed unit called the Airborne Geophysics Group. When he explained that he had never had a college geology course, she pointed out that other members of the unit also lacked that training.

Randolph Bromery took the first available trolley car to their office at Cabin John, Maryland, on the Potomac River north of D.C. Again, he was impressed by their warm welcome, and because of his training in mathematics and physics and his flying experience, he was immediately hired.

Six years after Randolph Bromery left Howard University, he went back to try to straighten out the confusion over his credit requirements. Fortunately, he and the university were able to reach a compromise. Bromery was required to take a course in English literature as a substitute for the missing physical education credits. The class was taught by the highly respected Professor Sterling Brown, who, as a jazz fan, could relate to Bromery's interest in his father's music. Finally in 1956, Randolph Bromery received his degree from Howard.

After his belated graduation, Bromery entered the graduate program in geology at American University in Washington, D.C. At the same time, he was invited to teach an evening course in geophysics at Howard. Therefore, while continuing to work days at the Geological Survey in nearby Maryland, Bromery taught a night course in engineering geophysics at Howard and took night courses in geology at American.

He was awarded his master's degree from American University in 1962. By that time, he had already authored or coauthored about 80 scientific reports published in the professional literature. Fortunately, Bromery had entered the fields of geology and geophysics at the beginning of a period of major advances. Scientists had demonstrated that they could detect—in a rapid and economical way—patterns of the earth's magnetism and variations in the earth's gravity from above the earth's surface. In 1950, not long after the development of the magnetic survey techniques, other measurement methods were also being tested. There was growing interest, for example, in the new ability to detect variations in atmospheric radiation. Some of this radiation occurs naturally as cosmic rays, but other radiation comes from atomic power plants and the testing of nuclear weapons. In addition, Randolph Bromery was conducting studies on how variations in the earth's magnetic field might indicate the locations of valuable minerals such as manganese.

In the process of preparing his scientific reports, Randolph Bromery was drawn to the work of Professor Ernest Cloos of Johns Hopkins University in Baltimore, Maryland. Cloos had come to the United States from Germany in the late 1930s—just before the outbreak of World War II. Now, in the summer of 1963, Professor Cloos was on the verge of retirement. When Randolph Bromery contacted him about the possibility of becoming his doctoral student, Cloos said that he no longer advised advanced students. Bromery wanted to talk to Cloos anyway and made an appointment to visit the professor at his office on the Homewood campus of Johns Hopkins. Two hours later, Dr. Cloos had been persuaded to take on one last doctoral student.

While continuing to work long hours for the U.S. Geological Survey, Randolph Bromery attended classes and collected data for his doctoral dissertation. The Survey recognized the strength of Bromery's dedication and awarded him an In-Service Training Grant to help cover the costs of his first year at Johns Hopkins. The officials of the university were also impressed and gave him a Gilman Fellowship to fund his second year.

While still a doctoral student, Randolph Bromery's dissertation research was used to help determine the best routes for high speed transportation lines between Washington, D.C., and Boston, Massachusetts. He received a special award for his work on this project from the U.S. Department of the Interior in 1967.

During this time, he was also working overseas on airborne radiation measurement techniques. Starting in 1964 and continuing for four years, he worked on a survey of magnetic variations and atmospheric radiation in Liberia. One of the goals was to determine likely sites for finding valuable minerals. This project was sponsored by the U.S. State Department through their Agency for International Development (USAID).

In 1967, while still working on his studies, Bromery spent significant periods of time as a part-time consultant to his employers, the U.S. Geological Survey and two mining companies. All three organizations were interested in the mineral resources of several African countries.

In the fall of 1967, several months before he completed his doctoral work, Randolph Bromery made an important career decision and joined the faculty at the University of Massachusetts in Amherst. He finished his dissertation while preparing to teach at Amherst. The same day—and on the same stage—that Bromery received his degree from Johns Hopkins, the university awarded Professor Cloos an honorary doctorate. The distinguished African American statesman, Senator Edward Brooke of Massachusetts, was the commencement speaker at the ceremony.

Career Highlights

By the time Randolph Bromery graduated with his doctorate from Johns Hopkins University, he had already had two careers—one as an aviator and one as an exploration geophysicist. Because he had almost 20 years of experience as a professional geologist, he was a leader in the field. In 1969, after just two years on the faculty of the University of Massachusetts, he was named full professor and chair of the department of geology and geography. After one more year, although still a member of the teaching faculty, he was made vice chancellor for student affairs. He became acting chancellor in 1971, and while still retaining the post as chancellor, he moved through the ranks from executive to senior vice president during the period from 1977 to 1979. In 1979, finally tired of administrative work, he returned to full-time teaching as the Commonwealth Professor of Geophysics.

By discontinuing his administrative work, Dr. Bromery was free to exercise some of his other talents. He helped to found and manage the Weston Geophysical International Corporation from 1981 to 1986, and he also founded the Geoscience Engineering Corporation in 1983. These organizations had international clients, but they were particularly active in various African nations. Also, as an extension of his interest in minority education, Dr. Bromery has worked to increase minority participation in the Earth Sciences through organizations such as the Geological Society of America. He has served on the boards of directors of several large corporations and still maintains that relationship with EXXON, NYNEX, Chemical Bank, and John Hancock Mutual Life Insurance Company.

Dr. Bromery took leave from the University of Massachusetts in 1988 to serve for two years as the acting president of Westfield State College in Westfield, Massachusetts. Later, he served as the interim chancellor of the Board of Regents of Higher Education for the whole state of Massachusetts during the school year of 1990–91. Finally, at the peak of his extraordinary career, he accepted the job of president of Springfield College, in Springfield, Massachusetts.

On a more personal level, Dr. Bromery will, in a few years, celebrate his 50th wedding anniversary—a union that produced five children.

Carolyn Branch Brooks

Born: July 8, 1946, in Richmond, Virginia

Status: Research Associate Professor and Interim Chair, Agriculture Department, University of Maryland Eastern Shore, Princess Anne, Maryland

Education:

Bachelor of Science degree, Tuskegee University, Tuskegee, Alabama, 1968

Master of Science degree, Tuskegee University, 1971

Doctor of Philosophy degree, Ohio State University, Columbus, Ohio, 1977

Research Area: Microbiology

Early Years

Carolyn Branch, her older sister, and her parents lived with her great grandparents on the north side of Richmond, Virginia, in a prosperous African American neighborhood. While her parents worked—her father was a truck driver, and her mother worked in an antique store—Carolyn was cared-for by her great grandparents and her older sister.

Since most of the other families in the neighborhood were comparatively well off, Carolyn's parents worked long hours to give Carolyn and her sister the same advantages enjoyed by their peers. Carolyn appreciated her parents' hard work, and she tried to repay them by doing well at school. She excelled in her studies, in sports, and in her social life, hoping her parents would feel that their investment was worthwhile.

In the 1950s, her parents moved to the west side of Richmond, a working-class neighborhood. The new situation eased some of their financial pressure; however, Carolyn continued to attend her old school on the north side of Richmond, traveling across town on the public bus. Every day, Carolyn simply got on, paid her fare, and sat behind the driver, without realizing that, according to the segregation laws of the time, she should have sat at the back of the bus. When the first civil rights demonstrations began in Richmond, she discovered that she had been an activist without knowing it.

Segregation was soon lifted from the Richmond school system, but Carolyn preferred to remain among her friends and the supportive atmosphere in her old school. Here, her teachers recognized her potential and encouraged her to do her best. They were aware that the social climate in the United States was changing. Soon, there would be good opportunities for well-prepared, young African

Americans, and they wanted their students to be ready to accept the opportunities.

To better prepare young African Americans, special programs had been designed, including a special summer school for science students. The sessions were held at Virginia Union University in Richmond. The goal of the program was to interest minority students in a future career in science. Students came from Richmond and all the middle Atlantic states. The program drew prominent scientists, who described their work to the students. One such guest speaker was a medical microbiologist. When he spoke, Carolyn was strongly impressed and decided she wanted to pursue a career in medical microbiology.

By the time Carolyn was in high school, her parents purchased a neighborhood grocery store. Even though there was not much money, her mother continued to support Carolyn's ambition to enter college as soon as she finished high school. Her father was less enthusiastic. He saw that young African Americans could find very respectable jobs without spending the money to go to college. The family tension on this point evaporated when Carolyn was offered scholarships at six different colleges. She chose Tuskegee University, in part, because she would be able to travel to a distant and very different part of the country.

Higher Education

In many ways, the experience at Tuskegee was a continuation of the supportive atmosphere that Carolyn Branch had enjoyed in high school. The students were a bit more competitive at college, but the science students were particularly respected at Tuskegee—possibly because of the heritage of George W. Carver (see p. 42).

As a biology major, Branch briefly considered going to medical school; however, she recognized that she would have severe regrets and possibly become depressed if she ever lost a patient. In the field of microbiology, however, Branch was able to make a contribution to human health without the emotional strain of clinical practice.

In the meantime, Carolyn Branch met Henry Brooks. He had majored in education and was about to graduate from Tuskegee with his teacher's credentials. At the end of her second year, Carolyn and Henry were married. Now, she had to decide whether she, herself, really needed to be a college graduate. She thought not, but her new husband and her professors thought otherwise. So, she stayed in the program while her first two boys were born. She received her degree from Tuskegee in 1968. A year after she graduated, those same people persuaded her to return to Tuskegee for an advanced degree. By 1971, she had her first daughter and had earned her master's degree.

After she graduated, Carolyn Brooks was offered a research position in the local Veteran's Administration Hospital. She was given the opportunity to work with other biologists on the sickle-cell disease that often affects African Americans. After she had worked at the hospital for a short time, Henry Brooks was offered a place in the doctoral program at Ohio State University in Columbus. Henry persuaded his wife to apply to the department of microbiology at Ohio State. She was quickly accepted and awarded a fellowship.

The transition from Alabama to Columbus, Ohio, was something of a shock. There were no Black faculty members and very few Black students in her department. The word minority began to take on new meaning. Carolyn Brooks's first lab partner was convinced that Brooks was there only because of the university's affirmative action program. He did little to hide his disdain, and this reminded Brooks of the insults she had suffered as a child. She resolved to prove that she deserved her position. Brooks, however, soon realized that it was unnecessary to prove her worth, and she was able to ignore insults of this kind. She also discovered that the science faculty at Ohio State was not so narrow. Brooks quickly found a new mentor to lead her through her dissertation research and examinations. He became as supportive as her African American teachers had been at Tuskegee.

Career Highlights

Brooks's dissertation research was concerned with how the guardian cells (T-cells) in the blood attack and destroy invading microbes. She showed how natural chemicals in the cell wall of the invading microbes permit the defenders to attach themselves to the invader. When attached, the defenders use other chemicals to dissolve the foreign microbe. Brooks completed this research and was awarded her doctoral degree from Ohio State in 1977.

After her graduation, she moved into other research areas. Her first job was at Kentucky State University in Frankfort, Kentucky. Dr. Brooks took the leadership role in a special program of community health studies, which brought together the resources of both the university and the statewide social service agencies in order to help improve the lives of rural Kentuckians. For three years, Dr. Brooks worked on the nutritional needs of the elderly. Dr. Brooks's concern was to assess the amount of essential minerals—such as iron and potassium—taken in by the elderly. The first step was to develop methods to measure the intake of these minerals that did not require verbal reports. Using laboratory animals, she found that the traces of minerals found in their hair correlated to the amount of such substances stored in the animal's tissues. This meant that tests on hair could be accurate indicators of the minerals consumed by these animals. After she had determined this correlation, she turned to the measurement of minerals in the diet of elderly people. Her examination of the test subjects' hair did indicate the amount of the mineral intake in their diets. In this way, medical problems caused by improper diet could be diagnosed. However, Dr. Brooks's research revealed that other, important medical problems of the elderly could not be detected by tests on the subjects' hair. In short, the logic behind the new tests was good but the practical consequences were limited.

In 1981, Dr. Brooks decided to take a position at the University of Maryland Eastern Shore (UMES) in Princess Anne, Maryland. Her job included conducting her own research and guiding the research of students. She would also be responsible for developing the organization of new research programs at UMES and guiding the project proposal through funding agencies in the government and the private sector.

The direction of her own research changed again when she moved to UMES. She focused on the relationship between certain microbes and the family of plants that includes peas and beans. Peas, beans, and other legumes typically welcome the presence of certain microbes in the outer layer of their roots. These microbes form colonies that force the roots to swell, making small root blisters or nodules. The microbes in these nodules absorb nitrogen from the air. This nitrogen is transformed by the microbes into compounds that the plant can absorb and use to construct amino acids in its cells. These amino acids are used to build plant protein and consequently make the plant more nutritious.

Farmers who grow these plants need to apply little additional fertilizer to the soil. In the case of legumes, such as soybeans, the crop is completely independent of outside sources of nitrogen. In fact, growing such crops actually enriches the soil rather than depletes it. Unfortunately, crops such as corn and wheat do not provide the right conditions to attract the helpful nitrogen-gathering microbes. Some of the crop plants can support these microbes, but the amount of nitrogen generated by the microbes in those plants is less than needed for their most efficient growth. Consequently, Dr. Brooks has worked on ways to increase the productivity of those microbes that draw nitrogen from the air.

During the academic year of 1984–85, she visited Togo and Senegal in West Africa. She conducted research on microbes found in the roots of a particular legume, one of the African groundnuts. Dr. Brooks helped to increase the ability of those microbes to capture nitrogen and, therefore, improve the food value of that plant. In early 1988, she spent time in Cameroon, also in West Africa. By using modern laboratory techniques, she was able to help local scientists and agronomists improve productivity of a whole range of food crops.

Dr. Brooks has also focused her research on the creation of crop plant species that have a built-in resistance to insects and other predators. She has sought to locate plants that have good insect resistance and to transfer that trait to crop plants. If the naturally resistant plant is of the same species as the valuable crop plant, selective breeding can sometimes provide the desired results. However, if the pest-resistant plant is of a completely different species, one must use genetic engineering, in which the genes with the desired trait are selectively transferred to the other plant. This is a difficult procedure because the key gene

or genes must be identified and separated from thousands of other genes. The key gene must then be implanted in a carrier, such as a virus, and be introduced into cells of a young plant. All this work is done at the submicroscopic level.

In some cases, insect resistance can be provided by microbes, which cause bacterial or other infections within the insect. Special bacteria, lethal to insects but harmless to plants or other animals, are encouraged to grow on plants that are vulnerable to insect attack. The bacterial microbes then can serve as a defence against these insect pests.

To perform such cutting-edge techniques requires constant study. Part of that study comes from reading the current scientific literature but some comes from pursuing further education. To improve her research skills, Dr. Brooks has regularly attended special short courses at the University of Maryland College Park, the Universities of Minnesota and Wisconsin, and other institutions in the Midwest.

Dr. Brooks has received a host of honors and awards for her community service as well as her research accomplishments. Her two most treasured awards recognize her ability as an outstanding mentor to her students. Because of the guidance and friendship that she received from her own teachers, Dr. Brooks is well aware of the importance of this support. In 1988, she received an award at a White House ceremony hosted by President Ronald Reagan. The ceremony was part of the first annual White House Initiative on Historically Black Colleges and Universities. Faculty members from these institutions were chosen for recognition because of their "exemplary achievements as educators, researchers and role models." The second award came in 1990 from the Maryland Association for Higher Education. Dr. Brooks continues to receive recognition for her exceptional ability to counsel her students and champion their concerns.

George Campbell, Jr.

Born: December 2, 1945, in Richmond, Virginia

Status: President, National Action Council for Minorities in Engineering, New York, New York

Education:

Bachelor of Science degree, Drexel University, Philadelphia, Pennsylvania, 1968

Doctor of Philosophy degree, Syracuse University, Syracuse, New York, 1977

Research Area: Physics

Early Years

During the holiday season of 1945, George Campbell's parents traveled to Goochland, Virginia, from their home in New York City to visit relatives. George was the Campbell family's early Christmas present. He was born in near-by Richmond, the closest city with a hospital that accepted African American patients.

When George was still in elementary school, his parents separated, and his mother took him and his younger brother, Robert, to live in Philadelphia, Pennsylvania. There, they found a large circle of supportive relatives, but they were extremely short on money. George's father provided no financial assistance, and his mother earned little as a domestic worker.

In Philadelphia, George experienced the tensions of street gangs and the conflicts between gang members and the police. He had problems with teachers and other students and began to develop a reputation as a "disruptive" child. In junior high school, he was suspended several times and only narrowly escaped being sent to a correctional institution for boys.

But George had three things going for him. First, he had a high level of natural ability and scored well on tests and examinations of all kinds. Second, his mother supported him whenever he was in trouble at school or with the police. Third, and perhaps the most important, George had an excellent relationship with his grandfather in Virginia. George spent many summers on the 120-acre farm owned by his mother's parents. His grandfather was a strong family patriarch, who had little formal education but an unquenchable thirst for knowledge. He was a powerful male role model for George.

George's mother was convinced that at least some of his behavior problems occurred because he was bored by school work that did not challenge him. She had George apply to the program established for talented and gifted students that was offered at Philadelphia's Central High School. Some of George's junior high school teachers were opposed to providing such an opportunity for a young man whom they regarded as disrespectful. In spite of this opposition, and probably because of his good test scores, George was accepted into the special program.

George fell in love with classic western literature and philosophy. He read everything assigned and more—from the writings of Homer to those of Robert Frost. He also discovered at Central the basis for an organized view of politics and modern history through the writings of Langston Hughes, Ralph Ellison, James Baldwin, Richard Wright, Martin Luther King, Jr., Malcolm X, and Kwame Nkrumah. George also won letters in track, cross country, and fencing. He was a distance runner on the city championship track team, and in 1963, he won a silver medal in the Pennsylvania State High School Fencing Championship Tournament.

Each year, Central High School was visited by a representative from the Bell Telephone Laboratories located in nearby New Brunswick, New Jersey. Bell Labs hoped to encourage Central students to consider careers in science or technology, and they arranged for one of their scientists to demonstrate the lab's new accomplishments. These science demonstrations had their intended impact on George. He saw his future career as one in which he utilized a combination of mathematics, physical science, and the visual arts.

Higher Education

Even though his family was still suffering from financial problems, George Campbell took it for granted that he would attend college. Fortunately, he won a four-year Simon Guggenheim Scholarship in 1963, which would pay tuition and fees at the college or university of his choice. For a number of reasons, Campbell chose Drexel University. He had decided that engineering would allow him to combine his special interests with his future career, and Drexel specializes in training engineers. Also Drexel is located in Philadelphia, Campbell's home town. He could save money by living at home. Finally, Drexel had a well-structured work-study program. University staff members helped students arrange internships with major industrial firms, where the students could earn money and learn new ideas in practical, real-world situations. Part of the internship had to be served during the regular school year, which extended the degree program at Drexel to five years rather than the standard four years.

After completing his first year of study with high marks, Campbell was hired as a "co-op" intern by the International Harvester Company of Chicago, Illinois. This company manufactures heavy construction equipment, farm machinery, and trucks. Campbell was given many different work assignments, each of which provided a valuable, learning experience. In one project, he worked on the design of a new diesel engine. In another, he investigated the methods used to control the flow of parts to the product assembly line. It is essential that the right parts show up at the assembly line in the right quantities at just the right time. If the timing is incorrect, production slows and the company can lose money.

In his third year at Drexel, George Campbell discovered that he had a strong interest in basic research. Consequently, he changed his major course of study from engineering to physics, which led his employers to reassign Campbell to the Corporate Research Center in Hinsdale, Illinois, a Chicago suburb. There, he conducted studies on the effects of stress, a condition which causes failure in the metal and plastic parts used by the company. During his final year, the International Harvester Company offered Campbell a permanent job, but he had already decided to begin graduate school as soon as possible.

George Campbell graduated from Drexel in 1968.

In the summer of 1968, Campbell became active in the antiwar and community development movements. Because of these concerns, he spent the summer working at the Young Great Society offices in Philadelphia on a community development project. At the end of the summer, he married Mary Schmidt, whom he had known since his high school days. The new Mrs. Campbell had graduated from Swarthmore College a few months earlier. Then, just as he was about to enter graduate school, he received his military draft notice. Campbell opposed the war in Viet Nam on moral grounds, and consequently, he applied for conscientious objector status. The rules that apply to a designation as conscientious objector include a requirement for two years of civilian service that "supports the national interest and makes a contribution to humanitarian causes." George and Mary decided that they would seek an assignment in Africa. They were offered teaching positions at the Nkumbi International College in Kabwe, Zambia. This facility is supported by the African American Institute of New York City and provides degree programs for young Africans, many of whom were refugees from political oppression.

George Campbell was assigned to teach in the mathematics department but soon saw that there was a greater need to strengthen the programs in physics and chemistry. He designed new courses of study and drew up the plans for a new laboratory. In his free time, he built a darkroom for photography in the chemistry laboratory and coached the college basketball team. Furthermore, he sought to give these young Africans an understanding of what was happening politically and economically in the third world and elsewhere. In 1970, his first son, Garikai, was born. Such an event is a major social occa-

sion in Zambian society, and the entire local community participated in the celebration of the birth.

In 1971, George Campbell and his family returned to the United States so that both George and Mary could begin their graduate studies at Syracuse University in upstate New York. He began his Ph.D. program in physics, and she began her Ph.D. studies in art history. The university had a distinguished faculty in both fields. In addition, the town of Syracuse and its university had a history of progressive ideas and politics. Around the time of the Civil War, Syracuse had been a center of the abolitionist movement and an important way station on the "underground railroad" that helped slaves reach freedom in Canada.

Although the physics department had not had a Black graduate student or faculty member until Campbell arrived, the atmosphere was already enlightened and international in tone. Because Campbell felt comfortable in that environment, he was inspired to spend some of his time painting in addition to studying. Soon, Campbell's work began to be included in museum exhibitions and to sell on the art market.

Meanwhile, George Campbell took his physics courses and tried to decide in which area of physics he wished to do his research. The scientific emphasis in the department was on the mathematical representations that are basic to modern theoretical physics. These mathematical "models" are particularly important to physicists, since they are the only way to describe the smallest objects known to exist, the elusive quarks and leptons. Quarks and leptons can be detected only by their reactions with other tiny particles called hadrons. These reactions can be produced only with a cyclotron. After an experiment is completed within a cyclotron, physicists try to understand the recorded observations by entering the measurements into the equations of a mathematical model. Campbell's first undertaking in this area of physics was conducted by a team that included Veronica Rabl, a post-doctoral student, and Professor Kameshar Wali, the team leader. The team's goal was to study the form of the mathematical model that would be needed if there were four quarks in nature rather than the three that had been identified. The outcome of the study was George Campbell's first published scientific report. This work turned out to be particularly timely because the physicists at Stanford Linear Accelerator Center in California and the Brookhaven National Laboratories in New York had just observed signs of the presence of a fourth quark in their experiments.

George Campbell wrote two more theory papers on the fourth quark under Wali's supervision. In 1977, he completed his research project and was awarded his doctoral degree from Syracuse. That summer, after his graduation ceremonies, he taught undergraduate physics courses at Syracuse, while he was negotiating the terms of a job at Bell Laboratories in New Brunswick, New Jersey. The opportunity was particularly appealing to Campbell for two reasons. First, he remembered his positive experience with the lectures by Bell Labs scientists when he was still a student at Central High School. Second, the laboratories were close to the Studio Museum in Harlem, where Mary had taken a job as the executive director.

Career Highlights

Bell Laboratories was one of the most unusual research organizations in the world when Dr. Campbell joined their scientific staff. Bell Labs is owned by the American Telephone and Telegraph Company which, at the time, provided almost all the local and long distance telephone services in the United States. Therefore, Bell Labs was will-

ing to invest in more research than similar companies that had to compete in the marketplace. Several of the most famous and most accomplished scientists in the world have worked at Bell Labs, and over the years their employees have won seven Nobel Prizes.

When Dr. Campbell joined this organization in 1977, he became interested in the physics of orbital space, an area 23,000 miles above the earth. At that great distance, the orbits of satellites—set to orbit on a 24 hour cycle—appear to be stationary when viewed from the earth. Before scientists could safely put a communications satellite into orbit, they needed to determine whether the natural radiation at that altitude would damage the delicate electronic parts of the satellite.

Dr. Campbell found that the weakest parts of the satellite were the solar cells that convert sunlight into the electrical power needed to run the systems. He determined that the entire power supply apparatus, including the backup batteries that become the power source when the satellite orbits into the earth's shadow twice each year, needed to be redesigned. Dr. Campbell and his team developed a power supply system that would work for at least ten years—three years longer than the former system. His power supply system proved successful in the Telstar 3 satellite and continued to function well beyond the ten-year target period.

Soon, Dr. Campbell's reputation was known to important government agencies. In 1980, he was selected by the National Science Foundation to serve as a visiting professor at Bowie State College in suburban Maryland. This college, just a few miles from Washington, D.C., has had a long tradition of serving minority students. At Bowie State, now a branch campus of the University of

Maryland system, Dr. Campbell was able to refresh and adapt some of the ideas about teaching that he had developed in Zambia.

Scientists from other countries were also becoming aware of Dr. Campbell's work. He was chosen to work with the telephone companies of Japan and Great Britain to help develop technical standards and methods of linking high capacity information channels across international boundaries. In a related activity, Dr. Campbell served his country as a delegate to the world body—now under the United Nations in Switzerland— that works to achieve worldwide agreements on international telephone calls.

In the mid-1980s, Dr. Campbell was selected by Bell Labs for the Leadership Continuity Program, a program designed to prepare well-qualified, middle-level managers for advancement into the highest levels of management. Part of the program entails participation in advanced management courses at Yale University, in New Haven, Connecticut. Dr. Campbell found this experience to be particularly valuable, and after completing the program, he was elected to represent his class on the Alumni Board of Yale's School of Organization and Management.

Dr. Campbell also became more and more involved in community activities in New Jersey and New York City. In 1989, he was introduced to the National Action Council for Minorities in Engineering, Inc., or NACME, by Dr. Morris Tanenbaum. Dr. Tanenbaum was a distinguished Bell Labs scientist who had become vice chairman of AT&T and was also a member of the NACME board of directors.

Founded in the early 1970s by a group of executive officers from major high-tech corporations, NACME's mission is to lead a national effort—in collaboration with the National Academy of Engineering and leaders of the minority communities—to increase the enrollment of under-represented groups in engineering education programs. By 1980, NACME had become the nation's largest non-government source of scholarships for minority students in engineering and was supporting 10 percent of all such students.

In 1989, NACME needed a new president, and Dr. Campbell was just the right person for the job. Previous attempts to help minority students succeed in engineering degree programs had focused on their financial problems. Dr. Campbell saw that financial aid alone was not enough to correct the situation. Psychological and social support was also needed. New methods of faculty orientation were developed, and as a result of these and other coordinated efforts around the United States, the number of minority students who stay in college has doubled in the past few years.

While these programs were being implemented, Dr. Campbell realized that other areas of minority science education needed further development. Research, information, and public awareness programs have expanded through the Public Broadcasting System, video tapes for broadcast and small audience presentation, and the publication of a new magazine. Dr. Campbell has recently made a major investment of NACME resources to produce science demonstration programs for use in elementary schools. He is aware that many minority students are lost to the scientific and technical professions before they reach high school. Direct efforts toward better vocational guidance for minority students need to be expanded to the elementary school level. It is vital that the significance of this vocational guidance be understood by parents, teachers, counselors, and, most important, by the young students, themselves.

George R. Carruthers

Born: October 1, 1939, in Cincinnati, Ohio

Status: Senior Astrophysicist, U.S. Naval Research Laboratory, Washington, D.C.

Education:

Bachelor of Science degree, University of Illinois, Champaign-Urbana, Illinois, 1961

Master of Science degree, University of Illinois, 1962

Doctor of Philosophy degree, University of Illinois, 1964

Research Area: Astrophysics

Early Years

George Carruthers was the oldest of four children. His father, also named George, worked as a civil engineer for the U.S. Army Air Corps (later known as the U.S. Air Force) during and after the years of World War II. When George was seven years old, his family moved to Milford, Ohio, a suburb just east of Cincinnati. It was in this small town atmosphere that George attended grade school and first became interested in science. George's initial interest in space exploration came from reading comic books. He was particularly inspired by Buck Rogers, the fictional astronaut who was the first comic book character to go to Mars.

George quickly expanded his interests and began to read his father's books on astronomy. George's father encouraged these interests and also tried to make sure that the young boy realized how difficult it would be to become a space explorer. He insisted that George study all parts of science and mathematics and bought him more books, so that he could go beyond the work in his science courses at school.

By the time he was ten years old, George began working on projects that were indicative of things he would study later in his career. His first big project was to build his own telescope. He used the money he earned working as a delivery boy to order lenses from a mail order company that advertised in boys' magazines. When the lenses arrived, he mounted them in a cardboard tube that he found around the house. He was delighted that the telescope worked so well. The more stars George could see through his homemade telescope, the more enthusiastic he became.

Unfortunately, when George was twelve, his father died. The financial situation for the family changed drastically. George's mother, Sophia, decided that it would be best for the family to move to Chicago, Illinois, where she had relatives. When they were settled in Chicago, Sophia went to work for the U.S. Post Office.

George enrolled in Englewood High School in Chicago. The faculty soon recognized George's potential. The science teachers, in particular, encouraged George's interests in science just as his father had done. They introduced him to the wide range of resources in the Chicago area such as the Field Museum, the Museum of Science and Industry, and the Chicago Planetarium. They also helped him with his telescope projects. Soon, George had designed and built a bigger model so that he could enter the local science fair competition. His new telescope won first prize.

Higher Education

In 1957, George Carruthers entered the College of Engineering at the University of Illinois in Champaign-Urbana. He took the basic courses in science and mathematics that enabled him to begin his study of aeronautical engineering. His mind leaped skyward. He hoped to combine the program in aeronautical engineering with the program in astronomy, so that he could study the subjects together. Scientists had just begun to question the possibility of studying astronomy from space, and there was already talk on television and in the newspapers about the prospect of launching both manned and unmanned artificial satellites into space. Carruthers saw that these satellites could serve as space-born astronomy stations. Telescopes of all kinds would work better outside the blanket of the earth's atmosphere, and the view of space would be clearer on all wavelengths. The officials at the College of Engineering agreed with Carruthers and helped him plan the combined program.

After completing his undergraduate degree, Carruthers continued in the graduate program at the University of Illinois. He now began to broaden his interests. For example, one of his first projects in graduate school was to experiment with a new type of rocket engine called a plasma engine. Plasma is a super-hot gas composed of only one kind of atom. Conventional rocket fuel burns when it is mixed with liquid oxygen, but Carruthers discovered that when electricity is used to heat helium to a very high temperature, the molecules of the helium gas begin to come apart. This gas, as plasma, would be expelled

through the engine, giving the space vehicle motive power.

Carruthers was also working on another problem of space craft design. When the space craft descends into the earth's atmosphere at high speed, the friction between the skin of the craft and the gases that make up the atmosphere creates enough heat to damage the outer skin of the craft. The gas molecules can become so hot they turn into a plasma such as is created in a plasma jet. Carruthers saw the connection between these conditions and began to analyze the problem of the super-hot gases.

While he worked on these projects, Carruthers was teaching a beginning course in astrophysics, and he determined to make the course as interesting as possible. He made a demonstration model of a plasma engine complete with a high-intensity electrical power supply, so the motor would actually work. Carruthers' professors were impressed with his model and with the way his knowledge of aeronautics and astronomy benefited the students.

Career Highlights

As soon as Dr. Carruthers graduated with his doctoral degree, he was hired by the U.S. Navy to work in Washington, D.C., at their Naval Research Laboratory, a famous site for high-quality research. He has been there ever since.

Dr. Carruthers's first project as a navy scientist was to design a new space camera that could measure ultraviolet light. Ultra-violet light is of particular interest to astronomers, because it can be used to determine which atoms and molecules are in the thin gas between the stars. For example, scientists can use ultraviolet light to identify the atoms and molecules in the gases that make up a comet's tail. Once the scientists have this information, they can determine which chemicals make up the solid portion of the comet by watching the way the sun's light is reflected off the gases in the tail.

It took Dr. Carruthers and a team of other scientists, engineers, and technicians several years to design and build this complicated camera; and once they had finished, the camera functioned exactly as they hoped it would. Even before all the tests on the new camera had been completed, Dr. Carruthers was presented with the Arthur S. Fleming Award for scholarly accomplishment by a local Washington, D.C., organization. And soon after the completion of this outstanding project, Dr. Carruthers was awarded the Exceptional Scientific Achievement Medal by the National Aeronautics and Space Administration (NASA). That same year (1972), the camera was taken to the moon aboard Apollo 16. Pictures taken of interstellar gases and the earth's atmosphere were read by a computer when the camera was returned to earth. For the first time, the concentration of the pollutants, such as carbon monoxide, in the air surrounding large cities could be determined for many cities at the same time.

The success of the Apollo 16 missions proved the value of a camera that could "see" ultraviolet light. In recent years, cameras designed and assembled by Dr. Carruthers's teams have been taken into space aboard the space shuttle, where they have been used to determine the thickness of the ozone layer in the stratosphere around the earth. It is important that the government officials have an accurate scientific measure of the amount of ozone in the atmosphere, because if the ozone layer, which filters out harmful portions of the sun's ultraviolet radiation, were not there, some plant growth would be stunted and people would be more likely to get skin cancer. Scientists believe the ozone layer is reduced by polluting gases that contain chlorine, the type of gases used in almost all air conditioners and refrigerators. Without these

measurements, the government cannot devise fair and efficient environmental regulations. The cameras made by Dr. Carruthers's teams are of great help in making these measurements.

Dr. Carruthers has also helped pioneer the development of electronic telescopes for use aboard satellites put into orbit by NASA. These telescopes use electronics to increase the intensity of the light that has come from distant stars and from the planets in our own solar system. When the light is transformed into electrical signals, the image can be transmitted back to earth and displayed on a television tube.

His newest cameras are computer controlled and the information that comes through the lenses can be read directly by the computer. Such a camera will also be used to help determine how new stars and planets are formed from the dust and gas that makes up most of the universe.

While Dr. Carruthers's main job is doing research and designing new cameras for use in space, he continues to teach. He recently spent a year teaching astrophysics at Johns Hopkins University in Baltimore, Maryland.

In pursuing his interests in education, Dr. Carruthers regularly visits high schools and grade schools in the Washington, D.C., area, encouraging young minority people to study mathematics and science. These visits further the work he is doing with an organization called SMART, an acronym for Science, Mathematics, Aerospace Research and Technology. The organization, most of whose members are from minority groups, sets up training workshops for both local students and teachers.

Dr. Carruthers works with other minority scientists and engineers through an organization called the National Technical Association. This organization provides career information and other forms of support for minority scientists around the country. During the 1970s, Dr. Carruthers served as the editor-in-chief of the magazine published by the association. This magazine has contributed to the establishment of a communication network serving to bind minority scientists into a community. In 1977, Dr. Carruthers was presented with the Samuel Cheevers Award sponsored annually by the association for his work to improve the mutual support among minority scientists.

In spite of all his achievements and awards, Dr. George Carruthers is noted by his colleagues as a shy and humble person. He would rather give credit to his team of coworkers than take credit for himself. His motto for himself and his students "Not even the sky is the limit to what a person can accomplish" has served both Dr. Carruthers and the world community in this space age.

Benjamin S. Carson, Sr.

Born: September 18, 1951, in Detroit, Michigan

Status: Associate Professor, Johns Hopkins Medical Institution, Baltimore, Maryland

Education:

Bachelor of Arts degree, Yale University, New Haven, Connecticut, 1973

Doctor of Medicine degree, University of Michigan, Ann Arbor, Michigan, 1977

Research Area: Physiology

Early Years

Ben Carson was eight years old when his father and mother divorced. Until that time, he had a happy childhood. His father had worked in an automobile factory and the family had been doing well financially. They owned their own home in central Detroit, Michigan. After the divorce, Ben's mother was given ownership of the house. However, without the father's pay coming in, Mrs. Carson could not afford the mortgage payments. She had to rent the house and use the rent money to pay the mortgage.

Ben, his older brother, Curtis, and their mother moved to Boston, Massachusetts, to live with Mrs. Carson's older sister. They lived in a poor neighborhood, and Ben was frightened by the rats that lived in the back alleys behind his home.

Ben's mother worked very hard as a housemaid for some prosperous families in Boston. Although she had had few educational opportunities, she believed in the importance of education for her children. She told her sons to concentrate on their school work. Mrs. Carson was also a religious person and took Ben and Curtis to church every week. One Sunday, Ben was inspired by a sermon about a missionary doctor. He decided then and there that he would become a physician.

After two years in Boston, the Carson family moved back to Detroit. They still could not afford to live in their own home and rented a small apartment in a racially mixed neighborhood.

In Boston, Ben and his brother had gone to a small church-sponsored school. When Ben returned to the Detroit school system, he was behind his classmates in all of his lessons. He received the lowest grades of any student in the fifth grade. Although he did not know it, one of his problems was his poor eyesight. He was very nearsighted and had difficulty reading the blackboard from his desk. Fortunately, the school system provided routine vision tests and Ben's problem was discovered. The school gave him his first pair of glasses. From then on, his grades gradually improved.

Ben began to read science books in his spare time. He especially liked to read about animals and other nature topics and learned to identify many different rocks and plants. The new glasses and his increased reading worked wonders. By the time he reached the seventh grade, his school work had improved dramatically. Ben had become the best student in his class.

Even though Ben was doing very well academically in junior high, he still faced problems. Some students, and even some teachers, were upset because an African American boy got the best grades. Another problem was his clothing. Ben did not have enough money to dress well, and other boys teased him about his out-of-fashion clothes. Eventually, his mother was able to give him some money to buy new clothes.

Ben wanted so much to be accepted that he started hanging out with a gang. His grades began to fall, and he had arguments with his mother. One day he got in a fight with a friend. He was so angry that he struck at his friend with a knife. Fortunately, the knife blade broke on the friend's belt buckle and nobody was hurt. Ben was ashamed. Even

though the fight had been over nothing, he had lost his temper and self-control. He turned to his family's religion for help and vowed never again to lose control of himself.

Ben's brother Curtis also provided help and support. Although Curtis was only two years older, Ben looked up to him for guidance. When Curtis joined the Reserve Officer Training Corps (ROTC) in high school, he did very well. Later, Ben decided to join and try to do even better.

The ROTC helped Ben develop leadership ability. After only three years, he became the highest-ranking student cadet in the Detroit area. The ROTC also helped solve Ben's problems with fashionable clothes because the cadets wore uniforms to school.

Higher Education

In the late 1960s, many colleges and universities began actively seeking talented black students. Because Ben Carson had done so well at school and in the ROTC, he was offered a scholarship to West Point, the U.S. Army's prestigious academy. He was also offered financial support at the University of Michigan. However, when the time came to apply for college, Carson had enough money for only one application fee. He chose to apply to Yale University in New Haven, Connecticut. He was very pleased when they accepted his application.

It took Carson a while to adjust to his new life at Yale. At first, he tried to follow the pattern of study he had used in high school, postponing serious study until he had to take a test. By using this method, he almost failed his first chemistry test.

Carson had always worked in the summer, and he continued to do so throughout his college years. After his first year at Yale, he found a job with the Wayne County Highway Department in Michigan. He supervised a crew of boys who collected trash along the edge of the main highway. Carson used his leadership skills, and as a result, his crew collected more trash than any other. They would fill their quota of trash bags before noon each workday and then spent the afternoon at a swimming pool.

In the summer of 1972, Carson worked on an auto assembly line. Even though he was only a summer employee, his work was so good he was given a job as an inspector. That same summer, he met Candy Rustin at a reception for new Yale students from Michigan. She started at Yale in the fall. Four years later, they were married.

Ben Carson graduated from Yale in 1973 and hoped to begin medical school that fall. This time, he applied to five schools. The University of Michigan in Ann Arbor was the first to admit him, and he accepted immediately. He thought Michigan would be the best school for him.

Carson continued to hold interesting summer jobs. Before starting medical school, he worked in a steel mill and learned to operate a large crane. The work helped give him confidence in his ability to handle delicate controls. After his first year in medical school, he worked as an X-ray technician. This experience later proved useful in his research projects.

In his third year of medical school, Carson completed a very important project. He developed an easier method for brain surgeons to locate hidden parts of the brain. Carson's technique reduced the time of a surgical operation. This success led him to think about becoming a brain surgeon.

In 1977, Ben Carson graduated from medical school at the University of Michigan and began his surgical internship. The standard surgical internship is two years but Dr. Carson was able to finish in only one. He then competed with 130 other people for the one available residency in brain surgery. He won the job and began a four-year residency at the Johns Hopkins University Hospital in Baltimore, Maryland.

In his last year, Dr. Carson began to do research on brain cancer. He developed a way to induce the growth of brain cancer in rabbits. Using this technique, various treatments could be tested on these animals.

Career Highlights

When Dr. Carson finished his residency in brain surgery, he was offered a position on the medical faculty at Johns Hopkins. He wanted to remain there, but he also wanted to see other parts of the world. One of his colleagues, a senior surgeon from the city of Perth, Australia, invited Dr. Carson to return to Australia with him and teach new interns at the Queen Elizabeth II Medical Center. This hospital was the only place in western Australia where difficult brain surgery was being performed.

At first, Dr. Carson was worried because Australia had a bad reputation for racial prejudice. However, he was warmly welcomed in Perth. He and his wife Candy attended church and soon made many friends among the congregation, and everyone was pleased when their first child was born in Australia.

When he was ready to return to the United States, he was uncertain about his next job. Although there was a position open at Johns Hopkins Medical Institution, Dr. Carson was worried that racial prejudice would keep patients away. He wanted to work with children, and he was afraid that other doctors and parents would not have confidence in his skill. Dr. Carson was also concerned about his age. After all, he was only 33 years old. In the end, however, he decided to accept the position at Johns Hopkins.

Dr. Carson soon found that his fears were unfounded. He was given more and more difficult cases. Soon he was helping young patients from all across the United States. He operated on children with brain cancer, severe epileptic seizures, and serious birth defects. For many of these children, Dr. Carson's intervention was their last chance for life.

In 1987, Dr. Carson performed his most famous operation. Earlier that year, a pair of Siamese twins had been born to a family in Germany. The two boys were joined at the backs of their heads and they shared a common network of veins and arteries. The two babies had only a single blood supply for both brains. The operation took 22 hours and the boys received 60 blood transfusions. During the procedure, the twins were cooled from their normal temperature of 98.6 degrees to 68 degrees. This decreased temperature slowed all their bodily functions. The babies were kept unconscious for almost ten days after the surgery. When they finally were allowed to wake up, it soon became clear that the operation had been a great success. The event was widely reported in the media, and Dr. Carson was interviewed on a nationwide TV news program.

Dr. Carson is not always so successful, however. Since he accepts cases which other physicians consider impossible, a small number of his patients do not survive. But over the years, his dedication and skill have offered hope to many families with critically ill children.

George Washington Carver

Born: Sometime in late 1860 or early 1861 near Diamond Grove, Missouri (adequate records not available)

Status: Died, January 5, 1943, at Tuskegee, Alabama

Education:
Bachelor of Science degree, Iowa State Agricultural College (now Iowa State University), Ames, Iowa, 1894

Master of Science degree, Iowa State University, Ames, Iowa, 1896

Research Area: Varied, including Plant Physiology and Biochemistry

Early Years

There are no good records covering the first few years of George Carver's life. He was born in perilous times just before the outbreak of the Civil War. His mother was a slave on the farm of Moses Carver, and his father was apparently a slave on a neighboring farm.

Missouri, a so-called border state, contained many people who were strongly against slavery. Sometimes, anti-slavery supporters would raid the farms of slave holders to help the slaves escape. Moses Carver wanted to keep his "property" intact, so he sent all his slaves to a friend's farm in Arkansas. George was still a baby when Carver's slaves traveled south. After the war, Moses Carver tried to find his slaves—perhaps out of some sense of responsibility. When he arrived in Arkansas, he found that his former slaves, now freed, had left. Only the boy, George, had been left behind, because he was ill with whooping cough. Moses Carver took the boy home to his Missouri farm and nursed him back to health. George stayed on that farm until he was about 12 years old.

Even though he recovered fully from his illness, George Carver's health was always delicate. He could not do much of the hard labor on the farm. Instead, as a way to earn his keep, he learned to cook, sew, and do laundry. During this time, George also learned to read by using an old spelling book, which he soon knew by heart.

George Carver also spent as much of his time as possible walking in the woods and fields, where he collected plants and studied the local animals. He loved to replant the wild flowers in his own hidden garden near the farm house. George had a very strong desire to learn, and he wanted to know about every flower, insect, bird, and animal that he saw.

When George Carver reached the age of twelve or so, his yearning for knowledge became almost overwhelming, but there were very few schools where African Americans were allowed to go. The closest school was in Neosho, Missouri, about a hundred miles from the farm. Even as young and frail as he was, George Carver walked all the way to the school by himself. He found a farmer who would provide him his meals and a place to sleep in return for work. So work he did—both on the farm and in the one-room schoolhouse.

After learning all he could at the little school, George Carver traveled from Missouri to Kansas to go on to high school. While in high school, he harvested wheat, cut wood, and did other jobs to survive. During this time, he continued to collect and study plants, and even began to sketch and paint them. George realized he needed even more education, so he applied to Highland University, a small college in Kansas. His application required comments from his teachers. These comments were so good and his grades were so high that Carver was admitted without an interview. When he arrived at Highland University, however, George was refused admittance because he was Black.

George Carver did not give up. He wanted an education, and he would find a way to get it. He worked on farms in Kansas and saved as much money as possible.

Higher Education

In 1890, at the age of thirty, George Carver was admitted to Simpson College in Indianola, Iowa. He studied biology, mathematics, chemistry, music, and art. His art teacher realized that Carver was very interested in and knowledgeable about plants. As a lucky coincidence, her brother taught botany, the scientific study of plants, at Iowa State Agricultural College. She suggested to George that he apply to that college before taking further courses at Simpson, because Iowa State had better teachers in botany and agricultural chemistry. She wrote a strong letter of recommendation for him, and he was admitted to the college (now Iowa State University) in 1891.

While taking as many science courses as possible, George Carver continued to paint plants and flowers. A few years later, in 1893, four of his paintings were featured at the World's Columbian Exposition in Chicago.

This important fair, a celebration of the 400th anniversary of America's discovery, was very well attended, and the display of Carver's work was good for both his and the college's reputation.

While a college student, Carver worked in the greenhouse and the agriculture laboratory to pay for his tuition. He was also hired as a tutor for Henry A. Wallace, the college president's young son, who, in adulthood, became the secretary of agriculture and, later, vice president of the United States. Their friendship later led to the first successful agricultural extension programs for the education of poor Black farmers in the southern United States, starting in 1900.

Meanwhile, Carver's grades were among the best in his class, and he graduated from Iowa State Agricultural College with high honors. Carver was the first African American to graduate from this college. The head of the botany department said that Carver was one of the most brilliant students he had ever taught, and he offered Carver a job working on agricultural experiments. Carver took the job and began graduate courses in mycology, the specialized study of fungus. George was particularly interested in finding ways to fight fungi that damage plants, and he identified new chemicals to stop the growth of harmful fungus. He was awarded his master's degree from the institution now known as Iowa State University in 1890.

Career Highlights

That same year, Carver received a letter from another famous African American, Booker T. Washington. Washington was the head of the Tuskegee Normal and Industrial Institute, in Tuskegee, Alabama, a school where Black students could earn degrees in many different subjects. Booker T. Washington's goal was to prepare African American students for employment when they graduated. Some studied conventional subjects, such as chemistry, mathematics, agriculture, and biology, while others worked on more applied skills like carpentry, carriage building, or woodworking. Washington asked Carver to be the head of Tuskegee's agriculture department, and in 1896, Carver left Iowa State to go to Tuskegee. Carver's greatest desire was to help Black students learn and advance in society. Toward this end, he taught at Tuskegee for the rest of his life.

When Carver arrived at Tuskegee, he found no test tubes, beakers, or other laboratory equipment. So, he and a group of his students made their own equipment. They used bottles, cups, cans, and whatever they could find. The year after Carver's arrival, the state of Alabama passed a special bill to fund an agriculture station at Tuskegee for the purpose of plant and soil experimentation. Carver was made director of the station and at last was able to buy better equipment for his laboratory. Unfortunately, he was a poor administrator and was forced to step down from the directorship. Carver was not depressed by this decision, because his true interests lay in his research and educational projects. He hoped to find solutions to some of the specific problems faced by African American farmers in the region.

Carver knew that most of the farmers in this part of the South had problems with their soil. He also knew that most farmers grew the same crops every year. The main crops, usually cotton or tobacco, used large portions of the nutrients from the soil, without replenishing them. Carver was aware that certain plants help return important nutrients to the soil. He told his students to teach the farmers to plant beans, peas, peanuts, or some other legume one year and then the regular crop the next two. Using this method, the farmers improved the health and yield of the regular crops. Carver also demonstrated which types of soil and combinations of fertilizers are best for each crop. His studies showed, too, that when the soil is plowed more deeply the plants grow better.

Carver taught these methods to the students at Tuskegee. He also traveled around the region, explaining his farming techniques to poor, uneducated farmers. In order to help as many of these farmers as possible, Carver wrote short pamphlets in simple language, explaining his farming methods. Starting in 1899, Carver and a Tuskegee graduate, who worked as his assistant, traveled further into Alabama to teach good farming skills. These activities became an official extension program the following year.

Not long after starting the extension education program, an insect called the cotton boll weevil migrated from Mexico into the southern part of the United States. This insect ruined so many fields of cotton that farmers were forced to switch to peanuts as their main crop. This change was good for soil restoration and defense against the weevil but not good for the peanut market. Soon there were more peanuts than people could use, and the price of raw peanuts dropped. Carver was concerned that the peanut prices might force the farmers to go back to growing only crops that hurt the soil. Instead of rejecting the peanut as a good source of income, Carver looked for ways to increase the demand for these vegetables. He began inventing products that could be made from peanuts. Some of the over 300 products he invented include peanut butter, vinegar, soap, cheese, milk, instant coffee, and face powder. Carver also invented over 100 products from sweet potatoes, including flour, dyes, ink, and rubber. Carver's creativity did not stop there. He made about 75 products from the pecan nut, found ways to use plant wastes—such as corn stalks—to make cardboard and other useful materials, and invented the means of making paper and insulation from cotton. He also produced many dyes, paints, and inks from

clay, and over 500 different dyes from various types of plants.

Carver received many awards and honors during his life. In 1916, he was elected to the Royal Society of Arts, Manufacturers, and Commerce in Great Britain, and in 1923, the NAACP awarded him the Spingarn Medal. In the early 1920s, Thomas Edison offered Carver a job that paid considerably more money than he was getting at Tuskegee, but Carver declined the offer. He wanted to stay at Tuskegee, where he thought he could do the most good.

Carver did, however, do some of his work outside the Deep South. He worked with Henry Ford in Dearborn, Michigan, developing plastic materials that Ford could use in his cars. Carver also took his educational extension ideas to Liberia, an African country founded by freed slaves from America.

As he grew older, Carver's honors increased. In 1935, he was appointed to help the U.S. Department of Agriculture with its research on plant fungus. Two years later, he was awarded the Franklin Roosevelt Medal for "Distinguished Research in Agricultural Chemistry." In 1940, the International Federation of Architects, Engineers, Chemists, and Technicians chose Carver as Man of the Year for his great work in science and his "distinguished service to humanity."

During his long career, Carver did not seem interested in making money. Out of about 500 products, Carver patented only three: one was a way to make cosmetics, and the other two were ways to make dyes and paints from clay. When he died, he left his life savings to start the George Washington Carver Research Foundation. He hoped that the foundation would provide a way for others to continue his research and programs of education. Although Carver was born in the middle of the nineteenth century, his major contributions to human knowledge and welfare came in the early twentieth century and, indeed, they continue to echo today—less than a decade from the beginning of the twenty-first century.

Emmett W. Chappelle

Born: October 24, 1925, in Phoenix, Arizona

Status: Physical Scientist, National Aeronautics and Space Administration

Education:

Associate of Arts degree, Phoenix College, Phoenix, Arizona, 1947

Bachelor of Science degree, University of California, Berkeley, California, 1950

Master of Science degree, University of Washington, Seattle, Washington, 1954

Research Area: Biochemistry

Early Years

In 1925, when Emmett Chappelle was born, Phoenix, Arizona, was a small town with only a few African Americans. Emmett, his two older brothers and younger sister, and his parents lived at the edge of town on a small farm where they grew cotton and tended a small herd of milk cows. The Chappelles made very little money, and the farm had no electricity until Emmett was 12 years old.

Emmett began school at a one-room country school, where all the students were African American. He then went into the city of Phoenix, where he attended a segregated school that was part of Phoenix Union High School district. He graduated at the top of his class of 25 students.

In 1942, immediately after he graduated from high school, Emmett was drafted into the U.S. Army. Because of his good grades in high school, Emmett was assigned to the Army Specialized Training Program. In this program, young men were given college-level courses in technical subjects. The army needed junior officers who knew some engineering. Unfortunately, the program was closed down before Emmett could finish his training, and he was reassigned to an all-Black infantry division.

This division, the 92nd Infantry Division, landed in Italy in 1944. The U.S. Army was fighting German Army units north of Rome on the Arno River. Emmett Chappelle was wounded twice as the division fought bravely to liberate Genoa, the city in which Columbus had been born 500 years before.

The war in Europe ended in the spring of 1945. Emmett's division stayed on as an occupation force in northern Italy, and he did not return to the United States until January of 1946.

As soon as he came home, Emmett entered a two-year program in electrical engineering at Phoenix College. The technical courses he had taken while in the army gave him a background for his studies, and he did very well at the college.

Higher Education

After Emmett Chappell finished his associate of arts degree in 1947, he married his childhood sweetheart, Rosemary Phillips. They both knew that Emmett would need more education to reach his career goals, so in the fall of 1947, he started his engineering studies at the University of California at Berkeley. The GI Bill of Rights, a government program which provides educational support for war veterans, paid his tuition and provided a small monthly income of $165.

To remain eligible for financial aid, Chappelle had to enroll in classes for every semester—fall, spring, and summer. The engineering courses in summer school were not attractive to Chappelle, because the short summer semester did not allow enough time to complete the assigned projects. Consequently, he took courses in other subjects during the summers. He began to explore course work in biology. He soon found that he enjoyed his biology courses far more than his engineering ones. He decided to change his whole program. To catch up with the other biology students, Chappelle worked an extra year to complete his degree. He graduated in 1950.

After finishing his degree program at the University of California, Chappelle took a teaching job at Meharry Medical College in Nashville, Tennessee. For two years, he taught biochemistry to nursing students and found time to continue his own research projects. Chappelle was studying the workings of red blood cells, especially how the iron from molecules in these cells is recycled. As a red blood cell dies, the iron molecules are released into the liquid part of the blood. When new cells are formed, these iron molecules are absorbed and reused by the new cells. Chappelle was able to trace the pathway of these molecules by using radioactive iron. The amount of this iron could be measured in the organs and bodily fluids at each stage of recycling.

He also explored the problem of anaphylactic shock, which is caused when a person or animal has a strong allergic reaction, and which can be fatal. Chappelle discovered that during anaphylactic shock the body releases a chemical that causes a reaction in the body similar to asthma. The air tubes in the lungs contract so that the victim cannot breath properly. In these studies, Emmett Chappelle again used radioactive iron as a way of tracing the steps in the biological process.

His reports were published in highly respected scientific magazines, and other biologists became interested in his work. He soon began receiving offers from graduate schools. Professor Harlan Wood invited Emmett Chappelle to come to Western Reserve University in Cleveland, Ohio. However, Chappelle chose the University of Washington in Seattle, so that he could study with Professor Frank Hunnekes, a famous biochemist.

Chappelle entered the graduate school at the University of Washington in the fall of 1952 and focused on new research projects. In particular, his research on the amino acids that form proteins when linked together, demonstrated that one amino acid can be converted into a different amino acid by the introduction of a particular enzyme.

Emmett Chappelle received his master's degree from Washington in 1954 and then continued his graduate studies at Stanford University in Palo Alto, California. He worked there for four years. In the last two years (1956–58), he held a full-time research job in Stanford's chemistry department. While there, he found a key enzyme for the production of the amino acid called glycine. Chappelle determined that this amino acid is produced both in plants and animals by exactly the same enzyme. He extracted the enzyme from cabbage leaves and compared it to an enzyme produced in the brain of laboratory white rats. They were identical.

While still at Stanford University, Emmett Chappelle also discovered a chemical that could split protein molecules in a predictable way. Proteins are long, twisted chains of amino acids, and Mr. Chappelle's chemical could clip off the amino acids at the tip ends of the chain. The clipped off amino acid molecules could then be changed from an amino acid to another form of molecule. These new forms were aldehydes that could be easily separated and measured.

When used carefully, the chemical clipper could help research scientists determine the weight and composition of a protein. It could also be used to find out whether the particular protein had one, two, or three twisted strands. While Chappelle did not receive a degree from Stanford, his work was recognized and applauded by others in the community of biochemists.

Career Highlights

In 1958, Mr. Chappelle decided to leave Stanford and focus on a new direction for his research. He and his family moved from California to Maryland, where he joined the staff at the Research Institute for Advanced Studies in Baltimore. The institute is a division of the Martin Marrietta Corporation. This corporation is famous for designing airplanes and space craft, in particular the space craft used to land men on the moon.

Mr. Chappelle's work at the Research Institute was aimed at the regulation of a safe air supply for the astronauts. The air in a space craft can be polluted by carbon monoxide, the same poisonous gas that comes from automobile exhaust pipes. Mr. Chappelle discovered that growing plants can absorb the deadly gas. He found that even tiny, one-celled plants, such as green algae, can transform carbon monoxide to carbon dioxide. These small, light-weight plants could be easily transported in a space craft, while at the same time maintaining a safe oxygen supply for the astronauts.

In 1963, Mr. Chappelle transferred to the Hazelton Laboratories in Falls Church, Virginia, an organization that held several research contracts with the National Aeronautics and Space Administration. The goal of one of their research contracts was to detect life on Mars. Mr. Chappelle worked with a team to design the instruments that would go to Mars aboard the Viking space craft. One of these instruments would be used to scrape up a sample of Martian soil. The soil would then be tested to detect any tiny, one-celled creatures.

Mr. Chappelle also devised a plan to analyze the Martian soil that had been retrieved. He designed a test using a combination of chemicals—two produced by fireflies and a third common to all living creatures—that gave off measurable light when mixed with material containing living cells.

In 1975, when the Viking probes were finally launched, no living creatures were detected in the Martian soil. Even though Mr. Chappelle's techniques were not used in the Viking probe, he soon adapted his ideas for use in other projects.

While working at Hazelton, he became interested in helping medical researchers detect certain kinds of cells that might be found in bodily fluids—for instance, cancer cells in the blood. Mr. Chappelle believed that under certain conditions the firefly chemicals might cause such cells to light up during an analysis. He fed the chemicals to bacteria in the laboratory. Each bacteria cell absorbed a tiny quantity of the chemicals and gave off a small amount of light. Using this method, a chemist could tell how many cells were present in a test sample by measuring the intensity of the light.

In 1966, Mr. Chappelle transferred jobs again. He took a position with the National Aeronautics and Space Administration (NASA) at the Goddard Space Flight Center in Greenbelt, Maryland. He continued to study how single-cell creatures give off small amounts of light. Sometimes such light can be seen without special instruments. For instance, small ocean creatures called plankton shine when they are stirred up by wave action, which is why ocean waves often appear to sparkle at night. Mr. Chappelle found that other single-cell creatures also shine by themselves. His studies showed that the number of bacteria in drinking water can be measured by the amount of light the bacteria give off. This technique is routinely used by Fremont, California, to ensure that their drinking water meets certain standards of purity.

Mr. Chappelle also discovered that even plants growing in a farmer's field give off light. The brightest light comes from the fastest growing plants and the dimmest light from the slowest growing ones. By measuring this light early in the growing season, farmers can determine the health of their new crops. It is also possible to map which crops are growing in which fields. Each variety of plant gives off a slightly different color of light, and large areas can be analyzed by using orbiting satellites. The pictures from space can show how productive the crop is or whether it has been harvested.

Soon, Mr. Chappelle added another concept to his technique of measuring light given off by plant cells. He found that by using a laser, chemists can take more accurate measurements. Lasers also cause some cells to produce more light. Apparently, the laser acts somewhat like an ocean wave, stirring up the cells, so more light is given off.

Later, Mr. Chappelle discovered that lasers can be replaced by other light sources. For example, bright flashes of light of different colors can make plants react. Inspectors from the U.S. Soil Conservation Service use flash generators mounted on trucks to determine which areas of a farmer's field are bare of plant cover. The inspectors can then predict the locations where heavy rain could wash away the exposed soil and cause erosion problems.

Starting in 1975, Mr. Chappelle spent two years working with other scientists at Johns Hopkins University in Baltimore, Maryland. He and his fellow researchers were particularly interested in finding early warning signs of cancer. They made some progress in this direction but were unable to develop a reliable indicator of the presence of cancerous tissue.

Mr. Chappelle has thirteen patents on his inventions. He continues to study how living plants give off light and is now working with agricultural scientists from the U.S. Department of Agriculture to develop new and easier tests that will tell farmers and crop specialists whether plants need more water or fertilizer. Mr. Chappelle's work should help improve food production all around the world.

Jewell Plummer Cobb

Born: January 17, 1924, in Chicago, Illinois

Status: President Emeritus, California State University, Fullerton, California

Education:

Bachelor of Arts degree, Talladega College, Talladega, Alabama, 1944

Master of Science degree, New York University, New York, New York, 1947

Doctor of Philosophy degree, New York University, 1950

Research Area: Cell Biology

Early Years

Jewell Plummer grew up in a family that valued education. Her grandfather had been a graduate pharmacist, and her father was a

encouraged to read about politics and the struggle for Black equality. She also read about current events and scientific discoveries. Her mother took her frequently to performances of ballets and musicals.

The family spent their summer holidays on a lake in northern Michigan. Other African American families had summer homes and cottages on the lake shore, and Jewell enjoyed being with the other African American teenagers.

Even though Jewell had an active teenage social life, she also had many serious ideas. When she was in her second year of high school, she decided to become a biologist. She was particularly fascinated by microscopic organisms. She strengthened her interest by reading books such as *The Microbe Hunters* by Paul DeKruif. This book introduced the young biologist to the pioneers in the study of bacteria. Jewell took extra courses in biology during high school, because she wanted to make sure she was prepared for further studies. Even though none of her friends were interested in science, Jewell's mind was made up. With her firm career plan and plenty of encouragement from her ninth grade biology teacher, she held fast to her ambitions.

medical doctor. After Dr. Plummer, Jewell's father, graduated from Cornell University in Ithaca, New York, he did his medical training at Rush Medical School in Chicago, Illinois. His office was on the south side of the city, near the old Chicago stockyards. Many of his patients were stockyard workers.

Jewell's mother also had strong views about the value of education. She was born in Augusta, Georgia, and later moved with her family to Washington, D.C. She studied dance at Sargents College, which was connected with Harvard University. After her marriage to Dr. Plummer, she taught dance in the Chicago public schools. When Jewell graduated from high school, Mrs. Plummer decided to reenter college. In fact, mother and daughter began their college studies in the same year and graduated at the same time. In 1944, Mrs. Plummer received her degree from Roosevelt University in Chicago and Jewell graduated from Talladega College in Talladega, Alabama.

When Jewell was growing up, her parents gave her many cultural advantages. Her father had a large library at home, and she was

Higher Education

After graduating from high school, Jewell Plummer enrolled at the University of Michigan. She chose Michigan because both the friends she had made during the summers and the famous Michigan Wolverine football team were there. But it was not a good choice. In 1941, the University of Michigan dormitories were still segregated and the social climate of this large, bureaucratic institution did not meet Ms. Plummer's needs. She decided she would be more at home in a smaller, Black college. At the end of the 1942 fall semester, she transferred to Talladega College in Alabama.

Talladega did not accept transfer credits from other colleges, and so Plummer had to start all over again, which upset her, since she was in a hurry to finish. By taking summer courses and special examinations, she was able to complete her degree program by 1944. She did all her college work in three years rather than the usual four. Because of World War II, only 31 students graduated along with Jewell Plummer. Most were women.

Jewell Plummer had applied early to New York University for admission to their graduate school. She also hoped for a teaching fellowship to help pay her tuition and expenses. New York University accepted her application, but they did not offer her any financial assistance.

Plummer would not give up. She traveled to New York City and made appointments to talk directly to university officials. They were so impressed by her record and by her positive attitude that they changed their minds. She was given a teaching fellowship that she held for all five years of her graduate studies.

During her graduate program at New York University, Plummer followed her original interest in living cells. She wanted to study how cells grow and multiply, so she developed methods to grow cells in the laboratory. Plummer knew that small samples of cells could be taken from a living creature without harming it. Therefore, she took a tiny piece of skin from a mouse and studied its growth and development. The cells from this little piece of skin were put in covered glass containers, nourished with special food, and analyzed as they grew and developed by themselves. It was easier to see how this process took place when the different kinds of cells were isolated. Therefore, she revised her procedure so that she could isolate and grow various types of cells in her laboratory. Since Jewell Plummer could study each particular type of cell separately, she could tell, for example, how a skin cell differed from a muscle cell.

Jewell Plummer received her master's degree in 1947 and began work on her Ph.D. In 1949, she was invited to spend a summer doing her own research at the famous Marine Biological Laboratory in Woods Hole, Massachusetts. She completed her doctorate in cell physiology in 1950 and was then awarded a post-doctoral fellowship by the National Cancer Institute (NCI), one of the National Institutes of Health. She spent two years doing research on cell growth. She also studied anti-cancer chemicals and traced the steps by which skin cells produce the compounds that give skin its color.

Career Highlights

After Dr. Plummer finished her post-doctoral studies, she spent some time away from her research projects. She married Roy Cobb in 1954 and their son, Jonathan, was born in 1957.

Even before Jonathan was born, Dr. Plummer Cobb had resumed working. She returned to New York University in the fall of 1955, where she taught courses in biology and renewed her career in research. She began to focus on the cells that determine skin color, and she grew colonies of such cells in the laboratory. Dr. Cobb believed that skin cells that contained a fair quantity of coloring material were more likely to show abnormal growth patterns than skin cells that had only a small amount of pigment. She felt confident that if she could control such growth in her laboratory samples, she could learn more about skin cancer. The National Cancer Institute once again funded her research.

Dr. Cobb worked closely with medical doctors on these studies. She was appointed to be head of the laboratory where cell growth research was done in the College of Medicine at New York University. Her research revealed that some X-ray treatment of skin cancer was not working. If the skin cells were extremely dark, only intense X-ray treatment could prevent the cancer cells from growing.

Dr. Cobb taught biology and supervised the research done in her laboratory until 1960, then she was made professor of biology at Sarah Lawrence College in Bronxville, New York. There she continued her research on skin cancer with the help of additional grants from the National Cancer Institute. She also began to take on administrative duties.

In 1969, she transferred to Connecticut College in New London, Connecticut, where she served as professor of zoology, director of the cell biology laboratory, and dean of the college. In the early morning hours, she worked in the laboratory; before midday, she saw to her administrative duties as dean; and in the late afternoon, she taught her students. Dr. Cobb kept up this heavy work load until 1976.

One of her most important accomplishments at Connecticut College was the establishment of a scholarship fund for premedical minority students. She was able to convince private donors to fund over 40 such scholarships. Her program has now been copied by other colleges across the United States.

In 1976, Dr. Cobb transferred to Douglass College in New Brunswick, New Jersey, the women-only branch of Rutgers University, the state university of New Jersey. At Douglass College, Dr. Cobb was named dean and professor of biological science. She had hoped that this move would allow her to lessen her work load. Unfortunately, this was not the case. Her duties at Douglass College were such that she had to give up the research that had made her famous.

Dr. Jewell Cobb had accomplished a great deal with her cancer research. She produced over 36 research articles and had tested many chemicals for the treatment of skin cancer. One such compound, methotrexate, was found to be useful in treating lung cancer and childhood leukemia, as well as skin cancer. In her effort to treat skin cancer, Dr. Cobb had also tested natural products such as the body's own hormones.

Dr. Cobb's early work on skin cancer helped other researchers and medical doctors understand how the skin is affected by ultraviolet radiation. Ordinarily, ultraviolet rays are absorbed by the ozone layer in the stratosphere, but, as many scientists believe, the amount of ozone is decreasing, because gases from air conditioners and refrigerators are attacking it. While the government has restricted the use of such gases, so much has already been released that the ozone layer is thinning out. Some of the ultraviolet radiation getting through the ozone layer can cause skin cancer. Once, it was thought that a tan was a sign of good health, but Dr. Cobb helped scientists understand that too much sun can be harmful to the human skin.

Ten institutions of higher education have recognized the merit of Dr. Cobb's research by awarding honorary doctoral degrees to her. U.S. government agencies have sent her overseas to study and teach in England, Russia, and Italy. Her research career spans over 20 years—from 1955 to 1976.

In 1976, Jewell Cobb adopted a new crusade. She became a voice for increasing the number of women and minorities in science and engineering, and she has written nine articles on this topic for important magazines.

In order to more directly influence the recruitment of women and minority students, Dr. Cobb became president of California

State University in Fullerton, California, in 1981. This university had about 24,000 students and over 1,000 faculty members when Dr. Cobb took charge. As president, she helped set up a new center for older citizens in Orange County, California; obtain money from the state government to build new laboratories and classrooms, and strengthen support for the university's engineering and science programs. Her biggest project, however, was to increase the diversity of the student body. Scholarship money and other forms of support were provided to help women and minority students attend the university, and a new multiethnic residence hall was built on the campus. It was named in Dr. Cobb's honor.

Now that Dr. Cobb has retired, her son, Jonathan, is continuing the family tradition of research and professional service began by Jewell's grandfather. Jonathan is a medical doctor, studying new ways in which radiation, like X rays, can be used to see inside the human body.

Thomas J. Craft, Sr.

Brooks Photographers

Born: December 27, 1924, in Monticello, Kentucky

Status: Retired, Academic Dean, Florida Memorial College, Miami, Florida, 1987

Education:

Bachelor of Science degree, Central State University, Wilberforce, Ohio, 1948

Master of Arts degree, Kent State University, Kent, Ohio, 1950

Doctor of Philosophy degree, Ohio State University, Columbus, Ohio, 1963

Research Area: Developmental Biology and Education

Early Years

When Thomas Craft's great grandfather, Henry Craft, and his wife, Kizzana, were freed from slavery after the Civil War, they worked as laborers on the farm of Walsh Guinn, several miles from Albany, Kentucky. After working a few years for wages, Henry Craft purchased ten acres of land from the Guinn family. He paid the $1200 purchase price by tending sick animals on the Guinn farm.

Their daughter, Dona, had a son, Thomas M. Craft (Tom's father), by one of the Guinn sons. The Guinn family, however, never formally acknowledged the child as their own.

Jacob Travis, Tom's mother's father, was born to a slave couple in 1862, shortly before the Civil War began. When Jacob was 30 years old, he and his wife, Nannie, went into business in Albany, baking and selling cookies. This venture soon led to the establishment of a general store.

Around that time, education was a major problem for the African American families in Albany. Public education for Black youngsters stopped at the second grade. Jacob Travis organized a protest movement that led almost all the Black families in Albany to move to nearby Monticello, Kentucky, where schooling for African American children continued through the sixth grade. Mr. Travis bought a large building on the town square in Monticello and again started a general store. This building is still owned by the family's heirs.

In 1920, Tom's father, Thomas M. Craft, married Jacob's daughter, Wonnie Alta, a teacher in the local segregated school system. Before the marriage, Tom's father worked several months each year in Milwaukee, Wisconsin. His wages were invested in land and cattle to expand the farm in Albany. Until the Great Depression, Thomas M. Craft continued to spend part of each year in Milwaukee, earning money to improve the farm.

Fortunately, before the depression, the Craft family had been awarded a permit to grow tobacco. The state controlled the tobacco market. They allowed only a specified amount to be grown each year, but anyone with a permit was guaranteed at least some cash income from their crop. Therefore, the Craft family remained relatively prosperous during the depression period. They were able to keep a crew of farm workers and even raised two children from a needy family. Consequently, young Tom grew up with three other children, his older sister and a foster brother and sister.

Tom started the first grade when he was only five years old. He had been reading for a year because he liked to study with his older sister, who had taught him to read. In 1932, when Tom was in the third grade, the major event in Monticello was the arrival of a new teacher, Charles Coleman. Coleman, who had a bachelor's degree from Louisville Municipal College, was not only a capable scholar and teacher in the arts and sciences but was also an ac-

complished athlete and musician. He provided a powerful role model for Tom and the other young people of the town. Ironically, someone with Coleman's credentials probably would not have come to such an out-of-the-way place as Monticello, Kentucky, if the depression had not caused high levels of unemployment around the whole country.

When Tom reached the eleventh grade, he was looking forward to attending his last year of high school at Lincoln Institute in Simpsonville, Kentucky, the school at which his sister had spent her last year. However, in 1940, the Monticello school board added the twelfth grade to Tom's high school, which meant that he would have to spend another year in Monticello rather than go on to the Lincoln Institute. Tom was depressed by this development. As a way to cheer him up, his uncle invited Tom on a trip to enroll his cousin, Oneth Travis, Jr., at Wilberforce University in Wilberforce, Ohio. After Tom saw the campus and buildings of this university, he didn't want to go back. Following some complicated negotiations, Tom moved to Wilberforce, took a part-time job on a farm, and attended the local high school. After he graduated in 1941, he kept his part-time job and enrolled in the university.

Higher Education

Wilberforce University was a hybrid institution. It had been founded by the elders of the African Methodist Episcopal (AME) church in 1856 to offer a program in the liberal arts. In 1887, the state of Ohio and the Wilberforce trustees made an agreement that the university would add certain vocational courses to the curriculum. In return, the state would subsidize the university with a yearly allocation of operating funds. For the next 50 years, the university had two boards of trustees, one from the AME church and one from the state.

Even as Thomas Craft entered Wilberforce, he knew his time in college might be short. The United States was rapidly mobilizing its military capabilities because of the outbreak of World War II in Europe. Therefore, many young, college-age men were being called into the military.

Craft received his draft notice in October of 1943. He hoped to go into the army because he had finished two years of Army ROTC at Wilberforce. However, after some confusion at the induction station, he volunteered to enlist in the marines instead. Because of his ROTC training, Craft did well as a marine recruit. He was named Honor Recruit for his unit, which led to a promotion to corporal and an assignment for further schooling as a drill instructor. He served in that position for over a year.

Tom Craft was assigned to a combat unit in March of 1945. After a brief stop in Hawaii, his unit was ordered aboard a ship that was carrying troops to the planned invasion of Japan. Before they reached Japan, however, the atom bombs had been dropped on Hiroshima and Nagasaki, and the war was over. Craft's marine unit was reassigned occupation duty rather than combat duty.

Craft was discharged from the U.S. Marine Corps Reserve in the spring of 1946. His benefits from the GI Bill of Rights meant that he could return to school without working long hours. He could now experience some of the campus activities which he had missed before.

After he returned to Wilberforce, Tom Craft was elected class president and asked to speak at the annual Founder's Day banquet. On the evening of the banquet, he had his first date with a young biology student named Joan Ruth Hunter. They soon fell in love and became engaged.

Not only did Craft's social life change after he returned to Wilberforce but his academic interests began to change as well. Initially, he had been taking a variety of science courses with the rather vague goal of achieving certification as a high school teacher. Now he began to give much more attention to his academic performance, and he put aside his interests in musical drama and athletics. He began to do volunteer work in the biology laboratory, which soon led to his appointment as a paid laboratory assistant.

Changes were also taking place at Wilberforce University. Historically, the AME board of trustees were responsible for hiring and firing the president of the university. The state board of trustees did not interfere. However, at the end of the 1946–47 school year, the AME trustees moved to dismiss a very popular and able president, Dr. Charles Harris Wesley.

Protests from faculty, students, and the state board were disregarded. Between the end of the spring term and the beginning of the summer term, Dr. Wesley was dismissed by a secret meeting of the AME Board. Consequently, the state withdrew its support of Wilberforce and created Central State University on the state-owned portion of the campus. The first president of Central State was Dr. Wesley, and Tom Craft persuaded his fellow students to transfer to the new institution.

Tom Craft finished his degree program at Central State in the spring of 1948, married Joan Hunter, and moved to Milwaukee to be near his parents. In spite of some vague ideas, he had no real concept of how to use his training in science. His father suggested that he take a factory job while he thought about his future. Although he did well at the job, he was soon laid off because of a seasonal decline in business. Next, he went to work for the U.S. Postal Service. These work experiences were not very satisfactory, and the idea of graduate school became more desirable. Soon, he applied for graduate school at Kent State University, in Kent, Ohio.

Craft began his graduate work in developmental biology at Kent State in 1949. Because of his relevant experience in the laboratory at Central State, he was given a job as a laboratory instructor. Together with his benefits as a war veteran, he and Joan were able to start a family. A son was born to them in their second year of residence in Kent.

Tom Craft selected mammalian anatomy as his major subject and was assigned Dr. Kenneth L. Kelley as his advisor. Dr. Kelley had recently come from the University of Pittsburgh, where pioneering work in organ transplantation was being done. Dr. Kelley suggested that Craft's thesis research concentrate on the rejection or retention of skin grafts. The problem of graft rejection occurred with great frequency when skin was transferred from one person to another or from one location to another on the same body. Skin grafts are often needed after a serious injury, accident, or burn, and it seemed possible that the body's own defenses—aroused by the serious condition—were making rejection more likely. Adult amphibians, which had received transplants of their own skin, were injected with the hormones produced by the body under stress. Craft demonstrated that the hormonal increase in the animal's bloodstream would heighten the likelihood that the graft would be rejected.

In 1950, Tom Craft received his master's degree in developmental biology. After his graduation from Kent State, he was invited to Central State to work as an instructor in biology. Craft knew that with only a master's degree, he could advance in rank at Central

State, but to reach the top of his field, he would need further study. Therefore, in 1955, he joined the research team at the Stone Laboratory of Hydrobiology at Ohio State University in Columbus, Ohio, as a summer employee. The team focused their studies on the behavior of mammals in a water environment. Craft became fascinated by the swimming behavior of brown bats. Such behavior was particularly interesting because the bat has specialized anatomical structures for flying, not swimming.

Because of the quality of his summer research at Ohio State, he was admitted into the doctoral program in zoology. He worked part time and summers on his degree at Ohio State and continued to teach during the school year at Central State.

Career Highlights

After completing the doctoral program at Ohio State University in 1963, Dr. Thomas Craft still continued his teaching duties at Central State. Then in the summer of 1966, he studied the history and philosophy of science at American University in Washington, D.C., under the sponsorship of the National Science Foundation.

After his experience at American University, Dr. Craft became increasingly interested in how science is taught at all levels of education, especially how young people are introduced to science both in and out of school. Dr. Craft volunteered as a district director of the Ohio Junior Academy of Science. Soon, he became involved with science education on an international scale. He went to India for three-month periods in 1967 and 1968 to help the Indian government train college-level science teachers.

Because of his interest in organ transplants and skin grafts, he served on advisory bodies for the National Institutes of Health and the state government in Ohio. He also continued a series of research projects, including one concerned with the properties of the tiny pigmentation granules that give skin its color. Dr. Craft had first become interested in these granules—found within the skin cells of humans and lower animals—during his research at Kent State. The granules contain several chemicals and are scattered throughout the skin cell in an arrangement that looks like each granule is a tiny subcell within the larger skin cell. The main chemicals in these granules are melanins. They serve a protective role in the cell by absorbing light energy that could otherwise be harmful.

Dr. Craft steadily progressed up the ladder of academic rank and became a full professor at Central State University. By 1980, his academic interests included administration, and he accepted a position as director of the Energy Program at Florida Memorial College in Miami, Florida. At first, he retained his association with Central State and continued to work on developing their training program for health care professionals. Soon, however, all his time and energy were given to Florida Memorial. He became director of the student loan programs as well as chairman of the Division of Natural Sciences and Mathematics. By 1982, Dr. Craft was the administrative cabinet secretary and acted as assistant to the college president. From 1984 to 1987, when Dr. Craft retired, he served as academic dean.

After his retirement, Dr. Craft returned to Ohio. He now continues to serve his community in a variety of volunteer positions. Dr. Craft's greatest interest is in improving the educational opportunities for young African American men and woman in the fields of science, medicine, and technology.

Marie Maynard Daly

Born: April 16, 1921, in Corona, Queens, New York

Status: Retired, Associate Professor of Biochemistry, Albert Einstein College of Medicine, Bronx, New York, 1986

Education:

Bachelor of Science degree, Queens College, New York, New York, 1942

Master of Science degree, New York University, New York, New York, 1943

Doctor of Philosophy degree, Columbia University, New York, New York, 1947

Research Area: Biochemistry

Early Years

Marie Daly's father was born in the British West Indies; then as a young man, he moved to the United States. Later, he applied for and won a scholarship to attend Cornell University in Ithaca, New York, where he hoped to study chemistry. Money, however, soon became a problem. Mr. Daly was not able to earn enough to pay for his room and board and had to drop out after the first semester. He took a job in New York City as a postal clerk, married a young woman named Helen Page, and settled down to raise a family.

Helen Page was originally from the Washington, D.C., area, and after Marie's birth Helen's parents moved to Queens, New York, to be closer to their daughter and granddaughter. These maternal grandparents encouraged Marie in her studies during her early years.

All the members of the Page family were avid readers. When Marie was a small child, her mother read her to sleep almost every night. Grandfather Page had an extensive library in his home and was pleased when Marie wanted to read his books. Marie enjoyed books about scientists and their work. Like another scientist in this book, Jewell Plummer Cobb (see p. 49), she was particularly interested in *The Microbe Hunters*, by Paul DeKruif, which heightened her own desire to become a scientist

Marie respected her father's ambition to become a chemist, even though he did not have the chance to complete his education. She thought it would please him if she someday became a scientist, thus partly fulfilling his desire for a professional career in science.

In the 1930s, Marie attended Hunter College High School, a school with an all-female faculty and student body in New York City. At that time, Hunter College High School and Hunter College, also an institution with an all-female student body, were connected to the City College of New York. The school's atmosphere supported the students' ambitions, and the teachers helped convince Marie that she could be a successful chemist.

Higher Education

Marie Daly wanted to live at home and save money, while attending college, so she enrolled at Queens College in nearby Flushing, New York. This school, part of the higher education system of New York City, has a park-like campus, which is rare for a college in New York City. This green campus was one of the qualities that made Marie so fond of her school. Later in life, she would remember her affection for Queens College when she started a scholarship fund at that school.

In addition to being close to home and having beautiful grounds, Queens College had been founded only a short time before Daly enrolled; therefore, the number of students in each course was small compared to other colleges in the city. Small classes are particularly advantageous to people taking laboratory courses, like chemistry. In lab courses, Daly rarely experienced long delays while waiting to use a particular piece of equipment. Therefore, she accomplished more work in each class.

Marie Daly graduated with honors from Queens College in 1942. She knew she needed more schooling to work as a professional chemist, but she also knew that graduate school is expensive. The faculty of the chemistry department at Queens College recognized her problem and offered her a fellowship to study chemistry and a part-time job as a laboratory assistant. This arrangement meant that she could afford to enroll in the advanced degree program at New York University, where it took her only one year to obtain her master's degree.

After receiving this degree, Marie Daly remained on the staff at Queens College for one more year, tutoring new chemistry students. This extra year at Queens allowed Daly to save money for her next graduate program.

In the fall of 1944, Marie Daly enrolled in the doctoral program at Columbia University. World War II was at its height, and women were beginning to find career opportunities in fields that previously had been reserved for men. Ms. Daly was able to obtain financial support from the university, which helped her study chemistry full time.

Soon, she was ready to start the research for her dissertation. She felt fortunate that there was a woman on the faculty who could direct her work. Dr. Mary L. Caldwell had finished her own doctoral work at Columbia University in 1921, and was now nationally recognized as a specialist in the chemistry of nutrition. At Columbia, Marie Daly studied how chemicals produced in the body contribute to the digestion of food. After three years, she completed her dissertation and was awarded her doctoral degree in 1947. She was the first African American woman to receive a Ph.D. in chemistry in the United States.

Career Highlights

During the last months of her doctoral program, Marie Daly consulted with her fellow students about her future career path. One of the students suggested she talk to Dr. A. E. Mirsky at the Rockefeller Institute of Medicine in New York City. The Rockefeller Institute, which became Rockefeller University in 1965, is an important center for research.

Mirsky was willing to accept Dr. Daly as a research apprentice; however, he thought she should obtain her own research funds. She applied to the American Cancer Society for a grant, and while she waited for her application to be reviewed, she took a temporary job at Howard University in Washington, D.C. There, she worked with Dr. Herman Branson (see p. 19) and taught an introductory course on the physical sciences.

In the fall of 1948, after she received the grant from the American Cancer Society, Dr. Daly returned to New York City and began a seven-year research program with Dr. Mirsky. This work focused on the ways in which proteins are constructed within the cells of the body. In particular, Dr. Daly and Dr. Mirsky were interested in the workings of the cell nucleus. About that same time, an important breakthrough in the field of genetics was made. The role of organic acids found in the nucleus of a cell was discovered, and in 1952, James Watson and Francis Crick were able to describe the structure of DNA (Deoxyribonucleic acid), the spiral molecules that carry the genetic code of every living thing. This breakthrough led to an immediate increase in the scientific study of the chemistry of the cell nucleus. Dr. Daly was fortunate to be in the right place at the right time. At the Rockefeller Institute, she was able to learn from fellow scientists, namely, Dr. Lenor Michaels and Dr. Francis Peyton Rous, about the revolutionary studies on DNA. Both men were widely respected scientists and knowledgeable in the field of biochemistry.

In 1955, Dr. Daly moved to the College of Physicians and Surgeons at Columbia University. She wanted to return to Columbia, the school where she had received her Ph.D., to work with Dr. Quentin B. Deming. Dr. Deming was famous for his work on how various chemicals influence the heart's mechanics. Dr. Daly and Dr. Deming began a long series of studies related to the underlying causes of heart attacks. They focused their research on the blockage of arteries that supply oxygen and nutrition to the heart muscle, and they soon discovered that cholesterol was part of the problem. Dr. Daly and Dr. Deming addressed basic questions about the production of cholesterol and the ability of cholesterol and related fatty products to clog the arteries. Dr. Daly also studied the effects of sugar and other dietary products on the health of the arteries. Later, she did pioneering work on the effects of cigarette smoke on the functioning of the lungs.

In the 1960s, two changes took place in Dr. Daly's life. She and Dr. Deming moved their research projects from Columbia University, and in 1961, she was married to Vincent Clark.

The new home for the research projects was the Albert Einstein College of Medicine at Yeshiva University in New York City. At Yeshiva, Dr. Daly continued her research and taught courses in biochemistry to medical students. She focused her work on the breakdown of the circulatory system caused by either advanced age or hypertension. She also became a leader in the efforts to increase enrollment of minority students in medical schools and graduate science programs.

Marie Daly and her research are honored in many ways. She was inducted into Phi Beta Kappa, a national honor society; she was made a fellow of the American Association for the Advancement of Science; and she served the New York Academy of Sciences as a member of their Board of Governors from 1974 to 1976. Dr. Daly also has started a scholarship fund for minority students who want to study physics or chemistry at Queens College, where she received her bachelor's degree. The scholarship is in memory of her father.

Dr. Marie Daly retired from Albert Einstein College of Medicine in 1986. She and her husband now spend the cold months of the year in Sarasota, Florida.

Christine Mann Darden

Born: September 10, 1942, in Monroe, North Carolina

Status: Aerospace Engineer, NASA Langley Research Center, Hampton, Virginia

Education:

Bachelor of Science degree, Hampton Institute, Hampton, Virginia, 1962

Master of Science degree, Virginia State College, Portsmouth, Virginia, 1967

Doctor of Science degree, George Washington University, Washington, D.C., 1983

Research Area: Mechanical Engineering

Early Years

Christine was the youngest of five children. Her father, Noah Horace Mann, Sr., and her mother, Desma Cheney Mann, were the youngest children of large families. By the time these two were ready for college, their older brothers and sisters were able to help finance their schooling. Indeed, the young couple met while they were attending Knoxville College in Knoxville, Tennessee. After graduating, Mr. and Mrs. Mann became school teachers in rural Georgia.

After teaching for a few years in Georgia, Mr. and Mrs. Mann moved to Monroe, North Carolina. Monroe, with a population of about 7,000, is a market town and the county seat of Union County. Much of the surrounding countryside is farmland on which cotton is cultivated. Christine's father took a job with a publishing firm in Monroe. Her mother taught at Winchester Avenue School, just across the street from the family home. After a few years, Mr. Mann found a better job with an insurance company, and the family prospered.

Christine started her schooling at a very young age. When she was only three years old, her mother brought her to the school where she taught. The little girl played at the back of the classroom, which eliminated the need for a baby-sitter. Soon, Christine was not satisfied to sit and play with toys. She began to learn the lessons along with the regular students. Consequently, she was ready for admission to kindergarten when she was only four.

While still in grade school, Christine developed a great curiosity about how things worked. She took things apart, if she could, to find their inner mechanisms. Sometimes, she was disappointed because there were no inner mechanisms. She once opened up her only doll to see if there was anything inside. She was surprised when she found nothing but cotton stuffing. As Christine became older, these explorations would often lead to interesting results. She was able to take her bicycle apart and repair the brakes with a coat hanger. Later, her father gave her lessons in car care. He taught Christine how to change tires, replace the battery, change the oil, and do other routine repairs.

In addition to her love of mechanical objects, Christine also loved sports—particularly roller skating and baseball. She was also interested in music and began piano lessons in the fourth grade, continuing them through high school.

When Christine reached the eleventh grade, she transferred from Winchester Avenue School to Allen High School in Ashville, North Carolina. Allen was a private girls school in the Blue Ridge Mountains. It had been founded by the Methodist Church to educate minority students who showed a high aptitude for college work. The Allen school had a relatively small enrollment—only about 100 students. All were expected to help with the maintenance of the school. There were moderate tuition fees, but young women from poorer families could do extra jobs to help finance their schooling.

Before Christine transferred to Allen, she had become very interested in literature. Her family always had books around the house, and she frequently visited the library at the local community center. In fact, Christine's favorite teacher at Winchester Avenue School was the English teacher. However, at Allen, her favorite teacher was the geometry teacher. Christine did so well in geometry that she developed a strong desire to study more mathematics. This interest proved to be the major influence in her future career.

Higher Education

Christine Mann was only 15 years old when she entered Hampton Institute in Hampton, Virginia. While her interest in mathematics continued, she majored in education. This decision resulted from the fact that, in the 1960s, there were very few job opportunities for a female, African American mathematician.

Aside from her studies, one of her most important interests was the Civil Rights movement. Christine Mann participated in the student "sit-ins," which aimed to create equal access to ordinary activities, such as being served at a lunch counter. Even more important than the protests were the voter registration drives. Movement leaders knew that if African Americans could increase their political influence through voting, it would help reduce other problems, such as job discrimination.

During the first year after she graduated from Hampton Institute, Christine Mann taught at a nearby junior high school. She continued her own schooling by taking evening courses in mathematics at Virginia State College.

She was married after she completed her first year of teaching, and after a one year break, she returned to teaching junior high school and took further mathematics courses. She began to believe that a career as a mathematician might be a real possibility. To that end, she stopped teaching and enrolled as a full-time graduate student at Virginia State.

Her previous record as a part-time student was sufficiently good to help her acquire a research assistantship in the physics department. Her supervisors were studying the use of powerful beams of light to detect the proportions of various gases, smoke particles, and water vapor in the atmosphere. By observing how the light was reflected, scattered, or absorbed, air quality and presence of specific kinds of pollutants could be determined. Christine Mann Darden was able to use some of her research findings as the basis for her master's thesis. She graduated from Virginia State in 1967.

Christine Darden's ambition to make a living as a professional mathematician was soon to be fulfilled. In fact, she received several job offers. She accepted a position with the National Aeronautics and Space Administration (NASA) at the NASA Langley Research Center in Hampton, Virginia.

At first, she worked as a member of a computer group. At that time, computers were nothing more than mechanical calculators. NASA engineers would assign the group members a particular mathematical problem to solve. The problem was then divided into sections, and each person worked on their part using the mechanical calculators.

When modern computers were introduced, new programs—known as software—were needed before these computers could be used. Darden was one of the first people assigned to develop such computer programs. At first, this work was an interesting challenge for her. However, she wanted to remain a mathematician, and people with very little mathematical training can learn computer programming. Consequently, to stay involved with her chosen field, Darden continued to attend upper-level mathematics courses.

George Washington University, which has its main campus in the District of Columbia, also has a branch campus in Hampton, Virginia. On this campus, Darden began her advanced, doctoral-level courses in both mathematics and engineering science. In a difficult course in fluid mechanics, she was the only African American in the class of eight students. This was her first experience in an integrated school situation. However, her success in this course bolstered her self-confidence and led her to enroll in the engineering program. At the time, there were few African American men and very few women of any race in engineering.

While working toward her doctorate in engineering, Darden continued to work full-time for NASA. In addition, she was raising her three children. Fortunately, Darden's work on her dissertation was directly related to her project at NASA, which concerned the environmental impact of the supersonic transport (SST) aircraft which was then being designed. Airplanes moving at speeds above the speed of sound create a wave of pressure in the air. When that pressure wave reaches the ground, people in the area hear a loud boom. Such booms can be powerful enough to shatter windows and damage structures. NASA officials were worried that the SST would produce a sonic boom beneath its flight path. Because of this and other concerns, the top officials of the United States government were uncertain as to whether the supersonic transport was a sensible idea. However, if it were ever built, they did not want the sonic boom to be a major issue. Consequently, NASA scientists were asked to study this problem.

Darden was asked to reproduce the effect of a sonic boom in a computer program. The program contained such factors as the speed and shape of the aircraft, which were represented by numbers. If these numbers were modified in certain ways, the computer program would predict the resulting intensity of the sonic boom.

Other NASA engineers built SST aircraft models that could be used in a high-performance wind tunnel. When they checked the results from the wind tunnel tests against the results from Darden's computer program, they found that the two tests gave almost identical results. Of course, the computer tests were much cheaper and faster.

By 1979, it was increasingly clear that government officials were not going to develop the supersonic transport. The officials thought the aircraft would cost more than it would be worth. Consequently, Darden's project at NASA was discontinued. Other related activities, such as wing design for high-speed aircraft, kept Darden busy at her computer. However, aircraft designers continued to have serious interests in the control of sonic booms. Military aircraft often fly at speeds higher than the speed of sound and may be required to fly over populated areas. Consequently, Darden was able to continue the study of sonic booms, a central element in her dissertation. In 1983, she finished the research and graduated from George Washington University with her doctorate in engineering.

Career Highlights

Dr. Darden had established a fine reputation by the time she finished her graduate studies. She remained at NASA and continued her career in engineering. With the end of the cold war and the breakup of the Soviet Union, government scientists made arrangements to cooperate with Russian engineers on the redesign of their supersonic transport. Dr. Darden worked on this international project.

Dr. Darden did not discontinue her habit of advanced study. She attended a series of management classes in a special program conducted for NASA staff members by the faculty at Simmons College in Boston, Massachusetts. Dr. Darden is now involved in other continuing education courses sponsored by her employers. The completion of this program will lead to a position as a research administrator—a high level NASA executive.

Dr. Darden is convinced that her youthful commitment to the study of mathematics and science was the key to her lifelong success. She recommends that all students gain practical experience along with their academic training. In this way, they can see the connection between their studies and their chosen career. Hopefully, this insight will give young people the willingness to invest their energy in the pursuit of knowledge.

Leodis Davis

Born: September 25, 1933, in Stamps, Arkansas

Status: Professor of Chemistry, University of Iowa, Iowa City, Iowa

Education:

Bachelor of Science degree, University of Kansas City, Kansas City, Missouri, 1956

Master of Science degree, Iowa State University, Ames, Iowa, 1958

Doctor of Philosophy degree, Iowa State University, 1960

Research Area: Biochemistry

Early Years

Leodis Davis and his younger brother, Leroy, lived with their mother's parents, Grandmother and Grandfather Anthony, in Stamps, Arkansas, until Leodis was four years old. Their parents, Mary Ann and Prentis Davis, had gone to Houston, Texas, in search of work. Stamps, where most members of the Davis and Anthony families lived, was not a very good place to find work in the 1930s. The Great Depression that was sweeping the country had its worst effects on small towns where jobs had always been scarce. In spite of the hard times, Mary and Prentis found jobs in Houston, and the family was reunited.

A year later, Leodis was enrolled in the local kindergarten. He disliked it so much that after being taken to school by his mother, he would wait until she was out of sight and then race back home. After two weeks of such antics, Mary Ann Davis and the school principal decided that Leodis was not yet ready for school. They kept him out for one more year.

In 1941, the threat of World War II caused an improvement in the job market. Leodis's parents, encouraged by the economy, decided to move again—this time to Kansas City, Missouri. As before, the children were put into the care of relatives in Stamps. Leodis spent the second half of the third grade at the Lafayette County Training School. A place later made famous as the elementary school attended by Maya Angelou, the prize-winning African American author who wrote the inaugural poem for President Clinton. The two boys rejoined their parents again that summer.

In Kansas City, Mr. Davis worked in the airplane manufacturing industry, and Mrs. Davis worked as a cleaning lady. Leodis and his younger brother attended the W. W. Yates Elementary School, R. T. Coles Junior High, and Lincoln High School in Kansas City. Each summer they would return to Stamps to help their grandparents run their farm.

Although his father had only gone through the fourth grade and his mother had stopped after the eighth grade, both parents were very supportive of the boys' interest in learning. Mary Ann Davis collected cast-off books and magazines from the homes in which she worked. Leodis read everything she brought home—particularly if it had anything to do with science.

His parents also bought him a chemistry set. He used materials from the set together with ingredients from the family's kitchen cabinet to conduct his "experiments." These experiments were successful enough to earn him a prize each year in the local science fair.

Later, when Leodis was in high school, he was strongly influenced by a biology teacher, Luke Ponder. Ponder organized activities for the young African American men at Lincoln High School. He founded the "Redael Club" that met in the afternoons after school— Redael is "leader" spelled backwards. This club was one of the first mentoring organizations for young Black men in America.

Ponder recruited his friends to act as "big brothers" to the high school-aged members of the club. These men planned activities that involved the members' families, such as father-son baseball games and mother-son church gatherings on Mother's Day and other holidays. These outings provided opportunities for the older men to show, by example, the proper clothing, behavior, manners, and conversation for various social situations.

The club members were also expected to give time to public service activities. Members helped the Red Cross and carried out fundraising drives for other local charities. They hosted large social events for their fellow students at Lincoln High School. Social concerns, however, were really secondary. The primary function of the club was to prepare the members for a successful college career.

Higher Education

In fact, Leodis Davis qualified for two college scholarships and barely missed a third— from Yale. He chose the Victor Wilson Scholarship that helped pay his way through the University of Kansas City (UKC)—now the University of Missouri at Kansas City.

When Davis entered the university in 1952, it had been recently desegregated. The change was accomplished in a much calmer manner than in Arkansas and elsewhere, and Davis enjoyed his first year. During that time, he struggled to choose between history and chemistry as his life's work. At the end of his first year, he decided that he would be more successful in chemistry. Leodis Davis also did well in mathematics and physics, thus balancing his background in the sciences.

He participated in student government, accepted the presidency of the local Student Chapter of the American Chemical Society, and worked part-time and summers for his expense money.

In 1956, as soon as Leodis Davis graduated from UKC, he entered the graduate chemistry program at Iowa State University in Ames, Iowa. Earlier in its history, Iowa State had awarded an advanced degree to George Washington Carver (see p. 42), and in the 1950s, it continued fostering a strong relationship with African Americans. Indeed, when Davis enrolled, there were sixteen African American students in his program.

Davis, who had taught during his senior year at UKC, was able to persuade the chair of the chemistry department at Iowa State to give him a graduate teaching assistantship. Apparently there had been some concern that Davis's inner-city accent would be difficult to understand by students from Iowa farms, but these fears were groundless, and Davis was soon attracting large numbers of undergraduate students to his courses.

At Iowa State, Leodis Davis continued the research on chelates he had begun at UKC. Chelates are carbon-based molecules that are able to combine with metal atoms. Hemoglobin is a type of chelate molecule that includes iron atoms to give blood its red color.

Scientists believe that after a metal atom and a chelate molecule unite, the metal atom within the molecule begins to vibrate. The rhythm of the vibration influences the light waves that strike the molecule and produce the color seen in dyes, hemoglobin, and other compounds.

Under the supervision of Professor David E. Metzler, Davis also began a study of the properties of Vitamin B-6, a carbon-based molecule that can combine with an atom of copper or other metallic atoms. This work led to a master's thesis and a report published in the *Journal of the American Chemical Society*. The project was extended for his doctoral studies to include research on a key enzyme from the liver, which works with Vitamin B-6 to help release the energy present in carbon-based molecules containing nitrogen. This energy helps sustain the life of all cells in the body.

Career Highlights

When Dr. Davis was awarded his Ph.D. in 1960, the job market was depressed. Consequently, he did not hesitate to accept the chance to do a post-doctoral year in Professor Metzler's laboratory. Dr. Davis was able to continue his own investigations and introduce new graduate students to innovative research techniques.

When the year was over, Dr. Davis received an invitation from an old friend, Sam Von Winbush (see p. 342). Dr. Von Winbush, a recent graduate in chemistry from the University of Kansas, had been invited to accept the chair of the chemistry department at Tennessee State University in Nashville. Dr. Von Winbush asked Dr. Davis to join him at Tennessee State and take over the direction of the biochemistry program in the department. The next year, the duo was joined by a third friend, Dr. Sam Anderson. Together, the three young chemists remade the chemistry program at Tennessee State.

In a short time, the team had laid out the plans for a new science building. However, the president of the university did not approve the plan. Soon after the new building plan was rejected, the team broke up because of other attractive career opportunities. Von Winbush was hired away by North Carolina A & T University, Anderson left for Norfolk State University in Virginia, and Dr. Davis was hired by Howard University in Washington, D.C.

While still at Tennessee State, Dr. Davis had applied for and won a research grant from the National Institutes of Health. He was the first faculty member at Tennessee State to have won such a competitive prize. Dr. Davis used the funds to continue his studies of the liver enzyme and Vitamin B-6. These studies led, in turn, to the Medical Faculty Award from the Lederle Pharmaceutical Company in 1967. That same year, Dr. Davis was promoted and given faculty tenure at Howard University.

In 1968, Dr. Davis decided to take a one-year sabbatical, a leave given periodically to teachers for their own study and research. He and Professor Fred Duke, a friend who had been his teacher at Iowa State, planned a joint research project at Dr. Duke's laboratory at Purdue University in Indiana. Before the research began, however, Professor Duke was hired away from Purdue by the University of Iowa, so he and Dr. Davis conducted the research there instead. After his one year at Iowa, the university invited him to stay as a regular faculty member, which he did.

Dr. Davis saw his mission at the University of Iowa as creating an outstanding graduate program of enzyme study in the chemistry department. He was able to do this with support from the National Institutes of Health and the National Science Foundation. Today, students who graduate from this program are employed by industry and academic institutions throughout the country. Also, there are now over 50 published research reports that have been generated by Dr. Davis and his students.

In 1979, when Dr. Davis took over the chair of the chemistry department, he was able to give strong support to professional career development among minority students. He was in an even better position to give this support when he was appointed acting dean of the graduate college and then made associate vice president for academic affairs. Finally, in 1993, his rapid succession of promotions culminated with his appointment as associate provost for budget and planning, one of the most influential administrative positions at the university. Even though Dr. Davis has experienced success in administrative work, he eagerly hopes to one day return to teaching chemistry and conducting research.

Linneaus C. Dorman

Born: June 28, 1935, in Orangeburg, South Carolina

Status: Senior Scientist, Dow Chemical Company, Midland, Michigan

Education:

Bachelor of Science degree, Bradley University, Peoria, Illinois, 1956

Doctor of Philosophy degree, Indiana University, Bloomington, Indiana, 1961

Research Area: Organic Chemistry

Early Years

Linneaus Dorman's father fought in World War I and was badly injured while serving in France. Later, after he had partially recovered from his injuries, he attended South Carolina State College and graduated in 1925. Linneaus's mother also attended college and became a grade school teacher, working most of her life in various county schools near Orangeburg, South Carolina.

Linneaus was named after the doctor who delivered him. The doctor had been named after Karl Linneaus, the Swedish botanist who invented the classification system used for all plants and animals.

Since both of Linneaus's parents were teachers, education was highly valued in the Dorman family. Linneaus wanted to go to school long before he was old enough to attend classes in Orangeburg, so when he was five, his mother taught him first grade lessons at the rural school where she worked. The next year, he was enrolled in the first-grade at the laboratory school connected with South Carolina State College. Here, Linneaus had an educational advantage over most African American children. In a laboratory school such as this one, college students who are studying to be teachers do their practice teaching. Experienced teachers serve as supervisors in these classrooms and ensure a high quality of instruction. Therefore, Linneaus had a good educational program and good role models at home, at school, and in his broader social community.

When Linneaus was still in grade school, a friend of his was given a chemistry set. The two boys enjoyed playing with the set and learning what could be produced from combining chemicals. From that time forward, Linneaus was fascinated by chemistry.

Later, when Linneaus was attending the high school connected with South Carolina State College, he took chemistry from Clemmie Webber. Ms. Webber was so dedicated to science that she later went on to obtain her doctoral degree in chemistry and join the faculty at South Carolina State College. Her enthusiasm inspired Linneaus and encouraged his interest in chemistry.

With teachers like Clemmie Webber and other equally devoted people, Linneaus's high school provided a good foundation for its students, but the school also had its weaknesses. Only one foreign language was taught, the offerings in mathematics were limited, the chemistry lab lacked equipment, and there were no courses in physics. Nevertheless, many of the students went on to college and did well in their studies.

In 1951, Linneaus began to think about college. One day he saw a pamphlet in the guidance counselor's office entitled "Do You Want to go to College?" It was published by the National Scholarship Service and Fund for Negro Students, an organization that tried to find the best college or university for each African American student. They learned about the student and matched the young person to a particular school. For example, if a student had relatives living in a college town, the advisors might suggest that the student consider applying to that college. The student could then save dormitory fees by rooming with his relatives.

For Linneaus, one consideration was that his father had served in World War I, and Bradley University in Peoria, Illinois, had a special scholarship reserved for children of World War I veterans. Bradley University also was certified by the American Chemical Society, making it more attractive to Linneaus than the colleges closer to home. The National Scholarship Service helped Linneaus submit his application to Bradley, and he was awarded the scholarship.

Higher Education

When Linneaus Dorman arrived at Bradley University, Peoria was a tough factory town. The few African Americans who lived there worked in the factories. Dorman missed the intellectual stimulation of the educated African American community at South Carolina State and made the Ward Chapel AME Church and its members the main source of social life. For a time, he even sang in the church's junior choir.

In the early 1950s, Bradley University had only a few African American students. One was Robert Lawrence, who became Dorman's roommate in the dormitory. They were both interested in chemistry and helped each other with their course work.

Soon, Robert and Linneaus decided to join an all African American fraternity. In their third year, the members of their fraternity had the highest average grades of all fraternity men on campus.

Robert Lawrence, like Linneaus Dorman, had a very interesting life. During college, he was in the U.S. Air Force Reserve Officer Training Corp, and after graduation, he rose in rank to be an Air Force major. He received his doctoral degree in chemistry from Ohio State University in Columbus, Ohio, and became the first African American to enter astronaut training. Sadly, he was killed in a plane crash before his first space flight.

Bradley University now honors Robert Lawrence by holding an annual lecture in his name. In 1990, Linneaus Dorman was the person who presented the Robert Lawrence Lecture.

While at Bradley, Dorman was greatly influenced by Dr. John H. Shroyer, the head of the chemistry department. Dr. Shroyer attempted to identify students who had the ability to be research scientists. He wanted to match the interests and abilities of such students with various programs of advanced training. Dr. Shroyer thought that Linneaus Dorman would do well in the graduate school at Indiana University, and he wrote letters in support of Dorman's ability. Linneaus was admitted to the university and awarded a graduate teaching assistantship. His job was to help teach the introductory courses in chemistry.

The summer before graduate school Dorman took a job as a chemist with the Northern Regional Research Laboratory of the U.S. Department of Agriculture to help finance his graduate studies. He continued to work there every summer from 1956 through 1959.

After his first year of graduate school, Linneaus Dorman married Ms. Phae Hubble. Phae and her family lived in Peoria, Illinois, and he had come to know them through his church activities while at Bradley University. Ms. Hubble had already received a master's degree in library science from Atlanta University, and she held a professional position in the Peoria Public Library system. She continued to work there after they were married, and Linneaus traveled back and forth between Peoria and his classes in Bloomington, Indiana. However, when their first child was born in 1959, Phae joined her husband in Bloomington.

As with all graduate students, income was very limited for the young family. Fortunately, Linneaus Dorman won a Dow Research Fellowship which paid more than his teaching assistantship. Combined with their savings, that money allowed Dorman to finish his program of study.

Dorman was only the second African American from Bradley University to attend graduate school at Indiana University. His research work at the Northern Regional Laboratory was also successful, and in 1960, he was cowinner of the Bond Award, given for the best paper presented at the national meeting of the American Oil Chemists Society.

As his graduation neared, Dorman began to think about his future career. He considered becoming a professor, perhaps at a college with many African American students. He also considered the possibility of joining one of the big chemical companies. He was worried, however, that these companies would not hire him because he was an African American.

Nevertheless, he signed up for an interview with a representative of the Dow Chemical Company. Because Dow had provided his graduate fellowship, Dorman felt that both he and the chemistry department would appear unappreciative if he did not show an interest in the company. He did not think, however, that Dow would actually offer him a job and was surprised when they did. They were the only company to do so.

Career Highlights

After accepting the position, Dr. Dorman and his family moved from Bloomington, Indiana, to Midland, Michigan, where the Dow Company had its headquarters and research center. Dr. Dorman was gratified to work for a company that fostered full-time research.

During Dr. Dorman's long career at Dow Chemical, he's worked on many different projects. In the early 1960s, the company was just starting to work on chemicals that could be used by medical doctors. Dr. Dorman's first studies were related to testing compounds that might prove useful in the treatment of mental illness. After a few years in this field, Dr. Dorman became strongly interested in compounds called peptides, the building blocks for proteins. Proteins are, in turn, the main building blocks that make up every living creature. Peptides also have commercial uses. For example, they are used in the artificial sweetener Equal.

Dr. Dorman worked to design new kinds of peptides for specific medical uses, such as slowing down the process of blood clotting. He developed one set of peptides for the treatment of asthma and another that could help determine pregnancy. Dr. Dorman worked on these problems for eight years and published many important reports that are still being used.

In 1980, he went to work on yet another type of problem. By this time, many scientists and members of the public at large had become concerned with the damage to the environment caused by agricultural chemicals. Dr. Dorman undertook research to determine, for example, what would happen if the active chemicals were mixed with other compounds, or if the chemicals were made into little pellets rather than sprays. He sought to find the best way to introduce an agriculture chemical into the roots of a plant or into the soil around it. He also wondered whether a water proof material could be sprayed on plants to protect them during their early growth stage. He found that when the agricultural chemicals such as insect repellants were made into pellets with a mixture of plastic binders, the chemicals were released slowly onto the plant and into the soil. The plastic binders acted like glue to hold the pellet together and also make the chemicals less concentrated. When delivered in this way, the agricultural chemicals do not wash so easily into the rivers and streams when a sudden rainstorm arrives.

These and many other issues concerning the environment were raised in the research effort. Dr. Dorman worked hard to find the answers that would help protect the environment.

Still later, he began to address an entirely new problem. Dr. Dorman sought ways to make artificial bone material, which could be used to replace natural bone when a person had been badly injured in an accident. Dr. Dorman was successful, and recently he was awarded a patent for his invention of an artificial ivory-type compound. This compound is very similar to bone in its strength and flexibility.

In the late 1980s and early 1990s, Dr. Dorman became involved in new research concerning, among other things, the study of elastic materials like rubber. His goal was to find materials that last longer and can be more easily recycled than ordinary rubber. In fact, rubber is so difficult to recycle that the use of new rubber may be less expensive than the use of recycled rubber. Dr. Dorman continues to work on this particular problem and is preparing new reports on his research.

The quality of Dr. Dorman's research has been widely recognized. He was honored as Inventor of the Year by the Dow Chemical Company in 1983. In 1988, he was awarded an honorary doctoral degree by Saginaw Valley State University in Saginaw, Michigan. The American Chemical Society recognized his outstanding service to the profession in 1990 at an award ceremony. In 1994, Dow promoted him again, this time to the rank of Senior Associate Scientist.

Dr. Dorman is also active in his local community. In particular, he has encouraged minority individuals to become scientists and engineers and has shown that minority people can succeed in industry as well as in academic research.

Charles R. Drew

Born: June 3, 1904, in Washington, D.C.

Status: Died, April 1, 1950, near Burlington, North Carolina

Education:

Bachelor of Arts degree, Amherst College, Amherst, Massachusetts, 1926

Doctor of Medicine and Master of Surgery degrees, McGill University Medical School, Montreal, Quebec, Canada, 1933

Research Area: Physiology

Early Years

Charles Drew was the oldest of the five children of Richard and Nora Drew. He had one younger brother and three younger sisters. Unfortunately, tragedy struck the young family when Charles's sister, Elsie, died of influenza. Perhaps it was this early experience with death that inspired Charles to choose a career in which he would help save lives.

Charles's father worked as a carpet layer and was a financial officer in the local carpet layer's union. He set a good example for Charles as an energetic worker, a careful planner, and a forceful leader. His mother did not work outside the home, because she was so busy with her large family.

As a boy, Charles always had a lot of energy. Following his father's example, he was able to channel that energy into constructive activities. For instance, Charles put together a group of boys from his elementary school, Stevens Elementary in Washington, D.C., to sell newspapers. They sold a large number of newspapers, because of their organization and industry.

When Charles was sixteen years old, his family bought a new house in a very pleasant section of Washington. The Drew family lived in the house for almost twenty years, and it is now a National Historic Landmark.

After the family moved, Charles transferred to Dunbar High School. Although all schools in Washington, D.C., were segregated at that time, Dunbar was one of the best high schools in Washington. Many African American students who graduated from Dunbar went on to college. In fact, more African American graduates from Dunbar went on to college than from any other high school in the country.

Charles was an excellent athlete and he played four sports in high school. In fact, he received a letter in each one. He also received a medal for the best all-around athlete in his junior and senior years.

In those days, the army sponsored a Reserve Officer Training Corps (ROTC) at the high school level. Charles joined, and by the time he was a senior, he was the captain of cadets. Charles graduated with high honors from Dunbar High School in 1922.

Higher Education

After graduating from high school, Charles Drew went on to Amherst College in Massachusetts. Because of his outstanding achievements in high school, he had received a scholarship. It did not pay for all his expenses, however, and Drew had to earn the extra money by working as a waiter.

In college, just as in high school, Drew was an excellent athlete. Here, his best sports were football and track. He won the trophy for most valuable football player during his junior year. When he was a senior, Drew won a trophy for being the best all-around athlete during his four years at Amherst. Because of his commitment to sports and the time required to earn his expense money, Charles Drew did not do very well in his studies during his first two years in college. In his third year, however, he began to concentrate on his class work. His work improved overall, but in particular, he began to get very high grades in chemistry and biology. His teachers had been worried that his devotion to sports prevented him from working up to his potential. Now, they were pleased to see that Drew could earn good grades and still be a good athlete.

In spite of his athletic prowess and good scholarship, Charles Drew still had to deal with racial prejudice in his day-to-day activities. For example, in 1925, Drew traveled to Rhode Island with the track team for a meet against Brown University. After the meet, the team stopped at a hotel for dinner. The hotel would not serve the Black members of the team. At that time, this kind of discrimination was common in hotels and restaurants all over the United States.

Drew was also excluded from certain groups on campus, because of the racist beliefs of the members. Indeed, he was passed over as captain of the football team, even though he was the most valuable player.

After graduating from Amherst in 1926, Drew took a job coaching football at a traditionally Black institution, Morgan State College in Baltimore, Maryland. At Morgan State, he also served as an instructor in biology and chemistry. He worked there from 1926 to 1928.

During the summers, Charles Drew worked as the manager of a large public swimming pool in Baltimore. He took pride in teaching young neighborhood children to swim.

Then, in 1928, Drew applied to medical school. He was not accepted at Howard Medical School, because he had only six credits of English from Amherst and Howard Medical School required eight. However, he was readily accepted into McGill University Medical School in Montreal, Canada.

Charles Drew worked exceptionally hard on his studies in medical school. While at McGill, he won a prize for his research on the structure and function of the nervous system, and he was also elected to the National Medical Honorary Society. Drew scored the highest grade in a competition with other excellent medical school students.

He graduated from McGill Medical School in 1933. In addition to his degree of medical doctor (MD), he received the degree of master of surgery. After his graduation, Dr. Drew completed a one-year internship and a year of residency at Montreal General hospital. As an intern and resident, he practiced under another doctor's supervision. After his residency, Dr. Drew passed the test of the National Board of Medical Examiners in 1935. Finally, he was able to treat patients without someone overseeing his work.

Career Highlights

In that same year, Dr. Drew was appointed an instructor in pathology at Howard University College of Medicine. He taught students about the causes, symptoms, and treatments of disease. Dr. Drew was very happy as a teacher of medicine, but he also wanted to learn more about surgery. In 1937, he decided to do a residency in surgery, so that he could become qualified as a surgeon. He did his training at Howard University and soon became an instructor in surgery and an assistant surgeon at Freedmen's Hospital, a part of Howard University Medical School.

In 1938, still hungry for more medical knowledge, Dr. Drew accepted a fellowship in surgery from Columbia University's College of Physicians and Surgeons to work on his doctorate in medical science. The topic for his doctoral research was the preservation of blood. At the time Dr. Drew was doing his investigation, it was difficult to store blood for long periods of time. Scientists knew that regular or "whole" blood is made of four parts: white blood cells, which fight infection; red blood cells, which carry oxygen; platelets, which help blood to clot; and plasma, the liquid part of blood which carries nutrients. Dr. Drew's research proved that plasma is easier to store and preserve than whole blood because the red blood cells in whole blood are easily spoiled. Consequently, quantities of stored plasma could be available for surgeons whenever needed. Since plasma can be used for most of the medical purposes for which whole blood is used, the supply for emergencies was now more dependable.

In a closely related investigation, Dr. Drew and a colleague did important research on patients who suffered from shock. Shock, which usually occurs when a person suddenly loses a great deal of blood, such as during surgery or after a severe injury, can cause unconsciousness or even death. Dr. Drew's study demonstrated that if plasma is introduced quickly into the patient's body, the problems of shock are lessened. Both Dr. Drew's work in preserving blood plasma and his research on preventing shock proved invaluable in saving lives a few years later during World War II.

In 1939, when Dr. Drew was traveling to Tuskegee, Alabama, for a medical conference, he took a brief stopover in Atlanta, Georgia. During his brief stay, Dr. Drew met Lenore Robbins. It was love at first sight, and they were married that same year. Charles and Lenore Drew eventually became the parents of four children.

The year after his marriage, Dr. Drew received his doctorate from Columbia University in New York City and moved back to Washington, D.C. He returned to Howard University Medical School as an assistant professor of surgery and to Freedmen's Hospital as a staff surgeon. In 1941, Dr. Drew received his certification from the surgical examination board. He scored so well on the certification test that he was made an examiner for the American Board of Surgery.

That same year, World War II raged in Europe. The Nazis bombed the city of London, and many people were injured and dying. It was very important that a large supply of blood be sent to England quickly. Dr. Drew was one of the first doctors engaged in the collection and preservation of blood to be sent to Europe. He became a leading authority on separating plasma from whole blood and on preserving it for later use. In 1941, Drew was made director of the first American Red Cross Blood Bank and assistant director in charge of blood for the United States Army and Navy. He also was the medical director of the "Plasma for Britain" program. Dr. Drew's system for collecting blood and preserving the plasma became the model for the national volunteer blood donor program of the American Red Cross. His work helped save the lives of thousands of soldiers and civilians during the war. Since then, it also has helped countless people throughout the world.

Dr. Drew worked on the Red Cross blood program for only seven months and then returned to Howard University Medical School. The American Red Cross separated the blood of Black and White people for storage. Dr. Drew was aware that there was no scientific reason for doing this. Blood is grouped into the blood types A, B, AB, and O, and they have nothing to do with race. Some people believe that Dr. Drew left the Red Cross because of its policy of segregating blood according to race.

When he returned to Howard, Dr. Drew was made professor and chairman of the Department of Surgery and chief surgeon at Freedmen's Hospital. From 1944 to 1948, he also served as the medical director of Freedmen's Hospital.

In 1944, Dr. Drew was presented the Spingarn Medal by the National Association for the Advancement of Colored People (NAACP) for his outstanding work in training African American doctors. In 1949, Drew was invited by the Surgeon General of the United States Army to work with a team of doctors on improving hospitals and medical care in postwar Europe. This was one of his last assignments.

On April 1, 1950, Dr. Drew and three other doctors were traveling to Tuskegee, Alabama. He had done several surgical operations the day before and was very fatigued. Very early that morning, Dr. Drew must have fallen asleep while driving. The car went off the road and rolled over three times. Since cars did not have seat belts at that time, Dr. Drew was thrown from the car and received very serious injuries. Dr. Drew and the other doc-

tors, who had suffered similar but less severe injuries, were rushed to a small hospital nearby. He was taken to the emergency room, where he was given a blood transfusion and other emergency care, but he died two hours after arriving at the hospital. After his tragic death, there was some talk that Dr. Drew had not been given proper care because he was an African American. These stories, however, were proven false by the statements of the other African American doctors who had been injured in the fatal crash.

Charles Drew will always be remembered as one of the great contributors to medical research and to humanity. His greatest joy was doing surgical research and teaching medical students, interns, and residents. Most of the African American surgeons trained between 1941 and 1950 received some of their instruction under Dr. Drew. He died in the prime of his life, and it seems certain that, had he lived, he would have made many more contributions to the medical profession.

James B. Drew

Born: April 6, 1922, in Charlottesville, Virginia

Status: Retired, Associate Dean and Professor of Physics, Montgomery County Community College, Blue Bell, Pennsylvania

Education:

Bachelor of Science degree, Virginia Union University, Richmond, Virginia, 1943

Master of Science degree, Howard University, Washington, D.C., 1947

Master of Science degree, Rutgers University, New Brunswick, New Jersey, 1954

Research Area: Physics

Early Years

James Drew was born in Charlottesville, Virginia, at his mother's ancestral home. It was a family tradition that each female member return to the original homestead to give birth to her first child. Shortly after he was born, James was taken to his parent's home in Harpers Ferry, West Virginia, where his mother and father were both on the faculty at Storer College.

Harpers Ferry, a small town on the Potomac River, is rich in history. The old part of town sits on the river's edge and has been made into a national park and historical monument by the U.S. Park Service. The town is especially famous for the unsuccessful raid staged by the abolitionist, John Brown, in 1859. Brown's act sought to demonstrate the intensity of anti-slavery sentiment in the United States and was immortalized in the "Battle Hymn of the Republic"—the anthem of the Union Army during the Civil War.

Storer College, one of the institutions established after the Civil War to educate young African Americans, was founded in Harpers Ferry in 1867. In 1906, Storer was the site of a critical meeting of civil rights leaders led by W.E.B. Du Bois, a meeting that ultimately led to the creation of the National Association for the Advancement of Colored People (NAACP), one of the most important civil rights organizations in the United States.

In the 1920s and 30s when James Drew was growing up, Storer College was a major center for creative African Americans. James's parents were visited by George W. Carver (see p. 42) and W.E.B. Du Bois, along with other leading African Americans. On one of George Carver's visits, he showed young James how to make paper from peanut shells. Carver crumbled the shells into fine bits and then mixed them with lye in water. After the soupy mix had been rinsed several times and the water squeezed out in a towel, the pulp was rolled out like a pie crust and then dried. James was fascinated by Carver's unusual way to make paper, although his mother was not very pleased with this new use of her cooking equipment.

James also enjoyed visits from W.E.B. Du Bois. Even though James realized that Dr. Du Bois was a great scholar, he was far more impressed with Dr. Carver's sense of excitement.

The children of faculty members at Storer College were strongly encouraged to study nature. When students or faculty members from the biology department netted butterflies, the specimens were properly mounted and labeled so that the young people could compare the different species. In addition, the evening astronomy lectures at the college were open to all, including the young children of the faculty members. James was also able to help his father build the equipment for the demonstrations in his physics classes. Seeing the demonstrations gave young James confidence that he could someday understand the principles of physical science.

In 1935, when James Drew was 13 years old, his father accepted the position of dean and professor of mathematics at Virginia Union University in Richmond, Virginia. This move was timely for the Drew family because Storer College did not survive the Great Depression of the 1930s.

In Richmond, James entered Armstrong High School, where he took his first physics course from a Miss Bowles. He graduated from high school in 1939.

Higher Education

It was both convenient and economical for James Drew to continue his education at Virginia Union University in Richmond. The same year he began college, World War II broke out. Two years later, in December of 1941, America entered the war. By then, James Drew was in his third year of college and, as a budding scientist, was deferred from being drafted into the U.S. Army.

During his fourth year of college, in addition to his regular classes at Virginia Union, Drew acted as both a student and a teacher at Virginia State University in Petersburg, Virginia. At Virginia State, he took advanced physics courses and taught an engineering science course in electronics to help prepare soldiers for their duties.

After he graduated from Virginia Union in 1943, James Drew entered the Army's Training School for Engineering Officers. He served on active duty in the Corp of Engineers until the war was over in 1945. After the war, he became a reserve officer in the 2901 Research and Development Training Group that was housed in the Pentagon near Washington, D.C. This unit surveyed all the research and development being done in science and engineering around the world, attempting to determine whether any of the ideas had possible military applications.

Then in 1946, James Drew enrolled in the graduate program in physics at Howard University in Washington, D.C., just across the Potomac River from the Pentagon. He completed his master's degree in 1947 but remained at Howard for an additional three years teaching and doing research as a member of their scientific staff. James Drew was particularly excited about his research project because it involved an unusual collaboration of medical researchers from Freedmen's Hospital—the teaching hospital associated with the Howard University Medical School—and physicists from the university's main campus. The topic of investigation was the use of radioactive materials in the treatment of thyroid cancer. In those days, interdisciplinary research was rare and the use of radioactive compounds for cancer treatment was in its infancy.

In 1950, Mr. Drew entered the graduate program at Rutgers University in New Brunswick, New Jersey. At Rutgers, he worked on his second master's degree in physics and specialized in the field of nuclear magnetic resonance. Scientists knew that atoms can be made to vibrate in a magnetic field when the magnet is rapidly turned off and on. Mr. Drew worked on the problem of determining the molecular structures of the samples being tested. He received this master's degree from Rutgers in 1954 and was the first African American to earn an advanced degree in physics from that university.

While still at Rutgers, Mr. Drew became involved with the Franklin Institute in Philadelphia, Pennsylvania—just across the Delaware River from Camden, New Jersey, where he lived. The association with this world famous institution evolved into a 14-year career as a research physicist.

Career Highlights

Even after he graduated from Rutgers, James Drew continued to take advanced courses in physics. This increased his level of expertise, allowing the scope of his work to include high-level deliberations on atomic energy and the proper uses of nuclear isotopes.

The range of his research projects had also increased. At this time, the main focus of his work was the physics of very thin magnetic films, such as those used as magnetic memory storage in computers. Mr. Drew studied the properties of such film from both theoretical and practical perspectives and presented his research at the International Magnetic Conference in Stuttgart, West Germany, in 1966. This work led to the award of a Lilly Foundation Fellowship at the University of Pennsylvania in 1980. Mr. Drew was also active in the national professional societies in physics and served as a chairman of professional meetings and as a reviewer of technical books for the *Journal of the Franklin Institute*.

Mr. Drew's interest in the welfare of students was fostered at an early age by his parents' enthusiastic interaction with their students. Mr. Drew's desire to assist African American students eventually drew him to Montgomery County Community College in Eastern Pennsylvania, a two-year institution about ten miles away from downtown Philadelphia.

When he arrived at Montgomery, which now has about 9,000 students, Mr. Drew took on the dual roles of associate dean of the college and professor of physics and mathematics. He taught both basic science and engineering technology courses. His students also built Earth Station Montco, a student-operated satellite-tracking station.

As associate dean, Mr. Drew was responsible for modernizing the courses in the technology-oriented programs, planning for the expansion of computer utilization in instruction and college administration, and acting as faculty representative to the Black Student Union.

Working with young people was not limited to the students at Montgomery County Community College. Mr. Drew also worked with the Congress of Racial Equality (CORE), the National Association for the Advancement of Colored People (NAACP), and other organizations in Camden County, New Jersey. He also served as assistant commissioner for the Boy Scouts of America in the Camden District. In 1992, the Camden City School Board named the physics laboratory at Hatch Junior High School after Mr. James Drew. Mr. Drew is now enjoying his retirement in rural West Virginia near his childhood home of Harpers Ferry.

Joseph C. Dunbar, Jr.

Born: August 27, 1944, in Vicksburg, Mississippi

Status: Professor, Wayne State University, School of Medicine, Detroit, Michigan

Education:

Bachelor of Science degree, Alcorn College, Lorman, Mississippi, 1963

Master of Science degree, Texas Southern University, Houston, Texas, 1966

Doctor of Philosophy degree, Wayne State University, School of Medicine, Detroit, Michigan, 1970

Research Area: Physiology

Early Years

Joseph Dunbar and his two sisters grew up in Port Gibson, Mississippi, in the beautiful Mississippi River valley. Joe's mother, Henrienne, was a school teacher in the local public school system. Both she and her husband had received their degrees from Alcorn College (now Alcorn State University) in nearby Lorman, Mississippi. Joe's father, Joseph, Sr., was the county agricultural extension agent for Claiborne County, Mississippi. His job was to inform the local farmers of the best farming practices reported by the U.S. Department of Agriculture and the local agricultural research centers.

As children, Joe and his sisters loved to roam the fields near their home. They spent hours investigating the wild plants and animals that abound in river valleys. Indeed, because of this early informal study, all three of the Dunbar children chose careers in biology.

Joe first attended school in a two-room school house. One room was for the first through fourth grades and the other contained the fifth through eighth grades. By the time Joe had completed the fourth grade, the two-room school houses in the entire area were consolidated into one large school at Port Gibson. He completed his elementary schooling at the new building.

Joe began his secondary schooling at Alcorn College High School but in 1959 transferred to the Port Gibson High School. In spite of the changes in the setting of his high school studies, Joe was able to take a full set of science courses, in all of which he did well. He graduated from Port Gibson High in 1960.

Higher Education

Attending Alcorn College in Lorman, Mississippi, was a family tradition. Both his parents and his older sister had graduated from this school. Lorman was just a few miles from Port Gibson, and Joseph Dunbar saved money by living at home. Since the school was relatively small, classes were uncrowded and students received individual attention. It was in one of these classes that Dunbar's biology teacher, Dr. Earnest Boykins, recognized and encouraged Dunbar's desire to become a research scientist.

In 1963, after Joseph Dunbar graduated from Alcorn College, he taught high school biology and served as school band director in Bassville, Mississippi. In the spring of 1964, as soon as school ended at Bassville, Dunbar enrolled in summer school at Texas Southern University. He had been accepted into the graduate program at Texas Southern and wanted to get an early start. His savings from his teaching job financed his summer program and a teaching assistantship supported him during his further study.

After he completed his degree in 1966, Joseph Dunbar was invited to remain at Texas Southern as a regular faculty member. He decided that it would be a good idea to stay for one year and expand his teaching experience before continuing his graduate work. As a regular faculty member, he was assigned a student assistant to help him set up laboratory experiments. Joseph Dunbar quickly fell in love with the young woman who took the job, Agnes Estorge, and they were married at the end of the school year.

In the fall of 1967, Dunbar entered the doctoral program at Wayne State University in Detroit, Michigan. He was awarded an assistantship to help conduct research programs on diabetes. During his earlier research, Dunbar had studied gland functions, and he knew that this program would be relevant to his interest.

Diabetes is caused by a disorder of the gland in the pancreas that produces the hormone insulin. Insulin, in turn, controls how much sugar is released into the blood stream and how quickly it is used. Most people with diabetes do not produce enough insulin and, therefore, need a daily injection of pure insulin. Often, diabetic patients are allowed to administer the insulin themselves, but there are obvious dangers in such a procedure. For example, too large a dose of insulin can be as bad as too small. Also, some patients have bad reactions to pure insulin. Scientists, therefore, have searched for ways to control the natural production of this hormone.

Joseph Dunbar hoped to discover whether any chemicals other than insulin would be beneficial to victims of that disease. He was particularly successful in developing new ways to test such drugs. Joseph Dunbar finished his dissertation and was awarded his doctoral degree from Wayne State in 1970.

Career Highlights

After receiving his doctorate, Dr. Dunbar continued his studies as a post-doctoral fellow at Sinai Hospital in Detroit. At Sinai Hospital, he worked with Dr. Piero Foa on research, investigating how the pancreas gland reacts when it receives an injection of insulin. The two scientists wanted to know whether the normal function of the gland would decline if an outside supply of insulin was introduced.

Dr. Dunbar also studied how other glands work, such as the small, saliva-producing glands under the tongue. He was interested, too, in the effects of medicines and other organic compounds on gland functions. Another of his concerns was whether excess body weight was detrimental to the pancreas' function of regulating the storage and use of sugars.

Dr. Dunbar was invited to join the faculty at Wayne State School of Medicine as an assistant professor in 1972. His first daughter, Andrea, was just a year old when he began his teaching duties in the Department of Physiology. Now he had to balance his time among research projects, teaching assignments, professional obligations, and family duties. However, even with this heavy work load, Dr. Dunbar found the energy to teach one evening class in physiology and anatomy at the Harper Hospital Nursing School.

Dr. Dunbar's post-doctoral research at Sinai Hospital had been so valuable that he was asked to continue his affiliation with the hospital, an affiliation that continued nine years after his appointment to Wayne State. The connection with Sinai allowed Dr. Dunbar to continue his research projects and increase his publication productivity. In 1978, when he was awarded tenure at Wayne State and promoted to associate professor, he had 13 major research reports to his credit.

Dr. Dunbar's continuing study on the workings of the pancreas and the problems of diabetes included an investigation on the aftermath of a pancreas transplant into a healthy laboratory animal. Even more central to his theme was a study on whether other hormones, besides insulin, can influence sugar use and storage in the body. One such hormone is glucagon, also produced in the pancreas, but whose functions are directly opposite to those of insulin. Dr. Dunbar investigated the possibility that some forms of diabetes might be caused by an oversupply of glucagon rather than an undersupply of insulin. He thought that perhaps a person with diabetes would fare best if both insulin and glucagon were regulated by treatment. His research, while very fruitful and interesting, has not yet answered these questions to Dr. Dunbar's satisfaction.

Soon, Dr. Dunbar began to explore the connection of the pancreas to other organs of the body. For example, the liver stores the sugar-like materials that provide energy resources for the body, while the pancreas controls the availability of these materials in the blood stream. Other organs, such as the heart, can be negatively affected by insulin, which heightens blood pressure level. Also, if the pancreas produces an oversupply of insulin, blood sugar is reduced sharply, which seriously affects the brain, possibly causing the patient to lose consciousness. This condition, called insulin shock, can produce serious side effects or even death.

By the time Dr. Dunbar was promoted to the rank of full professor, his older daughter was 14 and his younger daughter was 10 years old. He greatly enjoyed watching his girls become lovely young ladies. Dr. Dunbar also enjoyed knowing that his years of teaching and research had influenced a whole generation of students to investigate the pancreas and the disabling disease of diabetes. He had supervised six master's degree projects and seen five doctoral students through their dissertation research. Government and private donors had awarded him continuous research grant support. In 1989, he won a Minority Achievement Award, and in 1992, he won the Charles Gershenson Distinguished Faculty Fellowship.

Dr. Dunbar continues his research into the mystery of gland function and disfunction and anticipates more discoveries in this important field of science.

Irving Wesley Elliott, Jr.

Born: October 21, 1925, in Newton, Kansas

Status: Professor and Chair, Department of Chemistry, Fisk University, Nashville, Tennessee

Education:

Bachelor of Science degree, University of Kansas, Lawrence, Kansas, 1947

Master of Science degree, University of Kansas, 1949

Doctor of Philosophy degree, University of Kansas, 1952

Research Area: Organic Chemistry

Early Years

Newton, Kansas, at the time of Wesley Elliott's birth, was a quiet railroad junction and farming center. Newton was also a major Mennonite center. Mennonites follow religious creeds that put high value on independence, nonviolence, and hard work. After the Civil War, the railroad arrived in Newton, and the town became the stopping point for cattle drives from Texas. The cattle drivers would receive their pay when they brought the cattle herds into Newton, and the conservative Mennonite farmers were shocked by their behavior. After 1870, when the railroad was pushed south and west, Newton quickly returned to its natural, quiet condition. Newton, however, was still a railroad town. In fact, Wesley Elliott's father spent his life working for the Santa Fe Railroad Company.

Elliot was the middle of three children, and the only boy. His older sister was taking chemistry at their high school when Wesley was a freshman. She complained that the textbook was too hard to understand. A typical younger brother, Wesley did not believe her. During the holiday season, he read the chemistry textbook from cover to cover, and, as he had suspected, it was not too difficult for him.

Later that same year, all the students in Wesley's speech course were given an assignment to prepare a short talk on their chosen future profession. Wesley's parents hoped he would become a lawyer. Since Wesley had no strong ideas about his future career, he was willing to follow his parents' wishes. However, when he did research for his speech, he found that everything on law had been used by another student. Among the materials that remained were those covering one of the fields of chemistry, so he started to prepare a speech as if he wanted to become a chemist. The more he read about chemistry as a career, the more interested he became. By the time he presented his speech, he had decided he would indeed become a chemist someday.

Wesley continued to read more and more about chemistry and eventually built his own chemistry laboratory in the basement. After earning money doing odd jobs in the summer, he bought test tubes, beakers, and some basic chemicals. He also bought a textbook on organic chemistry and the laboratory manual that went with it.

Wesley began to do his own experiments in his basement laboratory. He liked to conduct projects that were entertaining for his friends. He made hydrogen sulfide, which smells like rotten eggs, and dissolved pennies in nitric acid. He also enjoyed projects that were a bit risky and, from time to time, caused small explosions. His parents were not very happy, but Wesley was learning some good chemistry lessons on his own.

When Wesley completed high school in 1943, the United States had entered World War II. His mother wanted him to have some college credits before he was drafted, so she helped him enroll at the University of Kansas in Lawrence, Kansas, for the 1943 summer session.

Higher Education

Because of his poor eyesight, Wesley Elliott was never drafted. He was able to go straight through four years of college without interruption and complete some creative research projects with his chemistry professor, Dr. Calvin Van der Werf. Dr. Van der Werf was interested in a particular problem concerning the chemical compounds that come in both "right-handed" and "left-handed" versions. The arrangement of the atoms in the two versions are mirror images of each other. If they are mixed, they are almost impossible to separate because they have the same boiling point and melting point. However, each version can react with other chemicals in its own way. This can be important because the left-handed sugar molecule might be easy for a human to digest, while the right-handed version might not.

Elliott thought this work presented an interesting challenge. The problem for chemists is that the different versions cannot easily be separated. They have the same boiling point so distillation will not separate them. Also, it is very difficult to assemble molecules that are all of one type by synthetic methods in the laboratory.

Elliot worked with Professor van der Werf on these difficult problems with modest success. However, the work was good enough to strengthen ties of mutual respect so that van der Werf became a steady participant in Elliot's training during all three of his degree programs.

Elliott's activities included more than just school work. He was a very good runner and participated in track and field sports all through his college years. Unfortunately, he was not allowed to be a regular member of the track team. Other universities in his athletic conference still practiced segregation in college athletics and would not allow Elliott to compete in their events. Elliott, however, won many events in local campus competitions.

Students on campus wanted to have Wesley Elliott and other African American students as regular members of the university's sports teams. The students circulated petitions and held protest meetings. Eventually, the rules were changed. However, it was too late for Elliott to gain recognition for his athletic abilities. Nevertheless, he helped open the door for others. In later years, the University of Kansas was able to attract many outstanding African American athletes such as Wilt Chamberlain, Gale Sayers, and Jo-Jo White.

Wesley also had to deal with segregated student housing. There were no dormitory rooms for African American students at the University of Kansas in the 1940s. Most Black students had to find lodgings with African American families that lived in Lawrence, and there were very few such rooms available.

Many White students did not live in a dormitory. They formed cooperative housing groups. Two of Elliott's White friends belonged to such a group, and they invited him to join them, even though the group had never before included an African American member. The situation worked out to everyone's advantage. Again, Wesley Elliott had opened a door. By living in the co-op house, he showed that members of the two races could get along together for mutual benefits. In recognition of his accomplishments, he was awarded a grant from the William A. White-Hillel Foundation for his work to improve race relations. A year later, he was elected to a national society that honored students for their good scholarship, leadership, and moral character.

When Wesley Elliott finished his undergraduate degree, he went directly on to graduate school at Kansas. Dr. Van der Werf introduced Elliott to Dr. William E. McEwen, who had just come to the University of Kansas from Columbia University in New York City and had brought many new and difficult research problems with him.

Dr. McEwen asked Elliott to assist him in his research. He gave Wesley the problem of putting two atoms of nitrogen into a molecule that had very similar properties to the molecule that gives cinnamon its taste and smell. The project was interesting, because the presence of nitrogen tends to make natural compounds that have a strong effect on the human body—like nicotine and caffeine—very active.

Dr. McEwen and Wesley Elliott hoped their research would lead to the creation of a new compound that might possess unique biological effects. The experimentation involved placing the nitrogen atoms in exactly the right place in the molecule. Dr. McEwen and Elliott, however, only had partial success. Even so, it was a good step forward.

During the previous summer, Elliott had taken a temporary job with the Eastman Kodak Company in Elmira, New York. There, he learned many practical lessons, such as how to conduct more than one experiment at a time. He also studied new ways to see the actual structure of tiny molecules. These new techniques used various kinds of radiation such as X rays and infrared and ultraviolet light rays. Years later, Elliott was able to use this information in more advanced research projects.

He received his master's degree from Kansas in 1949 and immediately wanted to begin working toward his doctoral degree, but the university would not give him a teaching assistantship because of his race. He did not have enough money to continue his education on his own, so he decided to look for a teaching job elsewhere. A fellow African American student knew of an opening at Southern University in Baton Rouge, Louisiana. Wesley Elliott applied for this job and was accepted.

The situation at Southern University, however, was depressing. The Deep South was still burdened with total segregation. The students at Southern University were not well prepared for college, and their motivation was poor. The laboratory was poorly equipped, and Wesley Elliott had no one to help set up and supervise the laboratory assignments.

Some good things did happen, however. Wesley Elliott was introduced to Joan Louise Curl, a young woman who taught German at the university. Later, she became Elliott's wife and the mother of their two children. He also received a small research grant from the Carnegie Foundation, which allowed Elliott to continue the research he had started

at the University of Kansas on the effects of nitrogen in the cinnamon-type molecule.

To speed the reaction of the chemicals in his experiments, Elliott used a strong acid. One evening, he mixed his ingredients and observed the reaction. Soon, the process was complete—or so he thought. He closed his office and went to dinner. After he had eaten, he went to the library, where he was met by a campus security officer. His experiment had exploded.

Wesley Elliott's office was wrecked, and his desk and chair were completely destroyed. The explosion knocked down the wall between his office and the next one. Little pieces of glass and metal had spread through the room like shrapnel. The president of the university came to look at the damage. Although he did not say much to Elliott, Elliott anticipated that his contract would not be renewed for a second year. He was correct.

Wesley Elliott decided that the best thing he could do was to go back to the University of Kansas and continue working toward his doctoral degree. He rejoined his friends at the cooperative house. He also began a new set of research projects with Dr. McEwen. This time their goal was to change compounds that already contained a nitrogen atom. They started with one of the building blocks of quinine, a medicine that comes from the bark of a tree and is used to treat victims of malaria.

The research projects with Dr. McEwen went well. Progress toward the doctoral degree, however, was slow, because Elliott had to work part-time in the chemistry laboratory of the Kansas Geological Survey to support himself.

The situation began to improve, however, when Dr. Van der Werf and Dr. Ray Brewster were awarded a new research grant from the U.S. Army. The grant gave them money to hire a research assistant. Since the government did not allow racial discrimination in the awarding of grants, Wesley Elliott was chosen for the job. Fortunately, Elliott was able to use the results of the studies for part of his doctoral research. In August 1952, he passed the final oral examination on his dissertation. As soon as he had passed this last test, he married Joan Louise Curl. She had been teaching German at Florida A&M University in Tallahassee, Florida, and she used her influence there to get her new husband a job in their chemistry department.

Career Highlights

After only one year as a faculty member at Florida A&M University, Dr. Elliott was made the head of the combined departments of chemistry and physics and was promoted to full professor. While the other teachers were older, Dr. Elliott was the only person in physics or chemistry to have a doctoral degree. As head of the department, he could choose the courses he wished to teach and continue work on his research projects. He was soon able to publish his first independent research report in 1954.

Dr. Elliott was also able to choose the equipment for a newly constructed science building. He chose to install the type of research tools he had seen at the Eastman Kodak Company. This equipment gave Florida A&M a better research capability than many other universities in the southern United States.

The activism of some of his students drew Dr. Elliott into the local Civil Rights movement. Along with his wife and sister-in-law, he participated in the bus boycott of Tallahassee in 1955.

The civil rights situation had calmed down somewhat when Dr. Elliott received a National Science Foundation Faculty Fellowship. The fellowship allowed Dr. Elliott to study for a year at Harvard University, where he had the use of even more advanced re-

search tools than he had at Florida A & M. He studied the structure of pure organic compounds by seeing how the atoms vibrated in a magnetic field. This work led to more published reports in highly respected chemical journals.

After his year at Harvard, Dr. Elliott was offered a teaching position at Fisk University in Nashville, Tennessee. He accepted this offer and was soon awarded grant support for his research from the Petroleum Research Fund. He also inherited a collection of rare natural chemicals. Some of these chemicals had been provided by Dr. Percy Julian (see p. 197), when he had been associated with Fisk University. The chemicals were all carbon based with one or more nitrogen atoms attached. They were just the type of compounds with which Dr. Elliott had always worked. He began to expand the scope of his research projects.

He also began to travel more extensively. In the summer of 1964, he went to Dearborn, Michigan, as a visiting scientist at the Ford Motor Company. In 1965, he spent a year as a visiting professor at Howard University in Washington, D.C. In 1969, he studied at the University of Copenhagen in Denmark and Lund University in Sweden. His studies taught him more about the use of radiation to determine the structure of carbon-based molecules. In 1984, he was a visiting professor at Wellesley College in Massachusetts.

While he continued to explore many kinds of chemical reactions, he was most interested in materials that could affect human cells. In 1988, he and a group of his students discovered a new compound that, Dr. Elliott thinks, might be of use in the battle against AIDS. Dr. Elliott holds a patent on this chemical, and it is now being tested by the National Institutes of Health. If the tests show that this new chemical is effective, it will be a boon to Dr. Elliott, to AIDS victims, to health care providers, and to the citizens of the world.

Herman Eure

Born: January 7, 1947, in Corapeake, North Carolina

Status: Professor of Biology, Wake Forest University, Winston-Salem, North Carolina

Education:

Bachelor of Science degree, University of Maryland Eastern Shore, Princess Anne, Maryland, 1969

Doctor of Philosophy degree, Wake Forest University, Winston-Salem, North Carolina, 1974

Research Area: Parasitology

Early Years

Herman Eure was the seventh of ten children in the Eure family. His father, Grover T. Eure, served as a skilled pipefitter at the Norfolk Naval Shipyard in Portsmouth, Virginia. His mother, Sarah Goodman Eure, served as a domestic worker, while raising five boys and

five girls. Ella, the oldest girl, was the first person in the Eure family to attend college. She graduated from what is now North Carolina Central University in Durham, North Carolina, and later became a member of the Metropolitan Opera Company in New York City.

The four youngest children were boys, and Herman was the oldest of this group. They played schoolyard basketball and other sports and explored the rural countryside around Corapeake. Their favorite spot was the forest behind their home. This forest is part of the Great Dismal Swamp, which extends many miles from Norfolk, Virginia, into North Carolina and abounds with wildlife of all kinds. The four brothers explored the area and observed the many different kinds of animals that lived in the swamp. These experiences motivated Herman's later interest in biological science.

Because Corapeake was a very small farming town and had no schools, the Eure children went to T. S. Cooper School in Sunbury, North Carolina, for their first eight grades. During Herman's early years, the Cooper School was both an elementary school and a high school. In 1961, however, when Herman had finished the eighth grade, the school was reorganized as a grade school, and Herman transferred to Central High School in Gatesville, North Carolina. A school bus picked up Herman and a group of students at the Cooper School and then collected other young people along the route. Herman considered the daily bus ride to be an exciting adventure because it brought together young people from all over the county.

Herman was an excellent student and class member. He was class president for two years and president of the student government in his senior year. He also excelled in athletics, captaining the track team during his final two years in high school and the basketball team in his senior year. The high school fielded its first football team while Herman was at Central, and he served as one of that team's captains. Since the football team was new, its record of wins and losses was not outstanding; however, Herman had the distinction of catching the first pass thrown by a Central quarterback in a varsity game.

Herman graduated at the top of his class and won a scholarship named after Sam Ervin, a famous U.S. Senator from North Carolina. He was also offered a track scholarship by Maryland State College, now the University of Maryland Eastern Shore (UMES), in Princess Anne, Maryland, which he gladly accepted.

Higher Education

Herman Eure did as well in college as he had done in high school. Again, he was active in student government and won several awards for his contributions to student affairs. Eure continued to enjoy sports and played on his fraternity's intermural basketball team. He also spent many joyful afternoons just hanging out with his friends in the backyard of his fraternity house.

Herman Eure won a Ford Foundation Fellowship for his graduate studies. He returned to his home state of North Carolina to attend Wake Forest University in Winston-Salem.

Before beginning his program of study, Herman Eure spent the summer developing his research skills at the U.S. Department of Agriculture's research station in Hamden, Connecticut. He studied the inherited characteristics of the weevil that infests white pine forests in the New England states. The department's biologists sought to develop methods for controlling this pest by gaining knowledge of its ancestry and reproductive capabilities.

As his main research topic at Wake Forest, Herman Eure chose to study the parasites that attack fresh-water fish. His mentor in this

field of study was Professor G. W. Esch. Together, they studied the intestinal worm that infects largemouth bass. Their research question centered on a link between environmental pollution and the degree to which these fish might be infested with the parasite. In particular, Eure focused his attention on whether heat pollution in the water might increase the level of infection of largemouth bass by intestinal worms. Even more specifically, Eure wanted to know how well the bass fared when they lived in the reservoirs that are heated indirectly by industrial use. Eure chose the reservoir called Par Pond that has built up behind a dam on the Savannah River as the site for his study. The water in this reservoir is used to cool nuclear reactors that make plutonium for the government and produce electric power as a by-product.

The native fish were not harmed by the warm water. In fact, they seemed to like it. They congregated in clusters close to the outlet pipes from the plant. Consequently, catching fish to study was always easy. For the fish, so-called heat pollution was a good thing—they grew faster and were more productive in the warm water than they were in water at normal temperatures.

As a field biologist, Herman Eure had many other outdoor adventures, including contact with some stubborn alligators. A team led by graduate students from the University of Georgia was capturing and banding these animals when one refused to become a captive. The alligator simply uprooted the whole tree to which it was chained and headed back into the swamp. It took several students to grab the uprooted tree and prevent the escape.

Career Highlights

As soon as Dr. Eure finished his graduate studies, he joined his former teachers at Wake Forest as a teaching colleague. He continued to work on the parasites of fish, but other topics began to catch his interest. In particular, Dr. Eure became active in the selection and recruitment of minority people into advanced scientific training and scientific occupations. He focused this interest through the channels provided by organizations such as the National Science Foundation (NSF) and the Ford Foundation. The NSF is responsible for making sure government support of research projects is managed in such a way as to give minority applicants a fair chance of being funded. There are also legal requirements placed on the colleges and universities that receive NSF grants to ensure that faculty hiring is fair to minorities and women candidates.

Along these same lines, Dr. Eure has worked with the officials of educational institutions that have a tradition of serving African American and other minority students. One of the goals of his efforts has been to make sure that these institutions acted on the opportunities provided by new federal programs.

Also of great importance, Dr. Eure provides advice and direction to the people who develop, administer, score, and report on the tests that are used to evaluate the aptitudes of candidates for admission to colleges, graduate schools, and medical schools around the country. It has long been believed that some of these tests are not in balance from a cultural perspective. The effort to bring them back into balance is being aided by people like Dr. Eure.

All this work has resulted in Dr. Eure's participation in two relatively new enterprises. One is the Society for the Social Study of Science. The other is called the Graylyn Group. This organization is dedicated to the mission of placing minority women in science, mathematics, and engineering careers. Dr. Eure's participation in this project has led, in turn, to his collaboration on the book, *Blacks, Education and American Science*, edited by Dr. Willie Pearson and published by Rutgers University Press in 1989. On a more personal level, Dr. Eure now serves as a mentor for minority students on the scholarships that he, himself, helped bring into being at Wake Forest.

Back on the research front, in 1987 Dr. Eure was able to get a grant to support his studies. This led to a semester in England, where he worked in the laboratory of Professor Clive Kennedy at the University of Exeter. Here, Dr. Eure caught up on the study of fish parasites and expanded his research to include trout in addition to largemouth bass.

Dr. Eure was promoted to full professor at Wake Forest in 1991. Now, one of his main activities outside of teaching and research is the monitoring of the quality of the reports resulting from Ford Foundation Fellowships that support both pre- and post-doctoral scientific research. This work is coordinated through the National Research Council in Washington, D.C.

Slayton A. Evans, Jr.

Born: May 17, 1943, in Chicago, Illinois

Status: Kenan Professor of Chemistry, University of North Carolina, Chapel Hill, North Carolina

Education:
Bachelor of Science degree, Tougaloo College, Tougaloo, Mississippi, 1965
Doctor of Philosophy degree, Case Western Reserve University, Cleveland, Ohio, 1970

Research Area: Organic Chemistry

Early Years

When Slayton Evans was born in Chicago, Illinois, the United States was deeply engaged in a war with Japan and Germany. A few months after Slayton's birth, his father

chemistry set. On others days, he studied the insects and plants he collected near his home. After observing each specimen carefully under his small microscope, Slayton would draw its picture on an index card. He labeled the drawings and wrote down questions about the objects. Later, he would consult the books and encyclopedias at his school to find the answers.

Slayton and his younger brother and sister attended a segregated school run by the Roman Catholic Church in Meridian. His parents, who had both received some college training, wanted Slayton to be prepared to go to college—and graduate school, if possible. They were certain that the nuns at St. Joseph's School would give Slayton a solid foundation.

Something exciting occurred in the fall of 1957, just as Slayton was starting the ninth grade. The Soviet Union launched Sputnik, the first artificial satellite. Like many other young people at the time, Slayton became very interested in space exploration. He wanted to learn more about the subject and found a book about rocketry at his library. After reading the book, Slayton decided to build his own miniature rocket.

The nuns gave him permission to buy the chemicals needed to make dry rocket fuel. However, he found that the type of charcoal he needed was not readily available. Slayton had to invent a way of making his own. He used a test tube to make a miniature kiln and used a cork with a small hole punched through it as a stopper. Without the hole, the heated air could not have escaped and the test tube would have exploded. Next, wooden match sticks with the heads removed were placed in Slayton's kiln and it was heated over a laboratory burner. The wood charred but did not burn. Burning requires the presence of air, and the heated air in the test tube had been driven out through the hole in the cork. When the test tube and its charred con-

was called into military service. When Mr. Evans returned home, the family moved from Chicago to Meridian, Mississippi. Even though Meridian is the second largest town in Mississippi, its population is under 50,000. Mr. Evans was hoping to find a more congenial atmosphere in this smaller city.

Shortly after they arrived in Meridian, the Evans family moved into a segregated public housing project. In this city, the social relationships within the African American community were much more open and informal than in Chicago. Indeed, people in Slayton's neighborhood were like a large, extended family. In this supportive community, the boy's ambitions were encouraged by both family and friends. Special support also was given by his grandparents, who lived nearby.

Slayton's father worked as a stockroom manager for the local J. C. Penney store. The pay was low, but Mr. Evans was able to follow his own style of life. He rose very early so he could read or meditate before setting off for work. Young Slayton began to imitate his father. He, too, would get up early in the morning. Some days, he played with his tents had cooled, Slayton used marbles to crush the blackened match sticks in a bowl. Finally, he mixed the homemade powdered charcoal with the other ingredients to make his rocket fuel.

To construct his rockets, Slayton used aluminum foil to line cardboard tubes. Then for each launching session, his carefully prepared rocket fuel was poured into the tube. During his first launch attempt, the rocket did not leave the launching pad, but rather blew an eight-inch crater in the ground and brought out the local fire department. Of the six homemade rockets that Slayton built, only two achieved liftoff.

Because he did not go to a public school, Slayton's parents had to pay tuition for his education. As soon as he could, Slayton contributed to the effort. At first, this meant mowing lawns on weekends. Later, when he reached the eighth grade, he became the junior-assistant janitor for the elementary school. Later, he did the same sort of work at the high school cafeteria. His jobs paid for his own and his younger sister's tuition and helped the family's finances.

During his third year in high school, Slayton began to think about college. He knew his family could not afford the costs. Since his ambition was to become an astronaut, he thought of enlisting in the Air Force. By doing this, he could earn veteran's benefits for college and perhaps even qualify for the Air Force Academy. However, he was too tall to qualify for flight training.

The backup plan was to try for some sort of scholarship support. His parents and teachers were confident that he could win a scholarship. After taking several competitive examinations, Slayton was awarded an academic scholarship at Tougaloo College. St. Elmo Brady, the first African American to earn a doctorate, had spent his teaching career at this highly regarded school. The college, located in Tougaloo, Mississippi, also offered Slayton an athletic scholarship for basketball. With the financial aid from both scholarships, Slayton was able to begin his higher education in the fall of 1961.

Higher Education

Slayton Evans found the competition much more difficult at Tougaloo College than it had been at St. Joseph's High School. Many of the students were veterans of the Korean war. They were older and more serious about their studies than the younger students.

Even though Evans had taken all the mathematics and science courses offered by his high school, he was not as well prepared in these subjects as many of the other students. Fortunately, Evans's chemistry teacher was supportive and gave him extra help when he needed it. In addition, Evans and a friend, who was an engineering student, studied mathematics together. These study sessions were very helpful. At the end of the first year, Evans got the highest marks of all the freshman chemistry students.

Evans soon found that he was gaining knowledge of both science and the Civil Rights movement at Tougaloo. In the early 1960s, the freedom riders were beginning to come into Mississippi and Alabama. Tougaloo became one of the favorite stop-over places. As a private college, it could be protected from invasions by anti-civil rights groups. In other words, Tougaloo was a safe haven.

During this same period, Evans met a woman exchange student from an eastern school. Her father was a senior scientist at Abbott Laboratories in Chicago, Illinois, a major producer of medicines. After the father met Evans, he offered to help the young man find summer employment at Abbott Laboratories. The job was excellent training for Evans because he could see the practical applications of what he was studying at school. The experience also strengthened Evans's resolve to become a research chemist.

His first jobs at Abbott were relatively easy. He was asked to create specific chemical compounds by selecting the proper ingredients from a designated assortment of raw materials. Since he knew that the compounds would be used in the manufacture of medicines, Evans worked with great care and accuracy. His concern went beyond the standard requirements for the job. For example, he studied the compounds to see if they could be made with less expensive raw materials.

When he was invited back to Abbott for a second summer, he was given more challenging projects. He was asked to identify the underlying steps through which some chemical reactions take place. The professional chemists at Abbott Labs soon took an interest in Evans. They assured him that he had the ability to attend graduate school. However, Slayton Evans was worried that he could not pay for further education. He had worked after class and every summer since he began college. Graduate school might be so demanding that he would not be able to work. The chemists at Abbott suggested that Evans attend the Illinois Institute of Technology (IIT) in Chicago. Then, he could continue to work part-time at Abbott Labs.

He was admitted to the graduate program at ITT, but it did not work out. One of his teachers suggested that he might feel more at home at Case Western Reserve University in Cleveland, Ohio. He accepted this advice. Evans applied to Case Western and was offered a research assistantship. With this financial aid and some outside employment, he was able to begin his graduate studies.

His research assistantship turned out to be a multiple blessing. While still in his first year of graduate school, he got a draft notice to serve in Viet Nam from his draft board in Meridian, Mississippi. However, Evans's re-

search project was crucial to the war effort. He was working on the development of a medicine that could be used to control the disease, Schistosomiasis. This disease, caused by a parasite, is common in Viet Nam and elsewhere in southeast Asia. The officials at Case Western communicated the importance of Evans's research to his draft board. Evans was taken off the list of people eligible for the draft. He now felt secure enough to set a wedding date. Slayton Evans and his fiancée were soon married.

Career Highlights

Slayton Evans finished his course work at Case Western in the fall of 1969. However, his degree would not be conferred until the spring of 1970. Nevertheless, he accepted a postdoctoral fellowship at the University of Texas in Arlington. By the time he received his doctorate, the new Dr. Evans had already made a professional name for himself. Before the fall of 1970, he had been invited to begin a second postdoctoral fellowship. He would be conducting research at the University of Notre Dame in South Bend, Indiana.

For the two years at Notre Dame, Dr. Evans worked with the acclaimed chemist, Professor Ernest L. Eliel. Under Dr. Eliel's tutelage, he learned the delicate techniques for assembling molecules that can bend light to the left or to the right. The direction of the light depends on how the individual atoms are arranged in the molecule. A molecule can be either right-handed or left-handed. In three dimensions, these near-twin molecules look like mirror images of one another.

In medical usage, the biological effect of the molecule can depend on its handedness. For example, a particular molecule that bends light to the left makes a person's heart beat faster. The very same molecule's right-handed twin might have little or no effect on the heart rate. Dr. Evans became an expert in the positioning of atoms in molecules to control the light's direction. This field of chemistry—stereochemistry—has become Dr. Evans's most important specialty.

When Dr. Evans completed his fellowship research, he joined the faculty at Dartmouth College in Hanover, New Hampshire. However, Dartmouth did not have the laboratory resources he needed to continue his research. Therefore, Dr. Evans was pleased when he was invited to join the faculty at the University of North Carolina at Chapel Hill. At North Carolina, Dr. Evans was rapidly promoted and reached the rank of full professor in just ten years.

Among his most successful accomplishments at Chapel Hill has been the creation of a research team that is composed of graduate and undergraduate chemistry students from around the world. The exact composition of the team changes as students graduate and new ones arrive. However, the spirit and style as well as the scientific mission of the team remains constant because of the dedication of Dr. Evans.

During the 1980s, Dr. Evans expanded the scope of his research activities to include other countries. A Ford Foundation Fellowship allowed him to build a strong relationship between his research team and a similar team at the Université Paul Sabatier in Toulouse, France. Later, a Fulbright Fellowship allowed Dr. Evans to strengthen ties with other groups in France, Germany, Poland, Greece, Russia, and Mexico.

In addition to his teaching and research, Dr. Evans has served on the review committees of the National Institutes of Health and the National Science Foundation in Washington, D.C. He has been active in recruiting minority members to study science at institutions across the country, and in April 1994, he received the Tanner Award for Teaching Excellence at the University of North Carolina.

Angela D. Ferguson

Born: February 15, 1925, in Washington, D.C.

Status: Retired, Associate Vice President for Health Affairs, Howard University, 1990

Education:

Bachelor of Science degree, Howard University, Washington, D.C., 1945

Doctor of Medicine degree, Howard University, 1949

Research Area: Physiology

Early Years

Angela Ferguson's father was a "man of many parts"—as the old saying goes. He was a teacher at Samuel Armstrong School, a segregated school in Washington, D.C., that taught teen-aged African American students the so-called manual arts: carpentry, metal working, and mechanical drawing. Mr. Ferguson also worked as an architect and had established his own architectural business. At the same time, he was a reservist in the U.S. Army with the rank of lieutenant colonel. Yet, in spite of all these positions, the

Fergusons, a family of eight, lived on the edge of poverty. In part, the family's financial condition was due to the deep economic depression in the 1930s.

When Angela was in grade school, she worked in the cafeteria in exchange for her school meals. At home, dinner might be limited to a serving of boiled potatoes or hot cocoa made with water. Sometimes even water was not easily available because the family had no money to pay the bill.

When Angela was ready for high school, she had to decide which school to attend. Her choices were Samuel Armstrong School, Dunbar High School, and Cordoza High School. She did not want to attend Armstrong because her father taught there, and she was afraid of being labeled a teacher's pet. Dunbar was considered a college preparatory school, and since Angela was not thinking of going to college, she decided Cardoza was the most sensible choice. Cardoza's courses focused on business skills but they also provided a strong general educational program.

During her second year of high school, Angela took the basic science courses to meet her graduation requirements. She had not studied science before and was surprised to find that she liked her science courses very much. She was particularly fascinated by chemistry. Her ability to solve chemistry problems by the use of mathematics was a revelation to her, and she began to see herself as a future scientist.

Because she originally intended to take only the minimum number of science courses, Angela was behind those students who were science majors. Therefore, she had to make up during summer school the courses she missed.

While in high school, Angela also participated in extracurricular activities, such as cheerleading, serving as the drum majorette in the marching band, and playing the French horn in the school orchestra. Angela graduated from Cardoza High School in 1941.

Higher Education

Angela Ferguson wanted to continue her education and pursue a career in science, so she applied to and was accepted by Howard University in Washington, D.C. Her parents had saved enough to cover her college tuition and fees for the first year, and since she lived at home, she had few extra expenses. After her first year, Ferguson's tuition and fees were covered by scholarship money. She was able to pay her extra expenses from the money she earned during the summer months at the laboratories in Freedmen's Hospital—the teaching hospital connected to the Howard University Medical School.

Meanwhile, her interests were changing. In her first year, chemistry and mathematics were her major subjects. In her second year, biology began to have more appeal. Chemistry and mathematics seemed too dry. She now found such courses as comparative anatomy to be far more to her liking. Also, in her biology classes, she met and became friends with several students who were preparing for medical school. In their conversations, these friends praised the medical profession and the quality of medical training at Howard. Angela gradually decided that she would like to become both a scientist and a medical doctor. Medical training was now her strong ambition. Her faculty advisor agreed with this decision and gave Ferguson the academic support she needed.

Anglea continued at Howard University for her medical training. Her most enlightening class in medical school was a course in pediatrics, the medical care of infants and children, taught by Dr. Roland Scott. The subject matter and his teaching style strongly appealed to Ms. Ferguson, and she resolved to make children's health care a part of her career plans. She finished her course work and was awarded her medical degree from Howard in 1949.

Career Highlights

Dr. Ferguson did her internship in general medicine at Freedmen's Hospital. Consequently, she worked in all areas of the hospital—obstetrics, pediatrics, surgery, and emergency care among others. After a year as an intern, Dr. Ferguson continued her training as a hospital resident, specializing in pediatrics.

After completing her residency and passing her board examinations, Dr. Ferguson started her own private pediatrics practice. As a doctor, she was expected to answer parents' questions related to the developmental stages of their children, e.g., when a baby should begin to cut its teeth, when a baby should be expected to take its first steps, and if a baby was overweight or underweight. But Dr. Ferguson was unable to answer these questions. Up until that point, the research done on developmental physiology had been based solely on children of European heritage—not African.

Her mentor at the Howard University School of Medicine, Dr. Scott, agreed that more research should be done on developmental physiology using African American children. Dr. Scott was able to bring Dr. Ferguson onto the staff of the medical school as a research associate, and he obtained the funds necessary to support the new research project.

The doctors realized their best source of child development information would be the well baby clinics around the country. These clinics had been established to encourage parents to follow a regular schedule of medical examinations and immunizations for their children. Therefore, detailed records were available on thousands of children—including those of African heritage. With these records, the researcher could follow an individual child's progress over several years or compare the observations on many children at exactly the same age. Statistics such as height and weight could be averaged to provide a good estimate of the expected size at each age level.

But before the new norms had been completely calculated, Dr. Ferguson identified a new problem. A large number of African American children suffered from sickle-cell anemia, a hereditary disease that causes the red blood cells to function improperly. Healthy red blood cells are donut shaped, but the diseased red blood cells are folded into a strange, sickle shape, thus preventing the easy flow of blood in the veins and arteries. Under ordinary conditions, the disease is not fatal, but if a person suffers an injury or gets an infection, the proportion of the sickle-shaped cells in the blood increases, which tends to clog the blood vessels. Usually, this clogging leads to serious pain and swelling, but the symptoms go away once the injury heals or the infection is cured. In severe cases, however, the blood pressure rises and the patient can die.

As with many medical conditions, early diagnosis is very important for successful treatment. Dr. Ferguson's first goal was to develop a method for detecting the disease in young children. Unfortunately, the early symptoms of the sickle-cell condition closely resemble a host of other medical conditions. In infants, the symptoms of sickle-cell anemia resemble those of arthritis; between the ages of two and six years, the symptoms look like a shortage of certain vitamins in the diet; between six and twelve years, most children show no symptoms or only very mild ones; and after twelve years of age, the disease can return— with skin ulcers as the most common symptom. Dr. Ferguson made a study of hundreds of cases of sickle-cell anemia and discovered the telltale symptoms. Her findings were published and distributed to doctor's all over the country.

Now that doctors had a good method to diagnose the disease, Dr. Ferguson turned her attention to the development of better treatments. She examined and organized the experiences of many victims and observed that if a sickle-cell patient had to undergo surgery, the stress could bring on severe problems. These problems could be reduced, however, if the patient were given extra oxygen after coming out of the anesthesia. For active five-year-olds, relief from severe symptoms could be obtained by the simple act of drinking extra water every day—especially water with a small amount of baking soda dissolved in it. Undoubtedly, the most important change instituted by Dr. Ferguson was the practice of giving each newborn African American a blood test so that the condition, if present, could be detected at the earliest possible time.

In the 1960s, Dr. Ferguson decided to shift her focus to administrative work. In 1965, the federal government offered to build a new teaching hospital at Howard University to replace the outdated Freedmen's Hospital. Because of her position on the medical school faculty, Dr. Ferguson was asked to develop plans for the children's wing of the new hospital. Then, in 1970, she was requested to take charge of the University Office of Health Affairs, which put her in charge of all facility development, student health services, research, and advanced instruction for all degree programs at Howard Medical School. In this new position, she was responsible for determining the facilities needed by each department under her jurisdiction and integrating those needs into the plans for the new hospital.

Dr. Ferguson also had to contend with members of the United States Congress, who wanted to control government spending on the new hospital building. The senators and

representatives' lack of medical expertise made it difficult for them to understand, for example, why there needed to be several feet of extra space around patients' beds. Dr. Ferguson explained that this is a necessity in a teaching hospital because a group of students must be able to gather around their instructor, a physician, while he lectures about the patients' particular medical problems.

In spite of the reluctance of some government officials, Dr. Ferguson saw to it that the budget was large enough to construct a building suitable for the purposes of a teaching hospital. The new, well-equipped Freedmen's Hospital opened in 1975. In 1979, Dr. Ferguson was named as the university's associate vice president for health affairs, and she held that position until she retired in 1990.

Dr. Ferguson's pioneering work in the health care of African American children and her research on the diagnosis and treatment of sickle-cell anemia have put her in the vanguard of American physicians.

Lloyd Noel Ferguson

Born: February 9, 1918, in Oakland, California

Status: Retired, California State University, Los Angeles, California, 1986

Education:

Bachelor of Science degree, University of California, Berkeley, California, 1940

Doctor of Philosophy degree, University of California, Berkeley, California, 1943

Research Area: Biochemistry

Early Years

Lloyd Ferguson is a third-generation Californian. His grandparents moved to California in the 1870s after the Civil War, and both his mother and father were born in that state.

His mother's father, William A. Johnson, worked in Oakland, California, as a bank teller, and his father, Noel S. Ferguson, worked for an insurance company in Oakland. His mother worked full-time as a house maid for a local medical doctor. Until the Great Depression in the 1930s, the family had plenty of money. Then, like so many other people, Noel Ferguson lost his job, and he and his wife had to sell their house. Since both his mother and father worked, Lloyd was raised mainly by his grandmother, who lived only a block from his home.

When he was just seven years old, Lloyd almost died of a complicated case of diphtheria and pneumonia. The medical doctor for whom his mother worked saved his life. It took Lloyd a long time to recover from his illness and he missed a whole year of school, but this misfortune made a powerful impression on Lloyd and later influenced some of his career decisions.

Before and after his illness, Lloyd liked going to school. He enjoyed being a hall monitor and doing chores for the teachers. In those days, a person could skip grades by passing tests and Lloyd skipped two grades while in grade school. One skip made up for the year he missed and the other put him a year ahead. He graduated from high school at the age of 16.

When Lloyd was about 12 years old, he bought a chemistry set. This began his life-long love of chemistry. He built a shed in his backyard, so he could do his experiments away from the house. He was more systematic than most children his age and kept a record of each of his experiments. Therefore, when Lloyd started high school, he already knew the nature of many of the more common chemicals.

After Lloyd Ferguson learned some new ideas from his high school chemistry class, he began to make more complex and useful products in his backyard shed. Lloyd made a handy moth repellant, spot remover, silver polish, and lemonade mix, and sold them in his neighborhood. In fact, he still makes and uses his own silver polish.

Because of money problems in his family, Lloyd held various jobs during the 1930s. Each day he delivered over one hundred copies of the *Oakland Tribune* to local residents, and during high school, he became the laboratory assistant for the chemistry course which paid 25¢ an hour. His chemistry teacher was very supportive, and she encouraged Lloyd to go on to college.

When Lloyd finished high school, however, he did not have enough money for college. Even though he kept his paper route, he knew that he had to find a regular job, so Lloyd went to work for the Works Progress Administration (WPA), a program the government had set up to find jobs for the unemployed. The WPA hired him to help build a new set of docks in Berkeley, California.

Lloyd did not remain a manual worker for very long, however. After a few months, he took a job as a porter for the Southern Pacific Railway Company. This job also allowed him to give up his paper route.

Myra King, the man in charge of the porters, was always on the lookout for bright young African Americans. He thought working as a porter would help the young men finance their college careers. The income from the new job did allow Lloyd to save money for college and also to help his family. After two years, he enrolled at the University of California at Berkeley.

Higher Education

Lloyd Ferguson continued to work as a porter while he was a student at the University. His work involved the transfer of luggage from Oakland to San Francisco by ferry boat across San Francisco Bay. Fortunately, he could study during the 20-minute boat ride. Since the hours were flexible, he could work in the morning before his classes began and in the evening after they were finished. He lived at home during this time and continued to help his family with the extra money that he made.

No one in Lloyd Ferguson's family had ever gone to college; therefore, he was forced to adjust to this new situation without much help from them. And since there were only a few African Americans enrolled at the university, he could not expect much advice from his fellow students. Ferguson realized that he did not know how to study at the college level. At first, he thought that he could succeed by simply attending his classes and reading his textbooks—that was how he had achieved good grades in high school. Unfortunately, this was not enough. There are higher standards in college.

After his first year, Ferguson decided that he must raise his academic standards. He and some fellow students formed a study group to work on physics and mathematics problems. The leader of the study group was an outstanding young man named Pat Fuller. Fifty-five years later, Pat Fuller and Lloyd Ferguson are still friends. Of more importance is the fact that the new study arrangement worked well. All the young men who joined received higher grades. Some, like Ferguson, rose to the top of the grade lists.

When he finished college, Lloyd Ferguson wanted to study the chemistry of rice. He wrote a letter to George Washington Carver (see p. 42) at Tuskegee Institute, hoping Dr. Carver would accept him as a research assistant, but Dr. Carver advised Ferguson to go on for graduate studies. Dr. Carver thought Ferguson should finish his education before trying full-time research. Lloyd Ferguson took the advice and applied for advanced training at the University of California.

Most universities have rules against accepting their own students into graduate programs. Educators are afraid that a student does not gain a broad view of his field if he attends both undergraduate and graduate school in the same institution. Ferguson, however, had done so well in his undergraduate work that an exception was made. Therefore, after receiving his bachelor of science degree from the University of California at Berkeley, he was accepted into Berkeley's own graduate program in 1940.

At first, he continued to work as a porter. But, after only two months in graduate school, one of the senior professors offered Ferguson a job in the Donner Radiation Laboratory at the University. This job paid less than working as a porter, but it was a good way for Ferguson to get professional experience. In the laboratory, his task was to isolate radioactive compounds. This was risky work, because the material had been exposed to beams of radiation from a cyclotron.

A few months later, another opportunity appeared. A young faculty member, Dr. Melvin Calvin, was working on a national defense project. He was looking for a material that could produce oxygen in an emergency and could be transported easily and safely by a submarine on patrol. Space is limited on a submarine and only a few oxygen tanks can be carried aboard; therefore, the scientists hoped to develop a space-saving material that would give off oxygen only when needed. Then, when the emergency was over, this same material would reabsorb oxygen from the outside air and be ready for reuse.

The team of Melvin Calvin, Lloyd Ferguson, and other students worked on the project. After many false starts and a year of experimentation, they finally found the right answer. They developed a material similar to hemoglobin in red blood cells. This crystalline material was encased in tubes through which air could be blown. The crystals change color (from red to black) as oxygen is absorbed. When the crystals are heated, they release the oxygen back into the surrounding atmosphere.

The team's ideas were turned over to the Monsanto Chemical Company and large quantities of the material were manufactured. This material was used on naval ships during the final years of World War II. However, the need for such a capability declined after the adoption of the snorkle systems for submarines. Snorkles allowed submarines to take in air from above the ocean's surface even when the submarine was submerged.

Lloyd Ferguson also worked on theoretical ideas. He studied the construction of molecules that are composed mainly of carbon atoms. This subject eventually became the focus of his doctoral research. His research was so important that his report was published in the *Journal of the American Chemical Society* in 1944. Lloyd Ferguson was the first African American to obtain a Ph.D. in chemistry from the University of California at Berkeley.

Career Highlights

When Dr. Ferguson completed his graduate studies, no major university was hiring African American faculty members. The only offer came to him from North Carolina Agricultural and Technical College (now University) in Greensboro, North Carolina, an institution that played a very important role in the local Black community.

As soon as his dissertation was nearing completion and his new job in Greensboro was secure, Lloyd Ferguson got married to Charlotte Welch. His wife was from Arkansas and had attended Wiley College in Texas. After she had finished her degree from this Black institution, she had taken a job in Oakland, California, and moved in with her brother and sister-in-law. Her new home had been only a block away from Lloyd's parents' house. Soon, the young couple had become acquainted and fallen in love.

After a year in Greensboro, Dr. Ferguson received two new job offers. One was from the Tuskegee Institute in Alabama and the other from Howard University in Washington, D.C. After much thought, he decided to go to Howard, the most outstanding Black university at the time. It had many famous faculty members and a growing set of graduate programs in scientific subjects.

When he first arrived at Howard, Dr. Ferguson was mainly concerned with teaching, not research, but he had a backlog of unfinished projects from his years in California and so published two reports on these projects in 1946. Gradually, he made time for more research. During the late 1940s and throughout the 1950s, he continued to focus on the basic problem of the structure of carbon-based molecules.

In 1952, the first of his textbooks was published. It was quickly translated into Japanese. He would go on to publish six more textbooks. Two of these were also translated into Japanese, and one was translated into Hindi for use in India.

In the meantime, there were other exciting events. In 1953, Dr. Ferguson was awarded a Guggenheim Fellowship, which he used to do research at the Carlsberg Laboratory in Copenhagen, Denmark. This laboratory was famous for its studies on the processes of fermentation.

In 1958, Dr. Ferguson was made head of the chemistry department at Howard University. In that role, he built the first doctoral program in chemistry at any Black college or university.

In 1960, Dr. Ferguson obtained a National Science Foundation Fellowship. Again he traveled to Europe and taught for a year at the Swiss Federal Institute of Technology in Zurich, Switzerland.

After he came back from Switzerland, Dr. Ferguson began to study the sense of taste. He hoped to show that some features of molecular structure led to specific taste sensations. In particular, Dr. Ferguson wanted to know why materials taste sweet or sour and why one kind of molecule sets off the taste buds in the tongue. He also was interested in learning why some similar molecules have no taste at all. Dr. Ferguson worked on answers to these questions for twenty years.

In 1965, Dr. Ferguson was asked to join the chemistry faculty at California State University in Los Angeles. He chaired that department from 1968 to 1971. Then for the next year, he served as a visiting professor at the University of Nairobi in Kenya.

In the 1970s, Dr. Ferguson renewed an interest in recruiting young minority people for careers in science. Between 1946 and 1981, he wrote many articles for high school teachers and students, as well as a chapter in a book on career guidance, stressing the opportunities that scientists have for world travel. He used his own experiences as examples of such opportunities. A series of thirteen such articles were published in the *Journal of Chemical Education*.

Another way in which Dr. Ferguson helped young African Americans was his support of Project SEED. Project SEED stood for Support of the Educationally and Economically Disadvantaged. The project was started in 1968 and was the idea of a small group of members of the American Chemical Society, which supported the undertaking. The main goal of the project was to allow minority students to study at top-ranked universities in the summer months. In addition, some students were given summer jobs in the laboratories of major chemical companies.

In 1972, Dr. Ferguson took charge of a new program at California State University. It was called the Minority Biomedical Research Program (MBRP) and was sponsored by the National Institutes of Health in Washington, D.C. The goals of the program were to teach minority students research methods and to encourage them to stay in school. It was thought that these students would be more likely to seek advanced degrees. The program at California State University helped Asian Americans and Hispanic Americans as well as African Americans. Faculty members from the university gave talks at regional high schools. These faculty members would then ask the high school teachers to nominate promising science students. These young people were encouraged to apply for scholarship money from the program funds.

Dr. Ferguson was also a founder of the National Organization of Black Chemists and Chemical Engineers, an organization that helps young African American scientists move forward in their careers.

As part of his research and community activities, Dr. Ferguson has studied the chemistry of cancer, especially the materials that might cause cancer and also those that might help cure it, and has been an advisor on such issues to government groups both in the U.S. and abroad.

Throughout his career, Dr. Ferguson has been offered many opportunities. He has eagerly accepted each one and has been able to study, teach, and conduct research in many parts of the world. He has become a leader in both research and education and has also given much of his time and energy to encourage minority students to choose science as their major field of study. Through the programs and organizations that he sponsors, he has made it possible for many of these young people to achieve rewarding careers in science.

Gregory L. Florant

Born: August 31, 1951, in New York, New York

Status: Professor of Biology, Colorado State University, Fort Collins, Colorado

Education:

Bachelor of Science degree, Cornell University, Ithaca, New York, 1973

Doctor of Philosophy degree, Stanford University, Palo Alto, California, 1978

Research Area: Animal Physiology

Early Years

Gregory Florant was raised in Englewood, New Jersey, and Palo Alto, California. His family moved from New Jersey to California when Greg was ready to enter the first grade. Greg enjoyed his new home and its unspoiled natural surroundings. He especially enjoyed the family's monthly trip to Yosemite National Park, where Greg developed a keen interest in birds of prey.

As soon as he was old enough, Greg bought and trained his own birds, and when he reached the eighth grade, he joined the North American Falconry Association, where he was able to gain information from experienced falcon breeders. One such mentor was Dick Chandick, a curator at the Palo Alto Junior Museum. He gave Greg a part-time job at the museum and helped him learn more about birds and other animals.

Another important person in Greg's young life was Professor Robert Risebrough at the University of California at Berkeley. During Greg's senior year in high school, he worked with Dr. Risebrough on a research project to capture wild birds in their natural surroundings—a sometimes risky enterprise. They discovered a disturbing fact during their work with the wild birds. Some of them, who lived well away from regular contact with human activities, were contaminated with PCBs, a synthetic chemical used mainly in electrical equipment. Greg and Dr. Risebrough publicized their findings in hopes that the users of PCBs would try to find less harmful substitutes.

One day, while doing research in the library for Dr. Risebrough, Greg found himself talking with a visiting professor from Cornell University. As they discussed PCBs and the industrial uses of the chemical, the Cornell professor asked Greg about his plans for college. When he found that Greg was uncertain about his direction, he suggested that Cornell would give Greg a warm welcome. Greg knew that Cornell had one of the best programs of bird research in the United States, so he acted upon the professor's suggestion and applied.

In the meantime, his report on the research done with Dr. Risebrough was published in a scientific magazine. This research paper was a major factor in Greg's nomination as the outstanding member of the senior class at Palo Alto High School.

Higher Education

Greg Florant was accepted at Cornell and began his college career in 1969, just after his eighteenth birthday. Because of his interests in biology, he enrolled in the College of Agriculture and Life Sciences, a school that has produced more than its share of Nobel Laureates.

Even though Florant's experiences at Cornell were positive ones, his experiences in Ithaca were mixed. He enjoyed and benefited from his work with Drs. Cade, Keeton, and Brussard from the Cornell faculty, but there was an unpleasant climate in Ithaca—due to uncomfortable weather and bad race relations. While Florant was at the university, racial tensions at Cornell were unusually high. To maintain his morale, Florant concentrated even harder on his school work. Fortunately, his money problems during the years at Cornell were eased by a university scholarship.

One of the main questions during Gregory Florant's early years at Cornell was whether he should become a scientist or a medical doctor. Dr. Peter Brussard was particularly influential in helping his student make this important decision. During the summer after Florant's second year, Dr. Brussard led a group of young faculty members and students in field research based at the Rocky Mountain Biology Laboratory in Gothic, Colorado. The team's primary interest was the study of butterflies. Since Florant had some interest in this insect—and in Rocky Mountain scenery—he decided to join the group. While in Gothic, he was able to participate in some ongoing studies related to the golden eagle, as well as enjoy the mountains. Most important, Greg Florant met and worked with Paul Ehrlich, the world-famous biologist, who became one of his mentors. These summer experiences helped him settle on science as his future career.

Gregory Florant was among the few African Americans to graduate in biology from Cornell's School of Agriculture prior to the 1970s. After graduation, he was awarded a Ford Foundation Fellowship to continue his graduate studies at the school of his choice.

Florant's choice of graduate school was strongly influenced by Dr. Ehrlich's suggestion to apply to Stanford University in his home town of Palo Alto, California. Dr. Ehrlich told Florant that, in his view, Stanford had the best graduate school in biology in the world.

After his acceptance at Stanford, Gregory Florant worked with Dr. Ehrlich on bird biology. They wanted to understand how birds with black coloration had adapted to survive in both hot and cold climates. The color black absorbs heat. It seems logical, therefore, that desert birds, to avoid overheating, would be lighter in color. However, some black crows thrive in the desert, where daytime temperatures can reach well into the 100s.

Unfortunately, the colony of birds that Florant had established for his research project escaped one night before the study was finished and no firm conclusions could be drawn. Florant was so disheartened that he decided to discontinue his bird studies for a while. He needed new inspiration. Dr. Craig Heller, a biologist doing work on animal hibernation, gave Florant a new direction for his research. Dr. Heller was observing the hibernation adjustments of ground squirrels, and he wanted to include in his study other species, such as the marmot. There was some evidence that these animals could not regulate their body temperature during hibernation, and Dr. Heller wondered how marmots could survive in particularly severe winters if this capability were impaired.

The main obstacle in doing marmot studies is the animal's ability to avoid capture. Even though there are many wild marmots in the Sierra Nevada Mountains, Dr. Heller had managed to trap only a few each year. Florant needed a sizeable colony of these animals to be sure that the observed hibernation activities were consistent with those of the entire species. Dr. Heller, worried that his student would be unable to capture the animals quickly enough, reminded Florant that his Ford Foundation Fellowship lasted only four years. Gregory Florant solved the problem of capturing marmots by thinking like a marmot. He asked himself what food would be most appealing to a marmot after being asleep all winter and losing a significant amount of body weight. He decided that marmots would be attracted to fatty foods, so he baited his traps with bacon grease poured over oatmeal. After just one night, Florant and his student assistant had caught ten marmots. Dr. Heller was amazed.

During his studies, Florant examined many facets of hibernation. For example, he was interested by the seeming magical quality of bears, who not only live off the fat stored in their bodies during hibernation but also give birth and produce milk for their nursing cubs. Florant was interested in the mechanism that triggers the onset of hibernation and whether a drop in body temperature would cause vital functions to slow. Conversely, he sought to understand why there is a periodic awakening for some animals, and what stimulus causes springtime arousal.

With the help of his faculty advisor, Dr. Heller, Florant began the studies that led to his dissertation. Among his findings, he showed that marmots do, indeed, control their body temperature during each of the stages of hibernation. Gregory Florant finished his dissertation and graduated from Stanford in 1978.

Career Highlights

After graduation, Dr. Florant spent two years doing research at the Montefiore Hospital in New York City, his birthplace. When Dr. Florant first arrived at Montefiore Hospital, he directed his work at improving the understanding of the basic cycle of sleep and wakefulness that most animals experience each day. His main supervisor on this research was the late Dr. Elliot Weitzman.

Dr. Florant's attention was also drawn to the research projects of Dr. Rosalyn Yalow, a 1977 Nobel Prize winner. She was using the marmot to study how the body regulates the storage of sugars and fats. She was particularly interested in how the glandular hormone, insulin, might affect an animal's tendencies to become overweight. Insulin is known to regulate sugar levels in the blood and might act on the animals appetite for sweets or other fattening foods.

Dr. Florant's work with Dr. Weitzman and Dr. Yalow greatly increased his potential as an important research scientist. He was offered a job by the officials at Swarthmore College, a famous Quaker school near Philadelphia. Since World War II, Swarthmore had been famous for the quality of its biology faculty. Dr. Florant and other young Stanford graduates were seen as possible successors to the senior researchers who had retired or moved on to other institutions. Dr. Florant and his collegues' reputations suggested that they could bring in research grants from the government and philanthropic organizations, a quality that is very attractive to college and university officials.

Dr. Florant surpassed the expectations of the Swarthmore administrators. Shortly after arriving on the campus, he was awarded a grant from the Research Corporation of Tucson, Arizona. The grant was renewed for a second year in 1981. By the time that support was finished, Dr. Florant had received a two-year grant from the National Science Foundation. Altogether, he produced 16 project reports in the nine years he was at Swarthmore.

During this time, Dr. Florant was named Distinguished Minority Alumnus of the Year by the faculty of the College of Agriculture and Life Sciences at Cornell. The following year, he was selected as one of six outstanding young research scientists by the Philadelphia Physiological Society. Then in 1983, he served as a Fulbright Scholar at one of the world's great biological laboratories near Graves, France. Here, he renewed his study of how certain hormones, such as insulin, influence the functioning of hibernating mammals.

In 1984, he was given a National Research Council Fellowship to spend the summer in Alaska doing research on arctic ground squirrels and marmots. Over the Christmas break in 1986–87, Dr. Florant traveled to Germany to collaborate on research projects that were related to his work in the U.S. This connection led to a winter season at Phillips University in Marburg, Germany, where he ob-

served hibernating animals and studied the deposits of brown fat that, in many animals, are the key to survival during the hibernation period. In recognition for his research, Dr. Florant was made a fellow of the American Association for the Advancement of Science in 1989.

In the fall of 1990, Dr. Florant joined the faculty of Temple University in Philadelphia. Temple, a truly urban university, has about 20,000 full-time students and a large number of part-time students. Temple appealed to Dr. Florant because, unlike Swarthmore, it has a graduate program in the sciences, and he wanted to assist in the education of the next generation of research scientists. Each year, in this new position, Dr. Florant produced about four major research reports and acted as thesis director to one new master's degree student.

His new research projects have integrated several of his long-held ideas. He has undertaken research on the practical problem of human obesity by trying to determine why some people put on weight even when they are careful about their food intake. Since an animal's control of fat is crucial to the hibernation process, he reasoned that some of the same controls might determine whether or not a human became overweight. Dr. Florant proposed that human obesity might be solved by studying hibernating mammals. In 1990, reports on his research were presented to groups of research colleagues in Japan. By 1992, Dr. Florant received a major increase in the funding provided by the National Science Foundation for his studies of how sugars, starches, fats, and oils are absorbed, stored, and used by mammals. This grant should allow him to continue his important research at his new position as Professor of Biology at Colorado State University. Luckily, the region has a plentiful supply of marmots.

Joseph S. Francisco

Born: March 26, 1955, in New Orleans, Louisiana

Status: Professor of Chemistry and Earth and Atmospheric Sciences, Purdue University, West Lafayette, Indiana

Education:

Bachelor of Science degree, University of Texas, Austin, Texas, 1977

Doctor of Philosophy degree, Massachusetts Institute of Technology, Cambridge, Massachusetts, 1983

Research Areas: Chemical Physics and Atmospheric Chemistry

Early Years

Joseph Francisco was raised in Beaumont, Texas, by his grandparents, Merlin and Sarah Walker. His grandfather drove a truck for the Pyramid Pipe Company in addition to owning and operating a real estate business with his wife. As soon as Joseph was old enough, he was recruited as a bookkeeper for

the business. He dealt with the accounts and balanced the ledgers once a week, which helped him gain and develop skill in mathematics, an ability that he would use later in life.

As a child, Joe loved animals. When he was a teenager, he owned thirteen dogs, two cats, two rabbits, and ten chickens. His grandparents decided that Joe should pay for the pet food, so he found a job in the neighborhood as a janitor at Fowler's Pharmacy. The pharmacist, Dr. Alan Fowler, and Joe got along very well. Soon, Dr. Fowler began to teach Joe some of the details of the pharmacy business. Joe also developed an interest in chemistry from watching the pharmacist compound prescriptions. Dr. Fowler, a patient man, answered all of Joe's questions about the properties of various medicines. During his four years at Forest Park High School, Joe worked in the pharmacy after school and during his summer vacations.

Joe also pursued his interest in chemistry at home. When it came time to plan a project for a school science fair, Joe wanted to exhibit something in the field of chemistry. He spent the summer between his junior and senior years reading chemistry and physics books in order to find an interesting project.

One afternoon, late in the summer, he was riding his bike through the campus of Lamar University in Beaumont. As he passed the chemistry building, he decided to go inside and look around. He was wandering through the halls idly reading the notices on the bulletin boards when he was confronted by Professor E. A. Eads. After Joe told the professor about his interest in chemistry and his search for a science fair topic, the two sat down in Eads's laboratory for a five-hour chat about chemistry. Eads finally suggested that Joe might develop a good project by building a gas chromatograph. This is an instrument used by chemists to separate and identify the various chemicals in a mixture. Joe was very excited by the suggestion.

Joe spent the rest of the summer as well as the fall semester doing research on the gas chromatograph, finally coming up with a design that could be built for less than $20. With some help from John Flannery, a young apprentice teacher at Forest Park High School, Joe's design began to take form. After demonstrating that the instrument worked properly, Joe wrote a project report describing the idea, the scientific principles employed, the testing procedures, and the test results. His science teachers were very impressed with his project and helped him enter the competition. He won first prize in the regional science fair and third prize at the state level.

During his visits to Lamar University, Joe also became acquainted with Dr. Richard Price. Dr. Price had just finished his doctorate at the Ohio State University and was beginning his teaching career at Lamar. Before meeting Dr. Price, Joe had little idea about the competition he would encounter in a large university setting. After Dr. Price talked about the chemistry program at Ohio State, Joe realized that he had some weaknesses in his background. They decided to work out an informal tutorial program in mathematics to give Joe an advantage over other college freshman.

During Joe's last years in Beaumont, many people reached out to him and helped him with his education, including his high school physics teacher, who took him to visit the major universities in Texas. Such interest undoubtedly helped Joe to gain admittance to the state's flagship institution, the University of Texas at Austin, in 1973.

Higher Education

Joe Francisco liked the large size of the university. He hoped to remain anonymous in this setting and be judged only by his learning ability. His excellent test scores in chemistry, however, did not allow him to remain anonymous for long. Soon, his teacher, Dr. Raymond Davis, recognized Francisco's ability and invited him to work on a research project in X-ray crystallography. In this technique, a sample of crystal material is exposed to X rays. The resulting picture usually looks like a fuzzy snowflake. The image can be interpreted to determine the physical structure of the crystal. After much practice, Francisco made his first interpretation at the end of his freshman year.

After his second year of college, Joe Francisco accepted an invitation to a summer research program for students at the Argonne National Laboratories near Chicago, Illinois. Argonne Labs is managed by the University of Chicago for the U.S. Department of Energy. A major research effort was then underway to determine how some materials can, at very low temperatures, conduct electricity with no resistance. Some of these "super-conductors" are in the form of very thin films. For this project, Francisco was assigned to work under the supervision of Dr. Jack Williams, and he was to formulate and identify the structure of new materials which were similar to known super-conductors. This was a difficult research project but Francisco enjoyed the challenge.

In 1977, just two weeks before he was to graduate from the University of Texas, Francisco was informed that his grandfather had died, leaving the family with financial problems. Francisco had to postpone his entry into the graduate program at the Massachusetts Institute of Technology in order to help out his family. He quickly took a job with the Monsanto Chemical Company in Texas City, Texas. The commute from Beaumont to Texas City was 100 miles each way. This was a difficult time, but it gave Francisco the opportunity to enjoy some independence and a good income. These advantages forced him to reconsider the prospect of leaving Monsanto and entering one of the toughest graduate degree programs in the world. However, Francisco soon realized that he had no desire to continue as a technician. More education was absolutely necessary if he wished to succeed. After one year at Monsanto, Francisco's financial problems had improved, and he applied to graduate schools for a second time. He was admitted to both the Massachusetts Institute of Technology (MIT) and the University of California at Berkeley. He chose to enter the MIT program in the fall of 1978.

At first, Joe Francisco felt very isolated at MIT. He was the only African American in the physical chemistry program. Soon, however, he joined a group of students under the leadership of Professor Jeffrey Steinfeld. These students were conducting research on the use of lasers to control chemical reactions. They sought to discover whether the light energy from a laser beam could be tuned to break some—but not all—chemical bonds in a given molecule. This was time-consuming, trial-and-error research but the results were important to the development of the field. To better understand the effect of the lasers on the test molecules, Francisco was sent to study with some Australian scientists. He visited Professor Robert Gilbert at Sydney University in New South Wales and Professor Keith King at Adelaide University in South Australia. They introduced him to the theory that when a molecule absorbs light energy from a laser, specific chemical bonds can be split open. Joe Francisco brought these innovative ideas back to MIT, giving his research group a more complete understanding of laser-initiated chemical reactions.

Career Highlights

In 1983, as soon as he finished his graduate program at MIT, Dr. Francisco went to England for postdoctoral studies and worked with Dr. Ian H. W. Smith at Cambridge University on the reaction of individual molecules to the energy generated by light, heat, or both. During his second year at Cambridge, Dr. Francisco worked with Dr. Ian H. Williams on the structure of unusual, man-made molecules.

In 1985, Dr. Francisco returned to MIT to work with Dr. Steinfeld. While he continued his research in laser chemistry, he co-taught a course in chemical kinetics with Professor Steinfeld. This collaboration led to the creation of a textbook that was published in 1989.

Wayne State University in Detroit, Michigan, recruited Dr. Francisco as soon as he had completed his third year of postdoctoral study. Dr. Francisco joined the teaching faculty in 1986.

This position called for a new direction in Dr. Francisco's research efforts. While in England, Dr. Francisco had studied a report by two University of California chemists. The now classic report demonstrated that inert gas used in aerosols and air-conditioning systems released chlorine atoms into the atmosphere. The separate chlorine atoms would then attack and destroy some of the ozone molecules that form a thin layer of gas in the stratosphere. Ozone is a molecule composed of three atoms of oxygen rather than the two atoms of oxygen found in the earth's lower atmosphere. In the stratosphere, ozone serves as a shield against some of the sun's ultraviolet radiation. This particular ultraviolet radiation can be harmful to plants and animals if they get too much exposure. In fact, this radiation is thought to increase the likelihood of skin cancer in humans.

Dr. Francisco was curious about these chemical reactions. There appeared to be many strange intermediate steps as the atomic chlorine and the ozone reacted with each other. Also, these interactions seemed to depend on the sun's energy. The observations agreed with Dr. Francisco's previous studies of the chemical effects of the light energy from lasers. His theory also included the idea that the chemical reaction which destroyed ozone molecules was effected by both the free chlorine atoms and other molecules from the aerosol gas. His research won a Presidential Young Investigator Award from the National Science Foundation and a Research Fellowship from the Alfred P. Sloan Foundation in 1990.

In addition to his teaching and research, Dr. Francisco had another mission in life. He wanted to spare young African Americans from some of the problems he had faced during his years of training. At Wayne State, he established the first student chapter of the National Organization for the Professional Advancement of Black Chemists and Chemical Engineers. Under the sponsorship of the new organization, advanced undergraduate and graduate students tutored newly arrived students through their critical first-year science courses. In addition, Dr. Francisco encouraged graduate students to serve as mentors to undergraduates during their whole undergraduate experience. Through the Baptist Church in Detroit, college students also reached out to high school students who were interested in science. Furthermore, funds were contributed by students to bring prominent Black scientists to the campus for special seminars on their research. In recognition of the positive changes that he initiated, Dr. Francisco was given the Outstanding Teacher Award by the American Baptist Church, U.S.A., in 1992.

In 1994, Dr. Francisco was invited to join the faculty at Purdue University. He and his family now reside in West Lafayette, Indiana, where Dr. Francisco continues his busy schedule of teaching, research, and community service.

Renty B. Franklin

Born: September 2, 1945, in Birmingham, Alabama

Status: Professor of Physiology, Dental School, University of Maryland, Baltimore, Maryland

Education:

Bachelor of Science degree, Morehouse College, Atlanta, Georgia, 1966

Master of Science degree, Atlanta University, Atlanta, Georgia, 1967

Doctor of Philosophy degree, Howard University, Washington, D.C., 1972

Research Area: Physiology

Early Years

Renty Franklin's parents owned and operated a small grocery store in Birmingham, Alabama. Renty's mother, Pinkie Smith

Franklin, and his uncle worked in the store during the day. Renty's father, George Franklin, worked during the evening hours after he had spent a full day as a miner or steel mill worker. When they were old enough, Renty and his younger brother also worked in the family store.

On Sundays, when the store was closed, the Franklin family spent their time in religious observances. They took their religion very seriously and, as a group, attended church as many as three times each week.

Renty's mother had been a school teacher before becoming the owner of a grocery store. When business was slow and during the evening, she gave the two boys lessons in the basic skills of reading, writing, and arithmetic. Consequently, both boys were allowed to skip grades in elementary school. In fact, Renty entered high school two years earlier than his classmates. During his first two years of high school, his age did not present a problem in either his school work or his social life. In spite of his relatively young age, Renty also was able to participate in the school's athletic program—particularly in track and baseball. However, during his last two years in high school, he experienced some very awkward moments in his dealings with the young ladies in his school. They were less than excited about dating someone two years younger than they were.

Renty also concentrated intently on his studies. He became focused on his courses in science and mathematics for which he had both high interest and aptitude. Because of his good grades in science, Renty was invited to a special summer session at the Tuskegee Institute. Many talented young people from all around the state of Alabama attended the session. For the first time, Renty experienced real academic competition. Instead of being the top student among his classmates, he now found himself near the middle of this group. Renty wondered how some of the others had gained so much more knowledge than he had acquired. He was motivated to work even harder at school.

Higher Education

Because of the peculiar scheduling procedures in the Birmingham school system, Renty Franklin finished his high school work in January rather than in the more standard May or June. Shortly after his graduation in the winter of 1962, he traveled to Atlanta, Georgia, to enter Morehouse College. He was just 16 years old but considered himself to be a self-directed and independent person.

When Franklin first entered the biology department at Morehouse, his career goal was to become a physician. At that time, however, the Civil Rights movement had gained momentum in Atlanta and throughout the South, and Franklin's enthusiastic involvement in the movement caused his grades to suffer. After his advisor, Dr. Roy Hunter, saw his grade report, he told Franklin that such mediocre grades would prevent his admission to medical school. This admonition convinced Franklin to give less time to the Civil Rights movement and more time to his studies.

Dr. Hunter's words had other effects on Franklin's thinking. Dr. Hunter emphasized the unsolved problems in the biological sciences—not those already solved. A focus on unanswered questions is typical of a research scientist. Franklin soon saw the connection. He became intrigued by the research procedures and methods used by the leading scientists to obtain new information. Franklin began to consider the field of scientific research rather than that of medical practice as his career goal. By the time he finished his college work, that consideration had become a certainty.

Because Renty Franklin had begun college in mid-year, he finished his undergraduate program at Morehouse in January. Although his formal graduation did not take place until spring, he immediately entered the graduate program at Atlanta University. Renty Franklin was awarded a graduate research assistantship that paid his tuition and some of his living expenses.

At Atlanta University, Franklin came under the benign influence of Drs. George E. Riley and Lafayette Frederick. They not only taught him biological science and research procedures but also instilled in him the proper demeanor for a scientist. He began to understand what a scientific career would entail.

Dr. Riley became seriously ill while Franklin was attending Atlanta University, which meant that someone would be required to take over Dr. Riley's courses. Franklin was chosen to fill in for the emergency period. He was even asked to lead a graduate seminar, which is an unusual assignment for a graduate student. Because of this experience, Franklin developed a strong desire to teach at the graduate level. He adjusted his career goals once again. This time, they included upper-level teaching as well as research.

Although he wanted to pursue his doctoral degree, his economic needs required that he temporarily postpone his studies. Consequently, after completing his master's degree at Atlanta, Renty Franklin joined the faculty at St. Augustine's College in Raleigh, North Carolina, as an instructor. St. Augustine's was one of the first schools founded after the Civil War to provide higher education for African Americans.

In 1969, after teaching at Raleigh for two years, Franklin was financially able to begin his doctoral studies. He chose one of the flagship institutions of African American scholarship, Howard University in the nation's capital. In his first years at Howard, Franklin supported himself by another graduate research assistantship. In this position, he studied under Dr. Edward Hawthorne, who then chaired the department of physiology at Howard.

Franklin did his dissertation research under the supervision of Dr. L. C. Costello. Dr. Costello directed Franklin's interest toward the ability of the body to mobilize its energy resources. Franklin sought to determine which natural chemicals support this process. Scientists understand that these chemicals, know as enzymes and hormones, usually come from glands. Franklin's research looked at how the enzymes and hormones were produced. The influence of other chemicals, such as specific vitamins or minerals, on the production of these hormones was also studied. Franklin, too, investigated the possibility that glands are vulnerable to particular diseases.

For his later doctoral research on enzymes and hormones, Renty Franklin received a predoctoral fellowship from the National Science Foundation. In 1971, in Atlantic City, New Jersey, he presented a report on his findings to a large meeting of research biologists.

Renty Franklin completed his dissertation and received his doctoral degree in 1972. His dissertation was concerned with how a hormone from the parathyroid gland in the throat affects the workings of the kidneys. One of the main functions of the kidneys is to rid the body of surplus biochemicals. For example, the citric acid that comes from eating oranges and grapefruit is of little use to the body; therefore, it is removed from the blood and expelled in the urine. Franklin's research examined how this process is controlled.

Career Highlights

At the same time that Renty Franklin received his doctorate, the medical school at Howard was in need of someone to teach a basic science course in physiology. The course was designed for medical students, pharmacy students, and those in the allied health professions, such as physical therapy. Dr. Franklin accepted the position as assistant professor in the medical school in 1972, just after his graduation.

In 1974, after two years at Howard, he was awarded a research fellowship by the Porter Foundation, an organization that supports advanced medical research. Dr. Franklin was invited to Harvard University Medical School to spend the fellowship year. This was a particularly fruitful period. The time allowed Dr. Franklin to concentrate on one of his main research questions, the role of minerals in bodily functions. He was able to study the relationship between high levels of calcium in the blood and the onset of diseases, such as cancer.

Two years after Dr. Franklin returned from Harvard, he was promoted to the rank of associate professor and awarded permanent tenure by Howard University. However, another opportunity to expand his research horizons soon appeared. Dr. Franklin was offered a tenured position on the faculty of the dental school of the University of Maryland in downtown Baltimore. He accepted this position in 1980. Dr. Franklin expanded his studies of glandular functions—particularly of the prostate gland, which is a major health hazard to older men. Although his research productivity was already high, he now began to complete two or more major research reports each year. In addition, Dr. Franklin published shorter reports and presented many papers at scientific meetings.

Dr. Franklin was soon acknowledged as a world expert in the functions and medical problems of the prostate gland. The National Cancer Institute awarded Dr. Franklin and his colleagues at the University of Maryland a series of research grants. These grants have totaled over $1.5 million during the time Dr. Franklin has been in Baltimore. In 1994, Dr. Franklin was also honored by the Howard Hughes-Morehouse Distinguished Scientist Award.

The successful research program at the dental school could be considered a career in itself; however, Dr. Franklin also teaches classes in undergraduate physiology and graduate-level courses in glandular functions and reproductive physiology. He supervises the thesis and dissertation projects of graduate students, as well.

Dr. Franklin is also concerned with the recruitment of young minority members into careers in science and technology. Dr. Franklin advises major federal agencies, such as the National Science Foundation, in the development of workable programs to bring more minorities into these scientific professions.

Dr. Franklin also indulges himself a bit. For relaxation, he coaches football and baseball for the county recreation department. He also served as vice president and then president of a local track club. Evidently, his youthful interest in athletic activities has never faded away.

Bertram Fraser-Reid

Born: February 23, 1934, in Coleyville, Jamaica, West Indies

Status: James B. Duke Professor of Chemistry, Duke University, Durham, North Carolina

Education:

Bachelor of Science degree, Queen's University, Kingston, Ontario, Canada, 1959

Master of Science degree, Queen's University, 1961

Doctor of Philosophy degree, University of Alberta, Edmonton, Alberta, Canada, 1964

Research Area: Organic Chemistry

Early Years

Bertram Fraser-Reid is the youngest of six children. His father was the principal of an elementary school and his mother, who died before Bertram was a year old, was a teacher in Coleyville, Jamaica.

The school system in Jamaica, established when Jamaica was a British colony, follows the British system of education. Therefore, the Jamaican equivalent to a U.S. high school provides a more intense and longer educational program. By the time Jamaican students finish a British-type "secondary school," they are at least as advanced as second-year college students in the U.S. Consequently, when Bertram Fraser-Reid finished secondary school, he was able to begin his teaching career immediately. Indeed, he took a job as a sort of working apprentice or "junior master" under the supervision of a "senior master" at the secondary school from which he had just graduated.

Over the next few years, while Bertram was learning how to teach and was taking more responsibility for his courses, he realized that he was not happy with his job. He had always enjoyed playing the piano and other keyboard instruments, and he began thinking about a career in music. Before he could act on this possibility, however, fate intervened.

A young man named Stanley Shepherd, who had just returned from studying science in Great Britain, joined the teaching staff at Bertram's school as a mathematics, physics, and chemistry instructor. Stanley liked teaching mathematics and physics, but he loathed teaching chemistry. The two young men frequently talked about Stanley's intense dislike for chemistry, and Bertram became curious. He purchased a book entitled *Teach Yourself Chemistry* and became fascinated that one could combine two or more chemicals and produce an entirely new product, and that this product could be of practical use. Bertram then began to study chemistry on his own, and the more he read, the more interested he became.

Higher Education

Bertram Fraser-Reid's formal study of chemistry began at Queen's University in Kingston, Ontario, in 1956. He had considered applying to schools in the U.S. but had decided that, since the U.S. was experiencing difficult racial problems at the time, it would be better for a young Black man with a foreign accent to attend school in Canada.

At Queen's, Fraser-Reid found a job in the laboratory of Professor J.K.N. Jones, a noted organic chemist who was focusing his research on the chemistry of sugar and chemically related substances. The basic building block in sugar chemistry is glucose, a molecule whose chemical structure is a chain of six carbon atoms with hydrogen and oxygen atoms attached. This relatively simple molecule has several very interesting properties. The basic chain structure of the molecule can fold around to form a loop, and then that loop can attach itself to a similar loop. When a glucose loop links with a fructose—fruit sugar—loop, the result is sucrose—regular table sugar. Starch and cellulose, the main chemical structure of all the higher plants, is formed when the glucose loops are linked in longer strings. Consequently, sugar and its relatives make up most of the organic chemicals in the world.

The other critical property of sugar-based materials is that they are burnable in the bodies of animals. That is, sugar can be oxidized to provide animals with energy. Humans and some other animals cannot digest the very long strings of sugar chains that make up cellulose, but cows, sheep, and other grazing animals derive nutrition from the cellulose in grass and fodder. Even though humans cannot break down cellulose, they can break down starch. Consequently, the starch in grain and potatoes provides good nutrition for humans.

While still in college, Bertram Fraser-Reid became recognized as an unusually astute scientist because of his research on sugar chemistry. In his third and final year of undergraduate studies, he was awarded the Susan Near Scholarship as well as an additional university scholarship at Queen's University. These paid for his tuition and living expenses. Fraser-Reid graduated in 1959.

He began working on his master's degree at Queen's the following year, when he was awarded the Reuben Wells Leonard Graduate Fellowship. With this financial aid, he was able to dedicate himself to his research in Professor Jones's laboratory and to the preparation of his thesis.

When Bertram Fraser-Reid finished his master's degree in 1961, he wanted to continue his graduate studies. He enrolled in the doctoral program at the University of Alberta in Edmonton, Canada. At Alberta, he worked with Professor Raymond U. Lemieux, a pioneer in the use of nuclear magnetic resonance (NMR), to determine the fine structure of complicated molecules. In this procedure, a pure sample of a material is placed into an NMR machine, and then strong magnets are turned on and off in a regular rhythm. The magnetic force moves some of the electrons in the material being tested. When the magnet is turned off, the electrons that were shifted by the magnetic force immediately move back to their original positions. Those shifting electrons release a tiny electrical charge that can be detected and recorded. The pattern of the recording is different for each type of material; therefore, NMR can often be used to detect which atoms are in an unknown material and identify how the atoms are arranged.

Meanwhile, a young woman Fraser-Reid had known casually when both were students at Queen's University, had come to Edmonton to accept a nursing position in a local hospital. When they renewed their friendship, it developed into a more serious relationship. Lillian Lawrynyuk and Bertram Fraser-Reid were married in 1963, while Bertram was preparing for his final year of doctoral study.

Career Highlights

After completing his doctoral degree in 1964, Dr. Fraser-Reid was awarded a two-year fellowship by the National Research Council of Canada to do post-doctoral research at the Imperial College in London, England. He worked under the supervision of Professor Sir Derek Barton, who was later awarded the Nobel Prize for chemistry. Dr. Fraser-Reid did not produce any earth-shaking research reports during his two-year stay in England, but he was able to observe how internationally famous chemists did their work and published their papers. He also came to understand the strategies required to carry on a sustained research program.

In 1966, Dr. Fraser-Reid returned to Canada to accept a position at the newly created University of Waterloo near Toronto. Using the ideas he had gained while in London, he began to explore the processes by which a basic building block—the simple sugar molecule—could be used to construct more complicated materials.

It took almost 10 years of research, but ultimately Dr. Fraser-Reid demonstrated that sugar could be used as the raw material for making almost every sort of medicine, plastic, paint, insecticide, and other carbon-based chemical. In 1977, his work was recognized when Dr. Fraser-Reid was awarded the Merck, Sharpe & Dohme Award for outstanding contributions to chemistry. The crucial, practical significance of Dr. Fraser-Reid's research demonstrated that the chemical industry was no longer dependent on petroleum as a raw material. In the future, when most of the world's oil reserves are depleted, industry should be able to use sugar cane and sugar beets to help keep factories running.

Dr. Fraser-Reid was also able to integrate his research on the sugar molecule with insect chemistry. In 1975, he had become interested in pheromones, the complicated chemicals that insects use to communicate with one another and to attract members of the opposite sex. Dr. Fraser-Reid realized that the structure of the Pine Beetle sex pheromone could be duplicated by using sugar as the raw material. This synthetic pheromone could then be used for pest control.

Meanwhile, Dr. Fraser-Reid gained an excellent reputation as a very productive research scientist. Several universities in the United States were interested in his work, but he was reluctant to leave Canada because he appreciated the support given to him over the years. However, he knew that he needed to test his ability to meet new challenges. So, in 1980, he moved to the University of Maryland at College Park, where he stayed for three years, working on the structure of cancer-fighting materials.

Dr. Fraser-Reid was then offered a named professorial chair at Duke University in Durham, North Carolina. He promptly went to work on his sugar-based compounds, and he and his students invented new ways of assembling and reassembling the building blocks. Lately, he has focused on the sugar-based materials that single-cell organisms, such as viruses, use in constructing their cell membranes. These viruses adjust their sugar coating when they are about to attack and invade another cell. A virus can multiply only inside another cell; therefore, if a chemical can be designed to interfere with this adjustment process, the virus would be disarmed. Research on this matter is currently underway in Dr. Fraser-Reid's laboratory.

Dr. Fraser-Reid has been a very productive scientist. By 1990, he had already published over 250 scientific reports on his research findings. He also continues to travel the world, giving about 20 speeches every year to international audiences.

Meanwhile, Dr. Fraser-Reid has worked diligently to give minority students positive experiences in the field of chemistry. Each summer, three high school students and three college students are invited to work alongside the chemists at the Paul M. Gross Laboratory at Duke University. While there, these minority students not only practice some of their research skills, but also gain an understanding of the hard work required to achieve scientific excellence.

A. Oveta Fuller

Born: August 31, 1955, in Mebane, North Carolina

Status: Assistant Professor, Department of Microbiology and Immunology, University of Michigan Medical School, Ann Arbor, Michigan

Education:

Bachelor of Arts degree, University of North Carolina, Chapel Hill, North Carolina, 1977

Doctor of Philosophy degree, University of North Carolina, 1983

Research Area: Microbiology

Early Years

Oveta Fuller grew up on her family's farm near Yanceyville, North Carolina. Her older brother was three when Oveta was born and her younger brother arrived eleven years later. Oveta's mother, Deborah Woods Fuller, taught junior high school most of her adult life, and her father, Herbert R. Fuller, operated the family farm. Oveta's paternal grandmother, Lillie Willis Fuller Graves, was in charge of the farmhouse.

The farmland had been purchased many years before by Mollie Fuller, Oveta's paternal great-grandmother, who had been a licensed midwife in the years following the Civil War. After her death, her property was inherited by her children. Oveta's grandfather, Randolph Fuller, received 50 acres. Later, he added another 50 and willed it all to his wife, Lillie, and their three children. After Randolph's death, Lillie remarried and had four more sons. The sons lived on the farm while Oveta was growing up.

The farm provided most of the food for the extended family. They grew their own fruits, vegetables, and grain and also raised cattle, pigs, and chickens. The cash crops were cattle and tobacco. The teaching job held by Oveta's mother also increased the household income.

When Oveta was four, she and her family moved into a new house that her father and uncles had built a short distance down the road. Oveta continued to spend much of her time with her grandmother while her parents were at work. She relished the days with her grandmother, who encouraged the inquisitive and active little girl to "work" with her on many domestic chores. For example, when the grandmother was sewing, Oveta was allowed to cut and sew her own fabric.

Grandmother Lillie Fuller Graves suffered from diabetes and mild arthritis. As a child, Oveta noticed that there were specific treatments for the diabetes but few for the arthritis. But the mysteries of medicine weren't really dramatized for Oveta until her grandmother was bitten by a water moccasin. The child knew that snakebites could be life threatening, and she was very worried when her grandmother was rushed to the local doctor in her father's truck. Of course, Oveta was relieved when her grandmother returned home in "fine" condition, having been given a medicine know as an antivenin. Oveta learned that medicines were not only specific to certain conditions but that some were very powerful—strong enough to counteract the bite of a deadly snake.

At her young age, Oveta did not consider these experiences to be the groundwork for a career in science. She was expected to do well in whatever she chose to do, but no one suggested that she think about her future career. In high school, however, she did have inspiring science teachers—Ms. Elam in beginning biology and Mr. Majette in advanced biology. Even so, she did not consider herself a future scientist.

During her junior year in high school, Oveta's guidance counselor nominated her to attend the highly regarded North Carolina Governor's School at Salem College in Winston-Salem, North Carolina. The school is a summer program which brings together selected students from all over the state. Even though Oveta's summer program was focused on the study of mathematics, the exchanges among the teachers and the students ranged from music to all forms of literature.

Higher Education

After graduating from high school, Oveta Fuller was awarded a full four-year Aubry Lee Brooks Scholarship to the University of North Carolina (UNC) at Chapel Hill, only an hour's drive from her home. She majored in biology but did not restrict her studies to a rigid premedical curriculum. English literature, English composition, and journalism were her favorite subjects. Fuller also greatly enjoyed working for one of the college newspapers.

Because of her biology major, it was assumed that Fuller was planning a career in medicine, but she felt the need to explore all her career options. During the summer break before her senior year, she took a job as an apprentice in a local health clinic. She worked half the time as a physician's assistant and the other half as a laboratory assistant. The clinic served many elderly patients who were chronically ill. The only available medical response was to provide good cheer and minimize their pain. In contrast, the laboratory environment was far more lively, and the young scholar began to see herself as a research scientist.

During Fuller's senior year at Chapel Hill, there was an outbreak of an illness now known as "Legionnaire's Disease." At first, the cause of the disease was unknown. After several fatalities, a microbe was identified, but the path of infection was still a mystery. Later, Fuller wrote an extensive research paper on the detective work done by the bi-

ologists, public health specialists, and physicians who finally solved the puzzle. After this experience, Fuller could see herself as a biologist on a team of scientific detectives or as the author of feature articles on medical mysteries.

Oveta Fuller's general curiosity about the world at large influenced her decision to travel. After she graduated from UNC in 1977, she traveled to Louisiana for a summer job with a national publishing company. There, she marketed children's reference books. In the meantime, she had decided to begin her graduate studies in biology. Several college possibilities were open to her because of her excellent academic performance at UNC. Howard University and Georgetown University in Washington, D.C., and the University of Illinois were all taken into consideration. However, UNC—her undergraduate school—was the best and most practical choice for her graduate training. The program in microbiology at UNC was outstanding, and she would not have to move from Chapel Hill. At UNC, there were also several current research projects in microbiology as well as easy access to the interesting research at North Carolina State University, North Carolina Central University, and Duke University. All of these institutions are in the Research Triangle area, which is full of government laboratories and private research organizations.

Fuller received a graduate fellowship from the university, which relieved her parents from any burden of supporting her through her graduate program. Fuller also worked part-time to supplement her income from the fellowship and to maintain her ties to the local community.

In the summer after her first year of graduate study, she resumed her work in the publishing business, and during the academic year, she tutored high school students in science and mathematics. Fuller also worked with college students in the Upward Bound program at the university.

In addition to these activities, Fuller became involved with professional organizations. She was a founding member of a regional chapter of the National Technical Association, which had been established to bring together and provide visibility to African American scientists and engineers affiliated with the larger academic institutions.

Fuller's doctoral project at UNC was concerned with the biological actions of two plant toxins. One toxin was Abrin, an eye irritant that comes from the pealike plant, abrus, and the other was Ricin, a blood coagulant made from castor oil beans. Her studies of these materials led to her doctoral degree and graduation from UNC in 1983. Now, she was eager to move on to the study of viruses and cell surface chemistry, which had become much more interesting to her.

Career Highlights

After graduation, Dr. Fuller pursued her research interests on a full-time basis. She accepted postdoctoral research support from the Anna Fuller Cancer Fund, which is administered by a relatively small, private philanthropy similar to the more widely known Damon Runyan Cancer Fund. This award and others funded Dr. Fuller's work on Professor Patricia G. Spear's research team at the University of Chicago.

The focus of her studies was the behavior of the herpes virus, which causes cold sores, fever blisters, and genital inflammations. The virus attacks the soft linings of various parts of the body. Such diseases can be recurrent and are often transmitted by intimate contact. Dr. Fuller sought to determine how the virus penetrates the cell wall or plasma membrane, the cell's outer protection. She questioned whether the cells of soft tissues have a particular molecular structure in their plasma membrane that allows the herpes virus to attach itself to the membrane. Once attached, the virus slips through to the inner part of the cell. The research also examined the likelihood that the virus could be engineered to introduce new genetic material when it invades the cell. In addition, Dr. Fuller studied the possibility of preventing the herpes virus from entering the cells. Some cells have a natural immunity, and Dr. Fuller and Dr. Spear were able to identify some of the molecules that appear to help bring about at least a partial immunity. In spite of this work and others' discoveries of some useful medicines for herpes, there are still no true cures for the diseases caused by the herpes virus.

Dr. Fuller's work with Professor Spear's research team also investigated other viruses. She conducted important studies that compared the similarities between the chemicals of the virus and the chemicals of the defensive cell membrane. She was able to demonstrate that each pairing of virus and host cell involves a specific combination of chemicals which contain amino acids—the building blocks of protein. If the host cell chemicals are not "right," the virus cannot infect the cell. This finding might explain why viruses and other microbes infect some people and not others, and why humans seldom are infected with animal diseases. It is possible that such new information about viruses can help find a control for the AIDS virus.

Although heavily involved with her research, Dr. Fuller continued to teach. In 1984, she taught an introductory course in genetics at the University of Chicago and, in 1986, an advanced course in human genetic disorders.

Dr. Fuller spent almost five years at the University of Chicago with Professor Spear. For the first three years, she was a research fellow. In addition to the support from the Anna Fuller Cancer Fund, research support came from the U.S. Public Health Service and the National Institutes of Health. Then, in 1987, Dr. Fuller received a prestigious fellowship from the Ford Foundation. Her title changed to research associate, and she was no longer considered a student. She soon became a fully independent scientist.

In 1988, Dr. Fuller joined the faculty of the medical school at the University of Michigan. This position provided Dr. Fuller an opportunity to pursue her research interests and to teach in the medical, dental, and graduate schools. The largest portion of her time, however, is still given to her own research. Shortly after going to Michigan, Dr. Fuller began to generate her own grant support. At first, the funding came from within the university, but soon, it also came from outside sources, such as the National Institutes of Health and the National Science Foundation. In addition, Dr. Fuller is now guiding the efforts of her own apprentice researchers. After she arrived at Ann Arbor, she soon had several doctoral students as well as several part-time undergraduates on her research team.

Also, institutions at home and abroad began to request that Dr. Fuller lecture about her research. Indeed, in 1992, she was co-chair of a technical session at an International Herpes Conference in Edinburgh, Scotland.

Research continues to be the focus of Dr. Fuller's professional life. She and her research team have prepared many major reports and have more in progress. Each successive research report represents new information on how viruses attack body cells. Eventually, such knowledge may provide the means to control all viral diseases.

Cornelia Denson Gillyard

Born: February 1, 1941, in Talladega, Alabama

Status: Associate Professor of Chemistry, Spelman College, Atlanta, Georgia

Education:

Bachelor of Science degree, Talladega College, Talladega, Alabama, 1962

Master of Science degree, Clark Atlanta University, Atlanta, Georgia, 1973

Doctor of Arts degree, Clark Atlanta University, Atlanta, Georgia, 1980

Research Area: Organic Chemistry

Early Years

The relatively small town of Talladega, Alabama, where Cornelia was born, is part of an iron- and metal-working community that is centered about 40 miles away in Birmingham. It is also the home of Talladega College, a private liberal arts institution with a long tradition of serving the African American community.

After working at a variety of jobs, Cornelia's father, Frank Denson, became a foundryman in a factory that made iron and steel castings. Eventually, he was promoted to the position of shift foreman.

Cornelia's mother worked as a part-time, private duty nurse for terminally ill patients. In addition to homemaking and raising Cornelia and her two younger sons, Mrs. Denson also spent a large portion of her time as a volunteer in community betterment organizations, including the local Parent-Teacher Association.

When Cornelia was in grade school, the family moved from town to town in central Alabama so that her father could find work. Moving from school to school was confusing to Cornelia and sometimes for school officials as well. Often, Cornelia was placed in classes with older children. Since she kept up with these older students rather easily, she was officially allowed to skip the second grade.

Cornelia was always eager to learn. In one of the schools, she was given a new world history book. Cornelia read the entire book before coming to class the next week. She wanted to be sure she was progressing as rapidly as the teachers thought she should. Even when she made mistakes, the teachers were always supportive. This support gave her self-respect, which made it relatively easy to have respect for others.

The home environment was also supportive. Cornelia's mother was active in church work, and Cornelia attended Bible school every weekend. Her mother also taught her the traditional homemaking skills, and Cornelia learned practical skills from such organizations as the 4-H Club—of which she was an eager member.

Cornelia went to the Ophilia Hill High School in Talladega. This school had classes from the eighth grade through the twelfth. Starting in the eighth grade, Cornelia began to study and

enjoy science and mathematics. During the eleventh grade, she became fascinated by the things she learned in her chemistry class. Her teacher recognized her interest and aptitude and gave her advanced tutoring in chemistry during the study hall periods.

Cornelia liked other science subjects as well. For a science fair competition, she and another student built a wooden replica of the human skeleton. On a panel mounted in front of their skeleton, they listed the names of the bones. By each name was an electrical push button. When a small light was lit next to one of the wooden bones, viewers could push the button next to the name they considered to be the correct one. If they were right, a bell rang. She and her partner won a prize for this project.

Cornelia also enjoyed other school activities, such as singing in the school chorus and serving as a cheerleader for the athletic teams. She graduated as valedictorian of her class in 1961.

Higher Education

Cornelia Denson's choice of college was limited by the segregationist policies in most Alabama institutions. She chose Talladega College for several reasons. First, it had an excellent reputation and was recognized by academic centers outside of Alabama. Consequently, the college had a good record for placing its students in graduate schools around the country. Several of Denson's most admired high school teachers had also gone to Talladega College, and they encouraged her to attend. Also, it was close enough to home that Cornelia could save money on living expenses. Finally, she was given a scholarship by the school, which helped resolve her difficult financial problems.

At first, Denson chose biology as her major subject. However, she did so well in her first college chemistry course that the teacher convinced her to change her major to chemistry. Cornelia Denson soon found that advanced-level chemistry courses are quite difficult. In high school, she read the assigned chapters one time and then passed her examinations with high marks. She realized that in college, however, she needed to review the material carefully before taking a test. She also found it wise to discuss the more complicated ideas with some of her classmates.

In their last year of college, all students at Talladega were required to complete a major independent research project. Denson chose a difficult problem in the chemistry of nutrition. She wanted to be able to determine the relative amounts of protein, which is essential to human growth, in different kinds of nuts. She also wanted to be able to compare the amount of protein to the percentages of fats, oils, fiber, and other nutritional elements in each kind of nut.

Her research method required that she crush each sample of nutmeats so that the chemicals could be extracted. The sample was then tested for its nitrogen content. The amount of nitrogen in a nut is proportional to the amount of amino acid in the nut. All amino acids contain nitrogen, while fats and carbohydrates do not. Also, when the amount of amino acid is known, the amount of protein can be estimated because amino acids are the building blocks of all protein.

At the end of the year, Denson and the other senior students turned in reports on their research. A few days later, they were tested by oral examination on what they had learned. Cornelia Denson passed easily and graduated in the spring of 1962.

Denson was still a bit uncertain about her career goals. She was attracted to the field of human health, but she did not have the financial resources to attend medical school. In fact, she needed to increase her savings before making any career commitment.

During the summer of 1962, she lived with her aunt in Columbus, Ohio, and explored her job prospects. She found employment at the Ohio State University Hospital, where she was assigned to the nuclear medicine laboratory. The function of the lab was to prepare materials for injection into the blood of patients being readied for major surgery. The radioactive material in the blood could be detected by mechanical radiation scanners. In this way, the volume of blood flowing to vital organs would be revealed. The surgeons could watch the flow of blood on a TV screen and be able to react quickly to any problems that might arise.

As chief laboratory technologist, Cornelia Denson was given special advanced training in nuclear medicine at another nearby hospital. She learned how to direct the injection of radioactive iodine into the blood vessels of patients with thyroid diseases. Iodine is taken up by the thyroid gland in the neck. If the thyroid is diseased, that fact is revealed by the pattern that the radioactive iodine shows on X rays. Modern medicine uses many radioactive substances, such as iodine, iron, cobalt, and potassium. Denson learned the procedures for using each of these materials.

After two years at the university hospital, Denson moved on to Children's Hospital in Columbus, where she helped plan and develop their new radio isotope laboratory. The field of nuclear medicine was growing rapidly and many experimental techniques were being tried. Denson was a partner in several of these experiments and co-authored the reports that described these studies. Her colleagues recognized that she had a gift for research. They encouraged her to continue her work and to consider getting an advanced degree.

Denson saw the wisdom of this advice and applied for admission to Clark Atlanta University. At first, her goal was to earn a master's degree in organic chemistry and then teach—perhaps at the college-level. She hoped that she could finish her studies quickly and go back to work. She asked to be given credit for the experience she had gained in teaching medical students at Ohio State about the techniques of nuclear medicine, but that credit was denied. Nevertheless, she resolved to continue.

The research for her master's thesis was supervised by Dr. Thomas W. Cole, who is now the president of Clark Atlanta. The study was aimed at an improved understanding of the chemistry of vitamin B-12. This vitamin acts as a catalyst in the production of red blood cells. A shortage of vitamin B-12 leads to a reduction of red blood cells and makes humans more susceptible to anemia.

In 1973, Denson finished the program and received her master's degree from Clark Atlanta. She had several job offers from major chemical companies and drug manufacturers around the country. However, she chose to return to Columbus, Ohio, to work for the Battelle Memorial Institute, a prestigious, nonprofit research organization near Ohio State University. One of her most interesting projects was the search for compounds that could be used in the construction of solar energy collectors. She sought materials that might be able to turn sunlight directly into electrical current. She did find some, but they were very costly and so were not competitive with other methods of generating electricity.

In 1974, Denson married and returned to Atlanta, Georgia, to be a homemaker. After a few years, she decided to resume her career in science and in 1977, re-enrolled at Clark Atlanta University. She entered a new program in chemical education, which was specially designed to prepare people to teach chemistry at the undergraduate level. While she was still working on her doctoral research project, she began teaching courses in general and organic chemistry at Spelman College in Atlanta, a highly regarded women's school. She also taught a course in chemical

science for Spelman students who were not science majors. Many colleges have such courses so that students in other fields can fulfill their degree requirements without competing against science majors.

Among the courses she taught at Spelman, her favorite was an honors seminar for chemistry majors. Students were required to choose a current problem in the field. After reviewing the scientific literature, they prepared a major paper and gave an oral presentation of their findings. Denson Gillyard and her students all learned many new ideas from the course.

Career Highlights

Dr. Gillyard received her doctoral degree from Clark Atlantic in 1980. As soon as she graduated, she joined a team of scientists at Spelman who were working on the problem of arsenic contamination in natural waterways. The arsenic comes mainly from the drainage of farm fields that have been treated with insecticides or herbicides. The Spelman project was aimed at evaluating the introduction of microorganisms into the contaminated waterways. The scientists hoped that the digestive process of these micro-organisms could change the toxic arsenic compounds into harmless material. Dr. Gillyard studied the amount of each chemical produced by the digestion of the substances containing arsenic. In this way, she and her colleagues could find out which microorganisms were most efficient in improving the quality of the water.

In addition to her teaching and research, Dr. Gillyard has been working with the National Aeronautics and Space Administration (NASA) on the recruitment of African American women into science careers. For many years, the NASA-sponsored program has provided four- or five-year scholarships to ten to twelve incoming Spelman students who are majoring in physics, chemistry, mathematics, computer science, or engineering. Special activities for these female students start the summer after they finish high school. For six weeks, chosen students are tutored in science and mathematics so that they will be fully ready to compete at the college-level when the fall term begins. In each successive summer, the students are assigned to various NASA laboratories around the United States. In this way, they can acquire practical experience to complement their classroom studies at Spelman. Dr. Gillyard is the associate director of this program and director of the summer activities.

A somewhat similar program is conducted under the sponsorship of the National Science Foundation (NSF). The NSF program provides funding for two-year research projects that students initiate at the beginning of their third year at Spelman. Each research project is monitored by a faculty director and is designed to generate a report that can serve as the student's senior honor thesis. The report might also be published as part of the general scientific literature. Dr. Gillyard serves as codirector on this program.

Mack Gipson, Jr.

Born: September 15, 1931, in Trenton, South Carolina

Status: Professor of Geology, University of South Carolina, Columbia, South Carolina

Education:

Bachelor of Arts degree, Paine College, Augusta, Georgia, 1953

Master of Science degree, University of Chicago, Chicago, Illinois, 1961

Doctor of Philosophy degree, University of Chicago, 1963

Research Area: Structural Geology

Early Years

Mack Gipson grew up on his grandmother's farm near Trenton, South Carolina. His parents, Mack Gipson, Sr., and Artie Mathis Gipson, worked another small farm near Augusta, Georgia, where the owner of the land received one part of the crop and the Gipsons received the other part. This arrangement, called sharecropping, is still practiced in parts of the United States.

Mack's grandmother was also a sharecropper but she had other family members to help her. Consequently, she had the time and energy to look after Mack and his sister, Margaree. As the children grew older, they also helped with the farm work.

Mack attended a small elementary school in the country, and then in 1943, he went into the town of Trenton for junior high school. At about this time, just as he was becoming interested in nature, he read his first science book, *The Earth and Life upon It*. Although he had experienced nature in many forms while living on the farm and helping with the work, he had not been particularly interested in science. Now, in junior high school, he found himself wondering how rocks were formed and what caused the different layers in the earth. *The Earth and Life upon It* showed him that the study of science was a way to answer his questions.

In the rural South during Mack's childhood, most young African Americans went no farther than the tenth grade in school. Some did not even go that far. In many cases, public schools for Black students did not extend beyond the sixth grade. Mack's school did extend to the eleventh grade. Even so, he wanted to go further and improve his life.

When he was in his last year of public school at Trenton, Mack told his grandmother that he wanted to finish high school. He said they should move to Augusta, Georgia, where his parents lived and where there was a high school for Black students. He would go to school during the day and work at night. To his amazement, his grandmother agreed. His parents, who already lived near Augusta, were able to find a place for Mack, his sister, and his grandmother to live. The older woman and the two young people moved to Augusta in December, 1947.

Mack enrolled in the Augustus R. Johnson High School on January 2, 1948, and graduated in the spring of 1949. The year after he graduated, the school was reorganized and renamed the Lucy C. Laney High School.

Higher Education

Mack Gipson's family agreed with his ambition to continue his education. However, they had very little money. After trying other ways to find money for Mack's tuition fees, his mother borrowed $100 from a local moneylender. In those days, this was enough to cover tuition and other fees at Paine College, a nearby institution. Fortunately, Gipson could save money by living at home.

In his agreement with his family, Gipson worked part-time, so he could pay his tuition for each spring semester, while the family paid the tuition for each fall semester.

Gipson's part-time jobs included working in a restaurant, shining shoes, and cutting hair in a barbershop.

Mack Gipson first chose English literature as his college major. However, his interest in science, begun in junior high school, caused him to think about becoming a high school science teacher. So, after his first year of college, he changed his major to science and mathematics.

Immediately after Mack Gipson finished college in 1953, he found a job teaching at Pearl High School in Madison, Georgia. In the country towns of those days, young African Americans went to school in July and August and stayed home in September and October to help harvest the farm crops. Therefore, Mack Gipson, who had received his college degree in June, was required to begin his teaching career the very next month.

After he completed his first year of teaching, he returned home to Augusta. He was immediately offered a job at Lucy C. Laney High School, the same school where he had done his own high school studies. He taught mathematics there for the 1953–54 school year.

In June 1954, Mack Gipson was drafted into the United States Army. Because of his science background, he was given training as a radio technician. After this schooling, he was assigned to a U.S. Army post in southern Germany near the town of Neu Ulm, Bavaria. There, his duties were relatively light. He had spare time to study on his own and think about his future career.

One of his friends in the unit had taken a course in geology at Boston University before being drafted. Mack Gipson began to think that geology might be an interesting subject for his own advanced studies. Working outdoors as a field geologist interested him much more than being confined to a laboratory or classroom. He began to read as many books as he could get on geology. The more he read, the more he liked the idea of becoming a geologist.

Mack Gipson completed his military service in June 1956 and returned to Augusta, Georgia. He was not yet ready to apply for graduate school, because be had some other items on his agenda. The first was to marry Alma D. Gadison. Gipson had met Alma while he was a senior at Paine College, where she was in training to become a psychiatric nurse.

He then needed to improve his modest financial situation. He decided to take a job teaching mathematics at a local junior high school during the 1956–57 school year. That spring of 1957, he applied to graduate schools. He was accepted at Colorado State University in Fort Collins, Colorado, and at the University of Chicago in Chicago, Illinois. He chose the University of Chicago because his wife, Alma, was more likely to find a good job there than in Fort Collins. He had another financial reason for choosing the University of Chicago. The state of Georgia had a very strange arrangement for African American students. At that time, Blacks were not allowed to enter the University of Georgia. However, if a student enrolled in a university located east of the Mississippi River and took a course of studies that was also offered at the University of Georgia, the state would pay the student a small amount of money. Since Chicago is east of the Mississippi River and Fort Collins is not, Mack Gipson would be eligible for that money only if he went to Chicago.

The University of Chicago had a reputation for welcoming African Americans (see Ernest E. Just, p. 201). However, only one African American had ever studied geology there. That student had enrolled twenty years earlier and had never finished his degree program.

Even with his wife's salary and the small payment from the state of Georgia, the Gipsons did not have enough money to survive in an expensive city like Chicago. Mack Gipson went to work part-time, doing whatever jobs he could find. After three years, he was awarded a small scholarship, but he still had to continue his extra jobs. Gipson never had a single month that he could devote entirely to his graduate studies. He always had to split his time between employment and schooling. Fortunately, his work soon became more related to his studies. After his fourth year, he became a research assistant on a project supported by the U.S. Office of Naval Research.

In his last year, he took a job as a geologist with the Walter H. Flood Company. His duties included testing samples of soil obtained by using a special machine. The machine drove a metal sleeve into the ground. When the sleeve was withdrawn and opened up, the geologists would have a sample of the layers of soil. Such a sample is called a core. One of Gipson's projects was to test cores during the construction of the runways at Chicago's O'Hare International Airport.

The research for his doctoral degree, however, was in a different area of geology. Gipson was studying the deeply buried rock layers near the coal fields of central Illinois. Since such research required expert knowledge in chemistry and physics, as well as in geology, his work was overseen by three advisors—one in each field. All of these advisors gave the finished project their strong support.

Career Highlights

When he completed his degree, Dr. Gipson stayed on at the University of Chicago for six months. They needed his help on a project that included the study of samples of clay and rock taken from the bottom of the sea. Such samples were important in showing how the oceans evolved over millions of years.

Then in June 1964, Dr. Gipson was invited to join the faculty at Virginia State University. At that time, none of the African American colleges or universities had a well-rounded program in geology. No degrees in this subject were offered by these schools, and any courses in geology were taught by scientists from other fields of specialization. The officials at Virginia State University saw that the lack of a geology program was a problem, and they turned to Dr. Gipson to solve that problem.

Dr. Gipson founded the first Department of Geological Science in a traditionally Black university. As its chairperson, he led the development of this pioneering program from 1964 to 1973. Many students who graduated from the program went on to teach earth science in high schools. Some even went on to receive advanced degrees in geology. Thus, Dr. Gipson helped to make the study and research of geology possible for African American scientists.

During his nine years at Virginia State University, Dr. Gipson continued his own research. One of his projects was supported by the National Aeronautics and Space Administration, which asked Dr. Gipson and his colleagues to solve the mystery of the pyramid-shaped formations on Mars. Some thought that such regular shapes had to have been produced by creatures possessing high intelligence. He and his team discovered that sandstorms, prevalent during different seasons of the Martian year, gradually had smoothed the sides of extinct volcanoes. Thus, the perplexing mystery of the Martian pyramids turned out to be a case of wind erosion.

Dr. Gipson was also interested in the development of energy resources. In 1973,

he left Virginia State and went to work for the Exxon Company to investigate territories that might hold hidden petroleum deposits. He studied possible oil fields in Alaska, Florida, Mexico, Czechoslovakia, and Pakistan. Then in 1982, Dr. Gipson transferred to ERCO Petroleum Services, Inc., of Houston, Texas. With ERCO, he worked on all parts of oil exploration and extraction, effectively improving the production levels of both oil and gas wells.

In 1986, Dr. Gipson returned to teaching. He joined the faculty of the University of South Carolina, where he continues his research in support of locating new oil fields in Czechoslovakia, Pakistan, and Tanzania. Furthermore, he is once again leading the way toward bringing more minority students into the study of geology.

Meredith C. Gourdine

Born: September 26, 1929, in Newark, New Jersey

Status: President, Energy Innovations, Inc., Houston, Texas

Education:

Bachelor of Science degree, Cornell University, Ithaca, New York, 1953

Doctor of Philosophy degree, California Institute of Technology, Pasadena, California, 1960

Research Area: Engineering Physics

Early Years

Meredith Gourdine, the oldest of five children, has three younger brothers and a younger sister. While he was still very young, both of his parents left the family home in Newark, New Jersey, to work in New York City. During this time, he was raised by his grandmother.

When Meredith was nearly six, his father found a position as a superintendent of several large apartment buildings in the Harlem district of New York City. The children moved back in with their parents, and Meredith's mother, a devout Catholic, who at one time thought of entering a convent, enrolled Meredith in St. Joseph's parochial school in Harlem,

In 1940, Meredith's father took a high paying job at the Brooklyn Navy Yard, and the family moved across the East River to Brooklyn. There was no parochial school nearby, so Meredith entered Public School no. 67 in Brooklyn. The standards at School no. 67 were less strict than they had been at St. Joseph's, and Meredith spent less time studying and more time getting into trouble. He and a friend even had to serve a three-week sentence in the New York Juvenile Hall.

Luckily, he was rescued by his mathematics teacher, Mr. Novotny. This teacher challenged Meredith and his friend to a boxing match. He took on both boys at the same time, knocked both of them down, and then dared them to try a different contest. Mr. Novotny bet them he could correctly figure out the square root of any number they gave him. He won and then showed the two boys his mental tricks.

After he had captured their interest, Mr. Novotny challenged them further with a variety of mathematical problems. He did not reveal that these problems were taken from old examinations used by the New York City School Board. Mr. Novotny's work with Meredith and his friend paid off. When the boys took their examinations in 1941, both received high marks and were admitted to the Brooklyn Technical High School.

Meredith's friend did not complete high school with him. Unfortunately, the boy had retained some of his old bad habits. He broke into a theater building and was caught. When he tried to run away, he fell from the balcony level and broke his spine. The friend spent the rest of his life in a wheelchair.

At Brooklyn Technical High School, Meredith was a good student and a top athlete, excelling as a swimmer and broad jumper. In fact, he was given the nickname "Flash" by his schoolmates for his speed and skill. In his last two years of high school, Meredith not only worked hard at his studies and athletics, but also at a part-time job. He was saving his money for college.

Higher Education

At the end of high school, Meredith Gourdine was offered an athletic scholarship to the University of Michigan, but for some unknown reason it was withdrawn. Fortunately, the coaching staff at Cornell University in Ithaca, New York, knew about Gourdine's athletic ability, and even though it was past the deadline for admission, they helped him enter the physical science program at Cornell. Because Gourdine had missed the deadline for financial aid, the money he had saved from his high school job was his main source of support during that first semester of college.

Meredith Gourdine soon switched his major from physical science to engineering physics, a program that takes five years to complete at Cornell. Because of his excellent grades in high school and his performance during his first semester, he was offered a scholarship that provided money for his tuition and fees plus room and board at a house set aside for outstanding students.

Everything went well for Gourdine during his first three years at Cornell. During his fourth year, however, he was forced to make a difficult decision about his priorities. He had become interested in competing in the 1952 Summer Olympic Games and, after much thought, decided to apply for a place. Meredith qualified for the U.S. Olympic Broad Jump Team. Of course, it took serious dedication to prepare himself for the Olympic Games, and sacrifices had to be made.

This dedication to athletics took its toll on Gourdine's academic standing. That spring, he was in the middle of some of his most demanding physics courses, but his practice sessions didn't allow him to study like he needed to. Even though he went on to win the silver medal in the broad jump for the U.S. Olympic Team, he scored an F on his final examination in solid state physics and lost his scholarship.

Without his scholarship, he had to find a part-time job to support himself. Frustrated, Gourdine took a position on a research team headed by Professor Arthur Kantrowitz. The Kantrowitz team was studying the effects of sudden blasts of air on various structures. Gourdine was given the job of building a device called a shock tube, a metal sleeve that is pumped full of air. When the air pressure is high enough, a rubber insert gives way to allow a blast of air to escape. Gourdine's shock tube didn't work. The rubber insert failed to break under pressure, and the devise became a compressed air bomb. He had neglected to put a safety valve in the shock tube, and another engineer had to be called in to solve the problem. Meredith Gourdine was harshly criticized by Professor Kantrowitz, who said that Gourdine had to show more dedication to the work, if he hoped to retain his position.

Meredith Gourdine needed a better way to manage his life. He knew that he wanted to be a well-rounded individual with many interests, so he began centering his complete concentration on each of his interests in turn. For example, in one part of the day, Gourdine would focus his attention on his course work and in another part, he would concentrate on his athletics. Other interests would also have their turns.

His plan worked so well that his scholarship was restored by the end of the fall semester. In addition to this funding, Meredith Gourdine received support from the Naval Reserve Officer Training Program. After graduating from Cornell in 1953, he served two years as a Naval Officer on an aircraft carrier, where he earned practical experience by working with electronic systems.

When Gourdine finished his military service in 1955, he married Carolina Baling from Zamboanga City in the Philippines. He also enrolled in the doctoral program at the California Institute of Technology, a move that had already been arranged by Dr. Theodore Von Karman, a man whom many considered to be the father of modern aeronautics. Von Karman, a visiting teacher during Gourdine's last year at Cornell, had been so impressed with Gourdine's abilities that he recommended him for a graduate fellowship from the Guggenheim Foundation. Because of Dr. Von Karman's support, Gourdine was awarded the fellowship.

The doctoral program at the California Institute of Technology was troublesome in several ways. First, Meredith Gourdine had a difficult relationship with his advisor, Dr. Hans Liepmann. Liepmann had an unusual style of presenting his ideas to students, and Gourdine thought it would be amusing to adopt this style when he made a presentation about his research plans. Dr. Liepmann was not amused.

Later, Meredith had problems in designing a research project that would solve a practical problem. He knew that airplane wings and helicopter rotor blades work best if the airflow around them is smooth. Gourdine wanted to study ways of smoothing airflow that had become bumpy and swirling under bad weather conditions. He duplicated these adverse atmospheric conditions inside a tube in the laboratory. He then tried to produce a magnetic field in the tube that would help smooth the airflow. Unfortunately, his idea was stolen by someone visiting his laboratory and Gourdine had to find a new project.

His advisor, Dr. Leipmann, suggested a project that involved studying the effects of a magnetic field on a falling object. The experiments did not achieve any results, but it took Gourdine six months of hard work to come to this decision.

Next, Meredith Gourdine decided to do a project based on mathematics, so he asked Dr. Julian Kohl, an expert in mathematical theory, to be his new advisor. This time the research was successful. Gourdine became the first to discover that an object moving in a magnetic field creates a type of bow wave. Like a ship moving in water, the object bends the magnetic field in front of it. The successful study led to Meredith Gourdine's doctoral degree in 1960.

Career Highlights

By the time Dr. Gourdine had finished his graduate work, he and his wife, Carolina, had four children. He had worked during his last year of school at the Jet Propulsion Laboratory, a facility operated by the California Institute of Technology. This job helped support his growing family. However, he was unhappy at the laboratory, because the work was not demanding enough.

In 1960, Dr. Gourdine went to work for Plasmadyne Corporation where he was named director of their aerospace laboratory. Then, in 1962, he decided to accept a position as chief scientist for aeronautics with the Curtis Wright Corporation in New Jersey, where he was in charge of a project to develop spaceship engines.

Soon, Dr. Gourdine found that he did not enjoy working for a large organization. He decided to start his own company, and in 1964, he founded Gourdine Systems, Inc. At last, Dr. Gourdine could be a full time inventor. He took theoretical ideas from engineering physics and used them to develop practical applications. He invented instruments to clear fog from airports, a machine to help clean the smoke from incinerators, and a method to evenly spray paint onto peculiarly shaped objects.

Dr. Gourdine also has invented new devices that generate electrical power and conserve energy. These devices are based on the concept of a fuel cell. Two gases are introduced into a reaction chamber from separate sources. The reaction chamber contains a catalyst that helps the two gases react with one another. Their reaction generates an electrical current. The by-product of the process is as harmless to the environment as pure water. Dr. Gourdine's contribution to the development of this technology was the design of a reaction chamber in the form of a set of specially shaped tubes. These tubes allow the gases to react over a larger space and increases the efficiency of the electrical generation. Unfortunately, the power generated by even the most advanced fuel cells costs three to four times as much as power from conventional power plants, so the use of fuel cells is restricted to special purposes such as providing electrical power for space vehicles.

Although Dr. Gourdine greatly enjoyed inventing these products, he did not enjoy the manufacturing, marketing, or selling of his inventions. He closed his first company, Gourdine Systems, in 1974.

Dr. Gourdine then went on to found a new company in Houston, Texas. This new company, Energy Innovations, allows him to continue the work that he enjoys the most—inventing. Indeed, Dr. Gourdine's genius for invention has netted him over 70 U.S. and foreign patents. Many of these patents are used under licensing agreements with other companies.

His own company provides the setting for improvement of these licensed technologies and further research and development activities. Energy Innovations is linked to three affiliated organizations that pursue the commercial applications of devices such as Dr. Gourdine's airport fog removal system.

As a student at Cornell University, Meredith Gourdine was forced to develop a method by which he could channel his energies amongst his many interests. Because of this accomplishment, Dr. Gourdine has achieved excellence as a scholar, an inventor, and an athlete.

Evelyn Boyd Granville

Born: May 1, 1924, in Washington, D.C.

Status: Sam A. Lindsey Professor of Mathematics, University of Texas, Tyler, Texas

Education:

Bachelor of Arts degree, Smith College, Northampton, Massachusetts, 1945

Master of Arts degree, Yale University, New Haven, Connecticut, 1946

Doctor of Philosophy degree, Yale University, 1949

Research Area: Mathematics

Early Years

Evelyn Boyd was the second daughter of William Boyd and Julia Walker Boyd. She and her sister, who was older by eighteen months, attended the segregated schools of Washington, D.C., during the Great Depression.

Evelyn's father, William Boyd, worked as a janitor in big apartment buildings when Evelyn was growing up. He also worked, from time to time, as a chauffeur and messenger for government agencies. Because of the depression, however, Evelyn's family was still dependent on public welfare during some of her childhood.

Evelyn did well in school from the first. Her major problems were social. Although she had many school friends, she considered herself a "wallflower" because she had no talent for easy banter at school parties and other social events. She spent a good portion of her free time in the libraries and great museums that are open to the public in Washington, D.C.

About the time Evelyn entered Dunbar High School, her mother and father were separated. In addition to the emotional trauma, the family's financial situation looked bleak. However, Evelyn's mother found a government job at the Bureau of Engraving and Printing as a technician in their quality control unit. This job gave the family a degree of financial security.

Evelyn was always encouraged by her mother, her teachers, and her friends to become a professional person. At first she was called to teaching. She thought she would teach mathematics and science at the high school level. Such a vocation would give her solid status in the community. However, because of superior performance in mathematics courses, her own high school teachers advised her to consider other, more challenging, career possibilities.

Dunbar High School has a tradition of sending their graduates to the best universities in the East. In line with their ideas about the level Evelyn could reach, her teachers suggested that she apply to some of the outstanding women's colleges. Smith College in Massachusetts accepted her application for admission but did not award her any financial aid. With only her mother's modest income, it was impossible for Evelyn to pay the high cost of tuition at Smith. However, Evelyn's mother's sister was very concerned about her niece's progress, and she volunteered to pay half of the tuition. The other half was covered by a scholarship from a national organization of female African American teachers.

Higher Education

Evelyn Boyd entered Smith College in the fall of 1941, just a few months before the United States was drawn into World War II. Student bodies and faculties at most colleges and universities around the country were decimated, as young men were called into military service, but Smith, the largest women's college in the United States, was barely affected during the early months of the war. For Ms. Boyd, the war was actually a boon because she was able to find good summer jobs in Washington. She worked as a mathematician at the National Bureau of Standards (now the National Institute of Standards and Technology) every summer after her first year at Smith.

The Smith faculty was quick to recognize Ms. Boyd's abilities. They soon helped her obtain financial support from the college's administrators to cover her tuition and fees. In effect, Smith College paid Evelyn Boyd to study there.

Smith College has very high standards of scholarship and recruits students from all over the United States and abroad. Ms. Boyd never felt discouraged by the competition. If anything, her training at Dunbar High School had given her an edge over her fellow students. Her plan of study was to do the required courses in languages, literature, and history as early in the four-year sequence as possible. Then, during her third and fourth years, she could concentrate on the mathematics, physics, and astronomy courses she liked best. Her career goal was to teach mathematics at the high school level.

By the time Evelyn Boyd reached her fourth year at college, however, her vision of the future changed. She began to view herself as a teacher at the college or university level, which would require further study. She applied to the University of Michigan and to Yale University and was accepted at both. She chose Yale because they were willing to give her some financial aid. With additional scholarship money from the Smith Student Aid Society, Ms. Boyd was able to go directly into her program of graduate studies. Later at Yale, she also won fellowships from the Julius Rosenwald Fund and from the U.S. Atomic Energy Commission.

Her program of study at Yale was influenced by many teachers but the most important one was Professor Einar Hille. Dr. Hille helped Ms. Boyd understand the complicated mathematics invented by a Frenchman named Laguerre in the mid-1800s. This mathematician showed how two positive numbers, x and y, could be combined in a particular equation whose product would always be zero—regardless of the original values assigned to x and y. Evelyn Boyd did her dissertation research on this equation. She finished the work for her degree and graduated from Yale in 1949. That year, Evelyn Boyd and Marjorie Lee Brown from the University of Michigan tied as the first African American women to earn doctorates in mathematics.

Career Highlights

After graduation, Dr. Boyd took a job at the Institute of Mathematics at New York University in New York City. This position allowed Dr. Boyd to teach college-level students on a part-time basis. She found teaching so enjoyable that she soon took a full-time teaching job at Fisk University in Nashville, Tennessee.

Nashville, still following southern traditions in education, was very different from New York City. Despite the adverse attitudes held by some people, Dr. Boyd was able to identify and encourage several outstanding young African American women during her short stay at Fisk. Indeed, several of her students, such as Eta Zuber Falconer, were destined to gain doctoral degrees in mathematics at other institutions of higher learning.

Dr. Boyd missed the rich academic and cultural climate of Washington, D.C., and returned there in 1952, where she found work with the National Bureau of Standards. The group to which Dr. Boyd was assigned was attempting to solve the problem of calculating the ideal settings for the fuses installed in ballistic missiles. Dr. Boyd's group was soon transferred out of the Bureau of Standards and into the Department of the Army, where it was given a new name, the Diamond Ordnance Fuse Laboratory. Other mathematicians in this laboratory were beginning to explore the use of electronic computers to help them solve complicated equations. This work appealed to Dr. Boyd, and she began to study the workings of computers and the methods for writing computer programs. This interest led her to join the International Business Machine (IBM) Company in 1956. She stayed for one year in Washington, D.C., where she wrote programs for the newest IBM computers. She then transferred to New York City, where she was assigned to work as a trouble-shooter with IBM customers who needed help with their computer programs. When IBM was awarded a contract from the National Aeronautics and Space Administration (NASA) to calculate orbits for space vehicles, she requested an assignment to that work team, which was based in Washington, D.C.

Around this time, Dr. Boyd took a business trip to California, where she met the Reverend G. Mansfield Collins at a friend's house. The young preacher was not intimidated by a woman with an advanced degree in mathematics, instead he was rather impressed. They were married in Washington, D.C., in the fall of 1960 and immediately moved to his parish in Los Angeles, California.

In Los Angeles, Reverend Collins was in the process of founding a new parish called the All Saints Community Church. Dr. Evelyn Boyd Collins suddenly had a ready-made family of three young step-children to look after as well as responsibilities as a minister's wife to fulfill. She not only accepted these responsibilities but soon was back at work part-time as a professional mathematician at the Space Technology Laboratories in Los Angeles. There, she continued her pioneering work on orbit computations for manned space vehicles.

When the work of setting up her husband's new parish was nearly completed in 1962, Dr. Boyd Collins went back to work full-time with the North American Aviation Corporation. Soon, North American and other aerospace firms were awarded contracts by NASA to help design the space vehicle for Project Apollo. Dr. Boyd Collins would now have the chance to help put human beings on the moon. She stayed with the Apollo program until 1967, even though her place of employment switched from North American Aviation to IBM, her former employer. IBM lost their government contract in 1967, the same year that Dr. Boyd Collins's marriage ended. She decided she needed to find a position with more flexibility, so she accepted a job as assistant professor of mathematics at California State University, Los Angeles. There she taught pure mathematics in a course on numerical analysis and applied mathematics in a course on computer programming. She also taught a special mathematics course for people who were preparing to be grade school teachers.

Working with young people who were training to be teachers raised Dr. Boyd Collins's interests in the problems of teaching mathematics to children. She joined a statewide project to place college mathematics teachers into elementary classrooms so that they could see where the problems lay. For one school year, Dr. Boyd Collins taught one class of second graders and one class of fifth graders each day. Her experiences in a grade school classroom led her to coauthor a book on teacher training that was published in 1975.

In 1970, Dr. Boyd Collins married for the second time. Her new husband, Edward V. Granville, was a successful real estate broker in the Los Angeles area. She adopted the name of her new husband and became known as Dr. Boyd Granville.

In 1983, Dr. Boyd Granville was ready to retire. She and her husband bought a house near Tyler, Texas—where Mr. Granville had spent his childhood—and moved in 1984. Shortly after moving to their new house, they became acquainted with a member of the local school board. He discovered that Dr. Boyd Granville had taught grade school mathematics and was also an expert in computer programming. He asked if she would be willing to teach computer literacy to eighth graders. In the fall of 1984, she was scheduled to teach three sections of computer literacy, one section of eighth-grade math, and one section of ninth-grade algebra. The enterprise turned out to be a mistake. Teaching at this level was so unlike her previous teaching experience that by Thanksgiving, she had given up the entire project.

For some people, this experience would have spelled the end of any future teaching ambitions, but Dr. Boyd Granville was undaunted. She soon accepted a part-time teaching position at the University of Texas in Tyler in their mathematics department. She now teaches state-of-the-art computer science courses, which she has designed, and is in a good position to keep up with the new developments in her rapidly changing field.

Judith L. Gwaltney

John L. Gwaltney

Born: September 25, 1928, in Orange, New Jersey

Status: Retired, Professor, Syracuse University, Syracuse, New York, 1992

Education:

Bachelor of Arts degree, Upsala College, East Orange, New Jersey, 1952

Master of Arts degree, New School for Social Research, New York, New York, 1957

Doctor of Philosophy degree, Columbia University, New York, New York, 1967

Research Area: Anthropology

Early Years

John Gwaltney grew up surrounded by a large family, which included not only his brother, sister, and parents, but also his cousins, aunts, and uncles. John's mother relied on the family members willingness to help one another, since her husband was a merchant seaman and often gone on long voyages. The help and support of the family, however, became even more crucial after John's birth. John was born blind.

When he was small, his mother Mabel Harper Gwaltney, tutored him, hoping to improve his understanding of the world. Mrs. Gwaltney made cardboard cutouts to show John the shapes of animals, objects, and letters of the alphabet. She kept a piano in their house and encouraged John to practice as much as possible. She hoped John would become a preacher or a musician, because she thought these were the only jobs open to a blind African American.

John's mother was determined to do everything possible to help her son. Doctors said that medical science could not cure John's blindness, so his mother tried other methods. She visited religious healers and used old-fashioned remedies made of roots and herbs. Nothing worked but she continued her quest.

When John was ready to start school, Franklin Roosevelt was president of the United States. Mrs. Eleanor Roosevelt, the president's wife, had been trying to establish a government program to provide special education for handicapped children. She wanted these children to have a better chance in life.

John's mother took a bold step. She wrote a letter about her son to Mrs. Roosevelt. The president's wife was able to help, and John was soon enrolled in a special school program for blind children.

Mabel Gwaltney was concerned that her son be able to do things for himself. When he was nine years old, she sent him to summer camp. Initially, John was afraid he would get lost in the woods or die of snakebites, but he ended up loving the camp, and returned there each summer until he was sixteen.

In his last year of high school, John bought an old second-hand car and that purchase allowed him more freedom than he had ever had before. His brother or his friends drove John and his mother to the countryside where they had many happy outings. Unfortunately, the old car was soon to be employed as an ambulance. John's mother became very ill from diabetes, and they used it to rush her to the hospital. After Mrs. Gwaltney was admitted, the young people used the car to make many trips back and forth to the hospital.

In spite of the fact that her son had serious disabilities, Mabel Gwaltney was convinced that John should go on to college. He enrolled at Upsala College in East Orange, New Jersey, so he could stay as close to her as possible during her illness. Unfortunately, Mabel Harper Gwaltney died shortly before her son graduated in 1952.

Higher Education

Although John Gwaltney's choice of a college had been determined by his mother's illness, his choice of subject matter was decided by other factors. When John was in grade school, he had acquired a love of geography from two of his teachers, Lee Belmont and Althea Nichols. They helped him develop an interest in people from all parts of the world. Gwaltney's father helped, too, by telling him stories of his travels. As a merchant seaman, Mr. Gwaltney visited the big port cities in Europe, Asia, and Latin America. John Gwaltney thought it would be fascinating to learn about these far-away places, and he imagined himself visiting as an explorer.

When Gwaltney was about ten years old, he listened each week to a special radio program called the Columbia Broadcasting System's School of the Air. One of the speakers was Professor Margaret Mead, a famous anthropologist. In her radio broadcast, she described how people lived in traditional societies all over the world. Through her talks, she gave Gwaltney a sense of how exciting it is to learn about different groups of people. By 1947, when Gwaltney entered Upsala College, he had decided to pursue a career in the social sciences.

After graduating from Upsala in history and sociology, John Gwaltney moved to New York City to study for a master's degree in political science and sociology. He had been awarded a scholarship provided by the presidents of both his undergraduate school, Upsala College, and his present college, the New School for Social Research.

In graduate school, John soon became interested in the problems of colonialism in Africa. He was particularily interested in the Mau Mau uprising, a bloody and only partly successful war for independence in Kenya.

When he finished his master's degree in 1957, he took a job teaching at the Henry George School of Social Science in New York City. This high school tries to attract good students who plan to study one of the social sciences in college. John Gwaltney was able to improve his teaching skills and earn money to finance his future graduate studies.

In 1959, John Gwaltney entered the final stage of his formal education. He enrolled in the graduate school at Columbia University in New York City. There, he had many excellent professors, such as Morton H. Fried and Conrad Arensberg. The most influencial professor, however, was Dr. Margaret Mead.

In 1960, Dr. Mead took John Gwaltney under her wing and helped him plan his major research project. It must have been a strange experience to meet the person who, twenty years earlier, had influenced his career decision. Gwaltney had always wanted to do field anthropology and live among the people he was studying. Dr. Mead was confident that he could do so. She supported his wish to study the Indians who lived in the village of San Pedro Yolox in southeastern Mexico.

This almost inaccessible village could only be reached by mountain trails. Anthropologists knew that the people of San Pedro Yolox were special in several ways. They were descendants of the Chinantec Indians and spoke that language rather than Spanish. These people also suffered from a condition known as New World River Blindness. One out of every twenty villagers had the disease, which is carried by a black fly that breeds in tropical rivers.

One of the purposes of John Gwaltney's research was to find out how these native people were able to maintain their society when so many of their number were blind. The inhabitants of this area also had another serious problem—the shortage of level, fertile land. The steep slopes around the village actually provided four separate climate zones. High up, the weather was always chilly, and the villagers used this location as a source of timber. Lower down, the climate was moderate, and at this level, they planted corn. Still lower, the climate was semitropical, and here, they grew coffee, a crop that brought in small amounts of money for the villagers. In the deep valleys, the climate was tropical and the land level. There, they grew citrus fruit and bananas in the rich soil. Unfortunately, black flies, the enemies of the villagers, lived at this level as well. The farmers knew that if they cultivated this fertile land, they risked getting the infection and going blind.

The people of San Padro Yolox had accustomed themselves to their difficult existence. They treated the blind people with great respect. Young children served as guides for each blind villager, a responsibility the children saw as an honor. The villagers also believed that supernatural forces protected the blind people from dangers such as poisonous snakes.

John Gwaltney spent more than a year living among the people of San Pedro Yolox. He was partially supported by a fellowship grant from the National Institutes of Health, which was interested in finding out more about the nature of New World River Blindness. Gwaltney returned to New York City in 1966 to prepare his reports. He completed his dissertation and received his doctoral degree from Columbia in 1967.

Career Highlights

After graduation, Dr. Gwaltney joined the faculty at the State University of New York at Cortland, and in 1969, he was promoted to the rank of associate professor. His research interests began to expand. In 1969, he studied the Shinnecock and Poospatuck Indians of Canada, and later, he became interested in studying the culture of African Americans in the United States.

In 1971, Dr. Gwaltney transferred to Syracuse University in Syracuse, New York, where he began a series of biographies of African Americans who lived in the major industrial cities in New York and neighboring states. He focused on the idea that there is a core Black culture. Dr. Gwaltney perceived the main institutions in that culture to be the family and the church. He saw that in African American culture, the family is a group consisting of parents, sons, daughters, grandparents, aunts, uncles, and cousins and defined by mutual support, not just marriage and kinship.

These studies led to the book, *Drylongso,* published in 1981. Drylongso means ordinary or nothing unusual. Dr. Gwaltney believed that most people, including social scientists, did not understand Black culture. The media reports only Black problems and unusual happenings in the African American community. But in reality, most Black people live their lives in harmony with their community. In his book, Dr. Gwaltney told the stories of many ordinary African Americans and showed the true nature of African American culture.

In 1980, Dr. Gwaltney returned to the village of San Pedro Yolox. He found that some things had changed but others had stayed the same. Most changes were for the good. The River Blindness disease was under control. The Mexican government had sent in teams of public health specialists, who had learned to cure the infection when it was detected early enough.

The government had also expanded the public school system and brought in teachers who spoke both the Chinantec and Spanish languages. New roads, electric power, and even television were now found in San Pedro Yolox. Unfortunately, inflation had caused the price of farm tools and other commodities to increase more rapidly than the price of the coffee beans sold by the villagers. Even with the improvements in their condition, most villagers still had little money and little power over their lives.

When he returned to the United States, Dr. Gwaltney began a new research project—rebels in society. His idea was that dissenters help a society stay in touch with reality. Using his research skills, he interviewed dozens of revolutionaries from every walk of life. He put their stories together in a book entitled *The Dissenters*. It was published in 1986 and nominated for the Robert F. Kennedy Book Award in 1987.

Dr. Gwaltney is now retired from teaching and spends his time creating works of art. His interest in art began when he was eight years old and his mother gave him a piece of wood to carve. She wanted to increase his sense of his own creative abilities. In 1983,

his carving of an African dala, a ceremonial staff, won the Best of Show prize in an art exhibit at Syracuse University. Dr. Gwaltney's art is an important way of representing his own mental images, as well as his African American heritage.

Lloyd Augustus Hall

Born: June 20, 1894, in Elgin, Illinois

Status: Died, October 29, 1971, in Pasadena, California

Education:

Bachelor of Science degree, Northwestern University, Evanston, Illinois, 1916

Doctor of Science degree (honorary), Virginia State College, Petersburg, Virginia, 1944

Research Area: Chemistry

Early Years

Lloyd Hall's parents, Augustus and Isabel Hall, put a very high value on education. Both of them had graduated from high school, which was unusual for young African Americans in the years just after the Civil War.

In 1908, Lloyd entered East Side High School in Aurora, Illinois, where he was quickly attracted to science. He especially loved chemistry and saw it as a subject in which he could excel. During high school, he did very well in all his academic courses and won awards for his athletic performance in track and baseball. Lloyd not only found the time to study and to perform athletics, but he also managed to work part-time. During his senior year, he rose at dawn to deliver the morning newspapers in his neighborhood. In 1912, this hard-working young man graduated among the top ten students in his class.

Higher Education

Lloyd Hall had done so well in high school that he received offers from several universities. He accepted a small scholarship from Northwestern University in Evanston, Illinois. While in college, he continued working at odd jobs to pay his living costs.

Chemistry continued to be his main area of study. In one of his courses, he shared his laboratory work bench with a young man named Carroll L. Griffith. They became good friends and Hall helped Griffith with the laboratory projects. Ten years later, this friendship would lead Lloyd Hall to his chosen career.

Hall graduated from Northwestern in 1916, but he continued as a part-time student at the University of Chicago and the Chicago branch of the University of Illinois. Although he would have preferred to remain in school, he knew that he must get a full-time job. He was low on funds, and there were viturally no scholarships for African American students at this time.

Career Highlights

Mr. Hall had a difficult time finding a job after his graduation. Many companies did not hire African Americans, but finally, he got a job with the Chicago Department of Health, where he tested food products for purity. Mr. Hall did excellent work, and after just one year on the job, he was promoted to the rank of senior chemist.

In 1919, he accepted a better-paying job in Dubuque, Iowa, as chief chemist at a well-known company that produced hams and bacon. Now that his income had increased, he could think about starting a family of his own. He married a school teacher from Macomb, Illinois, named Myrrhene E. Newsome.

Two years later, he was offered the job as chief chemist at Boyer Chemical Laboratory in Chicago, and the young family moved back to Illinois. Mr. Hall was gradually gaining confidence in his ability to make a successful career in the food industry. Consequently, in 1922, he decided to begin work as an independent consultant.

One of his clients was Carroll Griffith, his college friend. The Griffith family owned a company that sold flavorings to meat packers. Mr. Hall's work proved so helpful to the Griffith company that he was asked to become their chief of research. He held this position until his retirement almost thirty years later.

The combination of Griffith's business sense and Mr. Hall's technical abilities was very fruitful. Together, they worked on inventing and selling new products, including a better way to preserve meat.

For hundreds of years, meat was kept from spoiling by storing it in brine, a concentrated solution of salt and water. Meat stored in this manner—a process called curing—can be kept for several months without spoiling. Other curing compounds were developed over the years, such as those containing sodium and nitrogen, which give meat an attractive pink color and a much better taste, but also cause the meat to turn soft and spongy.

Many people had tried to find a mixture of plain salt and nitrogen compounds that would retain the good qualities of each method, but nothing had worked very well until Mr. Hall invented a new technique. He dissolved both plain salt and a small amount of the nitrogen compounds in water. The solution was then sprayed on hot metal rollers. The heat quickly evaporated the water, and as the rollers turned, the dried salt mixture was scraped off. The mixture was then dissolved in water to make a better curing solution.

This method of mixing plain salt with the nitrogen compounds worked very well. The plain salt bound the nitrogen compounds so that the meat stayed firm. The process also allowed enough of the nitrogen compounds to be released at the proper time so that the meat acquired good color and taste. Mr. Hall also found a way to keep the mixture from caking or turning into a solid mass after it was packaged.

His methods also helped reduce the cost of food production. For example, Mr. Hall developed a new and faster way to cure bacon and ham by injecting the curing liquid directly into the meat, which saved both time and money and gave the meat a better quality. He was awarded several patents for these inventions.

Mr. Hall was also aware of another difficult problem facing the food industry. Spices such as cinnamon and cloves were sometimes harvested in a careless manner and then transported thousands of miles before being processed. Germs and insects could get into the containers, contaminating them. Most people

in the food industry thought it was impossible to disinfect these raw spices properly before they were put into food. If the spices were heated high enough to kill the bacteria and insects, their flavor and color would be lost.

Mr. Hall developed a method to overcome this problem. The raw spices were placed in a large revolving drum. Then, all the air was sucked out of the drum to create a vacuum which dried the spices without heating them. Next, a gas called ethylene oxide was piped into the drum and while the drum revolved to stir the spices, the gas killed all the micro-organisms.

The Griffith Company was so happy with the idea of germ-free spices that they started a new line of business. Previously, they had sold their products only to meat packers and others in the food industry. Now, they began to package pure spices in small containers for home consumption. Mr. Hall's method of sterilization was also adopted for other materials beside spices. The raw materials used in medicines and cosmetics were treated by the Hall technique. For example, baby powder could now be made germ free, as could the bath powder used to keep the skin dry in humid weather.

Another of Mr. Hall's major contributions was the development of a method to prevent fats and oils from spoiling. Fats and oils, such as those used to make butter substitutes, normally absorb oxygen from the air, which makes the oil or fat turn rancid and develop a very unpleasant taste. To combat this problem, Mr. Hall experimented with mixtures that contained tiny amounts of a metal called gallium, which is similar to aluminum. He found that gallium and certain other metals could capture the oxygen before it was absorbed by the fat or oil. In practice, the metal compound was mixed with plain salt and some other ingredients. Then, this mixture was used in the preparation of fatty or oily foods—like potato chips—to prevent spoilage. Soon, potato chip makers began using salt that contained a very tiny amount of the gallium compound. Their packaged chips stayed fresh for a longer time.

The kind of challenge that Mr. Hall liked best was to transform low-cost raw materials into higher-priced products. He had studied the ancient alchemists who tried to transform lead into gold, and he knew that their dreams had not come true. Trying to find lower-priced substitutes for costly flavoring compounds, however, would prove to be a more down-to-earth project for a modern chemist. Hall and his fellow workers discovered which basic chemicals were present in expensive flavoring agents such as oil of sage. They then analyzed other natural materials that contained these same chemicals and attempted to isolate the desired materials. Mr. Hall found that by the process of distillation, he could separate the costly flavorings from the less expensive ones in many natural materials. For example, a good sage oil could be distilled from the oil of eucalyptus.

During his career, Mr. Hall also worked on the chemistry of petroleum, soap, and rubber compounds. For example, during World War II, he helped develop the self-sealing gasoline tank. Used in U.S. combat aircraft, the tank was lined with a plastic that could flow into a bullet hole and seal it. It was this work that led to Hall's honorary doctorate degree from Virginia State College. By the time that Mr. Hall retired from Griffith Laboratories, he had been awarded more than 100 different patents in the United States and abroad for his work with the chemistry of food and raw materials.

Lloyd Hall, a tall, slender man, was a commanding figure. His philosophy of equal opportunity for all gave him added stature. During his long tenure at Griffith Laborato-

ries, he always showed his fellow workers—men and women of varied races and religions—the respect with which he himself wished to be treated.

Don Navarro Harris

Born: June 17, 1929, in New York, New York

Status: Consultant on Human Resources, Bristol-Myers Squibb Pharmaceutical Research Institute, Princeton, New Jersey

Education:
Bachelor of Arts degree, Lincoln University, Lincoln Pennsylvania, 1951

Master of Science degree, Rutgers University, New Brunswick, New Jersey, 1959

Doctor of Philosophy degree, Rutgers University, 1963

Research Area: Biochemistry

Early Years

Don Navarro Harris's parents, John Henry and Margaret Vivian Harris, met and married in Louisa County, Virginia, an area of rolling hills between Charlottesville and Richmond. They moved from Virginia to Washington, D.C., in the mid-1920s and from there to the Sugar Hill Section of central New York City. Don's father worked as an electrician, and his mother worked as a seamstress in New York's garment district.

In the summer of 1929, when Don was born, New York City was a vibrant and exciting place. People were getting rich in a hurry by buying and selling stocks on the New York Stock Exchange. Sadly, only four months after Don was born the stock market crashed. The stock prices lost as much as half their value overnight. Many people not only lost their savings but found themselves deeply in debt.

Don's parents were hurt by the crash and had to struggle through the crisis by working much harder. They were lucky to have solid skills and to be able to find work when others were unemployed.

Don attended integrated public schools in New York City. By the time he reached junior high school, he was competing with his fellow students for the best grades. This was a challenge because many of his classmates were very bright and went on to successful careers in law, medicine, and the entertainment industry. It was during this time that Don decided to pursue a career in science.

When Don was 15, he enrolled at George Washington High School, an integrated high school in Manhattan. At George Washington, he made good grades, particularly in his science courses. He was also successful on the track and cross-country teams.

The next year, his parents bought a new home in the St. Albans section of Queens on Long Island, but Don remained at George Washington High School. He wanted to continue in a setting where he was enjoying success

in both his classes and on the athletic fields. He did his homework on the train during the two-hour subway commutes to and from the city.

Higher Education

Lincoln University in Pennsylvania is not many miles from New York City but it has a very different atmosphere. The setting is rural rather than urban, the university was only one-fourth the size of George Washington High School, and Lincoln's student body was almost entirely African American. Don Harris chose Lincoln because he and his parents had heard very positive accounts of the college. The Harris family doctor was a graduate of the school as were several of Don Harris's older friends.

One of the advantages of a modest-sized institution, such as Lincoln University, is the opportunity a student has to receive a reasonable amount of individual attention from the instructors. Harris was fortunate to receive such attention from the late Professor Harold F. Grim. Grim inspired a special kind of loyalty among the young people who were considering careers in the sciences. Indeed, the group of students, advised and mentored by Professor Grim, became a sort of club and called themselves "Grimlins" to show their respect and affiliation with this teacher.

As with other students at Lincoln, Harris had to work part-time to pay for some of his expenses. He worked in the cafeteria and for Dr. Toye Davis in the student infirmary, where he was able to gain experience relevant to his courses in chemistry and biological science.

After Don Harris graduated in the spring of 1951, he had no particular plans to continue his education. The job market was fairly active at the time, and Harris was able to find employment as a professional chemist with the city of New York, state agencies, and various medical laboratories.

Then in 1953, just after the Korean War, Harris was drafted into the U.S. Army. At first, he was stationed at Brooke Army Hospital at Fort Sam Houston in Texas as a medical technician. While there, he met and married his wife, Regina. Soon after his marriage, he was shipped overseas to the Army General Hospital in Croix Chapeaux, France. He was separated from his new bride but, at least, was someplace where he could continue to learn. When he came back to the United States in 1955, he was able to return to the type of job he had left two years before. He and his wife went back to New York City, where he accepted a job with the city's Public Health Service.

Harris could have kept his good government job as a laboratory technician, taken his civil service promotions and salary increases, and lived a comfortable life, but he wanted to do something more challenging. He decided to go to work for the Columbia University Research Service, where he joined a research team headed by Professor Erwin Mosbach. The team members were studying the properties of cholesterol and were beginning to understand how cholesterol might be a cause of arterial obstructions and heart attacks. This research determined Don Harris's future career. The team generated a report on cholesterol that was published in the scientific literature, and Harris was listed as one of the authors.

The experience of doing such successful research and the encouragement of Professor Mosbach helped Don Harris decide that he wanted to pursue a career as a research scientist. He applied to Rutgers University in nearby New Brunswick, New Jersey, and entered their graduate biochemistry program in the fall of 1958. In his first year, he had to rely on the veteran's benefits from his military service and from the help of his family to finance his education. His graduate work was so successful, however, that he completed his master's degree in one year, and after that first year, Harris was awarded a research assistantship in the Department of Biochemistry, which provided financial support during his Ph.D. studies.

Don Harris's doctoral research was guided by Professor Frank F. Davis. Harris and his mentor were studying DNA and RNA, the molecules that control the growth and development of all biological cells. They were trying to discover how some forms of RNA controlled the construction of proteins that make up the body's living cells. The research was difficult and took a long time to complete; however, Don Harris enjoyed the collaboration with his teacher and the other graduate students working on similar projects.

Before Harris graduated in 1963, he and the other team members were able to show how the molecular codes in the RNA directed the construction of specific amino acids.

Career Highlights

In general, young scientists must decide between a career in basic, theory-oriented research or one in applied research which has more immediate practical consequences. Dr. Harris was fortunate enough to do both during his career. His doctoral research had been very basic, but his first job after he finished his degree focused on applied research. Dr. Harris went to work for the Colgate-Palmolive Company in their Research Center at Piscataway, New Jersey, where he supervised two younger scientists in a study of dental cavities and plaque. The team hoped to find compounds that might be added to toothpaste to help prevent cavities and plaque build-up near the gum line. The use of fluorides in toothpaste had already proved successful, and many toothpaste manufacturers were hoping to produce a new product with different additives such as compounds based on peroxides used as bleaches, that might improve their share of the market.

After one year of applied research at Colgate-Palmolive, Dr. Harris decided to return to the basic research he had done on the chemistry of the individual cell. In 1964, he went back to Rutgers University on a one-year appointment as an assistant research specialist in the Bureau of Biological Research. He was assigned a graduate student to assist him in the testing of a variety of methods for separating and characterizing the very small, complicated molecules of a cell's nucleus. These small molecules are the building blocks for DNA, which conveys genetic information, and RNA, which controls the assembly of the molecules that compose the cell.

In the late summer of 1965, after the completion of his Rutgers appointment, Dr. Harris made the most important career decision of his life. He joined the research staff of the Bristol-Myers Squibb Research Institute. At one level, his job consisted of supervising a biochemical research laboratory staffed by five or six younger scientists. At another level, his work focused on developing new methods of separating and detecting the structural design of complicated molecules. This work took Dr. Harris into the new technique of using radioactive elements to determine the fine structure of biologically active molecules. At still another level, Dr Harris's work was directed at understanding the submicroscopic activities of these molecules. He sought solutions to such diverse questions as how sex hormones influence the development of cells throughout the body, and whether certain enzymes can control high blood pressure and affect the formation of blood clots. Finally, at still another level, Dr. Harris's work involved the integration of the skills and ideas of many scientists. He often took the role called "area team chairman," where he and his colleagues deliberated over strategies for integrating scientific skills to solve specific medical problems, such as the development of a particular kind of medicine.

Many of the research reports co-authored by Dr. Harris are recorded in the pages of more than 60 scientific articles. He also helped produce over 50 short articles—or abstracts—and is the holder or coholder of 5 U.S. patents on various curative compounds.

Meanwhile, Dr. Harris has not forgotten his community responsibilities. He has been active in many organizations that work for racial equality and that promote educational opportunities for minority youth who are interested in careers in science or medicine. He also serves as an adjunct faculty member in the Temple University School of Medicine, where he can reach out to African American students with guidance and encouragement. As a consultant to the human resources department of the Bristol-Myers Squibb Pharmaceutical Research Institute, he helps his company to identify, recruit, and support young, minority scientists.

Mary Styles Harris

Born: June 26, 1949, in Nashville, Tennessee

Status: Chief Executive Officer, BioTechnical Publications, Claremont, California

Education:
Bachelor of Arts degree, Lincoln University, Lincoln University, Pennsylvania, 1971
Doctor of Philosophy degree, Cornell University, Ithaca, New York, 1975

Research Area: Genetics

Early Years

Mary Styles's father was in medical school at Meharry Medical College in Nashville, Tennessee, when he met and married her mother, Margaret. Mary Styles was born just before her father finished medical school. Only a few months later, the young family moved to Miami, Florida, where the new doctor set up his practice in the African American section near the center of the city. Mary's mother had taken her degree in business administration at Tennessee State University, but decided to stay at home and raise Mary and her two siblings.

Mary was encouraged to read at an early age by both her parents. Through her reading, she began to develop an interest in science. Some of this early interest was centered on medicine because of her father's profession; she asked him endless questions. Soon, he showed Mary how to find her own answers to many of her questions. Even at that early age, she enjoyed doing scientific research.

Unfortunately, Mary's father died when she was only nine years old. His death was a major crisis for the family, but it didn't dampen Mary's desire to continue her scientific education. When she entered high school in 1963, the schools in Miami were just beginning to desegregate, and she was among the first African Americans to attend Miami

Jackson High School. Although Miami Jackson was a public school—theoretically open to all young people in the district—Mary's mother had to fill out a formal application before Mary could be admitted.

In spite of the adjustment problems Mary encountered as one of the first African Americans at Jackson, she excelled in her school work. When she graduated in 1967, she was ranked twelfth out of the 350 graduating seniors.

Part of her good performance was probably due to her activities outside the regular classroom. She entered the local science fair each year, and in the evenings and on weekends, she served as a volunteer at the first Black-owned medical laboratory in Miami. In return for her time, various members of the laboratory staff showed Mary how to use the technical equipment and how to do routine biological tests, such as counting the red cells in blood samples. Mary worked hard to integrate ideas from her schoolwork with the techniques she learned in the laboratory and the research experience she gained from her science fair projects.

Higher Education

Just as Mary Styles had been one of the first African Americans to enter Miami Jackson High School, she was one of the first women to enter Lincoln University in Pennsylvania. Her mainly male classmates seemed surprised to find Ms. Styles in courses such as advanced algebra and organic chemistry. She spent most of her time with pre-med students, and at first, they assumed that Ms. Styles hoped to attend medical school. Colleagues of her father had arranged, through a minority recruitment program, to reserve a place for her at the University of Miami Medical School, but Mary did not accept the place. Her fellow students found it hard to believe that anyone would reject an opening in medical school—the goal toward which they were all struggling. However, she had her own plans. Ms. Styles did not want to treat patients, she wanted to do research. Because of her good grades and outstanding academic performance, she was awarded a prestigious Ford Foundation Doctoral Fellowship for the study of molecular genetics.

Shortly after Ms. Styles graduated from Lincoln University, she married Sidney Harris. Harris, who had just graduated from Morehouse College in Atlanta, Georgia, had been accepted in the graduate engineering program at Cornell University in Ithaca, New York. Since Cornell was a famous center for research in molecular genetics, Mary decided to pursue her graduate studies at that university, as well. Years before, Cornell had spawned two winners of the Nobel Prize in biology. One of these winners, Dr. Barbara McClintock, did pioneering studies on the genetics and embryology of corn. Dr. McClintock was still a frequent visitor at the Cornell laboratories when Mary Harris was a student there. In fact, Mrs. Harris's faculty mentor and advisor, Dr. Gerry Fink, worked closely with Barbara McClintock over many years.

When Mary and Sidney arrived in Ithaca, the university's Graduate Student Housing Office helped them find a small apartment near the center of the city. At first, their landlord seemed a little startled to discover that his new tenants were African Americans. However, by the time the young couple finished their degrees, they had been accepted as part of the landlord's own family.

When Mary graduated with her doctorate in 1975, the study of genetics was becoming very exciting. In particular, geneticists were just beginning to understand the full meaning of the structural genetic codes in DNA (deoxyribonucleic acid). Mary was awarded a post-doctoral fellowship by the National Cancer Institute to do research on the chemical composition of viruses. She chose New Jersey University of Medicine and Dentistry as the institution at which to do her research. She wanted to study the most basic virus structures and to determine how new discoveries could be used to improve people's health. Meanwhile, Dr. Sidney Harris took an excellent job with the Bell Laboratories, one of the great research centers in the United States.

Career Highlights

At the New Jersey College of Medicine and Dentistry, Dr. Harris took over an ongoing project to discover materials that would retard the growth of viruses. To acquaint herself with the project, she began to redo some of the experiments that had been completed by her predecessor. Soon, Dr. Harris became troubled about the results of her experiments on the test materials. She was unable to reproduce the earlier positive conclusions. The project directors knew that such problems would raise questions on the validity of the research that had seemed so exciting. Indeed, they still hoped that their test materials would not only be of benefit to curing viral diseases but might also slow or stop the growth of cancer cells. This project had the potential to bring large grants to the university.

Dr. Harris continued to work for several months in a frustrating effort to get her experiments to duplicate the earlier conclusions. Finally, it was determined that the previous researcher had used contaminated materials in all of the experiments. It was a great disappointment to everyone involved in the project.

Dr. Harris took on a new project dealing with the chemical structure of viruses and genetically important molecules. Even though she was able to do successful studies on this topic, she did not want to continue a career in grant-supported basic research. After two years in a biology laboratory, she needed a complete change. When she was offered the job of executive director of the Sickle Cell Foundation of Georgia, she quickly accepted. The move to Georgia was good for Dr. Sidney Harris as well. He was invited to join the faculty of the Business School at Georgia State University.

Dr. Mary Harris knew there would be a variety of responsibilities in her new administrative position. Part of her time was spent raising money to combat sickle-cell anemia, a condition found mainly among people of African descent. She also had to learn the political aspects of directing an organization dedicated to public service. She did not lose sight of her scientific fundamentals, however. Mary Harris knew that she must integrate scientific advancements with the practical problems of improving public health. She met this challenge so well that she was chosen by the National Science Foundation for a Science Residency Award. This award, which is similar to a research fellowship, gave Dr. Harris the opportunity to work with broadcasters to produce a series of television documentary programs on the relationship between science and medicine. Dr. Harris appeared as the host on several of these programs, and later, because of them, won *Glamour Magazine's* Outstanding Working Woman Award. The award ceremonies, which took place during the presidency of Jimmy Carter, were conducted at the White House and led by the president.

When Dr. Harris completed her Science Residency in Washington, D.C., she was asked to become State Director of Genetics Services for the state of Georgia, a newly created position. This position allowed her to influence public health policy not only in Georgia but across the entire nation. Soon, public health authorities in other states began to seek her advice and guidance. She was also teaching part-time at the Medical School of Georgia and at Morehouse Medical School. In the midst of this very busy schedule, her daughter was born.

The next few years proved to be equally hectic. She spent three years as director of Genetic Services and then two years as the project coordinator of a seven-state program of genetic screening of newborn infants. With her heavy work load and her child to care for, Dr. Harris was beginning to feel that she needed a short break. Consequently, she welcomed the news that her husband had been offered a professorship at Claremont College's School of Business in California.

Dr. Harris's break was, indeed, very brief. Shortly after arriving in California, she founded her own consulting company. Many new companies, busy developing products based on genetic engineering, needed help in explaining their activities to the general public, to prospective customers, and to various government officials. Dr. Harris's experiences provided a near perfect background for helping these new companies build their reputations.

More recently, she has won grant support from the National Cancer Institute to produce a new series of television programs covering the particular health problems of African Americans. Her company is also producing audio-visual educational materials that cover a broad range of health care issues faced by women and minorities. Finally, she is doing a series of radio features that cover a number of public health topics.

She did not enjoy a typical California holiday by moving from Atlanta to Clarement; however, she is happy that her husband was made Dean of the Business School at Claremont College and that her daughter is doing well in high school. Dr. Harris is also grateful for the support provided by her family and friends so that she can continue to address such important issues as the excessively high rates of African American infant mortality. She continues to deal with such diverse concerns as her consultations with biotechnology companies and her plans for information programs concerning good health practices and health care resources.

Wesley L. Harris

Born: October 29, 1941, in Richmond, Virginia

Status: Associate Administrator for Aeronautics, National Aeronautics and Space Administration (NASA)

Education:

Bachelor of Aeronautical Engineering degree, University of Virginia, Charlottesville, Virginia, 1964

Doctor of Philosophy degree, Princeton University, Princeton, New Jersey, 1968

Research Area: Aeronautical Engineering

Early Years

Wes Harris is one of three children born to William and Rosa Harris, both of whom worked in Richmond's tobacco factories.

As a child, Wes loved airplanes. His brother and sister used to tease him because he built so many different models. Some of his airplanes were made of balsa wood and others of plastic. Some were powered with rubber bands and some had tiny gasoline engines. In the forth grade, Wes won an essay contest about career goals with a paper on how he wanted to become a test pilot.

Wes's family truly believed in education. His parents thought that education would give their children an entry into a better life. His mother and his grandmother, Alice Minor, were especially supportive. They always made sure Wes studied hard, and they instilled in him a love of learning for its own sake.

Wes was lucky that he had such good teachers at Richmond's Armstrong High School. Many of them had advanced degrees from northern universities, such as Pennsylvania State College and Columbia. Because of the segregation in Virginia during the 1950s, these highly educated African Americans could not teach in Virginia's White colleges, and many of them found jobs in the city's segregated high schools.

Two of Wes's teachers had a great effect on his high school performance and also influenced his later career choices. Wes excelled in the mathematics classes taught by Roselle

Diamond and the physics classes taught by Eloise Washington. Ms. Washington, a strict teacher with strong educational beliefs, would not allow her students to obtain extra help from tutors. She insisted that they master physics on their own, so that the hard-won knowledge would stay with them for the rest of their lives.

Another strong influence on Wes during his high school years was Maxie Robinson, Sr., the Armstrong High football coach. Mr. Robinson was also a strict disciplinarian, often making his players practice until after dark. The long practice sessions made them very tired but also very strong. The coach required Wes and his teammates to work hard, instilling in them the philosophy that they must be able to endure hardships and never give up in any situation.

While Wes was still in high school, the Soviet Union launched the first earth satellite, Sputnik I. This great advance in science was seen as a huge challenge to the United States. The U.S. government responded by improving science education. Money was provided to local schools, so that they could hire more science teachers, purchase more laboratory equipment, and buy more science books for their libraries. The Soviet satellite was also a personal challenge to Wes. He knew that opportunities in aviation and astronautics would increase, and he became even more determined to make a place for himself in these fields.

Higher Education

After graduating from Armstrong High School in 1960, Wes Harris decided to go to the University of Virginia in Charlottesville. Although he wanted to study physics, in those days the university did not allow African Americans to major in those subjects. His only option was to enter the program in aeronautical engineering. Although this program came close to fitting his career goals, Harris had hoped for more training in basic research.

Other aspects of college life were also frustrating for the young man. He had married in 1960 and now had family responsibilities, limiting his time for social activities. He was often lonely, because there were only five or six other African Americans at the university. To make things worse, most facilities in Charlottesville were still segregated, and there were only a few places Black students could go.

Fortunately, two of Harris's professors attempted to make his time at the university more pleasant. Dr. John Scott, Jr., was known as a tough, domineering educator. However, he saw Harris's potential and decided to take a special interest in him. Dr. George Matthews was just as committed to helping Harris achieve success in school.

During his last year at Virginia, Wes Harris received some welcome encouragement. He demonstrated in his senior research project that when air flows over an airplane's wings, the flow changes from smooth to turbulent. For his efforts, he won an award from the American Institute of Aeronautics and Astronautics (AIAA), a prominent professional association. Harris was also the first African American to become a member of the Jefferson Society, the University of Virginia's famous debating group.

Another high point of Wes Harris's college days came when Dr. Martin Luther King, Jr., was invited to speak at the University of Virginia. Harris was thrilled, because he was invited to have dinner with Dr. King and to introduce him to the campus audience. The entire crowd—Whites and African Americans alike—were inspired by Dr. King's presentation.

When he graduated from the University of Virginia, Harris decided that he wanted to become a university professor, which meant that he must attend graduate school. Since Professors Scott and Matthews had received their doctorates from Princeton University in New Jersey, they strongly advised Harris to apply there, and he did.

Wes Harris led a quiet life as a Princeton student. He had to work and study hard to maintain the university's high standards of excellence. This was the first time Harris had been outside the South, and in his free time, he made brief visits to New York and Philadelphia. He developed new perspectives and enjoyed discussing the future of America and Africa with other African American graduate students.

When he received his doctorate in 1968, Wes Harris decided that the best way for him to make a real impact on the education of African Americans was to return to the South. He applied for a teaching position at the University of Virginia and was surprised and pleased when they hired him.

Career Highlights

For his first two years at Virginia, Dr. Harris was an assistant professor of aerospace engineering. He was also a pioneer of sorts, although he didn't see himself in that way. Dr. Harris was the first African American to receive a regular professorial appointment at the university and was also the first to teach engineering at that school.

While still working for the University of Virginia, Dr. Harris took a one-year leave of absence to teach physics at Southern University in Baton Rouge, Louisiana, a university that enrolls mainly Black students. Dr. Harris felt strongly that Black educators should use their skills to encourage promising African American students.

When Dr. Harris returned to Virginia as an associate professor, he met a man who would be his counselor and mentor over the years. This person was Leon Trilling of the Massachusetts Institute of Technology (MIT) in Cambridge, Massachusetts. In the mid-1960s, Trilling had started a program to take some students from Boston's inner city areas and place them in suburban schools. He persuaded Dr. Harris to take another "temporary" leave of absence from the University of Virginia in 1972. Then in 1973, MIT offered Dr. Harris a position as a full-time associate professor of aeronautics, astronautics, and ocean engineering. Dr. Harris accepted this position at MIT and remained there until 1979.

While at MIT, Dr. Harris had a warm relationship with his students. They appreciated the fact that he always made sure their names came before his on their jointly published technical papers. Dr. Harris's interest in his students was apparent, too, when he founded MIT's first Office of Minority Education in 1975. The goal of this office was to help MIT's African Americans and other minority students earn better grades and decrease their dropout rate. To this end, Dr. Harris created methods to measure the students' achievements and developed ways in which the school could help them improve their performance. He also started a program to acquaint other faculty members with the special needs of African American students.

Dr. Harris took a break from MIT in 1979 to work at the National Aeronautics and Space Administration (NASA) headquarters in Washington, DC. There, he pioneered the use of computers to solve problems concerning very high-speed air movement. His success with such complicated problems paved the way for NASA to acquire more powerful supercomputers.

By 1985, Dr. Harris felt he had achieved his original goal of becoming a respected university professor, and he decided he was ready to focus on a new challenge. Consequently, he accepted a position as dean of the School of Engineering at the University of Connecticut in Storrs, Connecticut.

During his five years at Connecticut, Dr. Harris forged a strong partnership between the school and local companies, namely, Pratt & Whitney, an aircraft engine maker, and United Technologies, an aerospace giant. He also established the university's first research center for grinding metals and an institute for environmental research.

As he had done in his previous posts, Dr. Harris made a special effort to help minority students. When he went to Connecticut, the School of Engineering recruited only five or six African American or Hispanic students each year. When he left in 1990, the number of new minority students accepted each year was about 40.

A year later, Dr. Harris became vice president of the University of Tennessee Space Institute (UTSI) in Tullahoma, Tennessee. The president of the university was Mr. Lamar Alexander, the onetime governor of Tennessee. Dr. Harris respected Mr. Alexander because he had supported minority education as governor. Later, Mr. Alexander was named secretary of education under President George Bush. Dr. Harris didn't move to Tennessee just because he thought it would be interesting to work with Mr. Alexander, it was also a family decision. His second wife, Sandra, had three sisters who lived near Tullahoma.

During his years as a teacher and as an administrator, Dr. Harris continued to work on his research projects. Each of these projects sought to demonstrate what happens when an object travels at or above the speed of sound. Dr. Harris studied, for example, how the shape of the object would influence its high-speed movement through space.

He also investigated other effects—such as noise—generated by very high-speed travel. If an airplane crosses the sound barrier, it generates a shock wave. This shock wave, called a sonic boom, sounds like an explosion on the ground and can be strong enough to break windows. Humans, animals, and even buildings can suffer from repeated sonic booms.

The problems of air flow in supersonic conditions can be very serious. When an airplane's wing is moving faster than sound, the air flowing over and under the wing swirls and forms bubbles. The wing needs a smooth flow to provide the lift that keeps the airplane flying. A similar difficulty can be observed when the tips of the rotor blades on a helicopter go faster than sound. The swirling air at the tips causes a slapping sound and makes the helicopter hard to control. Dr. Harris studied these problems for many years. He has written more than 100 reports on his research and has been recognized by professional organizations and engineering institutions for his unusually high research output.

In 1992, Dr. Harris received one of the highest honors awarded to an aerospace professional. The American Institute for Aeronautics and Astronautics (AIAA) named him a fellow for his research and writings on the topics of helicopter rotor noise, air flows just above and below the speed of sound, and the advancement of engineering education.

Toward the end of 1992, Dr. Harris was inspired by NASA administrator Dan Goldin's call for a rebirth of aviation studies in the United States. Dr. Harris decided to accept Goldin's invitation to return to NASA as head of the agency's aeronautics program.

As NASA's aeronautics chief, Dr. Harris is in charge of many exciting projects, including research on technology for a new supersonic transport plane. Also, he is supervising work to improve subsonic airliners and to create computers a thousand times faster than today's models. He also directs the National Aero-Space Plane (NASP) program, which is developing an aircraft that will be able to climb to orbital altitudes under its own power.

Dr. Harris feels very strongly that America must lead the world in aviation advances, and that NASA is the best agency to manage that effort. Dr. Harris is helping to build new respect for this organization by making sure NASA's scientists conduct aeronautical research of the highest quality.

Faye Venetia Harrison

Born: November 25, 1951, in Norfolk, Virginia

Status: Associate Professor, University of Tennessee, Knoxville, Tennessee

Education:

Bachelor of Arts degree, Brown University, Providence, Rhode Island, 1974

Master of Arts degree, Stanford University, Palo Alto, California, 1977

Doctor of Philosophy degree, Stanford University, 1982

Research Area: Anthropology

Early Years

Faye Harrison's grandmother, Tola Harper, was the daughter of ex-slaves. She had once been a teacher in a one-room school house in rural North Carolina, and she knew, from her own experience, that her children needed to receive a better education than was available in that part of the country. Tola's husband, Arthur, shared her goal of improving the children's opportunities. Therefore, in the 1920s, the young family moved to the port city of Norfolk, Virginia. Arthur was able to find a good job, and not only did the children obtain a much better education in the city but the family's standard of living also improved.

When Faye was seven years old, the family moved into a house whose previous occupants had left a closet full of old *National Geographic* magazines. She studied the wondrous photographs of far-off places and peoples and read the treasured magazines over and over again. Her sights were raised beyond the narrow views of Norfolk and tidewater Virginia, where racial problems were common. The magazines revealed that in other counties, people held different views about racial matters. She wondered why a country such as Brazil was seemingly free from the racial tensions found in the United States, and she marvelled at the relaxed way of life in places such as Polynesia. The more Faye studied other cultures, the more she wanted to know. She was curious about how cultural attitudes combine with different economic and political systems around the world, and whether these cultural attitudes could be changed by different political systems. Even though Faye was quite young, she began to think about these questions in an organized and scientific manner.

As early as the fifth grade, Faye began carrying on the family tradition that each new generation should become better educated than the previous one. She was an industrious student, and her teachers recognized her diligence, curiosity, interests, and capabilities. They encouraged Faye with her various projects and guided her efforts to write short stories. In these stories, Faye tried to capture her fascination with other people and societies. Her teachers praised her work and gave her many opportunities to share her ideas, stories, and projects with her classmates.

Later, in junior high school, Faye's efforts were focused on developing some basic ideas about how a society is influenced by its geography. She was interested in whether the soil fertility of a country helps determine how rapidly its society progresses. Faye also wanted to know if climate was a factor in molding a people's culture. By the time Faye was ready to begin high school, her questions were directed toward understanding the workings of political and economic systems, such as the one adopted in Soviet Russia. She wanted to find out, for example, whether people in the United States could learn from the experiences of the Soviet people and if they could learn from us. These were very serious questions for a young teenager to be asking. Fortunately, there were teachers who continued to support Faye's curiosity and her interests in foreign cultures.

Faye realized that in order to conduct her future research she would need to be fluent in the languages of her proposed subjects. She studied the major languages of South America and the Caribbean Islands—Spanish, Portuguese, and French—because she decided that the cultures of Latin America would be the most interesting area of investigation. One of her high school teachers recognized Faye's ambitions and tutored her in Hispanic literature. Faye did so well in her Spanish studies that her work was recognized by the members of a local African American sorority, who provided her with scholarship money to travel to Puerto Rico with a group of fellow language students.

Higher Education

Faye Harrison's excellent performance in high school allowed her to attend Brown University in Providence, Rhode Island, on a full university scholarship. She began at Brown in 1970, and after taking beginning courses in archeology and cultural anthropology, she realized that anthropology—which includes archeology, cultural studies, linguistics, and biophysical anthropology—would provide her with the best background for answering her questions about different societies. She became interested in how people of African descent were both shaping and being shaped by their cultural environment. In order to pursue these ideas to the fullest extent, Faye Harrison was allowed to take graduate courses in anthropology.

In her senior year, she was given the opportunity to undertake an independent research project, in which she examined the attitudes and opinions of a special group of high school students whose forebears had come to the United States from the Cape Verde Islands off the coast of Africa. This immigrant community had struggled over the years to maintain its particular identity. She was curious about the retention of their original language—Portuguese—and about whether they no longer regarded themselves as Cape Verdeans but as African Americans.

When Faye Harrison graduated from Brown University in 1974, she was awarded the Samuel T. Arnold Fellowship. The fellowship money allowed Harrison to spend a year in London, England, where she studied the lives of a group of West Indians from the Caribbean Islands, who had immigrated to England in search of a better life. Harrison was able to observe how the beliefs and behaviors of the Caribbean people differed from those of the English. Young teenagers of Jamaican parentage were often torn between the cultural views of their parents and those of their English classmates.

The experience of doing such anthropological research strengthened Harrison's desire to study at the graduate level. She applied to Stanford University in Palo Alto, California, and was awarded a one-year, full-university fellowship in 1975. After organizing and polishing the notes from her research on the West Indian youths in London, she decided to use that study as the basis of her master's thesis. Faye Harrison's work was influenced by the ideas of St. Clair Drake, the noted African American anthropologist. Dr. Drake, one of Harrison's mentors at Stanford, had done pioneering research on multiethnic communities in Great Britain, and his work provided a prototype for Harrison to follow.

While finishing her thesis, Faye Harrison worked with Professor Leo Kuper from the University of California at Los Angeles on the problems of plural societies. A plural society is one in which members of a particular racial or ethnic group move into an area populated by members of a different racial or ethnic group. European colonization of Africa and of North and South America are prime instances of the formation of a plural society. Professor Kuper's research was concerned with the kinds of conflicts that resulted from such situations and also in the ways the conflicts were resolved.

Faye Harrison earned her master's degree from Stanford in 1977 and immediately began work on her doctoral program. During these studies, she received support from the Danforth and Wenner-Gren Foundations. She chose as her next research project—a follow-up to her London study—an investigation of West Indian families living in the West Indies. Her courses at Stanford covered such matters as the industrialization of an agrarian society and how that change leads to the migration of rural populations into cities. These changes were taking place in Jamaica, and she used her new knowledge to guide her research on Jamaican society. Harrison was fortunate to receive funding for her important work from the Fulbright-Hays Program.

Her field observations were recorded in the slum areas of Kingston, the capital of Jamaica. Harrison focused on the everyday life of the families living there. She saw how these people, who were often unemployed in the formal economy of the country, earned a living within an informal or "underground" economic system. These slum-dwelling families bought and sold material goods between themselves and also provided goods and services to the larger community on an informal or casual basis. Some informal economic exchanges were even taking place across international boundaries. In other words, the conditions of life in the Kingston slums were very complex. Instead of being idle and unemployed, many slum residents were, in effect, running their own businesses. These surprising findings were presented in Faye Harrison's doctoral dissertation, and she was awarded her Ph.D. from Stanford University in 1982.

Career Highlights

In the fall of 1983, Dr. Harrison joined the faculty of the University of Louisville in Kentucky. During the school year, she taught a variety of introductory and advanced courses in cultural anthropology. In the summers, she returned to Kingston, Jamaica, to continue her field research.

By maintaining the continuity of her studies from summer to summer, Dr. Harrison was able to detect trends in the everyday life of the Kingston slum dwellers. She showed how the informal trade, which had been part of the daily activities in the 1970s, gradually shifted into illegal drug dealing in the late 1980s and early 1990s. In a similar manner, the semistructured groups originally formed for sports and other worthy goals, were transformed into "posses" that engaged in smuggling drugs and guns. Dr. Harrison's research indicates that both economic and political forces caused these unfortunate changes in Jamaican society.

Dr. Harrison believes that women, who frequently are the sole providers for their children, are exploited in Jamaican society. She also believes that the economic and social activities of these exploited women are a major factor in the ability of their neighborhoods and, indeed, of the entire country to resist both internal and external disintegration.

In 1989, Dr. Harrison was invited to join the faculty of the University of Tennessee in Knoxville and is now an associate professor at that institution. With this new appointment, Dr. Harrison has been able to expand her professional scope and the directions of her research. She holds a position on the board of directors of the American Anthropological Association and has written a major scholarly work entitled *Decolonizing Anthropology*. The book, published in 1991, deals with her struggle to understand the relationships between peoples of different ethnic heritages.

More recently, Dr. Harrison has begun a series of studies which concern her own heritage. She is collecting the oral history of her ancestors who lived in North Carolina and

Virginia. Because of her professional training, she can define the patterns of behavior that are continued from generation to generation. Dr. Harrison now understands how conversations at family gatherings and formal reunions help clarify the social and racial identities of the family members. She is pleased that this research project presents to her kin an understandable example of her professional interests. The members of her family can comprehend how her research reveals that the decisions and actions of their ancestors helped determine the character of their present-day family.

Robert W. Harrison III

Born: October 13, 1941, in Natchez, Mississippi

Status: Chief, Division of Endocrinology and Metabolism, University of Rochester School of Medicine and Dentistry

Education:

Bachelor of Science degree, Tougaloo College, Tougaloo, Mississippi, 1961

Doctor of Medicine degree, Northwestern University School of Medicine, Chicago, Illinois, 1966

Research Area: Endocrinology

Early Years

Robert Harrison was born in Natchez, Mississippi, a famous port on the Mississippi River. Over many years, much of the cotton grown in southern Mississippi was shipped from this port. The mood of the townspeople rose and fell with the price of cotton. Robert's parents, therefore, chose to settle in the calmer atmosphere of Yazoo City, Mississippi, where they were surrounded by their relatives. His mother worked as a school teacher, and his father was a dentist.

There was never any question about Robert's future education. His parents expected him to go to college and complete an advanced, professional degree. When he was 13, he was sent to Tougaloo College to attend high school. Tougaloo was a center for teacher training and maintained a high school where apprentice teachers did their practice teaching. Everyone—students and teachers alike—was highly motivated to do well. The high school program was designed to prepare the students for college.

Robert chose Tougaloo for his high school education partially because his father had graduated from Tougaloo College. Also, he liked the fact that the school is located near Jackson, Mississippi, the state capital, less than 40 miles from Yazoo City. After graduating from high school at Tougaloo, Robert entered their undergraduate program.

Higher Education

At about the same time that Robert Harrison began college, the social and political situation in the United States began to change. In 1959, during Robert's second year of college, U.S. Army corporal Roman Duckworth was shot dead by a Mississippi police officer when Duckworth refused to move to the back of a Trailways bus. It was revealed that Duckworth was on his way to his wife's sickbed on compassionate leave from his army base. The "Jim Crow" practices in the South suddenly came under intense criticism from the rest of the country

The next year the Congress of the United States began considering major civil rights legislation. Southern senators tried to stall these actions by means of a record-breaking filibuster. However, a voting rights act was passed in spite of this dramatic form of opposition. Another breakthrough came when restaurants in Greensboro, North Carolina, were desegregated after six months of sit-in demonstrations.

In 1961, during Harrison's last year of college, the freedom riders began to arrive in the South. These freedom riders were northerners who, under the auspices of the biracial Congress of Racial Equality (CORE), came south to participate in the demonstrations. Tougaloo College provided a safe haven for many of the participants.

Harrison graduated from Tougaloo in the spring of 1961. During his years in college, he had changed his career goals from chemistry to medicine. After graduation, he found a summer job near Chicago, Illinois. Northwestern University, the school from which his father received his dentistry training, has a main campus in Evanston, Illinois, a suburb of Chicago, but its professional schools are located near the center of the city. After a visit to this campus, Harrison was convinced that he should follow in his father's footsteps and take his medical training at Northwestern. Robert Harrison received his medical degree from Northwestern in 1966.

Career Highlights

When physicians receive their degrees, they are far from finished with the formal requirements for the practice of medicine. They first must complete an internship and usually one or two medical residencies. Dr. Harrison did his internship and his first residency at Chicago Wesley Memorial Hospital.

After a one-year residency, Dr. Harrison was ready to fulfill his military service obligation with the U.S. Navy. He was commissioned as a lieutenant senior grade and became a destroyer squadron medical officer. This was an interesting two-year period because it gave Dr. Harrison experiences similar to those in a large general medical practice. Indeed, he saw a wider range of medical conditions than he could have seen in a civilian hospital. Moreover, the situation was rewarding because Dr. Harrison was able to visit many foreign countries.

In 1970, Dr. Harrison put his naval uniform aside, but he remained a member of the inactive reserve for the next 10 years. He chose to do his second residency at Hartford Hospital in Hartford, Connecticut, because he wanted see another part of the United States. At Hartford, he again treated patients with a wide variety of illnesses. In addition to his hospital duties, he studied diligently for his medical board examinations. In 1972, after the two-year residency, he passed the examinations and received his certification in internal medicine.

Now he had to face another major decision. Dr. Harrison could open his own medical practice, join the practice of an older physician, or become affiliated with a health maintenance organization. Another course would be to seek a position in a medical research or teaching institution, which would allow him to contribute to the knowledge of all medical practitioners. Dr. Harrison chose this last option because of his intense curiosity about the human body. He was particularly interested in studying the diseases of the glands that produce hormones.

In order to pursue his research goals, Dr. Harrison joined the faculty of the Vanderbilt University Medical Center in Nashville, Tennessee. Just one year later, while still at the rank of instructor, he became codirector of the Steroid Receptor Core Laboratory in the Center for Population Research and Reproductive Biology at Vanderbilt. While in this position, he produced a flood of research reports. His reports concerned the hormones and related biochemicals that control the sexual and reproductive functions in animals and humans.

His studies then became focused on chemicals called glucocorticoids. These hormones are produced by the outer covering of the adrenal glands that lay next to the kidneys. The glucocorticoid hormones include the familiar cortisone and have a strong influence on the way the body uses its energy resources. When infection or cancer attacks the covering of the adrenal gland, the usual symptoms include muscular weakness and general loss of vigor. Dr. Harrison conducted research to compare the pattern of effects from various diseases of the adrenal gland.

In 1974, Dr. Harrison was promoted to assistant professor of medicine and, in 1977, became a Howard Hughes Medical Institute research associate. This connection with the Hughes Institute was important to Dr. Harrison. The financial support from the institute generates some of the most advanced medical research in the world.

In 1978, Dr. Harrison accepted an additional appointment with the department of physiology in the school of medicine at Vanderbilt. This position allowed Dr. Harrison to work with specialists from many fields of medicine. In addition, Dr. Harrison had contact with medical students at an early stage in their training. He could, therefore, better advise them on their future study programs.

In 1980, Dr. Harrison took a year-long sabbatical leave. He was invited to spend this period with Professor Isadore Edelman in the department of biochemistry at the Columbia University College of Physicians and Surgeons in New York City. At Columbia, Dr. Harrison learned to isolate and purify some of the important biochemical molecules that help the glucocorticoids function in individual cells. During this research project, Dr. Harrison discovered which gene controls the production of these particular molecules. He was able to clone that gene and produce the molecules in the laboratory.

Dr. Harrison then returned to Nashville and remained there for four more productive years. In 1985, he was offered a totally new challenge at the University of Arkansas in Little Rock. He was named associate dean for special projects in their medical sciences unit. This position was designed to support the university's efforts to diversify its faculty and student population.

Although this job was very demanding, there was no decline in his research productivity. In fact, Dr. Harrison became the director of the Clinical Endocrine Laboratory at the same time that he was made associate dean. However, the focus of his work broadened to include the hormonal aspects of infectious diseases. The target diseases now included conditions such as AIDS that involve the immune response and have raised new problems in the field of hormonal biochemistry.

Dr. Harrison's tenure at Arkansas lasted eight years. During this time, he had been productive in both research and teaching. In 1993, Dr. Harrison received an offer from the school of medicine and dentistry at the University of Rochester in upper New York State. As chief of the division of endocrinology and metabolism, Dr. Harrison has assembled a strong research team of human physiologists who study individual biochemical molecules. This team is currently developing an im-

proved understanding of hormonal functions in the human body.

Walter Lincoln Hawkins

Born: March 21, 1911, in Washington, D.C.

Status: Died, August 20, 1992, in San Marcos, California

Education:

Bachelor of Science degree, Rensselaer Polytechnic Institute, Troy, New York, 1932

Master of Science degree, Howard University, Washington, D.C., 1934

Doctor of Philosophy degree, McGill University, Montreal, Canada, 1939

Research Area: Organic Chemistry

Early Years

From an early age, Walter Lincoln Hawkins was called Linc by friends and family. In the early years of this century, his family lived in what was then a well-to-do neighborhood near the campus of Howard University in Washington, D.C. Linc's mother was a science teacher in the District of Columbia school system, and his father was a lawyer who worked for the United States Census Bureau.

Linc showed an early interest in mechanical devices. He often took apart one kind of mechanical toy and reassembled the parts to make another kind of toy. One of his favorite projects was making toy boats powered by spring-wound motors that came out of mechanical clocks. He liked to test his creations in the famous reflecting pool in front of the Lincoln Memorial.

Linc and his friends also attempted to design a machine that, once started, could run forever. They spent hours trying to perfect their invention, but had to finally give up the project and admit failure.

Linc was also interested in radios. He acquired the plans for a simple radio that worked with a set of earphones. After he built the radio, he listened to the broadcasts of the old Washington Senator's baseball games. He used the radio on the local playground and relayed the action to his friends as the game went on.

In 1924, Linc entered Dunbar High School, one of the three segregated high schools in Washington, D. C. It was the only high school in the city, however, that prepared young African Americans for college. The other schools were focused on vocational training, such as bookkeeping or carpentry.

As a student at Dunbar, Linc noticed that his physics teacher drove a very expensive car. Linc discovered that the physics teacher had invented a self-starter, which, in those days, was installed only in the most expensive cars. Other cars had to be hand cranked in order to be started. The company that built the cars gave the physics teacher a new car each year as a gesture of thanks for his invention. Linc learned that the teacher, who had a doctoral degree, also received royalties for his inven-

tion. Linc soon made a connection between this advanced degree and the possibility of financial success and community respect and decided that he, too, would one day pursue a doctoral degree.

During his years at Dunbar, Linc also was taught about the ancient African empires and centers of science and learning and about the lives of older African American scientists and inventors. These lessons gave Linc confidence that he could succeed in a science or engineering career if he chose to pursue such a goal.

Higher Education

Troy, the home of Rensselaer Polytechnic, is a relatively small town in rural New York State. This school has long been regarded as one of the best, small engineering schools in the country. When Linc Hawkins arrived in Troy to begin his college studies, he found very few African Americans in the town. Soon, he realized that there were even fewer among the faculty and student body at Rensselaer. Even though Hawkins had little difficulty doing well in his studies, he was lonely during the four years of preparation for his engineering career.

In 1932, Linc Hawkins graduated from Rensselaer near the top of his class in chemical engineering. However, jobs for young Black engineers were hard to find—particularly at the height of the Great Depression, when about 30 percent of the work force of the country was unemployed. Hawkins's best option was to continue his education. He enrolled at Howard University near the family home in Washington, D.C., and began a graduate program in organic chemistry.

After receiving his master's degree from Howard in 1934, Hawkins began teaching at a small trade school. Unfortunately, the students were uninterested in science, and Hawkins began to feel very frustrated. One of his professors from Howard University learned of his distress and advised him to return to school to earn his doctoral degree. In the bad economic climate of the mid-30s, however, this did not seem possible. Then, a friend and teacher from Howard, Professor Harold Blatt, told Hawkins about a special scholarship program at McGill University in Montreal, Canada. The scholarship, however, could not be awarded until a candidate had shown outstanding performance for a one-year period. This meant that Hawkins would have to leave his job and endanger his savings on the hope of getting that fellowship. Since he intensely disliked his job, he decided to risk all he had and enroll at McGill. He won the fellowship after the first year and went on to receive his doctorate in 1939. His doctoral research concerned cellulose, the basic building block for all green plants in the world. For his work on cellulose, he won a postdoctoral fellowship at McGill. Linc Hawkins continued to work and teach at that university until 1941.

In that year, Dr. Hawkins was invited to continue his research at Columbia University in New York City. His appointment was financed by a fellowship provided by the National Research Council. He was next recruited by the Bell Laboratories of the American Telephone and Telegraph Company, one of the most powerful scientific institutions in the world.

Career Highlights

World War II was at its peak in 1942 when Dr. Linc Hawkins joined the staff at the Bell Laboratories. The Japanese had overrun most of Southeast Asia and cut off the supply of raw rubber to the United States. Chemists all over the country were frantically trying to find a workable substitute for this natural product that came from the sap of trees.

Dr. Hawkins's previous research on the sugar-like compounds that link together and form starch and cellulose, proved useful in his attempts to invent synthetic plastics that might be used as substitutes for rubber. In this effort, his past research experiences were vital because many plastics are made up of chains of molecules just as starch is made of a chain of sugar molecules. In a relatively short time, the contributions of Dr. Hawkins together with those of many other chemists led to the development of a successful rubber substitute made from petroleum raw materials.

Dr. Hawkins was the first African American to join the technical staff at Bell Laboratories. This opportunity was partially due to the war effort and the wartime shortage of trained scientists and engineers. However, the recruitment of minority scientists, like Dr. Hawkins, for professional positions soon proved very beneficial to organizations like Bell Labs. In the years since the war, Bell Labs and many other progressive firms have made sure that minorities are reasonably represented at all levels of their work force.

During the war years, much of Dr. Hawkins's work was secret and, therefore, could not be published. As soon as the the war ended, however, he went to work on a nonsecret project of great consequence. Dr. Hawkins sought to find a new way to insulate telephone cables. Before the war, heavy duty telephone cables that run for long distances underground or underwater were insulated with fiber wrapped by lead sheathing. Unfortunately, the lead would eventually give way and the copper wires in the phone cables would begin to corrode. Replacement of these underground or underwater cables was difficult and expensive. Therefore, scientists began to consider plastic, a material improved during the war, as a more durable substitute for the fiber and lead. Dr. Hawkins invented a stabilizer for plastic insulation so that it could outlast lead or any other material. Over the next 10 years, a long series of studies led to continued improvements in the insulation of the copper wire used in all telephone cables. The substitution of plastic for fiber and lead as an insulating material benefited all telephone users. Plastic proved to be less expensive, lighter in weight, and longer lasting—a life of 70 years. These advances made it possible to install telephone lines in rural areas that were otherwise too expensive to serve. Also, the reduced costs of installations made phone service affordable to many city residents who had previously considered telephones a luxury.

In 1963, Dr. Hawkins was made supervisor of applied research at Bell Labs. He was named a department head in 1972 and assistant director of the Chemical Research Laboratory in 1974. In the meantime, Dr. Hawkins's research interests had expanded to include issues in environmental protection and recycling. Plastics are a problem for environmentalists because they are nearly indestructible. Indeed, many plastics are even resistant to bacterial consumption. Since Dr. Hawkins was an expert in making plastics last longer, he had good ideas about shortening their lives, as well.

One of Dr. Hawkins's main efforts outside the laboratory was to induce more minority members to consider a career in the sciences or engineering professions. He helped set up the programs used by AT&T and Bell Labs to recruit African Americans. Dr. Hawkins was also a founder and first chairman of Project SEED, a program of the American Chemical Society designed to bring more minority people into scientific work. Dr. Hawkins was also active in the National Action Council for Minorities in Engineering.

After he retired from the Bell Laboratories in 1976, Dr. Hawkins began his second career as a teacher. He served as an adjunct faculty member at the Polytechnic Institute of New York and as a trustee of Montclair State College of New Jersey. He also taught courses in the corporate education program for the Western Electric Company, another branch of AT&T.

Dr. Hawkins was elected as the first African American member of the National Academy of Engineering, an honor reserved for less than one percent of all engineers. In June of 1992, he was invited to a ceremony in the Rose Garden at the White House in Washington, D.C. President George Bush presented Dr. Hawkins and seven other recipients with the prestigious National Technology Award. Just over two months after he was honored at the White House, Dr. Hawkins died at his home in San Marcos, California. During his lifetime, he had helped produce some 55 major scientific research reports, 3 books, and 19 U.S. patents.

John K. Haynes

Born: October 30, 1943, in Monroe, Louisiana

Status: David Packer Professor and Chair, Department of Biology, Morehouse College, Atlanta, Georgia

Education:

Bachelor of Science degree, Morehouse College, Atlanta, Georgia, 1964

Doctor of Philosophy degree, Brown University, Providence, Rhode Island, 1970

Research Area: Biology

Early Years

John Haynes, or JK, as he came to be known to family and friends, was born in Monroe, Louisiana. Monroe, a medium-sized town in the north-central section of the state, lies between Shreveport on the Red River and Vicksburg on the Mississippi.

JK's mother, Grace Ross Haynes, was a teacher who had received a graduate degree from Atlanta University, and his father was the principal of Lincoln High School, a segregated, comprehensive school with grades from one to twelve in Ruston, Louisiana, the next major town in the direction of Shreveport. Mr. Haynes was able to convince the first grade teacher to take JK as a student when the boy was only four years old.

Two years later, the family moved to Baton Rouge, Louisiana. JK entered the third grade at the Southern University Laboratory School, where education students did their practice teaching. Although JK liked his teachers, he was not a very conscientious student until he reached the tenth grade, when he decided to become a medical doctor. He began to work harder at school and participate in other school activities. At that time, English was his favorite subject, and he competed in the statewide academic rallies during his last two years in high school. He became involved in student government and was elected president of the senior class. JK also became interested in sports. He made the football team and was named most valuable player in baseball in his senior year.

Higher Education

John Haynes entered Morehouse College in Atlanta, Georgia, just two months before his seventeenth birthday. His parents had both done either their undergraduate or graduate work in Atlanta and were well aware of the high quality of Black education in that city. Dr. B. R. Brazeal, then dean of Morehouse College, and his wife were family friends of the Haynes. Before starting college, John Haynes had been very impressed that the dean had been willing to talk to him about coming to Morehouse. Indeed, Dean Brazeal arranged a partial scholarship, which Haynes was delighted to accept.

John Haynes had many excellent teachers while at Morehouse, including his chemistry professor, Henry McBay (see p. 242). However, the strongest influence on Haynes was his comparative anatomy and embryology teacher, Professor Roy Hunter. Haynes was so enthralled by the embryology course that he decided then and there to study developmental biology in graduate school. When Haynes announced his decision to Professor Hunter, the professor advised his student to apply to Brown University where Hunter, himself, had done his graduate work. But Haynes also continued to hold his original ambition to become a medical doctor. Consequently, during his junior year at college, Haynes applied to several medical schools but to only one graduate school in pure science—Brown University. Some of the medical schools offered him a place, but not the ones that he preferred. Brown accepted him, and so he enrolled in their graduate program in biology.

As an undergraduate at Morehead, Haynes had worked with one of the biology professors, Dr. Frederick Mapp, on a project sponsored by the National Science Foundation. Haynes had assumed that his work on this project had acquainted him with a good understanding of the research process. However, once he started the biology program at Brown, he began to understand for the first time how the discovery of new information can fit into the whole structure of scientific knowledge. He found the excitement of discovery so compelling that he never again considered applying to medical school.

In his second year at graduate school, Haynes made a crucial connection with the people at the Marine Biology Laboratory at Woods Hole, Massachusetts. During a summer at Woods Hole in 1966, he took a course in embryology with Professor James Ebert. It was a productive summer, and he made contacts with some of the top biologists in the world. Afterwards, for more than a dozen summers, John Haynes returned to enroll in a summer course at Woods Hole. In this way, he could revitalize his research skills and enjoy the company of an international group of eminent scientists.

Haynes's dissertation research at Brown was done under the supervision of Professor Donald Kimmel. The project was directed toward a better understanding of the earliest stages of a frog's life. It was designed to reveal how the activity of one particular enzyme was controlled by other enzymes in the cells of the growing frog. The enzyme in question helps regulate energy use by the frog. Haynes developed a way to measure very accurately the amount of the enzyme in a tissue sample. He found that the enzyme is present in all parts of the frog embryo but is confined to the liver in the adult frog.

Haynes completed his dissertation and was awarded his doctoral degree from Brown University in 1970.

Career Highlights

After his graduation, Dr. Haynes was invited to spend an additional year at Brown doing research. In this first post-doctoral year, Dr. Haynes began a new research project under the supervision of Professor Seymour Lederberg. The goal was to strengthen his knowledge of the new field of molecular biology and its impact on the older field of embryology. The focus of the research concerned the process in which a particular virus can invade only certain kinds of bacteria. Dr. Haynes sought to understand why some bacteria have a defense system that renders them immune from viral attack.

During this year at Brown, only modest progress was made toward an understanding of this complicated problem. In the meanwhile, the topic of sickle-cell anemia began to receive attention in both scientific circles and in the mass media. Sickle cell is a condition of the red blood cells that mainly afflicts people of African descent.

Dr. Haynes realized that his recently acquired knowledge could be utilized in studying this disease. While still at Brown, he began a collaborative research project with some medical doctors at Meharry Medical School. They tested a new drug that the Meharry people thought might be able to return red cells that had taken the sickle form back to their original shape. Some drugs were already being used to do this but these established drugs caused bad side effects. The tests showed that their new drug did restore the red blood cells with less harm to the patients.

After his first post-doctoral year at Brown and the collaboration with colleagues from Meharry Medical School, Dr. Haynes accepted an invitation to go to the Massachusetts Institute of Technology (MIT) for two more years of advanced study of biochemistry. At that time, there was a heady atmosphere in the biology department at MIT, partly because of the presence of Professor Salvador Luria, Nobel Prize winner and co-founder of the field of molecular biology.

During both years of the program, Dr. Haynes was able to serve as research partner with

Professor Vernon Ingram, another distinguished biological scientist whom he had meet at Woods Hole. Dr. Haynes's first published report in a scientific magazine was co-authored with Professor Ingram. The subject of this report was a method—discovered jointly by Dr. Haynes and Professor Ingram—for screening large numbers of people for the sickle-cell gene. Later, Dr. Haynes worked on methods for diagnosing the disease in unborn babies. He also investigated the nature of the disease by doing a microscopic study of red blood cell membranes.

After three years of post-doctoral research, Dr. Haynes was ready for a permanent position. He accepted a joint appointment as a junior faculty member in the department of genetics and molecular medicine and in the department of anatomy at Meharry Medical School in Nashville, Tennessee. Dr. Haynes spent five years teaching and doing sickle-cell research at Meharry.

Scientists had discovered that the sickle-shaped red blood cells can clog the capillaries in the circulatory system. This condition causes the symptomatic pain, swelling, and organ damage in a victim of the disease. Scientists had also discovered that the rigidity as well as the shape of the unhealthy blood cells were responsible for this blockage. Dr. Haynes's study focused on the cause of the rigid condition of the diseased cell. A key factor of the problem appeared to be a surplus of calcium in the sickle-shaped cells. This surplus reduced the cell's ability to change shape while passing through the small capillaries in the circulatory system.

Even though his sickle-cell anemia research was not complete, Dr. Haynes returned, in 1979, to Morehouse College in Atlanta. He was assigned the usual teaching chores for a young associate professor of biology but was also given responsibilities as director of the Office of Health Professions at the college.

Dr. Haynes was now responsible for the education of those Morehouse students who wanted to pursue one or another of the health professions. The job included the placement of students in medical and dental schools all over the country. Among the projects supervised by Dr. Haynes was the development of a course which gave students experience in taking standardized examinations. Dr. Haynes also instituted a project in which high school students planning to take the pre-medical curriculum in college could get a preview of what their program would be like.

In keeping with his new responsibilities, Dr. Haynes became increasingly involved in recruiting minority students into the fields of science and health care. Shortly after he returned to Atlanta, Dr. Haynes arranged for a grant of almost $385,000 from the Robert Wood Johnson Foundation. This funding was used to strengthen the training of health care professionals in minority-oriented institutions in the Atlanta area. Subsequently, Dr. Haynes helped to foster minority recruitment programs sponsored by such agencies as the National Institutes of Health, the National Science Foundation, the National Academy of Sciences, the National Research Council, professional societies, and philanthropic foundations. Altogether, Dr. Haynes has overseen the raising of more than $4 million in grant funds for institutions in the Atlanta area.

In 1985, Dr. Haynes was named to the endowed David E. Packard Chair in Science at Morehouse and also became chairman of the biology department. In his new capacity, he worked to improve teaching and research in his department. A new curriculum was developed for the undergraduate biology major that included more emphasis on laboratory work. New courses in plant science, ecology, and biological evolution were also added to the program.

Dr. Haynes also took action to improve the department's physical facilities. In 1989, a new building was opened to house both the chemistry and biology programs. A grant from the National Science Foundation funded the construction of another new building—completed in 1994—to provide additional space for the biology department.

Dr. Haynes temporarily stopped his research projects in 1987 so that he could concentrate on his administrative duties—such as the building projects. By 1991, he was more than ready to resume his research studies, and therefore, took a sabatical leave, given to scholars so that they can investigate the latest achievements in their field as well as conduct their own research.

During his leave from Morehouse, Dr. Haynes returned to Brown University to conduct research with Dr. Leon Goldstein. Dr. Haynes hoped that Dr. Goldstein's specialty in how cells regulate their own size would supply important answers to his questions about sickle-cell anemia. He believed that it was time to reenter the struggle toward a better understanding of that problem.

Dr. Haynes had known for some time that sickle-cells contain a surplus of calcium. He also knew that the unhealthy cells contain insufficient water and lack some of the small organic molecules present in healthy red blood cells. In a sense, the sickle-cells had dried out and become rigid. Dr. Haynes and Dr. Goldstein hoped to discover how certain necessary molecules pass in or out of the cell membrane. They found that the proteins which make up this membrane can change shape and position to form little passageways through the membrane. If this process is not working properly, a cell might be unable to replenish its required supply of small organic molecules and water. An oversupply of calcium might complicate the situation by combining with some of the water retained by the red blood cell. This would compound the water shortage inside the cell and make it rigid. Dr. Haynes believes that this theory is correct and is continuing his investigations into why the passageway proteins fail to function as they should.

James H. M. Henderson

Born: August 10, 1917, in Falls Church, Virginia

Status: Chair, Natural Sciences Division, Tuskegee University, Tuskegee, Alabama

Education:

Bachelor of Science degree, Howard University, Washington, D.C., 1939

Master of Arts degree, University of Wisconsin, Madison, Wisconsin, 1940

Doctor of Philosophy degree, University of Wisconsin, 1943

Research Area: Plant Physiology

Early Years

James Henderson was named after his grandfather, James Henry Meriwether, a descendent of Meriwether Lewis, who was the co-leader of the famous Lewis and Clark expedition that explored the northwestern United States in 1803. James's grandmother graduated from Oberlin College in 1868 as one of their first Black graduates, and his mother's sister married Booker T. Washington's son, David E. Washington. Therefore, James is the grand-nephew of Booker T. Washington, the founder of the Tuskegee Institute.

James's father, Mr. E. B. Henderson, was a civil rights pioneer in the field of athletics. He was the first professional physical education teacher in the Washington, D.C., area as well as a published author. He wrote many sports articles for the *Washington Post* and the *Washington Star* and books about African Americans in sports. He was also a founder and the second mayor of Highland Beach, Maryland. The first mayor was Haley Douglass, grandson of Frederick Douglass, the great Black abolitionist of the Civil War era.

James grew up in Falls Church, Virginia, but attended Garrison Elementary Demonstration School, located in the District of Columbia, just across the Potomac River. This school, used for practice teaching by education majors from local colleges, was a testing ground for new teaching methods. Therefore, the quality of instruction was particularly good. A similar educational situation existed at Garnett-Patterson Junior High School, which James attended from 1928 to 1932. In 1932, he enrolled in Paul Lawrence Dunbar High School. At the time, Dunbar was the most advanced segregated school in the United States. It was famous for its high academic standards and its successful sports teams. James made the teams in football, baseball, and swimming, as well as the National Honor Society.

Higher Education

In 1935, James Henderson entered Howard University in Washington, D.C., as an honor student. He graduated in 1939—still at the top of his class—with majors in biology and chemistry.

In part because of his good grades, Henderson immediately entered the graduate program at the University of Wisconsin in Madison. He completed his master's degree in one year and went directly to the doctoral program. His doctoral studies were focused on the basic sciences of chemistry and biochemistry and the practical subject of plant physiology. Henderson's major research project concerned the means by which the tomato plant can control the water and nutrients taken up by its roots. A report of this research was later published in the *American Journal of Botany,* an important science magazine. The report describes how chemicals commonly produced by plants—such as citric acid in lemons—can act to increase (or sometimes decrease) the rate of energy utilization by the plant cells.

While James Henderson was a graduate student, the United States had entered World War II. He contributed to the war effort by working at the Badger Ordinance Works near Madison, Wisconsin, during his last year in school. This organization conducted research on gun powder and similar materials used as rocket propellants.

Henderson earned his doctoral degree from Wisconsin in 1943 and then went to work as a chemist at the University of Chicago's Toxicity Laboratory. This work was sponsored by the National Defense Research Committee of the Office of Scientific Research and Development. He worked there for two years, studying the natural poisons plants produce to ward off predators.

Career Highlights

Two themes have guided Dr. Henderson's research. One is the question of growth. He has sought to discover if plants can control their own growth and if they produce growth hormones similar in chemical structure to those produced by animals. We now know, partly due to Dr. Henderson's research, that plants do produce growth hormones—in the form of complicated, carbon-based, acidic compounds. Similar compounds can now be produced artificially and used to increase plant growth.

The second theme of Dr. Henderson's research is usefulness. He hoped to determine whether the chemicals found in plants could be beneficial to humans. Specifically, he studied whether the chemical found in plant hormones, used by the plant to control growth, could be useful to stop the growth of cancer cells.

In 1945, as soon as the war was over, Dr. Henderson joined the Carver Research Foundation at Tuskegee University, where he began his life-long study of the sweet potato and where he taught courses at both the graduate and undergraduate levels in biology and chemistry. In his first three years at Tuskegee, he taught his regular courses, did his own research on plant growth regulation, and directed three students through their thesis projects.

Dr. Henderson took a two-year leave from the Carver Research Foundation in 1948 to accept a special research fellowship that allowed him to work and study at the California Institute of Technology in Pasadena, California. While there, he used his new techniques on the study of plant growth to investigate other plants, such as the sunflower. He found that tumors of the sunflower plant can continue to grow when essential enzymes are withdrawn because the tumor cells can make their own enzymes as replacements.

After returning to Tuskegee, he continued his teaching and research and, in 1957, was named professor and head of the biology department. Then in 1961, Dr. Henderson was awarded a Senior Faculty Fellowship by the National Science Foundation. This award allowed him to spend a year at a research center in France, where he continued his analyses of the regulators of plant growth called auxins. During the following years, he and his coworkers were able to test a wide range of natural and synthetic chemicals for their power, either to aid auxins in promoting plant growth or to prevent the auxins from working.

A few years after his return to Tuskegee, he was named director of the Carver Research Foundation and served in this position until 1975. He was then appointed senior research professor in biology and chair of the division of natural sciences, a position he still holds.

Dr. Henderson has traveled widely in Europe, China, Russia, and Africa. As recently as 1986, he spent six months teaching classes and guiding research at Isbadan in Nigeria. He has also published over 50 articles in scientific magazines during his career.

In addition to his scientific research, Dr. Henderson has been a leader in his community. During the Civil Rights movement of the 1960s, he helped supervise the voter registration drives in the South. In 1972, he was active in obtaining a Holiday Inn franchise for Tuskegee. This was the first such franchise to be owned by African Americans. Dr. Henderson also serves as a member of the board of trustees of Stillman College in Tuscaloosa, Alabama.

Dr. Henderson has also encouraged young people to pursue careers in science. He developed a special summer program at Tuskegee, which brings talented high school students to the university and gives them an understanding of the demands and joys of scientific research. Many of these young people have gone on to higher education in the field of science.

In the 1970s, Dr. Henderson led a similar summer program for high school science teachers, sponsored jointly by the National Science Foundation and the Atomic Energy Commission. This program allowed teachers to earn a salary while they learned about the rapid advances in their own field of science.

In spite of many achievements and awards, Dr. Henderson is proudest of his work with young African Americans, especially as a member of the Boy Scouts of America. He has played a leading role in organizing scouting programs in the state of Alabama and was presented with the Silver Beaver Award for this work in 1961. Dr. Henderson is still involved in his most important leadership role. He is the director of the Minority Biomedical Research Support Program at Tuskegee, sponsored by the National Institutes of Health. Over 300 young people have benefited from this program, which helps support the college education of promising students.

Warren E. Henry

Born: February 18, 1909, in Evergreen, Alabama

Status: Semiretired, Professor, School of Engineering, Howard University, Washington, D.C.

Education:

Bachelor of Science degree, Tuskegee Institute, Tuskegee, Alabama, 1931

Master of Science degree, Atlanta University, Atlanta, Georgia, 1937

Doctor of Philosophy degree, University of Chicago, Chicago, Illinois, 1941

Research Area: Physical Chemistry

Early Years

Warren Henry's father, Nelson E. Henry, and his mother, Maddie McDaniel Henry, were both graduates of Tuskegee Institute and both school teachers. At that time, school teachers were highly respected, but poorly paid, members of the community. Many teachers found it necessary to farm during the summer to make an adequate living. The Henry farm was near the small village of China, Alabama. Even though Warren was born at the farmhouse, his birth was registered in Evergreen, Alabama, a market town about eight miles from China.

Warren was the oldest child of the Henry family. As soon as each was old enough, the five boys and two girls helped with the farm work. The family raised potatoes, corn, beans, and other vegetables for their own table. They also raised cotton and peanuts as cash crops. When he was 10 years old, Warren learned to plow the corn and cotton fields with a team of mules. He picked cotton for his parents and, to make a little money, helped other cotton farmers in the area.

Warren's father was a very effective farmer. His training at Tuskegee had introduced him to modern farming methods. George Washington Carver (see p. 42), who taught at

Tuskegee at that time, was a strong advocate of modern farming methods, such as crop rotation and the use of natural fertilizers. Carver was also a pioneer in the methods of extension education. Teachers of the new farming techniques visited farmers at their homes rather than making the farmers travel to a central location.

Warren's father was chosen by Dr. Carver to be one of the new extension agents. During the summer months from 1915 to 1920, Mr. Henry traveled by horse cart throughout his region of Alabama.

The school where Warren's parents taught was near their home. Mr. Henry had actually built the two-story school with his own hands. Money for materials had been provided by church donations from the northern states. When Warren was only three years old, his parents took him to their school each day. He was seated in the back of a classroom and given toys and books to keep him amused. His parents would look after him while they taught. Warren liked to pretend that he was a pupil like the older children. Indeed, he was a very good "pretender." He surprised everyone, including his parents, by learning to read before he was four.

Warren's elementary school had no science instruction. In the seventh grade, he transferred to the Lomax-Hannon School, run by the local African American church in Greenville, but Warren still could not take courses in science. The Lomax-Hannon School went to the eleventh grade, and once again, Warren was required to transfer. In order to earn his high school diploma, he spent his senior year at Alabama State Normal School in Montgomery, Alabama. This residential school was originally designed as an institution for training elementary school teachers. It was here that Warren received his first formal science education.

Warren's mother strongly encouraged him to enroll in as many science courses as possible. In the summer before he left home to attend high school, she gave him the chemistry textbook she had used at Tuskegee. Warren eagerly read this book and later enrolled in a chemistry course at his new school. He did so well in the course that the teacher invited Warren to become her laboratory assistant.

Higher Education

When Warren Henry was 18, he enrolled at the college his parents had attended, Tuskegee Institute. Although he was contemplating a career in science, the school officials did not encourage early specialization. Their goal was to give their students a broad background in the liberal arts and in practical skills, such as carpentry and brick laying. Henry took courses in English and modern languages along with mathematics, physics, and chemistry.

As one might expect, Henry needed to work while he was in college. During his first term, he was employed as a night watchman at the school. In his second term, he worked in the pharmacy at the Tuskegee Hospital. All through his last three years in college, Henry was the laboratory assistant in the chemistry courses.

During the summer months, he worked on the Tuskegee experimental farm, where studies of insecticides and fertilizers were being conducted. His job was to spray the cotton plants from a horse-drawn wagon. The researchers were looking for the best way to control the cotton boll weevil.

In 1931, after he received his bachelor's degree, Henry found a job as a teacher and high school principal in Atmore, Alabama. However, he still was interested in research. During the summer after his third year at Atmore, he attended a summer program at Atlanta

University as a way to refresh both his teaching skills and his scientific knowledge. The science course was a review of general chemistry, and Henry did very well. At the end of the term, the head of the chemistry department offered Henry a scholarship if he would enroll as a graduate student. He accepted the invitation.

During his time at Atlanta, the funding from the scholarship helped, but Henry needed more money for his living expenses. In his first year, he accepted a part-time teaching job at nearby Spelman College, a renowned school for African American women. After he finished his course work, he concentrated on completing his thesis research. At the same time, Henry returned to Tuskegee as an instructor in their chemistry department. In 1937, he received his master's degree in organic chemistry from Atlanta University.

Shortly after he graduated, he taught a course in psychology at Tuskegee and then went on a long trip. The purpose of his travels was to see the scientific research facilities in industrial laboratories throughout the northern part of the country. He visited laboratories in New York City, Chicago, Detroit, Pittsburgh, Philadelphia, and Washington, D.C.

The following summer, he enrolled in an advanced chemistry course at the University of Chicago and worked in the chemistry laboratory as an assistant. Again, he made a very favorable impression on the faculty and was invited to remain as a doctoral student. During his first year, the faculty arranged for him to tutor undergraduate students. He also worked as a hat-and-coat checker in the restaurant in his dormitory building, and he conducted door-to-door surveys. Fortunately, he was invited to be a teaching assistant during his last two years of doctoral studies, for which he received free tuition and a small salary to cover living expenses.

Henry's dissertation concerned the testing of his own invention. His device measured very small changes in temperature resulting from an ongoing chemical reaction. The temperature detector was placed directly in the midst of the reaction and measured changes as small as one ten-millionth of a degree.

Career Highlights

After receiving his doctorate from Chicago in 1941, Dr. Henry returned to Tuskegee as an assistant professor of chemistry. Because of his broad program of studies at Chicago, he was also qualified to teach physics. He was asked to teach special physics courses to the young men who were training to be Army Air Corps officers. These young men would ultimately form the 99th Pursuit Squadron and become world famous as the Tuskegee Airmen of World War II.

In the summer of 1943, Dr. Henry again taught courses in chemistry and physics at Spelman. Soon, he moved to the Massachusetts Institute of Technology (MIT) in Cambridge to take a crucial job in the war effort. He joined the team that was working to improve the performance of radar systems. In early radar displays, the signals were presented on a scope similar to a computer or television screen. These signals looked like wiggly lines on a graph and were hard for the operators to understand. Dr. Henry's work, which was classified as top secret, involved filtering and strengthening the radar signal to make it clearer on the radar screen. He invented a device called a video amplifier that worked faster and better than anything else at that time.

Dr. Henry's radar designs were intended for use in permanent radar installations on land. However, while he was at MIT, he was presented with an emergency request. The navy needed more compact radar systems for use aboard the warships in the Pacific theater of combat. Dr. Henry worked without stopping for 36 hours to finish the design of a special amplifier that would work as part of the new system. From the day it was installed aboard ship, the device worked perfectly.

After the war was over, Dr. Henry returned to the University of Chicago and its Institute for the Study of Metals. At this time, jet aircraft were beginning to be used by the military. However, there had been several crashes of jet military aircraft, and investigators reported that the main wing spars seemed to have failed. A spar is the main wing support that runs from the body of the aircraft to the tip of the wing. Researchers in England discovered that repeated flexing—up-and-down movement—of the wings at high speed gradually wore out the main spar at the point where the most flexing occurred. They said the failures were due to "metal fatigue."

Both designers and mechanics wanted to be able to predict in advance when a main spar might fail so they could replace the wing support before an accident occurred. However, they did not want to replace the spar too soon because such replacements were expensive.

Dr. Henry found an answer to this problem by using information from his doctoral research on small temperature changes. When metal flexes, it tends to get warmer. The faster the heat builds up, the sooner the metal will break. By testing sample spars made of various metal alloys, Dr. Henry showed which alloy would last the longest and just how long it would last.

In 1947, Dr. Henry joined the faculty at Morehouse College in Atlanta as professor and acting head of the physics department. One of his projects was to provide special tutoring for students who were fall-

ing behind in their physics classes. He did much of this tutoring himself. The students complained that he expected too much work from them. Dr. Henry called the students together and showed them articles from the latest journals on physical science. He explained that because of the rapid progress in the sciences, students and, indeed, senior scientists, had to strive to keep up with the advances. Hard work was the price of being a scientist.

In 1948, Dr. Henry moved again, this time to the Naval Research Laboratory just outside of Washington, D.C. The main focus of his research was superconductivity. Some materials, mainly alloys of copper, loose all their electrical resistance when cooled to near absolute zero (minus 460 degrees Fahrenheit). This characteristic could help in the efficient transmission of electricity. Scientists sought to discover precisely why the materials became superconductive. The long-range goal was to identify materials that would act as superconductors at somewhat higher temperatures—if possible above 70 degrees absolute. That is the temperature of liquid nitrogen, a coolant which is easily available from commercial suppliers.

Dr. Henry and other scientists also studied the problems in one of the practical applications of superconductive materials. The property of superconductivity is lost when the materials are put into a strong magnetic field. Since it would be desirable to use the superconductive materials in the construction of powerful magnets, system designers hoped to be able to overcome this limitation. They had only limited success, and this is still a serious problem in the practical applications of superconductors.

Dr. Henry left the Naval Research Laboratory in 1960 to join the engineering staff at the Lockheed Missile and Space Company in California. By using his experience in magnetics, he was able to design electronic guidance systems for missiles, detection systems for finding enemy submarines, and techniques for saving people from disabled submarines. He also helped guide a major breakthrough in electronic astronomy by developing a device that could measure magnetic fields in outer space.

After Dr. Henry was transferred to Washington, D.C., in 1968, he taught night courses at Howard University. At first, he served as an adjunct professor. Soon, his potential was recognized, and he was offered a full professorship in the physics department. Later, he taught courses on nuclear systems in the school of engineering. His main pleasure, however, came from guiding doctoral students in their research.

In 1977, Dr. Henry began to think about retirement. However, he had to attend to unfinished business. He had been working for some years with a program called Minorities Access to Research Careers, or MARC. MARC gives students in their third and fourth years in college an opportunity to conduct research in a teamwork situation. During summer sessions, the students visit other colleges and universities, where they increase their research experience. Dr. Henry holds seminars for MARC students at Howard and gives them individual help with their research projects.

Because of his many achievements, Dr. Henry has traveled the world to give talks to fellow scientists. During his long career, he has been honored in many ways, including the Carver Award from Tuskegee in 1978. Now that he is semiretired, he feels most honored by the many students who are following in his footsteps.

Walter Scott

Walter A. Hill

Born: August 9, 1946, in New Brunswick, New Jersey

Status: Dean and Research Director, School of Agriculture and Home Economics, Tuskegee University, Tuskegee, Alabama

Education:

Bachelor of Arts degree, Lake Forest College, Lake Forest, Illinois, 1968

Master of Science degree, University of Chicago, Chicago, Illinois, 1970

Master of Science degree, University of Arizona, Tuscon, Arizona, 1973

Doctor of Philosophy degree, University of Illinois, Champaign-Urbana, Illinois, 1978

Research Area: Plant Physiology

Early Years

When Walter Hill was in grade school, his parents moved from New Jersey to North Little Rock, Arkansas. His mother was a school teacher, and his father was a minister of the African Methodist Episcopal Church. Shortly after they arrived, his father began to reach out to the Black families on the farms around the town. Ordinarily, the children of these families would stop going to school after the eighth grade because there were no high schools for Black children in those rural areas, but Walter's father valued education and wanted to improve the opportunities for young Black people. He succeeded in developing a plan so that the rural children could go to high school in North Little Rock. These young people were invited to live in the town with members of his parish during the school term. Without the help of Rev. Hill, most of the young people from the surrounding rural areas could not have attended high school.

Walter was inspired by his father's example and by the books he read about the work of Black scientists. George Washington Carver (see p. 42) was his favorite. Walter decided early in his life that he wanted to be both a teacher and a scientist, as Carver had been. In particular, he wanted to carry on Carver's work of finding new uses for and products from common plants. He also wanted to work on problems of plant growth and improve the way food was cultivated. For example, many farmers still did not practice crop rotation. To maintain fertility and to reduce the dangers of crop diseases and insect pests, a field should be planted in a different crop every year or so. Walter wanted to carry on Carver's program of extension education for African American farmers.

Higher Education

Walter Hill earned such good grades in high school that he received a scholarship to Lake Forest College in Lake Forest, Illinois. The college, a small, liberal arts school, is a few dozen miles north of Chicago on the shores of Lake Michigan. At Lake Forest, Hill took every chemistry course that was offered,

along with many other science courses. He received his degree in 1968.

Walter Hill moved to Chicago and accepted a job teaching high school chemistry, physics, and general science. During the summer, he took advanced chemistry courses toward a master's degree at the University of Chicago. He also studied at night and on weekends during the school year. In 1970, Hill was awarded a master's degree in chemistry by the University of Chicago.

Walter Hill wanted to continue his education, so he began to investigate the graduate programs at several universities. He decided that the University of Arizona in Tucson would best fit his needs and interests. Hill liked the fact that this university had both its agricultural experiment station and its agricultural extension service located on its main campus. He also appreciated the fact that the university offered him some financial assistance.

Hill had earned his first graduate degree in chemistry, but at Arizona he chose to study soil science. He wanted to understand the details of how plants grow, especially about how plants take chemicals from the soil for their growth. He also wanted to know how plants change these chemicals into material that becomes food for humans and animals.

Because his previous studies were in basic science, Hill had to start his degree program at the beginning level. He realized he would have to prove his ability, even though he had already earned a master's degree.

To pay his way, he worked in the research laboratories in the School of Agriculture. He washed test tubes and filled bottles of chemicals for the advanced students and faculty members. He worked hard to demonstrate his dedication to his studies. Fortunately, the faculty in agricultural science soon recognized his ability, and Hill was quickly transferred into the advanced degree program, where he received his second master's degree in 1973.

Walter Hill's teachers at Arizona were so impressed with his ability that they encouraged him to continue his education. His major professor, Dr. H. Bohn, suggested he continue his studies at the University of Illinois in Champaign-Urbana, Illinois. The University of Illinois has a world-famous College of Agriculture, where much of the pioneering research in corn and soybean culture had been done in the 1930s and 1940s

Again, Hill had to work to pay his expenses. In 1978, after five busy years, he was awarded his doctoral degree in soil science from the University of Illinois.

Career Highlights

After completing his Ph.D., Dr. Hill had many job offers. He could have chosen a job with a high salary in one of the private companies that grow seeds or manufacture chemicals for farmers, or he could have taken a job in a government laboratory that would provide him with job security for the rest of his life, but he chose to teach. The institution that most appealed to him was Tuskegee University in Tuskegee, Alabama. In a way, this was a return to the roots of his interest. Tuskegee University had been founded by Booker T. Washington in 1881 and was the place where George Washington Carver—his boyhood hero—built an agricultural extension service for the struggling Black farmers of the area. It was at that institution that Carver had done his world famous research on the peanut and other crops. Fortunately, there was an opening for a specialist in soil science, and Dr. Hill joined the faculty at Tuskegee in the fall of 1978.

He quickly began an intense program of work. In addition to the beginning course in general soil science, Dr. Hill taught five other

courses during his first year at Tuskegee. He taught soil chemistry, soil physics, soil classification, soil and water conservation, and soil microbiology.

He also sponsored and led several student clubs and began his own research program. Dr. Hill particularly wanted his students to join with him in the research. That way they could learn about science by doing science, as well as increase their confidence in their abilities. By 1991, his students had won 17 awards for their research projects.

Hill also won awards for his teaching. He was named a Danforth Associate in 1980 by the Danforth Foundation, an award that recognized his performance in teaching beginning students. His own students gave him an award as an outstanding faculty advisor in 1982, and in 1988, he was recognized in a White House ceremony with other Black educators through a program authorized by President Reagan. The American Society of Agronomy presented him with the Outstanding Education Award in 1990, and he has also been praised in media such as *Black Enterprise Magazine* and the Public Broadcasting System.

Dr. Hill's research activities follow a similar pattern to the work of Carver. His favorite research subject is the sweet potato. At Tuskegee, he examined the way the sweet potato plant used nitrogen from fertilizers. He also studied whether sweet potatoes, like some plants, could make their own fertilizer, naturally. These plants provide a home for bacteria that capture nitrogen from the air. The bacteria then provides the nitrogen to the plant. The research goal was to help the sweet potato roots become attractive to this type of bacteria. If that could be done, farmers would need to use less artificial fertilizer in growing sweet potatoes. Dr. Hill's research was successful, and in 1983, he received the Plucknett Award of the International Society of Tropical Root Crops in Lima, Peru, for his work on sweet potatoes.

After a successful beginning, Dr. Hill was eager to do more research on the sweet potato. His timing was good. Money to support his research became available from an unusual source, the National Aeronautics and Space Administration (NASA). As early as 1978, scientists at NASA laboratories had decided to develop a new system of life support. They knew that all the food, air, and water needed by astronauts could not be carried on very long missions. There had to be a way to recycle waste materials. Growing plants are ideal for such recycling. They can transform waste material into food to eat, oxygen for breathing, and purified water for drinking.

In 1985, NASA scientists began to ask research people in colleges and universities to help them work on the project. Dr. Hill saw the sweet potato as a particularly good plant for use in a recycling system. He believed that sweet potatoes could be grown in tanks of water without being planted in soil, and thus be easily transported on a spacecraft.

Dr. Hill wrote down his ideas and sent them to the NASA scientists. They were impressed. In 1986, Tuskegee University was awarded $600,000 to develop new ways to grow sweet potatoes. A few years later, the grant was increased to $1,000,000.

The job was not easy. Other plants such as the cucumber and the tomato could be grown in tanks of water, but they are not root crops. The most important part of the sweet potato is the root, and no root crop had been grown successfully in a water tank before Hill began to work on it. He had to invent a new recipe of minerals to put into the water tank, light and temperature had to be carefully controlled, and ways had to be found to support the stem of the plant. Hill and his stu-

dents solved all these problems, and his procedure was awarded a U.S. patent.

He was also correct about the advantage of the sweet potato compared to other green plants. For example, the sweet potato plant will grow well in zero gravity, which is an unusual property among green plants. The sweet potato is also versatile. Using Dr. Hill's method, the plant grows rapidly—twice as fast in the water tanks compared to growth in a farmer's field. The potato part, or tuber, provides vitamins as well as energy food, and the leaves can be eaten like spinach. Dr. Hill and others are now thinking that his method would also help farmers. Sweet potatoes grown in water tanks could provide good food in regions where soil fertility is low.

Dr. Hill has fulfilled the ambition he imagined as a young student. He has taken the start made by George Washington Carver into the future of human space exploration.

William Augustus Hinton

Born: December 15, 1883, in Chicago, Illinois

Status: Died August 8, 1959, at Canton, Massachusetts

Education:

Bachelor of Science degree, Harvard University, Cambridge, Massachusetts, 1905

Doctor of Medicine degree, Harvard University, 1912

Research Area: Microbiology

Early Years

William Hinton's parents were born into slavery in North Carolina. Soon after the end of the Civil War, they emigrated to Chicago, Illinois, where they were able to find work but were unable to find decent living conditions. When William reached school age in 1889, his parents moved to Kansas City, Kansas, hoping to find good schools for their children.

Young Gus, as William was known to his friends, attended Kansas City public schools for his elementary schooling, a parochial Catholic school for the middle grades, and back to public school for high school. From his middle school years on, he helped the family finances by delivering newspapers, raising chickens to sell, and doing whatever odd jobs he could find. When he graduated from high school in 1900, he was only 16 years old, the youngest graduate in the history of the school.

Higher Education

Gus Hinton made excellent academic progress after entering the University of Kansas. During his first year, his biology teacher, a specialist in physiology, influenced Hinton to prepare for a medical career. When Hinton started his second year, he entered into the premed program. He had a heavy course load in his first year and continued with a heavier-than-normal load during his second year. In this way, he was able to finish three years of college work in two years' time, and because

of faculty connections, officials at Harvard University in Cambridge, Massachusetts, invited Hinton to finish his college work there.

But he did not have enough money. Hinton had to stop classes for a year and go to work. Although his savings were still small, he was able to enter Harvard in 1903. The money was sufficient for the first year, and by working summers and winning a small scholarship, he was able to complete his second year, graduating from Harvard in 1905.

Hinton's work in the classroom brought him to the attention of some of the leading senior scholars at Harvard, including William James, the founder of the study of psychology in the United States; the philosophers George Santayana, Josiah Royce, and Hugo Munsterburg; and the second American to win a Nobel Prize, the chemist, Theodore W. Richards. In spite of the positive impressions he made on these people, however, he was unable to go directly into medical school.

Hinton's first job after graduation was teaching biology courses at Walden University in Nashville, Tennessee. He also worked as an adjunct instructor at Meharry Medical School in Nashville. During the summers, he would travel north to study bacteriology and pathology at the University of Chicago. In 1908, he left Walden to join the faculty of Oklahoma Agricultural and Mechanical College in Langston, Oklahoma. There he met Ada Hawes, another young faculty member. They were married the next summer, and Gus entered Harvard Medical School that fall.

Hinton's years of teaching various subjects related to medicine, plus the courses he had taken at the University of Chicago, allowed him to pass his second-year medical examinations at the end of his first year. In effect, Gus Hinton "skipped" a year of medical school. Although his wife earned some money and Hinton worked part-time for two prominent medical researchers, finances continued to be a problem. Harvard Medical School offered Hinton a scholarship set aside for African American students, but he did not want what he considered to be charity. He chose, instead, to compete on a completely open basis for other scholarships. Gus Hinton won the competition for the Wigglesworth Scholarship two years in a row and, in his final year, won the coveted Hayden Scholarship.

While still a medical student, Gus Hinton became interested in the diagnosis and treatment of syphilis, the notorious venereal disease. The interest was fostered by two mentors, Drs. Richard Cabot and Elmer Southard. These men were already working on a better understanding of the disease when they recruited Gus Hinton to help them in their research. One target of their studies was the problem of diagnosing the disease. The main tool for diagnosis of syphilis in those days was the Wasserman test, which often gave false positive results. At that time, the treatments for syphilis tended to be long and painful and included heavy metals, such as arsenic and mercury salts. These metals would accumulate in vital organs, such as the kidneys, and could do the patient more harm than good. In those days, a patient falsely diagnosed as having syphilis might be killed by the unnecessary treatment. Today, antibiotics such as penicillin are effective against the disease and harmless to most patients.

The other negative aspect of being falsely diagnosed was the social penalty. Like AIDS now, individuals who were infected with, or thought to be infected with, syphilis were shunned and could easily lose their employment.

On the other hand, it was necessary to detect the disease when it was actually present. Syphilis is a disease that progresses through three distinct phases. If the disease is correctly diagnosed while it is still in the first phase, the chances of controlling or curing the disease are high. In those days, if it reached the second or third stage, the situation was virtually hopeless. Gus Hinton entered into the study of syphilis with enthusiasm and resolved to find a way to help the victims of the dreaded disease. These initial studies took place during his final year in medical school. They fit in with the formal curriculum at that stage. Consequently, he was able to graduate with honors with his doctor of medicine degree from Harvard Medical School in 1912.

Career Highlights

Ordinarily, after the award of the M.D. degree, the new medical doctor completes an internship and hospital residency to polish his or her clinical skills. Three years is the typical duration for these practical studies. On the technicality that he was married and, therefore, could not live at the hospital, Dr. Hinton was denied a posting at Massachusetts General Hospital. On less official but more significant grounds, the hospital officials were afraid that their patients would react negatively toward an African American physician. Therefore, instead of a clinical internship, Dr. Hinton served for three years as a volunteer assistant in the pathology laboratory of the hospital. He also worked afternoons in the Wasserman Laboratory at Harvard Medical School. In addition to supervising diagnostic testing, he was soon teaching medical students how to do the Wasserman test and other diagnostic tests on the blood and spinal fluids of patients.

After three years in this unusual internship/residency arrangement, he began his first full-time professional job as a physician. In 1915, he was appointed assistant director of the division of biological laboratories at the medical school. He was also "loaned out" to the Massachusetts State Wasserman Laboratory in Boston, where, for all intents and purposes, he was the manager.

Scientists knew that the spinal fluid of patients with syphilis was chemically different from that of disease-free individuals; however, it was not known how this fact could be put to use as a diagnostic tool. What Dr. Hinton sought was a test that was quick and sensitive and gave a diagnosis that could be read with complete certainty. He found the solution to the problem when he combined pure forms of beef protein, cholesterol, common table salt, and water. When a small sample of spinal fluid from a diseased person was added to this mixture at just the right temperature, the cholesterol in the mixture came out of suspension, and the murky looking liquid turned perfectly clear.

Dr. Hinton was still not satisfied. He kept testing variations and making improvements. He soon had an advanced version of the Hinton Test that needed only microscopic amounts of spinal fluid from the patient. He continued to work diligently to make the test easier and cheaper. Dr. Hinton was also especially interested in how the microbes that caused the disease attacked the central nervous system when the disease was in its advanced stage. A form of insanity often affected patients who carried the microbe in their bodies for many years. Dr. Hinton discovered that the microbe destroys nerve cells and the other cells in the brain called glia cells that serve as structural supports in the brain. When the front parts of the brain are destroyed by the microbe, the patient can no longer control his or her behavior. This mental disease is called paresis.

In 1936, all Hinton's research, and the findings of others as well, were put together in a medical textbook called *Syphilis and Its Treatment*, written by Dr. William Augustus Hinton. He also published many separate research reports in the medical periodicals.

In the meantime, Dr. Hinton was carrying out his role as a teacher. After being appointed as director of the laboratory department of the Boston Dispensary, he began to develop a program to train young people—who could not afford to attend college—as medical laboratory technicians. Now such arrangements are common, but in the 1930s, Dr. Hinton's ideas were highly innovative.

Dr. Hinton maintained a close connection to the Harvard Medical School. He served as a part-time faculty member for over 30 years, teaching mainly courses in bacteriology and immunology. He also taught on a part-time basis at Harvard School of Public Health, Simmons College, and the Tufts Medical and Dental Schools in Boston. Finally, in 1949, he was awarded a full professorship at Harvard Medical School—the first African American to hold such a prestigious position.

By the time Dr. Hinton retired in 1953, over 100 laboratories modeled on the Wasserman Laboratory that he developed had been founded around the country. Laboratories under his direct supervision were performing over 2,000 diagnostic tests a day—not just for syphilis but also for other diseases, such as rabies.

University of Maryland Baltimore County

Freeman A. Hrabowski III

Born: August 13, 1950, in Birmingham, Alabama

Status: President, University of Maryland Baltimore County, Baltimore, Maryland

Education:

Bachelor of Arts degree, Hampton Institute, Hampton, Virginia, 1970

Master of Arts degree, University of Illinois, Champaign-Urbana, Illinois, 1971

Doctor of Philosophy degree, University of Illinois, 1975

Research Area: Statistics

Early Years

Freeman Hrabowski's parents were both educators, and they encouraged educational excellence in their family. Therefore, Freeman was expected to do well in school. Fortunately, he loved his studies. His ambition was to become a teacher, like his parents, and perhaps even an administrator.

One of the most significant moments in Freeman's young life came when he was 12 years old. Because of his participation in a civil rights demonstration, he spent a week in a Birmingham jail with Dr. Martin Luther King, Jr. From this experience, Freeman learned about civil protest and the importance of taking responsibility for one's own actions. He came to understand how the nation could be changed by highly motivated people involved in political and social activities.

Freeman had already completed his first year in high school when he met Dr. King. Freeman was advanced in his education because he had skipped two grades in elementary school—under the watchful eye of his mother, who knew what the problems of being underage might be.

Higher Education

After Freeman Hrabowski graduated from high school at the age of 15, he entered Hampton Institute (now Hampton University) in Hampton, Virginia. This private school, founded just after the Civil War, has a tradition of service to the African American community.

Even though he was younger than most of his classmates, Hrabowski volunteered to serve as "big brother" to other students at Hampton Institute. He became the special mentor and mathematics tutor for hearing impaired students.

While a student at Hampton Institute, Hrabowski spent a year studying abroad in Cairo, Egypt. The program was sponsored jointly by Hampton Institute and the Ford Foundation to promote international understanding. At Cairo University, Freeman took courses in mathematics and physics and special studies in Arab cultures. In addition to his formal studies, he took advantage of the local attractions, visiting the ancient pyramids and the sphinx. He also rode a camel across a stretch of the desert and stood on the banks of the Nile River. Freeman remembered that this river was a major factor in the rise of the first great human civilization. The Nile was also the river of the Bible story of Moses, and he recalled the emergence of Judaism, Moses's great religion. He remembers, too, his amazement at seeing a Coca Cola machine in the middle of the desert.

After Hrabowski returned to the United States, he began to think about graduate studies. One of his professors, Dr. Geraldine Darden (see p. 60), was a graduate of the University of Illinois, and she suggested that Hrabowski apply there. He did and was promptly accepted.

Once settled in Champaign-Urbana, Freeman pursued his well-developed interest in tutoring. He quickly established a tutorial center that specialized in mathematics instruction for minority students. Despite the time invested in his tutoring activities, Freeman Hrabowski was able to complete all the requirements for his master's degree in mathematics in only one year.

Hrabowski decided to remain at the University of Illinois for his doctoral studies. For his dissertation research, he chose to use mathematics to study the effects of race in education. With the help of his advisor, Dr. Ernest Anderson, he focused on mathematics instruction in higher education. Using statistical methods of research, Hrabowski compared the mathematical performance of two groups of African American students. In one group were those who had studied mathematics at historically Black colleges, and in the other were those that had studied at predominantly White colleges.

His talents in mathematics and educational administration began to pay dividends, even before Hrabowski began his dissertation research. In 1974, he was named assistant dean for student services at the University of Illinois. Hrabowski was also given responsibility for two major undertakings at this large state university. The first of these efforts was Project Upward Bound, of which Freeman Hrabowski served as director. Upward Bound attempted to encourage low-income high school students to attend college. Hrabowski believed that motivation to succeed involved both the expectations of the student and the support provided by family and friends.

Hrabowski's second project was the Educational Opportunities Program (OEP), which provided information and support for minority students after they arrived at college. Many of these students found themselves facing situations for which they had no background or experience. OEP staff helped them resolve their confusion and doubts.

Partly because of low expectations, many of these students had had few challenging experiences in school before coming to college. In fact, many had poor study habits and had to be taught to prepare for their classes and exams. They also needed to learn good interpersonal communication skills in order to work well with their teachers and fellow students. The efforts of the two programs—Project Upward Bound and OEP—gave Freeman Hrabowski the opportunity to make a positive difference in the lives of minority students.

These projects, along with regular courses and research, created a heavy workload for Freeman Hrabowski. Even so, the following year, he also accepted the job as assistant professor of statistics in the department of educational psychology. In that academic year of 1975–76, he taught, worked as a university administrator, and studied night and day. He finished his doctoral studies at the University of Illinois and earned his degree in the spring of 1975.

Career Highlights

The following fall, Dr. Hrabowski found himself working in a totally different setting. From a large Midwestern school with over 20,000 students, he went to a small Southern school with less than 4,000 students. Dr. Hrabowski served as associate professor of statistics and research and as the associate dean for graduate studies at Alabama A&M University.

At Alabama A&M, in the small town of Normal, Alabama, he taught statistics to high school counselors and classroom teachers. In his classes, Dr. Hrabowski used the findings from his research on the issue of minority students in higher education. He showed educators the nature of the special problems faced by teachers, students, and their parents in rural Alabama.

The following year of 1977, Dr. Hrabowski accepted yet another challenge. He undertook a position at Coppin State College in Baltimore, Maryland. Like Alabama A&M, Coppin State had been founded as a training school for teachers. However, like many other "normal schools," Coppin State's faculty and administrators had ambitions to offer a complete curriculum in the arts and sciences and become a full-fledged university. While Dr. Hrabowski was on the faculty, Coppin State made progress in developing and broadening its programs. Later, through a major reorganization of higher education in Maryland, Coppin State became part of the eleven campus University of Maryland system.

At Coppin State, Dr. Hrabowski was appointed professor of mathematics and dean of arts and sciences in 1971. Then, in 1981, he was appointed vice president for academic affairs, the second highest position on the campus. His greatest challenge was understanding the problems of students from inner-city Baltimore. He was most impressed by the motivation of students from low-income homes. Many of these students had parents who did not support their child's desire to earn a college degree. He saw that these students had the courage to persist in seeking their goal against formidable odds.

The next great challenge for Dr. Hrabowski was to assume the job of vice provost at the University of Maryland Baltimore County (UMBC). This institution opened its doors to students in 1966 and has grown rapidly from that date.

In 1988, Dr. Hrabowski began working with the Baltimore philanthropists, Robert and Jane Meyerhoff. They created the Meyerhoff Scholarship Program for talented African American undergraduates in science and engineering. The program was designed to address the shortage of African American students in these career fields. Students who participate in the program are known as "Meyerhoff Scholars" and are competitively selected. The program now includes over 150 exceptional young men and women from across the United States. During the sum-

mers, these students are invited to work in research laboratories at universities and private companies throughout the nation. Through these experiences, the young people strengthen their research skills and capabilities. After receiving their bachelor's degrees, the Meyerhoff Scholars are typically admitted to some of the United States' best universities, where they continue their education in science, medicine, and engineering.

After serving for three years as vice provost at UMBC, Dr. Hrabowski was named executive vice president in 1990. He served as interim president during the school year 1992–93 and was named president of the university in 1993. While serving as president of UMBC, he continues his efforts to strengthen the education of minority students, particularly in the sciences, mathematics, and engineering. These efforts are supported by the Meyerhoff Scholarship Program and the information gained from his own research on minority students in colleges and universities. His statistical research describes, in elegant detail, how providing students with strong support and encouragement can improve the successful completion of their higher education.

Shirley Ann Jackson

Born: August 5, 1946, in Washington, D.C.

Status: Chair, United States Nuclear Regulatory Commission, Washington, D.C.

Education:

Bachelor of Science degree, the Massachusetts Institute of Technology, Cambridge, Massachusetts, 1968

Doctor of Philosophy degree, Massachusetts Institute of Technology, 1973

Research Area: Theoretical Physics

Early Years

Shirley Ann Jackson was born in 1946, one year after the end of World War II. She was the middle daughter of the three Jackson children. Shirley's mother was a social worker, and her father was a supervisor in the U.S. Postal Service. Both parents encouraged Shirley and her sisters to do well in school. Her father, in particular, encouraged her interest in mathematics and science. He also helped Shirley and her sisters build their own toys by providing tools and consultation.

In her first few years of school, Shirley attended Parkview Elementary School in the District of Columbia. At that time, the public schools in the District were still segregated. However, by the time Shirley was ready for the third grade, the Supreme Court had determined that segregation was unconstitutional. Shirley then transferred to Barnard Elementary School, which had a diversified student body. Her teachers soon realized that she was very adept at mathematics. They all suggested that Shirley follow a program oriented toward math and science.

Her teachers at MacFarland Junior High School and Theodore Roosevelt High School also encouraged her interest in science and mathematics. In fact, Shirley began her study of Latin in junior high in order to learn and understand the scientific names for plants, animals, and parts of the body. In high school, she was enrolled in the advanced placement courses in science and mathematics. She also competed regularly in science fairs. For one of her entries, Shirley studied the effects of various foods on the health and vigor of white mice. In this project, her father helped her build the cages for the mice.

Shirley did well in all her courses and received high honors in the science fair competitions. When she graduated from high school in 1964, she had the best grade record in her graduating class.

Higher Education

Shirley Jackson's good grades and the backing of her teachers helped her gain admittance to the Massachusetts Institute of Technology (MIT) in Cambridge, Massachusetts. Even as an undergraduate, Jackson had two four-year scholarships. One was from the Martin Marietta Company and the other was from the Prince Hall Masons, a charitable organization. Even so, she needed to make additional money to help pay her tuition and living expenses. To do so, she worked in the nutrition and food science laboratory at MIT as a technician. Her earlier research on the diets of white mice proved helpful in this job.

The general atmosphere at MIT is highly competitive and not very supportive. Historically, there have been few African Americans and few women of any ethnic heritage at the Institute. In 1964, when Shirley Jackson entered MIT, there were only 43 women in the freshman class and roughly 20 African American undergraduate students. Jackson was the only Black woman undergraduate in the physics program. Fortunately, there was a Black sorority at MIT that provided Jackson with some support.

At first, Shirley Jackson was not enthusiastic about joining an organization that sometimes showed discrimination based on family income. However, at MIT, the young women who joined the sorority needed each other's help in their stressful academic situation. The women students also enjoyed the support and sense of accomplishment provided by the older MIT graduates who had belonged to the sorority—many of whom lived nearby and continued to participate in sorority activities. Jackson's sorority, in turn, provided help to the local young people. The sorority members carried out a tutoring program for high school students in nearby Roxbury and also provided college counseling services. Shirley, who had never considered sorority membership before arriving at MIT, was elected president in her senior year.

In that same year, she began a major research project on superconductivity. Ordinarily, copper or aluminum wires conduct electric current with a moderate amount of resistance. When metals that have high resistance are used to conduct electric current, they become hot from the resistence. An electric stove is an example.

Some metals, particularly alloys of copper and mercury, can lose all their resistance to electric current under special conditions. When an electric current is introduced in a circuit of superconducting material at a very low temperature, it will continue going around forever, provided the temperature is kept constant.

People have known about superconductors for many years, but the challenge has been to find materials that take on the property of superconductivity at somewhat higher temperatures. This was the challenge that Jackson accepted. No great breakthroughs came from her research, but she was able to add to the growing knowledge about materials that *might* be usable. Shirley Jackson completed her research on superconductors and received her bachelor's degree from MIT in 1968.

As a graduate student at MIT, her money situation improved. She received a traineeship from the National Science Foundation for the first three years and several Ford Foundation Fellowships to complete her program. Even though Jackson could have transferred to another graduate school, she decided that MIT would provide the most interesting set of conditions.

As an undergraduate, Shirley Jackson had worked with the Black Student Union (BSU) to persuade the administrators to do more to recruit and retain minority students. She continued this effort as a graduate student in the role of an advisor to the BSU. The number of minority students and women began to improve during Jackson's time in the program. Some years later, in 1976, she was elected to MIT's Educational Council and the board of trustees of MIT a few years after that. Thus, she was able to continue her efforts to increase the enrollment of minorities and women at MIT over a long period of time.

Shirley Jackson's dissertation research concerned the forces that hold the parts of an atomic nucleus together. The phrase "splitting the atom" refers to how the nucleus of the atom is wrenched apart. This happens when the powerful forces that keep the nucleus intact are overwhelmed by an external force, usually intense radiation. When the atomic nucleus is wrenched apart, it can send out new radiation that will tear apart other neighboring atoms, causing a chain reaction. In an atomic explosion, millions of atoms come apart at the same time—releasing their energy and radiation very quickly.

Shirley Jackson sought to describe the workings of these forces by using a compact set of mathematical equations. She received the help of her advisor, Dr. James Young, the first

African American to become a full professor of physics at MIT. Jackson was also given support by colleagues at the International School of Subnuclear Physics on the Italian island of Sicily. In 1973, she finished her project and was awarded her doctorate from MIT.

Career Highlights

The next three years of Dr. Jackson's life were spent in the continuing study of high-energy physics. The first year, she did research at the Fermi National Laboratory (Fermilab) in Batavia, Illinois. Then, she spent a year at an international facility for nuclear research, known as CERN, in Geneva, Switzerland. Finally, she returned to Fermilab for another year. Dr. Jackson was able to establish her reputation by adapting her theoretical models of atomic forces to actual scientific observations made during high-energy experiments at CERN and at Fermilab.

In 1976, Dr. Shirley Jackson began her career as a theoretical physicist at the AT&T Bell Laboratories in New Jersey. Her research projects now became more diversified, but they exhibited a common theme. Her work focused on the problem of how one can understand the behavior of large bodies of matter by studying only the properties of the smallest parts. This field of research is known as condensed-matter physics. The term "condensed-matter" includes a variety of materials from ordinary glass to the mysterious substance that makes up a hyper-massive neutron star. However, some of the most interesting examples of condensed-matter are plasmas, gases made up of atoms from which a part of their outer shell has been stripped. The sun's atmosphere, for example, is a plasma.

In plasmas, some of the electrically negative electrons that circle the electrically positive nucleus are separated from the atoms of the gas. This condition makes the gas act like an electrically conducting fluid. Because of this characteristic, the gas can be controlled in space by a magnetic field. One possible future application of this property would be controlled atomic fusion. In this condition, atoms are fused together under great heat and pressure. Controlled fusion would allow electric power to be generated without nuclear contamination of our environment.

One of Dr. Jackson's first major research projects at Bell Laboratories was similar to one she conducted as an undergraduate at MIT. Her research was focused on the possibility that ceramic materials, which are condensed-matter substances, could act as superconductors of electric currents.

Again, progress was slow. However, some of the related research on condensed matter has been very successful. Practical applications of condensed matter physics include the liquid crystals used in digital watches, transistors, and the integrated circuits used in computers. Many ideas generated through the study of condensed-matter physics have had a stimulating effect on other branches of science. Thus, the study of condensed-matter physics has been widely beneficial. Dr. Jackson has welcomed the opportunity to be a contributor to these prospective advances.

In 1985, the governor of New Jersey, Thomas Kean, appointed Dr. Jackson to the state's Commission on Science and Technology. A major goal of this commission was to foster constructive relations between state institutions of higher education and private industrial organizations. The committee of experts was to work together on common problems, such as the disposal of hazardous materials and the improvement of manufacturing methods.

During her years at AT&T Bell Laboratories, Dr. Jackson continued to be active in community and professional affairs. She pressed for the inclusion of more women and minorities in the scientific and technological occupations. In support of these views, Dr. Jackson has worked with the National Academy of Sciences and the American Association for the Advancement of Science. She has been on the governing boards of the American Physical Society and the American Institute of Physics. Dr. Jackson also served a term as the president of the National Society of Black Physicists. She has served as a member of the board of trustees of both Rutgers University and MIT. Her service as a trustee for Lincoln University in Pennsylvania and its lesser-known division, the Barnes Foundation, is particularly interesting. The Barnes Foundation, a private museum in the suburbs of Philadelphia, owns important examples of African sculpture and French paintings from the late 1800s and early 1900s. It was, for a time, also a special showcase for the works of African American artists.

In 1991, Dr. Jackson became a professor of physics at Rutgers University. At Rutgers, she taught both undergraduate and graduate students and pursued her own research. Her recent projects included inquiries into how very thin layers of a given substance, placed between other materials in a sandwich arrangement, can influence the passage of light or electricity from one sandwich face to the other. For example, some of these ceramic and metal sandwiches can act as storage places for electrical energy, and a quick burst of this energy can be released by a low-power electrical signal sent to the inner layer.

In July of 1995, President Clinton appointed Dr. Jackson as head of the Nuclear Regulatory Commission. Dr. Jackson now supervises the 3,000 federal workers who are responsible for the safety of all nuclear power plants in the United States.

William M. Jackson

Born: September 24, 1936, in Birmingham, Alabama

Status: Professor of Chemistry, University of California, Davis, California

Education:

Bachelor of Science degree, Morehouse College, Atlanta, Georgia, 1956

Doctor of Philosophy degree, Catholic University of America, Washington, D.C., 1961

Research Area: Physical Chemistry

Early Years

As a young girl, Bill Jackson's mother lived in Selma, Alabama. In 1919, her father died in Selma during an influenza epidemic. After his death, Bill's mother and her sister went to live with their mother in California, where his grandmother worked as a maid for some of the famous Hollywood stars, such as Carol Lombard and Ann Southern. Bill's mother graduated from Santa Barbara Junior College in California and later worked for the U.S. government in Birmingham, Alabama. After World War II, she took a job as a program director for the only African American radio station in Birmingham.

Bill's father's father, who had prospered as the owner of the only icehouse in Birmingham, died while Bill's father was in college. Consequently, Bill's father had to work so that he could finish his education. He graduated from the Tuskegee Institute (now University).

The family tradition of hard work led Bill's father to relative financial success. He owned and operated a taxicab company in Birmingham. He also taught automobile mechanics and algebra at Parker High School. Although the Jackson family lived in relative financial comfort, young Bill faced many hardships. He contracted polio when he was just nine years old and was forced to miss a year of school. Before his illness, Bill excelled in his school work. When he was able to return to his classes, however, things were very difficult. He was teased by the other children because of his disabilities. In his anger and frustration, he began to lash out at his classmates and was involved in fights. Then, four years after his recovery, his parents divorced, and he had to move with his mother to Mobile, Alabama.

In Mobile, he entered Central High School. Soon, his teachers recognized that Bill was one of the brightest students in his class. Consequently, no one was surprised when Bill was awarded a Ford Foundation Scholarship and was accepted at both Fisk University in Nashville, Tennessee, and Morehouse College in Atlanta, Georgia.

Higher Education

Bill Jackson entered Morehouse College in 1952. He had chosen Morehouse because it had a four-year program, while Fisk's program lasted five years. Jackson wanted to finish his education as quickly as possible.

At first, he wanted to follow in his father's footsteps and major in mathematics. However, he soon changed his mind. Some of his older friends challenged him to take a course in chemistry from Professor Henry McBay (see p. 242), whose classes were thought to be some of the hardest at Morehouse College. Jackson soon realized that he loved chemistry, even though he did not get the best grades. He found Professor McBay to be as tough as his reputation had indicated. However, by his last year at Morehouse, Jackson had convinced Professor McBay that he was a serious and talented student.

Professor McBay thought that Jackson should stay in Atlanta and continue his study of chemistry at Atlanta University before going to a large northern school. This option, however, did not agree with Bill's desire to move ahead as quickly as possible. Also, some of his other teachers encouraged him to go directly to graduate school.

Jackson applied to about a dozen high-status graduate schools and was accepted at several, including Northwestern University in Evanston, Illinois, and Purdue University in West Lafayette, Indiana—two of the best schools for chemistry. Unfortunately, he did not receive financial aid or fellowships from any of the graduate schools. The response of the Admissions Committee at Northwestern's department of chemistry is representative of Bill's problems. He was informed that the three fellowships for Black students had been awarded. If he wished, he could enroll, prove his ability, and try again for financial aid. This was a kind of "Catch 22" because Bill needed the financial aid before he could enroll and prove his ability.

After this disheartening experience, Bill Jackson decided that he should take a break from schooling, get a job, and save some money. He went to Washington, D.C., where he could board with a cousin. Jackson went to various government agencies to inquire about jobs, and at each agency, he also asked the senior chemists about the quality of D.C.-area graduate programs in physical chemistry. Almost all the chemists replied that Catholic University had the best graduate chemistry program in the region.

In the late summer, just before school was to begin, Jackson walked the 10 blocks from his cousin's house to the campus of Catholic University. He went to see the chairperson of the chemistry department and asked if he could enroll in night school. Jackson was told that Catholic did not offer an evening program in chemistry. Of course, he was discouraged. However, since he was with the chairperson, Jackson decided to ask for a brief evaluation of his undergraduate work. When he showed the transcript that listed all his courses and grades from Morehouse College, there was a pause in the conversation. Then the department chairperson said that he still had some fellowship money available and that Jackson could begin regular classes the following Monday.

In 1957, after his first year of graduate study, Bill Jackson began a long and fruitful association with the U.S. government. He accepted a summer student trainee position at the Harry Diamond Laboratory, a part of the U.S. Army. Bill was assigned to work on problems related to the physical properties of molten salt compounds. His work focused on how these compounds react to electric currents.

When he returned to Catholic University after a successful summer experience, he was ready for the comprehensive examinations. He easily passed the exams in mathematics and physics but failed the exams in chemistry. This was a serious blow to someone who was studying toward a doctorate in chemistry. In the face of this setback, Jackson decided that it might be wise to change his

major to physics, which would mean that he would have to take additional physics courses. Returning to the classroom instead of the laboratory was a depressing option, but it was something he was committed to doing. After just one semester, however, he received some news. Jackson's young wife had become pregnant. Jackson decided to drop out of school for a while and earn money to support his growing family. He talked to one of his professors about his problem. She suggested that he apply for a job at the National Bureau of Standards (now the National Institute of Standards and Technology).

After he began his new job, Bill was greatly influence by Dr. James McNesby, the head of his research team. Dr. McNesby saw that one of his research projects might provide the topic for Bill's dissertation research. He recommended that Bill use the time away from classes as a opportunity to study before retaking the comprehensive examination in chemistry. This suggestion worked well. Bill retook the examination in the spring of 1960 and passed it. In the fall of 1961, Bill also finished the dissertation research that had been suggested by Dr. McNesby. His research revealed some of the minute chemical details of what happens when gasoline burns at the high temperatures found in an automobile engine. By knowing such details, it was hoped that new gasoline additives could be developed to make the fuel more efficient in generating energy but less harmful to the environment.

Career Highlights

Dr. Jackson's first job after finishing his doctoral studies in chemistry was with the famous aerospace firm, Martin-Marietta Company of Baltimore, Maryland. His projects were related to the protective materials used to keep missiles from self-destructing when they reenter our atmosphere at high speed. Dr. Jackson found this work to be less than fascinating and began to look for other opportunities.

In 1963, he returned to the National Bureau of Standards (NBS) as a postdoctoral research associate. This position allowed Dr. Jackson to gain more research experience and to continue to look for a challenging job. During the stay at NBS, Dr. Jackson studied how radiant energy influenced chemical structures. He was particularly interested in what effects radiation has on the coatings put on the metal parts of space vehicles. He used high-energy beams of radiation to try to break the chemical bonds that attached the coating material to the metal surface. For this work, Dr. Jackson designed and built his own molecular beam-generating apparatus.

After a year, an interesting, permanent job opened up at Goddard Space Flight Center (GSFC), which is part of the National Aeronautics and Space Administration (NASA). At the GSFC in Greenbelt, Maryland, Dr. Jackson continued his research on how certain molecules break down when they encounter various forms of energy. The research revealed that some of the strange chemicals found in comets are produced by the action of sunlight on molecules in the comet's surface. The scientists were surprised because the original molecules are normally very stable and resist chemical change of any kind. They found it remarkable that sunlight alone could break the molecules apart and keep the parts from rejoining one another.

In 1969, Dr. Jackson took a temporary leave from NASA to spend a year teaching and doing basic research at the University of Pittsburgh in Pennsylvania. Two regular faculty members, Professors Wade Fite and Ted Brackman, were of great help. They tutored Dr. Jackson in research procedures and gave him a new understanding of how to predict whether an experiment could be done successfully.

His work in a university setting caused Dr. Jackson to consider a career in teaching. He realized that a job that combined teaching and research might satisfy his ambitions. It is not easy, however, to move from a job in government or private industry into a university position. Faculty members prefer that other faculty come up through the ranks rather than from outside the academic community. Therefore, Dr. Jackson returned to his job at Goddard Space Flight Center for another four years. During that time, he designed a device using laser beams to detect the unusual chemicals called free radicals. Free radicals are incomplete molecules formed when sunlight or other beams of energy hit certain chemicals such as those of the surface of a comet.

In the winter of 1974, one of Dr. Jackson's friends and professional colleagues died suddenly. His friend had been a part-time chemistry teacher at Howard University in Washington, D.C. The head of the chemistry department was desperate to employ someone as a replacement teacher. Although distraught at the death of his friend, Dr. Jackson nevertheless agreed to teach for the remainder of the term. When the semester ended, the departmental chair announced that the part-time position had become a permanent appointment. Dr. Jackson was unanimously approved for the job, and he became a professor of chemistry at Howard University.

In 1982, Dr. Jackson accepted a dual appointment in the chemistry and physics departments at Howard. The new position allowed Dr. Jackson to advise and supervise graduate students in both departments. This was wise, because Dr. Jackson's research included both fields of science.

Then, just a few months later, Dr. Jackson was appointed as the graduate professor of laser chemistry in the chemistry department, a post that gave Dr. Jackson the rank equal to a departmental chairperson. It also reflected his continuing interest in how chemical reactions are influenced by light and how these reactions can be studied by the use of lasers.

Other opportunities soon opened up for Dr. Jackson. In 1985, he was invited to join the chemistry faculty at the University of California in Davis, California. At one time, this branch campus of the California system of higher education was noted mainly for its research in the science of agronomy. However, it has now become a center for basic research in all the sciences and rivals the other branches, such as those in Los Angeles, San Diego, and Berkeley.

Dr. Jackson was saddened to leave Howard University, where he had helped many minority students begin their careers in science. Indeed, many of his former students had already risen to prominence. However, Dr. Jackson felt that his new position at the Davis campus would give him more opportunities to assist minority students.

By this stage of his career, Dr. Jackson was already an active champion for the cause of minority scientists. He had proclaimed to government policy makers that support for minority scientists is morally correct and in the best interests of the United States. Over the years, Dr. Jackson has written, spoken at public meetings, and testified before congressional committees on these matters. As a way of reaching more people, he agreed to serve as associate dean for academic personnel at the College of Letters and Sciences at UC Davis from 1990 to 1993. Dr. Jackson has now returned to his regular faculty position, even though he continues to be the director of a project funded by a $1 million government grant. The goal of the project is to increase minority participation in the fields of mathematics and the physical sciences.

Ambrose Jearld, Jr.*

Born: March 6, 1944, at Annapolis, Maryland

Status: Chief, Research Planning and Evaluation, Northeast Fisheries Science Center, United States Department of Commerce, Woods Hole, Massachusetts

Education:

Bachelor of Science degree, University of Maryland Eastern Shore, Princess Anne, Maryland, 1965

Master of Science degree, Oklahoma State University, Stillwater, Oklahoma, 1970

Doctor of Philosophy degree, Oklahoma State University, 1975

Research Area: Marine Biology

Early Years

When Ambrose was three months old, he went to live with his grandmother on her farm

---

* In the area of North Carolina populated by Ambrose Jearld's family, the name is spelled Gerald.

near the small village of Orrum, North Carolina. His father was in the Navy and the country was at war. His mother was working and trying to raise his older sisters at their home near the Naval Academy in Annapolis, Maryland. In many ways, the move to the old family homestead was a boon for everyone, but particularly for Ambrose.

He was the only child in a household that included two uncles who attended North Carolina A&T College and two aunts who were teachers in the local school. The immediate family also included a farmhand who had been hired to work on the farm when Ambrose's grandfather died two years before.

Other uncles, aunts, and cousins lived along Wire Grass Road that led into Orrum. Most of the uncles were farmers but also worked at other jobs. On their farms, they raised grain for livestock and cotton and tobacco as cash crops. Almost all of his aunts were school teachers.

The nearest town of any size was Lumberton, North Carolina, where several of his uncles worked. One owned and ran the local filling station, one owned a shoe shop, and several were independent brick masons. Another worked for the railroad as a signalman in the larger town of Fayetteville, 39 miles from the family center. Family forebears had founded churches and schools and had built and owned the local saw and grist mills. In short, the Jearlds and their relatives were a large, solidly established and self-sufficient family. They supported each other while maintaining easy and constructive relationships with those who were not related to them.

The countryside around Orrum is low lying and wet. Many streams run through the territory, and it is dotted with lakes, ponds, and extensive blackwater swamps. For a future biologist, it was an ideal place to grow up. The large pond at the edge of the family's property contained blackbass, catfish, and pickeral, plus frogs, salamanders, and snakes. The swamp behind the pond provided feeding grounds for green and great blue herons, turtles, raccoons, and other wildlife. Blackberries, persimmons, and hickory nuts grew wild. The vegetable garden produced greens, sweet corn, tomatoes, and root crops including peanuts. The orchard had pears, peaches, apples, figs, plums, and pomegranates, plus black walnuts and pecans. In the yard roamed dogs, cats, and chickens, and in the barn lot were horses, mules, dairy cows, and pigs—many pigs. Indeed, Ambrose had many plants and animals to study.

Ambrose spent hours observing the domestic animals and learning the habits of the creatures of the swamp. He was particularly curious about the wild quail because they nested near the house and mingled with the chickens and other animals in the yard. One of his favorite activities was finding wild flowers and tree seedlings that could be replanted in the yard around the family home. Trees that he planted over 40 years ago are still alive today.

In the summer, family members set off in a cavalcade for the ocean at Atlantic Beach, South Carolina. The uncles netted fish, which were salted down to preserve them. Ambrose was most impressed by the occasional sightings of dolphins arching out of the water just off shore.

When Ambrose was in grade school, his ambition was to become a farmer like his uncles. He participated in the 4-H Club and the Future Farmers of America activities. He was always assigned to tend the plants that were grown in the classroom. After the first grade, he was enrolled in a new consolidated school in Proctorville, North Carolina. In this school, his aunts were often his classroom teachers.

In 1954, when Ambrose was 10, his father, one older and one younger sister, and two younger brothers came to Orrum to visit the family and to retrieve Ambrose. He remembers being excited about the train trip back to Annapolis, Maryland, but was worried about fitting in. Ambrose also wondered if he would enjoy being away from the countryside and in the city of Annapolis, capital of the state and the home of the famous Naval Academy. Indeed, he had to make many adjustments after moving from a very rural setting where many of the people were his kin. Now he lived in an apartment building in a small but sophisticated city where almost everyone was a stranger.

However, there were compensations for living in Annapolis. One was the blue crab; a native of the Chesapeak Bay. For Ambrose, the blue crab was a curious form of life but also the source of a tasty meal. Ambrose studied the way that the blue crab swims and how it finds and captures its prey. He observed the crabbers as they built their traps and penned in the young crabs so that they could be caught easily in the summer months. During the summer, the young crabs shed their hard shells and are known as soft shell crabs. These young crabs are quickly caught and fried because many people especially enjoy eating them. Ambrose also watched when older crabs were steamed in spicy water, and he learned how to pick the delicious crab meat from the shell.

The grade school for African Americans in Annapolis was Stanton Elementary. Ambrose's mother and grandmother had gone to school there, too. His sixth grade teacher was Ms. Elouise Duvall, who had the reputation of being strict but fair. During the year, she took her class to Washington, D.C., to visit the Smithsonian Institution. The class particularly enjoyed the Museum of Natural History, which houses the biological exhibits. Ambrose never forgot that trip and later made sure his own students and his own child had the same experience.

When Ambrose reached junior high school, he joined the Boy Scouts. Scouting fit in well with his interests of nature study and science. The Scoutmaster was Mr. Dallas Pace, who was also the chemistry teacher at the Wiley H. Bates High School. Ambrose was very pleased when he earned the title of senior patrol leader. This meant that he could go to the Broad Creek Memorial Boy Scout Camp one week earlier than the others in his troop. He also joined other organizations for young people at the First Baptist Church, the Hi-Y, and the NAACP Youth Group.

In addition to his other new interests, Ambrose decided that he wanted to earn his own spending money. At first, the work was mainly running errands for the older people who lived in his apartment complex. The next step was selling newspapers and magazines. When he entered his second year of high school, he began to help out at a neighborhood drugstore. The owner and pharmacist, "Doc" Clark, gradually gave Ambrose more responsibilities for running the store. While learning some management skills, the young man also became familiar with medicines. Later, Ambrose took a job as an orderly at the Ann Arundel Hospital. His experience at the drugstore helped him to receive a good salary at the hospital. While working as an orderly, Ambrose observed that there was a relationship between a patient's medical condition and the diet the patient was permitted to eat. Ambrose learned about the dietary needs of patients from a professional nutritionist who saw that he was interested in all aspects of his job. The knowledge he gained from these jobs proved helpful in his science classes. His other part-time job at a restaurant frequented by college students helped him learn about people and their attitudes.

Higher Education

After Ambrose Jearld graduated from high school in 1961, he entered what was then called Maryland State College in Princes Anne, Maryland. Maryland State was the branch of the University of Maryland that traditionally served the African American community. In the late 1980s, the Maryland higher education system was reorganized and Maryland State became the University of Maryland Eastern Shore.

Even though tuition and fees at Maryland State were relatively low, Ambrose had to work his way through school. He was fortunate to find a job on the campus. He was doubly fortunate that the nature of the work benefited his educational program. Ambrose became the assistant in the biological science laboratory. Since he kept this same job for his full four years in college, he became a skilled laboratory technician.

During his years in the laboratory, he worked with Dr. Marion Richards Miles on her research on fava beans. She evaluated the effects of various chemicals on the growth of fava bean roots at different stages of the plant's life. Ambrose was delegated to take samples of the root tips at precise times and to prepare these samples for microscopic examination. He did much of the microscope work and learned to record his observations in a clear and disciplined manner. This effort resulted in winning him the Senior Biology Achievement Award.

After graduating from Maryland State in 1964, Ambrose realized that he needed more formal education if he wanted to work at the professional level. However, money was a problem. Therefore, he looked for a job where he could make some money and learn some new skills at the same time. Fortunately, he found such a position at Publickers Industry, Inc., a chemical company in Philadelphia, Pennsylvania. On this job, Ambrose learned about analytic chemistry by helping to develop new chemical apparatus for the separation and identification of carbon-based compounds.

After two years in Philadelphia, Ambrose had saved some money and his self-confidence had improved. He enrolled in the graduate program in biological science at Oklahoma State University in Stillwater, Oklahoma. He knew of this school because some of the science faculty at Maryland State had taken their degrees there.

Most people would not think of Oklahoma State as a place to study the biology of fishes. However, the state has many reservoirs, and the university had a major fisheries research effort supported by the U.S. Fish and Wildlife Service. Ambrose joined this research project as a research fellow as soon as he arrived at school. The goal of the research program was to protect the wellbeing of fish and game that lived in or near the lakes formed by major dams on the Arkansas River and its tributaries. In particular, the biology students and faculty from Oklahoma State worked at nearby Lake Carl Blackwell and the Keystone Reservoir, about 40 miles east of Stillwater. People in the state government wanted an accurate census of the fish population and a picture of their general state of health. The research teams knew that any drop in the fish population would indicate pollution or some other adverse condition. With the help of the ongoing fish census, problems could be quickly detected. Then, actions could be taken to save the fish from total destruction.

Ambrose was given the job of supervising a team of students who captured and tagged samples of fish. Some of the fish were retained for laboratory examination. The general health of the fish, growth potential, feeding habits, and reproductive capacities were carefully studied. This comprehensive demonstration of a field biologist's work lasted for almost two years and allowed Ambrose to accumulate a wealth of experience. However, in August of 1969, his program was interrupted when he was called upon to fulfill his obligation for military service.

The war in Viet Nam was raging at the time, and many young men were being quickly trained and sent into combat. Then, Ambrose's scientific experience was noted by the U.S.Army, and officials decided that his talents were better suited to research than to carrying a rifle. He was assigned to the Medical Research Laboratory at Edgewood Arsenal in Maryland—not too far from his old home town of Annapolis. At Edgewood, he continued to conduct biological research. In his free time, Ambrose finished his thesis on the feeding behavior of channel catfish. Luckily, he was also able to take some courses in psychobiology at Johns Hopkins University in Baltimore, Maryland. In short, Ambrose Jearld continued to enlarge his knowledge of biological science even while fulfilling his military obligations.

As soon as he completed his military service, Ambrose returned to Oklahoma State to begin work on his doctoral degree under the supervision of Dr. Rudy Miller. He again found a job with the zoology department—as a teaching assistant for several biology courses. He also received a research assistantship grant from the National Science Foundation. This time, his own research projects were more tightly focused on animal behavior. Specifically, he began a major study on the sexual behavior of the Honey Gourami. This fish can actually breath air as well as take oxygen from the water. The Honey Gourami has lung-like organs in addition to standard fish gills. Ambrose Jearld presented the results of this research for his doctoral dissertation in 1975.

While still enrolled in his final year of graduate studies, Ambrose began another job. He worked nearly full-time at the Techrad Company at a site not far from Stillwater while he finished the work on his dissertation. In a sense, this work was similar to his master's project because it involved a fish census in the waters of the Arkansas River. The particular emphasis was on potential water pollution problems and the possible effects on fish populations.

Career Highlights

In the fall of 1975, Dr. Jearld moved back East to take a position on the faculty at Lincoln University outside Philadelphia, Pennsylvania. He taught the usual undergraduate courses in biology but was given other challenging responsibilities as well. For example, Dr. Jearld was put in charge of developing a new program of biological studies for first-year students. The idea was to emphasize independent study so the student could set his or her own pace. A large set of new instructional materials, such as audio and video presentations, had to be created to support this program. In addition, Dr. Jearld became involved with the University Cluster Program. The purpose of this program was to establish productive relationships with regional business and industrial companies. Specific actions included arrangements for student internships and special scholarship grants from private sources.

In the summer of 1976, Dr. Jearld was again involved in field biology. This time the site was San Francisco Bay, and the key animal was the anchovy. Of particular concern was the prospect that industrial waste—especially waste that contains copper—was being dumped in the Bay and harming the anchovies. Dr. Jearld was again out on the water collecting samples of fish, fish eggs, and fish embryos. Captured fish were placed in tanks at the Lawrence Livermore Laboratory, a part of the University of California at Berkeley. Small amounts of copper were dissolved in the water of the tanks, and the fish were tested to determine their resistance to this type of pollution.

The next summer, Dr. Jearld worked at a new site with a new animal. The site was the wetlands on the coast of New Jersey. The animal was the grass shrimp, and the sponsoring organization was the U.S. National Fisheries Service. Again, the underlying problem was environmental pollution.

In the fall, Dr. Jearld began teaching at Howard University in Washington, D.C. For a year, he was the typical assistant professor. He taught classes, developed new courses, and pursued his own research on the impact of pollution on fish populations. He happily renewed his acquaintance with the Smithsonian Institution and introduced his students to the Museum of Natural History.

The summer of 1978, Dr. Jearld made a fateful decision. He accepted a summer appointment as a research biologist at the Northeast Fisheries Center in Woods Hole, Massachusetts. Dr. Jearld soon realized that Woods Hole was a place where his career could thrive. The atmosphere is mentally stimulating, and advanced research is always underway. Indeed, famous biologists and other scientists gather there every year. Dr. Jearld decided that he wanted to stay at Woods Hole past the summer months.

He took the job of chief of fishery and biological investigation at the National Marine Fisheries Service. His duties included managing the research of other professional biologists as well as planning his own studies. Much of the work of the Fisheries Service is done with college students and faculty people. The management of such programs is difficult since the students are involved for relatively short periods of time. However, Dr. Jearld found that these arrangements also provided opportunities to conduct outreach efforts. He was able to support minority hiring programs and the training of minority

scientists and engineers. This was a part of the job that Dr. Jearld particularly enjoyed.

After seven years in his original job, Dr. Jearld was promoted to be chief of research planning and evaluation. He became the regional coordinator of all fisheries research in the northeast region of the country.

Dr. Jearld receives information from researchers and those who have responsibilities for basic operations in the fishing industry. He also works with people in state and national organizations which protect the fish from environmental hazards and overfishing. He has received many awards for his work, including the Distinguished Alumnus Award from the University of Maryland Eastern Shore in 1995.

If you like to eat seafood from time to time, it is good to know that your future menu is in the hands of Dr. Jearld and his associates. They help maintain the supplies of cod, flounder, and shad that are shipped from the Atlantic fishing grounds to your dinner table.

Mae C. Jemison

Born: October 17, 1956, in Decatur, Alabama

Status: Teaching Fellow, Dartmouth University, Hanover, New Hampshire

Education:

Bachelor of Science degree, Stanford University, Palo Alto, California, 1977

Doctor of Medicine degree, Cornell University Medical School, New York, New York, 1981

Research Area: Physiology

Early Years

Mae Jemison was only three years old when her family moved from Decatur, Alabama, to Chicago, Illinois, where her father went to work as the maintenance supervisor for the United Charities of Chicago and as an independent contractor in roofing and carpentry. Mae's mother took a job at the Beethoven Elementary School in Chicago and taught there for over 20 years.

From a very early age, Mae Jemison wanted to know about all areas of learning from science to dance and the arts. While still in grade school, she became fascinated with the idea of space exploration, and she read all the astronomy books she could find. Part of her interest in space travel came from the adventure fantasies all children have; however, another part of her interest was linked to the idea of outer space as a source of new knowledge.

During these early years, Mae's father took her along on hunting and fishing expeditions, which gave her confidence in her ability to do anything she wanted to do. He also welcomed her into his work place, where she learned carpentry and other construction skills. Later, Mae used these skills to build equipment for her school science projects. Her uncle Lewis was also supportive. When Mae was only six or seven years old, he tutored her in the fundamental scientific ideas,

convincing her that she could understand basic science, even at her young age.

Mae was only 16 when she graduated from Morgan Park High School in 1973. She had received excellent grades and high scores on college aptitude tests and, therefore, decided to submit applications for several scholarships. In the spring of 1973, AT&T Bell Laboratories awarded her a National Achievement Scholarship. She also received an offer of a partial scholarship from the Massachusetts Institute of Technology (MIT). When Mae talked to the MIT admissions people, however, they proposed to reduce their portion of the funding because of her scholarship from Bell Labs. They said any lack of money could be made up by Mae's participation in their work-study program. Ada Jemison, Mae's older sister, questioned the wisdom of MIT's proposal because she knew that the work-study program would reduce Mae's time for studying. Mae agreed. She was certain that there were other good schools where administrators would work out a better financial arrangement and would also provide a more accepting and collegiate atmosphere. Mae chose Stanford University in Palo Alto, California, because of her strong interests in the arts, sciences, and social sciences. She wished to expand her knowledge in all of these areas, and Stanford had the range of programs to allow her to do so.

Higher Education

Mae's welcome to Stanford went beyond the formal and official. As soon as she arrived at school, she was met by her new roommate, Janet Waggoner. They became lifelong friends. However, some problems did arise. The difficulties that Mae Jemison met at Stanford came mainly from some of the less progressive members of the engineering faculty. They did not demonstrate obvious disrespect, but they made it clear that they thought an African American woman engineer was an outrageous idea.

Jemison determined to use the emotional energy generated by this disrespect in a positive way. She began working on independent research projects under the modest supervision of some of the more sympathetic professors. She widened her scope of knowledge, as she had hoped she could, by taking a separate major in African studies through the political science department. She also made contact with the people in drama, music, and dance both within the university and in the local community. Consequently, in her senior year, she scripted, produced, directed, and performed a dance program with a modern jazz theme that she called *Out of Shadows*. Jemison was particularly pleased with this full-fledged production because she realized that the time and opportunity for this type of endeavor might never come again.

Indeed, some demanding commitments were already on the horizon. An old friend of Jemison's, Sam Denard, was a graduate student at Stanford when Mae was in her last year. Sam had applied to the National Aeronautics and Space Administration (NASA) to train as a mission specialist and had been accepted. He was full of enthusiasm and suggested that Jemison apply immediately for the same kind of position. Jemison was encouraged by the fact that NASA was fulfilling its promises to recruit African Americans and women into the space program. However, Jemison was committed to completing her education program before taking on the overpowering commitment that the space program would require. Consequently, she followed her plan to enter Cornell University Medical School as soon as she completed her undergraduate degree.

Mae Jemison graduated from Stanford in 1977 with a double degree in chemical engineering and African studies and immediately enrolled in Cornell University Medical School in New York City. She hoped to conduct biomedical engineering research in a developing country such as Cuba or Cambo-

dia and was given that chance during one of her early semesters in medical school. The International Traveler's Institute for Health Studies sponsored Jemison to spend time studying the problems of health care delivery in the remote areas of Kenya, Africa. The lessons she had learned in her African studies program and her ability to speak some Swahili were put to good use.

Career Highlights

In 1981, Mae Jemison graduated from Cornell Medical School. She did her internship at the University of Southern California Medical Center in Los Angeles, and after completing this training, she worked briefly in Los Angeles as a doctor for a health maintenance organization. She then went back to Africa as a Peace Corps physician—this time to Sierra Leone in eastern African. Her work actually spread over several countries in the region because she tended Peace Corps volunteers and other Americans under the auspices of the U.S. Embassy. Dr. Jemison had been placed in charge of a major medical practice that included the management of all medical supplies and materials, patient education, prevention programs, and research.

Dr. Jemison returned to the United States in 1985 and joined another health maintenance organization in southern California. In a short time, she felt ready to make the serious step of applying for astronaut training. Even the news of the *Challenger* tragedy in January 1986 did not alter her ambition. Dr. Jemison applied to and was accepted into the program in 1987.

The training period lasted about a year, but the analysis of the *Challenger* accident and the testing of new procedures caused many mission delays. Finally, Dr. Jemison was scheduled to conduct the biological research activities for the *Endeavor* mission—the fiftieth shuttle flight. This flight would be significant because the crew would conduct studies concerning the proposed orbital space station. The Japanese government had decided to provide part of the money to build and operate the space station, and they sent their own astronaut to gain firsthand information from these studies. Therefore, the mission not only put the first African American woman but also the first Japanese in space.

When the day arrived for the shuttle launch, large numbers of media representatives appeared to witness an African American woman become an operational astronaut. Dr. Jemison was not always pleased with the attention she received, and she looked forward to the day when such events would be commonplace.

Early in the morning of September 11, 1992, the *Endeavor* lifted off successfully. Once in orbit, the crew was divided into two teams. The Red Team included the Japanese astronaut and undertook projects related to the space station. These studies had top priority as a courtesy to the Japanese government. Other studies conducted by the Red Team concerned the development of chemical crystals in a weightless environment and the effect of weightlessness on certain pieces of equipment. The Blue Team, led by Dr. Jemison, was mainly concerned with biological research. One project was directed at testing various ways to prevent harmful changes in the circulation of blood under weightless conditions. Another experiment determined whether normal biological processes, such as fertilization of frog eggs and growth of frog embryos, would proceed successfully in space. The Blue Team also tested methods to control or prevent space sickness that comes from the disorientation of weightlessness. Finally, the team was responsible for broadcasting lessons down to earthbound classrooms in the United States.

After seven days in space, the shuttle made a dramatic landing. A few days later, the city of Chicago organized a major celebration in honor of their hometown heroine. Emotions ran particularly high when Dr. Jemison visited her beloved Morgan Park High School. She told the students how they must resist being stereotyped—they must believe that they can qualify for any job and can function in any position in society. When she finished her talk to the student assembly, she joined the Morgan Park cheerleaders in a spontaneous cheer.

In the weeks following the *Endeavor* mission, Dr. Jemison did some serious thinking about her future goals. She knew that most of the former astronauts remained at NASA and were promoted to senior technical or administrative positions, but her interests were in the fields of scientific research and education. Therefore, in 1993, after she resigned from NASA and the shuttle program, she returned to university life. Now, at Dartmouth University, she continues to define her own challenges.

Frederick M. Jones

Born: May 17, 1893, in Covington, Kentucky

Status: Died, April 15, 1961, in Minneapolis, Minnesota

Education:
Completed sixth grade in Covington, Kentucky

Research Area: Mechanical Engineering

Early Years

When Fred Jones was only a few months old, his mother packed her bags and left her husband and her new baby. After that, Fred and his father, John Jones, lived on the edge of poverty. John was able to get temporary jobs in Covington and in Cincinnati, Ohio, just

After his father's death, Fred continued to live at the rectory. However, by the age of 10, Fred was becoming tired of being a servant and thought that school had become repetitious. He had learned to read and could do some algebra. He liked to learn but thought he could discover more things on his own.

At this time, automobiles were gaining in popularity. When wealthy parishioners arrived at church in their luxury vehicles, Fred rushed to help their drivers clean and polish the cars. He became fascinated with cars and cut his school classes to spend time at a local garage, watching the mechanics and handing them their tools. At age 11, he dropped out of school, ran away from the rectory, and found a job as a mechanic's helper in Cincinnati, Ohio.

At first, his new life was difficult. Fred worked at other jobs in addition to the one at the garage. He worked as a pin setter in a bowling alley and as a janitor in a grocery store and a pool hall. Some of his earnings were used to buy books and magazines about cars and other mechanical devices. In this way, Fred taught himself how to be an automotive technician. When he was only 14, he was skilled enough to be hired as a full-time mechanic. At 15, Fred was made foreman of the team of auto mechanics at the garage.

The owner of the garage built and drove racing cars. Fred became interested in auto racing and helped build the cars. He also wanted to be a race car driver, but the owner thought he was too young. Fred strongly disagreed. During his working hours, the young man began going to the racetrack to learn about race car driving. This led to a dispute with the owner of the garage. At age 19, Fred was fired and went on the road.

His first stop was St. Louis, Missouri, where he got a job on a Mississippi steamboat as a boiler tender. He saw little of the river because most of his time was spent shoveling

across the Ohio River. However, it was very difficult to work and care for a baby. The two stayed in one rooming house after another, and John paid the landladies to look after his child. In this kind of life, Fred grew up fast.

In spite of Fred's family problems, it was soon evident that the boy had unusual abilities. When he was just five years old, he used small tools to take a watch apart and used mechanic's tools to take apart a wagon. His father was convinced that the boy needed a better chance in life and began to look for a foster home for his son. In those days, there were no orphanages for Black children in southern Ohio or north-central Kentucky. John Jones, therefore, turned to the Catholic Church for guidance. A kindly priest, Father Ryan, gave Fred a place to live in the rectory of his church in Covington. The boy attended the parish elementary school and worked for his keep. He helped the cook, washed dishes, and scrubbed floors. When he was a bit older, he mowed the lawn in summer, and in the winter, he shoveled coal into the furnace and snow off the sidewalks. When Fred was nine years old, the parish priest told him that his father had died. Now, he was truly an orphan.

coal into the steam boiler. The paddlewheel steamer was mainly used for vacation cruises, and it did not operate during the winter months. Therefore, Fred was soon looking for another job. Since he couldn't find one, he became a "bum," hopping freight trains from one town to another. Fred took whatever work he could find, often going hungry.

In 1915, when he was 23 years old, he found a job as a janitor and general handyman in a hotel in Minneapolis, Minnesota. The owner of the hotel was Walter Hill, a member of the family that owned a large share of the Great Northern Railroad. Mr. Hill recognized that Fred was an exceptionally good worker and offered him a permanent job on his 30,000 acre farm in northern Minnesota.

Higher Education

Fred Jones had no formal education beyond the sixth grade. However, as a mechanic on Mr. Hill's large farm, Jones received firsthand experience by repairing many types of equipment. Now that he had more stability in his life, he began to take correspondence courses in electrical engineering. Jones soon learned the basic principles of electrical circuitry and electric motors.

Career Highlights

In 1915, Walter Hill sold his large farm. Once again, Fred Jones was out of a job. However, he was well known in the nearby town of Hallock, Minnesota, and quickly found work as an auto mechanic. At the garage, he began to design and build snowmobiles that ran on skis and used an aircraft propeller for propulsion.

When the United States entered World War I in 1917, Fred was 24 years old and had been on his own for 13 years. He was certain that he could learn more in the army than in a small town garage, and he joined the service.

After a brief basic training, he was sent to France and was assigned as an orderly to a front-line division, but since he already had a reputation as an excellent mechanic, the top officers soon asked him to rewire the whole divisional base camp. When he had successfully finished that job, other camp commanders wanted his help. He was asked to maintain the telephone and telegraph systems near the front. Jones repaired the X-ray machine at the base hospital and served as an auto mechanic for the trucks and motorcycles used by the division. Before many months had passed, he was promoted to the rank of sergeant—about as high as a Black person could get in the army in those days. In his spare time, he organized classes to teach other soldiers about electrical circuitry.

When Fred Jones returned to Hallock, Minnesota, after his discharge from the army, he wanted to be his own boss. He used his savings to found a local radio station. The station was very successful, partly due to Jones's improvements to the microphones used in the studio. Because of his inventiveness, the amount of static was reduced, and the clarity of the sound was increased. Indeed, his station had better sound quality than most radio stations in the big cities.

People began to realize that Fred Jones was exceptionally talented. They asked for his help with their mechanical problems. In the early 1920s, a local medical doctor was unhappy that the X-ray machine at the local hospital was too large and bulky to be transported. There was no way to get an X-ray picture without bringing the patient to the hospital. The doctor wanted to know if Mr. Jones could design a portable X-ray machine. After studying the machine at the hospital, Fred Jones built a transportable machine that actually made better images than the larger one.

About this same time, Fred again became interested in racing cars. He designed a very fast car, and in 1925, he was invited to Chicago by the International Motor Racing Association. He drove the car himself. Unfortunately, it crashed during a race and, thus, ended Fred Jones's racing career.

As the 1920s came to a close, sound movies began to replace the silent movies. Many theater owners found themselves in financial trouble trying to keep current with the changing technology. The theater owner in Hallock could not afford to buy the equipment that coordinated the sound with the picture. He turned instead to Fred Jones. Indeed, Mr. Jones was able to develop several successful adaptations of the motion picture equipment. As the production methods changed in Hollywood, the local theater owner's equipment was always up-to-date. Fred Jones's reputation soon spread throughout the region.

In 1930, he was invited to become an employee of the Ultraphone Sound Systems Company in Minneapolis. His good contacts with theater owners and operators throughout the region alerted him to many new technical problems and opportunities. For example, owners were annoyed when their patrons had to stand in long lines to wait for their tickets and change. Fred Jones saw the opportunity and invented equipment that would automatically—by the use of buttons—dispense both the proper tickets and the correct change. This was Fred Jones's first major patent.

The work on his next important patent began in an interesting manner. As the story goes, Fred's boss was once entangled in an argument with two associates. One was a long-haul trucker, and the other did air conditioning for moving picture houses. Fred's boss, Joseph Numero, hinted that he knew an inventor who could solve the problem of food spoiling as it was transported over long distances. Both his associates were skeptical. The air conditioning man could not imagine a refrigerator that was light enough, small enough, rugged enough, and efficient enough to keep the food cold as the truck bounced along the roads.

Fred Jones went to work on the problem. By 1935, after much study and some design failures, he had a working model. Again, he applied for patents. This time, the invention had so much potential that Joseph Numero suggested he and Fred Jones, as partners, form a new, separate company. Numero would provide the money and business experience, and Jones would provide the technical expertise and inventive imagination. The company, called the U.S. Thermo Control Company, was a success from the outset.

After World War II broke out in 1939, there were many needs for advanced refrigeration technology. Fred Jones and his new company responded by inventing ways to preserve blood and blood plasma for use under battlefield conditions. He also developed new, lightweight refrigerators for food storage at positions near the front lines. In 1944, Fred Jones was elected to membership in the American Society of Refrigeration Engineers—an honor usually reserved for people with advanced degrees in engineering. After the war, he served as a regular consultant to the Department of Defense and the National Bureau of Standards.

During his career, Fred Jones was granted 61 patents. His inventions have saved producers and transporters of perishable materials millions and millions of dollars. Mr. Jones's inventions have also changed the foods that people eat. Refrigerated trucks and boxcars allow fresh food to be shipped to distant markets—in all seasons of the year.

Percy Lavon Julian

Born: April 11, 1899, in Montgomery, Alabama

Status: Died April 19, 1975, at Oak Park, Illinois

Education:

Bachelor of Arts degree, DePauw University, Greencastle, Indiana, 1920

Master of Arts degree, Harvard University, Cambridge, Massachusetts, 1923

Doctor of Philosophy degree, the University of Vienna, Vienna, Austria, 1931

Research Area: Organic Chemistry

Early Years

Percy Julian's father, James Julian, was a railway mail clerk with a great love for reading, mathematics, philosophy, and education. It was important to him and his wife that their six children go to college, and they made many financial sacrifices to make sure their children were given that chance to succeed.

In the early years of this century, the nearest public high school for Black children who lived in Montgomery, Alabama, was in Birmingham, Alabama, 90 miles away. So, when Percy, who lived in Montgomery, was ready for high school, the only available option was the local, privately-supported State Normal School for Negroes. This school had been established to prepare young people for teaching positions in segregated elementary schools. Percy had hoped that his high school courses would give him a broad background in science, but he soon found that the science curriculum—and, indeed the entire curriculum—was very limited. Even after completing the full program of study, Percy was not really ready for college, but he applied to Depauw University in Greencastle, Indiana, anyway, and he was accepted.

Higher Education

The exact conditions of Percy Julian's admission to DePauw are not known. His status was called "sub-freshman," and he was required to take make-up courses at a nearby high school in addition to his college course work. Not only did he have to do the extra course work, but he also had to work each day to support himself.

This complicated schedule should have delayed his progress, but it did not. Julian graduated with a degree in chemistry from DePauw in 1920, at the top of his class and in the prescribed four years. Although he had fulfilled his childhood ambition to become a scientist, he knew that he needed more schooling to become a professional chemist. However, he wasn't accepted into Harvard University's graduate program as he had hoped, so after graduation, he accepted a teaching position at Fisk University in Nashville, Tennessee.

In 1923, after two years at Fisk, Percy Julian applied again and was accepted into Harvard. Not only was he admitted, he was also given an Austin Fellowship to help pay

It took him just one year to earn a master's degree in chemistry—again with top grades—after which he expected a good university to offer him a faculty position. Once again, he was disappointed. Harvard did encourage him to some degree. They gave him a position as a research assistant to Professor E. P. Kohler, one of the most widely known chemists of that time. Although Percy Julian would have preferred to work on his doctorate and teach students, the research job turned out to be a blessing in disguise. It provided Julian with the opportunity to do his first serious research on complicated, carbon-based molecules.

The research apprenticeship at Harvard lasted for three years. In 1926, Julian was invited to West Virginia State College—a school with a predominantly Black student body—as a full professor of chemistry. Then, after one year, he went on to Howard University in Washington, D.C., to become the head of the chemistry department.

In 1929, Percy Julian received his first really big break. The General Education Board of the Rockefeller Foundation offered Julian a scholarship for doctoral studies at the school of his choice. He chose the University of Vienna in Austria for two reasons. He saw Europe as a place less troubled by racial prejudice than the United States. Also, there was a strong tradition among American science students to spend time at one of central Europe's great institutions of higher learning.

In some ways, the two years in Vienna must have seemed a release to Julian. As a Rockefeller scholar, he actually had more money than most of the other advanced students at the Chemische Institut. Indeed, he had brought laboratory equipment from the United States with which the Austrian students were unacquainted. There were many cultural benefits for Julian as well. He was able to attend the opera and other entertainments that most students could not afford. He became very proficient in the local version of the German language and hosted parties, for which he provided the piano music. In short, he became a celebrity in the circle of university intellectuals that lived in Vienna at that time.

The scientific training was even better than the social life. Julian's advisor was Professor Ernst Späth, a notoriously domineering individual. In spite of this haughty attitude, strong mutual respect grew between student and teacher. Years later, after the end of World War II, Julian was notified that Späth had died. The Austrian scientist had lost everything because of the war and had left no money. Julian returned to Vienna, paid for Späth's funeral, and commissioned a portrait bust of Späth, which is still displayed in the foyer of the Chemische Institut.

Späth's main scientific interest was the chemistry of natural products. He was especially interested in material from plants that are biologically active. For example, he was interested in the chemical nicotine, a powerful poison in the family of compounds called alkaloids, which is a product of tobacco plants. Other alkaloids, such as ephedrine and caffeine, also interested Späth. Caffeine comes from the coffee plant, and ephedrine comes from several plant sources. It is a chemical similar to the natural human hormone, adrenaline, that is released when a person is frightened. Späth directed Percy Julian's attention to the soybean and the Calabar bean as sources of alkaloid compounds, namely eserine. Eserine is useful in medicine because when applied as drops to the eye, it relieves symptoms of glaucoma, a disease that can cause pressure within the eyeball. Julian's dissertation identified the molecular structure of eserine—a necessary step toward the artificial production of the compound.

Career Highlights

In 1931, Dr. Julian passed his final examinations and received his doctoral degree from Vienna. He then returned immediately to Howard University to continue his commitment to the expansion of their science program. Research on the artificial production of eserine was also important to Dr. Julian. He knew that the project would be difficult, and he convinced the officials at Howard to hire two of his Vienna classmates as research associates. Meanwhile, he designed a new chemistry building and supervised the beginning stages of the construction. He also continued to work on further improvements in the chemistry curriculum.

However, Dr. Julian's plans for chemical research and instructional development were not implemented. Apparently, the Howard officials decided the costs of Dr. Julian's improvements were too expensive. Consequently, there was a painful parting, and Dr. Julian's hopes of synthesizing the compound eserine had to be put aside. Rescue came from his former mentors at DePauw University. By convincing some wealthy donors of the importance of Dr. Julian's research, Professor Blanchard, a colleague from DePauw, was able to raise funding for the project. This money paid the salary of Dr. Julian and one of his Viennese colleagues, Dr. Josef Pikl.

The project became a race with time because money was available for only two years. During that period, Drs. Julian and Pikl had defined two of the main ingredients needed to make eserine but had not quite finished their research on the manufacture of the synthetic material. The project was rescued a second time by a large donation from the Rosenwald Fund. Confident that his job was secure, Dr. Julian and Anna Johnson of Baltimore, Maryland, were married. She, too, was a scholar and had received her doctorate in sociology from the University of Pennsylvania in 1937.

Only one more year was needed to produce the artificial eserine; however, there were immediate doubts about the validity of the process. Researchers in England, working under the direction of a famous chemist, Dr. Robert Robinson, reported a very different procedure for making eserine. The reports seemed to indicate that the Julian/Pikl method was incorrect. Robinson was a powerful voice in the community of chemists, and Dr. Julian was warned not to challenge the findings. However, Percy Julian was confident of his findings and publicly stated that he could prove his procedure was correct and that Robinson's was wrong. In February of 1935, the crucial test of matching the artificial eserine with the natural compound—taken from the Calabar bean—was performed in the laboratory. It showed conclusively that the work done at DePauw—and led by Dr. Julian—was valid.

If Dr. Julian had lost, he would have been disgraced and might have been forced to leave the profession of chemistry altogether. However, the challenge had been so dramatic that when the DePauw scientists had won, the news quickly spread around the world. Dr. Julian's rewards for his victory, however, were a long time in coming. The faculty and the president of DePauw University, G. Bromley Oxnam, attempted to give Dr. Julian a full professorship, but the board of trustees was not ready for such a progressive act. They declined to approve the appointment, as did the directors at the University of Minnesota, where a similar opening was available. Dr. Julian was then offered a job as a senior researcher at the Institute for Paper Chemistry in Appleton, Wisconsin, but he could not accept it because a racist local ordinance prevented him from living in Appleton.

Finally, Dr. Percy Julian was offered an excellent opportunity by the Glidden Company. W. J. O'Brien, a vice president at Glidden, offered Dr. Julian the directorships of Glidden's soybean products division, its fine chemicals division, and the research division of Durkee Famous Foods, a Glidden subsidiary. This was the first time an African American had been given a supervisory position over large teams of scientists and engineers of all ethnic backgrounds.

The expectations of those who backed this appointment were quickly fulfilled. New ideas and discoveries came swiftly—ranging from new food supplements derived from soybeans to a fire-fighting foam that could be used on gasoline or oil fires. Even so, the best was yet to come. Dr. Julian's experience with soybeans in Austria led him to develop new ways of extracting the raw materials for progesterone and testosterone, key female and male hormones, respectively. Further work with progesterone by other scientists led eventually to the development of the birth control pill.

In 1948, research from the Mayo Clinic in Minnesota showed that synthetic cortisone was useful in combating the inflammation symptoms of arthritis. This material was, however, far too costly for most patients. A cheaper way of making the artificial version was badly needed. Dr. Julian discovered that by combining soybean oil with natural cortisone, he could greatly increase the amount of artificial cortisone. What had cost hundreds of dollars per dose could now be purchased for pennies a dose.

By 1950, Dr. Julian's position at Glidden allowed him to buy a new home in Oak Park, Illinois, just outside of Chicago. He was the first African American to move into this upper-middle class neighborhood. Soon after they were settled, when the members of the Julian family were away from home, an arsonist attacked the house and tried to burn it down. Neighbors quickly spotted the fire and called the local fire department in time to prevent major damage. A year later, a bomb was thrown from a passing car while the Julian's two children were in the house. No one was injured, but this act aroused the neighbors to publicly denounce such violence. Now, years later, the town of Oak Park celebrates Dr. Julian's birthday as a civic holiday.

In 1953, Dr. Julian left Glidden to found his own company. This venture was also a success, mainly because Dr. Julian discovered new ways of making drugs from common plants like the Mexican sweet potato. In 1961, he sold the company for over $2 million. Now that he had decreased his work load, he was able to devote more of his time to civic affairs, such as the revitalization of the Legal Defense and Educational Fund in Chicago. This organization played a key role in the Civil Rights movement over the succeeding years.

As a scholar and scientist, Dr. Julian's fame is assured by his authorship of over 100 patents and more than 50 major scientific reports, and in 1960, he was elected to the National Academy of Sciences in Washington, D.C. Dr. Julian also received 19 honorary doctorates and an appointment to the board of trustees at Depauw University—the body that had once rejected his faculty appointment. Eighteen years after his death, he was honored by the U.S. Postal Service. A first-class stamp, bearing the portrait of Dr. Percy Julian, was issued in 1993. Dr. Julian has joined a select group of African Americans to be honored in this way. Some of the honorees include Sojourner Truth, Jackie Robinson, and Martin Luther King, Jr.—fitting company for a courageous and pioneering scientist.

Ernest Everett Just

Born: August 14, 1883, in Charleston, South Carolina

Status: Died, October 27, 1941, in Washington, D.C.

Education:

Bachelor of Arts degree, Dartmouth College, Hanover, New Hampshire, 1907

Doctor of Philosophy degree, University of Chicago, Chicago, Illinois, 1916

Research Area: Marine Biology

Early Years

Ernest Just was the third child of Charles and Mary Just. When he was born, his father was a construction worker at the Charleston, South Carolina, docks, and his mother worked as a seamstress. Tragedy struck the young family before Ernest was a year old. His older brother and sister both died. For a short time, Ernest was the only child in the family. Then, after two years had passed, his mother gave birth to a boy, who was named Hunter. The next year, Inez, the last of the children, was born.

Unfortunately, problems continued for the Just family. When Earnest was four years old, his grandfather died. He had lived with the Justs and helped support the family. The boy had been very close to him. A few months later, an even greater tragedy occurred when Ernest's father died. Earnest's mother suddenly became the sole support of the family.

At first, she taught in a small grade school for African American children in Charleston. In the summers, she did backbreaking work as a laborer at a phosphate mine on nearby James Island. While working on the island, she saw plenty of vacant land that could be made into small farms at low cost. She soon persuaded a group of African American families to move from Charleston to the island. There, they founded a new town called Maryville, in her honor. Maryville was the first town in South Carolina to be governed entirely by African Americans.

Mary Just managed Maryville's business and ran their school. For a time, all went well. Then, when Ernest was six years old, he became very ill with typhoid fever, which affected his ability to learn and retain information. Fortunately, a few months after recovering from the fever, his ability to learn came back.

Mary Just wanted Ernest to follow her example and become a teacher. She liked working with students and thought that Ernest would also enjoy the profession. She scraped up enough money to send Ernest to an all-Black boarding school in Orangeburg, South Carolina, when he was 13 years old. This school taught trade skills, such as brick laying and carpentry, to young African American boys, and it also prepared some of the young people to teach in all-Black grade schools.

Ernest graduated from the boarding school when he was 16 years old. He had completed his teacher preparation studies in only three years and was qualified to teach in a grade school. However, both Ernest and his mother thought he was too young to begin his teaching career. They agreed that he should pursue further training.

Mary Just had read about a school in New Hampshire called the Kimball Union Academy that was supported by an organization called the Christian Endeavor World Unity Group. This school offered scholarships for exceptional students. Mary wrote to them about her son and asked that he be considered for one of the scholarships. Before the family had received a reply, Ernest set out to visit the school.

The family had no money for his transportation, so Ernest had to find work along the way. Initially, he found a job on a small ship sailing from Charleston to New York. He received $5 as his total salary when he left the ship in New York City, and that was not enough to pay his fare to New Hampshire. So he took a job as a cook in a New York City restaurant, and after working there for just a month, he had enough money to buy a train ticket to New Hampshire.

When he arrived at Kimball Union Academy, Ernest discovered that he had been awarded a scholarship and that he could begin his studies immediately. He realized that he had been very fortunate, and this inspired him to work especially hard on his studies. He did so well that he was able to complete the four-year program in only three years. Ernest, the only African American student in the school, graduated in 1903 with the highest grades in his class. Unfortunately, his mother passed away during his second year at the academy and did not see him graduate.

Higher Education

Because of his excellent work at Kimball Union, Ernest Just was admitted to Dartmouth College in Hanover, New Hampshire, and began his studies in the fall of 1903. Just first studied the history of ancient peoples and took languages such as Latin and Greek. However, in his second year, he became more interested in the field of science. Biology, the study of plants and animals, became his favorite subject. He had acquired this interest from his early nature studies on James Island. Just was inspired and helped in this interest by his biology teacher, William Patten.

Ernest Just received the first of many awards when he was in his third year of study at Dartmouth College. He was named as a Rufus Choate Scholar, the highest award for a Dartmouth student.

He graduated first in his class from Dartmouth in 1907 and became a member of the famous honorary society, Phi Beta Kappa.

Career Highlights

After graduation, Just found a job teaching at Howard University in Washington, D.C. At first, he did not teach biology. His job was teaching English composition to new students. Even though Just considered this job to be a temporary arrangement, he wanted to do his best. While he was there, Just organized the first student drama group at Howard. The creation of the student group led, a few years later, to the founding of Howard University's new drama department.

Meanwhile, other changes were being put in place by Howard University's forceful new president, Wilbur P. Thirkield. Dr. Thirkield wanted to modernize all departments of the university. This modernization included a strong emphasis on the natural sciences. Thirkield needed someone to lead the development of a degree program in biology, and in 1908, after teaching one year at Howard,

Just was made head of the biology department.

He soon found that the demands of this new position left little time for his own research. Fortunately, his friend and former professor at Dartmouth, William Patten, introduced Ernest Just to Frank R. Lillie. Professor Lillie was the head of the biology department at the University of Chicago. He was also the chief of the Marine Biological Laboratory at Woods Hole, Massachusetts. Woods Hole, as it is known to scientists, is a famous research center. There, top biologists from around the world spend their summers doing research and exchanging scientific ideas.

Dr. Lillie invited Ernest Just to spend the summer of 1909 at Woods Hole as his research assistant. This arrangement had an extra incentive for Just. At Woods Hole, he could earn course credit for a graduate-level degree at the University of Chicago without actually moving to Chicago. In 1912, Just published his first research report based on his studies at Woods Hole. It described the first few minutes in the life of a sandworm. During his lifetime, he continued to study and write about the first moments of life of many marine animals.

Later that same year, Ernest Just married Ethel Highwarden, a young language instructor at Howard University. They had three children: Margaret, Maribel, and Highwarden.

Each summer, Just would travel to Woods Hole and do research projects with Professor Lillie. Soon, Lillie suggested that Ernest complete his degree work in biology. In 1915, Just took a leave of absence from Howard University to attend advanced courses on the campus of the University of Chicago. The next year, he received his doctor of philosophy degree from Chicago. Afterwards, he continued to teach at Howard University and to do research work at Woods Hole.

Even before he finished his studies at the University of Chicago, many people recognized Ernest Just as an outstanding young scientist. In 1915, he was awarded the Spingarn Medal by the National Association for the Advancement of Colored People (NAACP) for his work in biology.

After obtaining this honor and earning his advanced degree, Dr. Just hoped to be asked to join the faculty of a top university in the United States. He received some offers but none that fit his ambitions. Dr. Just had also hoped to arrange a steady income that did not require him to teach all the time. He wanted to spend more of his time doing research. He was able to obtain research grants from organizations such as the National Research Council, the General Education Board, and the Carnegie Corporation, but these grants provided support only for short periods of time, requiring Dr. Just to teach at Howard University for part of each year. One of his grants, from the Julius Rosenwald Fund, was intended to encourage Dr. Just and the officials at Howard University to continue the expansion of their biology program. In particular, Mr. Rosenwald wanted Howard to establish graduate-level instruction in the sciences.

Meanwhile, Dr. Just had become an internationally respected biological scientist. In particular, his work on small water creatures was judged outstanding by biologists in Germany and France. In fact, he was more respected in Europe than in his own country. Dr. Just felt that prejudice against his race was holding him back in the United States; therefore, he stopped spending his summers in Woods Hole and began to spend more and more time in Europe. In 1929, he worked at a research center in Naples, Italy. The next year, he was the first American to be invited to the Kaiser Wilhelm Institute in Berlin, Germany. He spent six months at the institute during 1930 and returned each year until 1933 when he took up residence in Germany. While he was in Germany in 1931, he met a young woman, Hedwig Schnetzler. In 1939, they were married.

After 1933, Dr. Just did most of his research work in Italy and at the Sorbonne, the famous educational and research institution in Paris. Although he was still employed by Howard University, he spent as much time as possible in Europe. In 1938, he was able to move permanently to France, and he began to think of that country as his home.

While he was living in France, his masterpiece, *The Biology of the Cell Surface*, was published in Philadelphia, Pennsylvania, in 1939. This important book summarized his life's work on small marine animals and provided new knowledge for people interested in biological research.

Unfortunately, Germany invaded France in 1940, a year after the beginning of World War II. Ernest Just was arrested by the Germans in Paris and put in prison for a short time. Since the United States was not yet at war, U.S. State Department officials were able to free Dr. Just, and he returned to the U.S. in September of 1940. Dr. Just had been very ill for many months before his arrest, and his condition worsened while he was in prison and on the trip to the United States. By the time he arrived back in the United States, he was too ill to continue his work. He died of cancer a year after his return.

Earnest Just faced and conquered many challenges throughout his life. His accomplishments show that with self-confidence, determination, and hard work, even the most ambitious goals can be realized.

James King, Jr.

Born: April 23, 1933, in Columbus, Georgia

Status: Director of Engineering and Science, Jet Propulsion Laboratory, Pasadena, California

Education:

Bachelor of Science degree, Morehouse College, Atlanta, Georgia, 1953

Master of Science degree, California Institute of Technology, Pasadena, California, 1955

Doctor of Philosophy degree, California Institute of Technology, 1958

Research Area: Physical Chemistry

Early Years

When Jim King's older sister started first grade at the age of six, she took Jim to school with her. Jim's mother used this as a method of low-cost baby-sitting. The teacher allowed some of her students' brothers and sisters to stay in the back of the classroom during the school day. The older child could continue with school work and, every once in a while, check on the younger child.

It soon became apparent to the teacher that young Jim was learning the lessons along with his older sister and the other first graders. The following year, when Jim was four, he was officially enrolled in the first grade. His older sister, now in second grade, was able to look after Jim because the first and second grades shared a room.

Jim had further opportunities to skip grades during his elementary school years. However, there were problems being younger and smaller than the other children in his classes. When his parents were offered the chance to skip Jim from fourth to sixth grade, they declined. His comparative youth was already having some bad effects on his morale. The problem became more painful when Jim reached high school, with its proms and school parties. Most of the girls in his class saw him as too young to be a suitable escort. Nevertheless, while he sometimes felt awkward and out of place, he continued to do very well in his studies. Jim graduated from his segregated high school—which did not go past the eleventh grade—in January of 1959. He was only 15 years old, at least two years younger than his classmates.

During his free time, Jim enjoyed taking apart watches and clocks to see how they worked. He convinced himself—if no one else—that he could put them back together. He was often in trouble with his father, however, because of the destroyed watches, but Mr. King felt more kindly about his son's intense curiosity when Jim won a full scholarship to Morehouse College in Atlanta, Georgia.

Higher Education

Jim King entered Morehouse College in August of 1959 when he was still only 16 years old. His studies were centered on his ambition to become a medical doctor, but that still left him time for other activities. He tried out for the football team his freshman year, even though he weighed only 175 pounds, and made the team as a center. The two guards who played on either side were very big. The left guard was 275 pounds, and the right guard was 240 pounds. He felt well protected between the two.

Playing on the football team was of major importance to King. So, when he was given the choice of majoring in chemistry or biology as a premed student, he chose chemistry because the laboratory schedule made a better match with the the football practice schedule.

Another influence that helped to change his choice of careers was his success in mathematics. His mother had helped him have a positive feeling about arithmetic when he was a small child. Now, he feared that his high school preparation in mathematics was not very good. In spite of his worries, he wanted to learn more mathematics and, therefore, enrolled in every course that was open to him. To his surprise, he did well.

In his third year of college, King took advanced courses in biology to meet the requirements for his premed program. He soon discovered he disliked dissecting animals, which was required in his comparative anatomy course. At this point, he decided that he would rather earn an advanced degree in chemistry than pursue a career in medicine.

Jim King graduated from Morehouse in 1953, just two months past his 20th birthday. Because of his record at Morehouse College, he was awarded a one-year General Education Board Scholarship by the Rockefeller Foundation and a Danforth Foundation Fellowship to complete his graduate studies.

King chose the California Institute of Technology for graduate school because of its outstanding reputation in physical chemistry. No one from Morehouse had ever gone to Cal Tech, which is known as one of the most competitive institutions in the country. In fact, some of his teachers and advisors at Morehouse were worried that King might fail in this high-stress environment. King was also worried about failure, but he felt that his youth gave him a definite advantage. He could always transfer to another institution if he did not do well at Cal Tech. Even if he waited two years to change schools, he would still be the same age as other graduates.

Of course, he did not fail. He did so well in his first year of graduate studies that the officials at Cal Tech set up a new scholarship specifically for Morehouse graduates. Consequently, another graduate of Morehouse, William Hutchinson, was enrolled at Cal Tech when King started his second year of graduate studies.

At Cal Tech, Jim King soon began to learn advanced methods of chemical research under the tutelage of Professor Norman R. Davidson. Early in his program, King's interests were focused on the chemistry of iron. In particular, he studied how an iron atom changes as it forms compounds with different quantities of oxygen. Rust is the compound that comes from the chemical marriage of iron and oxygen. However, there are two kinds of rust. Red rust is the most common. In this form, one iron atom combines with one oxygen atom. The other form of rust, which is blackish in color, is formed when two iron atoms combine with three oxygen atoms. This type of rust coats a piece of iron and prevents other rust from developing. King's first major research project dealt with how red rust transforms into black rust when placed in weak acid solutions. The report of this study was published in a major scientific magazine.

Later, under the supervision of Professors Davidson and Harlen M. McConnell, King began a series of studies focused on how metals such as iron react with complicated organic molecules found in living cells. Probably the best example of such a combination is the iron-organic compound called hemoglobin, which gives blood its red color.

In this type of research, organic molecules containing metals are placed in an apparatus that generates a strong magnetic field. The magnet is turned on and off very rapidly, and a pattern of electrical activity is created. The electrical patterns formed by the current give the researchers clues about how the molecule is constructed. Since different molecules give different patterns, scientists can also determine the identification and construction of an unknown substance. Jim King used this type of apparatus to solve some basic questions about the chemical behavior of subatomic particles. In 1958, he finished his dissertation and received his doctorate from Cal Tech.

Career Highlights

After his graduation, Dr. King accepted a position with a company called Atomics International. His first project, however, was closer to the field of physics than to chemistry. He was asked to develop a technique to determine the temperature inside an atomic reactor because no ordinary thermometer could survive in such an environment. Dr. King devised a temperature scale based on the speed at which a special gas passed through a ceramic partition. The faster the passage, the higher the temperature. The device was calibrated in the laboratory so that the specific temperature at each speed level was known. After the device was installed in the reactor, a nuclear technician could record the speed and read the temperature from a chart.

In the 1960s, Dr. King was recruited by a new company that was attempting to develop an electric automobile engine. They hoped to devise a solar-powered automobile, one that would run on electricity generated by the sun. This was an important project because gasoline was in short supply due to the Middle East oil crisis. When the energy crisis of the 1960s was over, however, the interest in solar-powered automobiles ended and Dr. King was let go.

Fortunately for Dr. King, some of his old friends at Cal Tech badly needed his help. He accepted a position with the Jet Propulsion Laboratory, a government-sponsored organization that is managed by Cal Tech. Dr. King was assigned to work on the physical chemistry of atomic hydrogen, the simplest of all elements.

While conducting his research, Dr. King developed a new way to separate the various kinds of atomic hydrogen. While hydrogen appears to have only one form, it actually has several. Tiny variations in the electrical charge and initial energy state of the hydrogen atom can make a significant difference in how the atom reacts with other elements. Being able to separate the different kinds of hydrogen led Dr. King to study the different ways that hydrogen and other gases work in the human body. In particular, the patterns of behavior of the different types of hydrogen gave Dr. King new ideas about anesthetic gases. Anesthetics are those gases used to put people or animals to sleep during surgery. Dr. King was soon able to build a whole new theory of gas anesthesia from the results of this research. In the pages of *Science*, the weekly journal of the American Association for the Advancement of Science, he described how anesthetic gases could enter the human body through the lungs by means of the small, natural level of static electricity in the molecules making up the lining of the lungs. Before Dr. King's studies, scientists had thought that the anesthetic molecules had to form new chemical compounds with the moisture in the lining of the lungs. However,

Dr. King and his colleagues showed that such compounds are not stable at body temperature. His explanation was better and simpler.

From this time forward, the chemistry of both natural and artificial gases was central to Dr. King's research. He investigated the strange electrical effects that take place when otherwise unreactive gases are bombarded by subatomic particles in a cyclotron. He studied how ethylene and acetylene are formed when ethane is bombarded by charged particles. He also showed by experimentation how unreactive gases such as xenon or helium could influence other chemical reactions, even if they did not themselves enter directly into the newly formed chemical molecules.

About that same time, Dr. King began to study gases made from carbon combined with chlorine or fluorine or combined with both gases. He showed how difficult it was to make the carbon atom give up its attachment to fluorine in particular. Years later, however, scientists have come to believe that such gases that combine carbon and chlorine *can* release chlorine and cause a decline of the stratospheric ozone shield.

By 1969, Dr. King was named manager of the physics section of the Jet Propulsion Laboratory. Then in 1974, he was transferred into government service on a sort of lend-lease arrangement. Dr. King became the director of the space shuttle environmental effects program in the Office of Manned Space Flight of the National Aeronautics and Space Administration in Washington, D.C. His knowledge of the chemistry of both natural and synthetic gases was very valuable to the government. The directors wanted to ensure that the gases produced by the space shuttle would not harm the atmosphere during either the shuttle's launching or its orbiting of the earth.

After two years in this bureaucratic position, Dr. King was ready to return to the Jet Propulsion Laboratory in California. When he returned, he managed, in sequence, several programs of research: atmospheric science, astronomy and astrophysics, and finally, general space science and its applications to practical problems. Dr. King, who was known as an excellent manager, was asked to direct the work of many different experts, such as those in astrophysics. It is a tribute to Dr. King's administrative skills that he was able to manage a group of scientist who were experts in fields Dr. King knew little about.

By the fall of 1984, Dr. King was ready to move into still more varied enterprises. Under a special arrangement with the Jet Propulsion Laboratory, he took a two-year leave of absence and returned to his home school, Morehouse College in Atlanta, Georgia. There he helped the college officials and faculty build an entirely new program of teaching and research in the area of atmospheric science. This project was aided by his extensive knowledge of the chemical reactions of natural gases found in the atmosphere and the synthetic gases that can pollute it.

When Dr. King returned to his work in Pasadena, he continued to move into more and more responsible positions. By 1988, he was the senior technical manager for the Space Science and Applications Program. In this capacity, he was supervising the expenditure of $40 million a year. Finally, in 1993, Dr. King was promoted to director of science and engineering at the laboratory. That same year, he was honored by the National Technical Association of the United States with the presentation of the Technologist of the Year Award.

In his role as director of an important division of the country's space program, Dr. King focuses on reducing the pollution that often comes with advances in technology. Scientists know that spacecraft generate some atmospheric pollution. This must be balanced against the benefits of space exploration. Dr.

King's knowledge of atmospheric science assists the space program's research in reducing the pollution inflicted by our shuttles and other space vehicles. Dr. King also volunteers his time as a member of the Scientific Committee of the Los Angeles Air Pollution Control District. When the smog in Los Angeles is finally eradicated, many believe that Dr. James King will have been a major contributor to the effort.

Flemmie P. Kittrell

Born: December 25, 1904, in Henderson, North Carolina

Status: Died, October 1, 1980, in Washington, D.C.

Education:

Bachelor of Science degree, Hampton Institute, Hampton, Virginia, 1928

Master of Science degree, Cornell University, Ithaca, New York, 1935

Doctor of Philosophy degree, Cornell University, 1940

Research Area: Nutrition

Early Years

Flemmie Kittrell was the seventh of nine children born to James L. Kittrell and Alice Mills Kittrell. Flemmie was very involved with her family as a youngster. Her mother was her best friend, and her father often read stories and poems to the family in the evening. He is also said to have praised his children for each and every one of their accomplishments.

As a student in the Henderson public schools, Flemmie enjoyed learning from the time she entered first grade. Her favorite teacher was a woman named Sally Thomas Eaton, who taught that first grade class. Flemmie was a little concerned, however, when she discovered that Sally Eaton would be her teacher again in the third grade. The child was not sure that someone who could teach first grade actually knew enough to teach a third grade class. Luckily, Sally Eaton was a good third grade teacher. Flemmie did very well all through her school years and graduated from high school with honors.

Higher Education

Flemmie Kittrell was accepted at Hampton Institute in Hampton, Virginia. Her teachers were soon impressed with her outstanding ability in home economics and general science. In fact, Professor Thomas Wyatt Turner encouraged Flemmie to consider graduate school at Cornell University in Ithaca, New York.

At first, Kittrell was not enthusiastic or particularly interested in graduate school. Even before she graduated from Hampton Institute (now University), she had accepted a teaching position at Bennett College in Greensboro, North Carolina. This position gave her the chance to increase her financial resources and to practice being on her own. When urged to continue her schooling,

Kittrell replied that she would be a stranger in a strange land up north in New York State. Furthermore, the only graduate program open to her at Cornell was in the field of nutrition, which she liked the least of all the topics related to home economics.

At that time, there was a scarcity of female graduate students and an even greater scarcity of African American graduate students at Cornell. Kittrell eventually decided to confront the challenge and attend graduate school. The fact that she was awarded an Anna Cora Smith Scholarship also helped change her mind about going north to Cornell.

As soon as she arrived at Cornell, she went to register for a dormitory room but was told that she would have to find off-campus housing in the town of Ithaca. She promptly went to the office of University President Fearon. After a brief meeting, she was given a letter—affixed with the president's official seal—to take to the dean of women. This letter directed the dean to find a place for Kittrell in the women's dormitory.

Another example of Kittrell's composure in the face of challenges occured during her oral doctoral examination. She was asked an irrelevant question about some trees on the campus that had blown down in a severe wind storm. She was tempted to give an angry reply. Wisely, she retained her composure and responded that the death of the trees was an example of poor stewardship. The trees had been planted by humans, and consequently, these humans should give the trees proper care. This was symbolic of the human tendency to start projects and later abandon them if the work became too difficult. It was a lesson in responsibility. Even the rather superior-acting professor who had posed the question was impressed with this response. Kittrell was promptly awarded her doctoral degree.

Career Highlights

Dr. Kittrell returned to Bennett College in 1940 shortly after she graduated from Cornell. However, she was soon called to her home institution, Hampton Institute, to serve as head of the department of home economics and dean of women.

The status of home economics in a university setting has always been controversial. Some see the subject matter of home economics as watered-down chemistry, biology, and psychology. Others see it as a field allied to agriculture because of the historical linkage with agricultural extension programs and the stress on nutrition. Basic agricultural extension helps farmers improve cultivation and animal husbandry, and home economics extension programs reach out to the farmers' wives to help improve homemaking. Dr. Kittrell saw home economics as a field of research where results should apply to the solution of practical problems. From this perspective, home economics is most akin to the problem-solving tradition of engineering and medicine.

Dr. Kittrell realized that trained home economists should be particularly concerned with low-income and minority families in small towns and rural areas. She knew that community and individual services were very important to these families. Indeed, research programs in support of outreach services were the guiding principle of Dr. Kittrell's career.

She saw the prospect of being able to assume leadership in this field when she was invited to join the faculty at Howard University in Washington, D.C. In 1944, she accepted the position after the university president, Dr. Mordicai Johnson, promised that the university would construct a new building dedicated exclusively to home economics. She waited for almost 20 years for that promise to be fulfilled. In the meantime, she was a leader in her field in the United States and abroad.

At Howard, she established cooperative arrangements with other departments in the university. This was good for both cost savings and politics. The home economics department began providing courses in support of the offerings of other departments, and indeed, those departments began assisting Dr. Kittrell's students. Another local accomplishment was the strengthening of her own program. Nine of Dr. Kittrell's master's degree students went on to receive doctorates at highly rated universities in the United States and Canada. Indeed, by the time Dr. Kittrell retired, Howard University offered its own doctorate in nutrition.

Probably her most important contribution was the development of the nursery school program at Howard. This school served as both a training site and a laboratory for research in human development. Her carefully controlled studies of child development were instrumental in opening the way for programs such as Head Start. In fact, her influence as a member of the executive committee for the White House Conference on Children and Youth in 1960 was critical to the creation of Head Start. This program is now recognized by all public officials as a truly successful project of social services operated by the federal government.

Dr Kittrell's international involvement in the field of nutrition began shortly after she arrived at Howard University. In December of 1946, the U.S. Department of State asked Howard to give Dr. Kittrell a leave of absence. She was invited to lead a field survey of nutritional practices and needs in the West African country of Liberia. In this country, Dr. Kittrell found widespread deficiencies in the intake of protein and vitamins. The six-month project led to recognition of a condition known as "hidden hunger," in which a person might have a full stomach but be severely malnourished. The project participants worked hard to understand and overcome this condition. They set up a series of programs to give Liberians a balanced diet of easily obtainable foods that were grown and processed in their own country.

The field survey, conducted in the bush country outside the larger cities, had some adventurous moments. Many of the rural tribespeople were not accustomed to seeing women in positions of authority. One chief was particularly upset to see a woman wearing *trousers* and accused Dr. Kittrell of being a bad woman. He quieted down when she explained that she was a "Missionary Ma." Bringing harm to a missionary is tabu in that part of the world.

The broad significance of Dr. Kittrell's study on "hidden hunger" was soon recognized by the international community. The concept was vital to nutrition specialists concerned with the improvement of health and living standards in developing countries. Dr. Kittrell allied herself with religious organizations as well as government bodies that wanted to improve these conditions, and these religious groups, particularly the Methodist Church, allowed Dr. Kittrell to voice her views to an international audience.

In 1950, the State Department sought Dr. Kittrell's help on a project in Baroda, India. The project was to create a new college-level training program for home economists. Dr. Kittrell was asked to design both facilities and research programs to study the problems of nutrition. In August of 1953, she returned to India as a Fulbright Scholar and took part in the first graduation ceremonies at the new school.

Dr. Kittrell was also in demand as a lecturer in nutrition and child development in countries across the African continent, Southeast Asia, and the Pacific Rim. At the height of the Cold War, the Soviet Union invited Dr. Kittrell to tour Russia in the interests of peaceful co-existence.

In 1962, after the Belgian Congo achieved independence, she was invited by a team of Methodist missionaries to establish new facilities for higher education in the Congo. One of their goals was to ensure that schools like the Congolese Polytechnic Institute in Leopoldville would admit women students. The creation of a College of Home Economics within the Polytechnic Institute achieved this goal, and Dr. Kittrell's expertise was needed to plan and initiate the new college.

Dr. Kittrell also designed a program for Howard University to support the recruitment of students from other countries. With financial support from many sources—public and private—she developed a series of seminars on the latest research in nutrition and child development. International leaders in these fields were invited to attend the meetings. Soon, Howard University was known as the site of worldwide home economics programs.

During her lifetime, Dr. Kittrell was awarded honorary degrees and prizes for her research and humanitarian accomplishments. The one which may have touched her the most was the creation of a scholarship in her name by the American Home Economics Association Foundation. This award was created to support outstanding minority students. As a young woman, Dr. Flemmie Kittrell had been one herself.

Wade M. Kornegay

Born: January 9, 1934, in Mount Olive, North Carolina

Status: Head, Radar Measurements Division, Lincoln Laboratory, Massachusetts Institute of Technology, Lexington, Massachusetts

Education:

Bachelor of Science degree, North Carolina Central University, Durham, North Carolina, 1956

Doctor of Philosophy degree, University of California, Berkeley, California, 1961

Research Area: Engineering Physics

Early Years

Wade Kornegay lost both his parents at an early age. His father, a tenant farmer, died first, and his mother died when he was six years old. Nine children were left orphaned. Wade, the five older children, and the three younger ones went to live with their maternal grandmother. The family lived in a small country town in North Carolina.

All the Kornegay children attended segregated schools where the teachers were interested in providing a good education for their students. Indeed, Wade wanted to learn as much as he could. To this end, he read many books. Wade also was not reluctant to reveal what he knew to anyone who would listen. His nickname at home was "Mister Know-it-all."

Although Wade liked to show off for his classmates, he was sometimes unsure of himself. When he was in the sixth grade, his teacher selected him to play the leading male role in the class operetta. Wade protested that he could not sing very well. The teacher told him that he could chant the words if he could not sing them. When performance time came, all went well and Wade sang his songs. The success of this production was a big morale booster for Wade Kornegay.

Wade was fortunate that his teachers, even at the grade school level, respected their students' ambitions and career plans. The teachers carefully explained the connection between education and a career. They described the work of scientists, mathematicians, and other educated people. The students were told that someone with a college degree was accorded respect by members of the community.

When Wade reached Carver High School, he again found teachers who encouraged their students. Unfortunately, the resources of the school were very limited. There were few science courses and no courses in advanced mathematics. Nevertheless, Wade's desire to become a scientist remained strong.

Higher Education

As soon as Wade Kornegay finished high school, he took a summer job as an attendant at a school for the mentally retarded in rural New York State. When he arrived at the school, he found the situation to be more difficult that he had expected. Indeed, Kornegay had had no prior experience in this kind of work and there were few coworkers or patients who were African American. He found that he was uncomfortable in the situation and was relieved when the summer was over.

Kornegay then enrolled at North Carolina Central University in Durham. This school had a good reputation for serving members of the African American community and was not far from his home town. University officials awarded Kornegay a two-year scholarship, and his savings from the summer job covered expenses for the first semester. He soon found a job in the college dining hall to help pay for the rest of his undergraduate education. Kornegay did exceptionally well in his studies and was elected class president in his first year.

In spite of his limited college preparation, Kornegay was adept in his major subjects—mathematics and chemistry. He also gave particular attention to broadening his horizons by taking courses in art history, music, and German.

In 1956, Wade Kornegay graduated with high honors from North Carolina Central. His study of German was soon put to practical use. He won a Fulbright fellowship and spent a year at Bonn University in the capital of the former West German Republic. Naturally, the classes were taught in German, but after a little practice, Kornegay was able to speak and understand the language. Even though he concentrated intently on his main course of study, chemical physics, he was able to travel widely in Western Europe, visiting Spain, France, Switzerland, Austria, Italy, and Yugoslavia, as well as Belgium, Holland, and England.

When he returned to the United States at the end of the summer, Wade Kornegay visited his family in North Carolina and married his childhood sweetheart, Bettie Joyce Hunter. Shortly after their wedding, the young couple took a long bus ride to the University of California at Berkeley, where Kornegay had won a Danforth Graduate Fellowship.

In the late 1950s and early 1960s, Berkeley offered a wide variety of new research projects and innovative ideas. Kornegay became interested in studying the conditions that lead to chemical reactions. One way to study the separate steps in this process is to observe how inert gases enter into reactions with other elements. Inert gases, such as argon, xenon, and krypton, must be heated to a high temperature before they will become active and form compounds with other elements. When the heat is raised to over 6,000 degrees Fahrenheit, the atoms of the inert gases begin to shed their outer ring of electrons. Under normal conditions, these electrons circle the nucleus of the atom. When some of the negatively charged electrons are driven off by the heat, the nucleus of the atom with its remaining electrons can enter into chemical reactions.

Chemists knew that after the transformation of these inert substances into active substances occurred, the formation of new molecules took place very swiftly. Kornegay was able to create conditions in the laboratory so that the heating and the subsequent chemical reactions could take place in a few thousandths of a second. His technique allowed many observations to be made of these rare events. The reports of this research were widely publicized by the scientific media. In 1961, soon after Kornegay had completed his research on chemical reactions, he was awarded his doctorate by the University of California at Berkeley.

Career Highlights

Dr. Kornegay remained for a year as a postdoctoral fellow at Berkeley. Under the sponsorship of the National Science Foundation, he refined his research skills and conducted studies on how certain compounds, such as nitric oxide gas, can absorb heat energy. This research required a beam of infrared light almost as long as a football field. Dr. Kornegay was able to produce such a beam by using the reflective quality of mirrors in a space only a few yards in length.

When his fellowship was completed, Dr. Kornegay joined the staff of the Lincoln Laboratory at the Massachusetts Institute of Technology (MIT) in Lexington, Massachusetts. This organization was founded during World War II to further improve the design of radar, which had been developed into a useful device in England early in the war. When World War II was finally over, the cold war with the Soviet Union began. Consequently, the work of the laboratory continued with funding that came mainly from the U.S. Defense Department.

During the 1950s, great strides were made in the computerization of radar signals, especially in the systems used to detect enemy bombers and to direct interceptor/fighter aircraft. When detected by radar, targets were given special identification by the computer. In this way, radar operators could keep track of each individual aircraft in a large formation. Computers could also calculate the likely course of the aircraft, even if the radar did not always continue to register the enemy plane.

By the time Dr. Kornegay joined the staff at the Lincoln Laboratory, ballistic missiles—not enemy aircraft—were the main threat. Scientists sought to discover if the flight of these missiles could be detected far above the earth's atmosphere. They also wanted to discover whether defensive action was possible after the nose cone carrying the bomb had separated from the rocket that had carried it beyond the stratosphere. The staff also studied whether defensive missiles could be directed at the relatively small and rapidly moving incoming reentry devices.

As time passed, both sides in the cold war began to use more and more advanced technologies. Rockets were designed to carry more than one bomb. Also, some rockets were equipped with fake bombs. This meant that defensive actions would be wasted and real bombs might get through to their targets.

Dr. Kornegay was particularly interested in how our missile defense systems could tell real bombs from fake bombs. The fake bombs might reflect the radar beam in peculiar ways. When this happens, the target is said to have a signature. Perhaps using both radar and high speed computers, these signatures could be recognized. If so, early defensive actions could be set in motion to target only the real bombs. During his time at the Lincoln Laboratory, Dr. Kornegay worked on these and other difficult problems.

In the meantime, he and his wife raised their three children. In addition, he reached out to minority students interested in professional careers in science and engineering. In the 1960s, Dr. Kornegay served for three years as a top official in the Task Force on Youth Motivation. This organization was founded by Vice President Hubert H. Humphrey. Later, Dr. Kornegay was a moving force in the statewide Pre-Engineering Program for Minority Students in Massachusetts. He served, too, as a director for the National Consortium for Black Professional Development. In 1969, Dr. Kornegay was awarded an honorary doctoral degree from Lowell University in Massachusetts for both his research accomplishments and his community service activities. He also has been a lecturer for the Visiting Scientist Program of the American Institute of Physics and remains active in civic organizations in the Boston area. In 1980, he was awarded the Martin

Luther King Award by MIT for his service to minority education. Then, in 1990, he was named Scientist of the Year by the Society of Black Engineers.

Samuel Lee Kountz

Born: October 20, 1930, in Lexa, Arkansas

Status: Died, December 23, 1981, at Kings Point, New York

Education:

Bachelor of Science degree, Arkansas Agricultural, Mechanical and Normal College, Pine Bluff, Arkansas, 1952

Master of Science degree, University of Arkansas, Fayetteville, Arkansas, 1956

Doctor of Medicine degree, University of Arkansas, 1958

Research Area: Physiology

Early Years

Samuel Kountz was the oldest of three boys. His father was the minister in the local Baptist church, and both of his parents put a high value on education.

Sam's early education was in the Black school system of the small Arkansas town of Lexa. At the age of 14, he graduated from the Morris Booker College High School, but his parents knew that he would need more training if he wanted to go to college, so they sent him to boarding school at the Baptist Academy. This school educated young people, many from low-income families, for religious careers, something Sam thought he might want to pursue.

The Baptist Academy faculty enforced rigid discipline, and Sam soon learned how to work under harsh conditions. Unfortunately, his courses were very abstract and focused mainly on religious ideas, instead of the basic education that he wanted. Consequently, in 1948, Sam failed the entrance examination for the Arkansas Agricultural, Mechanical and Normal College. He was allowed to enroll, however, on the merit of the strong recommendations from his former teachers and excellent character references from important people in the area. He spent his first year at college on probation, which meant that he had to earn good grades in order to continue.

Higher Education

Sam Kountz did very well in his science classes from the beginning, and his teachers encouraged him to become a medical doctor. In order to pursue a medical career, Kountz decided to major in biological science and minor in mathematics.

Kountz became a student leader and was elected president of the Honor Society and the Science Club. He was also the vice president of the Student Government Association and participated as a member of the college debating team. Indeed, he enjoyed the social part of college as much as the academic part.

In 1952, Arkansas senator William Fulbright visited the college. Sam Kountz was assigned as the senator's student host. While Kountz guided the senator around the campus, the senator asked him about his career plans. Kountz told the senator that he had applied to two Black medical schools but had been rejected by both. Although he ranked near the top of his class, stiff competition for admission had made acceptance very difficult. Senator Fulbright proposed a radical scheme to gain Kountz's admission to medical school. He suggested that he first earn a graduate degree in chemistry. The senator believed that an advanced degree would make Kountz's application to medical school seem more attractive to an acceptance committee. Furthermore, in spite of the fact that the school was still segregated, the senator proposed that Kountz apply to the graduate chemistry program at the University of Arkansas. Before becoming a senator, Mr. Fulbright had been president of that university, and he promised strong backing for Kountz's application.

Senator Fulbright proved true to his word, and Sam Kountz was admitted to graduate study in chemistry at the University of Arkansas. During his first two years in graduate school, Kountz worked as a teaching assistant in the chemistry laboratory. The job helped pay his tuition and expenses and provided a good foundation in basic science and research techniques. Kountz soon found that this preparation also helped open the door to medical school. He was accepted into the medical school at the University of Arkansas even before he finished his science degree. He started his medical studies in 1954, while he was finishing the research project for his thesis. The report of this research was Kountz's first published paper. It described

how plants remove carbon dioxide gas from the air to produce sugar and starch. This research helped Kountz understand how various creatures utilize raw materials from their environment.

Once in medical school, Sam Kountz was able to show his real talent. At first, he continued to teach chemistry and conduct research in the chemistry department. Then he was named as a U.S. Public Health Service Fellow in the summer of 1955. In line with his future career plans, he became a research assistant in the department of neurology during his final year of medical school. He passed his state board examinations and was given his license to practice medicine in the summer of 1958.

Career Highlights

In that same year, Stanford University Medical School was conducting a special intern training program at San Francisco General Hospital, which included research as well as patient care. This combination seemed interesting to Dr. Kountz because he wanted to employ both his training as a chemist and his skills as a doctor. He was very pleased when Stanford accepted him into the program.

After one year as an intern, Dr. Kountz wanted to enter Stanford's surgical resident program. Such an appointment was highly competitive, and Dr. Kountz encountered problems because of his race. However, he received the strong support of Dr. Roy Cohn, a professor of surgery at Stanford Medical School. Dr. Cohn was also a supervisor of the surgical resident program and helped Sam Kountz gain a place in the program— as his own student.

Dr. Kountz had previously worked on a wide variety of research projects, but by 1958, he was focusing his attention on cancer research.

He was concerned that some cancer patients suffer from more than one cancer at the same time and that certain people might inherit cancer problems from their parents. During the resident program, however, Dr. Kountz became involved with Dr. Cohn's study of tissue transplants. Years before, doctors had begun to transplant skin from one part of the body to another. This procedure was done most often with patients who had suffered severe burns. In the 1950s, Sir Peter Medawar, a doctor from India, showed that skin could be transplanted from one person to another. This finding encouraged doctors to begin research on organ transplants. Dr. Cohn thought that it might be possible to transplant a kidney, and he and Dr. Kountz worked for years on possible methods. Although not all their ideas were successful, they finally found a set of procedures that seemed to work.

At first, the only kidney transplants that succeeded were between identical twins. Generally, transplanted kidneys were rejected by the body of the recipient. The body reacted to the transplanted organ as if it were an invader, such as a germ or virus. But in 1961, the team of Cohn and Kountz made history when they successfully transplanted a kidney from a mother to her child.

This work made both doctors famous. The next year, they went to England to work with another pioneer, Dr. William Dempster. The three doctors did basic research on the most effective way to prepare patients to receive a donor's kidney. They also worked on how to keep the kidney alive after it had been removed from the donor's body.

In 1963, after returning from England, Dr. Kountz was appointed to the faculty of Stanford Medical School as an instructor. The following year, he was given a Fulbright Professorship, which enabled him to travel to Egypt. Egyptian doctors had invited Dr.

Kountz and Dr. Dempster to help supervise the opening of a new medical research center in Alexandria.

For the next few years, Dr. Dempster and Dr. Kountz were often in Egypt working together or alone. During one of the times Dr. Kountz was working by himself, he was asked to perform emergency surgery on two patients who were dying of kidney failure. Dr. Kountz performed the operations and was praised for his quick action in the local newspapers.

But Dr. Kountz had done the emergency surgery using equipment brought to Egypt by Dr. Dempster, and Dempster, who thought no one should use his equipment without his permission, was extremely angry when he heard about the incident. He accused Dr. Kountz of taking credit for work that he, Dempster, had done and tried to have Dr. Kountz thrown out of Egypt. The worldwide medical community stood solidly behind Dr. Kountz, however, and Dr. Dempster's attack was diffused. This confidence in Dr. Kountz was echoed by his rapid promotion at Stanford Medical School.

In 1966, Kountz left Stanford for the University of California, where he was made a full professor. At about this time, he began to receive awards and honors. In 1967, he earned the Lederle Medical Faculty Award, and in 1970, was awarded an honorary doctoral degree by the University of San Francisco. In 1972, Dr. Kountz was named chairperson of the department of surgery at the Downstate Medical Center in New York City. The center, part of the State University of New York, is located in a multiethnic neighborhood. This new position allowed Dr. Kountz to help minority patients and teach minority students.

At Downstate Medical Center, he continued his research while fulfilling his teaching and administrative duties. Dr. Kountz was able to increase the success of kidney transplants as well as develop the idea that transplanted organs should be replaced at the first sign of failure. He also wanted to transplant kidneys from chimpanzees to human patients, a procedure that, if successful, would help overcome the shortage of human organs.

In 1976, in an attempt to increase the amount of donated organs, Dr. Kountz performed a kidney transplant operation for a network television broadcast. Because of the program, almost 20,000 people contacted their local organ banks to donate one of their kidneys.

In 1977, Dr. Kountz was invited to visit South Africa to help train people to perform organ transplants. He worked for two months at the University of Cape Town, but he felt very uncomfortable because his travel papers designated him as an honorary White person. He did not want that label and therefore stayed in South Africa for only a short time.

A few months after his return to the United States, Dr. Kountz was stricken with a rare nerve disease from which he never recovered, and in 1981, he died at the relatively young age of 51.

Dr. Kountz never gave up in the face of disappointment. He overcame his early education problems with diligent study. He had difficulty being accepted into college and then into medical school, but he found ways to gain admission. He experienced an attack on his integrity, but the entire medical community rallied behind him. Dr. Kountz was not stopped or slowed by these events because he believed, as he told his friends, that once he had earned his college degree, he attained control over his destiny.

Joseph Mehling, Dartmouth College Photographer

George M. Langford

Born: August 26, 1944, in Roanoke Rapids, North Carolina

Status: Ernest Everett Just Professor of Natural Sciences, Dartmouth College, Hanover, New Hampshire

Education:

Bachelor of Science degree, Fayetteville State University, Fayetteville, North Carolina, 1966

Master of Science degree, Illinois Institute of Technology, Chicago, Illinois, 1969

Doctor of Philosophy degree, Illinois Institute of Technology, 1971

Research Area: Cell Biology

Early Years

George Langford was born in the small town of Roanoke Rapids, North Carolina. He grew up, however, in the even smaller town of Potecasi, North Carolina, just south of the border between Virginia and North Carolina.

George's family lived on a small farm, where he first became interested in biology. As a child, he was so curious about animals on the farm that he one day opened the barn gate to see them better, and they began to pour through. George's mother heard some strange sounds from the garden where she had been weeding. She came around the corner of the house and let out a loud scream. George picked up a sizable stick and tried to chase the animals back into the barn yard. When George used the stick on a gray horse's back legs, the horse kicked George in the stomach. The boy went into the air and landed unconscious on the ground.

His family rushed to his aid, taking him to the doctor's. Fortunately, the doctor found no serious damage. George had just had the wind knocked out of him. His family was relieved, but they never let him forget about the trouble he had caused.

By the time George was a student at W.S. Creecy High School in Rich Square, North Carolina, he knew that he wanted to be a scientist. All the teachers were African Americans and were among the best teachers in the state. The chemistry and algebra teacher, Ms. Clark, became a mentor for George. She encouraged him to work up to his capabilities. George's geometry teacher was also an important influence. In his senior year, she selected George for the school prize in mathematics. He was pleased with the prize, but more importantly, it confirmed that he could do well in a difficult subject.

George was also involved with extra-curricular activities in high school. He played on the football team in his freshman year. Later, he played the piano and sang in the school chorus. In 1962, he graduated near the top of his class of 40 students.

Higher Education

George Langford entered Fayetteville State University that fall. Fayetteville State was an institution dedicated to training African Americans for teaching positions. Langford was pleased with his school for several reasons. The biology program at Fayetteville was particularly strong, and since he wanted to be a science teacher, a sound background in biology was of particular importance. Langford also found that the science faculty related to him as an individual—not just someone occupying a seat in a classroom.

During his college years, George Langford was a good student but not an excellent one. Without the encouragement of science teachers such as Drs. Joseph Knuckles and F. Roy Hunter and the calculus teacher, Dr. Eldridge, he might have changed his mind about a career in science.

Langford found that the laboratory facilities at Fayetteville were not very modern or extensive. Students could not become involved in substantial research because none of his teachers were conducting research projects. Indeed, grants for African American scientists at small state schools were almost impossible to obtain in those days. Even with these drawbacks, the high level of teaching and individual attention gave Langford a good preparation for his chosen field.

His three major professors were instrumental in persuading him to attend graduate school. In fact, Dr. Hunter used his influence to arrange a teaching assistantship for Langford at the Illinois Institute of Technology (IIT) in Chicago, Illinois. Langford graduated from Fayetteville State in June of 1966 and in the fall headed north to Chicago.

George Langford experienced the same good fortune in graduate school that he had had as an undergraduate. His teachers were supportive and helped him develop the research skills that he had not yet acquired. His thesis advisor, Dr. Teru Hayashi, who was the department chair, was patient with the young man as he learned how to conduct a research project. George was assigned as an assistant to Dr. Jean Clark Dan, a visiting faculty member. She, like many of George's teachers, took a strong interest in his future.

Ironically, Langford's initial weakness in research methods did not keep him from choosing one of the most difficult research areas, cell biology. Langford wished to investigate nerve and brain cells, the most mysterious cells in the body. Furthermore, to add to the complexity, he proposed to study the functions of the very tiny structures within these mysterious cells. Langford earned his master's degree from IIT in 1969 and remained at that school to continue his graduate studies.

During George Langford's last year in graduate school, he was awarded a graduate research fellowship from the Argonne National Laboratory, one of the research centers operated by universities under the sponsorship of the U.S. Department of Energy. The funds from this fellowship allowed George Langford to work full-time on his doctoral research project, which sought to describe the chemical stages in the breakdown of sugar compounds in the bodies of single cell green plants called *euglena*.

Career Highlights

After Dr. George Langford received his doctoral degree from IIT in 1971, he was given a two-year appointment as a postdoctoral fellow at the University of Pennsylvania in Philadelphia. Dr. Langford worked closely with the director of a laboratory in which the physical properties of individual cells were being studied. His project, in collaboration with Dr. Shinya Inoue, was the beginning point of his research career. In fact, this project concerned the central problem of cell biology. The scientists sought to explain how key materials, produced within a given cell, can relocate inside that cell to keep it functioning. Work on this project continued for many years.

When Dr. Langford completed his postdoctoral studies, he accepted his first regular faculty position in the biology department at the University of Massachusetts in Boston, where he taught cell biology and pursued his research.

During the summer of 1976, Dr. Langford joined the research team of Dr. Raymond E. Stephens as the Josiah Macy Scholar at the Marine Biological Laboratory at Woods Hole, Massachusetts. Dr. Langford wanted to use this break as a chance to learn new techniques in biochemistry. This was the beginning of a long and profitable association that led to Dr. Langford's service on the board of trustees of the Marine Biological Laboratory and of Dartmouth College.

In the fall of 1977, Dr. Langford joined the faculty of the College of Medicine at Howard University in Washington, D.C. While there, he continued to work on the problems of material transport within individual nerve cells. Dr. Langford also taught young medical students the basic sciences of cell structure and neuro-anatomy.

In 1979, Dr. Langford transferred to the School of Medicine at the University of North Carolina at Chapel Hill, one of the top research universities in the country. He spent the next 12 years teaching cell physiology and continuing his study of the inner workings of the nerve cell. Dr. Langford spent a year's leave of absence as program director for cell biology at the National Science Foundation in Washington, D.C. The National Science Foundation brings together top scientists from all over the country. Thus, it can be a great learning experience for beginning and established scientists.

When Dr. Langford completed his short stay at the National Science Foundation and returned to Chapel Hill, he found that he had been promoted to a full professorship in the School of Medicine. However, Dr. Langford did not remain long at Chapel Hill. In 1991, he moved on to Dartmouth College and its medical school, which was the home school of Dr. Ernest E. Just (see p. 201). The trustees at Dartmouth had set up a professorship in Just's name and invited Dr. Langford to fill the position. It was an offer that was almost impossible to refuse.

This appointment could have easily provided the high point in Dr. Langford's career. However, because of his affiliation with the Marine Biological Laboratory at Woods Hole, Dr. Langford maintained his summer appearances there. The laboratory was in the process of encouraging more multicultural collaborations in research projects, and this strongly appealed to Dr. Langford. He teamed up with a scientist from Germany and one from Russia, and together they worked during the summer in cell biology at Woods Hole.

In the summer of 1992, a breakthrough occurred. The partners found a totally new and unexpected method used by cells to transport key particles from one place to another within the cell. Scientists had know for years that tiny elements called microtubules transported key particles within the cell. The team of George Langford, Dieter Weiss, and Sergei Kuznetsov had suddenly discovered a supplemental "roadway" system in the nerve cell composed of filaments or threads of a material called actin. Microtubules serve as the main highway for material transfer, while the actin threads support local crosswise transport of materials. This finding could become more and more important as researchers, such as Dr. Langford and his partners, learn how to direct or control the transportation activity of the cell. Once this control is understood, steps can be taken to ensure the health of vital cells. Indeed, this research may someday lead to the control of such cellular diseases as cancer.

Margaret Morgan Lawrence

Born: August 19, 1914, in New York, New York

Status: Retired, Harlem Hospital and Columbia University Medical School, New York, New York, 1984

Education:
Bachelor of Arts degree, Cornell University, Ithaca, New York, 1936

Doctor of Medicine degree, Columbia University, New York, New York, 1940

Master of Science degree, Columbia University School of Public Health, New York, New York, 1943

Research Area: Psychiatry

Early Years

Margaret Morgan's parents were Sandy Alonzo Morgan and Mary Elizabeth Smith Morgan. About a year before Margaret's birth, her parents' first child, a boy, had died in infancy from unknown causes. Mary Morgan thought her son had died because of the poor medical care found in the rural South, the area in which they lived. Consequently, she traveled to New York City shortly before

Margaret was born. Her grandmother and several aunts lived in the city and looked after her and her newborn child.

Margaret's father was a minister in the Episcopal Church. In those days, ministers moved often from parish to parish. When Margaret was born, her father had a parish in Portsmouth, Virginia. The next year, the family was in New Bern, North Carolina. Two years later it was Widewater, Virginia, and then on to Mound Bayou, Mississippi. Because of these frequent moves, Mary Morgan became depressed, and her health suffered. However, by the time Margaret was ready to begin school, the family made a final move to Vicksburg, Mississippi. Mrs. Morgan was much happier in this city.

Margaret's father's work went well in Vicksburg. He was generously supported by his parishioners and other, more prosperous citizens. Many of them were interested in furthering the church's work in the city. Mary Morgan blossomed under these improved conditions and became a respected teacher and community leader.

Every summer while Margaret was growing up, she and her mother would travel to New York City to visit their relatives. They both enjoyed the cultural resources that the big city provided. It is not surprising that Margaret proposed to move to New York when she was ready to attend high school. She wanted to live with her mother's sisters and attend one of the elite schools. Everyone approved of this plan, and Margaret enrolled in the Wadleigh High School in the fall of 1928. She did extremely well in her studies, and when Margaret told her teachers that she wanted to study medicine, they all encouraged her to continue her education.

Higher Education

Since Wadleigh High School was a girl's school, Margaret Morgan applied to two women's colleges: Smith College in Northampton, Massachusetts, and Hunter College in New York City. She also applied to coeducational Cornell University in rural New York State because of its strong reputation in the biological sciences. All three colleges accepted Morgan for admission. However, she chose Cornell, in part because of a generous scholarship offer.

Margaret Morgan began her college program in 1932. It turned out to be a demanding experience. This was the first time she had not had the support of other women—particularly African American women. In fact, in her first year at Cornell, she was the one and only African American undergraduate student. Even under these trying and lonely conditions, she did very well in her studies.

Since the scholarship covered only her tuition and fees, finances were difficult for Morgan. She also faced other problems. She was not permitted to live in the dormitory with the other female students. Morgan lived with a family in Ithaca and worked as their maid for her room and food. After her third year, she was able to stop working as a maid because she found a job as a laboratory assistant in biology. Fortunately, this work was interesting, and she learned new skills. One of her jobs was to prepare tissue specimens for microscopic study. Morgan learned to use delicate equipment, such as a microtome, to prepare very thin slices of material.

One of Morgan's reasons for choosing Cornell was the outstanding reputation of its medical school. After excelling in her college studies, she applied for admission to the Cornell Medical School. She believed that she would be strongly welcomed. She was wrong. Cornell Medical School had, a few years before, conducted an "experiment" by admitting an African American man to the program. Morgan was told that the "experiment" had not been successful and that, consequently, no African Americans were being admitted. Fortunately, Morgan had applied to other medical schools in addition to Cornell. She was accepted at Columbia Medical School and was the third African American to enter their program.

Morgan's medical program was guided in part by the unexplained—and perhaps unnecessary—death of her infant brother over 20 years before. She had long resolved to study pediatrics so that she would be able to prevent unnecessary deaths of children. Her dream was finally realized when she graduated from the medical school of Columbia University in 1940. However, her medical training was not finished. She still had to complete her internship and her residency. Probably because of her race, she was not allowed to do her internship or residency at such institutions as the reputable Babies Hospital in New York City. Instead, Morgan continued her training at Harlem Hospital in the northern part of Manhattan.

While she was still in medical school, Margaret Morgan had married Charles Radford Lawrence II. She had met him during the summer between her first and second years at Cornell. At that time, he was a student at Morehouse College in Atlanta, Georgia. Since his family lived in Vicksburg, Mississippi, near her family home, the young couple saw each other every summer vacation.

After their marriage in Vicksburg in 1938, Lawrence returned to Atlanta to work on his graduate sociology degree at Atlanta University. Margaret returned to her medical training in New York City. For several years, the young couple saw each other mainly during school vacations.

While Dr. Margaret Lawrence completed her residency at Harlem Hospital, she continued her formal education at Columbia University. She received a master's degree in public health in 1943. At Columbia, she met and worked with the famous Dr. Benjamin Spock.

He helped her recognize the connections between a child's emotional well-being and its physical health. Later, these links would be the theme of much of Dr. Lawrence's research.

Career Highlights

When she had finished all her formal medical training, Dr. Margaret Lawrence was invited to join the faculty at the premier medical school for African Americans, Meharry Medical College in Nashville, Tennessee. Her husband, Dr. Charles Lawrence, had been invited to join the faculty at Fisk University—just across the street from Meharry. At Meharry, Dr. Margaret Lawrence taught pediatrics and public health courses for four years. When she left Meharry in 1947, she had reached the rank of associate professor.

Dr. Lawrence found that she could not forget her experiences with her young patients at Harlem Hospital and the ideas she had gained while working with Dr. Spock. She strongly believed that a child's mental health was one of the keys to its physical health. To expand her training in the field of mental health, she accepted a fellowship from the National Research Council that allowed her to return to New York in 1947. After a year of study at Babies Hospital, she began a program of psychiatric and psychoanalytical training at Columbia University. She became certified as a psychoanalyst in 1951.

The main bases for her research and clinical work were Harlem Hospital and Columbia Medical School. In the meanwhile, Dr. Charles Lawrence was making a distinguished career as a teacher of sociology at Brooklyn College.

Dr. Margaret Lawrence's years of study deepened her belief that poverty and class discrimination lead to emotional problems in children. These problems lead, in turn, to lowered resistance to physical disease. She collaborated with Dr. Kenneth Clark on studies which had been inspired by Dr. Spock. Dr. Lawrence strove to aid Dr. Clark in his efforts to persuade government officials that racial prejudice and economic deprivation were bad for the country as a whole. Even after school desegregation, Drs. Clark and Lawrence contended that more must be done to improve education for all young people. They argued that many children were still being poorly taught in ramshackle schools.

In order to address the problem of children's emotional health, Dr. Margaret Lawrence advocated that mental health professionals should be employed by school systems. These people could function in much the same way as the nurses and doctors who provide medical services within school buildings. Dr. Lawrence's first book, published in 1971, describes how visiting teams of mental health specialists could serve within the schools.

In 1973, Dr. Margaret Lawrence and Dr. Charles Lawrence spent a year studying children in economically disadvantaged communities in the United States and in Africa. They sought to identify patterns of mental characteristics that help children overcome economic handicaps and thrive in depressed situations. While organizing her observations from these field studies, she finished her second book. It was based on her prior study of Black families in inner city settings. Her third book balanced the picture by portraying young people from rural situations in the United States and Africa. In these studies, she recorded similarities among the problems faced by children in very different settings. These comparisons are one of Dr. Margaret Lawrence's main contributions to the science and practice of pediatric psychiatry.

After retiring from her positions at Harlem Hospital and Columbia University Medical School in 1984, Dr. Margaret Lawrence continued to practice medicine in Rockland County, New York. She also continued her crusade to improve mental health care for economically disadvantaged children. In 1987, at the age of 74, she gave a paper before the annual meeting of the American Academy of Psychoanalysis. This is a rare honor for someone who has "officially" retired from her profession.

Bachrach Studios

Carroll M. Leevy

Born: October 13, 1920, in Columbia, South Carolina

Status: Distinguished Professor of Medicine, New Jersey Medical School, Jersey City, New Jersey

Education:

Bachelor of Arts degree, Fisk University, Nashville, Tennessee, 1941

Doctor of Medicine degree, University of Michigan, Ann Arbor, Michigan, 1944

Research Area: Physiology

Early Years

Even though Carroll Leevy's grandparents were freed slaves, both his parents pursued and completed college degrees. His father graduated from Hampton Institute, and his mother graduated from South Carolina State College. They both took teaching jobs in South Carolina as soon as they finished college.

After they were married, Carroll's parents founded a department store in Columbia, South Carolina, a town which was still rigidly segregated. The department store catered to the African Americans of that community and was very successful until the Great Depression of the 1930s.

When he was four years old, Carroll caught the flu and developed pneumonia. He had a high fever and could not breathe properly. Fortunately, Carroll's fever broke, but he did not recover fully for many weeks. The boy believed that his doctors had saved his life because they had watched his progress so carefully. A few months later, one of his aunts developed stomach cancer. She moved from the country to Columbia where she could be treated, and she lived for a time with Carroll's parents. When she died, Carroll told his father that she had needed a better doctor.

When Carroll was in high school, his father started an undertaking business and owned both a mortuary and funeral parlor. Carroll became aware of the large number of young Black men who were dying in his community. His father explained that most of the deaths could have been prevented by better medical care. Then his younger sister developed tuberculosis and was placed in a special hospital called a sanitarium. When Carroll visited her there, he saw many other African Americans who suffered from this disease. After his sister's death, Carroll became determined to pursue a career as a physician.

Carroll attended Booker T. Washington High School in Columbia—a school his father had helped to establish. The chemistry teacher encouraged Carroll's interest in medicine. He also showed Carroll how to do chemical analysis, a way to identify the various substances in a mixture or compound. For example, a chemist can take something like a piece of cake and determine its contents. The chemist can tell how much of the cake is starch, how much is sugar, how much is oil, and so on. Carroll saw how science could unravel medical puzzles and provide new knowledge about disease.

At this time, Carroll became interested in learning about the history of medical research and the lives of medical scientists. He knew that he wanted to progress beyond the great discoveries of the pioneers and make his own important contributions.

Higher Education

Carroll Leevy graduated from high school at the top of his class. With his good record, he had no trouble earning admission to Fisk University in Nashville, Tennessee, an all-Black school that has provided leadership in the arts, the social sciences, and the natural sciences. Fisk also has a strong program in religion.

Leevy was influenced by the religious program at Fisk. He became a leader in the Student Christian Association and the Young Men's Christian Association (YMCA). The YMCA held summer conferences, and in 1940, Leevy was a delegate to the conference in Lisle, New York. Because this conference was racially integrated, it was an important experience for Leevy. He saw for the first time how people of different racial and cultural backgrounds are able to successfully work together.

Carroll Leevy, who was president of his senior class, graduated from Fisk with honors in 1940. He was elected to the Advisory Committee of the National Youth Administration, an organization that supported job training for young people during the hard times of the Great Depression. Even though President Franklin D. Roosevelt hoped the program would help minority people, most of the money was used for segregated training projects. Leevy realized that he could do little to change the situation and resigned from the Advisory Committee. He decided the he could spend his time better by beginning his medical training. So, in 1940, he enrolled at the University of Michigan in Ann Arbor.

Leevy had to borrow money and work part-time during his first two years in medical school. However, conditions changed after the United States entered World War II on December 7, 1941. In the fall of 1942, Leevy entered the Army Specialized Training Program. This program provided financial support for students who were studying science and medicine. There was a shortage of physicians during the war and government programs provided the means to train more people.

In medical school, Carroll Leevy was again encouraged to become a research specialist. His professors also suggested that he should consider becoming a teacher. They hoped that he would stay in Michigan and arranged for his hospital training at Wayne County Hospital in Detroit. This hospital mainly served the African American community in Detroit. However, Leevy wanted to develop his skills in a more integrated setting. He chose Jersey City Medical Center, a large hospital with a very good reputation.

Career Highlights

At the medical center, Dr. Leevy learned that some physicians did not treat African American doctors as equals. He worked hard to overcome the prejudice. Other physicians soon found that he was an excellent problem solver and often asked him to work on a difficult diagnosis.

The research team that he joined at Jersey City showed how a high-salt diet was bad for patients with heart disease. The report of this research was published in the *Journal of the American Medical Association*. Partially because of this study, Dr. Leevy was asked to remain at the center for a second year.

World War II ended while Dr. Leevy was still an intern. Consequently, he did not need to go directly into military service. He was made chief resident at Jersey City Medical Cernter in 1947. At this time, the hospital needed specialists in all areas of medicine, especially in the area of liver diseases. Doctors often dislike this speciality because many of the patients are also alcoholics. With alcoholic patients, sometimes the disease is untreated for so long that it cannot be cured. However, Dr. Leevy wanted to help the hospital, and he volunteered to work with these patients.

In his work with liver diseases, Dr. Leevy tried innovative techniques. He adopted an almost painless method of obtaining tiny samples of a patient's liver. By studying the liver samples under a microscope, Dr. Leevy developed new ways of diagnosing the problems. In this capacity, he fulfilled his ambition to be a teacher, training advanced medical students in his new procedures.

In 1951, he was awarded a grant from the American College of Physicians. This support allowed him to travel to the University of Toronto in Canada, where, he worked with Dr. Charles Best, who had helped develop new treatments for diabetes. Dr. Leevy became interested in the connections between diabetes and liver disease. In his research, he demonstrated that diabetes could cause problems in the liver's blood supply.

This work led to another research grant. With Dr. Leevy's help, the National Institutes of Health decided to establish a new research organization at the Jersey City Medical Center. This decision was one of the initial steps toward the development of New Jersey's first medical school.

Dr. Leevy still had to fulfill his obligation to serve in the U.S. Armed Forces. In 1954, he was assigned to the U.S. Naval Hospital in St. Albans, New York. At first, he was asked to look after patients with lung diseases. However, he soon convinced his superiors that he would be better employed in his special field of liver disease. In two short years, he made the Naval Hospital a center for research on this problem. Also during this time, Dr. Leevy finished his first book on his speciality. It was regarded as a model for clear writing about a complicated subject. Also, at this same time, Dr. Leevy married Ruth Secora Barboza.

While Dr. Leevy was at the Naval Hospital, arrangements were underway for the establishment of a medical school at the Jersey City Medical Center. The medical school was to be part of Seton Hall University. Problems arose, however, because Seton Hall is a private, Roman Catholic school and the medical center is a government institution. The government is forbidden by our constitution from supporting religious organizations. Dr. Leevy helped to solve the problem. He worked to create a feeling of cooperation between university and government administrators. In 1965, the state simply purchased the assets of the medical school from Seton Hall and renamed the institution as the New Jersey College of Medicine and Dentistry (NJCMD). Meanwhile, Rutgers, the state university, established a partial,

two-year program in 1966. This facility, located in new Brunswick was merged with the NJCMD and moved to Jersey City in 1970.

After Dr. Leevy completed his duties for the U.S. Navy, he received another grant. This money came from the National Institutes of Health and allowed Dr. Leevy to spend a year at Harvard Medical School in Cambridge, Massachusetts. He was accompanied by his wife, Ruth. She had been trained as a chemist, and they went to Harvard as a team.

At Harvard, Dr. Leevy observed how physicians were trained at a world-famous medical school. He also gained information about Harvard's new research in his special field, liver disease. In collaboration with his new wife and other colleagues, he began researching various aspects of his speciality. They studied how different chemicals can affect the liver and how dietary habits might damage that organ. The team also investigated whether environmental pollutants could also cause liver diseases. Optimistically, the scientists also studied various compounds that might help the liver repair itself.

When he returned from Harvard, Dr. Leevy began teaching at the new medical school in Jersey City. Soon, he was promoted to the rank of professor of medicine. Dr. Leevy also became director of the department that studies nutrition and liver diseases.

In 1984, Dr. Leevy accepted the post of the scientific director of the Sammy Davis, Jr., National Liver Institute. The next year, 1985, he was joined at the institute by his son, Dr. Carroll Barboza Leevy. Together, they began studies of liver cancer. Their research centered on whether children of cancer victims are likely to develop the disease. Such studies are still underway.

Over the years, Dr. Leevy has written 4 major textbooks on liver disease and over 500 scientific articles on the subject. He is recognized worldwide as a expert in the causes and cures of liver disease. Dr. Leevy also has been a leader in bringing attention to the work of African American scientists. His example has shown how people can achieve success when they work together. Perhaps most important to Dr. Leevy, he has taught medicine and medical research to over 3,000 students of every race and creed.

Photographic Services of Lawrence Berkeley Laboratory

William A. Lester, Jr.

Born: April 24, 1937, in Chicago, Illinois

Status: Professor, University of California, Berkeley, California

Education:

Bachelor of Science degree, University of Chicago, Chicago, Illinois, 1958

Master of Science degree, University of Chicago, 1959

Doctor of Philosophy degree, The Catholic University of America, Washington, D.C., 1964

Research Area: Theoretical Chemistry

Early Years

Bill Lester grew up in the city of Chicago, the third largest city in the United States. He has one older and two younger sisters. Bill's mother, Elizabeth Lester, was a talented seamstress who made clothes for her daughters. She also made dresses that were sold to local wholesale companies. She worked at home until the youngest girl entered school. She then took a job as a secretary for a physician.

Mr. Lester was a mailman. After working for the postal service for a few years, he was promoted to the position of supervisor.

Bill's grandparents also lived in Chicago. Both his mother's and his father's families had moved to the city from Atlanta, Georgia, between 1910 and 1917. Bill's father's father died before the boy was born but the other three grandparents were alive while Bill was growing up. All the grandparents provided Bill and his sisters with guidance and inspiration.

His father's mother was a practical nurse. She had worked during the day and gone to school at night in order to learn her profession. Bill's maternal grandmother had attended Morris Brown College in Atlanta. After she moved to Chicago, she became a successful real estate agent. Her husband was a lawyer who had worked his way through law school. He liked to joke around with young Bill. However, he also had a serious side and taught Bill to finish any job or project that he started.

Bill attended segregated elementary schools. When he was about 11, his parents moved to the far south side of Chicago. There, his older sister, Florence, was in the first group of young African Americans to attend the local, desegregated high school. Bill followed his sister a year later. He began high school when he was only 12 because he had skipped two earlier grades.

Even though he was two years younger than his classmates, Bill played both football and basketball in high school. Fortunately, he was big for his age. Even so, it took him three years to make the basketball team. He was a good outside shooter and became a starting guard in his senior year.

During high school, he always worked part-time. First, he delivered newspapers. Then he found a job working for a food market and delivered fish and poultry on his bicycle. When he was older, his godfather gave him a job as a clerk and clothes presser in his tailor shop. Bill's godfather provided him with new clothing as well as paying him a salary. During his final year of high school, Bill also worked as a clerk in a hardware store.

During the summer between his third and fourth year in high school, Bill worked at the University of Chicago in the physics department. He was assigned to type research reports and became familiar with the vocabulary that is necessary to the study of physical chemistry. Also, Bill was able to meet some of the professors. At that time, the physics department was headed by Professor Robert S. Mulliken, who would soon win a Nobel Prize for chemistry.

Higher Education

In spite of his interest in chemistry, Bill Lester was awarded a scholarship for the study of history. He had done particularly well in that subject. A former librarian at his high school had funded a scholarship for the study of history, and accepting this scholarship was the only way that Lester could finance his education at the University of Chicago.

After his first year of college, Lester was able to concentrate on his two favorite activities, basketball and chemistry. His basketball career actually started in his first year. He started every basketball game but one during his four years of eligibility. He was team captain for three years and held single-game and career scoring records for over 20 years. Lester also won the Amos Alonzo Stagg Medal for the best scholar-athlete of the year and the university's "Man of the Year" award in his senior year.

During his years at Chicago, Lester learned a great deal about chemistry. He also learned about computers. In 1957, he began to write his own computer programs on chemical reactions.

Lester wanted to go to graduate school as soon as he received his degree from Chicago in 1958, but he had applied to very competitive schools and had not been accepted by any of them. His faculty advisors suggested that he stay at the University of Chicago for one more year. By doing so, he could earn his master's degree and prove that he could succeed at the graduate level. This tactic worked. After completing his graduate work at Chicago, he was accepted as a doctoral student and offered a teaching assistantship by Washington University in St. Louis, Missouri.

He started his doctoral studies at Washington University in the fall of 1954. At Christmas time, he married Rochelle D. Reed. When he returned from his honeymoon, he was faced with two difficult problems. Lester learned that his chosen faculty advisor would be unavailable to direct his dissertation research. He also discovered that his current research project had developed difficulties.

Lester had been trying to grow crystals with specific properties. The effort had failed.

He decided that Washington University was not the best place for him. He realized that he could do better work in the field of theoretical chemistry. In that area of science, he could use his talents in chemistry, mathematics, and computer programming. However, he knew he would need special guidance in his graduate program. He chose to work with Professor Virginia Griffing, who taught at the Catholic University of America in Washington, D.C. Lester and his young wife moved to Washington in the fall of 1960.

At Catholic, Lester was awarded a teaching assistantship that provided some financial support, and his first semester began well. Fate stepped in once again, however. Soon, he and his wife learned that they were to become parents. It was clear that he would need more money than his salary as a teaching assistant. He began to look for a better job. A former Catholic University student told Lester that summer jobs were available at the National Bureau of Standards (NBS)—now the National Institute of Standards and Technology. Lester was offered one of the jobs for the summer of 1961 and began to work with Dr. Morris Kraus.

In addition to his work at NBS, Lester attended graduate school on a part-time basis. He had just begun to think about his dissertation topic. Unfortunately, his advisor, Professor Virginia Griffing, died in 1962. Her death left Lester without an advisor for his dissertation research. His connection with the Natural Bureau of Standards saved the day. Dr. Kraus arranged a full-time job for Lester in the summer of 1962. Together, they planned a research project that could be accepted as a dissertation topic at Catholic University. Lester worked on this research for two years and received his doctorate from Catholic in 1964.

While at the National Bureau of Standards, one of Dr. Lester's colleagues was Dr. Frederick Miles. The two young men functioned as a team under the supervision of Dr. Kraus. The situation was a good one for Dr. Lester. He was introduced to many more aspects of chemistry than he would have learned as a full-time graduate student. This experience also helped Dr. Lester receive a postdoctoral fellowship at the University of Wisconsin at Madison, for which he took an educational leave from the National Bureau of Standards. He, his wife, and their two children moved to Madison at the end of 1964. At Wisconsin, he worked with Professor Richard Bernstein at the Theoretical Chemistry Institute.

Career Highlights

Dr. Bill Lester's research was now focused on the problems of high-velocity molecular collisions. He sought to discover what factors controlled the rate of such collisions and if the shape of the molecule's electronic shell made a difference in its behavior. He did research, too, on whether the collision of two molecules formed a new compound or caused them to bounce off each other. Other studies concerned the distance and direction taken by the scattering effect when several molecules of one kind collided with a stream of another kind. Dr. Lester was required to use advanced mathematics to accomplish this research. He found that the answers he sought were often best expressed as mathematical averages or proportions. Dr. Lester was, therefore, also working on new and exciting ideas about the use of statistics in physical chemistry.

After eight months of doing research at the Theoretical Chemistry Institute, Dr. Lester was asked to become assistant director. He was aware that this position would reduce the time that he could spend on research.

However, he wanted to learn about the administration of the organization. While still working as assistant director of the institute, he was made a lecturer in the chemistry department of the university.

In 1968, Dr. Lester and his family moved West. He took a job with IBM and joined their staff at the IBM Research Laboratory in San Jose, California. In this position, he was able to conduct research on a full-time basis.

The years between 1968 and 1975 were very productive for Dr. Lester, and in 1975, he was appointed to the Technical Planning Staff of the Director of Research for IBM. He and his family moved to the T. J. Watson Research Center in Yorktown Heights, New York. In 1976, they returned to California, when he was invited to become manager of a research group at the IBM laboratory in San Jose.

In 1978, Dr. Lester was selected from many applicants for a job at the Lawrence Berkeley Laboratory. This laboratory is operated by the University of California for the U.S. Department of Energy.

Dr. Lester was chosen to manage a project called the National Resource for Computation in Chemistry (NRCC). The project had several goals. One was to develop new methods in which to use mathematics in the field of chemistry. Another was to write new computer programs and design specific chemical research projects to demonstrate the value of mathematics. These new techniques were then communicated to working chemists all over the country. The NRCC program was the first organized attempt to bring all the new information together. Dr. Lester needed all his skills as chemist, teacher, mathematician, and manager to direct this project.

Dr. Lester has written more than 130 research reports and book chapters. He is also a coauthor of a very advanced book on theoretical chemistry. Dr. Lester's scientific abilities have been recognized in many ways. He has served as advisor to government agencies and the National Academy of Sciences. In 1979, he won the Percy L. Julian Award for Pure and Applied Research. In 1983, the Catholic University of America's Alumni Association awarded him the Alumni Achievement Award in Science. Perhaps the best acknowledgment for his years of hard work, however, was the Outstanding Teacher Award from the National Organization of Black Chemists and Chemical Engineers. This tribute was presented to Dr. Lester in 1986.

Jon Gilbert Fox

H. Ralph Lewis

Born: June 7, 1931, in Chicago, Illinois

Status: Professor of Physics, Dartmouth College, Hanover, New Hampshire

Education:

Bachelor of Arts degree, University of Chicago, Chicago, Illinois, 1951

Bachelor of Science degree, University of Chicago, 1953

Master of Science degree, University of Illinois, Champaign-Urbana, Illinois, 1955

Doctor of Philosophy degree, University of Illinois, 1958

Research Area: Theoretical Physics

Early Years

Ralph Lewis grew up in Chicago, Illinois. From his earliest childhood, he was aware that his family placed great emphasis on education. His father, Harold R. Lewis, had a bachelor's degree in electrical engineering. His mother, Lena V. Lewis, was trained as an elementary school teacher. While still in elementary school, Ralph became very curious about technology and the physical world. He read a great deal and asked his teachers and family endless questions.

Ralph's curiosity, dreams, and initiative began to shape his life as a boy. They made him studious and inquisitive and led him to speculate on such diverse things as how radios work and the distance to the farthest star. Although he was interested in many subjects, Ralph decided during his senior year of high school that basic physics research would be the best career for him. He was helped toward that decision by the many different people who supported his hard work and his spirit of inquiry.

Higher Education

Following his graduation from high school in January of 1948, Ralph Lewis spent one semester attending Wilson Junior College in Chicago. During that semester, he accepted a scholarship to attend the University of Chicago, an institution renowned for its excellent program in physics.

The undergraduate school of the University of Chicago was called The College. The administration of the university required that the program of study in The College include a very broad range of subjects. Courses in history, physical science, biological science, and social science were required of every student, even those who intended to specialize in a specific subject, such as physics. This requirement worked well for Lewis. Being involved with a broad range of studies before specializing had a very important and positive impact on Lewis's view of his own life. It helped him see his place in the world, and he became much more aware and interested in the broad scope of human activity.

Ralph Lewis received two degrees from the University of Chicago: a bachelor of arts degree from The College and a bachelor of science degree from the department of physics. He then attended graduate school in physics at the University of Illinois in Champaign-Urbana. At that institution, he earned a master's of science degree in 1955 and a doctor of philosophy degree in 1958. Among the faculty members of the department of physics at Illinois were a number of outstanding research physicists. Lewis was fortunate to join the group of one of the most active researchers. His group focused on the investigation of radiation from atomic nuclei (nuclear physics) and the use of such radiation to study properties of solid materials (solid state physics). The subject of Lewis's Ph.D. dissertation was the use of nuclear radiation to measure magnetic fields within certain special materials called superconductors. Scientists knew that when a superconductor is cooled below a certain critical temperature, it loses all of its electrical resistance and allows electricity to flow very easily through it. However, magnetic fields can reduce this capability. Dr. Lewis's research sought answers to this difficult problem.

Career Highlights

After receiving his Ph.D. from the University of Illinois, Dr. Lewis was eager to continue in basic scientific research. Even though his Ph.D. dissertation had been in experimental physics, Lewis had also taken courses to prepare him for a dissertation in theoretical physics. Because he was still interested in theoretical physics, he sought a post-doctoral position in which he would have an opportunity to work in that field. He was fortunate to receive a fellowship which allowed him to work for two years in Germany at the Institute for Theoretical Physics at the University of Heidelberg. Those two years were very valuable to him. Not only did he profit by learning more about physics, he also expanded his cultural horizons. He became fluent in the German language, and a few years later, he collaborated with a colleague to translate into English six books of lectures by the famous German physicist, Wolfgang Pauli.

Dr. Lewis returned to the United States in 1960 to join the faculty of the department of physics at Princeton University. In addition to teaching, he continued his experimental research in nuclear physics. He remained at Princeton University for three years. During that time, he decided to change his field of research to the newly developing area of plasma physics, the study of ionized gases. Dr. Lewis became interested in plasma physics because he wanted to understand the recently discovered "radiation belts" that circle the earth. He also wanted to take part in the international effort, begun in the early 1950s, to develop a source of electric power that is based on thermonuclear fusion reactions. These reactions are responsible for the energy generated by stars like our sun. They also provide the explosive energy released by the hydrogen bomb. A source of electric power based on thermonuclear fusion reac-

tions is called a thermonuclear fusion reactor. Such a reactor would be very safe and would not produce any radioactive waste materials. Although such a reactor has not yet been achieved, intense international research and development on this project is still underway.

In 1963, Dr. Lewis joined the thermonuclear fusion project at the Los Alamos National Laboratory as a research physicist. The Los Alamos National Laboratory in Los Alamos, New Mexico, is a very large and important organization for scientific research and development. It was formed in 1943 during World War II to develop a weapon based on nuclear fission, the atomic bomb.

Dr. Lewis remained at Los Alamos until 1990. During his long career there, he made significant contributions to basic and applied research in various aspects of theoretical and computational physics. His research activities led to collaborations with scientists in universities and research laboratories in the United States and other countries. At various times, he was associated with the teaching faculties at the University of Wisconsin, the University of New Mexico, Pennsylvania State University, and the University of the Witwatersrand in Johannesburg, South Africa. For two years, Dr. Lewis was on temporary assignment at the United States Department of Energy, where he assisted in the management of the national thermonuclear fusion program. He also helped in the management of national supercomputer resources.

After leaving the Los Alamos National Laboratory, Dr. Lewis was a member of the faculty of St. John's College in Santa Fe, New Mexico, for one semester. He then moved to Dartmouth College, where he has been a professor of physics since 1991.

John W. Macklin

Born: December 11, 1939, in Fort Worth, Texas

Status: Associate Professor, Department of Chemistry, University of ·Washington, Seattle, Washington

Education:

Bachelor of Arts degree, Linfield College, McMinnville, Oregon, 1962

Doctor of Philosophy degree, Cornell University, Ithaca, New York, 1968

Research Area: Physical Chemistry

Early Years

By December 1939, Germans conquered Poland and World War II had broken out in Europe. America was far removed from the fighting, but many people sensed that the United States would soon be involved in the war. John Macklin was born during this uneasy time in our history.

When John was very young, his father died, and the boy went to live with his grandmother in Fort Worth, Texas. Even before he entered school, John gained a reputation for having an intense curiosity about how things were built and how they worked. If he discovered an unattended mechanical object, he would try to take it apart and put it back together. This curiosity extended to a baby chick that he discovered. Fortunately, the chick was rescued before John could begin the disassembly work. His grandmother, not wanting to frustrate his curiosity, supplied him with numerous mechanical gadgets.

When John was seven years old, he joined his mother, stepfather, and younger sister in Seattle, Washington, where his stepfather had a good job. During his grade school days, John's hobby was to design and build model airplanes and boats. When he was older, John became a newspaper carrier and saved his money to purchase two chemistry sets. He liked to imagine himself as an alchemist—a chemist who produces ancient magical spells and potions. He assembled his two chemistry sets on a laboratory bench that he had built in his bedroom. This arrangement was mainly for show because real experiments took too much time for such a young man.

When John reached high school age, he was interested in woodworking and began to design and build full-sized furniture from plans and ideas in *Popular Science* and *Popular Mechanics.*

John was on the high school football team and, during the off season, played saxophone and clarinet in the marching band. He also sang in the church choir and played in a dance band. In school, John majored in chemistry and mathematics. His dreams of being an alchemist had not completely disappeared.

Higher Education

John Macklin chose Linfield College in McMinnville, Oregon, for his undergraduate studies. One of the recruiters had visited his high school and, because of Macklin's good grades and athletic ability, had persuaded him to enroll. The small liberal-arts college, founded by the Baptist church, has approximately 2,000 students of whom about 400 have a minority background. Admission standards are high.

At first, Macklin chose chemical engineering as his major field of study but soon decided that he preferred to major in basic chemistry. He took a minor program in music and sang in the school choir. He also continued his interest in football and played on the varsity team for three years.

Linfield College has a good record for placing its students in prestigious graduate schools. The faculty suggested that John Macklin apply to Cornell University, in Ithaca, New York. Cornell offered John a research assistantship, which he retained for the full six years of his graduate program.

When John Macklin arrived at Cornell, his advisor, Professor Robert A. Plane, helped him plan a research project in the field of analytical chemistry. One of the main goals of analytical chemistry is the accurate identification of various substances, sometimes from very small samples. John Macklin's doctoral research was aimed at developing techniques of analysis that used tools such as lasers. During this complex research, Macklin relaxed by singing with the Cornell University Glee Club and a local group that performed the comic operas of Gilbert and Sullivan. In 1968, Macklin finished his dissertation and received his doctorate from Cornell.

Career Highlights

After his graduation, Dr. Macklin returned to the West Coast. He had been invited to join the faculty of the University of Washington in Seattle. During the 1970s, Dr. Macklin's research concentrated on how laser beams are used to determine the identity of the atoms in a molecule and demonstrate how they fit together. His main technique was Raman Spectroscopy—named after the scientist from India who developed it. In this technique, a scientist shines a laser beam through a sample of the material to be iden-

tified. The beam causes individual atoms in each molecule of the sample to move a very small distance from their original positions. This shift in location also changes the energy level of the atoms and causes each atom to release its own color of light. When the amount and tint of each new color is observed, the pattern of light identifies the atoms and their location in the molecule.

Starting in the 1980s, Dr. Macklin began a collaboration with scientists from the National Aeronautics and Space Administration (NASA) and from Stanford University in California. The goal was to determine whether meteorites and cosmic dust particles from outer space contained complicated carbon-based molecules. This research led to a consideration of whether carbon compounds from outer space could have interacted in the Earth's primeval oceans to produce the original building blocks of living creatures.

Scientists knew that carbon compounds of local origin existed on Earth before the advent of living creatures. They questioned whether these relatively simple molecules could have combined to form the more complicated molecules that are essential to life. Dr. Macklin's studies demonstrated that tiny crystals in ordinary clay can use the sun's energy to support the construction of complicated carbon-based materials. The kind of research done by Dr. Macklin may someday solve the mystery of how the first primitive, one-celled creatures came into being.

The quest to find carbon-based molecules in cosmic dust generated a need to test smaller and smaller samples. In the mid-1980s, Dr. Macklin and his colleagues designed and developed a light meter that functioned on a microscopic scale. They fashioned a device that recorded the pattern of intensity in the different colors of light reflected from the cosmic dust. This information was fed into a computer that attempted to identify the composition of the cosmic dust by matching the patterns of light with similar information from known materials. This new technique speeded the study of interplanetary dust particles.

It soon became apparent that the ability to analyze very small amounts of material had other interesting applications. For example, this method may prove useful for detecting very small amounts of materials—such as powerful chemicals—that can contaminate the environment when released into the air or water. Dr. Macklin is now working on this application.

In addition to his teaching and research, Dr. Macklin has served as the spokesperson for minority graduate students in their relations with administrators at the University of Washington. Most significantly, Dr. Macklin has been a leader in various programs designed to bring a higher quality of science teaching into the grade schools and high schools in Washington State. If he is successful, it will leave a lasting mark on the education of young people of all ethnic backgrounds.

Walter E. Massey

Born: April 5, 1938, in Hattiesburg, Mississippi

Status: Director, The National Science Foundation, Washington, D.C.

Education:

Bachelor of Science degree, Morehouse College, Atlanta, Georgia, 1958

Master of Science degree, Washington University, St. Louis, Missouri, 1966

Doctor of Philosophy degree, Washington University, 1966

Research Area: Theoretical Physics

Early Years

Walter Massey's father worked as a laborer in a local chemical factory, and his mother was a grade school teacher. They did not have much money, but they were proud of their family.

His mother always encouraged Walter and his younger brother to work hard at school and to stay out of trouble. In his second year of high school, Walter's good work was rewarded. He received a Ford Foundation Scholarship that would pay for his tuition and expenses in college.

In the 1950s, the Ford Foundation had a project aimed at finding young African Americans from the southern part of the United States who would benefit from a college education. The foundation knew that many young African Americans could not even think about college because they lacked the financial support.

Each year, the Ford Foundation arranged for selected high school seniors, who had been nominated by their teachers, to take a series of tests. Those who did well were sponsored for admission to either Morehouse College in Atlanta, Georgia, or Fisk University in Nashville, Tennessee, where all their college expenses were paid.

In 1953, the nominees who lived in Mississippi were requested to go to Jackson, Mississippi, to take the tests. Walter's mother volunteered to drive the students from Hattiesburg. She asked Walter, who was in his second year of high school and therefore too young to be nominated, to help her with the driving. Since he liked to drive, he agreed to accompany her.

When the group arrived at Jackson, the students gathered in a large classroom to take the test. Walter and his mother waited outside. The school officials, seeing that Walter had nothing to do, suggested he take the test as well. Later, he learned that he had earned the best score of any student from Mississippi. In fact, he had done so well that the Ford Foundation awarded him a scholarship, even though he was two years too young.

Walter did so well on the test because he wasn't nervous about it and because of the high quality of teaching at Royal Street High School in Hattiesburg. Many of his teachers had advanced degrees from famous universities. They taught in the all-Black high school because there were few opportunities elsewhere.

Walter graduated from high school in 1954 and became a sponsored student of the Ford Foundation. He was admitted to Morehouse College in Atlanta, Georgia, at the age of 16.

Higher Education

Because Walter Massey was starting college two years early, he had some problems. He lacked confidence in his ability to succeed in any of his college classes. He actually expected to do poorly. His college career was saved by one of his teachers, Dr. Hans Christiansen. Dr. Christiansen had faith in Walter and believed he showed great promise. He became Massey's mentor and refused to allow him to fail.

Such extensive help from a teacher was not uncommon at Morehouse College. It was founded in 1867 by members of the American Baptist Mission Society, who were dedicated to helping young African Americans achieve a better life. In the 1950s, the faculty still had their roots in the Baptist Church and were commited to the academic excellence of their students.

Since Dr. Christiansen taught physics, he encouraged Walter Massey to take courses in that subject. The effort was successful. Even though he had never heard of the study of physics before 1954, he graduated with honors in physics in 1958.

Walter was now just 20 years old. He knew that he would need further education to become a professional physicist, but he did not feel ready for the intense competition of graduate school. He thought he needed more experience in life—more maturity. The teachers at Morehouse were sympathetic, and they invited him to stay an extra year at Morehouse College and do some teaching.

When his extra year was finished, the teachers at Morehouse helped Walter Massey arrange a year of advanced study at Howard University in Washington, D.C. There, he learned more about physics in a relatively relaxed setting at a highly respected Black university.

The two-year break helped build Massey's confidence. After his year at Howard, Dr. Christiansen helped Massey get accepted into the graduate program at Washington University in St. Louis, Missouri. Both were confident of his success. However, when Massey took his first examination in mathematics, he scored only 9 points out of a possible 100. Luckily, an older graduate student named Henry Jackson came to his rescue. Henry became his friend and tutor and helped Massey with his studies.

As his understanding of physics and mathematics expanded and his confidence increased, Walter Massey's grades quickly improved. However, he soon began to worry about his ability to cope with one of the requirements for his advanced degree. He knew that to earn a Ph.D. in physics, each student was required to design and carry out an original research project. Such a project requires creative imagination and a great deal of persistence. When Walter Massey faced this challenge in his second year of graduate training, he became discouraged again. He was sure that he had the perseverance but was uncertain that he could plan a worthwhile project. He told his advisor that he wanted to quit school.

For a third time, a mentor came to his aid. Dr. Eugene Feenberg, Massey's dissertation director, steered Walter into a new and exciting field of research called cryogenics, the study of materials kept at very low temperatures. Walter Massey's main research topic concerned the effects of very low temperatures on helium.

Helium is a very unique substance. Normally, it is a gas that is lighter than air, and therefore, commonly used in balloons. It is very safe to use because it will not burn and only rarely reacts with other materials. Helium gas, however, has very peculiar properties when it is sharply cooled. It does not liquify until it is very cold—only a few degrees above absolute zero (minus 460 degrees Fahrenheit)—but when it does, it becomes a superfluid that can leak through the glass walls of a container. Liquid helium also appears to defy gravity. If an empty test tube is cooled and held upright in a pool of liquid helium, the helium will creep up the outside of the test tube, enter the tube, and flow into it until the level inside is even with surface level of the pool.

The peculiar properties of liquid helium can be used to test various ideas in basic physics. Liquid helium can also be used as a coolant while conducting practical research on the flow of electricity, making it useful to both physicists and engineers.

Career Highlights

As soon as Dr. Massey completed his doctoral studies, he moved 200 miles north from St. Louis, Missouri, to Chicago, Illinois. He became a full-time researcher at the Argonne National Laboratory and held the position of post-doctoral fellow for two years.

Argonne National Laboratory is one of seven national laboratories that are supported by the U.S. Department of Energy. This research center is owned by the federal government but is managed by the University of Chicago.

The link to the University of Chicago goes back to the 1940s and World War II, when the first nuclear chain reaction was produced at the University of Chicago in 1942. This gave Chicago priority in basic nuclear research. From a small group of faculty researchers and students who worked on the Chicago campus, the laboratory, now located in a suburb south of the city, has grown to over 4,000 workers.

At Argonne, Dr. Massey continued his studies of liquid helium and other materials at very low temperatures. He was quickly promoted to staff physicist. When he finished his two-year research program at Argonne, he was invited to join the teaching faculty at the University of Illinois at Champaign-Urbana, Illinois.

His next move was to Brown University in Providence, Rhode Island. At Brown, where he accepted a permanent position, he was involved in important new research on sound waves in liquid helium. He was able to explain why liquid helium acts to muffle sound waves passing through it.

Also at Brown, Dr. Massey founded a project called the Inner City Teachers of Science. He organized science students from the university to act as tutors in inner city high schools. For this work, he received the Distinguished Service Citation from the American Association of Physics Teachers in 1975. That same year, he was promoted to full professor and was appointed dean of the college. Later, he worked to encourage private companies to create scholarships for young Black college students to study physics.

In 1979, Dr. Massey was asked to return to Argonne National Laboratory as director. The government sponsors were uncertain about the goals and mission of the laboratory, and many people were worried about the safety of nuclear energy and about the prospects of designing and building new types of nuclear power plants. Experts in nuclear physics were worried about losing their jobs, because some physicists thought more attention should be given to solar energy and less to nuclear energy.

After he became the director at Argonne, Dr. Massey soon restored worker morale and defined new programs of basic research. He was able to persuade people in different government departments that the staff at the laboratory was sensitive to their needs. He helped to show leaders in industry how projects done at Argonne, such as research on increasing the efficiency of coal-burning power plants, could benefit them in terms of cost-cutting and improved performance. To further this cooperation, he started the Argonne National Laboratory/University of Chicago Development Corporation. Called ARCH for short, its purpose is to transfer ideas from research findings into new products and services. In recognition of this success, financial support

from the U.S. Department of Energy was increased.

In 1983, Dr. Massey was made vice president of research at the University of Chicago. In that position, he remained responsible for managing the Argonne National Laboratory along with other university duties. He was particularly active in working with African American students. He wanted to support their studies as he had been supported by older students and faculty members when he was a student.

Dr. Massey also took time to work with local leaders in the Chicago area. He served as director of the charitable organization United Way and served as a trustee of both the Chicago Symphony Orchestra and the Museum of Science and Industry.

On the national and international level, Dr. Massey has given his time to various projects of the National Academy of Sciences and the National Academy of Engineering. With support from these academies, he has worked to help develop science and technical education in African countries.

In 1987, he was elected president of the American Association for the Advancement of Science (AAAS). The AAAS, founded in 1848, has the largest membership of any science organization in the United States, and Dr. Massey was the first African American scientist to serve as its president.

In 1990, Dr. Massey was made director of the National Science Foundation, the second African American to serve in this capacity. (See John Slaughter, p. 292) The National Science Foundation is part of the United States government and was created in 1948 by an act of Congress to support all forms of basic research as well as science and mathematics education. It does so by distributing more than two billion dollars a year in grants to colleges and universities for research and educational projects. It is the most success-ful organization of its kind in the world, and its director has a strong voice in all the sci-entific research activities done in the United States.

Samuel Proctor Massie

Born: July 3, 1919, in North Little Rock, Arkansas

Status: Professor Emeritus, U.S. Naval Academy, 1994

Vice President for Education, BINGWA Multicultural Software Co.

Education:

Bachelor of Science degree, Arkansas Agri-cultural, Mechanical and Normal College, Pine Bluff, Arkansas, 1938

Master of Arts degree, Fisk University, Nash-ville, Tennessee, 1940

Doctor of Philosophy degree, Iowa State University, Ames, Iowa, 1946

Research Area: Organic Chemistry

Early Years

Samuel Proctor Massie was called Proctor or "Proc" by his immediate family because his father was also named Samuel. Proctor's parents had met at Shorter College in North Little Rock while they were both studying to become school teachers. Shorter College, a small school with about 350 students, was founded in 1886 by the local parishioners of the African Methodist Episcopal Church. As a child, Proctor attended nursery school at the college.

When Proctor was still very young, his fa-ther taught at the North Little Rock High School. In those days, a married couple could not teach in the same school system. There-fore, Proctor's mother had to teach outside their hometown. She taught in a rural, one-room school in Keo, Arkansas, about 18 miles away.

As was fairly common in those days, Proc-tor began to accompany his mother to her school when he was four years old. Proctor's mother supervised him as he sat in the back of the classroom with his toys and books. He loved to copy the older children and study along with them. At six, when he began first grade in North Little Rock, he could already read, spell, and do arithmetic at the third grade level. In the first grade, he completed a whole year's work each semester and en-tered the fourth grade when he was just seven. By the age of nine, he had already finished the seventh grade.

In 1929, when Proctor was 10 and starting his second year of high school, he transferred to a new facility, Paul Lawrence Dunbar High School. Proctor had excellent teachers in this segregated school—including his father, who was his biology teacher.

At age 13, Proctor graduated from high school with the second highest grades in the class. He had mild regrets about missing some of the social activities because of his young age. His parents wisely decided that he was too young to go straight into college. Also, this was during the depth of the Great Depression, and money was scarce.

Proctor decided to stay out of school for a year because of his age and the difficult financial situation. He found work in a grocery store and learned important lessons about the differences in people. The next year, 1934, he enrolled in Dunbar Junior College in Little Rock, Arkansas, and spent two years broadening his grasp of mathematics and the liberal arts in general. In 1935, his classmates elected him student body president.

Higher Education

Samuel Proctor Massie entered Arkansas Agricultural, Mechanical and Normal College (Arkansas A, M & N) in 1936. This college, now the University of Arkansas at Pine Bluff, is about 40 miles south of Little Rock and has an enrollment of about 3,000 students.

Massie was too young and still too small to become involved in competitive sports. Instead, he joined the debating team and revived the long dormant college yearbook called *The Lion*. In his role as editor of *The Lion*, he learned some valuable lessons in team leadership.

As usual, Massie put most of his energies into his studies and carried extra courses each term. At age 18, he graduated at the top of his class, with a major in chemistry and minors in mathematics and French. Massie wanted to continue his education in the sciences. He hoped that by studying chemistry, he would find a cure for asthma, a condition from which his father suffered.

While still at A., M. & N. College, Massie had met some key faculty members from Fisk University, a school in Nashville, Tennessee. They knew of his scholastic ability and welcomed him into the Fisk graduate program. One of his connections was Dr. William J. Faulkner, a dean and head of student employment at Fisk. Dr. Faulkner made arrangements for Massie to receive a National Youth Administration Scholarship grant from the federal government. This made it possible for Massie to attend classes full time. He was awarded his master's degree from Fisk in 1940.

In the fall of 1940, Sam Massie returned to Arkansas A., M. & N. College to teach mathematics for a year. However, World War II was well underway by then and Sam was eligible for the draft. For a while, he obtained a deferment by enrolling in the doctoral program at Iowa State University in Ames, Iowa. However, because of his race, Massie could not be given a teaching assistantship or allowed to live in a college dormitory. To make things worse, he was assigned a dank laboratory space in the basement of the chemistry building.

When Massie was nearly finished with his doctoral studies, his deferment was revoked by the draft board in Pine Bluff, Arkansas. He had already been invited by Dr. Henry Gilman, his graduate supervisor, to join his special research team. The team was part of the Manhattan Project, which was working secretly on the atom bomb. By accepting Dr. Gilman's offer, Massie had to cease his doctoral studies but could continue to work at Iowa State. His acceptance also allowed his draft deferment to continue. As soon as the war was over, he went back into the doctoral program and graduated from Iowa State in the spring of 1946.

Career Highlights

When he had graduated, Dr. Massie's old friends at Fisk University offered him a faculty position as a chemistry instructor. Although the appointment at Fisk was an important step, other events soon became more significant to Dr. Massie. During the academic year of 1946–47, he met and married Gloria Thompkins, president of the Fisk Class of 1947. The result of this union was three sons, all attorneys, and five grandchildren.

Later in 1947, a compelling offer came from Langston University in Langston, Oklahoma. This relatively small school had been founded in 1897 as a state college under the federal land grant system. Consequently, even though small, it was an integral part of the State University System of Oklahoma. Dr. Massie accepted the position as head of the chemistry department and received a full professorship. He began to build and strengthen their teaching and research programs. With the help of colleagues at Langston and other institutions around the state, he arranged for a national conference on chemical education to be held at the college.

In 1953, Dr. Massie was elected to the presidency of the Oklahoma Academy of Science. This was an unusual happening in a Southern state at this time. However, Dr. Massie would not remain long in Oklahoma. A short time after his election, he was invited to return to Fisk as chair of the chemistry department.

At Fisk, Dr. Massie gathered together a group of students to form a research team to study the chemical phenothiazine. He mobilized the team to complete a line of research he had begun at Iowa State while still a graduate student himself. A first step in the new project was to conduct a comprehensive literature review, catching up with new findings and integrating the whole body of knowledge about this chemical. Phenothiaz-

ine is an organic chemical molecule made of three rings. The two outside rings are each composed of six carbon atoms. These two carbon rings are joined by an atom of sulfur and an atom of nitrogen to form an inner ring. The atom of nitrogen helps phenothiazine react easily with other chemicals. It had been used for some years to produce interesting products such as colorful dyes, animal medicines, and insecticides.

Their review article was accepted for publication in a major scientific periodical. Within a few months, a developmental breakthrough was announced by a team of French scientists. They had shown that phenothiazine could be used as the main building block in the production of thorazine, an important drug for treating psychiatric patients. A flurry of additional research was generated, and Dr. Massie's review paper became one of the key resources for scientists around the world.

The focus on phenothiazine included consideration of its use in cancer therapy as well as in mental health. This interest led to Dr. Massie's invitation to speak at a major scientific conference in Zurich, Switzerland, in 1955. There, Dr. Massie stood out from the crowd as the only African American present. He was able to informally communicate to many prominent individuals about the quality of the science programs at Fisk. Interchanges were set up whereby well known research people came to Fisk as guest lecturers. In turn, a number of Fisk students received fellowship offers from the home institutions of these visitors.

In addition to his research and writing, Dr. Massie began to organize another conference on chemical education, modeled after the meeting at Langston. He hoped that Fisk might host one of the national research conferences sponsored by the American Chemical Society. After two years of planning and some help from the Ford Foundation, the conference took place. Prominent chemists from around the country spoke at the meeting—including the Nobel Prize winner, Linus Pauling. It was a good opportunity for many African Americans to demonstrate their scientific abilities. Very important Black scientists, such as Percy Julian (see p. 197) and Lloyd Ferguson (see p. 94) presentations on their research. This was the first such major scientific conference to be hosted by an historically Black institution, and it was a gratifying success.

In 1960, Dr. Massie moved on to the National Science Foundation (NSF) in Washington, D.C. The following year, he received recognition for his work at Fisk from the Manufacturing Chemists Association. They named him as one of the six best college chemistry teachers in the country. A key ingredient in the recognition was the strengthening of the master's degree program at Fisk, which enabled many students to go on to complete doctorates at prominent institutions of their choice.

At the NSF, Dr. Massie served as associate program director for special projects in science education. In this position, he was able to bolster the effort of the government to help institutions of higher education improve their laboratory and library resources.

During his last year at the National Science Foundation, Dr. Massie took on a part-time position as the new head of the department of pharmaceutical chemistry at Howard University in Washington, D.C. After getting the program started at Howard, Dr. Massie was invited to become the president of North Carolina College at Durham. This institution, which was founded in 1909 as a state facility for African Americans, has recently become a key element in the state university system under its new name, North Carolina Central University.

In 1966, after three years in North Carolina, Dr. Massie received his most important invitation. He was asked to join the faculty of the United States Naval Academy in Annapolis, Maryland. The opportunity had many interesting aspects. Dr. Massie would again have time to conduct research. He would have access to the resources of coworkers, funding, and materials that are needed to do research of the highest quality. He would also have the opportunity to serve the national security of the United States as well as break some attitudinal barriers. There was a significant symbolic element in being the first Black science professor at the prestigious United States Naval Academy. In addition, Dr. Massie was the first Black departmental chairperson at the academy, a post he held from 1977 to 1981.

After he began his work at the Naval Academy, Dr. Massie looked for ways to help his community. His own early school experiences and his concern for minority education made him particularly alert to the problems of both public and private two-year colleges. Consequently, Dr. Massie joined the Maryland State Board of Community Colleges, where he served for 21 years, 10 as the chair. During his tenure on the board, he argued for more investment in the science curricula. In 1989, the board initiated the Massie Science Prize to be awarded each year to an outstanding science student from a Maryland community college. Another of his services to the state was an investment of six years as chair of the Governor's Science Advisory Committee.

Meanwhile, Dr. Massie continued his research. Two themes were central to his program of studies—human health and environmental protection. He developed foaming agents that would disperse poisonous gases and shield military personnel from their deadly effects. Dr. Massie also worked on anti-infection materials. In 1985, he and his coworkers were awarded a U.S. patent for a specific antibiotic for gonorrheal infections.

In the field of environmental pollution, Dr. Massie conducted a long series of studies on the properties of chemicals which are used aboard ships. For example, certain chemicals are used to help remove barnacles from the steel hulls of naval vessels. These chemicals are, of course, rinsed into the sea. Dr. Massie sought to determine whether these chemicals are harmful to marine life in general. He also studied the negative environmental effects of detergents and fire-retardant compounds after they are flushed into the ocean. Furthermore, he questioned whether trace amounts of toxic metals are released into the water after a ship is cleaned of rust and corrosion. Many such problems were studied by Dr. Massie and his colleagues. They did their research during the summer break when they could use the laboratories at the navy's David Taylor Research Center near Annapolis.

In recent years, Dr. Massie has served as principal speaker at many graduation ceremonies around the United States and has received honorary degrees. He has also been a visiting professor at many colleges and universities. Dr. Massie was recognized in 1980 by the National Organization of Black Professional Chemists and Chemical Engineers as the Professor of the Year. He won the Henry A. Hill Award for his research from that same organization in 1987.

After almost 30 years at the Naval Academy, Dr. Massie received more awards and recognition as he neared his seventieth birthday. For example, he was presented a National Lifetime Achievement Award at a White House ceremony in 1988 for his work in the field of minority education. In 1989, he was entered into the National Black College Alumni Hall of Fame. In 1990, he received the Faculty Achievement Award from the Naval Academy. In 1992, the National Naval Officers Association and the academy's African American alumni organization created the Samuel P. Massie Educational Endowment Fund. This fund was designed to help pay the college costs of minority individuals and women from the local area. In 1993, Dr. Massie became the second civilian and the first African American to become an honorary member of the National Naval Officers Association.

In 1994, a new program, "Science in American Life," was initiated by the Smithsonian Institution's National Museum of American History. Excerpts from Dr. Massie's biography are part of the permanent exhibits for this program. In that same year, Dr. Massie's portrait was selected to be hung in the marble corridors of the National Academy of Sciences' headquarters on Constitution Avenue in Washington, D.C.

In late 1994, a coalition of 100 of the country's largest companies plus 9 colleges and universities—each with a tradition of serving the African American community—and the U.S. Department of Energy created a Samuel P. Massie Professorial Chair of Excellence at each of the 9 participating institutions. Each school will receive a total of $1.6 million to support an outstanding scientist who will lead a research team in environmental studies.

After his nominal retirement in 1994, Dr. Massie continues to lead a very active life. He is working with the BINGWA Software Company to develop computer-based instruction. The programs, in mathematics and other subjects, use story problems and examples that reflect a multicultural orientation. His vast knowledge of science is now being repackaged in computer readable form to enhance learning activities in elementary school classrooms.

Henry C. McBay

Born: May 29, 1914, in Mexia, Texas

Status: Professor Emeritus, Clark Atlanta University, Atlanta, Georgia, 1986

Education:
Bachelor of Science degree, Wiley College, Marshall, Texas, 1934
Master of Science degree, Atlanta University, Atlanta, Georgia, 1936
Doctor of Philosophy degree, University of Chicago, Chicago, Illinois, 1945

Research Area: Organic Chemistry

Early Years

Henry McBay's parents lived in the small town of Mexia, Texas. When Henry was born, his father worked in a barber shop of which he was part owner. Hundreds of years ago, in addition to cutting hair, barbers performed other surgical operations, such as amputations. When Mr. McBay worked as a barber, barbering was still considered by many people to be a form of surgery. In some ways, Mr. McBay's interests represented the old connection between barbers and doctors. In his spare time, he studied human anatomy. He also worked part-time for a local undertaker, who taught him the art of embalming. Soon after Henry was born, his father passed the Texas state examination for licensed embalmers and went into business with one of his older brothers as an undertaker and funeral director. The next year, he and one of his younger brothers started a new drugstore in Mexia. Henry's mother worked as a seamstress and made dresses for the young African American women who lived in Mexia.

Henry's family life was enriched by other children. He soon had a brother and two sisters. A cousin, the daughter of Mrs. McBay's brother, also lived with the family. In spite of the father's many business activities and the hard work of both parents, money was always in short supply. After seeing that the richest African American in Mexia was the local doctor, Henry decided that he would become a doctor and never need to worry about money again.

When Henry's parents were young, there was no high school for African Americans in Mexia. Consequently, neither Henry's mother nor father had been able to attend school beyond the seventh grade. But by the time Henry finished grade school, there was a good Black high school in Mexia. The Paul Lawrence Dunbar School actually took in African American students from the fourth through the twelfth grades. When Henry enrolled, the school had 500 students and a staff of highly qualified teachers. Many of these teachers had advanced degrees from northern universities. The school principal, for example, had a master's degree from Northwestern University in Evanston, Illinois, and was able to build an outstanding program in the study of mathematics.

Such a school was very unusual for the southern United States. It had been made possible by the discovery of oil. A major oil deposit was located right under the town, and by the year 1920, Mexia was booming. Some African American families had oil wells in their back yards. Large amounts of money came into the community, and some of it was invested in the school and its teachers.

While the oil boom did not make his family rich, Henry did benefit from it. The good education—particularly in mathematics—that Henry received at Dunbar School gave him the necessary background to do well in his studies at college. He also profited from the opportunity to be part of a well-coached high school football team. In his senior year, Henry's school won the championship over other Black high schools in their regional conference tournament. Even though the school was still segregated at that time, the people in the town, both White and African American, were proud of Henry and the Dunbar team.

Higher Education

After Henry McBay's graduation from high school, he was accepted at Wiley College in Marshall, Texas. Even though Marshall, with a population of about 30,000, is similar in size to Mexia, McBay felt uneasy when he first arrived at the college. He was only 16 years old, his parents had been quite strict and protective, and he had had very little contact with people from different backgrounds. Segregation had kept him from even knowing many of the children of his own age in Mexia. His youth and lack of confidence made him shy and awkward in social situations.

As it turned out, Henry McBay had little time for socializing. He had to work part-time in the school's dining hall during his first two years of study to help pay his expenses. The dining hall manager saw that McBay was a good, dependable worker and helped him get a better job at the college post office at the start of his third year. The pay was still very low, but the work was less fatiguing.

Henry was fortunate, too, in the professors he met. Two of the best teachers at Wiley were his chemistry and mathematics professors, and he took as many courses with them as possible. He became particularly interested in organic chemistry. By the time Henry McBay graduated with top scholastic honors in 1934, he knew that he wanted to pursue a research career in the field of organic chemistry.

In order to qualify for a research job, Henry needed more education. With the help of his teachers, he applied for a scholarship at Atlanta University in Georgia. His scholarship application was approved, and he was accepted at the university.

When Henry McBay arrived in Atlanta, he had only $1.65 in his pocket. In desperation, he applied for a job at the college dining hall so that he would get enough to eat. Fortunately, after a few days, McBay's faculty advisor, Professor K. A. Huggins, discovered his situation. Huggins quickly arranged for McBay to work in the chemistry laboratory instead of in the dining hall.

Professor Huggins soon tried to interest Henry McBay in the research he was conducting. His study concerned new types of plastics that had properties similar to natural rubber. McBay became interested in the project and soon was doing his own analysis of the plastics. Huggins was conducting his research to complete his own graduate-level studies at the University of Chicago. When the project was finished, Henry McBay received his master's degree and Professor Huggins received his doctor's degree—based in part on the high quality of their research. This research, too, allowed Henry McBay to forge a link with the University of Chicago that later proved to be important to his career.

For the moment, however, money was once again of great importance. McBay's younger brother had already started college, and his youngest sister was ready to begin her college career. The family did not have enough money to pay the expenses of two college students. McBay felt that he should provide some help. He accepted a teaching position at Wiley College, where he had been a student only a few years before. Unfortunately, some of the faculty members at Wiley still saw Henry McBay as their student. They disregarded his research activities and his advanced degree from Atlanta University and gave him little respect.

In spite of his unhappiness, McBay stayed on the teaching staff at Wiley for two years until his brother finished his degree and his parents could finance his sister's education.

In 1938, he took a job at a junior college in the little town of Quindaro, Kansas, near Kansas City. Here, his pay was much better. At the end of the spring term, McBay enrolled at the University of Chicago in their summer school program. He earned good grades in his summer courses and went back to Quindaro in the fall of 1939. Unfortunately, a new principal had been appointed by the governor of Kansas. The new administrator began awarding teaching appointments to instuctors for political reasons and not for their ability as teachers. McBay's contract was nullified to make room for the new appointees. Suddenly, he had no money and no place to turn.

Finally, a high school teaching job opened up in Huntsville, Texas. One of Henry McBay's friends had been teaching there but left to accept a new job with the U.S. Postal Service. When school officials asked him who might take his place on such short notice, the friend gave McBay's name as a possibility. Henry accepted the job and taught mathematics in Huntsville for three semesters.

By that time, his fine work at Atlanta University had been recognized by other scientists. He was invited to join a research team that had been formed at Tuskegee Institute in Alabama. The purpose of the research was to find a substitute for the fiber obtained from jute, a plant grown in India. Large quantities were needed to manufacture industrial rope and sacking fabric, and shipments from India had been shut down because of the outbreak of World War II. The project at Tuskegee was indirectly in support of the early U.S. war effort.

The scientists investigated the possibility that high-quality fiber could be obtained from the okra plant. They hoped to devise a method by which they could harvest the mature okra for food and then crush the stems of the plant for fiber. They hoped that this fiber could be dried and spun into coarse threads. Unfortunately, good fiber could be obtained only from immature okra plants. If the plant were allowed to mature to the point where it could be harvested, the fiber would be too brittle to spin. One could have either food or fiber, but not both. When Henry McBay proved this fact with his experiments, he found that he had worked himself out of a job.

At this point, McBay was on the verge of being drafted into the U.S. Army. Coincidentally, his friends at the University of Chicago found him a special job as a teaching assistant in the chemistry department. McBay was finally able to re-enroll as a doctoral student. Since the government wanted as many chemistry graduates as possible, they did not draft McBay or any other young college-level chemistry teachers.

As a teaching assistant, Henry McBay had an opportunity to observe how courses were planned and organized by the faculty members of an important university. Soon, he began to develop his own ideas about designing the best possible chemistry course for first-year college students.

Meanwhile, the University of Chicago had become an early center for the development of the atomic bomb. The leaders of the bomb project needed good chemists and offered Henry McBay a position on the research team. It would have been a well-paying full-time job, but by accepting the position, McBay would have had to postpone his doctoral studies for the duration of the war. McBay decided that he had already lost too much time, and he rejected the job offer.

By 1944, Henry McBay was ready to start his doctoral research project, and he chose Professor Morris Kharasch as his research advisor. McBay was taking one of Karasch's courses at the time. The work in the course was highly individualized, and McBay's assignment was to learn some very specialized laboratory techniques in handling dangerous compounds. He was required to make very explosive materials that had great value as chemical building blocks.

Because of the nature of the research, Henry McBay was given a private laboratory in the chemistry building. His assignment led him to develop new ways of producing a dangerous compound from the common substance hydrogen peroxide. The total thrust of his work was so impressive that Henry McBay was awarded the Elizabeth Norton Prize for excellence in chemical research for both 1944 and 1945. This research also provided the main topic for McBay's dissertation. He was awarded his doctoral degree from the University of Chicago in 1945.

Career Highlights

Many people benefited from the work that Henry McBay had done in producing new materials from peroxides. Before the creative work of Kharasch and McBay, complicated peroxide compounds, so useful as building blocks in many chemical reactions, had been costly and in short supply. Now chemists all over the world could afford to do experiments using these compounds.

One of Professor Kharasch's favorite projects was the fabrication of a particular artificial hormone. This hormone, which is used in medicine, can be produces quickly and cheaply by using the peroxide materials developed by Henry McBay. Professor Kharasch obtained a valuable patent for the production process, and over the next few years, Kharasch showed his gratitude for Henry McBay's contribution by helping him obtain several important research grants. During this time, Dr. McBay returned to Atlanta after accepting a post as an assistant professor at Morehouse College in 1945. He was to maintain a relationship with Morehouse for the next 36 years.

After his initial appointment, Dr. McBay was quickly promoted. The college administrators made him an associate professor in 1948. In 1956, he became head of the chemistry department and was named the David Packard Professor of Chemistry. In 1982, he transferred from Morehouse to Atlanta University and became the Fuller E. Callaway Professor of Chemistry there. Altogether, Dr. McBay spent 41 years in the Atlanta University system. During this time, he taught courses at all three college campuses—Morehouse, Spelman, and Atlanta.

One of his main goals while at Morehouse was to give the chemistry program a national reputation for excellence. He pressed for better student preparation in mathematics and for all-day study sessions in chemistry. He wanted students to be able to complete longer laboratory projects than those assigned for the traditional two- or three-hour sessions. To help the students concentrate on such projects with as few distractions as possible, Dr. McBay often arranged for their lunches to be delivered to the laboratory.

Dr. McBay always tried to help his students see the wonder of chemistry. He loved to demonstrate how two materials could be combined to produce a new material, displaying completely different properties. One of his frequent examples was the combination of sodium, a metallic poison, and chlorine, a gaseous poison. Dr. McBay showed that the combination of these poisonous chemicals produces common table salt—a compound that is vital to human health. He regarded this and other chemical processes as minor miracles and wanted his students to share his wonder of chemistry.

Throughout the years, Dr. McBay's teaching and research abilities have become widely recognized. In 1951, the United Nations Education, Scientific, and Cultural Organization asked Dr. McBay to help develop a chemistry education program in Liberia, Africa. He has been invited to teach special courses at a number of important institutions, such as the University of Minnesota, Harvard University, and the University of Maryland. He has been welcomed as a top researcher at major industrial laboratories and at the Canadian government laboratory in Ottawa, Canada. Dr. McBay has received awards from many professional societies, and Emory University in Atlanta granted him an honorary doctoral degree in 1992. A teaching award and a student scholarship have been established in his name at Atlanta University, and a new science building at that institution has been named after Dr. McBay and two other notable educators. In 1991, he was appointed the Martin Luther King, Jr. Visiting Scholar at the Massachusetts Institute of Technology.

Although Dr. McBay has been honored by many awards and tributes, his greatest legacy is the scores of students he has inspired to achieve distinguished careers of their own.

NASA

Ronald Erwin McNair

Born: October 21, 1950, in Lake City, South Carolina

Status: Died, January 28, 1986, near Cape Canaveral, Florida

Education:

Bachelor of Science degree, North Carolina Agricultural and Technical State University, Durham, North Carolina, 1971

Doctor of Philosophy degree, Massachusetts Institute of Technology, Cambridge, Massachusetts, 1976

Research Area: Engineering Physics

Early Years

Lake City, where Ronald McNair grew up, is a medium-sized country town in east-central South Carolina. Ronald's father, Carl McNair, worked as an automobile mechanic who specialized in car body repair work. His mother, Pearl McNair, was a school teacher. He had two brothers—one a year older, and another, five years younger.

Books were a central feature of Ron's young life. He learned to read when he was only four years old. He was enrolled in kindergarten at that age and entered first grade when he was five. In addition to reading whatever was assigned for school, Ron loved to read comic books and stories about outer space explorations.

When he was in grade school, his father taught him about car repairs. Soon, father and son were working together as mechanics. Ron learned good practical engineering from these experiences, and the family gained badly needed money. During the summer months, Ron picked beans and cotton on the farms near town. Although the wages were very low, he was able to make a little extra money.

Education was more important than work in the McNair family. As soon as Ron's younger brother began school, his mother enrolled in graduate school. She earned a master's degree in education from South Carolina State University in Orangeburg, South Carolina. Ron's grandmother, who had been deprived of educational opportunities as a child, also went back to school. She was awarded her high school diploma when she was 65 years old.

Unfortunately, Ron's parents separated before he was 10 years old. His father moved to New York City, and Ron, his mother, and his brothers moved in with his grandparents. After the move, Ron helped in his grandfather's crate-selling business. He was soon keeping the accounts and the other business records. Meanwhile, Ron's father would return to Lake City for a while each summer and during holiday breaks to visit his children.

As Ron grew up, many important events were taking place. The Soviet Union put the first orbital satellite into space in 1957. Because there was great rivalry between the United States and the Soviet Union, the U.S. government increased the amounts of government money they invested in various programs of science education at all levels of instruction. New systems of fast communication were developed to help scientists learn about research being published in English and other languages. Indeed, the developments in the Soviet Union caused the U. S. to accelerate all aspects of space exploration. In fact, the United States had a small satellite in orbit only three months after the Soviets had launched Sputnik.

In spite of the programs to regain the lead in space technology, the United States government was disappointed once again. In 1961, the Soviets demonstrated their advanced capabilities by orbiting a human in space. The U.S. was again quick to respond. Alan Shepard ventured into space to test the worthiness of a space capsule in May of 1961. By February 1962, John Glenn was orbiting the earth inside an improved version of that space vehicle.

These dramatic events were exciting to young people around the world. Ron was no exception. He read about each accomplishment with great interest and began to dream about participating in space exploration.

In 1962, Ron entered Carver High School in Lake City. Carver was still segregated under the "separate but equal" doctrine. However, the definition of equal was not very clear. Books and laboratory equipment at Carver were often run down or completely unavailable. Fortunately, the quality of the teachers at Carver was very high. Their capabilities and inventiveness compensated to some extent for the lack of other resources. Certainly, their commitment was an inspiration to many of their students.

Although young for his grade and small for his age, Ron became a competent high school athlete and played all major sports. He was particularly noted as a hard-hitting linebacker on the football team. He also became a capable saxophone and clarinet player and, for a time, seriously considered making music his career.

Higher Education

In 1967, when Ron McNair arrived on the campus of the North Carolina Agricultural and Technical State University, he declared music as his major field of study. He soon decided to change his major to physics. The freshman guidance counselor—who saw McNair's potential as a physicist—had convinced him that he could succeed in that demanding field.

McNair and many of his fellow students, who also came from rural Southern schools, had deficiencies in their preparation for college-level studies. The problem resulted from the lack of interest and financial backing from the school systems, not from the efforts of their dedicated teachers. These deficiencies had to be corrected by taking extra courses. During his first two years in college, McNair studied almost continually. His only recreation was taking karate lessons. By the time he finished college, he had been awarded a black belt and had reached the fifth degree level. McNair reasoned that karate was the most efficient way to keep fit while using the least amount of his precious time.

McNair did not remain at North Carolina A&T for his third year of college. By then, his potential was widely recognized and he was chosen for a special one-year educational experience. The officials at the Massachusetts Institute of Technology (MIT) had established an exchange program with several Southern schools. Promising minority students from the schools were brought to MIT for one year. In exchange, some of MIT's faculty members taught for a year at those colleges.

Ron McNair found Cambridge, Massachusetts, to be rather cold in more ways than one. The faculty at MIT were generally welcoming, but there were very few African American faculty or students. After many years in all-Black schools, McNair was naturally a bit wary. Also, Boston citizens were struggling with the problems of school integration, and many people were uneasy about race relations. Even though confronted with these race problems, McNair enjoyed his year at MIT. He returned to North Carolina A&T for his senior year and graduated in June of 1971. During that year, he decided to apply to MIT for his graduate studies.

As a graduate student, Ron McNair again found that his previous education was incomplete. He took the necessary undergraduate classes while he was a graduate student. At the end of his second year of graduate work, McNair was required to pass a long and complicated examination before he could begin his dissertation project. The first time he took this exam, he did not pass. Again, in line with his steadfastness, he simply picked up the pieces and went forward. He studied even more intensely, and the next time the exam was given, he passed it.

A similar setback occurred when he was in the middle of his dissertation research. He misplaced the laboratory notebook that held all the records of his study on new ways to generate laser beams. Fortunately, he was able to repeat the work rather quickly. McNair received his doctorate from MIT in the spring of 1976. Less than two months later, he married Cheryl Moore. Ron McNair had met Cheryl, a school teacher, earlier that year at a church social in Cambridge.

Career Highlights

Very shortly, Ron and Cheryl headed West. After graduation, Dr. McNair had received several exciting job offers. He chose to work at the Hughes Research Laboratories in Malibu, California, near Los Angeles. The laboratories were part of the giant Hughes Aircraft Company that had been founded by Howard Hughes just before World War II. Most of the work done by the parent company and the laboratories was supported by defense contracts. The government was interested in using lasers to send messages from one orbital satellite to another. A network of satellites would provide the basis of a worldwide communication system.

To some extent, working on the satellite communication system was similar to being involved in space exploration—Ron McNair's boyhood dream. When Dr. McNair got a letter from the National Aeronautics and Space Administration (NASA), he thought his childhood prayers had been answered. The letter contained instructions for applying to the astronaut training program. With his wife's approval, Dr. McNair completed all the forms. When some of his fellow workers joked about his chances of acceptance, Dr. McNair expressed the same self-confidence and determination that he had used to earn his graduate degree in physics. He was right to be confident. In spite of the fact that there were over 10,000 other applicants, his request to join the space program was approved.

In 1978, Dr. McNair and his wife moved from California to the Johnson Space Flight Center near Houston, Texas. He was ready to undergo six years of advanced training to become a space shuttle crew member. A physicist was needed to perform space research projects in a near-zero gravity environment. For example, government scientists wanted to know if certain valuable crystals would form more perfectly if the crystal molecules were uninfluenced by gravitational forces.

After the first two years of training in Texas, the McNairs were blessed with a baby boy, whom they named Reginald McNair. A baby girl, Joy, was born two years later.

In February 1984, Dr. McNair made his first flight in the *Challenger*. The space shuttle orbited the earth 27 times in an 8-day period. Dr. McNair was responsible for sampling the very thin gases which surrounded the spacecraft. He was also responsible for testing the newest versions of solar cells that would be exposed to space in order to transform sunlight into electricity. The solar cells are typically mounted on large, flat panels so that each cell can absorb the sun's energy. The electric power could then be used in either a manned spacecraft or an unmanned orbiting satellite.

Dr. McNair's first space mission was marked by two important events. First, there was a malfunction of the rocket motors on the two satellites that were released from the shuttle. Later, while in space, two of the crew members, Bruce McCandless and Robert Stewart, successfully used their jet-propelled backpacks to maneuver themselves outside the space craft.

Perhaps the most important of Dr. McNair's jobs in the shuttle was to test the large crane-like mechanical arm that was mounted in the shuttle's large storage bay. When deployed, this mechanical arm could reach 50 feet from the shuttle to retrieve equipment or other objects in space. In fact, such an arm was used nine months later— by a different shuttle crew—to retrieve the satellites that had misfired during Dr. McNair's first mission.

Two years later, Dr. McNair was preparing for his second shuttle mission. In late January 1986, the *Challenger* was once again attached to its launch motors and stood erect at the Kennedy Space Center in Florida. The crew had arrived a few days earlier. The lift-off was delayed by poor weather conditions and a series of minor but annoying equipment problems. Rain squalls downrange from the launch site had delayed the lift-off. The rain would have ruined any attempt of an emergency landing—if one were to be needed. Another weather problem, unusually chilly temperatures at Cape Canaveral, did not cause any serious concern. It was so cold that ice formed each night on the power and fuel lines which stretched from the launch platform to the space vehicle.

Finally, after some frustrating delays, the launch was to go forward on the morning of January 28. Again, Dr. McNair was to have a crucial role. His job was to deploy the telescopic camera that would capture special scientific pictures of Haley's comet. The famous comet was swinging near the earth on its 76-year circle around the sun.

Although the cold weather caused the technicians, once again, to chip ice off the launch equipment, none of the space scientists were alarmed. Until many days later, no one knew for certain that the cold had greatly reduced the flexibility of the rubber gaskets that sealed the giant solid-fuel booster rockets. Less than two minutes after the launch of the *Challenger*, the seals broke and flaming rocket fuel burst out and destroyed the shuttle. Dr. Ronald McNair and the six other crew members perished without a trace.

This tragedy was made the more bitter by the loss of NASA's first civilian passenger, Christa McAuliffe. She was a young Boston-born high school teacher from Concord, New Hampshire. The other members of the "All-American Crew" included test pilots Dick Scobee, Michael Smith, and Hawaiian-born Ellison Onizuka. The two other engineer/scientists in the crew were Gregory Jarvis, a satellite designer who, like Dr. McNair, had come from the Hughes Aircraft Company, and Dr. Judith Resnick, the official flight engineer.

There were many consequences of the disaster. Nothing, of course, could make up for the loss of such outstanding young people. The many responses—great and small—demonstrated the emotional impact of the tragedy. After Dr. McNair's first mission, the townspeople of Lake City, South Carolina—his home town—had renamed the main street after him. Following the tragedy, they renamed their integrated high school after Ronald McNair.

Recognition was shown, too, by the faculty and officials at MIT. The large new structure housing their Center for Space Research was named the Ronald E. McNair Building. Perhaps most touching was a gesture made by the whole community of astronomers and space scientists. They named a moon crater after each of the astronauts who did not survive the launch of January 28, 1986.

Ronald Elbert Mickens

Born: February 7, 1943, in Petersburg, Virginia

Status: Professor of Physics, Clark Atlanta University

Education:

Bachelor of Arts degree, Fisk University, Nashville, Tennessee, 1964

Doctor of Philosophy degree, Vanderbilt University, Nashville, Tennessee, 1968

Research Area: Physics

Early Years

Ronald Mickens, the son of Joseph Mickens, a carpenter, and Daisy Brown Williamson Mickens, was born in Petersburg, Virginia,

amid the bustling activity of World War II. Petersburg is the site of Ft. Lee, a major U.S. Army installation and the source of much of the regional employment.

Like many youngsters of the time, Ronald grew up in an extended family that included his mother's parents, Mr. and Mrs. James Williamson. On hot summer nights, Ronald and his brothers, Carroll and Calvin, who were twins, would sit outside with their grandfather, listening to Br'er Rabbit tales. These stories were punctuated with facts about the planets, chemistry, and mathematics. Inspired and encouraged by his grandfather, Ronald developed a curiosity about the world around him at an early age. Therefore, it is not surprising that by the time he was eight years old, Ronald had decided to become a scientist. Mr. Williamson also taught his grandson to work hard to achieve his goals and to gain satisfaction from acquiring, using, and passing along knowledge. When Ronald and his grandfather played games such as cards and checkers, Mr. Williamson taught him to accept both winning and losing with dignity. The close relationship between Ronald and his grandfather continued until Mr. Williamson's death in 1956.

Ronald was fortunate to grow up in a community with a strong education system, and he took full advantage of the opportunities it afforded. His teachers not only helped him learn facts, they also taught him to reason and analyze.

In Petersburg during the 1950s, there was no shortage of capable, dedicated teachers in the Black school system, one of the few career choices open to bright, educated African Americans before the 1960s. Peabody High School, which Ronald attended, had especially strong mathematics and science programs. While at Peabody, he took two years of algebra, plane and solid geometry, biology, chemistry, and physics. Ronald also spent his summers taking extra courses, and he finished high school only a few months after his 17th birthday.

Higher Education

Ronald Mickens's excellent grades in high school and his exceptional scores on standardized tests, such as the National Scholastic Aptitude Test, helped him earn a full scholarship to Fisk University in Nashville, Tennessee. Fisk, a small liberal arts college, was founded after the Civil War to educate the children of freed slaves. The scholarship grant from Fisk enabled Mickens to receive the college education that his family could not afford to give him.

After enrolling at Fisk, he decided to major in chemistry. He then switched to mathematics and finally to physics. During his years at Fisk, he acquired a strong academic foundation in calculus, differential equations, nuclear physics, analytical mechanics, and complex function theory. In 1964, Ronald Mickens graduated from Fisk with one of the highest academic averages in the school's history, and he immediately began a Ph.D. program at Vanderbilt University, also in Nashville. While he was working toward his doctorate at Vanderbilt, Mickens taught undergraduate physics courses at Fisk.

By the time Dr. Mickens had received his Ph.D. from Vanderbilt in 1968, he had earned a number of awards. He was elected to Sigma Chi, a scientific honorary society, and Phi Beta Kappa, perhaps the nation's most prestigious honorary society. Dr. Mickens also won a Woodrow Wilson Fellowship, a Danforth Fellowship, and a National Science Foundation Postdoctoral Fellowship.

The National Science Foundation Fellowship, awarded in 1968, enabled him to study at the Massachusetts Institute of Technology (MIT) in Cambridge, Massachusetts. Dr. Mickens spent two years at MIT, carrying out research in elementary particle physics at the Center of Theoretical Physics.

Career Highlights

In 1970, Dr. Mickens accepted a full-time teaching position in the physics department at Fisk. Except for brief periods when he was conducting research at other universities and institutes, he continued to teach at Fisk until 1982. Since 1982, he has been a professor of physics at Clark Atlanta University in Atlanta, Georgia, and was named Callaway Professor of Physics in 1985.

Dr. Mickens has authored five textbooks for advanced students in mathematics. His book *Difference Equations*, published in 1987, gave mathematicians some of the basic tools for the study of chaos theory—a field that has practical applications in medicine and weather forecasting. This theory was just beginning to be tried in such scientific fields when Dr. Mickens made his initial contribution.

In 1990 and 1994, he produced revised and expanded treatments of the mathematics of difference equations. In 1990, he also edited a more literary work, *Mathematics and Science,* that brought together the philosophical ideas of 19 leaders from a wide range of scientific specialties. This work reflected a major scientific interest of Dr. Mickens. That interest has been to demonstrate the connection between pure mathematics and science. He supports the belief that scientific ideas can be best understood by using the language of mathematics. Also, he argues that mathematics is the most powerful tool for solving many practical problems. These problems range from improving the design of radios to understanding the workings of body organs.

To explain the role of pure mathematics in the field of science, Dr. Mickens has not only published 5 books, but has also authored approximately 100 abstracts and presented research results in more than 120 scientific papers. He has written for both technical and popular audiences.

Although he enjoys research, Dr. Mickens's first love is teaching. His greatest satisfaction has been the knowledge that through his teaching efforts, several hundred students have acquired an appreciation of the joy, mystery, and power of mathematics and the sciences.

Dr. Mickens has also been interested is the connection between science and society. In seeking to build an increased recognition of African American women in the sciences, he has written biographies on several women scientists.

During summers and other breaks from teaching, Dr. Mickens has done research in many places. He studied at Los Alamos National Laboratory in New Mexico and worked at the Stanford Linear Accelerator Center, the Lawrence Berkeley Laboratory, and the Lawrence Livermore Laboratory in California. Dr. Mickens has also spent time in Colorado at the Aspen Center for Physics and the Joint Institute for Laboratory Astrophysics at Boulder. In addition, he has studied at the European Organization for Nuclear Research in Geneva, Switzerland.

Dr. Mickens has been invited to participate in international physics conferences in England, Canada, Germany, and Japan. Government agencies that have funded his research include the National Science Foundation, the U.S. Department of Energy, the National Aeronautics and Space Administration, and the U.S. Bureau of Standards.

Earl D. Mitchell, Jr.

Born: May 16, 1938, in New Orleans, Louisiana

Status: Associate Vice President for Multicultural Affairs and Professor of Biochemistry and Molecular Biology, Oklahoma State University, Stillwater, Oklahoma

Education:

Bachelor of Science degree, Xavier University of Louisiana, New Orleans, Louisiana, 1960

Master of Science degree, Michigan State University, East Lansing, Michigan, 1963

Doctor of Philosophy degree, Michigan State University, 1966

Research Area: Biochemistry

Early Years

Earl Mitchell, the oldest of seven children, grew up in the New Orleans "projects." His father served in the U.S. military and, after the war, briefly attended college under his veteran's benefits. Earl's mother, also a high school graduate, was kept busy with her growing family.

In order to make ends meet, Earl's father worked two jobs. During the day, he worked as a claims adjuster for an insurance company. At night, he worked as a clerk for the U.S. Postal Service. During the work week, Mr. Mitchell rarely saw his children.

Earl did well in high school and was encouraged by Mr. Webster, his chemistry teacher, to enroll in the chemistry program at Xavier University in New Orleans.

Higher Education

During his time at Xavier, Earl Mitchell lived at home and worked to finance his education. For two summers, he was employed at a local hospital as an orderly and maintenance worker. Later, Mitchell worked as a park supervisor for the New Orleans Recreation Department.

In order to work for the post office during the holiday season, Mitchell maintained a difficult schedule each December. Until Xavier adjourned for the holidays, Mitchell went to school from 8:00 AM until 4:30 PM and then worked at the post office from 5:30 until 2:00 in the morning. Fortunately, Mitchell had friends who lived on campus and was able to take an occasional nap. Earl's hard work allowed him to earn the money necessary for his education.

Professor Peter Paytash was a major figure during Mitchell's years at Xavier. Although Paytash did not have a doctoral degree, he was a skilled chemist and took great care to involve his students in his research projects. The results of this teamwork produced reports published in the *Journal of the American Chemical Society*. Mitchell was impressed by Professor Paytash's collection of papers and reports prepared by his former students. Earl resolved to earn a graduate degree, become an important chemist, and publish his reports in the best science journals. Indeed, Dr. Earl Mitchell's own publications were later displayed by Professor Peter Paytash to new students at Xavier University.

During Mitchell's college years, two of his younger brothers were enrolled in the chemistry department at Dillard University in New Orleans. Of course, there was friendly competition among the brothers. Dr. Tyrone Mitchell now works for the Corning Glass Company in Corning, New York, and holds many patents—including several for silicone caulking compounds. Dr. Gerald Mitchell works for the National Institute for Standards and Technology in Washington, D.C., and specializes in the chemical properties of fire resistant materials.

Before Earl Mitchell finished his college degree, he married Bernice Compton. Their first child, Karen, was born in the spring prior to Mitchell's admittance to graduate school.

After Earl Mitchell graduated from Xavier in 1960, he was awarded a teaching assistantship in the chemistry department at Michigan State University in East Lansing. The late Professor Robert D. Schuetz supervised Mitchell's research on chemicals from natural plant sources. His master's thesis was a study of carbon and sulfur compounds that are found in certain green plants. For example, the strong taste and smell of onions and garlic come from carbon compounds that contain small amounts of sulfur.

After just one year as a teaching assistant, Earl Mitchell became a technician at Michigan State's Plant Analysis Laboratory. This job allowed Mitchell opportunities to perfect his research skills. His thesis research was completed in 1963, and he received his master's from Michigan State.

When Mitchell entered the doctoral program at Michigan State, he became more closely associated with the department of biochemistry. He was appointed to a research assistantship and came under the mentorship of Professor N. E. Tolbert, who encouraged Mitchell's interests in natural-product chemistry. The focus was again on biologically active compounds. Mitchell's dissertation research concerned the isolation of an active chemical in the juice of the sugar beet. When purified and applied to certain plants, the chemical tends to halt the development of seeds. Scientists hoped that the chemical might prove useful in the production of seedless fruits.

In his last year in graduate school, Earl Mitchell became a research associate in the department of biochemistry, which provided him more money and recognition for his achievements. He finished his degree requirements and received his doctorate from Michigan State in 1966.

Career Highlights

After graduation, Dr. Earl Mitchell accepted the position of research associate in the department of biochemistry at Oklahoma State University in Stillwater, Oklahoma. He joined a research team headed by Professor George R. Waller and worked on the famous study which isolated the chemical in catnip that makes the plant so attractive to the domestic cat. The team demonstrated how the chemical was absorbed and used by the cat's nervous system. The report of the research was published in the important magazine *Science* and was featured as their cover story.

In 1969, Dr. Mitchell was appointed to the position of assistant professor in the biochemistry department, and in 1972, he was promoted to associate professor. During this time, he continued to work on the catnip chemical and also began to study the processes by which animals digest starches. Dr. Mitchell worked to isolate and describe complicated molecules that might play a part in the digestive function of both plants and animals.

On the eve of his promotion to full professorship in the chemistry department at Oklahoma State, Dr. Mitchell accepted a position as assistant dean of the graduate college at that institution. He was immediately faced with the problems of understanding university finance, obtaining government support for research, and allocating scarce resources such as laboratory space.

Later that year, Dr. Mitchell became eligible for a six-month sabbatical leave. He chose to spend this period at the Cellular Metabolism Laboratory of the National Heart, Lung and Blood Institute, a premier research facility in Bethesda, Maryland. Along with Dr. Joel Avigan, Dr. Mitchell studied the compounds that produce the active ingredient in catnip. One of these compounds is identical to a substance that occurs naturally in humans and other animals and influences the production of cholesterol. The two scientists reported their findings on this important research in the *Journal of Biological Chemistry*.

In the mid-1980s, Dr. Mitchell began a series of studies on the genetic engineering of food plants. He became interested in this area because of his earlier studies on sugar beets. Genetic engineers had investigated the introduction of new genes into the next generation of plants by treating cells of the mature plant rather than by planting treated seeds. It was determined that most plants that are useful to humans are difficult to modify genetically in this manner.

For many years, Dr. Mitchell has been concerned with equal opportunity, affirmative action, and related matters. Since 1969, he has served as a member and as chair of the Oklahoma State Advisory Committee to the U.S. Commission on Civil Rights. In the mid-1980s, he chaired the committee that planned and inaugurated a new Black Studies program at Oklahoma State. More recently, he has chaired the Oklahoma Alliance for Minority Participation in Science, Engineering and Mathematics. This organization implemented a statewide program of minority student recruitment that is funded by the National Science Foundation at the rate of nearly $1 million per year. This important program is also under the auspices of the National Institutes of Health for Minority Biomedical Research Support and the National Science Foundation's Alliance for Minority Programs.

Since the early 1980s, Dr. Mitchell has been involved with the creation of the Oklahoma School of Science and Mathematics in Oklahoma City. After years of struggle, the school, closely affiliated with a new unit of the state government's Office of Science and Technology, opened its doors to students in 1990. The new school and the new government office will coordinate science research throughout the state and help attract high technology industry to Oklahoma. Dr. Mitchell has been a member of their board of trustees since they were chartered in 1986.

In addition to his duties as a university administrator, teacher, and program designer, Dr. Mitchell continues his research on plant genetics. He is currently working on methods to improve the cotton plant's resistance to disease by the introduction of disease resistant genes. Other research—such as his cholesterol studies—continues at a slightly slower pace.

James W. Mitchell

Born: November 16, 1943, in Durham, North Carolina

Status: Head, Analytical Research Department, Bell Laboratories, Murray Hill, New Jersey

Education:

Bachelor of Science degree, North Carolina A & T College, Greensboro, North Carolina, 1965

Doctor of Philosophy degree, Iowa State University, Ames, Iowa, 1970

Research Area: Analytical Chemistry

Early Years

James Mitchell was the oldest—and only boy—of the five children born to Willie Lee Mitchell and Eunice Hester Mitchell. Unfortunately, the parents divorced and Eunice Mitchell had to assume full responsibility for raising the children. Mrs. Mitchell felt it was important to give her children a sense of responsibility for their own actions—especially for their school behavior. Not surprisingly, money was a chronic family problem. Young James resolved to break out of this situation by earning a doctoral degree when he grew up.

James attended the segregated schools in Durham, North Carolina, where, in general, the quality of the teaching was excellent. James also did very well in the college preparatory program at Hillside High School; however, during his tenth grade chemistry class, he became confused and frustrated with the awkward method used to calculate measurements. James began to wonder whether chemistry was the well structured science he had expected. During this time, the National Science Foundation sponsored a special summer program for high school students with good science aptitudes. Students could chose to take a course—taught by a college instructor—in biology, chemistry, or mathematics at North Carolina Central State University in Durham.

James chose chemistry as his subject and had many enlightening experiences. He enjoyed the interesting laboratory projects such as the construction of a lead sulfate battery that generated enough electricity to light an ordinary bulb. However, James's most important experience was his teacher's use of straightforward, mathematical steps to calculate the measurements needed for their experiments. James saw that chemistry was based on logical principles that could be understood and depended upon. His choice of chemistry as a career was now decided.

Higher Education

In 1961, James Mitchell entered North Carolina A&T College (now the Agricultural and Technical State University of North Carolina) in Greensboro. His chemistry teacher, Professor James Pendergast, introduced Mitchell to interesting and challenging laboratory demonstrations in analytical chemistry. Mitchell was fascinated by the growth of single crystals from a concentrated solution of a pure compound in water. He observed color changes in the crystals as solutions were made more alkaline, by adding small amounts of caustic soda, or acidic, by adding small amounts of an acid.

James Mitchell also had the opportunity to work with Dr. Cecile H. Edwards in the university's undergraduate research program. The topic of her research was nutrition— particularly the role of specific proteins in the growth of animals. These studies taught Mitchell about new tests which used radioactive materials, and meters that record changes in the intensity of infrared light when passed through a solution of amino acids. These undergraduate experiences strengthened Mitchell's resolve to pursue a career in chemistry.

In the summer of 1964, James Mitchell married Alice Jean Kea. She had been his laboratory partner and research colleague for the first three years of the program. They graduated from college in 1965 and traveled to the Oak Ridge National Laboratory in Tennessee for summer internships. Some of the best scientists in the country work at Oak Ridge, a massive research organization operated under contract for the U.S. Department of Energy.

The young couple chose to attend graduate school at Iowa State University in Ames. Several of Mitchell's teachers had recommended Iowa State because the analytical chemistry program was highly regarded. Also, and not of minor importance, Iowa State offered Mitchell a research assistantship and summer employment at the Ames Laboratory, where pioneering work on the isolation of rare elements had been conducted.

At Iowa State, Jean Mitchell enrolled in the graduate program in nutrition and, in 1966, received her master's degree. In late 1966,

the Mitchells became the parents of a daughter, Veronica D. Mitchell. James Mitchell completed his dissertation under the direction of Professor Charles V. Banks and received his doctoral degree from Iowa State in 1970. His research had demonstrated the usefulness of new solvents for extracting and isolating rare elements from various mixtures.

Career Highlights

After his graduation, Dr. Mitchell accepted a position at Bell Laboratories, which has a strong, world-wide reputation for supporting both basic and applied research as well as engineering design, development, and testing. Bell Laboratories is also noted for allowing its highly qualified, professional staff freedom to define their own projects.

Dr. Mitchell joined the team that was working on the problem of developing glass-like fibers—called optical wave guides—that are used to carry light pulses (flashes of energy) over long distances. This technology has many practical applications because light pulses can carry more information than radio waves or microwaves in the same amount of time.

The materials used in the central core of an optical wave guide must be free of chemical contamination or the device will not function properly. Dr. Mitchell sought to develop methods to detect and remove any contaminants from the raw chemicals used in the central core. He developed a new analytic technique by focusing radioactive rays on the substances used in the core and recording the electronic reactions of the foreign chemicals. Dr. Mitchell also designed a new way of purifying the raw chemicals. He began this process with the material in liquid form, chilled it to a solid form, repeatedly heated it to the exact boiling point of each required chemical, and collected the vapor of those chemicals on a cold surface to liquify them again.

Because each chemical has a specific boiling point, only one chemical would vaporize at a given temperature. The chemical impurities were left behind.

During his work on this project, Dr. Mitchell was promoted to be the supervisor of a team that focused on noncarbon based chemicals—substances with no carbon atoms. In 1975, he became head of the whole Analytical Chemistry Department. In 1976, he received a patent on his purification method, and shortly thereafter, he and a colleague, Dr. Morris Zief, published a book on the subject.

As head of the Analytical Chemistry Department, Dr. Mitchell sought to improve its capabilities for analyzing carbon-based compounds, and he actively recruited outstanding organic chemists. He also improved the procedures for chemical analyses by using new measuring equipment. When light from a laser beam is shown through a vassal holding a liquid, a portion of the light is absorbed by each chemical compound. Since the amount of absorption is unique to each compound, the recorded patterns can be measured so that very small amounts of impurities can be detected.

Currently, Dr. Mitchell is exploring new ways to use his ultra-precise measuring procedures to detect trace amounts of various contaminants in our air and water. Very small quantities of some materials can cause serious problems, including cancer.

Dr. Mitchell's scientific accomplishments have been recognized in many ways. He received the Pharmacia Industrial Analytical Chemistry Award in 1978 and the Percy L. Julian Research Award in 1981. In 1982, Dr. Mitchell was awarded the IR-100 Award for industrial research and, in 1985, the prestigious Bell Laboratories Research Award. In 1989, he was honored with a second IR-100 Award and was inducted into the National Academy of Engineering—a distinction reserved for the best engineers in the country.

Dr. Mitchell lectures on scientific topics in the United States and abroad. When he speaks to young audiences, he stresses that science can be an enjoyable and rewarding career in which good communication is almost as important as good research. Dr. Mitchell believes that a scientific career also requires several kinds of dedication—to the field of science, to the community of scientists, and to one's own family who provide the essential support.

Harry L. Morrison

Born: October 7, 1932, in Hall's Hill, Virginia

Status: Professor, University of California, Berkeley, California

Education:

Bachelor of Arts degree, The Catholic University of America, Washington, D.C., 1955

Doctor of Philosophy degree, The Catholic University of America, 1960

Research Area: Theoretical Physics

Early Years

In the late 1800s, it was illegal in Virginia to teach a Black person to read. So Mr. Morrison, Harry Morrison's great-grandfather, and his brother established a church in the Shenendoah Valley that was used as a secret school. Mr. Morrison made sure that his son and his son's son could also read and write.

When Harry's father, Charles Morrison, was young, he developed a life-long interest in machinery. He sketched his new designs on the inside wall of a barn on the family farm in Virginia. Charles's father approved of the drawings and would not allow anyone to erase them.

When Charles was about 20 years old, he moved to Washington, D.C., found a job as a cook, and soon got married. His wife Ethel had grown up in a segregated village called Hall's Hill in Arlington, Virginia. Hall's Hill was originally the slave quarters of a large plantation. After the Civil War, the plantation owner sold the area to his former slaves and many of the present residents are direct descendants of those families.

Soon after Ethel and Charles were married, the Depression caused the economy to deteriorate. They took positions as servants on a large estate next to Hall's Hill, and Harry was born while they were employed there.

Charles Morrison had continued his interest in machinery, particularly the design of aircraft engines. Soon, both Charles and Harry were enjoying *Popular Mechanics, Popular Science*, and other technical magazines. Charles and Harry also visited airfields in northern Virginia and learned more about aircraft engines from the mechanics.

Harry—and his mother before him—attended the segregated John M. Langston Elementary School near Hall's Hill. The school, which had six grades in a four room building, was not an ideal setting for a serious student. Harry's parents taught him reading, writing, and arithmetic at home by giving him extra assignments. In his well equipped home workshop, Charles taught Harry about machinery and built him a gas engine for his model airplanes.

When Harry was about 10 years old, his father left his job as a cook on the estate, and the family moved into their own house in Hall's Hill. Charles Morrison started an auto repair shop, and Harry learned more about machinery by watching his father work.

Harry had some difficulty in taking school seriously because his parents had been so involved in his education. His grades up through the sixth grade were mediocre. Fortunately, Claudia Pitts, the district supervisor of African American schools, recognized Harry's potential. She gave him a set of standardized tests to evaluate his achievement. When Harry scored at the top on these tests, she recommended that he continue his education past sixth grade—the highest grade in the segregated, Virginia schools.

Harry's father located a school for African American students near Washington National Airport in Virginia. Here, Harry met more bright, creative young people than he had ever known before. Even though he was impressed with the school and its students, he transferred after eighth grade to a more academic high school in the District of Columbia.

Harry enrolled in Armstrong Technical High School, which had two programs of instruction, vocational education and—Harry's choice—college preparation. In spite of the motivation that he had gained in his previous school, Harry did not do well in his first year in high school. During his second year, he became fascinated with geometry but later lost interest and was given a failing grade. Harry had never failed before, and the grade was a major shock to him and his parents. His mother and father explained how strongly they felt about his future education. This was a turning point for Harry. He retook the course and earned an A plus grade. After this experience, he received an A in each of his mathematics courses. Indeed, during his third year in high school, he did well in all his subjects. Harry had come to appreciate the high quality of his education at Armstrong.

Higher Education

After his graduation from high school, Harry Morrison's parents did not have enough money to send him to college. Since he needed to earn money for his education, he first took a job as a janitor and then later a much better job at the Library of Congress.

When he learned that one of his high school friends wanted to attend Catholic University in Washington, D.C., Morrison decided to visit the campus. As he was looking around, he saw Laurence Burwell, his high school homeroom teacher. After Mr. Burwell realized that his promising, former student was not enrolled in college, he insisted that Morrison immediately fill out and submit an application for Catholic. Morrison's application was accepted for the fall of 1951.

Money was still a problem when he began college, and he worked overtime at the Library of Congress to pay his bills. Later, Morrison joined the Reserve Officers Training Corp (ROTC) to help finance his education. At Catholic, Harry Morrison majored in chemistry and took many courses in mathematics and literature. In fact, he combined his interests by writing an English term paper on the subject of nuclear reaction theory.

When Morrison graduated in 1955 with a degree in chemistry, mathematics, and philosophy, he was commissioned as a second lieutenant in the U.S. Air Force. He was scheduled to be sent to a training base in Florida to take instructions as a jet fighter pilot. However, Morrison was now interested in conducting research and made arrangements for a job at the National Institutes of Health (NIH) in Bethesda, Maryland. The work supported government programs, and Morrison was allowed to defer his military service. The arrangement with NIH also allowed him to use the findings from his research to help meet the requirements for an advanced degree at Catholic. He went to class early in the morning, then to his job in nearby Bethesda, and back to the university for classes in the evening.

At NIH, Morrison studied how individual living cells absorbed nutrition and dispelled waste products through the cell membrane. Although the movement of the substances through the membrane was invisible, the progress could be detected by the radiation of radioactive chemicals that had been introduced into the cell's environment.

After 15 months at NIH, Harry decided to become a full-time doctoral student. Again, the government was sufficiently interested in Morrison's work to defer his military service. Morrison's doctoral research concerned one of the most difficult aspects of physical chemistry and used a set of mathematical ideas called Quantum Theory. The theory allows scientists to predict the interactions between individual atoms as they combine to form molecules. The theory can also be used to predict how strong the connections between the atoms will be.

Harry Morrison completed his dissertation based on this study and was awarded his doctoral degree in 1960.

Career Highlights

After his graduation, Dr. Harry Morrison accepted a post-doctoral fellowship at the

National Bureau of Standards (now the National Institute of Standards and Technology). Dr. Morrison used his knowledge of Quantum Theory to study the states of physical matter at very low temperatures.

In 1961, the U.S. Air Force wanted Dr. Morrison to begin active duty. He was not sent to flight school but was assigned to the Air Force Academy in Colorado as an assistant professor of physics.

Dr. Morrison finished his tour of duty in 1964 and accepted a position with the Lawrence Radiation Laboratory (now the Lawrence Livermore National Laboratory), which is managed for the government by the University of California at Berkeley. Using Quantum Theory, Dr. Morrison continued to investigate how substances react at very low temperatures. For example, liquid helium takes on strange properties such as the ability to flow upwards over the walls of a glass container. Dr. Morrison discovered that these properties could also be partly accounted for using Quantum Theory.

Before joining the staff at the Lawrence Laboratory, Dr. Harry Morrison married Harriett Brock. In 1969, the couple had a daughter, Vanessa. In that same year, Dr. Morrison transferred to the Berkeley campus of the University of California, where he became a professor of physics. He also assumed the associate directorship of the Lawrence Hall of Science—a science education center. This position allowed Dr. Morrison to improve science instruction in grades K through 12. To further his goal, he developed a series of hands-on laboratory exercises for students in elementary and middle school.

In order to better prepare minority high school students for their college science courses, Dr. Morrison helped found a program called MESA (Mathematics, Engineering and Science Achievement). The program has grown from the original 18 students to the present 20,000 participants.

In addition to his teaching and research, Dr. Morrison has recently accepted the position as an assistant dean for the College of Letters and Science. His responsibilities now include overseeing courses in literature and philosophy. Dr. Morrison is grateful that his own college curriculum was broad enough to include these subjects.

Sandra Murray

Born: October 7, 1947, in Chicago, Illinois

Status: Associate Professor, Department of Cell Biology and Physiology, School of Medicine, University of Pittsburgh, Pittsburgh, Pennsylvania

Education:

Bachelor of Science degree, University of Chicago, Chicago, Illinois, 1970

Master of Science degree, Texas Southern University, Houston, Texas, 1973

Doctor of Philosophy degree, University of Iowa, Iowa City, Iowa, 1980

Research Area: Cell Biology

Early Years

Sandra Murray was the middle child in a family of three daughters. Her family owned and operated the Murray Brother's Moving Company in the heart of the Black ghetto on Chicago's south side. Muggie Wise-Murray, Sandra's mother, was the accountant, secretary, purchasing agent, and maintenance chief for the moving business. Mrs. Wise-Murray, who spoke with a soft Southern accent, was an extraordinarily busy woman. She not only managed the family business but also took complete care of the family home and ran several small business ventures on the side.

Sandra's father, Charles Murray, bossed the moving crews. He also made Sandra's favorite toys out of scraps of things left behind by the families he moved. For Muggie, these scraps were the source of spare parts that could be used to remake a toaster or radio that could be sold at the outdoor market on Maxwell Street.

When Sandra was a bit older, these discarded pieces were adapted to form components for the scientific apparatuses she exhibited at school science fair competitions. By then, Sandra had learned that someone else's junk could be turned into a treasure trove. She was strongly motivated to create new science projects because science fair participation gave her a week away from the regular classroom, a break she thoroughly enjoyed.

Sandra had been born with a piece of her shoulder bone missing and underwent corrective surgery while still in grade school. It did not go well, however. She temporarily lost control of her right arm and hand and the neck muscles on her right side. This aroused Sandra's curiosity about the workings of the human body. She begged to see the photos taken during her surgery that were used to instruct the interns who visited her hospital room. The more these people tried to hide her chart and photographs, the more curious Sandra became. Ultimately, some of these professionals recognized that her goal was to learn, not to frighten herself. While she recovered, they taught her some of the vocabulary of anatomy. One of the medical doctors who was retiring also gave her some professional books from his office library. The books were added to those that Sandra and her mother had been collecting for years from the stacks people left behind during their moves.

When Sandra returned to school after three months in the hospital, she was pleased that she had learned so much about biology and especially about human anatomy. She realized that she wanted to discover as much as possible about biological science.

While still in high school, she was accepted into a special biomedical research program that allowed selected students to attend Saturday science courses at the University of Chicago. Most of the students came from the wealthy Chicago suburbs, and Sandra was a little fearful of competing with them. Indeed, she was told by one of her high school guidance counselors that she should not aim too high. Sandra had asked the counselor about taking a course in Latin. She had learned in her special Saturday course that Latin words were used in the vocabulary of science. The counselor told Sandra that she would have no use for such knowledge because she was "colored, and a girl." Sandra realized from this and other instances that she would look foolish if she aspired to a career in science and then could not attain it.

Even though she was uncertain about her ability to do well in higher education, Sandra continued to look for new ways to learn about biology. While still in high school, she worked summers and Christmas breaks at the anatomy laboratory at the University of Illinois School of Medicine. One of the scientists in the laboratory, Dr. Lucille Wentworth, tutored Sandra on the preparation of tissue samples and the use of the high-powered microscopes. Being able to see the detailed structures of body cells opened up a new world to Sandra.

This extra work was good preparation for college. However, Sandra was still so uncertain about her own abilities that she did not register as a science major.

Higher Education

In the fall of 1964, just before her 17th birthday, Sandra Murray entered the University of Illinois at Navy Pier in Chicago. Even though Murray continued to live at home, she had to earn enough to finance her tuition and fees.

Murray did not take her first course in biology—her favorite subject—until her second year of college. The books for this course answered all the questions she had been asking since childhood. Murry was so encouraged by her ability to grasp the subject matter that she finally overcame her fear of failure. She now knew that she could become a scientist. Because of her outside work and her indecision about majoring in science, it took Murray six years to complete the four-year program.

In 1970, as soon as she graduated from the University of Illinois, Sandra Murray entered the graduate program in biology at Texas Southern University in Houston, Texas. During her first two years, she worked as a teaching assistant in the biology department. At first she proctored examinations, graded papers, and helped students in the biology laboratory. However, in her final year, Sandra became an instructor in the department and had complete responsibility for her courses.

Very shortly after Sandra Murray began her program of graduate training, she also be-

gan to win awards. She earned awards for leadership within the university community and for her research. In 1973, Murray completed her program and received her master's degree from Texas Southern.

In the fall of 1973, Sandra Murray began her doctoral program in anatomy at the University of Iowa in Iowa City. She worked as a teaching assistant until she was ready to begin the major research project for her dissertation. Fortunately, she received a Ford Foundation Fellowship at this time. The award meant that she could concentrate on her research and not be distracted by other responsibilities. She had chosen a difficult and important topic for her project. Murray studied how a hormone can affect the growth of cancer in the very gland that produces that hormone.

Career Highlights

In 1980, after completing her doctoral program at Iowa, Dr. Murray accepted a postdoctoral traineeship at the University of California at Riverside. This branch of the University of California is noted for investigations on how the chemicals of inheritance, deoxyribonucleic acid and ribonucleic acid (DNA and RNA) affect various organs of the body. This research has been especially concerned with the effects of DNA and RNA on the glands that produce the hormones which regulate many bodily functions.

Dr. Murray's interest in the problems of glandular cancer was relevant to her faculty appointment at the medical school of the University of Pittsburgh. She taught first- and second-year medical students human anatomy, cell biology, and endocrinology, the study of glands and the hormones they produce. Meanwhile, she continued her research on glandular cancer and other aspects of cell biology.

Dr. Murray spent her summers from 1986 through 1990 conducting research and studying with other biologists at the Marine Biological Laboratory at Woods Hole in Massachusetts. During the school year of 1991 to 1992, she was invited to do research at the Scripps Research Institute on Molecular Biology at La Jolla, California. She worked with Dr. Norton B. Gilula and his team of researchers on the precise quantitative measurements of chemicals that influence life functions and the effect of these chemicals on the individual cell.

Shortly after Dr. Murray returned to the University of Pittsburgh in the fall of 1992, she transferred her affiliation to the department of cell biology and physiology in the medical school. Now, she was able to integrate her research interests and activities more easily with the courses that she taught.

Dr. Murray has long been interested in increasing the number of minority students in the fields of science and technology. She vividly remembers how some of her teachers tried to discourage her from a career in science. With her busy schedule of teaching and research, she realized the difficulties in trying to achieve her goals as a scientist and as a champion of minority science students.

Dr. Murray, however, has found a partial solution to her problem. By scheduling substantial visits to institutions with high minority enrollments, she can encourage, educate, and energize students who hope to enter careers in science. In 1986, she spent a period of time at Florida International University in Miami and at Morgan State University in Baltimore, Maryland. In 1989, she again visited two schools, her old school, Texas Southern University in Houston, Texas, and Spelman College in Atlanta, Georgia. More recently, in 1994, Dr. Murray spent her time visiting Selma University in Selma, Georgia. This strategy seems to be working well because her visits can be scheduled in advance so they do not interfere with her

teaching and research. Also, since these visits are sponsored jointly by the Federation of American Societies for Experimental Biology and the National Institute of General Medical Science, they do not place a financial burden on the University of Pittsburgh. By dividing her time between her university career and her responsibilities to minority students, Dr. Murray is advancing the spread of knowledge in the fields of science and technology.

Ivory V. Nelson

Born: June 11, 1934, in Curtis, Louisiana

Status: President and Professor of Chemistry, Central Washington University, Ellensburg, Washington

Education:

Bachelor of Science degree, Grambling State University, Grambling, Louisiana, 1959

Doctor of Philosophy degree, University of Kansas, Lawrence, Kansas, 1963

Research Area: Analytical Chemistry

Early Years

Ivory Nelson was born in Curtis, Louisiana, a very small town near Shreveport, a port city on the Red River. He was born during the worst part of the Great Depression when unemployment was very high. A great many people were jobless and had little hope of ever finding employment. Fortunately, Ivory's father was a minister of the African Methodist Episcopal Church and the family had a small but relatively steady income.

In those days, many of the rural preachers moved from town to town every year or so. Until he finished the fifth grade, Ivory lived in a series of small towns in Louisiana and Mississippi and attended a different school each year. That summer, his mother died. His father could not care for the children on his own. The motherless family moved to Shreveport where other relatives could help with the children. In this more metropolitan setting, the quality of his education improved. Even so, Ivory was not particularly focused on science—or any subject—during his early school days. He, like most of his classmates, did the least possible amount of school work.

When Ivory finished high school, the Korean War was in full swing. He had been 11 years old when World War II ended and had followed the events of that war with great interest. In a way, the Korean War was an extension of the final days of World War II. The Selective Service Act was still in effect, and Ivory was eligible to be drafted. However, Ivory did not wait to be drafted. He enlisted in the U.S. Air Force as soon as possible.

When Ivory took the aptitude and placement examinations given by the Air Force, he always received high scores. Therefore, Ivory was placed in the highly regarded Air Force Security Service. All the other young men assigned to the Security Service had had some college training and were almost always White.

In the late days of World War II, President Harry S. Truman had signed the laws that strictly prohibited racial segregation in the armed forces. However, bringing such ideas into reality took some time. Ivory Nelson was almost always the first Black person to desegregate the units to which he was assigned.

In 1955, after the end of the Korean War, Ivory was given the rank of staff sergeant. During this time, he did exciting work for the Air Force Security Service. He intercepted and decoded enemy radio messages and put our own messages into codes that the enemy could not read.

When he neared the finish of his enlistment, Ivory Nelson applied for flight training in the Air Force. He easily passed the aptitude examinations but was not allowed to transfer into the flight program. Unfortunately, he had no college credits and two years of college was a requirement. While his experiences in the Air Force had been interesting, educational, and enjoyable, he did not want to remain an enlisted man. He wanted to be a flight officer, but that goal was blocked. He was glad to be finished and returned home early in 1955. It was time for him to make some critical decisions about his future. One such decision was to get married and another was to enroll in college.

Higher Education

Ivory Nelson applied to both Southern University and Grambling State University. He was accepted at Grambling for the fall of 1955. Since it was still early in the year, Ivory decided to get a head start by enrolling in a local college for the summer session. He applied and was accepted at Centenary College in Shreveport. When the officials of this previously all-White college discovered that Ivory Nelson was Black, a "great hullabaloo broke loose." Ivory decided to delay his education until the fall.

In a sense, Grambling State University is just down the road from Shreveport. It is in the town of Grambling in north-central Louisiana about 60 miles east of Shreveport. It is best known nationally as a training ground for professional athletes—particularly football players. However, this reputation obscures the fact that Grambling turns out its share of scholars, thinkers, and scientists.

For Ivory Nelson, both of these factors came into his decision to study there, but the main factor was that Grambling was not that far from home. If he felt the need, it was no big deal to hitchhike home for the weekend.

After his first year at Grambling, Ivory Nelson won the Omega Psi Phi Award for the best scholastic performance by a freshman. He was pleased, of course, but did not realize the extent to which this award pointed the way into his future career. At this stage of his education, he was receiving some support from the government as part of his benefits as a war veteran. He was also working during the summers of 1957 and 1958. These sources of funds were helpful, but he was nevertheless very happy to receive the T. H. Harris Scholarship for his senior year at Grambling.

When Ivory Nelson started at Grambling, he wanted to become a medical doctor. Consequently, he took the traditional pre-med program that includes a heavy emphasis on chemistry. He thought that if there were barriers to becoming a physician that could not be overcome, he could fall back on a career as a teacher of science—particularly chemistry—at the high school level.

During his senior year, with the enthusiastic help of his teachers at Grambling, he sent off applications to both medical schools and to graduate schools that offered training in the pure sciences. He soon found that monetary support for a medical education is almost impossible to find but that such support is available for science education at the graduate level. Consequently, Ivory found himself enrolling in the graduate program in chemistry at the University of Kansas in the fall of 1959.

The group of students entering along with Ivory Nelson numbered about 50. The University had a practice of using the qualifying examinations at the end of the first year of graduate study as a means of weeding out the excess numbers of students. Since there were gaps in the training Ivory had received at Grambling, he had to work on closing the gaps every weekend from Friday night until Monday morning for the whole year. Then, on Monday it would not be remedial material but rather all new information to learn and digest. When Ivory came to take the year-end qualifying examinations, he passed three out of the four in the first cycle of exam taking. He was then allowed to retake the fourth exam in a second cycle of testing that was the University's standard procedure. On this cycle, Ivory passed the examination in physical chemistry that he had failed in the first cycle. He could now go forward to the doctoral level. The students who had not passed at least two exams in the first cycle and two more in the second cycle were awarded master's degrees and then dropped from the program.

The person with the strongest influence on the development of Ivory Nelson as a scientist was Professor R.T. Iwamoto. He led Ivory Nelson to focus on the general problem of solubility. Why is one material readily soluble in another, like salt in water, while others like wax and water are not? What properties must be shared between two materials so that they will dissolve in one another? Can the addition of a third compound make the two original materials more or less soluble in one another? In particular, how can the chemist influence the solubility of metals such as copper in water or in other liquids that are not similar to water such as gasoline? Ivory Nelson began a series of research projects in this general area almost as soon as he finished the first year of his graduate training program. He published his first professional scientific report in collaboration with Professor Iwamoto in the fall of 1961. His doctoral research was about the electrical properties of solvents that do not mix well with water. A report of this research was published a year after he graduated.

Meanwhile, Ivory Nelson was not neglecting the other side of his training to be a college professor. In the summer of 1961, he went back to his beloved Grambling University to teach the beginning course in chemistry to incoming freshmen. He also served as a teaching assistant for the chemistry department at the University of Kansas from 1959 to 1962 and won the Dupont Teaching Fellowship in 1962. The money that went with this award helped carry his expenses for his final year at the University of Kansas. Before that final year got underway, however, Ivory Nelson also was able to sample the conditions of work in private industry. During the summer session of 1962, he worked as a research chemist for the American Oil Company and got a feel for the commercial side of chemistry.

When Ivory Nelson graduated in 1963, he was the first Black to receive a Ph.D. in analytical chemistry from the University of Kansas. His honors included memberships in Phi Beta Kappa and the Society of Sigma Xi—among others. He received offers from several large companies to join their research staffs. However, he had seen enough of the business side of chemistry and now sought an academic career. However, he admits that

he was not so high-minded as to take anything less than the offer that had the highest salary.

Career Highlights

As soon as he finished his degree, Dr. Nelson returned to Louisiana. He had been offered and had accepted a position on the faculty of Southern University in Baton Rouge, Louisiana. Southern University is one unit of a state-supported, three-unit system. There is another four-year institution, Louisiana State University, and a two-year college in Shreveport. Southern University has a tradition of serving the Black community, while LSU did not admit Black students until the mid-1960s.

At Southern, Dr. Nelson taught analytical chemistry to young science majors and continued his research on the solubility of metal salts in solvents other than water until 1966. That summer, he was invited by the administrators at the Universidad Autonomous de Guadalajara in Mexico to help them develop their teaching program in science. Dr. Nelson was awarded a Fulbright Scholarship by the U.S. Department of State to help cover the costs of this activity.

Guadalajara is, perhaps, the second largest city in Mexico. It is about 200 miles west of Mexico City and sits among the mountains of central Mexico's coastal range. The nearest ocean-side resort towns are at least 160 miles to the southwest. It contains one large state-supported university that claims to have over 200,000 students. The Autonomous University, however, is privately funded and has only about 6,000 to 7,000 students.

The chemistry department that Dr. Nelson helped to create has now become a school of chemical science with its own director. The program has a strong orientation toward research that was imparted to some degree by the visitor from north of the border by means of the tutoring he provided to the seven people who made up the core faculty in chemistry.

Dr. Nelson returned to Baton Rouge that fall of 1966 to resume his regular teaching duties at Southern University. However, he was beginning to get a taste for university development work, so he accepted an assignment to help expand the operation in Shreveport into a full four-year program. Then, as a way to further broaden his background, Dr. Nelson took a visiting faculty position at Loyola University at the request of the chair of their chemistry department. All of this was essentially preparation for the next major move, which was to become chairman of the division of natural sciences at the new campus of Southern University at Shreveport. In a sense, this move was a homecoming for Dr. Nelson. However, it was also an episode in pioneering because the new school needed almost everything an experienced science faculty person could provide. A key goal was to achieve accreditation at the end of the first year of operations—and this goal was reached. Dr. Nelson created the departments of mathematics, biology, and physics. He established a science library for all the natural sciences. He even persuaded the people in the chemistry department to launch a long-term research program in his favorite problem area—nonwatery solvents. Such a commitment to research is not common in the setting of an institution that specializes in awarding two-year degrees.

Dr. Nelson pulled together all these loose ends at Shreveport and was then eager for still newer challenges. His next move was to the neighboring state of Texas. There, he joined the staff at Prairie View A&M University at Prairie View, Texas. At first, he served as professor and assistant dean for academic affairs. In 1971, he moved up to be vice president for research and special programs. While still continuing his research projects, he began to formulate specific goals for the development of the University. One of his most pressing goals was to develop the means to help disadvantaged young people improve their basic skills in language and mathematics so they would not fail or just drop out during their first year at college. A closely related goal was to provide students at all levels with better and more accessible study materials. This was accomplished by the establishment of a new Learning Resources Center that contained nonprint and electronic materials as well as traditional books and magazines.

In 1979, Dr. Nelson was able to enjoy a brief interlude where his work on the development of new programs took him to Liberia in Africa. With support from the U.S. Agency for International Development, a project was initiated to transform a traditional Liberian high school into a school that would prepare the Liberian students for advanced learning in the sciences and particularly in engineering technology.

Back home, the chronic problem for all institutions of higher learning was money. Minority-oriented institutions have a larger than normal share of such problems. Consequently, Dr. Nelson sought to improve the flow of funds into the Prairie View University for all kinds of development programs as well as for scientific research projects. By 1982, he had increased the yearly flow of money from federal government sources alone to nearly $10 million from the under $2 million that had been the rate when he started.

He also acted to improve the communication flow between administrators and faculty. At the same time, he recognized and encouraged faculty research work by starting a campus magazine that contained reports of faculty research activities. Finally, Dr. Nelson believed in the usefulness of comprehensive, long-range planning. He saw to it that such plans were prepared and that they included consideration for the money it would take to make the plans come true. This discipline worked well when Dr. Nelson was appointed as acting president of the University in 1982.

Like the Southern University system in Louisiana, the A&M system in Texas has several units; in the Texas case, there are five. The headquarters for the whole system is in College Station, Texas. College Station is a small but important town about 90 miles northwest of Houston. The system is directed by a chancellor who makes his office in College Station. In his next move as a developer of college and university programs, Dr. Nelson moved to College Station as executive assistant to the chancellor. In this role, Dr. Nelson was able to further his own goals and improve the operation of the whole system by means of a regular mechanism of review, criticism, and revision of University policies and procedures.

In 1986, Dr. Nelson was ready to take over top command of a system of institutions of higher education. The system was what is called a community college district. Specifically, his system was the Alamo Community College District with three separate college campuses and a special projects center, all managed from offices in San Antonio, Texas. At the time, the system as a whole had 32,000 regular students and 20,000 older students in what are called "continuing education" programs. The total budget was over $100 million per year. In this setting, Dr. Nelson was able to use his planning and executive skills to provide a greater range of educational services to a larger population of citizens with

a reduction of tax money spending while still giving faculty and staff higher incomes. His performance in a racially integrated situation made Dr. Nelson a legitimate candidate for another position in higher education; the presidency of a major four-year university. Such an appointment was not long in coming. In 1992, Dr. Nelson was invited to take over the presidency of the Central Washington University in Ellensburg, Washington. It is of middle size, having about 7,000 students in residence.

Dr. Nelson is now in the process of putting his ideas to work in this new setting. As is common across the country, he is being forced to confront serious budget limitations. His procedures for planning and financial control will be put to a difficult test. In the meantime, Dr. Nelson remains true to his goal of helping to provide the highest-quality education to all who desire to learn—regardless of race, gender, or any other attribute.

Joan Murrell Owens

Born: June 30, 1933, in Miami, Florida

Status: Associate Professor, Department of Biology, Howard University, Washington, D.C.

Education:

Bachelor of Arts degree, Fisk University, Nashville, Tennessee, 1954

Master of Arts degree, University of Michigan, Ann Arbor, Michigan, 1956

Bachelor of Science degree, George Washington University, Washington, D.C., 1973

Master of Arts degree, George Washington University, 1976

Doctor of Philosophy degree, George Washington University, 1984

Research Area: Marine Biology

Early Years

Joan Murrell's father was a dentist, which allowed him and his family to live comfortably even during the Great Depression days of the 1930s. Dr. Murrell liked to fish, and took his wife and their three daughters on weekend fishing expeditions near their home in Miami.

Joan loved the sea and was fascinated by all its creatures. As a child, she spent hours watching the changes in the colors of the water. Over the years, she became acquainted with many water animals. She enjoyed watching the big, gentle manatees, the relatively small but aggressive Florida alligators, and the frisky river otters.

By the time Joan was in junior high school, she had begun reading books about the sea and the scientists who were studying it. One of her favorite books was Jacques Cousteau's *Silent World,* and years later, she became a charter member of the Jacques Cousteau Society. During high school, Joan began to dream of a career in marine biology.

Higher Education

In 1950, when Joan Murrell entered Fisk University, she was disappointed to discover that neither women nor African Americans were welcome in the marine sciences. She faced the problem of finding a second career choice. Murrell's mother suggested that she prepare for a career in teaching. Murrell considered majoring in mathematics, psychology, or art. Finally, she kept her options open by majoring in fine art, earning a double minor in psychology and mathematics, and taking education courses.

When she graduated with honors from Fisk in 1954, she was still uncertain about her future career. She was admitted to the graduate commercial art program in the School of Architecture at the University of Michigan in Ann Arbor. Soon, Murrell realized that she did not enjoy the program and needed to chose a new area of graduate study—preferably at the University of Michigan.

While walking on the campus, she happened to meet Leonard Spearman, an acquaintance from her high school days in Miami. Leonard was a graduate student in the School of Education. He suggested that Murrell might enjoy a program in the Bureau of Psychological Services, a part of the School of Education. She soon found that she had a special talent for working with brain damaged and emotionally disturbed children. Even before she finished her master's degree in 1956, she began to teach reading to the children at the Children's Psychiatric Hospital that was connected to the university.

In 1957, after two years at the hospital, Murrell was invited to join the staff of the English department at Howard University in Washington, D.C. She taught incoming students who did not have the reading skills needed to succeed in college. She designed and conducted a program that would improve their skills in the shortest possible time.

In 1964, her husband's job took her to Massachusetts, and she went to work for Education Services, Inc., in Newton, Massachusetts. She developed new procedures and programs for teaching English to educationally disadvantaged high school students. Her teaching concepts later served as the model for the Upward Bound programs.

Two years later, Joan Murrell Owens began to design college remedial programs for the Institute for Services to Education, Inc.—at first in Newton and later in Washington, D.C. Over the years, she had dealt with reluctant learners at every school level, from elementary through college. Now was time for a reappraisal of her future.

Owens had never really stopped dreaming of a career as a marine biologist. Almost 15 years after receiving her master's degree, she seriously considered returning to school to prepare for a new career. She turned for guidance to a friend and colleague, Dr. Phillip Morrison, a renowned physicist. He believed that Owens's interest and commitment were strong enough to ensure her success and encouraged her to pursue her dream.

When Owens returned to Washington, D.C., in 1970, she decided to begin her studies. Unfortunately, none of the many colleges in and around D.C. had an undergraduate program in marine science. She discussed her problem with an old friend Conrad Snowden, then assistant provost at Princeton University. He pointed out that a major in geology and a minor in zoology would be the equal of a formal program in marine science. With the approval of the chair of the geology department, Joan Owens enrolled at George Washington University in Washington, D.C.

After taking courses, including paleontology, oceanography, marine geology, and evolution in the geology department, and zoology, marine biology, and ecology in the biological sciences department, she was awarded her bachelor of science degree in 1973. She immediately entered the graduate program at George Washington in geology—with a specialization in paleontology. Owens received a fellowship from the Ford Foundation, which paid her tuition, fees, school expenses, and a small stipend for living expenses. She received her master's degree from George Washington in 1976.

Joan Owens remained at George Washington for her doctoral program. To help her decide on a dissertation topic, her advisor, Dr. A. G. Coates, suggested that she confer with some prominent marine scientists. Dr. Stephen D. Cairns of the Smithsonian Institute in Washington told Owens about a little-known family of deep-sea corals that biologists at the Smithsonian wanted someone to study. Unlike most corals that live near the surface of the ocean, these corals live at depths well below the layers penetrated by sunlight. They do not form colonies like other corals, and each animal—the size of a smallish button—lives alone.

The Smithsonian had a large collection of the beautiful and delicate internal skeletons of these animals. Owens was fascinated by the collection and immediately decided that the coral would be the subject of her dissertation studies.

Ordinary reef corals support microscopic plants within their bodies. These plants thrive on the shallow water sunshine and provide the coral animal with calcium carbonate and other minerals that reef corals need for their existence. Such plants are known as symbiots because both the plants and the coral animals benefit from the relationship. The little button corals have no such relationships and must compete for minerals with other sea creatures. Although the subject of Owens's research lives only in deep water, other types of button coral live elsewhere in the ocean.

Before finishing her dissertation studies, Owens took a teaching job at Howard University in the department of geology and geography. Her course preparation allowed her to study the whole range of marine organisms—both modern and extinct. By teaching an introductory course in oceanography, she extended her knowledge of ecology and human influence on sea life. In 1984, Joan Murrell Owens completed her research on the button corals and received her degree from George Washington University. She was the first African American woman in United States history to earn a doctorate in geology.

Career Highlights

Dr. Owens's career began before her doctoral degree was awarded. She had already taught geology courses at Howard University and presented scientific papers. Her first paper, concerning evolutionary changes in the skeletons of button corals, was given at an international meeting of marine scientists in 1983. Her paper received favorable comments. Dr. Owens perceived an attitude change in geologists and marine scientists toward the acceptance of women and African Americans into their fields. She had been a pioneer in establishing a more open community in the marine sciences.

Such community support led Dr. Owens to pursue additional research projects. She has redefined the classification of button corals and has discovered a completely new species which she named *Letepsammia franki* after her husband, Frank Owens. Funds to support her on-going research come from major oil companies as well as from Howard University faculty research grants.

Dr. Owens continues to teach at Howard University. She particularly enjoys teaching beginning science courses, where she is able to show students that science can be interesting and relatively easy. When such a student decides to become a science major, she is very pleased. Dr. Owens also finds satisfaction when her science majors receive outside recognition.

In addition, Dr. Owens teaches and lectures at other institutions. Audiences of all ages are fascinated when she explains how fossils can display what happened on earth millions of years ago. In addition, Dr. Owens is involved in the Science Discovery Day program sponsored by the American Association for the Advancement of Science. Each spring, minority women scientists give presentations at junior high schools. The goal of the program is to generate interest in science and demonstrate that both gender and ethnic disadvantages can be overcome.

When Howard University eliminated the department of geology and geography a few years ago, Dr. Owens transferred to the biology department. She now teaches marine biology—her youthful dream—and advises her students to keep their own dreams alive.

Hildrus A. Poindexter

Born: May 10, 1901, in Memphis, Tennessee

Status: Died, April 21, 1987, in Clinton, Maryland

Education:

Bachelor of Arts degree, Lincoln University, Lincoln University, Pennsylvania, 1924

Doctor of Medicine degree, Harvard University, Cambridge, Massachusetts, 1929

Master of Science degree, Columbia University, New York, New York, 1930

Doctor of Philosophy degree, Columbia University, 1932

Master of Public Health degree, Columbia University, 1937

Research Area: Bacteriology

Early Years

Hildrus Poindexter was the sixth of eleven children born to Frederick and Luvenia Poindexter. Although his birth was registered in Memphis, Tennessee, Hildrus had been born on his parents' farm. He was a big baby and soon was given the nickname, Gus.

His parents were tenant farmers in Delta Country about 15 miles up the Mississippi River from Memphis. Their main cash crop was cotton, and they used the cash to pay the rent on the farm. In good years, there were a few dollars left after the rent was paid. Luckily, they needed little cash for food because the family grew or raised almost everything that they ate.

In those days, there were few publicly funded schools for young African Americans in rural Tennessee. The owners of the big plantations controlled the school system and were not enthusiastic about investing tax funds in education for Black children. Consequently, the local African American families had to help themselves, and the church was one of the main forces for the improvement of Black education. Reverend Henry L. Peterson served the Black community near the Poindexter farm as both their pastor and the principal of the local school. Fortunately, Rev. Peterson was broadly educated in the classics and instructed young Gus in Latin, Greek, and mathematics. He also provided guidance and inspiration to his students. However, Rev. Peterson did not always have the funds to hire the necessary teachers. Consequently, formal education for Gus and the other children was an on-again, off-again situation. Indeed, Gus wasn't ready for high school until he was 15 years old.

As a teenager, he once found himself in deep trouble with his father. He had neglected one of his chores because he was playing a tightly fought game of sandlot baseball. Before his father could punish Gus with a leather strap, the boy decided that he had enough and ran away from home. He ran miles to an uncle's house, and the uncle allowed him to remain. He soon registered for school in his new neighborhood. He was surprised to find that he knew more about mathematics than the regular teacher. She promptly hired Gus as her assistant, and he earned $13 per month from his first teaching job.

The next fall, Gus returned home. He and his father called a truce and tried to ignore one another. After a while, Gus decided to leave east Tennessee altogether and seek more education and a better life. Rev. Peterson encouraged him in his plan because he hoped that Gus might eventually decide to become a Presbyterian minister.

Two years passed before arrangements could be made for Gus to enter the Swift Memorial College in Rogersville, Tennessee. This Presbyterian school offered remedial courses at the upper grade school level and traditional courses at the high school level. The instruction also included a specialized program in teacher training, which allowed the school to be called a college.

Poindexter's irregular educational background forced him to take remedial courses in English, history, and geography, which he took at the same time he was also enrolled in regular high school courses in algebra, Latin, and Greek. His teachers were confused because this new student, with little background in English, could readily translate Bible passages from the original Greek. Gus gladly worked two part-time jobs to cover his tuition and expenses at Swift.

During his first summer, the County Board of Education certified Gus to teach elementary school because of his prior experience as a teacher. The board then promptly assigned him as an assistant teacher in the worst school in the county. Soon after he arrived, the senior teacher gave up trying to enforce discipline. After Gus proved that he could keep order, the board gave him full responsibility for the school. Consequently, Gus earned a regular teacher's salary of $50.00 a month for the two-month summer session.

By January of 1919, Gus had completed all of Swift's requirements for both a high school diploma and a teaching certificate. His teachers had arranged for Gus to enter Lincoln University in Pennsylvania in the fall. The pressure to save money for his education was even stronger than before. With the help of some friends, Gus moved to Detroit, Michigan, and found work. Soon he was working full-time at both the Studebaker automobile factory and the Timkin Detroit Axle Company. By working two jobs a day and doing odd jobs on weekends, Gus was able to repay all his school debts and save a small amount of money.

Higher Education

When Gus Poindexter enrolled at Lincoln University, it was a small, all-male, almost all-Black school run by the Presbyterian Church. It was linked to Princeton University through the church connection. In fact, the nearly all-White faculty tended—rather unrealistically—to use Princeton students as models for academic and social standards.

Poindexter still suffered from some academic deficiencies, so his admission to the college was probational. By the end of the first semester, however, he had done well enough to have the probation removed. Poindexter was now a regular student. His program was a peculiar mixture of Latin, Greek, and Bible studies with a smattering of liberal arts, such as literature, and some sciences, such as organic chemistry.

During the school year, Gus Poindexter worked at everything from tutoring students in Greek and Latin to carrying out the ashes from the big coal-burning boilers. In his first summer, he earned little money but learned much from the racism he experienced as a dishwasher in Atlantic City, New Jersey. During his second summer, he worked for the Pullman Company as a porter. He enjoyed this opportunity to travel and to receive an education in geography. He continued to work for Pullman each summer and returned even after he graduated from Lincoln University.

During the school year, sports, especially football, were Poindexter's favorite activities outside the classroom. In his third and fourth years, he made conference All-American. He also set records in the 16-pound shot put. Gus Poindexter met his future wife when she attended one of Lincoln's baseball games. He married Ruth Viola Grier in June of 1924, the same month that he graduated from Lincoln.

Poindexter knew that he needed to save some money before he could afford to enter medical school. Mary Potter High School in Oxford, North Carolina—another Presbyterian institution—hired both Gus and Ruth. Gus Poindexter taught general science and Latin and was the coach and athletic director. The latter positions were the most important to the school officials and the surrounding community. He soon had a winning team in football, a competitive team in basketball, and a championship team in baseball. His sandlot sports—which had gotten him in trouble with his father—finally became positive experiences.

At the end of the school year of 1924–25, Poindexter had earned enough to pay his accumulated debts and save a small amount of money. He was also able to acquire more savings from his summer work with the Pullman Company. In the fall, he began two years of premedical studies at Dartmouth College in Hanover, New Hampshire.

Finally, after the two years of preparation, Poindexter enrolled in Harvard Medical School in 1927. While at Harvard, he came to the attention of Mrs. Elizabeth A. Mason, a philanthropist. Mrs. Mason had given much financial help to the development of health care education at Tuskegee Institute in Alabama. She became Poindexter's unofficial sponsor at Harvard. When he graduated from medical school in 1929, she persuaded him to go to Alabama for his internship. Mrs. Mason wanted him to work at the John A. Andrew Memorial Hospital, named in honor of her grandfather. The internship was an unpleasant year for Dr. Poindexter because he had not wanted to return to the Deep South. It was even more unpleasant for Ruth, who had never experienced Southern culture.

Dr. Poindexter asked his friends for help. They arranged for him to complete his internship and residency requirements at the Columbia University of Physicians and Surgeons in New York City. Dr. Poindexter was also accepted to work toward additional university degrees at Columbia. Indeed, he received a master's degree in bacteriology in 1930, just before passing his board examinations in medicine and surgery.

Career Highlights

Dr. Poindexter was now qualified to practice medicine in 45 states and many foreign countries. However, he decided that he would prefer a career in teaching. He joined the faculty of the Howard University Medical School in Washington, D.C., in July 1931. He was given a wide variety of teaching and administrative duties. These included service as an unofficial medical ambassador, both inside and outside the United States. For example, he was one of the participants in the preventive medicine programs sponsored by the Rockefeller Foundation in the southern part of the country. Dr. Poindexter spent part of 1934 and 1937 in Alabama and Mississippi studying the distribution of various chronic diseases among the rural population.

These projects fit in well with the basic theme of Dr. Poindexter's research interests. He wanted to understand all causes, routes of infection, symptoms, and effective treatments for diseases that occur in tropical climates. Most of his research was focused on the microscopic blood parasites that are usually transmitted by insects, such as malaria and African sleeping sickness. Dr. Poindexter fought against these illnesses during most of his lifetime.

While some of his studies were conducted by examining hundreds of human patients, his most significant contributions came from work in the laboratory. During his dissertation research, Dr. Poindexter made thousands of observations of white rats and mice. He studied how the parasites that cause sleeping sickness move through the body and concentrate in certain locations. Based on these studies and others, Dr. Poindexter earned an additional doctorate in bacteriology and parasitology in 1932 from Columbia University. In 1937, he was awarded a master of science degree in public health and tropical medicine from the same school.

In late 1941, the United States was drawn into World War II. Dr. Poindexter registered for the military draft but he was deferred because he was training other physicians. However, expertise in one of his medical specialties, tropical medicine, was soon to be in great demand. One of the first campaigns of the war was fought in North Africa, a tropical area. At that time, few specialists in this field of medicine were eligible for military service. Therefore, two high-ranking officers in the Army Medical Corp tried to persuade their colleague, Dr. Poindexter, to enlist as a volunteer. He was offered the rank of captain in the medical corp, but Dr. Poindexter declined this rank. He knew that several of his Harvard classmates had already volunteered and had been awarded higher ranks—those of major and lieutenant colonel. Finally, in May of 1943, the army offered Dr. Poindexter an appointment at the rank of major.

By the time the slow-moving military bureaucracy had decided on Dr. Poindexter's first assignment, the campaign in Africa was over. Dr. Poindexter was then given a variety of minor assignments. He attended a class in military protocol and a refresher course in tropical medicine, which was taught at the Walter Reed Army Hospital in Washington, D.C. After spending some unpleasant weeks at Fort Huachuca in Arizona, Dr. Poindexter sailed to the South Pacific. In mid-February 1944, he landed on the beach at Guadalcanal, one of the Solomon Islands. The battle for Guadalcanal—between U.S. and Japanese forces—had recently ended, and small bands of Japanese soldiers were still active in the jungle. Luckily, Dr. Poindexter was removed from the island after just one day.

His next assignment was more promising. Dr. Poindexter joined the headquarters unit of the 93rd Infantry Division as division malariologist. He traveled with them as they sailed northward and stopped at many islands in the Solomon and Bougainville groups. During this assignment, Dr. Poindexter instituted a program which greatly reduced the rate of malarial infection in the troops. He was awarded the Bronze Star for his work. Dr. Poindexter also received a unit citation for being part of the medical battalion which fought off a suicide charge by the Japanese on the island of Bougainville. In January of 1947, Dr. Poindexter left the army as a lieutenant colonel and joined the United States Public Health Service.

His first assignment with the Public Health Service was in the African country of Liberia. Dr. Poindexter worked for the new foreign aid program which had been developed under President Harry S. Truman. His task in Liberia concerned every aspect of health care. He studied the training of health providers, disease prevention (the general population was being instructed in hygiene and related practices), treatment, and research. His research included conducting health surveys to determine patterns of illness in the population and the study of specific diseases such as leprosy. For about two years, Dr. Poindexter managed all these activities. Then, from November 1948 until July 1953, he served as senior medical officer at the U.S. Embassy in the capital city of Monrovia.

His next tour of duty for the Public Health Service was spent in Viet Nam. At the time, it was still a "protectorate" of France. He was stationed first in the north at Hanoi and later in the south at Saigon. Not long after his arrival, he was made responsible for the health of refugees from the battle of Dien Bien Phu, which led to the withdrawal of the French Foreign Legion and the division of the country into North Viet Nam and South Viet Nam. The North became a communist republic. The South was organized as a parliamentary democracy with both an emperor (Boa Dai) and a president (Ngo Dinh Diem). This awkward political situation finally resulted in military involvement by the United States and the tragedy of the Viet Nam War.

However, during most of the time that Dr. Poindexter was in the country, there was little military activity. He carried out a public health program similar to the one which he had conducted in Liberia. In this setting, he was able to direct new research on the problem of intestinal parasites. Fortunately, Dr. Poindexter left Viet Nam in April of 1956 before the fighting began to escalate.

In order to extend his knowledge of tropical medicine, Dr. Poindexter next sought an assignment in South America. To improve his chances, he attended a short course at the Center for Disease Control in Atlanta, Georgia. This course concerned the latest research on infectious diseases. Soon after, he was assigned as chief public health officer in the U.S. Embassy in Paramaribo, the capital of Surinam. Dr. Poindexter's studies determined that parasite infection of the intestinal tract was the most common illness among all segments of the Surinam population. This highly curable condition is mainly a consequence of poverty.

The Bushnegros, which make up 10 percent of the Surinam population, are descendants of escaped slaves whose ancestors participated in slave revolutions in the 17th and 18th centuries. They tend to live in the remote interior rain forests, and their lives have changed little from the original West African practices. The Bushnegros fascinated Dr. Poindexter. In his relationship with the tribal people, he functioned as both an anthropologist and a physician.

Dr. Poindexter's next assignment was Iraq. Unfortunately, his transfer to this post came at the time of the revolution, lead by officers of the Iraqi Army, which overthrew the King. Dr. Poindexter's travel papers had been stamped with the royal seal in Washington. When he arrived in Baghdad, the seal was taken as a sign of counter-revolutionary be-

liefs. For a while, Dr. Poindexter was denied official entry into the country. After he was allowed to enter, his short visit gave him little time to work for public health. His one contribution was a scheme for the control of the local sandfly, a pest which transmits a variety of diseases.

The short stay in Iraq was followed by a regular two-year assignment in Libya. This tour led to field work in Egypt, the Sudan, Ethiopia, Aden, and Somalia. After his work in Africa, he spent six months in Jamaica, where he conducted research on the latest methods of malarial eradication. Following these studies, he returned to Africa for a final three-year tour in Sierra Leone.

In 1965, after Dr. Poindexter retired from the U.S. Public Health Service, he reestablished his old position at Howard University Medical School and continued his study of human diseases. Indeed, Dr. Poindexter did not stop working until his death in 1987 at the age of 86.

Kennedy J. Reed

Born: May 24, 1944, in Memphis, Tennessee

Status: Physicist, Lawrence Livermore National Laboratory, Livermore, California

Education:

Bachelor of Science degree, Monmouth College, Monmouth, Illinois, 1967

Master of Science degree, University of Wisconsin, Superior, Wisconsin, 1971

Doctor of Philosophy degree, University of Nebraska, Lincoln, Nebraska, 1976

Research Area: Theoretical Physics

Early Years

Kennedy Reed's great-grandfather, Ephraim Gator, was a slave on a Mississippi plantation. The son of the plantation owner, who was about Ephraim's age, broke the state law and taught Ephraim to read and write. Ephraim, in return, helped him each evening with his homework.

After the Civil War, Ephraim became a teacher and worked with church-sponsored teachers to educate former slaves. Ephraim Gator also helped found Rust College in Holly Springs, Mississippi. The college, sponsored by the United Methodist Church, now has about 1,200 students and a traditional liberal arts program that serves the African American community. Ephraim's commitment to education was passed on to his daughter (who lived to be 113 years old) and to his granddaughter, Lula, Kennedy Reed's mother.

Lula McClain Reed took her teacher's training at LeMoyne College in Memphis, Tennessee. She married Earl Reed just before the United States entered World War II in 1941. The family moved from Memphis to Chicago, Illinois, when Kennedy, the second of six children, was three years old. His father worked as a mechanic for the Ford Motor Company, and his mother taught elementary school. Unfortunately, the parents divorced after a few years, and the financial situation became difficult, as Kennedy's mother provided for the six children on her modest teacher's salary. The family lived in one of the giant Public Housing Authority apartment buildings on Chicago's south side.

Kennedy began school at Dolittle Elementary, a segregated school in a Chicago ghetto. Regardless of the crowded, imperfect conditions, Kennedy and his friends enjoyed learning. They particularly liked to study nature—especially snakes—in the nearby fields.

When Kennedy was about 10 years old, more public housing was built in his neighborhood. The large excavations were good sites for various games, and Kennedy noticed many unusual rocks in the deep holes. He and his older brother started a rock collection that they expanded by combing the sandy shores of Lake Michigan to find new rocks and fossils of sea animals.

Their schoolmates became interested in the collection and questioned the boys about the rocks. In order to answer all the questions, Kennedy and his brother began to study geology books—and other science books—that they borrowed from the Chicago public libraries. These books told of specific test procedures for determining the chemical composition of their rocks, and, soon, the boys' bedroom was transformed into a chemistry laboratory. Their mother encouraged their interest and took the boys to the Museum of Science and Industry and to the Field Museum of Natural History in Chicago.

When Kennedy was in the sixth grade, the brothers entered their rock collection in the local science fair. They were gratified when one of the judges, a high school science teacher, gave them some unusual rocks from his own collection.

As Kennedy became more interested in geology, he began to study the earth and the other planets in the solar system. When he was 14, he had saved enough money to buy a simple telescope. In order to study the stars and planets, he got up at four or five o'clock in the morning and took his telescope to the roof of his apartment building.

When Kennedy was ready for high school, he wanted to attend a nearby school with his friends. However, his mother insisted that he enroll in Tilden Technical High School—an integrated public school that prepared students for careers in science and engineering. At Tilden, Kennedy received well-rounded, basic education and guidance in finding college scholarships.

In spite of the educational opportunities at Tilden, Kennedy was often an indifferent student. He did not regain his early enthusiasm for learning until his senior year when his chemistry teacher took an interest in Kennedy's accomplishments. She encouraged his interest in research by allowing him to use the school's chemistry laboratory after school hours. These extracurricular study sessions increased Kennedy's motivation, and by the time he graduated in January 1962, he had received several scholarship offers.

Higher Education

Of the scholarships he'd been offered, Kennedy Reed accepted one from Monmouth College. Because of his mid-year graduation, he enrolled as a nondegree student at the Chicago campus of the University of Illinois during the spring term. He took college chemistry, calculus, and other mathematics and science courses to prepare him for more advanced work at Monmouth.

Monmouth is a liberal arts school in the small town of Monmouth, Illinois. Because there were few African Americans living in the town or enrolled in the college, Reed was more conscious of his race than ever before—he could not even get a haircut in the town.

He first chose chemistry as his major subject but soon became interested in the theory of quantum mechanics—the mathematical explanation of chemical reactions. The use of this theory allows chemists to determine the atomic makeup of a substance by observing the patterns of light given off by the substance when heated to a very high temperature. Since this theory is included in the study of physics, Reed transferred his major from chemistry to physics.

In 1967, as soon as he graduated from Monmouth, Reed married his childhood sweetheart. That fall, he began teaching physics at one of Chicago's inner-city high schools. He enjoyed his job but soon realized the need for more education and accepted a National Science Foundation fellowship for his graduate studies.

In 1970, Kennedy Reed entered the University of Wisconsin at Superior. Because he had taken advanced night and summer courses while teaching high school, he was able to earn his master's degree in one year. His research project was on the physics of fundamental particles such as the proton, the stable, positively charged unit in an atom; the neutron, the neutral unit in an atom; and the electron, the negatively charged unit in an atom.

Reed continued his graduate training at the University of Nebraska at Lincoln. During his doctoral program, he worked with scientists who "smashed" atoms. Target atoms are "smashed" by being struck by electrically charged atoms that have been accelerated to a very high speed. These charged atoms, called ions, have been stripped of one of their electrons. They can be propelled in a specific path by a series of magnets along a channel and into the target atoms.

Kennedy Reed used mathematical equations to predict what would happen when ions with a known level of energy strike specific target atoms. Such equations require tens of thousands of mathematical steps, and to speed the process, Reed designed a computer program to calculate the solution. By the use of this program, he demonstrated how to control the spin rate of the particles—parts of the atoms that were split by the collision. The rapid spinning of the particles releases energy in the form of X rays. The team of scientists were among the first to produce the X-ray lasers used to study the structure of complicated crystal molecules.

Career Highlights

After receiving his doctoral degree from Nebraska in 1976, Dr. Reed accepted a faculty appointment at Morehouse College in Atlanta, Georgia. He continued his research on the mathematical aspects of atomic physics by using the computer facilities at Georgia State University and the Georgia Institute of Technology in Atlanta.

At this time, Lawrence Livermore National Laboratory in California, funded by the U.S. Department of Energy, had initiated an outreach program to the science faculties of historically Black colleges and universities (HBCUs). African American scientists were invited to spend a summer term at the laboratory, and Dr. Reed was chosen to attend after his first year at Morehouse. The relationship between Dr. Reed and the research workers at the national laboratory—based on shared interests in ion-atom collisions—was so strong that Dr. Reed was invited back the following summer. In 1979, he returned to the laboratory during a two-year leave from Morehouse and accepted a regular staff appointment there, when his leave from Morehouse expired.

Soon, Dr. Reed's work focused on the difficult analyses of collisions between ions and electrons. The observations of such collisions provide information that is relevant to the Einstein theory of relativity. This famous theory predicts that the faster you move, the slower time passes. Such changes in the rate of time could be demonstrated by Dr. Reed's analyses.

Dr. Reed's research also revealed that the reactions between ions and electrons are important in the possible generation of electric power by atomic fusion. In fusion, two atoms combine to make a third element, and heat—but no new radiation is produced. At present, nuclear power plants use fission. In this process, a large atom divides into two different elements plus heat; in this case, however, harmful radiation is generated. Consequently, fusion reactors would be much safer than fission reactors. So far, fusion reactors are too costly to be used to produce large amounts of electrical power.

Dr. Reed also helped discover new ways in which elements could be easily ionized. The resulting ions could be used to generate X rays of the kind needed for X-ray lasers. These lasers are useful in the study of living cells because they can form three dimensional images of the tiny structures inside a cell. There is a strong demand for more advanced research on the workings of these X-ray lasers.

Because of his knowledge of ionization, Dr. Reed has been invited to visit research centers in Germany, Belgium, England, Northern Ireland, and West Africa. He has given lectures and worked with scientists on the magnetic control of high temperature ion plasmas—electrically charged gasses.

Over the years, Dr. Reed has made a regular practice of inviting science faculty and students from Morehouse College—where he once taught—to visit Lawrence Livermore Labs. His guests receive valuable experience in advanced scientific research.

Dr. Reed also helped found the National Physical Science Consortium, a group of about 30 colleges and universities that provides physics fellowships for women and minority students. Dr. Reed has also been active in the American Institute of Physics and the National Science Foundation. Additionally, in 1991, he traveled to the Bouchet Conference in West Africa to encourage collaboration in physics research between African and African American scientists.

Carl A. Rouse

Born: July 14, 1926, at Youngstown, Ohio

Status: Founder, Rouse Research, Inc., Del Mar, California

Education:

Bachelor of Science degree, Case Western Reserve University, Cleveland, Ohio, 1951

Master of Science degree, California Institute of Technology, Pasadena, California, 1953

Doctor of Philosophy degree, California Institute of Technology, 1956

Research Area: Astrophysics

Early Years

Carl Rouse grew up in a large family. He had two older brothers and four younger sisters. Two young cousins, children of his mother's sister, also lived with the Rouse family.

Before Carl was born, the family had moved from South Carolina to Youngstown, Ohio, a center of the steel industry. During World War I, there was a shortage of steel workers, and Carl's father was able to earn a good salary working in the mills. Many of Mr. Rouse's older relatives also moved to Youngstown to work in the steel industry. After the war, Carl's father, who was a very talented mechanic, started his own auto repair shop.

The neighborhood where the Rouse family lived was called Haselton. Although close to large steel factories, it was not an unpleasant place to live. Indeed, Carl learned to swim in the lovely, clean stream that flowed near his home. Later, he worked as a lifeguard in a nearby park.

There was always activity in the neighborhood because the steel mills stayed open day and night. The shops, food stores, and neighborhood recreation centers were busy all the time. Carl learned photography and woodworking in one of these centers. He also learned to build model airplanes, which he powered by rubber bands attached to the propellers. If his models were properly designed and built, they would fly for more than a minute.

As a youngster, Carl learned to play baseball, football, and basketball. However, boxing was his favorite sport. Even though his eyesight was not perfect, he was a very good boxer. Later, when he was in high school, he won the regional Golden Gloves championship in his weight class.

His work with photography and model airplanes gave Carl an introduction to science. He also acquired technical knowledge by helping his father in their auto repair shop.

His father told him about each auto part and how the various parts worked together, and this gave Carl a good practical knowledge of engineering.

Haselton was a multiethnic neighborhood. African American, Irish, and Eastern European families lived there. Almost all the men worked in the steel mills. Even though the children played together and went to school together, activities involving adults were segregated. When Carl joined the Boy Scouts, he was assigned to a segregated troop. There was also prejudice in the schools.

When Carl was in eighth grade, he entered a contest on current affairs sponsored by *Time* magazine. Carl was delighted when he won the prize, a one-year subscription to *Time* magazine. This experience helped improve Carl's self-confidence, since he discovered that he knew about a great many things.

After he entered high school, Carl's interest in science increased. He had good teachers, but it was his older brother who taught him about modern technology—his greatest interest. European countries were preparing for World War II, and Carl read about their new weapons, tanks, and aircraft. He and his brother were especially excited about the new combat aircraft. They both enjoyed building models of these advanced military airplanes.

In high school, Carl received very good grades in all his subjects. His chemistry teacher encouraged him to consider a career in science. His mathematics teacher, however, did not agree. He advised Carl to study law or another profession where he could have Black clients. He was afraid that Carl would not overcome the prejudice found in the fields of science or engineering. Probably many young African Americans have been advised to avoid scientific careers for this reason.

Indeed, Carl sometimes faced prejudice during his summer employment. While in high school, he took jobs outside the family business. He found that some bosses were honorable while others tried to pay Carl low wages because he was African American.

Higher Education

Carl Rouse graduated from high school in February 1944, one semester ahead of his classmates. World War II was reaching a new intensity. Since Rouse had passed the U.S. Army tests for advanced technical training, they sent him to Howard University in Washington, D.C., where he attended an accelerated course in engineering. In June, after that course was completed, he was sent to Pennsylvania State College (now University) for additional training.

As soon as Rouse reached 18 years of age, he was transferred to Fort McClellan in Alabama. There, he went through basic infantry training with a segregated company and was soon promoted to cadet platoon leader. Because Rouse was so young, he had to use his boxing skills to gain respect from some of the older recruits.

With the war in a crisis stage, the army had a shortage of ordinary soldiers. Most of the men in Rouse's unit were sent to Europe in December of 1944, which was the time of the famous Battle of the Bulge. At first, the battle was a grave setback for the U.S. Army, but the American soldiers finally held fast and turned the tide against the Germans.

Because of his outstanding grades at Pennsylvania State College, Carl Rouse was not sent to Europe. Instead, he was sent to New York University to study civil engineering. Rouse finished their entire program in one year. Fortunately, the war was over by the time he completed his course. He stayed in the Army for another six months and was discharged in July 1946.

Back home in Youngstown, Ohio, Rouse took a job making engineering drawings for the

Mahoning County government, but he really wanted to go back to school. The county engineer had a friend at Case Institute of Technology (later Case Western Reserve University) in Cleveland, Ohio. He supported Rouse's application to enroll in their physics department, and Rouse began the program in September 1947.

Unfortunately, none of the courses that he completed during his Army training were accepted for credit by Case Institute. However, Rouse's study of engineering made his difficult schedule much easier. During his freshman year, his teachers recognized that Rouse was talented in physics and mathematics and talked to him about graduate school. In fact, his good scholarship was widely recognized in 1950 when he was elected to two national honor societies, Tau Beta Pi and Sigma Xi. When Carl Rouse graduated from Case Institute in 1951, he was awarded the Physics Prize for his excellent grades.

During his time at college, Rouse, as a veteran, received money for his education under the GI Bill of Rights. He also worked every Saturday in the machine shop at Case Institute. Then, each summer, he would go back to Youngstown and work for the county engineer. He was pleased that he did not need to borrow money to finance his college education.

Because of his outstanding work at Case Institute, Rouse was accepted in the master's program at the California Institute of Technology in Pasadena and awarded a one-year institute fellowship. During the summer after his first year, he met a young woman named Lorraine Moxley, an employee of the Girl Scouts of America. Carl and Lorraine were married in 1955.

In his second year at the California Institute of Technology, Carl Rouse became a research assistant to Professor Carl D. Anderson. In 1932, Dr. Anderson had won the Nobel Prize for physics for his discovery of a new particle called a positron. This tiny subatomic particle was like an electron but had a positive rather than a negative charge.

Carl Rouse, guided by Professor Eugene W. Cowan, also conducted his own research. Rouses's primary project was to design a new type of particle detector. Atomic particles are far too small to be seen through the most powerful microscope. However, when a particle reacts with another material in a particle detector, tracks of the reaction are imprinted on a glass plate. The pattern of the tracks is photographed and physicists study the patterns. Scientists can determine how much energy the particle released when it reacted with the other material. Carl Rouse helped develop a machine that revealed different patterns of tracks that are characteric of different types of particles. After the completion of his dissertation, he was awarded his doctor of philosophy degree in June 1956.

Career Highlights

A doctoral degree in physics from the California Institute of Technology is highly respected by all scientists. Dr. Rouse could easily have obtained a job teaching in an excellent college. However, he knew that if he accepted such a job, he would be required to teach several courses. He liked to teach, but he really wanted to continue his research. In fact, he wanted to spend all his time doing research.

Dr. Rouse found a temporary job with one of the airplane companies in California, where he worked under government contract on the mathematics of guided missiles, but this was not his idea of real research. Dr. Rouse soon transferred to the Lawrence

Livermore National Laboratory, an organization which is managed for the U.S. government by the University of California.

Part of his work concerned the effects of the atomic bomb. When such a bomb explodes, temperatures near the point of detonation become so high that solid objects are instantly transformed into gases. Physicists call such transformations a change of state. The process can be seen by putting an ice cube in a pan over heat. The ice, a solid, melts into water, a liquid, and then the water becomes steam, a gas. Under normal conditions, these changes of state take several minutes. However, during the explosion of an atomic bomb, material such as iron can turn into gas in a fraction of a second. In 1957, scientists did not have the knowledge to fully understand this type of transformation.

Scientists also did not understand the extremely hot gases that make up the sun and other stars. For many years, Dr. Rouse's main goal was the understanding of this mystery. By late 1963, after carefully studying the writings of other physicists, Dr. Rouse knew that some of the accepted ideas were wrong.

Dr. Rouse continued his studies to explain the workings of our sun and other stars. He discovered a new way to measure the amount of helium in the sun's atmosphere. Helium is produced when four hydrogen atoms fuse together. This fusion releases energy that causes the sun to give off light and heat. Helium is somewhat like the ashes left by a fire. By examining the ashes, physicists can tell many things about the fuel that has been burned. Analysis such as this allowed Dr. Rouse to develop new theories about the workings of the sun.

By 1968, Dr. Rouse was able to calculate long tables of numbers for all the conditions of temperature and pressure in the sun's atmosphere. Interestingly, recent tables—produced with the help of new theories and high-speed computers—give almost the same results that Dr. Rouse obtained 22 years ago.

Many influential physicists, whose ideas were not accepted by Dr. Rouse, opposed his new theories about the sun's atmosphere. Because of these conflicts, Dr. Rouse was often assigned to routine projects at Livermore Labs. Therefore, he found it necessary to conduct much of his important research in his spare time.

To gain more freedom in his investigations, Dr. Rouse transferred to the General Atomic Company of San Diego, California, in 1968. There, his studies concerned the practical applications of atomic energy. This work was reasonably successful, and he was awarded a U.S. patent for improving the material used as shielding in nuclear power plants.

Finally, in 1986, he was able to use the supercomputer owned by General Atomic Company for his own personal projects. Consequently, his progress towards understanding the atmosphere of the sun and other stars has been greatly increased.

During his career, Dr. Rouse has edited four books on high-temperature physics, published many scientific reports, and given lectures in many countries around the world. He has enjoyed taking his wife, a psychologist in the San Diego school system, and his children on the international trips.

In 1992, Dr. Rouse founded his own research and consulting company in Del Mar, California. Through Rouse Research, Inc., he hopes to someday solve the mysteries of the sun's atmosphere.

Juanita Simons Scott

Born: June 13, 1936, in Eastover, South Carolina

Status: Dean, Division of Arts and Sciences, Benedict College, Columbia, South Carolina

Education:

Associate of Arts degree, Clinton Junior College, Rock Hill, South Carolina, 1956

Bachelor of Science degree, Livingston College, Salisbury, North Carolina, 1958

Master of Science degree, Atlanta University, Atlanta, Georgia, 1962

Doctor of Education degree, University of South Carolina, Columbia, South Carolina, 1979

Research Area: Developmental Biology

Early Years

Juanita Simons was born during the depths of the Great Depression. She grew up on a farm near Eastover, South Carolina, a small agricultural town about 15 miles east of Columbia, the capital of the state. Juanita milked cows, fed the farm animals, cultivated the vegetable garden, and weeded the corn and cotton fields. When she was a teenager, she helped her younger brother plow the fields with a mule.

When Juanita was in grade school, the farm had no running water or electricity. The family drew water from a spring about 200 yards from the house. They cooked on a wood stove, and the children did their homework by the light of a kerosene lantern.

There were 15 children in the Simons family. The parents placed great emphasis on family cooperation and mutual affection. Other strong family values included education and religion. At family prayer on Sunday morning, Juanita's father prayed that the children would always love one another. He also prayed that he would live long enough to see them finish their schooling and move on to independent lives.

Juanita joined in the family's religious life with enthusiasm. She taught Sunday School and, as a teenager, sang in the choir. She accompanied her father to district conventions of the Antioch African Methodist Episcopal Zion Church (AME Zion Church)—sometimes as far as 100 miles from home. She remains active in this church and serves both as a trustee and as secretary to the board. She acted as district director of Christian education for 13 years and is currently president of the AME Zion Church Missionary Society.

When Juanita was in school, the family participated in country-style recreation. They took walks through the woods to pick wild berries and nuts and cooked special treats at holiday time. There were some after-school sports, but organized recreation was usually in the form of 4-H Club meetings and preparing exhibits for the county fair. Juanita was allowed to start dating at 16. However, by that time she had already graduated from high school because she had begun first grade at the age of 5. She had started young only so that in her first year her aunt, who was just finishing elementary school, could walk with her the two miles to the school and back each day. In spite of her relative youth, Juanita did well in all her subjects at all grade levels though high school. During this early period of her life, however, she had no particular ambition to become a scientist.

Higher Education

Clinton Junior College in Rock Hill, South Carolina, was founded and supported by the AME Zion Church. Because of her family's deep involvement with the church, Clinton College, which is only 75 miles from Eastover, was a natural choice for Juanita Simons's undergraduate training. The district officials of the church offered her a partial scholarship, and the rest of her tuition and fees were covered by the sale of cotton grown on the family farm.

Juanita Simons discovered from her experiences at Clinton Junior College that she had a good capacity for learning. She also found that she did particularly well in her science courses. Simons was impressed by her young and energetic biology teacher, Ms. Leonora Chick. Consequently, she decided to major in biology. Her experiences on the farm made it relatively easy to relate to the study of plants and animals. Biology also appealed to Juanita's aesthetic interests because many of the assignments required drawings of the plants and animals.

Juanita Simons finished the two-year program at the top of her class and transferred to Livingston College in Salisbury, North Carolina. She was awarded another larger scholarship at Livingston. Since this institution was also connected with the AME Zion Church, the school setting changed, but the religious spirit remained the same.

Soon, Simons realized that she could combine her goal of becoming a teacher with her interest in biology. During the two years needed to complete her bachelor's degree, she majored in biology but also completed all the courses required for a teaching certificate.

Livingston College had strong rules about religious observation. Attendance was taken at chapel and vespers services. Chapel services were held three times a week, and vespers were observed each Sunday evening. When students missed four observances in a single semester, one credit hour was added to their graduation requirements. The addition of that one credit hour could mean that a student had to remain at Livingston an extra semester to take an additional course. Few students wanted to graduate a semester later than their classmates.

While at Livingston, Simons found it difficult to complete her science courses, her education courses, her other scholastic requirements, and her obligations to the church. Nevertheless, she made time to attend the home football and basketball games and to enjoy the not-very-frequent school dances.

When Juanita Simons graduated from Livingston in 1958, she accepted a job teaching biology and general science at Hopkins High School in Hopkins, South Carolina. Although Hopkins High was a relatively new school, it was segregated and not well funded. Consequently, supplies were sparse, and scientific equipment for the laboratory was not available.

Another challenge came from the fact that some of her tenth grade biology students were almost as old as Simons. Indeed, many were taller than she. Her strategy was to be firm but fair, and she soon earned the respect of her students. This respect came after she had been tested for courage by the inventive teenagers. One day they deposited a frog at her feet. Instead of being startled or repulsed, Simons picked up the frog and used the incident to demonstrate how such animals should be handled. The same response was used when she was challenged with a grass snake. She simply picked up the snake and showed the students how to distinguish harmless snakes from those that are poisonous.

After her first year at Hopkins High School, Juanita Simons married Robert Scott, her childhood sweetheart. The following year, Juanita Scott decided that she would like to prepare herself to be a research biologist. During the preceding summer break, she had participated in a special program for high school science teachers at Atlanta University. This program was sponsored by the National Science Foundation. The positive tone of this experience encouraged her to enroll in the graduate program at Atlanta University, one of the premier institutions for the advanced education of African Americans in the United States.

At first, Scott was a bit awed by the level of education and the sense of confidence that she perceived in her fellow graduate students. However, she soon realized that she could compete. Her confidence was bolstered by the help of Dr. Frederick E. Mapp. He served as mentor and advisor on her thesis project.

The main theme of that research project was inspired by the strange ability of some animals to regenerate lost limbs. Birds and mammals have lost this ability, but some amphibians, such as frogs and salamanders, are able to restore legs or tails lost by some mishap. Scott saw a connection between the ability to regenerate limbs, the process of healing, and the success of skin grafts and organ transplants from one individual to another. Her studies showed that the regeneration of a tadpole's tail could take place only after the tadpole had reached a certain stage of development. Her studies also showed that

transplants were far more likely to be successful between individuals of the same species than in transplants from other species.

In 1962, after she received her master's degree in biology from Atlanta, Juanita Scott was ready to teach at the college-level. In 1963, she accepted a position on the faculty of Benedict College in Columbia, South Carolina. Benedict College has always had strong ties to both the African American community and the Baptist Church. Mrs. Bathsheba Benedict of Pawtucket, Rhode Island, a strong abolitionist, founded the college for newly freed slaves in 1870.

Scott was hired to replace a teacher who had left the faculty in the middle of the school year. Her assignment was to teach the biological science survey courses that were part of the required curriculum for nonscience majors. Fortunately, one of the science faculty members, Robert Carmichael, helped Scott as she assumed the other teacher's classes.

In the spring, Juanita Scott's situation at Benedict became more difficult because she was about to give birth to her third child. The college had no maternity leave policy, and she was worried that she would not be re-hired in the fall. Indeed, after her child was born, Scott was fortunate to find another fill-in job at a neighboring institution, Morris College, in Sumpter, South Carolina.

Morris College, another Baptist institution, was only a few miles from Eastover, South Carolina, Scott's home town. She was pleased to be working so close to her family. She was also delighted to be teaching the core courses in biology. In fact, she was the only biologist on the faculty.

After a year as a fill-in teacher at Morris College, Juanita Scott returned, in 1968, to Benedict College as an assistant professor. In addition to teaching a full load of biology courses, she began to focus her attention on the problems of water pollution in the rivers and streams of South Carolina. It had become apparent that toxic industrial waste was being dumped into regional waterways. Among the major contaminants were mercury and other heavy metals, such as lead and cadmium. Scott's research concerned the manner and extent to which these materials were harmful to living creatures.

In the mid-1970s, Scott began to make arrangements to begin her doctoral studies as a part-time student at the University of South Carolina in Columbia, which was not far from Benedict College. Juanita Scott enrolled in the doctoral program in education and not biology because she felt that many college-level science teachers are so involved with the details of their subject that their teaching skills are weak. She reasoned that undergraduate science students would greatly benefit from the use of better teaching methods. Her doctoral research was focused on that assumption.

Meanwhile, she continued her research on the biological consequences of waterway contamination by heavy metals. By careful use of her time and energy, Juanita Scott finished her doctoral studies at South Carolina in 1979.

Career Highlights

After she received her degree, Dr. Scott was quickly promoted to associate professor at Benedict College, given tenure, and assigned new responsibilities. She assumed the job of planning a course of study for students who were interested in careers in medicine or in the allied health care professions. In 1981, she was promoted to full professor.

Although Dr. Scott added new interests and problem areas to her program of biological research, she continued her studies of the effects of water pollution. By the mid-1980s, she became particularly interested in the

microscopic characteristics of individual cells. Dr. Scott wanted to know how pollutants, such as lead, cadmium, and mercury, act on different structures within a cell. Her research has shown that some parts of a frog's skin cells are much more likely to react to metal contamination than other parts of the skin cells. She and her team of student researchers also found that a frog's skin not only repels some toxic compounds but also has some antibiotic properties. This research and other projects undertaken by Dr. Scott have been supported by research grants from the National Institutes of Health in Washington, D.C.

Dr. Scott's work in the 1980s and 1990s demonstrates her concern for the quality of science teaching in middle and junior high schools. This interest grew out of her observation that many students arrived at college or university with little knowledge of the sciences. These students frequently have the attitude that all science courses are "too hard."

Her first major program to combat this problem was the development of a series of hands-on science projects for students in upper elementary and middle school classes. These projects were designed to motivate the students and show them that science is fun, interesting, and not too difficult. One indication of their success was the frequency with which the students later designed their own projects for presentation at science fairs.

In 1987, Dr. Scott realized that she could influence more people by working with grade school and high school science teachers rather than with students. The National Science Foundation supported her work with fifth and sixth grade teachers in South Carolina. She sought to improve the quality of instruction at each level by making sure that teachers have a good feeling toward—and understanding of—basic scientific concepts.

The teachers who completed the science program conveyed the ideas to their home districts. In this way, a new attitude toward science education spread wider and wider throughout the region.

For several years, Dr. Scott has been involved with directing research, teaching biology, and conducting in-service training classes for science teachers. In addition, in 1987, Dr. Scott accepted the administrative responsibilities for the division of mathematics and natural sciences at Benedict College. In 1992, after a reorganization of the college's departments, Dr. Scott remained in charge of the department of biological and physical sciences.

In 1994, still more reorganization was initiated by a new president at Benedict College. Dr. Scott is now the dean of the division of arts and sciences and has administrative responsibilities for 10 academic departments.

John B. Slaughter

Born: March 16, 1934, in Topeka, Kansas

Status: President, Occidental College, Los Angeles, California

Education:

Bachelor of Science degree, Kansas State University, Manhattan, Kansas, 1956

Master of Science degree, University of California, Los Angeles, California 1961

Doctor of Philosophy degree, University of California, San Diego, California 1971

Research Area: Engineering Physics

Early Years

After the Civil War ended in 1865, Kansas, which joined the union as a free state in 1861, became a refuge for groups of freed slaves from the South. One such group included John Slaughter's forebears, who settled in the state capital of Topeka.

In 1954, after the Supreme Court decided that segregation was unconstitutional in the famous case of *Brown vs. the Board of Education for Topeka, Kansas,* the schools in Topeka began to integrate. However, when John Slaughter was a student in the public schools, they were still segregated.

John was the oldest of three children. His father was a used furniture salesman and a janitor at the famed Meninger's Clinic in Topeka. When John was a young boy, he dreamed that someday he would become an engineer—a designer and builder. His parents had little education, but they encouraged John to aim as high as he could.

Few people could see John as a future engineer. His high school coaches sneered at John's ideas. His teachers kept directing him into vocational courses. They thought that John should follow a program that would lead to a career as a mechanic or some type of electrical technician. Therefore, they did not guide John into the courses in science and mathematics that are required for acceptance into a degree program in engineering.

Fortunately, John developed ways of learning on his own. He used the technical training he received in high school and his own reading to develop the ability to repair radios. He taught himself the principles of electronics and soon understood how to relate theory to solving practical problems. When he had mastered these skills, he started his own radio repair business. However, John's life was not all work. He was very interested in sports. He was the top pitcher on his American Legion baseball team and won letters in track. In high school, John ran in half-mile and cross country events.

Higher Education

In 1951, after he graduated from high school, John Slaughter enrolled in Washburn University in his home town of Topeka. This institution, funded by the city government, is devoted to general education, teacher training, and prelaw programs. His choice of colleges provided Slaughter with two important advantages. First, he could finance his own education from his radio repair business. Second, he could follow a general science program and take the science and mathematics courses that he had missed in high school. Unfortunately, Washburn University did not offer a degree in engineering. After two years, Slaughter transferred to Kansas State University in Manhattan, Kansas. The reputation of this institution, with its fine engineering programs, helped its graduates find jobs in top industrial firms. Slaughter received his degree from Kansas State in 1956.

As soon as he graduated, John Slaughter married Bernice Johnson, a young woman he had meet in Kansas City. The young couple soon moved to San Diego, California, where he had accepted a job with the Convair Division of the General Dynamics Corporation.

General Dynamics is a large aerospace firm that specializes in the design and production of major military systems. Slaughter worked on many different projects in electronics but had little choice in his projects. He soon realized that if he wanted to pursue his own research interests, he would need further education to obtain a more rewarding job.

While still working for General Dynamics, Slaughter took night courses in an extension program provided by the University of California at Los Angeles (UCLA). He enrolled in advanced courses in electronics and control systems. Soon, he learned of an opening at the Naval Electronics Laboratory in San Diego. The navy was particularly interested in Slaughter's ideas about control systems. After Slaughter began his new job, the navy encouraged him to continue his advanced engineering program at UCLA. He worked part-time as he pursued his graduate studies and received his master's degree in 1961.

At this point, John Slaughter was interested in solving the design problems of electronic control systems, such as the automatic pilot that at times is used to fly multiengine military and commercial aircraft. Other types of automatic controls are used in automobiles, such as the antiskid braking system that automatically releases locked brakes so that a car does not skid.

In the 1960s, when John Slaughter began his studies of automatic control systems, the use of digital computers was in its early stages. Now, digital computers, which rarely break down or make mistakes, control almost all such systems. John Slaughter was one of the pioneers in the design of these computer-controlled systems. He led a small team of engineers and researchers at the Naval Electronics Laboratory who built and tested the new designs.

During his work in the field of engineering, Slaughter encountered some racial prejudice, perhaps partly because there were so few African American engineers. However, the navy scientists highly valued his work, and in 1965, John Slaughter was named Scientist of the Year by his employers at the Naval Electronics Laboratory.

The navy administration has an interest in assisting their people to continue with higher education. In 1967, Slaughter decided to finish his doctorate at the University of California at San Diego on a part-time basis. His supervisors at the Naval Laboratory encouraged him to do so. In his doctoral studies, he shifted his focus to theoretical physics. Thus, he became far more involved in basic research than in systems design. His doctoral research, for example, involved the use of a powerful computer program to solve a set of mathematical equations. Even though this set of equations originally came from mathematical theory, it also had proved useful in solving many practical problems.

The experience of working on his doctoral degree increased Slaughter's interest in two important aspects of higher education. He became more aware of the problems of managing institutions of higher learning. Also, he became more conscious of the low numbers of African Americans in all fields of science and technology, particularly in engineering. At times, John Slaughter had noted to others that he, himself, was the first African American engineer he had ever met. This was his way of pointing out that Black youth had too few visible examples of African Americans in the field of engineering.

Career Highlights

After earning his Ph.D. from the University of California at San Diego in 1971, Dr. Slaughter continued to work another four years for the navy. At the end of that time, he felt that he had made his contribution to the programs at the Naval Electronics Laboratory. Moreover, he had a growing interest in the administration of institutions of higher education and in the large-scale research activity conducted at such institutions.

In 1975, several opportunities were presented to Dr. Slaughter. The most promising was the position of director of the Applied Physics Laboratory at the University of Washington in Seattle. In this new capacity, he was an administrator in an academic institution but was able to maintain a connection with his previous work. Much of the research being done at the Applied Physics Laboratory was sponsored by the navy.

The new job also made Dr. Slaughter more visible to the leaders in the scientific community. Consequently, in 1977, he was invited to Washington, D.C., to serve a presidential appointment as assistant director at the National Science Foundation. Here, he led the directorate that was responsible for astronomy, geology, geophysics, oceanography, and the sciences concerned with weather and climate. This directorate is one of the largest and most important units of the National Science Foundation. The experience helped Dr. Slaughter broaden his perspective on how to integrate different branches of science. He also gained knowledge on how to encourage scientists from all the branches to work together.

After his experiences in management, Dr. Slaughter was ready to undertake the responsibility of the development of a major academic institution. He was invited to become the provost and academic vice president at

Washington State University in Pullman, Washington. Dr. Slaughter felt a kinship with his new setting because of his experience as an undergraduate at Kansas State University. He saw Washington State as an institution that was on the threshold of becoming an important center of scholarship and scientific research.

After working for two years to accomplish his goals, Dr. Slaughter was offered the position of the director of the National Science Foundation (NSF). The initial approach was made by a member of the science board who had known Dr. Slaughter when he was serving as an assistant director. Dr. Slaughter was not interested because he felt that his mission at Washington State had not yet been completed. However, the next approach was from President Jimmy Carter, and Dr. Slaughter felt that he could not refuse a direct appeal from the president.

Dr. Slaughter's appointment was quickly approved by the Senate. However, he needed several months to finish all of his outstanding projects at Washington State. Consequently, he did not begin his new duties in the nation's capital until late in November of 1980. By that time, Ronald Reagan was president-elect and Jimmy Carter was about to leave office. However, Dr. Slaughter had already made sure that the new administration would not interfere with the innovative programs planned for the NSF.

Since Dr. Slaughter had begun his career as an engineer, some scientists thought that he might be prejudiced in favor of practical applications. They feared that he would not fund the basic, theory-oriented research traditionally supported by the NSF. However, Dr. Slaughter had seen many times how theory and practice complemented each other. He knew that both approaches to science were important and needed gov-

ernment support. In particular, he knew that universities needed help from the government to modernize their research laboratories. Laboratories for engineering research especially needed assistance because universities could not afford the advanced equipment being purchased by industrial and government laboratories. Dr. Slaughter also realized that the NSF should provide support to improve science facilities at traditionally African American colleges and universities.

Again, Dr. Slaughter worked hard to accomplish his goals as quickly as possible. He knew that the political climate could change without much warning. Indeed, during his second year as director of the foundation, he had to testify at congressional hearings in favor of decisions with which he did not agree. No honest person can tolerate such political compromise for very long, and Dr. Slaughter decided to resign from the directorship. Ironically, it was at this time that Dr. Slaughter was elected to the National Academy of Engineering, one of the highest honors an engineer can receive.

Happily, he was now able to return to college administration, a position he enjoyed. He accepted the post as chancellor of the University of Maryland at College Park. At Maryland, he saw some of the same challenges and opportunities that he had seen at Washington State University. Indeed, there were some especially positive features at Maryland. The state tax base was increasing, so there were resources for initiating new programs, such as enrolling more minority students. Dr. Slaughter saw that the area from which the university drew its students had a high proportion of African American families. Therefore, the recruitment of talented Black students presented few problems. As chancellor, his avowed goal was to "blend quality with equality." He worked toward the realization of this goal for six years.

At that time, the stresses involved in administering a large university became apparent. A star basketball player, Len Bias, died in his university dormitory room from a drug overdose. This added to the serious tensions that had already developed between faculty members, coaches, and prominent alumni about academic standards and the quality of education provided to talented Black athletes. Dr. Slaughter found it necessary to replace the head basketball coach and other athletics department personnel and to introduce a series of reforms for the university's athletics programs. These reforms helped restore the proper emphasis on learning and research at the university.

Balance between alternative goals became a high priority for Dr. Slaughter. In 1988, he was offered the position as president of Occidental College in Los Angeles, California. He saw Occidental as a place which had the proper balance between athletic and academic programs. Although Occidental College has a vigorous sports program and often wins the conference title in football, it offers no athletic scholarships. Alumni express their desire to achieve success in all the intercollegiate sports but do not become too emotional about victories or defeats.

Dr. Slaughter also saw the chance to emphasize balance in academic programs. Ideas he had pursued at Washington State again became prominent in his plans. For example, cooperation between the arts, the humanities, the social sciences, and the natural sciences could be accomplished to everyone's benefit. Finally, he saw the chance to achieve a better balance in the racial composition of the student body. The Los Angeles area has a rich ethnic diversity, and Dr. Slaughter has worked to achieve the same level of diversity on the Occidental College campus.

Clarence F. Stephens

Born: July 24, 1917, in Gaffney, South Carolina

Status: Retired, Chair, Department of Mathematics, the State University of New York at Potsdam, 1987

Education:

Bachelor of Science degree, Johnson C. Smith University, Charlotte, North Carolina, 1938

Master of Science degree, University of Michigan, Ann Arbor, Michigan, 1939

Doctor of Philosophy degree, University of Michigan, 1943

Research Area: Mathematics

Early Years

Clarence Stephens was the fifth of six children. He had three older sisters and an older and younger brother. His birth certificate states that he was born in Gaffney, South Carolina. Years after his birth, members of Clarence's family told him that he really had been born in Macon, Georgia, where his parents had been visiting friends. However, his parents waited until they returned home to Gaffney to register his birth. They wanted all their children to have the same home town.

Clarence moved frequently during his young life. His mother died a few months after his younger brother, Samuel, was born. Clarence was only two years old. His father, who was a railroad worker, wanted to keep the family together after this tragedy. However, he was away from home much of the time, and there was no one to care of the younger children.

Finally, the family had to separate. The sisters stayed in Gaffney and looked after the oldest boy. Clarence and his younger brother went to live with their grandmother and her brother near Charlotte, North Carolina. When Clarence grew older, he was able to rejoin his father, sisters, and older brother in Gaffney.

Misfortune soon struck again. In less than two years, Clarence's father died. Two of the sisters were old enough to stay with family friends in Gaffney and finish the school year. However, the youngest sister and the three brothers were too young to be on their own. They all returned to their grandmother's care. She was now living in the town of Charlotte, North Carolina. The children attended the Alexandra Street Elementary School.

At the end of the school year, the grandmother moved back to the farm. The next year, the children attended a two-room country school which was a long, two-mile walk from their home. Meanwhile, the two oldest sisters entered a teacher training program in Concord, North Carolina, not far from Charlotte.

The final tragedy struck in 1928 when Clarence was 10 years old. The hard-working grandmother became ill and died. Now the little group of brothers and sisters could no longer be kept together. Each went to live with a different set of relatives.

Clarence moved to the farm home of his great aunt Sarah and her husband near Harrisburg, North Carolina. Their grandson, Clarence's cousin Willis, also lived with them. The farm house, which had no indoor plumbing, contained a kitchen and two bedrooms. One of the bedrooms was occupied by two teachers from the local elementary school. The two boys and their two elderly relatives occupied the other bedroom. All school work, social life, and dining took place in the kitchen.

Unfortunately for the Stephens children, there was no high school for African Americans in Harrisburg. When the time approached for Clarence to begin high school, he did not know what to do. Although he was only 12 years old, he considered running away from the farm. He thought about moving to a northern city where he could go to school part-time and work part-time.

His oldest sister, Irene, saved the day. She arranged for Clarence and his older brother to attend Harbison Institute, a boarding school in Irmo, South Carolina. Harbison had been founded by missionary workers from the Presbyterian Church. Money to run the school came from the wealthy Harbison family who owned a steel mill in Pittsburgh, Pennsylvania.

In 1930, only male students were enrolled at Harbison. Each new student took an entrance examination to determine his proper grade placement. Clarence, who was 13 years old, was assigned to the eighth grade. Young men who were over 20 years old were also placed in the same grade.

Clarence knew he had a propensity for mathematics. This ability was recognized by his teacher, Dean Robert Boulware, and his fellow students. Dean Boulware was a dedicated teacher who wanted all of his students to understand the inner workings of mathematical problems. He often asked Clarence to go to the blackboard and show his classmates the steps for solving a problem. Soon, he began to help his fellow students with their mathematics homework. Clarence explained how to think about math problems, because he wanted them to be able to solve difficult assignments on their own.

Before long, all three Stephens brothers were enrolled at Harbison Institute. Their older sisters always paid the tuition for his first year. After that, the boys worked on the school's farm land each summer to earn the $100 school fee. During the school year, each boy worked part-time for his room and board. Clarence worked as a kitchen helper and also dusted and swept the classrooms every school day.

Social life for the boys centered on the school and its church. Although Clarence had been raised a Baptist, he soon joined the Presbyterian Church which ran the school and the church next door.

During his years at Harbison, Clarence was also active in sports. He was a good football player and was offered a football scholarship by a nearby college. He also played on the varsity baseball team. Clarence, who enjoyed many school activities, was elected class president in his senior year. He was also good at debating and was given a lead role in the senior play.

Higher Education

One of the advantages of attending Harbison Institute was its connection with the Johnson C. Smith University in Charlotte, North Carolina. This school offered tuition scholarships to the best students from Harbison Institute. When Clarence Stephens graduated at the top of his high school class in 1934, he was offered such a scholarship. Although Stephens knew he must finance all his other expenses, he wanted to accept this offer. To earn the necessary money, he decided to live with his father's relatives in Indianapolis, Indiana. He hoped to find a well-paying summer job.

Unfortunately, the only job he could find was as a shoe shine boy at a neighborhood barbershop. After working all summer, he was able to save only $100. This sum, of course, would not cover his necessary expenses. Therefore, his sister Irene arranged for him to live with relatives in Charlotte, North Carolina, during the school year. Luckily, they lived only a few blocks from Johnson C. Smith University, and Clarence could walk to his classes.

During his first year, he took mathematics courses with a professor named Douglas. Stephens was pleased that Dr. Douglas used individual and group problem solving as his teaching method. Clarence Stephens believed that the lecture method, which Dr. Douglas rarely used, was a poor way to teach mathematics.

Stephens found that he needed to work part-time to earn additional spending money. He became a delivery man for a neighborhood drugstore. The pay was $6.00 a week, and Stephens made another $6.00 a week in tips. At first, he had to walk to his customer's homes. However, in the fall of 1935, the job became easier when the drugstore owner purchased a bicycle for Stephens to use.

In the summer of 1937, Clarence Stephens and his older brother, Claude, went north to Atlantic City, New Jersey, where they hoped to find summer employment. They both applied for the same position as a night clerk in a hotel. Clarence was chosen for the job because he could solve a problem set by the hotel manager. He was able to calculate the room charges for guests who checked out at different times. Luckily, this job paid fairly well, and he did not need to work part-time during his last year of college. Claude Stephens, fortunately, had found his own summer job as a barber.

During his last year at college, Clarence Stephens took his mathematics courses with Professor Woodson. In the calculus course, each student was assigned 10 problems from a set of 58 problems. Clarence correctly solved all 58. Professor Woodson was impressed and encouraged Clarence to think about graduate school.

In the fall of 1937, Dr. T. E. McKinney, the dean of liberal arts at Johnson C. Smith University, had been a visiting teacher at the University of Michigan. When he returned to North Carolina, he was enthusiastic about his experiences in Ann Arbor. He told Clarence Stephens that the University of Michigan would be a good school for his graduate studies. Although Stephens had planned to teach high school when he finished college, he decided that getting more education would be a better plan. He graduated from Johnson C. Smith in the summer of 1938 and began his graduate program at Michigan in the fall.

Unfortunately, the university provided no financial support for Stephens's studies. By working part-time, he was able to support himself for two years. He finished his master's degree in just one year, and during the second year, began his doctoral program. Various faculty members tried to arrange financial help so that Stephens could continue his schooling. He was eventually nominated for a Rosenwald Fellowship, but the decision was too slow in coming. In order to earn some money, Stephens accepted a temporary teaching job at Prairie View A&M College in Texas in the fall of 1940.

While he was still at the University of Michigan, he had begun to worry about his doctoral research project. He needed someone on the faculty to sponsor and guide his work. However, he could not find a good match between his interests and those of the available faculty members. Finally, he settled for a compromise and chose a research topic about which he knew little. Stephens was then able to get help from a respected faculty member, Professor J.A. Nyswander. The topic he chose was difference equations. These are very complicated equations which, however, have many practical uses. For example, they are used to describe changes in the texture of motor oil under the differing conditions of heat and pressure in an engine.

Clarence Stephens felt very isolated while he was teaching at Prairie View A&M College. There was no one in the area with whom he could talk about his doctoral project. Fortunately, he was able to borrow books from the University of Texas at Austin and continue his research.

In the summer of 1941, Clarence Stephens returned to the University of Michigan to complete his required courses. Because of his reading, he was able to submit a plan for his research project before he returned to his teaching job in Texas.

His advisor, Dr. Nyswander, thought Stephens's topic was too difficult. Indeed, Stephens made little progress during September and October. Then in November, the solution to the problem suddenly came into his mind. After this breakthrough, Stephens required only two weeks to complete the calculations and write up the results. He sent the completed project to his advisor for review just after Thanksgiving. The following week, the Japanese attacked Pearl Harbor in Hawaii and the United States entered World War II.

In the spring of 1942, the Rosenwald Fellowship finally was approved. However, Clarence Stephens could not accept it because he had made a commitment to the U.S. Navy. He had signed up to teach mathematics to the young men who were training to become navy pilots.

These arrangements fell apart because of racial problems, and Stephens became eligible for the draft. While waiting for his local draft board in Texas to decide his status, he returned to the University of Michigan. He needed to prepare for the final examination on his research project. While there, he met his future wife, a high school teacher from Detroit, Michigan. She was in summer school to begin her own program of graduate studies. They were married in December of 1942.

In the fall before his wedding, Clarence Stephens took additional advanced mathematics courses in order to complete preparations for his exams. He took his final examinations that spring and was awarded his doctoral degree from Michigan in June 1943.

Career Highlights

After a series of problems about how best to serve his country in the war, Dr. Stephens enlisted as a specialist in the U.S. Navy. He was on active duty as a second-class petty officer until December 1945.

When Dr. Stephens completed his service, he returned to Prairie View A&M College. His first professional article was published that year. The same year, he was offered a professorship at Morgan State College in Baltimore, Maryland. When he arrived at Morgan State, he discovered that he was to be made chairperson of the mathematics department.

Dr. Stephens continued to work on mathematical research projects. His accomplishments as a mathematical scientist were recognized by a Ford Foundation Fellowship in 1954. This fellowship allowed him to accept an invitation to spend a year at the famous Institute for Advanced Study at Princeton University in New Jersey. Dr. Stephens was at Princeton during the same time that Albert Einstein was a permanent resident scholar.

In 1954, Dr. Stephens was awarded an honorary doctorate by the Johnson C. Smith University. In 1990, he was given his second honorary doctoral degree by Chicago State University in Chicago, Illinois.

While Dr. Stephens is an outstanding mathematical problem solver, his main effort during his long career was to improve the teaching of mathematics. He believed that students could learn mathematics on their own. His first priority was to teach students the proper way to read a mathematics textbook. Dr. Stephens believed in "learning by doing," and his students were required to work through all the calculations in his homework assignments. The advanced students were also requested to show all the steps in proving a mathematical theorem.

Dr. Stephens encouraged teamwork. He wanted teachers and students to work together on solving problems. He organized teams of students to compete for the best explanation for a particular problem or theorem. Dr. Stephens also encouraged students to help each other.

In 1962, he was invited to join the faculty at the State University College at Geneseo, New York. A few years later, he transferred to another New York state university. From 1969 until he retired in 1987, he was professor and departmental chairperson at the State University College in Potsdam, New York. During this time, he worked to make sure that women and minority students were given the best learning situations possible. Dr. Stephens knew that race and gender were considered barriers to a proper atmosphere for learning mathematics. He also knew that many students fail because they have been told that they have no talent. He spent his career trying to change the public's attitude toward the study of mathematics. Indeed, Dr. Stephens created new programs whereby students in liberal arts, such as history or language, could get a combined master's degree with a minor in mathematics.

Dr. Stephens's success as a mathematics teacher continues to be widely recognized. In 1991, he was presented with the Distinguished Teacher Award at Potsdam College. Even after his retirement, Dr. Stephens carries on his crusade to improve the teaching and perception of mathematics.

Gerald V. Stokes

Born: March 25, 1943, in Chicago, Illinois

Status: Associate Professor, Department of Microbiology and Immunology, George Washington University School of Medicine, Washington, D.C.

Education:

Associate of Arts degree, Wilson Junior College, Chicago, Illinois, 1962

Bachelor of Arts degree, Southern Illinois University, Carbondale, Illinois, 1967

Doctor of Philosophy degree, University of Chicago, Chicago, Illinois, 1973

Research Area: Microbiology

Early Years

Gerald Stokes was born in Chicago but grew up in Argo, Illinois, a very small suburb on the city border. Argo, with its huge starch factory, was an industrial community, but it also had open pastures, farmland, and wooded areas where young people like Gerald could enjoy nature.

Gerald and his younger brother were small boys when their parents divorced. After his mother remarried, he went to live with his mother's parents and his brother went to live with their father's parents. Eventually, Gerald had six younger brothers and sisters who lived with three sets of relatives. The extended family got along well together and remained closely knit.

Almost all the adult family members were factory workers, and none had finished high school. However, Gerald's mother and his grandparents put a high premium on education. They wanted Gerald to break the pattern and obtain as much schooling as possible.

Soon after he entered Argo Elementary School, Gerald began to show a fascination with science. Some of the interest came from watching TV programs like "Mr. Wizard." However, most of his interest was generated by exploring nature in the fields and streams near his home.

Gerald was also assigned interesting science projects by his elementary science teacher. His favorite topic was a long term weather study for which he recorded the daily temperature, wind speed, wind direction, and relative humidity. At the end of the period, he made a chart to show the day-to-day and month-to-month variations.

The activities of the Boy Scouts of America also interested Gerald. At that time, however, the Argo troop did not permit African American members. Undaunted, Gerald and a friend used the Boy Scout manuals at the public library. They copied the directions for the prescribed activities and did many of them on their own.

Gerald attended the integrated Graves Junior High School in Argo. In the classrooms, the African American students were assigned to sit in the back rows. Gerald had trouble seeing the blackboard and began to fall behind in his grades. He did not want to cause a fuss or admit that he needed help, so he tried various methods to get a better view of the board. He squinted and made a tiny space—like a pinhole lens— between his fingers so that he could read the words. Finally, the school nurse had his eyesight checked and found that he needed glasses. After receiving his glasses, Gerald had no more trouble with his grades.

During this time, Gerald continued to do science projects—some on his own and some as school assignments. He made his own barometer for measuring the air pressure, constructed a model volcano, and did chemistry experiments. He also enjoyed reading *Popular Science*, *Popular Mechanics* and *Boy's Life* to learn about space flight and astronomy.

By the time Gerald entered Argo Community High School, people knew about his in-

terests in science, and he was nicknamed "the Professor." Fortunately, his high school biology teacher had imaginative ideas that helped make learning fun. Students in the botany class were each assigned a particular plant. They were instructed to find local examples, bring the specimens into class, discuss the interesting features, and explain the origins of the plant names.

Gerald enjoyed all of his biology courses but was particularly interested in dissecting earthworms and frogs and in studying microbes—organisms that can be seen only under a microscope. Each of the courses were taught with enthusiasm, and these experiences were a turning point in his thoughts about the future. Gerald began to look past high school and think about attending college.

Once it was clear that college was a goal, the problem of financing his education became important. Gerald knew that his extended family could not raise the needed money, so he found part-time work and saved every cent. During his second year in high school, Gerald found a job unpacking boxes at the local grocery store. He was the first African American hired by the store owners. Gerald and the owners liked each other and he kept that same job during his years in high school.

Gerald did very well at Argo Community High School. During his third and fourth years, he was a member of the National Honor Society. Now, there was no question about the possibility of college—Gerald had the grades and the money.

Higher Education

After high school, Gerald Stokes enrolled at the University of Illinois in Urbana. He soon found that he was uncomfortable with the impersonal conditions and large classes.

In addition, he had to work part-time during the school year, which gave him less time to study.

That spring, he returned home, went to work at the starch factory, and saved his money for another attempt at higher education. After one year, Stokes was ready to try again. He enrolled at Wilson Junior College in Chicago, where he could commute and save on his living expenses. Stokes soon found that he enjoyed this school because classes were smaller and the junior college atmosphere was far more supportive. After two years, he received his associate of arts degree and was ready for a more ambitious undertaking.

Stokes applied to Southern Illinois University (SIU) in Carbondale. SIU has a much smaller enrollment than the Urbana campus and Stokes sensed a feeling of enthusiasm among the students. Even though SIU is small, it has had some famous faculty members such as Buckminster Fuller—the world famous designer and futurist who invented the geodesic dome. Stokes did well at SIU and received his degree in chemistry in 1967.

Because of his student status, Stokes had been deferred from military service. Now, at the height of the Viet Nam war, Stokes was eligible for the draft. Fortunately, he was offered a full-time job as a research assistant at the LaRabeda Hospital in Chicago and a part-time job at the Clinical Microbiology Laboratory at the University of Chicago, where he concerned himself with organ transplants. Before an operation could take place, he had to determine—by various tests—whether the donor and the receiver had the same blood type and were comparable in many other biological factors as well. This work was judged vital to the public interest, and Stokes's deferment was continued.

Because of his connection with the University of Chicago, Gerald Stokes was invited to apply to their graduate program in microbiology and was given a full scholarship. The topic of his research was the class of microorganisms called Chlamydia. These microbes cause many serious medical conditions such as venereal diseases, eye infections, some forms of pneumonia, and possibly some types of heart disease. Chlamydia are much smaller than ordinary bacteria, much larger than viruses, and can be controlled by antibiotics such as penicillin. Like a virus, they prefer to reproduce inside specific body cells of another living creature rather than in an artificial environment.

More knowledge was badly needed about these microbes but their virus-like characteristics made it difficult to grow new colonies in the laboratory. Stokes demonstrated that Chlamydia produces a certain chemical when a colony begins to grow and prosper. Scientists would now save valuable time by discovering quickly whether the laboratory prepared host cells were supporting the newly started colonies of Chlamydia.

During his final year of doctoral study, Gerald Stokes met and became engaged to Charlotte Eubanks, a graduate student in the history department. They were married in 1973, as soon as Stokes received his Ph.D. from the University of Chicago.

Career Highlights

After graduation, Dr. Stokes accepted a postdoctoral appointment at the University of Colorado in Boulder. For three years, he studied the vaccinia virus, a microbe which is closely related to both the smallpox virus and the cowpox virus. The vaccinia virus is used to provide immunity to smallpox, and its name is derived from its use as a vaccine. The vaccinia virus produces no bad side effects in the human body and is therefore an excellent candidate for use in genetic therapy. New genes can be naturally introduced into body cells if they are carried by this virus. Dr. Stokes also continued his study of the Chlamydia microbes, and by using an electron microscope, he was the first person to observe them.

When he finished his three year post-doctoral appointment at the University of Colorado, Dr. Stokes was well known in the scientific community for his productive research. He was offered faculty positions at Duke University in North Carolina and Purdue University in Indiana. However, he chose to join the faculty at Meharry Medical College in Nashville, Tennessee—an historically Black school—because he wanted to serve the African American community.

Then in 1978, Dr. Stokes accepted a position as an assistant professor at the George Washington University School of Medicine and Health Sciences in Washington, D.C. He was the first and remains the only African American to teach graduate level basic science in this institution. His faculty position allows Dr. Stokes to actively recruit African American students into the study of microbiology. Through his affiliation with the American Society for Microbiology, Dr. Stokes has launched a nation-wide outreach program to such students. A semiformal network of microbiologists advises minority students who show an interest in the biological sciences. This project maintains a computerized file of grants, scholarships, and other help that is available to minority students. In many cases, such aid has been under used in the past.

Dr. Stokes continues his studies of Chlamydia, specifically looking at the genes that program this microbe. He hopes to discover an effective vaccine against this dangerous micro-organism in the near future.

———————

Louis Wade Sullivan

Born: November 3, 1933, in Atlanta, Georgia

Status: President, Morehouse Medical School, Atlanta, Georgia

Education:

Bachelor of Science degree, Morehouse College, Atlanta, Georgia, 1954

Doctor of Medicine degree, Boston University, Boston, Massachusetts, 1958

Research Area: Physiology

Early Years

Lou Sullivan was born in the depths of the Great Depression, when over 25 percent of the nation's work force was unemployed. Ordinarily, Lou's father, Walter Wade Sullivan, worked as an insurance salesman and undertaker, and his mother, Lubirda Elizabeth Priester Sullivan, was a school teacher. However, times were so bad that Lou's parents decided to leave Atlanta and move to the small Georgia farming community of Blakely. The parents hoped that the nearby farms and their own garden could provide enough food for themselves and their two boys.

The parents had not, however, anticipated that their new community would be dominated by organizations such as the Ku Klux Klan. To achieve some degree of protection, Lou's father helped found a local chapter of the National Association for the Advancement of Colored People (the NAACP), in which the members pledged to help each other if one of their number were threatened. This strategy worked well on several occasions.

Another problem for African Americans in rural Georgia was the lack of schools for young people. Some provision was made for children in the first few elementary grades, but there was no schooling after the sixth grade. Therefore, Lou's parents decided to send their children to Savannah, Georgia, to stay with relatives during the school months. There, Lou attended the fifth grade. The quality of the segregated school system in Savannah, however, was very unsatisfactory, so the following school year, Lou's parents made arrangements for the two boys to attend school in Atlanta, a city with a strong tradition of quality education for African Americans. The boys lived with a capable and motherly woman, whose home was directly across the street from the Booker T. Washington High School. Both boys attended junior and senior high school there, and in 1950, Lou graduated at the top of his class. He had worked extremely hard because he knew that his parents had made many sacrifices to ensure that he received a good education.

Higher Education

After graduating, Lou Sullivan enrolled in the premedical program, which stresses basic science, at Morehouse College in Atlanta.

Sullivan had to work part-time, in addition to doing his studies, but he still received top grades in his difficult science program. He did so well, in fact, that he was awarded a rare scholarship for a medical school. After he graduated from Morehouse in 1954, he enrolled in and activated his scholarship support at the medical school at Boston University.

His years at medical school were relatively uneventful and pleasant, even though Sullivan had to work as a waiter and a library clerk to help pay his way. In spite of this extra work, he always got top grades and was elected president of his class in his second and third years at school. In 1955, full of confidence in a bright future, he married Eva Williamson, and they eventually became the parents of two boys and one girl. In 1958, Dr. Sullivan graduated third in his class of over 60 students. He was the only African American in the group.

Career Highlights

After his graduation, Dr. Sullivan had to complete three more years of medical training. He chose to do both his internship and residency at the Cornell University Medical Center in New York City. His teachers suggested that he do his residency in surgery, but Dr. Sullivan did not like the idea of having to work on his feet for hours at a time. He chose, instead, to do his specialization in orthopedics, the treatment of diseases and deformities of the bones. His main interest, however, was in pathology, the study of the causes of disease. He was particularly interested in diseases of the blood.

In 1960, Dr. Sullivan and his family returned to Boston, where he had been awarded a research fellowship to study at Massachusetts General Hospital, one of the major medical research centers of the world. The following year, he conducted research at Harvard Medical School with the support of additional research fellowships.

Now, the main focus of Dr. Sullivan's research was to explore ways to control anemia and other disorders associated with the production of blood cells. He thought that vitamin B-12 might be useful in controlling the production of blood platelets, the small cells that help clot the blood. He also studied whether alcohol in the blood might decrease the production of blood platelets. Patients with histories of heavy drinking were carefully studied to determine whether they recovered more slowly from injuries than light or nondrinkers. Dr. Sullivan did many experiments to test these ideas and reported his findings in the scientific literature. He showed that alcohol in the bloodstream interferes with the activity of vitamin B-12. The lack of activity by this vitamin reduces the production of red blood cells. Consequently, heavy drinkers are at significant risk of acute anemia. However, the condition is readily treated by cessation of alcohol intake and emergency doses of vitamin B-12.

Dr. Sullivan also wrote a number of essays on health problems among African Americans and on diseases common in the third world, such as malaria infections. In some instances, the health care—both preventative and curative—for African Americans was less effective than health care in third world countries. Dr. Sullivan began a quiet crusade to improve the medical care of African Americans.

As soon as he completed his medical training, Dr. Sullivan joined the faculty at the New Jersey College of Medicine in Newark. After two years, in 1966, Dr. Sullivan returned to his favorite campus, Boston University. He was soon awarded tenure, promoted to associate professor, and was appointed director of hematology at Boston City Hospital. In 1974, Dr. Sullivan was made a full professor of medicine at Boston University Medical School.

The following year, Dr. Sullivan was asked to establish a medical school at Morehouse—his undergraduate college—in Atlanta. No medical school designed specifically for African American students had been established in the preceding 70 years. Dr. Sullivan would have to take a reduction in pay and live in a different manner in the South. He took the position anyway, because it fit directly into his ideas about improving medical care for all African Americans—rich and poor alike.

During the first few years, the new school had limited scope and facilities. The students enrolled in a two-year rather than a standard four-year program and had to finish the remainder of their course work at other, more established medical schools. But the program soon expanded to the standard four years of schooling. Moreover, in line with Dr. Sullivan's ideas about the role of a first-class medical school, the faculty and students began major research projects. These research projects addressed the special health problems of African Americans, such as sickle-cell anemia, high blood pressure, and certain types of cancer, i.e., cancer of the prostate gland.

In the early 1980s, when one of the new medical school buildings was ready to be dedicated, Dr. Sullivan invited President Ronald Reagan to attend the celebration. President Reagan, unsure of how the visit would appeal to his Republican supporters but unwilling to alienate the African American voters, decided to send Vice President George Bush and his wife, Barbara, as the White House representatives. Upon their arrival, Mrs. Bush quickly understood the importance of Dr. Sullivan's project of increasing the number of African American doctors and the specific study of African American problems. She was so impressed by Dr.

Sullivan and the new medical school that she joined the school's board of trustees.

When the Vice President and his wife began to plan a trip to Africa as part of a general "good will" program, Mrs. Bush suggested that Dr. Sullivan be invited to join them. The visit would give him an opportunity to discern the most urgent medical problems in sub-Saharan Africa. Soon, the Bush family and the Sullivan family became more than professional acquaintances; they became friends. Consequently, after George Bush was elected president in 1988, he nominated Dr. Sullivan as Secretary of the Department of Health and Human Services, the largest department in the U.S. government.

Cabinet officers must be confirmed by the U.S. Senate, and Dr. Sullivan's confirmation was not without its problems. There was concern over Dr. Sullivan's views on abortion. In order to dispell any confusion, Dr. Sullivan firmly pointed out, "As an officer of government, my personal views are not important. I must simply enforce the law as it exists." Eventually, Dr. Sullivan's nomination was confirmed, and he became the first African American to hold a cabinet post.

As soon as he was sworn in, he was faced with many medical problems at the national level, the most crucial of which was the AIDS epidemic. During Ronald Reagan's presidency, AIDS had not received the attention it demanded, and by 1988, the situation was in a crisis from both a medical and a political point of view. Another potential crisis situation was the rising incidence of tuberculosis in people living in poverty. Dr. Sullivan mounted major programs to combat and defuse this situation before it got any worse. Along with Surgeon General Dr. C. Everett Koop, Dr. Sullivan also attempted to reduce tobacco and alcohol consumption among African Americans, who are more severely affected by these products than any other group of people.

During Dr. Louis Sullivan's position of leadership as the Secretary of Health and Human Services, it seems clear that he put more value on his science training than on his political training. Even though many of his goals were not achieved, all were worthy of being realized. After President Bush's defeat in the 1992 election, Dr. Sullivan returned to his position at the Morehouse Medical School, where he remains today.

Welton I. Taylor

Born: November 12, 1919, in Birmingham, Alabama

Status: Retired, President, Micro-Palettes, Inc., Chicago, Illinois

Education:

Bachelor of Arts degree, University of Illinois, Champaign-Urbana, Illinois, 1941

Master of Science degree, University of Illinois, 1947

Doctor of Philosophy degree, University of Illinois, 1948

Research Area: Microbiology

Early Years

Welton Taylor was born in Alabama, but he grew up in Illinois. Until he was 11, the Taylor family lived in Chicago in a pleasant neighborhood across from a city park. The year before Welton moved from Chicago, he had his first scientific experience. The boy who lived next door to him had captured some small snakes. While a group of other boys gathered around, the neighbor dumped the writhing bunch onto the yard. The other boys scattered, but Welton was more fascinated than frightened. After admiring the snakes, the neighbor boy wanted to recapture them. He asked Welton to help restore the snakes to the paper bag used as a transport cage. Welton was assured that the snakes were not poisonous but that they might bite, which turned out to be quite true. Fortunately, the bites were not painful, and they made him more interested than afraid.

Welton began to read about his new found interest, and soon he could identify all the local species. He wanted to find out which snakes were poisonous so that he and his friends could go on snake hunting expeditions. In the outskirts of Chicago, snakes could be found easily in the unspoiled prairie land. After observing the habits of the harmless snakes that he caught, Welton released them in the large park across from his house.

In 1930, when Welton was 11, his family moved to the town of Peoria, Illinois. The stock market crash of 1929 had begun a deep economic depression, and many people were out of work. His father hoped that in Peoria he could find a good job and a lower cost of living, both of which turned out to be the case.

On Welton's walk to school every day, he went by a rough limestone wall. His new school friends showed him that there were many different kinds of fossils in the limestone. With some patience, he pried off pieces of the stone with a pen knife. Welton soon had an extensive collection of fossil ferns, snails, and other small shellfish that had been buried millions of years ago at the bottom of some ancient sea.

Welton also became very interested in insects—particularly butterflies and moths. He learned to make bait by mixing stale beer with molasses. When this mixture was brushed on tree trunks in the woods beyond his back yard, it would attract butterflies during the day and moths at night. When the fragile creatures fed on this bait, the tiny amount of alcohol in the beer would make them groggy and easy to catch. Welton's father was always willing to help in this field research. He would hold the lantern at night so that Welton could gather the drunken moths.

One of the more interesting moth species produced adults that were as large as bats. Welton collected some of the cocoons from this species. In the spring, he was able to watch the insects shed their cocoons and emerge as adults. Welton released most of the moths and observed the full cycle of their development. The adults mated, eggs were laid, and caterpillars hatched under Welton's watchful eye. He also carefully preserved and mounted some of these large creatures, other moths, and their cousins, the butterflies. The collection of mounted insects still hangs on the wall of his study, 60 years later.

In 1936, when economic conditions had improved somewhat, the Taylor family returned to Chicago. Welton finished his last year of high school in the very neighborhood that he had left years before. Welton graduated at the top of his class. He was such an outstanding student that some of the more prosperous African American professional men financed Welton's tuition at the University of Illinois.

Higher Education

After the initial gift of tuition money, Welton Taylor had to work his way through school. He worked in the dining hall for his meals and at the Natural History Survey of Illinois to pay his other living costs. His salary from the survey was 43 cents an hour. The money came from a grant from the National Youth Administration, a large government program. Taylor's work involved preserving and mounting poison ivy plants. He had been the only applicant who was immune to the plant's irritating secretions.

Taylor's first choice for a professional career had been chemical engineering. However, in the fall of his second year of college he took a course in bacteriology. He liked the course so much that he changed his major.

While his career plans were unfolding, events in the larger world were shaping his fate. When he was ready to graduate in the spring of 1941, the war in Europe had been underway for 18 months. France had already been overrun by the German army, and the future looked grim.

Welton Taylor had joined the U.S. Army's Reserve Officer Training Program at the University of Illinois as a way to help cover his costs. He had hoped to be assigned to flight training but had failed the physical because of his eyesight. He was commissioned as a 2nd lieutenant in the field artillery and ordered to active duty at Fort Sill, Oklahoma. Even so, Taylor did not give up his desire to fly. In his spare time at Fort Sill, he took civilian flying lessons at a nearby airport. After a few weeks, he did his solo flight and received his private pilot's license.

In 1943, the Army needed pilots for the light aircraft used as observation planes for spotting artillery targets. A person could qualify for this job if his vision was completely correctable with glasses. This was true for Taylor. He became a liaison pilot in the 93rd Division, the first all-Black division to see combat in World War II. Taylor directed artillery fire from his aircraft. Until the end of the war, he flew missions in the Pacific war zone over islands such as Guadalcanal, New Guinea, and Morotai. During brief periods of free time, he enlarged his collection of butterflies and moths from the jungles near the flight strips. When he returned home, he added these specimens to those he had collected in high school in Illinois.

When the war was finally over, Welton Taylor was eligible for veteran's benefits under the GI Bill of Rights. The government paid his college tuition and living expenses. He was able to marry and return to the University of Illinois. Taylor completed his master's and his doctoral degrees in a total of just over two years. His doctoral research concerned the study of the microbe that causes botulism, the most deadly kind of food poisoning. He described the growth of colonies of these microbes under laboratory conditions and showed how the rate of growth and vigor of such colonies was related to the production of their deadly toxins. He received his doctoral degree based on this research in 1948.

Career Highlights

Dr. Welton Taylor thought that it would be easy to find a job as a research microbiologist in an industrial or commercial company, but he received no job offers. Since his young wife was pregnant, there was no time to wait for the right job to come along. Dr. Taylor phoned the University of Illinois Medical School in Chicago. He planned to apply for a laboratory technician job without mentioning the fact that he had a doctorate. Fate stepped in when the telephone operator mistakenly connected Dr. Taylor to the head of the bacteriology department. Dr. Taylor described his true background and capabilities and was invited to come in the next day to apply for a faculty position. The head of the department quickly invited him to become a bacteriology instructor at a higher pay rate than the average for this position.

In 1950, Dr. Taylor was promoted to the rank of assistant professor. In this position, he began to direct the research of upcoming master's and doctoral students in microbiology. For example, he designed a research program on the prevention and treatment of tetanus and gangrene—both life-threatening forms of blood poisoning. Specifically, he designed a new treatment for these diseases that combined antibiotics with pain killers so the patient could better tolerate the condition while treatment was underway. He also did experiments with eye drops containing boric acid as the germicide. He studied how this germicide could sometimes prevent the proper working of the body's cells that attack germs. He showed how some supposed cures could actually make matters worse— undermining the body's natural defences.

Soon, Dr. Taylor's students began their own research careers in institutions of higher learning and industry. One of his former students had a job with the giant meat packing firm, SWIFT and Co., in Chicago. The company was being confronted with a nationwide outbreak of food poisoning. They needed expert advice very quickly. The former student suggested that the firm's executives call in Dr. Taylor. He became their senior microbiologist, and was the first African American to hold such a high position in the company.

Even though this position paid quite well, Dr. Taylor decided to leave the world of commerce after five years. In 1959, he returned to a medical research position at Children's Memorial Hospital in Chicago. He quickly began to expand his interests by accepting part-time and advisory appointments in several institutions in the region. For example, in 1961, he became an associate in the department of pathology at the Northwestern

University Medical School on Chicago's north side.

Around this same time, Dr. Taylor was gaining an international reputation as an expert on food poisoning. Officials of the World Health Organization invited him to work with the scientists at the Pasteur Institute in Lille, France, and the Colindale Central Public Health Laboratories in London, England. This organization also funded his research on an international study of food poisoning from imported foods. A research fellowship from the U.S. National Institutes of Health supported these visits. He and his family lived abroad during the whole of the academic year 1961–62.

In 1964, he was named microbiologist-in-chief at the West Suburban Hospital in Oak Park, Illinois. In that same year, he rejoined his colleagues at the University of Illinois Medical Center as an associate professor. By 1969, his primary occupation was as a consultant on microbiological problems for hospitals, teaching institutions, and government agencies. Dr. Taylor also became a frequent expert witness in court trials concerning situations, such as food poisoning, caused by negligence in food processing.

Since first working for SWIFT and Co., Dr. Taylor sought to improve the detection of germs that can cause food poisoning. Organizations that process foods, particularly egg and meat products, test these products on a regular schedule to ensure that there is no contamination. However, the standard procedures were slow, costly, and inaccurate. Dr. Taylor wanted to be able to do these tests quickly and cheaply but with the highest level of accuracy.

In 1965, he developed new methods for the detection of bacteria that cause food poisoning. In 1970, these methods became the standard procedures required by the U.S. Food and Drug Administration to prove that food products were free of contamination. These methods were so successful that the test has been adopted around the world. The U.S. Centers for Disease Control in Atlanta, Georgia, named a newly found bacterial species, *enterobacter taylorae*, in honor of Dr. Taylor's accomplishment.

Dr. Taylor also sought to improve testing methods in the field of medical microbiology. In 1977, he invented and patented a line of diagnostic kits. The contents could be used to test any type of biological specimen such as a patient's blood or tissues. Dr. Taylor started his own company to sell the diagnostic kits in the commercial marketplace. Unfortunately, even though the new product was technically sound, the company did not succeed financially. At present, the company, Micro-Palettes, Inc., is used exclusively as a base of operation for Dr. Taylor's consulting activities.

Emmanuel B. Thompson

Born: March 15, 1928, in Zaria, Nigeria

Status: Associate Professor, University of Illinois at Chicago

Education:

Bachelor of Science degree, Rockhurst College, Kansas City, Missouri, 1955

Bachelor of Science degree, University of Missouri, Kansas City, Missouri, 1959

Master of Science degree, University of Nebraska, Lincoln, Nebraska, 1963

Doctor of Philosophy degree, University of Washington, Seattle, Washington, 1966

Research Area: Pharmacology

Early Years

Emmanuel Thompson, the oldest of five children, was born in Zaria in northern Nigeria. His father worked for the United Africa Company, an organization that purchased agricultural products, such as cotton and peanuts, from local growers. It also sold manufactured products such as tools and clothing. The company had trading stations throughout Nigeria, and Mr. Thompson was the manager of the station in Zaria. Each product that he bought or sold brought in a small commission, and the commissions added up to a modest and reasonably steady income. In the United States, his job would have been similar to the manager of a general store in a medium-sized town.

Emmanuel Thompson attended a Roman Catholic elementary school that had about 200 students. Even though Nigerians taught alongside the Irish priests who operated the school, the language of instruction was English. Discipline at the school was harsh, and students would be spanked with a stick if they disobeyed.

Emmanuel Thompson was proud of his country and felt a kinship with the plants and animals of the great open grassland near his home. This sense of kinship helped him enjoy the biology courses at his school. He was particularly inspired when Dr. George Washington Carver (see p. 42)

came from the United States to visit his school. Dr. Carver took time to demonstrate new uses for native materials and showed the students how to make perfume from local plants. Emmanuel was very impressed by Carver's ingenuity.

Emmanuel's parents had a great respect for education and were willing to make sacrifices to help him continue his studies. When Emmanuel finished elementary school, they sent him to a boarding school in Lagos, the capital of Nigeria, which is 800 miles from Zaria.

The school Emmanuel attended was Saint Gregory's College. It was similar to a Catholic boy's high school in the United States. His parents had to pay for his tuition, room, and board. Emmanuel's chemistry teacher, a priest from Brazil, encouraged Emmanuel to ask questions and think about scientific ideas. One of his native Nigerian teachers was also a strong influence. This man taught Emmanuel the basic facts about electricity and magnetism.

When Emmanuel finished high school, he took a bookkeeping job with the United Africa Company in Lagos. However, he soon became very bored and frustrated with this work. He was determined to find a job that allowed him to follow his interest in science.

Soon, he accepted a position at a government research station in Vom, a village in northern Nigeria. Emmanuel worked as a laboratory technician and conducted research on animal diseases. The government wanted to control diseases of cattle because raising cattle was a major occupation of the people who lived near Vom.

The director of the laboratory, a man from England, was not interested in helping the Nigerian workers learn about scientific research. Nevertheless, the experience was good for Emmanuel. He began to understand the connections between scientific research and benefits for living creatures.

After three months in this remote village, Emmanuel decided that he had learned all he could from the English director. He promptly resigned and took a job teaching general science and geography at Saint John's College in Koduna, Nigeria. The school, a high school similar to Saint Gregory's College, was newly built but poorly equipped. Even though Koduna was a regional center of government for northern Nigeria, the school buildings were cheaply constructed of cement blocks with corrugated iron roofs and were often much too hot.

At this point in his life, Emmanuel Thompson was still unsettled about his future career. He wanted to provide people with health care, but he also wanted to work as a scientist. He realized that working in the field of pharmacy would fit his ambitions. In 1951, he enrolled in the Yaba School of Pharmacy in Lagos, the oldest institution of its kind in Nigeria. He studied there for two years and was awarded a pharmacy technician's diploma in 1952.

Higher Education

That same year, Emmanuel Thompson was presented with a totally new option. He was offered a small scholarship to attend Rockhurst College in Kansas City, Missouri. The scholarship was arranged by Dr. Desmond Bittinger who had been a Quaker missionary in Nigeria for 10 years. By 1952, Dr. Bittinger was president of a Quaker college in McPherson, Kansas. Because of Dr. Bittinger, the Quaker congregation in McPherson had a tradition of sponsoring ambitious Nigerian students who wanted to attend college in the United States. Emmanuel Thompson eagerly accepted the opportunity. He remembered how impressed he had been when Dr. Carver had discussed his research and how he hoped to someday conduct research in the United States.

Adjusting to his new life was not easy. Not only did Thompson have to study long hours, but he also had to earn money for his room and board. His part-time job required that he work late each evening, and he soon found that a Black person could not buy food late at night. This kind of racial prejudice made Thompson very uncomfortable. Therefore, he decided to study even harder, and he finished his degree in biology in only three years. He was then prepared to begin his specialized studies in pharmacy science.

In 1956, he enrolled in the pharmacy school at the University of Missouri. Soon after, Thompson fell in love with Nova Garner from Great Bend, Kansas. After they were married, his new wife found a good job and they were able to rent a house near the university campus. Emmanuel Thompson's living conditions greatly improved. After three more years of hard study, Thompson was awarded a degree in pharmacy, which allowed him to practice anywhere in the United States as a professional pharmacist. Nevertheless, he felt that he still needed more education. To pay for this education, he had to build up a financial reserve. Consequently, in 1959 he took a job as a hospital pharmacist at the University of Kansas Medical Center. After one year, he transferred to the Queen of the World Hospital. At the same time, Thompson also worked for a local drugstore as a registered pharmacist.

After improving his financial situation, he resumed his higher education. In 1961, he entered the University of Nebraska in Lincoln, Nebraska, to study for his master's degree. At Nebraska, he began to learn about drug development, the discovery or invention of new drugs. The aim of pharmaceutical research is to find a compound that does a better job of curing or controlling a disease. These new compounds might come from synthetic chemicals or from natural sources such as plants or animals. For example, the first aspirin-type compound was extracted from the bark of the willow tree.

Thompson made a particular study of a plant related to garlic. Extracts made from this plant were thought to lower blood pressure. His research identified the active compound and possible injurious side effects. Emmanuel Thompson finished his master's studies at Nebraska in 1963. He immediately enrolled in the doctoral program at the University of Washington in Seattle, Washington. By now, Thompson's family included two young daughters. His family moved into a large university apartment building with about 100 other families. All the graduate students in the building were enrolled in health sciences.

For his doctoral research, Thompson continued to work on compounds that might control high blood pressure. Now, however, he focused on a group of synthetic compounds that affect the nerves that control the heart muscle. These compounds block-off messages that tell the heart to beat faster. In 1966, Dr. Thompson finished his research on the synthetic compounds. As soon as he completed his dissertation, he received his doctoral degree from the University of Washington.

Career Highlights

After completing his doctoral studies, Dr. Thompson—not surprisingly—felt the need to earn some money. In 1966, he took a job as a senior research pharmacologist at Baxter Laboratories, Inc., in Morton Grove, Illinois, a suburb of Chicago. While there, he helped develop several general anesthetics, materials used to put people to sleep during surgical operations. One of his anesthetics was adopted for use by surgeons in Japan.

In 1969, Dr. Thompson joined the faculty of the College of Pharmacy at the University of Illinois Medical Center in Chicago. He was a popular professor, and the senior class selected him as "Teacher of the Year" in 1971. In 1973, he was promoted to the rank of associate professor and began teaching courses in the School of Public Health, the School of Associated Medical Sciences, and the College of Nursing. He has also given special lectures at the Illinois College of Pediatric Medicine and the School of Nursing at Chicago State University. Dr. Thompson has designed new courses, such as one on drug development, for the College of Pharmacy. He also has written a textbook for this course entitled *Drug Bioscreening*. The first edition of the book was published in 1985 and a new edition came out in 1990.

Meanwhile, Dr. Thompson's research activities continued at a rapid pace. He has studied drugs that might help control sickle-cell anemia. There is no cure, but the body's production of abnormal blood cells can be reduced by treatment. He has also worked to develop compounds that can control high blood pressure. Both sickle-cell anemia and high blood pressure are common problems for African Americans. By 1992, Dr. Thompson had published over 45 reports on this research.

At a time when preindustrial countries need help to move ahead, Dr. Thompson's work on drug screening is particularly important. For example, many new drugs have been developed from tropical plants, and drug companies are beginning to sponsor exploration of tropical rain forests to find such materials. The quest will be lengthy because hundreds of plants with possible medicinal value remain to be tested. Ecologists and other scientists hope that the potential worth of these tropical plants will help prevent the destruction of the rain forests.

Dr. Thompson's techniques for screening possible new drugs are very practical. In his latest book, he shows researchers how to test new materials in a step-by-step manner. His ideas could make the testing of tropical plants faster and less expensive. This information will benefit the drug development companies, the tropical countries, and patients around the world.

J. Tyson Tildon

Born: August 7, 1931 in Baltimore, Maryland

Status: Professor of Biochemistry, University of Maryland School of Medicine, Baltimore, Maryland.

Education:

Bachelor of Science degree, Morgan State University, Baltimore, Maryland, 1954.

Doctor of Philosophy degree, Johns Hopkins University, Baltimore, Maryland, 1965.

Research Area: Biochemistry

Early Years

Curiosity is a natural, human characteristic. Some people, like Tyson Tildon, have more of it than others. When he was about six years old, Tyson began to disassemble things—like toys and toasters—to see how they were made. Sometimes, but not always, he could put the parts back together. Now and then, he was punished for yielding to his curiosity.

Even so, Tyson's parents both encouraged and suported his curiousity. When Tyson was in grade school, his parents bought him a chemistry set. He associated chemistry with magic and was fascinated by what he could do with the chemicals. He especially enjoyed making liquids change color. He also enjoyed discovering new things about nature, and his parents often took him to visit local farms so that he could see firsthand the interdependence of the natural world. He soon understood how plants feed animals and how the animals' manure provides fertilizer for the plants.

Tyson, who was a self-motivated student, was also stimulated by his science courses. The teachers responded to his enthusiasm by giving him individual attention and suggesting new ideas that might interest him.

When Tyson reached high school, he often attended weekly programs sponsored by the Maryland Academy of Science. In a small auditorium at the Baltimore Public Library, local scientists and engineers gave presentations on their research. Tyson took advantage of these science lectures to learn about new ideas. He saw connections between the topics covered and his science courses at school.

He was also impressed by the evident enthusiasm of the scientists and engineers making the presentations. They always appeared to be excited about their work. It was during this time that Tyson decided he wanted to become a scientist one day.

Higher Education

Tyson Tildon graduated from high school at the top of his class. Because of his good grades, he was awarded a scholarship to attend Fisk University in Nashville, Tennessee. Tildon began classes in the fall of 1950 with a heavy course load that included chemistry, mathematics, and philosophy. He did well at Fisk, but even with the scholarship, money soon became a problem. Tildon decided that he would spend far less money if he lived at home and went to a local college.

In the fall of 1951, he enrolled at Morgan State University in Baltimore. Like Fisk, Morgan State has a tradition of serving the African American community. Because of government funding, Morgan's tuition is low compared to that of the privately endowed Fisk, and Tildon found his education much more affordable. He graduated in 1954 with a major in chemistry.

Because of continuing money problems, Tildon did not immediately begin graduate studies. Instead, he found a job as a laboratory technician at Mt. Sinai Hospital in Baltimore. Under the supervision of Dr. Harry Gordon, Tildon focused on analyzing blood and urine samples from patients being prepared for surgery. The laboratory was also involved with research on nutrition. Dr. Gordon saw that Tildon was ambitious and encouraged him to start his own projects. Tildon was particularly interested in the consequences of vitamin deficiencies. Vitamin E had been recently identified, and Tildon wanted to know if specific medical problems were caused by too little Vitamin E in the diet. He found that animals developed tiny, internal sores near their windpipes if they did not get enough Vitamin E.

Unfortunately, one of the older technicians copied some of Tildon's research ideas and submitted them for publication in a scientific periodical. When Tildon discovered this plagiarism, he was very upset and went to Dr. Gordon for advice. Dr. Gordon cooled Tildon's anger by pointing out that those ideas would not be his last or his best scientific thoughts. The plagiarist was quietly asked to resign. In turn, Dr. Gordon, impressed by the quality of Tildon's scientific ideas and his positive attitude toward what had been a negative experience, recommended Tildon for a Fulbright Scholarship to study abroad.

In 1957, Tildon was married to Sania Amr. Two years later, he took his wife and baby daughter to Paris, France, for his year of study on the Fulbright Scholarship. At the Institute for Biology and Physical Chemistry at the University of Paris, he teamed with Professor J. Szulmayster. The two scientists studied the enzymes in bacteria that break up the phosphorus molecules vital to the cell's energy production. Their work succeeded in isolating one of these enzymes.

In 1960, Tildon returned to Mt. Sinai Hospital in Baltimore. The next year, with Dr. Gordon's encouragement, Tildon enrolled in the graduate program at the Johns Hopkins University in Baltimore. Under the tutelage of Professors Albert Lehninger and James Olgivie, he began a research project to identify the chemical reactions that take place in the cells of the body. In living cells, these reactions are difficult to detect and identify. Biochemists sought to isolate the key chemicals and use them to duplicate identical chemical reactions in a test tube. Using this method, Tildon isolated a particular protein from the clear, fluid portion of blood and demonstrated its reaction with other chemicals.

Career Highlights

When Tildon received his doctoral degree from Johns Hopkins in 1965, he was awarded a Helen Hay Whitney Foundation Fellowship. He chose to spend the two-year period at Brandeis University in Waltham, Massachusetts, a suburb of Boston. At Brandeis, he worked with Dr. Nathan Kaplan on the nature of cell division.

The details of how cells multiply and become specific parts of the body are crucial to the understanding of how cancers grow. Dr. Tildon and Dr. Kaplan sought to observe the details of cell division by isolating this process from other biological processes. They then demonstrated how specific foreign chemicals, in reaction with the cell's natural enzymes, either speeded up or slowed down cell division and specialization. This discovery proved to be the main theme of Dr. Tildon's research for the next 25 years.

To prepare for his future career, Dr. Tildon saw the need to strengthen his teaching skills. He accepted a one-year appointment to the faculty of Goucher College in suburban Baltimore in 1967. There, he developed courses in biochemistry and designed a course on the physical sciences for nonscience majors.

The next year, Dr. Tildon accepted a joint appointment in the department of pediatrics and the department of biological chemistry at the University of Maryland School of Medicine in the heart of Baltimore. His teaching duties included first year courses in biochemistry and third year courses in laboratory techniques for students specializing in the care of infants and children.

Meanwhile, Dr. Tildon's research efforts continued. He began a long series of studies to determine which chemicals provide energy sources for organs of the body. Ordinarily, animals and humans burn sugar in the form of glucose as their major source of energy. In Dr. Tildon's experiments, sugar was withheld from the diets of laboratory animals to find out what other raw materials were usable. He discovered that chemicals such as ketones, which give bananas their special odor, and glutamine, one of the building blocks of protein, can be sources of energy, particularly in very young animals.

In 1971, Dr. Tildon was promoted to associate professor and, in 1974, to full professor. The following year, he was awarded a special scholarship by the Josiah Macy Foundation, allowing Dr. Tildon and his family to spend the year in Holland, where he studied children's diseases at the University of Groningen. Dr. Tildon's reputation began to spread around the world. He was invited to give lectures in England, Switzerland, Denmark, Italy, and Greece, as well as in Canada and the United States.

After these experiences, Dr. Tildon's interests became focused on crib death or Sudden Infant Death Syndrome (SIDS). This mysterious condition tends to affect children from the age of 6 months to 24 months. Dr. Tildon saw a connection between some of the signs of the disease and his work on nutrition. Many SIDS victims had the tiny sores near their windpipes that he had observed in animals with a shortage of Vitamin E. He studied the possibility that a missing ingredient in a baby's milk or a flaw in its digestive system could lead to a vitamin shortage.

Dr. Tildon became one of the main authorities on SIDS and was made the director of research at the University of Maryland's SIDS Institute in 1980. This institute provides diagnosis and treatment for infants that might become victims and provides counseling and support for their parents. It also carries out programs of general public education so that child-care practices can be ad-

justed to minimize the risk of SIDS. Most researchers and medical doctors have come to the conclusion that there are many different causes of SIDS, including pure accidents such as a baby being smothered by its blankets.

In addition to teaching and research, Dr. Tildon is active in community projects that further better relations between the races. He wrote a book on this topic in 1972 entitled *The Anglo-Saxon Agony* in which he contends that the Black heritage has much to contribute to European culture.

Dr. Tildon is now a grandfather several times over, but his curiosity has helped him maintain a youthful outlook. He continues to search for new ideas and learning experiences.

Margaret E. M. Tolbert

Born: November 24, 1943, in Suffolk, Virginia

Status: Director, Division of Educational Programs, Argonne National Laboratories, Argonne, Illinois

Education:

Bachelor of Science degree, Tuskegee University, Tuskegee, Alabama, 1967

Master of Science degree, Wayne State University, Detroit, Michigan, 1968

Doctor of Philosophy degree, Brown University, Providence, Rhode Island, 1974

Research Area: Biochemistry

Early Years

Margaret Mayo was the third of six children born to J. Clifton and Martha Artis Mayo of Suffolk, Virginia. Margaret's mother was a domestic worker, and her father served in the U.S. Army during World War II. After his discharge, he worked as a landscape gardener around the town of Suffolk.

When Margaret was still very young, her parents separated. Her mother tried to support all six children by herself, but not long after her husband left the family, Mrs. Mayo died. The neighbors did not want to contact social services, fearing that the youngsters would be placed in different foster homes. For a time, therefore, the children were cared for as a group by one neighborhood family or another. This kept them together but was an unsatisfactory way to raise six children on a permanent basis. The situation was finally resolved when the children were given a home by their father's mother, Fannie Mae Johnson Mayo.

Because of these family problems, Margaret had difficulty in kindergarten but quickly improved when she began the first grade at the Ida V. Easter School. She realized, even at that young age, that education was the means for her to achieve a better life, and by the time she was ready for East Suffolk Junior High School, Margaret was at the top of her class.

Margaret walked two miles to reach her junior high school. Her route took her past a factory where peanuts were roasted and packaged. Dust from the peanut shells often clouded the air and settled in her hair. Margaret loved the taste and smell of the roasting peanuts. In fact, peanut aroma still reminds her of the happy times during her childhood years.

In her very early teens, Margaret had to work as a maid and baby-sitter for nearby families. During this time, her father died and her grandmother became ill. Mrs. Mayo, by then in her 70s, needed constant care and moved in with a daughter in Portsmouth, Virginia. There was no room for Margaret, her two younger sisters, and one younger brother. An older, married sister gave the four children a home. They received some money from their father's insurance, but the strain was so great that the sister's husband soon abandoned the family. Margaret now had to work even longer hours as a housemaid while she finished high school.

The Simon A. Cook family, one of the families for whom Margaret worked, virtually adopted the teenager. Margaret's high school teachers and the Cooks encouraged her to plan for college. The teachers arranged for Margaret to take advanced placement courses in mathematics and science, and the Cooks helped Margaret investigate college possibilities. They drove her to various colleges and talked to the college officials.

Higher Education

Margaret Tolbert enrolled in the Tuskegee Institute (now University) in Tuskegee, Alabama. She chose this school because it had a family atmosphere, her high school principal had recommended it, the Cooks had friends on the faculty, and she thought she might find new experiences far away from her home in tidewater Virginia.

Tuskegee gave her a small scholarship, which Tolbert augmented by working at every job she could find—on or off the campus. Family friends from her old neighborhood contributed what they could, and the Cooks helped with money and clothing. Several of the faculty families served as sources of support and friendship for Tolbert. Since she could not afford to travel to Virginia, she particularly needed their friendship during holidays and other breaks when few students remained on the campus. During these times, she was invited to dinners and parties at their homes. On such occasions, Tolbert listened as they told stories about Booker T. Washington, George Washington Carver (see p. 42), and other great African American leaders.

When she first entered Tuskegee, Margaret Tolbert's goal had been to study medicine. She soon realized, however, that the costs of medical school would be too high for her limited finances. She also realized that if she chose basic science as a field of study, there would be good prospects for receiving financial aid. Consequently, she decided on chemistry as her future career.

Many of the Tuskegee faculty were involved in research projects, and Tolbert was able to serve as a research assistant to Professors C. J. Smith and L. F. Koons during her time at Tuskegee. Among her other duties, she assisted in the study of how different chemicals, when placed in water solutions, conduct electricity with differing degrees of resistance. She learned that part of the difference in conductivity depends on the ease with which the molecules of a chemical solution come apart when dissolved in water.

To further expand her knowledge, Tolbert worked one summer as a research assistant at Central State College in Durham, North Carolina, on a variety of projects. Tolbert spent the next summer at Argonne National Laboratories as a member of the analytics group that was studying the various chemical combinations made by uranium. She did very well in her various research projects and her undergraduate studies, and in 1967, Margaret Tolbert was awarded her undergraduate degree from Tuskegee.

In the fall of that year, she enrolled at Wayne State University in Detroit, Michigan. At Wayne State, she focused on improving her skills in chemical analysis, and in 1968, after just one year of study, she received her master's degree. Margaret returned immediately to Tuskegee to serve as a professional technician on the very research projects she had helped conduct as an undergraduate assistant. She was also employed to teach a regular course in the mathematics department.

Many members of the academic community have worked diligently to increase the number of minority people in science. Tolbert, with her ability and her extensive background of experience, was viewed as a prime candidate for an eminent career in the field of chemistry. Consequently, she was recruited into the doctoral program in chemistry at one of the Ivy League colleges, Brown University in Providence, Rhode Island. Tolbert also won a scholarship from the Southern Fellowship Fund, which helped her finance her doctoral studies.

At Brown, she came under the tutelage of Professor John N. Fain, who directed her attention to biochemistry. She decided to focus her research on the biochemical reactions that take place in the liver. The energy bearing materials are stored, processed, and released by the liver in several complicated sequences of chemical reactions. Tolbert analyzed some of these reactions and demonstrated how they work.

In the meantime, she taught night school at the Opportunities Industrialization Center in Providence, where adults upgraded their employment skills. At the center, she taught basic science to nurses and mathematics to welders.

Career Highlights

After completing her doctoral research project, Tolbert left Brown before her dissertation was finished and accepted an appointment to the chemistry faculty at Tuskegee. After she had been awarded some grant money, they assigned her a work space at the Carver Research Foundation laboratory and she continued her experiments.

Dr. Tolbert finished her dissertation and was awarded her doctoral degree in 1974. She remained at Tuskegee until 1977, then joined the staff at the College of Pharmacy and Pharmaceutical Sciences at Florida A&M University in Tallahassee. Dr. Tolbert also conducted a summer research project at the Lawrence Livermore Laboratory near Berkeley, California. In addition to these projects, she taught part-time at Southern Vocational College in order to help others improve their employment prospects. Dr. Tolbert wanted to give support to the community that had helped her when she badly needed it.

In less than two years at Florida A&M, Dr. Tolbert was promoted twice and was chosen to become an associate dean of the School of Pharmacy, but she decided to accept a position spending five months doing research in Brussels, Belgium, at the International Institute of Cellular and Molecular Pathology. After she returned to the United States, she spent seven months at Brown University as a visiting associate professor. The work in Belgium and at Brown resulted in two major research reports on the biochemistry of the liver.

Dr. Tolbert then returned to Tuskegee as director of the Carver Research Foundation and associate provost for the entire university. During her eight year tenure in these positions, she was able to place the foundation on a sound financial base. Dr. Tolbert also built a communications network with institutions of higher learning in West Africa and with three of the great national laboratories maintained by the U.S. Department of Energy.

In 1987, Dr. Tolbert took a position in corporate planning with the research arm of the British Petroleum Corporation in Warrensville Heights, Ohio. Dr. Tolbert was a member of the team that brought about the merger of the technical interests of British Petroleum and the Standard Oil Company of Ohio. During her time there, she also busied herself with the development of science education, including programs in science museums.

By now, it was increasingly clear that Dr. Tolbert was particularly adept at science administration. She was able to expand the availability of resources to bring minority and disadvantaged people into careers in the field of science. It was in this capacity that Dr. Tolbert was recruited by the National Science Foundation (NSF) and served three years as program director for the Research Improvement in Minority Institutions Program. After leaving NSF, she worked for a short time with the Howard Hughs Medical Center to establish some international research programs in Eastern Europe. Currently, Dr. Tolbert is once more employed by the Argonne National Laboratories, where she coordinates all the high school and post high school programs in science education.

Charles Henry Turner

Born: February 3, 1867, in Cincinnati, Ohio

Status: Died, February 14, 1923, in Chicago, Illinois

Education:
Bachelor of Science degree, University of Cincinnati, Cincinnati, Ohio, 1891

Master of Science degree, University of Cincinnati, 1892

Doctor of Philosophy degree, University of Chicago, Chicago, Illinois, 1907

Research Area: Biology

Early Years

Charles Henry Turner was born two years after the end of the Civil War. His father, Thomas Turner, worked in Cincinnati, Ohio, as the custodian of a church. In southern Ohio, there was still a high degree of tension about the war and the status of former slaves. Mr. Turner had always been a free man because he was from Alberta, Canada, a country that had no slavery. Charles's mother, Eat Campbell Turner, worked as a nurse and was

a freed woman from Kentucky, a slave state before the Civil War.

Charles's parents were very interested in learning, and they encouraged their son to read and study. Indeed, they bought as many books as they could afford and kept a small library in their home. Charles, however, did not limit his learning to books. He was very interested in nature and spent many hours watching ants, bees, and other insects. He also asked his teachers many questions about insect behavior. Charles wanted to discover how bees know which flowers have nectar and how ants find their way back home. Cockroaches also fascinated him, and he questioned why they run around when lights are turned on in a dark room. By the time Charles was in high school, he already knew that he wanted to spend his life studying insects.

Higher Education

After graduating from high school, Charles Turner enrolled in the University of Cincinnati. While there, he married Leontine Troy. After graduating in 1891, he remained at the University of Cincinnati for an advanced degree. He received his master of science degree in 1892, after just one year of study. At this point, Turner realized that he could not continue his education until he saved some money. Therefore, he worked briefly as an assistant instructor in the biology laboratory at the University of Cincinnati.

Even though Turner knew that he wanted to teach biology, he was not sure whether he wanted to teach at the high school or the college-level. He decided to try college first, and from 1893–1895 Turner taught biology at Clark College in Atlanta, which had been founded just after the Civil War by the Freedmen's Aid Society, a part of the African Methodist Episcopal (AME) church. The

AME church was very active in improving the lives of African Americans through education. In 1895, while Charles Turner was teaching at Clark College, his wife, Leontine Troy Turner, died. She left five young children. Some years later, Turner remarried.

From 1896 to 1908, Turner taught in several different schools, but he was still uncertain about his future career. First, he taught biology in a public high school in Evansville, Indiana, and then at another high school in Cincinnati, Ohio, his old hometown. Next, he became the principal at a high school in Cleveland, Tennessee. He also taught biology in the Haines Normal and Industrial Institute in Augusta, Georgia. During all these years, Charles Turner continued to conduct experiments on insect behavior. He reported his observations in the scientific literature and was recognized by other scientists as an expert on insects.

Turner's original research and publications were important factors in his acceptance into the graduate program at the University of Chicago. In the early 1900s, African Americans were not often given the opportunity to get an advanced education. To receive a Ph.D. from Chicago, one of the best universities in the country, was an amazing achievement for an African American at that time. In 1907, Dr. Turner was awarded his doctoral degree from the University of Chicago.

In 1908, Dr. Turner moved to St. Louis, Missouri, and took a job teaching biology at Sumner High School. Here he had found his true calling and taught at this school for the rest of his life.

Career Highlights

From the time Dr. Turner attended the University of Cincinnati until the time of his death, he performed fascinating experiments with insects. He was most interested in those insects that showed complicated or unusual behavior.

Dr. Turner was interested in how ants find their way back to the ant colony. He hoped to demonstrate whether light clues, chemical smell, landmarks, or their own footprints guided them back home.

Dr. Turner devised some very clever experiments to determine which of these were important factors. He designed a small platform with a ramp on the right and another on the left. A nest of ants was placed at an equal distance between the two ramps and an electric light was placed near each ramp. The lights were wired so that when one light was on, the other was off. Since Dr. Turner's experiment focused on light as a factor, he soon realized that there was a problem with his initial design. The light bulbs gave off too much heat. Because it was impossible to tell if the behavior was influenced by light or by heat, the heat had to be eliminated. Dr. Turner set up heat filters on each light so that the heat was blocked but not the light. He also added a mirror in case he needed to see the ants that were crawling near the bottom of the platform.

Dr. Turner placed ants, ant eggs, and larvae on the platform. He knew that ants have a strong tendency to carry eggs and the worm-like larvae back to the nest as quickly as possible. To start the experiment, Dr. Turner turned on the light near the right ramp. Soon, ants began to carry the eggs and larvae from the platform to the nest, using the right ramp. After a few hours, Dr. Turner switched off that light and switched on the light on the left ramp. He noticed that, at first, the ants moved around in different directions as if they were lost or confused, but in less than an hour, the ants were using the left ramp. Dr. Turner concluded that ants use light in some way to guide them to and from their nest. We now know that these clever creatures use many clues to direct their actions. In particular, ants and other insects can excrete chemicals called pheremones that help them identify locations and other insects.

Dr. Turner was also curious about a certain type of bee. Unlike ants, who always live in colonies, a particular species of bee burrows underground and makes a solitary nest. He wanted to know how the burrowing bee can fly some distance from his nest, stay there for a long time, and then return to its tiny hole in the ground. Again, Dr. Turner set up an interesting experiment. He located the hole of a burrowing bee and waited for the bee to leave. While the bee was gone, Dr. Turner placed a piece of paper over the hole to disguise the opening to the burrow. He then cut a hole in the paper and lined it up with the hole in the ground. When the bee came back, it flew around and over the paper for about two minutes and then went into the hole. Later it came out, flew around the hole a few times, and then flew off. The next time it returned, it flew over the paper for about 30 seconds and then went into its burrow. When the bee left again, Dr. Turner dug a hole about four inches away from the original bee hole. The white piece of paper was placed over the new hole to confuse the bee. Finally, Dr. Turner poked a hole in a piece of watermellon rind and placed it over the real bee hole. The bee came back, flew around for about one minute, and flew through the hole in the watermelon to its burrow. Dr. Turner concluded that burrowing bees know the exact location of their hole by remembering the features of the area near the hole. Even though the look of the hole changed, the opening was still in the same place, and the bee could find it.

Dr. Turner was interested, too, in determining whether bees could tell the difference between colors. His research proved that they not only distinguish between colors, they also can detect different geometric patterns of a single color.

Later, he conducted research on the hearing of moths. First, Dr. Turner found that a certain species of moth would respond only to very high-pitched sounds. To determine how adaptable the moths were, he tried to train them to find food by using lower-pitched sound signals. Dr. Turner succeeded in training the moths. In this experiment, he proved that insects were much more adaptable and trainable than most scientists had thought.

Along similar lines, he began to train cockroaches. To do so, he used a simple maze that was screened at the top. Food was placed at one end of the maze and the cockroaches were put into a starting box at the other end. The cockroaches were a bit slow in learning. Indeed, it took them a full day to go through the whole maze without making any errors. Nevertheless, Dr. Turner demonstrated, again, that insects are not limited to instinctive behaviors. They can learn from experience just as other animals can.

Dr. Turner's experiments and discoveries were very important to other scientists who studied animal behavior. He published many papers based on his research, which were read and quoted by scientists in Europe as well as in America. Dr. Turner was the first to observe a peculiar circling movement made by some ants when they were disturbed. Some French scientists became very interested in this behavior and did many follow-up studies to test Dr. Turner's ideas. In their reports, this ant behavior became known as "Turner Circling," and this peculiar pattern of movement continues to bear his name.

It is particularly noteworthy that Dr. Turner did this significant work without the benefit of government grants or any form of outside support. Nor did he have research assistants or a well-stocked laboratory, such as is available to scientists on university faculties. He bought his own books and equipment on a very small salary.

During the many years that Dr. Turner was conducting his experiments, he continued to teach at Sumner High School. His knowledge of insects and other animals made his biology classes fascinating to the students. He told them about his experiments and shared the resulting observations. To make his classes more interesting, he brought live plants and animals into the classroom. His students could conduct experiments with them and observe them under the microscope. Dr. Turner often took his students on field trips into the woods. He would tell them about the plants and animals and explain the interdependence of all living things.

Dr. Turner's classes were always special because he loved biology, and his students learned to love it, too. Although Dr. Turner could have taught at a college or university, he chose to teach in a high school, where he thought he could do the most good.

But Dr. Turner was interested in more than teaching and research. Unfortunately, he died before finishing a novel and a book of nature stories for children. He did, however, complete more than 30 poems. Dr. Turner was also very active in working for the civil rights of African Americans, including helping improve the social services for Black people in St. Louis.

When Dr. Turner died in 1923, the St. Louis Board of Education opened a school for the physically handicapped and named it the Charles H. Turner School. This was a fitting tribute to a man who was a creative and dedicated scientist, teacher, and humanitarian.

Warren M. Washington

Born: August 28, 1936, in Portland, Oregon

Status: Director, Climate and Global Dynamics Division, National Center for Atmospheric Research, Boulder, Colorado

Education:

Bachelor of Science degree, Oregon State University, Corvalis, Oregon, 1958

Master of Science degree, Oregon State University, 1960

Doctor of Philosophy degree, Pennsylvania State University, State College, Pennsylvania, 1964

Research Areas: Meteorology and Atmospheric Physics

Early Years

Warren Washington's father, Edwin Washington, moved to Portland, Oregon, in 1928. He had just graduated from Talladega College near Birmingham, Alabama, and hoped to find a teaching position in Portland. However, even this far from the South, in a city of integrated schools, few were ready for a Black teacher.

Instead of teaching, Edwin Washington went to work as a Pullman porter for the Union Pacific Railroad. While not as genteel as teaching, Edwin Washington made more money as a porter. Soon, he and his wife were the parents of five boys, and they needed every cent. As soon as Warren was old enough, he began to work for his spending money. He delivered the *Oregonian* newspaper to the families in his neighborhood and later washed dishes at the Good Samaritan Hospital and Medical Center.

In 1949, when Warren was in high school, attitudes toward race were gradually beginning to change. Harry Truman was president of the United States and the Supreme Court's ruling on school integration was just a few years away. Even though open discrimination was prevalent, Warren Washington never felt race was a big factor in his young life. In fact, he was encouraged by almost everyone—family, teachers, and neighbors—to follow his dream of becoming a scientist. One exception was the high school guidance counselor who could not imagine an African American doing advanced scientific work. The counselor recommended that Warren attend a business school rather than a college.

In contrast, Warren's high school chemistry teacher was very supportive. One day in class, Warren asked this teacher why egg yolks were yellow. She turned the question around and challenged him to find the answer on his own. Warren speculated that the yellow color had to come from something that chickens eat. Ultimately, he discovered that specific sulfur compounds in grasses and grain were eaten and digested by chickens, which caused the storage of sulfurous materials in the yoke of the egg, giving it a yellow color. Warren was pleased to have solved a complicated puzzle through his own efforts.

He soon began to look for other challenges. Another of his high school teachers used the challenge of puzzles to get Warren interested in physics. Soon, he realized that he was fascinated by his courses in this subject as well. Indeed, he decided to make the study of physics his life's work. Warren wondered why some of his fellow students who were very good in science courses did not have a continuing interest in the field. He sensed that aptitude was not the only factor in making a career choice. Ambition, curiosity, and a combination of other considerations all helped to determine a person's future career.

Higher Education

Warren Washington chose to attend Oregon State University in Corvalis because it had an undergraduate program in physics. The school also was close to his home in Portland and had a reasonable tuition. At Oregon State, he was a minority within a minority. Physics programs did not attract many students, and most of Washington's classes were small. He also was the only African American in the small group of students majoring in physics. In fact, there were only about eight Black students on the Oregon State campus at that time. Most of them were enrolled in non-scientific programs related to sports or business.

Washington, like many other students, had to work to finance his college expenses. Fate stepped in when he found a position operating the weather radar on a mountain-top installation near Corvalis. Washington was fascinated by his new job. The purpose of the installation was to track storms coming from the Pacific Ocean. Weather radar was still a relatively new technology, and Washington felt that he was making a real contribution.

He was not only providing his home community with timely storm warnings, but he also was testing new methods of weather analysis and technology.

Meteorology, the study of weather, is traditionally associated with the field of physics. Thus, Washington did not leave the study of physics when he shifted to meteorology as a possible career. As soon as he had completed his first college degree in 1958, Washington continued his study of meteorology at the graduate level. While working on his master's degree at Oregon State, another opportunity presented itself. Washington was invited to use his applied mathematics skills to analyze weather conditions for a large project being conducted by the Stanford Research Institute in Menlo Park, California. This position afforded a pleasant change in location and some badly needed money.

After his time in California, Washington returned to Oregon to finish his graduate program, and he received his master's degree in 1960. Even though Oregon State offered a master's degree in meteorology, the school had no doctoral program at that time. Therefore, Washington chose to go east to Pennsylvania State University to finish his advanced education. At Penn State, Washington's interest in mathematics became increasingly important in his research. The faculty at Penn State were among the pioneers in the application of computer power to weather studies. A powerful computer can keep track of thousands of pieces of meteorological information and help scientists analyze this data. In the short term, the computer can record, examine, and predict weather conditions over several days. In the long term, scientists, with the help of even more powerful computers, will be able to foretell weather conditions for the immediate or distant future.

Presently, long term studies look at trends in the weather from year to year and over longer periods. Year-to-year weather can be influenced by many terrestrial events, such as the eruption of a volcano. Ash and dust can stay in the air for many months and decrease the amount of sunlight that reaches the earth's surface. Other trends involve man-made chemicals that can react with natural chemicals in the atmosphere and cause the protective ozone layer to shrink. Ozone, a gas that is composed of three rather than the normal two atoms of oxygen, acts as a shield against some of the sun's ultraviolet radiation. The resultant expansion in this radiation could increase the occurrence of skin cancer.

By conducting trend studies, it is even possible to see how the climate might change over tens or hundreds of years. Each year, humans burn more oil, gasoline, coal, and wood, which puts carbon dioxide into the air. While it is true some of the carbon dioxide gas is absorbed by the ocean or used by growing plants, more of this gas goes into the air than is removed. Carbon dioxide acts somewhat like the glass walls and ceiling of a greenhouse. It lets in the warming rays of the sun and then holds the heat in the air near the surface of the earth. Many scientists believe that the climate of the earth will gradually become warmer as humans continue to burn so much fuel. Some think this could lead to the melting of the ice caps around the north and south polar regions, which would raise the level of the oceans enough to flood coastal towns and cities.

Warren Washington confronted these perplexing problems as he pursued his studies at Penn State University. Government officials responsible for the environment were also facing these issues and seeking new solutions. To this end, Washington was invited to join a team of meteorologists at the National Center for Atmospheric Research at Boulder, Colorado, as soon as he graduated. In 1964, he completed his research and was awarded his doctoral degree from Penn State.

Career Highlights

At the center in Boulder, Dr. Washington began a collaboration with fellow scientist, Dr. Akira Kasahara. They generated a program of mathematically-based climate prediction that continues to the present day—over 30 years later. In the beginning, they used relatively simple equations that represented only a few weather and climate processes.

The limitations resulted partly from a lack of actual observations. In those days, the number of weather observatories was not large, and only a few of them were near oceans, where most weather events take place. Also, observations of temperature, winds, and humidity at high altitudes required expensive procedures, such as launching balloons with instruments that could report readings back to earth. Another problem was the limited capacity of the available computers. Ideally, basic information on temperature, air pressure, humidity, and wind should be available every few minutes for every square mile of the earth's surface and every thousand feet of altitude above that surface. Even today, the quantity of numbers generated would exceed the capacity of the most advanced computers. Consequently, the research team at Boulder had insufficient computer power to interpret all the necessary information.

As the years passed, the power of computers increased dramatically. So did the scope of the climate models developed by Dr. Washington and his colleagues. By the early 1970s, they were able to generate images of the an-

nual monsoon in India and to show how it relates to the large, high-altitude river of air called the jet stream as it flows across the Pacific Ocean. Dr. Washington and his co-workers expanded their analyses to include the effects of artic and antarctic events on the weather in Europe and North America. In more recent years, Dr. Washington has included the effects of human activities in his climate analysis.

Because of such efforts, it is possible today for meteorologists to make quite accurate five-day forecasts. Such forecasts are broadcast every day on the local television news. It is also increasingly possible to predict future general shifts in the global climate. The factors that influence climate are years in the making. Carbon dioxide gas, for example, makes up only a very small fraction of the air. The surplus gas generated each year by burning various fuels is another small fraction of the total carbon dioxide. It takes years for this accumulation to have an effect that is detectable by the most sensitive scientific instruments. However, by the time the climate has begun to change, it will be too late to prevent further deterioration from taking place. Therefore, meteorologists and researchers like Dr. Washington hope to be able to predict the distant future with a higher degree of accuracy. With these predictions available, scientists will be able to take the steps necessary to avoid environmental disaster. To this end, Dr. Washington strives to create the mathematical tools that will be used with powerful computers to make long range predictions of climate change.

In addition to his research activities, Dr. Washington is a member of many organizations. He recently became the first African American to be president of the American Meteorological Society. Dr. Washington also has served as advisor and consultant to each president of the United States since Jimmy Carter.

One of Dr. Washington's major goals is to interest young women and minority members in scientific or technological careers. Because of prejudice, some young people are still denied the opportunity to live up to their capabilities. The country, therefore, is denied the product of their talents. To help avoid this problem, Dr. Washington became a co-founder of BEST, the Black Environmental Science Trust. This organization provides the means for African Americans in the scientific community to encourage young people to chose a career in science. In addition, these established scientists also provide a support system for those students who have chosen to seek an advanced degree in environmental science.

William R. Wiley

Born: September 5, 1932, in Oxford, Mississippi

Status: Director, Pacific Northwest Laboratory, Richland, Washington, and Senior Vice President, Battelle Memorial Institute

Education:

Bachelor of Science degree, Tougaloo College, Tougaloo, Mississippi, 1954

Master of Science degree, University of Illinois, Champaign-Urbana, Illinois, 1960

Doctor of Philosophy degree, Washington State University, Pullman, Washington, 1965

Research Areas: Microbiology and Biochemistry

Early Years

When Bill Wiley was a boy in the 1930s, Oxford, Mississippi, was a completely segregated city. However, the African American families did not see themselves as living in a Black ghetto. They considered themselves an independent community with its own churches, schools, doctors, dentists, stores, and other retail services. As a young African American growing up in Oxford, Bill had few contacts outside the Black community. His life centered around his large, affectionate family, and segregation was only a minor annoyance.

Bill's father, William Russell Wiley, owned a shoe repair shop. His mother, Edna Threlkeld Wilson, was of Native American heritage and worked as the manager of a small cafe when Bill was born. Her father, a barber in Oxford, had taken college courses before learning his trade. The whole family had a high regard for education.

Bill, the Wileys's first child, was followed by three girls and another boy. As the oldest, Bill was given special attention by the family. Indeed, his mother's sister, who lived next door, tutored Bill in mathematics and science when he was in grade school. She had just graduated from Rust College in Hollow Springs, Mississippi, and wanted to practice her teaching skills. This aunt was the first to inspire Bill to follow a career in science. His mother also encouraged his interest in science and gave him a chemistry set as a birthday gift. Bill enjoyed doing chemistry experiments in his basement.

When Bill was still a youngster, one of his sisters accidentally swallowed some embalming fluid and was saved by the local doctor. After that incident, Bill knew that he too wanted to save lives. He decided to become a physician when he grew up.

Before beginning high school, Bill earned his spending money by doing odd jobs and delivering newspapers. When he reached high school, he and four of his older friends began a produce business. They formed a corporation, bought fresh vegetables from farms near Oxford, and sold them for a small profit in town. They ran this business successfully for two years. When the older partners completed high school, they closed the business and Bill went to work in his father's shoe repair shop.

In addition to his interests in school and making money, Bill was involved in the Boy Scouts and the Methodist Church. Bill's father was a scout leader, and the whole family was active in church affairs.

Bill's leadership ability was also apparent on the football field, and he was elected captain of his team for his senior year. In fact, he was offered a scholarship at Tougaloo College partly because of his football skills.

Higher Education

Tougaloo College, located near Jackson, Mississippi, is well known for its educational services to the African American community. In the 1950s, it was also well known for its premedical program. Since Bill Wiley was considering a medical career, Tougaloo seemed a wise choice for his education. The faculty was highly qualified, and each student received individual attention in the relatively small classes.

At first, Wiley concentrated on football and paid little attention to his course work. However, he soon realized that he needed to do well in his classes, and he began to focus his attention on his studies. His grades quickly improved and at the beginning of his second year, his biology teacher hired Wiley as her laboratory assistant.

Other teachers also were aware of Wiley's abilities. His anatomy teacher designed an independent study project on the subject of sickle-cell anemia. This disease mainly attacks African Americans, and although medicine provides some relief from the symptoms, there is no permanent cure. Wiley's project was to review the research done on the basic biochemistry of the condition. He was soon able to recognize the connections between biochemistry and the causes and treatments of sickle-cell anemia.

At about this time, Bill Wiley began to have doubts about a career in medicine. He had discovered that dissecting animals was a very unpleasant experience. Also, his chemistry teacher, Professor St. Elmo Brady, had proved to be a strong role model. Wiley prospered as Brady's student, and the experience convinced Wiley that he could fulfill his career ambitions as a research chemist.

When Bill Wiley had finished his third year of college, he married Myrtle Louise Smith, a fellow student at Tougaloo. His parents thought the couple was too young to marry, but his father-in-law, a physician in Hattiesburg, Mississippi, was supportive. Money was not a problem because Myrtle Louise was teaching in Hattiesburg while Wiley completed his senior year. He graduated with top honors in the spring of 1954.

After he received his degree from Tougaloo, Wiley was inducted into the U.S. Army. His military service was a productive experience for him. He gained a knowledge of electronics and served as a civilian instructor for two years after he completed his tour of duty.

While he was teaching electronics to young airmen at Keesler Air force Base in Biloxi, Mississippi, he read about the discovery of the structure of DNA (deoxyribonucleic acid) in *Scientific American.* The research of James Watson and Francis Crick allowed scientists to understand exactly how characteristics were passed from parents to children by means of the DNA molecules. Bill Wiley was excited by the fact that DNA carries the messages that control inheritance from one generation to the next. He decided that he wanted a career in science and was ready to go back to school.

Because of his good grades at Tougaloo, Wiley received a scholarship from the Rockefeller Foundation and, in 1958, was admitted to the graduate program in biochemistry at the University of Illinois in Champaign-Urbana. As luck would have it, the first lecture he attended was given by James Watson, himself. Wiley's good fortune continued. His advisor was Dr. Salvador Luria, one of the three founders of molecular biology. Luria later won the Nobel Prize in 1969 for work that laid the foundation for the development of genetic engineering.

Unfortunately for Wiley, Dr. Luria left the University of Illinois for a position at the Massachusetts Institute of Technology just after Wiley had finished his master's degree. Wiley then transferred to Washington State University in Pullman, where Dr. Jacob L. Stokes had recently become chair of the department of bacteriology and public health.

Bill Wiley's association with Dr. Stokes worked out well. Stokes and Wiley soon produced research reports on how microbes require a neutral or alkaline condition rather than an acid condition in order to generate energy. Wiley's dissertation project showed how the acid-alkaline balance in a microbe's environment affects it ability to take in nutrition through its outer surface. The dissertation led to the award of Wiley's doctoral degree in 1965.

Career Highlights

Washington State University has a good relationship with the Pacific Northwest Laboratory in Richland, Washington. This research facility is managed by the Battelle Memorial Institute for the U.S. Department of Energy. Battelle Memorial Institute is one of the largest independent research organizations in the world. With headquarters in Columbus, Ohio, near Ohio State University, Battelle has branches in several locations in the United States and overseas. One such branch is the organization at Richland, Washington.

After graduation, Dr. Wiley joined the staff at the Northwest Laboratory and continued the line of research that he had begun at Washington State. However, he shifted his work from the study of bacteria to the study of yeast and related organisms. Dr. Wiley demonstrated how yeast is able to ingest materials for the assembly of proteins within its cells. He also described how the raw materials were used once they were inside the cell. In 1970, he and Dr. R. P. Schneider, produced a general review of the research on how microbes take in nutrition from their environment. In that same year, he also reviewed the research on the specific enzymes that help the microbes in this activity.

Soon, Dr. Wiley was promoted to manager of the Cellular and Molecular Biology Section of the Laboratory's Biology Department. In this position, Dr. Wiley continued his own research and supervised a team of 25 other scientists. In 1972, he was promoted again and became the associate manager of the biology department. In that job, he directed the work of researchers in Columbus, Ohio; Geneva, Switzerland; and Frankfurt, Germany—as well as in Richland, Washington. The broad scope of his research included studies on the development of brain cells and on the growth of cancer cells. Dr. Wiley was also responsible for organizing conferences that brought together top scientists from around the world.

In 1974, Dr. Wiley was named manager of the biology department. He was now supervising more than 200 research scientists, and the range of his research topics continued to expand. His staff was involved in broad investigations such as how the nervous system works in a coordinated fashion. Dr. Wiley's own research at this time was focused on methods to strip away the sugar-like molecules that make up the outer shell of yeast cells. When this is done properly, the workings of the inner-cell membrane, made of fat and protein molecules, can be seen and studied under an electron microscope.

In 1979, Dr. Wiley was appointed to be director of research and his staff grew to over 1,500 people, mainly scientists and engineers. Finally, in 1984, Dr. Wiley was made director of the entire Pacific Northwest Division of Battelle Memorial Institute and was also made a senior vice president. In addition to the large facility at Richland, the division includes a research center in Seattle and a marine science laboratory on the Olympic Peninsula in Washington State. The division employs over 4,000 people, and the annual budget is over $400 million. Projects include waste management, renewable energy systems, and energy conservation studies.

As the manager of a large scientific organization, Dr. Wiley has been active in recruiting minorities into scientific careers. Each year the Pacific Northwest Laboratory provides scholarships and summer internships for minority students studying science at an historically Black college or university. Wiley and many of his coworkers give their time to younger students in after-school science activities in the Washington-Oregon area. Dr. Wiley has also established programs at Battelle that are designed to identify people who have management talents in addition to their research skills. This program allows more Battelle employees to gain promotions within the organization.

The quality of Dr. Wiley's work has been recognized in many ways. He has two honorary doctoral degrees—one from Gonzaga University in Spokane, Washington, and the other from Whitman College in Walla Walla, Washington. He serves as a scientific advisor to the state governor and is on the state economic environmental task force. In 1992, he was a participant in the economic conference held by President-Elect Clinton in Little Rock, Arkansas.

J. Ernest Wilkins, Jr.

Born: November 27, 1923, in Chicago, Illinois

Status: Distinguished Professor of Mathematical Physics, Clark Atlanta University, Atlanta, Georgia

Education:

Bachelor of Science degree, University of Chicago, Chicago, Illinois, 1941

Master of Science degree, University of Chicago, 1941

Doctor of Philosophy degree, University of Chicago, 1942

Bachelor of Mechanical Engineering degree, New York University, New York, New York, 1957

Master of Mechanical Engineering, New York University, 1960

Research Area: Theoretical Physics

Early Years

Ernest Wilkins was born into a relatively prosperous family. His mother, Lucille B. Robinson Wilkins, came from a family of distinguished church people; her father, John W. Robinson, had been a founder of the Saint Mark's Methodist Church in New York City. Lucille Robinson held a graduate degree in education and was a popular teacher in the Chicago city school system. Ernest's father had received an undergraduate degree in mathematics at the University of Illinois and had then taken a law degree at the University of Chicago. After building a successful law practice in the city of Chicago, the elder Wilkins had been appointed assistant secretary of labor by President Dwight D. Eisenhower in the early 1950s. He was the first African American to hold a subcabinet post in the national government.

With such parents, it is not surprising that Ernest showed early signs of unusual talents. He could read and do basic arithmetic by the time he was three. While in the early grades at Willard Elementary School, he was reading adventure books for young adults from the public library. Ernest was challenged by his father to solve mathematical puzzles when he was just seven years old. By the time he was 11, it was evident that his mathematical talents were unusual. His skills were not just computational. He was interested in the mathematics of all sorts of games of chance. For example, he became interested in the problem faced by gamblers when they play the game of Blackjack. In Blackjack, a player tries for a hand that totals as close to, but no higher than, 21 points. Therefore, if a player's original hand totals 16 points, should he ask to be dealt another card? If the new card is a 6 or higher, the hand is lost. To solve this problem, Ernest sat at the family's dining room table for several evenings in a row and dealt Blackjack hands. His test results proved—to his satisfaction, at least—that the best strategy was to "stay" with 16 points rather than to ask for another card.

Ernest was also a good athlete. He was talented in track and tennis and was the neighborhood champion in table tennis. He also played sandlot football and baseball but was too small for hard contact sports, such as high school football.

Any real interest in official, interscholastic sports, however, would have been pointless since Ernest graduated from Parker High School at the age of 13. With his accomplishments in all subjects, but particularly in mathematics and Latin, he was now ready to enter college.

Higher Education

While much of Ernest Wilkins's life was spent working as a physicist and an engineer, his primary subject in college was pure mathematics. He adored the subject and was specially adept at algebraic geometry and statistics. His first scholarly paper was published in the *Duke Mathematical Journal* in 1943 when he was just 20 years old.

It took Wilkins three years to get his first degree, less than a year to get his second, and an additional year to earn his third university degree. Ernest Wilkins received his doctorate from the University of Chicago in 1942 at the age of 18. He was invited to spend the remainder of the year at the Institute for Advanced Study at Princeton University, where Albert Einstein was a permanent resident scholar.

In the 1950s, Dr. Wilkins returned to school to earn two additional degrees. However, in 1942, Dr. Wilkins was ready to begin his career.

Career Highlights

Dr. Wilkins took his first job at Tuskegee Institute in Alabama, but he left there after just three semesters.

By the spring of 1944, as Dr. Wilkins was leaving Tuskegee, the United States was engaged in World War II. He had received pre-flight training at the University of Chicago, while he was a graduate student. It was clear, however, that he would make a greater contribution to the war effort as a physicist than as a pilot. He returned to the University of Chicago to serve as a mathematical physicist at the Metallurgical Laboratory. This laboratory was actually a part of the Manhattan Project, which developed the atom bomb. The work on the bomb was distributed over many locations. For example, the uranium was refined at Oak Ridge, Tennessee, and the actual assembly of the bombs was done at Los Alamos, New Mexico. The facilities at Chicago were used to test ideas about the chain reaction that split uranium atoms. It was at Chicago that the first controlled chain reaction was achieved. Of course, all the activities within the Metallur-

gical Laboratory were highly secret during the war. In fact, much of the research has still not yet been revealed publicly.

The scientists at Chicago felt that they had played a key role in the victory against Japan. They had also done exciting and highly challenging research—even if they could not openly discuss it outside the laboratory walls. However, once the war was over, many of the scientists wanted to work in an open environment and engage in more commonplace research. Dr. Wilkins soon accepted a job as a staff mathematician at the American Optical Company in Buffalo, New York.

One of the main challenges at the American Optical Company was the development of lenses for the large telescopes that look into the most distant parts of the universe. Dr. Wilkins worked on testing optical techniques that would improve the ability to pinpoint one object in a group, such as a specific star in a group of distant stars.

In 1950, Dr. Wilkins returned to the field of nuclear physics. Like many of the scientists who had worked on the Manhattan Project, Dr. Wilkins was inspired by the idea of developing peaceful uses for atomic energy. For example, the use of nuclear forces to generate electrical power now seemed possible. The newly formed United Nuclear Corporation of White Plains, New York, was attempting to design nuclear power plants and propulsion systems for ships and submarines, and possibly space vehicles. When Dr. Wilkins joined this organization, he was one of seven employees who were dedicated to the survival of their small company in this highly competitive field.

In the nuclear power business, there were very few people who understood both the basic science of nuclear reactions and the technology of power-plant design and operations. Many nuclear physicists found themselves working as engineers with no training in that field. Dr. Wilkins solved the problem by returning to school to study mechanical engineering. He realized that a background in this profession was necessary if he wished to design and develop nuclear power plants. So, in addition to his heavy workload at United Nuclear, he commuted from White Plains into New York City to attend classes at New York University (NYU). Ernest Wilkins, already a distinguished scientist with a doctoral degree, was only 32 years old when he went back to school. It is likely that he rarely mentioned his three degrees. In fact, so few of his fellow students knew of his previous scholarship that he was designated as the "senior who has demonstrated the greatest promise in his profession." He received his bachelor's degree in mechanical engineering from NYU in 1957. Dr. Wilkins did not believe in half-measures and continued on to complete a master's degree in 1960. At that point, he felt qualified to design and supervise the construction of nuclear power facilities.

In the meantime, the work at United Nuclear was going forward with considerable success. By the year after Dr. Wilkins received his first engineering degree, the company employed over 300 scientists.

Shortly after the degree was awarded, Dr. Wilkins was ready for a new challenge. In 1960, he joined the General Atomic Company in San Diego, California, as assistant chairman of the theoretical physics department. Over a 10 year period with General Atomic, Dr. Wilkins served in four key managerial positions. These included the directorship of the Defense Science and Engineering Center and the directorship of computational research.

By now, Dr. Wilkins had spent 24 years working in private industry—mostly involved with the problems of nuclear energy—and was ready to return to his favorite career, teaching at the university level. Howard University in Washington, D.C., offered him a special professorship to teach mathematics and physics to graduate students. After six years at Howard University, Dr. Wilkins was eligible for a long scholarly leave. He chose to return to Argonne National Laboratory at the University of Chicago—an outgrowth of the original group that conducted research on nuclear energy. His connections to industrial and government research led to an offer from EG&G Idaho, Inc., the company that operates the Idaho National Engineering Laboratory for the U.S. Department of Energy in Idaho Falls, Idaho. The mission of the laboratory staff was to develop new ways to use nuclear power and to help design low-cost nuclear power plants.

After working seven years for EG&G, he took another year's leave and returned to Argonne National Laboratory. Dr. Wilkins then announced his retirement at the age of 62. For slightly more that five years he managed to stay retired, but then he accepted a special professorship—this time at Clark Atlanta University.

Another facet of Dr. Wilkins's career can be seen in his steady involvement in organizations such as the Urban League with its agenda for racial equality. Perhaps even more important was the service he performed for the government as a delegate to a 1955 conference on the peaceful uses of atomic energy. He was also involved in the work of the Nuclear Regulatory Commission on reactor safety. In 1976, Dr. Wilkins was given the rare honor of being elected to the National Academy of Engineering. It is not surprising that this eminent scientist, scholar, and educator was awarded the Outstanding Civilian Service Medal in 1980.

Theodore R. Williams, Jr.

Born: October 23, 1930, in Washington, D.C.

Status: Professor, College of Wooster, Wooster, Ohio

Education:

Bachelor of Science degree, Howard University, Washington, D.C., 1952

Master of Science degree, Pennsylvania State University, State College, Pennsylvania, 1954

Doctor of Philosophy degree, University of Connecticut, Storrs, Connecticut, 1960

Research Area: Analytical Chemistry

Early Years

Ted Williams's father, Theodore R. Williams, Sr., grew up in South Carolina. As a teenager he moved to Washington, D.C., in order to find a job and help put his sister through college. During the day, he worked as an orderly at the Garfield Hospital, and at night, he took classes at Dunbar High School. By the time he received his high school diploma, his sister had graduated from college. He then enrolled in pharmacy school and graduated in 1929. His first child, a daughter, was born that year, and in October, the stock market crashed, setting off the Great Depression of the 1930s. It was not a good year for a young Black man to seek a job as a pharmacist. Ted's father finally found a job as a laboratory technician in the Infectious Disease Laboratory at the United States Health Service in the Georgetown section of Washington, D.C.

Later, the research arm of the Health Service was reorganized as the National Institutes of Health and moved to nearby Bethesda, Maryland. Mr. Williams worked for the National Institutes of Health for 25 years. During this time, his salary remained near the bottom of the pay scale, and he received few promotions.

Ted's mother was trained as a teacher, but she stayed at home while her children were young. However, she was able to earn a little money. There was a commercial laundry across the street from their apartment building, and Ted's mother made lunches to sell to the employees. As soon as her children reached junior high school age, she returned to full-time teaching.

Ted and his older sister attended Monroe Elementary School, a segregated grade school. Although Ted's parents did not push him, he did very well in school. The teachers at Monroe set very high standards for their pupils, and Ted wanted to meet their expectations. Because of his excellent work, the teachers soon realized the boy was gifted.

Ted first became interested in science while he was attending Banneker Junior High School. He did not like the school very well because he thought the teachers favored the sons and daughters of the wealthier, higher status families. However, he did like the fact that one of the teachers held special science demonstrations during the lunch period. Ted found that he enjoyed both the subject and the methods used by this teacher.

While still in junior high, Ted began to earn his own money. His first job was going door to door to sell *Liberty* magazine—now, no longer in existence. Later, he followed his mother's example and sold lunches to the laundry workers across the street from his home. Still later, he began to help the drivers load the trucks that delivered the laundry. He became familiar with the truck routes and learned how to pack the laundry for easy unloading at each stop. The drivers appreciated his ability to make their jobs easier.

After Ted entered Dunbar High School, he became interested in woodworking. He built his own workshop in the basement, using second-hand tools. His father's friend, a maintenance engineer at the Garfield Hospital, taught Ted woodworking techniques.

There was some favoritism at Dunbar just as there had been at Banneker Junior High. Ted rebelled against this situation, and his grades and attendance went down. Luckily, his homeroom teacher understood the problem and gave Ted the encouragement that he needed. Ted also had a good chemistry teacher at Dunbar. The class was small, and the teacher organized the course so that there was a high degree of student participation. The teacher assigned specific problems to each student, and the students gave oral reports on their research. The teacher also set up laboratory projects that the students could do independently.

Ted became so interested in chemistry that he went to the Library of Congress on Sundays to research his topics. The more he read on his own, the more interested he became. When his father became aware of his son's interest, he took Ted with him on Saturdays when he worked at the Infectious Disease Laboratory. As a senior technician, Ted's fa-

ther was conducting experiments to isolate viruses and bacteria from the tissues of experimental animals, such as mice and rabbits. The fact that his father's work might lead to new ways to prevent or control diseases was very impressive to Ted.

Higher Education

After he graduated from Dunbar, Ted Williams enrolled at Howard University in the District of Columbia. He had rejected a scholarship to Lincoln College in Pennsylvania. He preferred to attend Howard for several reasons. It was among the top institutions with strong historical ties to the African American community. Also, there were two important financial reasons to attend Howard. Williams had been promoted to a better paying office job at the laundry where he worked, and he could live at home and save money on food and lodging.

Williams immediately began the chemistry program at Howard. By his second year, he was ready to take two of the most difficult courses in his department—organic chemistry and analytical chemistry. Williams worked very hard to master his program in chemistry. He graduated in 1952 and won the award from the American Chemical Society for being the best chemistry student in his class.

By now, Ted Williams knew he wanted to be a teacher and realized that he needed an advanced degree. He chose Pennsylvania State University under the impression that an integrated student body would mean a liberal college community. When he arrived at Penn State, however, he found that he would have to travel 30 miles to find someone to cut an African American's hair.

Nevertheless, he decided to stay. From an academic perspective, the decision to attend Penn State had been a good one. In his first year, he had a teaching assistantship and helped teach a college course in analytical chemistry. In his second year, he was doing independent research on the reactions of organic chemicals with water. He became so involved in the content of his studies that he could almost ignore some of the negative social situations.

Williams's intense interest in chemistry led him to continue his education still further. In 1954, after he received his master's degree from Penn State, he was offered a place at the University of Massachusetts, but he decided to attend the University of Connecticut instead.

Ted Williams married in 1954, just as he was beginning his doctoral program. His new wife also became a graduate student at the university. She studied for a master's degree in public policy, while Williams worked on his doctorate.

One of the advantages of attending the University of Connecticut was the opportunity to teach undergraduate students. In effect, Williams learned how to teach as he was paid for teaching. During his last year at Storrs, he was the chief teaching assistant for the introductory survey course in chemistry, in which over 400 students were enrolled. He also assisted the senior faculty in the design of the laboratory portion of this course.

The focus of Williams's doctoral research was the study of the electrical properties of several organic compounds. His work on this topic resulted in a successful doctoral dissertation in 1960.

Career Highlights

Even before his degree was awarded, Dr. Williams was able to begin his teaching career at the College of Wooster in Ohio. In fact, he was able to start teaching there in 1959, the year before he received his doctorate. Dr. Williams was attracted to Wooster because the college faculty placed emphasis on a student's independent study. The departments also required that each student complete a significant research project before graduating. This approach echoed the rewarding experiences that Dr. Williams had had when he was a chemistry student in high school.

Dr. Williams knew that this method would demand large investments of time on the part of the teacher. Much of the work had to be done in small groups or individual discussions. In spite of the extra time and planning, Dr. Williams felt that this approach would be the best for him—and his students.

Dr. Williams's life experiences taught him that crucial career decisions often are made while a person is in middle school or high school. Consequently, he took a leadership role in developing outreach programs to engage Wooster College faculty with middle and high school students from the region. One such effort is called the College Visitation Program, supported by the Martha Holden Jennings Foundation. In this program, groups of up to 20 high school students are welcomed to the Wooster campus for a day of chemistry. They are given an introductory talk and then divided into teams of three or four members. All the teams are given the same fictitious problem. Each must decide whether the typewriter correction fluid consumed by a two year old child is poisonous. The purpose of this exercise is to familiarize the young people with the most modern electronic tools for chemical analysis. Samples of the fluid are put through a battery of tests to determine whether the compound has the earmarks associated with poisons. The students learn how to use instruments rarely seen in high school chemistry courses, and they see how to employ the test results to obtain a single, solid answer.

Another program pioneered by Dr. Williams and his colleagues is a summer science camp for seventh grade girls. The goal of this program is to raise their level of scientific interest and understanding. Dr. Williams plans and coordinates the hands-on research experiences in biology, geology, chemistry, and physics.

A new program of outreach to minority students initiated by Dr. Williams is called COSEN. The initials stand for the Carolinas and Ohio Science Education Network. The activities used in this project combine many ideas from earlier programs. Six small colleges in Ohio and North and South Carolina send minority students to Duke University in Durham, North Carolina. The students are divided into small teams and given independent research projects. The week-long projects are conducted at either Duke's main campus, its facilities at the Research Triangle, or its Marine Laboratory on the North Carolina coast. In order to participate in this program, science faculties at the member schools must agree to provide continuing, personal support to the participating students. This individual attention helps to ensure that the students will be fully ready for their future graduate studies.

While he engages in a host of professional and civic activities, Dr. Williams has not neglected his own research. To determine the composition of the liquid parts of the eye, he has done detailed analyses of the liquid material in the lens. His findings are crucial to the effective treatment of such eye conditions as cataracts. During his years of research, he has been responsible for more than 40 published reports in scientific periodicals. His leaves-of-absence from Wooster have allowed him to conduct research projects at Harvard, Carnegie Mellon, and Case Western Reserve Universities. One source of pleasure and excitement for Dr. Williams is investigating new research instruments. His continuing quest ensures that middle school,

high school, and college students are made aware of the most advanced equipment.

Dr. Williams has won numerous awards for his teaching activities. He was the Sloan Visiting Professor at Harvard University in 1969 and won the Sears-Roebuck Foundation Teaching Excellence and Campus Leadership Award in 1992. The Chemical Manufacturing Association and the analytical division of the American Chemical Society have also recognized his performance by means of Outstanding Teacher Awards.

However, the most rewarding tributes come from his students. Letters from former students, who are now mature research scientists, attest to the dedication and affection that Dr. Williams provided. They relate experiences of confusion and depression that were resolved by the personal attention given by their former teacher. Dr. Williams is pleased that his actions have provided a model for younger generations of chemistry teachers.

Willie Williams, Jr.

Born: March 24, 1947, in Independence, Louisiana

Status: Professor of Physics, Lincoln University, Lincoln University, Pennsylvania

Education:

Bachelor of Science degree, Southern University, Baton Rouge, Louisiana, 1970

Master of Science degree, Iowa State University, Ames, Iowa, 1972

Doctor of Philosophy degree, Iowa State University, 1974

Research Area: Solid State Physics

Early Years

Willie Williams grew up on a farm near Amite, Louisiana. His father, Willie Williams, Sr., farmed during the day and worked as a hospital orderly in Greensburg, Louisiana, during the evening hours. As a young boy, Willie saw little of his father during the workweek. He spent his time with his mother, Leaner Williams, and his grandmother, Annie Moore.

Willie began the first grade at the age of six in the segregated, one-room Woods Chapel School. All the grades, one through eight, were taught by the teacher. The children in each grade were grouped together. Every day, the teacher went from one group to the next so that each grade could receive instruction and a little special attention.

The school was about a mile and a half from Willie's home. When he was very young, his mother would walk half the long distance with him. Willie loved to learn and was very much at ease in school. Because he enjoyed listening to the older children recite their lessons, he was always ahead in his studies, particularly in mathematics. In fact, he often helped the older students with their homework assignments. They appreciated Willie's help, and he made many friends among his schoolmates.

When Willie was ready for the fifth grade, he went to a new school. The school served most of the students in the southern half of St. Helena Parish (in Louisiana, a county is called a parish). Because of the much larger classes, Willie and his old classmates had to make some adjustments.

In the ninth grade, Willie transferred again. He enrolled in Helena High School in Greensburg. He continued the helpful practices he had adopted in grade school and was soon elected to be a class officer. He did well in this school and his teachers encouraged his growing ambition to become a scientist or a mathematician. During his third and fourth summers in high school, he worked in the local land management office of the U.S. Department of Agriculture. This job allowed him to experience the technical aspects of agricultural research.

Higher Education

To fulfill his strengthened career goals, Willie Williams knew that he would need at least a college degree. He chose Southern University in Baton Rouge, Louisiana, a highly respected institution that had served the African American community for many years. It was only 50 miles from Willie's home.

Early in his college career, Williams had to chose which scientific discipline to study. He chose physics because the chemistry laboratory smelled and biologists used too many Latin words. Once he established himself as a physics major, he was quickly assigned to be an assistant in the physics laboratory. He was guided by Mr. Earnest Simon, the laboratory instructor who taught Williams how to use all the laboratory equipment. He soon met two young men who also had chosen to major in physics. The three decided to form a study group and remained partners during their years of college. After studying until late at night, they would go to a neighborhood diner for the best sausage sandwiches in town.

During his first year, Williams's dormitory arrangement was annoying. His roommate insisted on playing music until past midnight. Williams received good grades in spite of this distraction, but the next year he wisely moved to a different dormitory. There, he met Clayton Lewis, a residential counselor who helped Williams develop his leadership and organizational skills. These skills became important when he campaigned for president of the Men's Federation at Southern University. He won the post and became an activist leader. Williams started an organizational newsletter and established a Men's Recognition Week on campus. While Williams was in office, this special celebration included a visit from Mohammed Ali, the reigning world heavyweight boxing champion.

Williams sought to use his summer vacations as constructively as he had done in high school. Now, more options were open to him. He chose to work as a summer intern at the Ames Laboratory at Iowa State University in Ames, Iowa. Iowa State had an excellent history as an institution that welcomed Black students. However, African Americans made up only a tiny fraction of the 20,000 students enrolled at the time. After years in all-Black schools, Williams had some adjustments to make during the two-month summer break. He was helped through the adjustment period by Dr. John Stanford, a faculty member in the physics department. During the summer months, Dr. Stanford and Williams worked together on the effects of electrical attraction on metal atoms in metal alloys. Dr. Stanford also helped Williams's morale and sense of self-worth by inviting him to accompany his family to church and to attend family dinners. It was natural, after these good experiences, for Williams to choose Iowa State for his advanced train-

ing in physics. He moved to Iowa for full-time study in the fall of 1970.

Willie Williams's doctoral studies were focused on the problem of magnetism. He sought to determine why certain metals become magnetized in a strong magnetic field that is generated by an electrical coil and others do not. He also investigated the mysterious property of antiferromagnetism. This property is exhibited when a magnetized metal looses its magnetism after being removed from the magnetic field and warmed above room temperature. Pure metals which show antiferromagnetism can be made into permanent magnets when alloyed with certain other metals. This property is thought to be linked in some strange way to certain alloys which conduct electricity with zero resistance at very low temperatures. This condition is known as superconductivity. Willie Williams and other scientists hope that a better comprehension of antiferromagnetism will improve their understanding of superconductivity.

As soon as Williams felt confident about his dissertation, he began to look for some part-time job opportunities. One such opportunity came from Drexel University in Philadelphia, Pennsylvania. Willie was hired as a part-time visiting professor to advise the faculty on how to accommodate more minority students in their classes. The Drexel faculty needed reassurance about their dealings with African American students. The officials at Drexel also felt that they could advance toward their goal of improving minority education by forging strong ties with an historically black college or university (HBCU). They chose Lincoln University, just outside Philadelphia, for their first project of cooperation. Willie Williams was asked to help in the negotiations with the Lincoln officials.

When Williams returned to Iowa State, he found that he was the only remaining African American graduate student in the physics department. The one other African American had transferred to another institution. Williams was soon asked by the physics faculty to help recruit African Americans to study advanced physics. He was disheartened when his search revealed that very few students were interested in this field of science. He decided to work at an HBCU for four years after his graduation from Iowa State in the hopes of encouraging young Black men and women to consider physics as their career choice.

Williams choose Lincoln University to carry out his pledge. Williams received his doctoral degree in the spring of 1974 and joined the Lincoln faculty that fall. The original four year commitment eventually was to be extended to more than twenty years.

Career Highlights

Dr. Williams joined Lincoln University in the fall of 1974 as an assistant professor of physics and the director of their preengineering program. From his first days on the job, Dr. Williams became an administrator as well as a teacher and researcher.

He spent his second summer after graduation in Washington, D.C., as a research physicist at the National Bureau of Standards, now the National Institute of Standards and Technology. He renewed his collaboration with Dr. Mike Lind, who had been a member of Dr. Williams's study group at Iowa State. Together, they worked on techniques for using lasers to transmit information. The two friends studied the use of silver alloys to capture the signals coded into a beam of laser light. Laser beams can carry much more information than other electromagnetic waves.

Dr. Williams's heavy workload continued during his third year at Lincoln. In that year, he was made the chair of the physics department. He did not drop any of his other jobs.

In fact, he also accepted the co-chair of the committee to coordinate program planning in science and engineering between the faculties at Cheney State University, Temple University, and Lincoln. One goal of the combined faculties was to solve a problem experienced by students of these institutions when they wanted to transfer to other colleges or universities. Specifically, preengineering students at Cheney State and at Lincoln were often denied full credit for their courses when they transferred to the fully-accredited engineering degree program at Temple. The faculty at Lincoln and Cheney State wanted to be sure that their students were given the proper credit for their work. The negotiations took much of Dr. Williams's time.

His heavy schedule continued into the next academic year, that of 1976–77. At that time, Dr. Williams did some consulting work for the Mobil Oil Corporation. Mobil was interested in developing a minority outreach program and establishing good internal management procedures for the activation of equal opportunity safeguards.

By the fall of 1977, things began to ease a bit. However, it was not long before Dr. Williams received a research grant from the National Aeronautics and Space Administration (NASA). The agency was particularly interested in the properties of various composite materials in which graphite and metal fibers were bound together in a ceramic mixture. The NASA engineers wanted to know which composite materials would stand up best to the intense vibrations and heat stress generated by vehicles reentering the atmosphere from outer space. On this research grant, Dr. Williams worked with the research team at Lewis Research Center near Cleveland, Ohio. Together, they made good progress toward the design of the heat shield for the space shuttle.

In 1979, Dr. Williams was promoted to associate professor. He also continued to chair the science and mathematics division in the university. At this time, he began to spend his summers working as a research physicist for the U.S. Department of Defense. The work was based on Dr. Williams's experience with using light beams to carry large amounts of information over long distances. The new research was focused on the study of materials that could be used for high-speed communications in outer space.

In 1982, Dr. Williams's duties at Lincoln began to expand again. In that year, he helped organize a new program called the Lincoln AeroSpace Engineering Recruitment Program (LASER). The objective was to take advantage of Lincoln's location in the center of many aerospace development organizations. For example, Boeing-Vertol Aerospace Corporation is not far from the Lincoln campus. Good support was also available from regional institutions such as Temple and Drexel Universities and the Franklin Institute in Philadelphia. These organizations could provide advanced laboratory facilities, internships, and work-study opportunities for Lincoln students. Dr. Williams knew that practical experience served to increase students' motivations to study scientific and technological subjects.

The name of the program was changed in 1986 but the original initials were kept to maintain continuity in public information efforts. The name became the Lincoln Advanced Science and Engineering Reinforcement Program. The new idea was to build better capabilities within Lincoln to meet the needs of its students. In this way, the science faculty did not need to rely on the resources of the neighboring institutions. In 1992, another program, Early Alert: Young Scholars Program, was added to Dr. Williams's array of activities. The objective of this program is to identify promising young people as early as possible and to make sure that they considered the *pros* and *cons* of a career in science or engineering.

As the decade of the 1990s progresses, Dr. Williams has been able to resume his own research. Recently, he has been studying the properties of certain metallic alloys, including those of copper. Dr. Williams's earlier research showed that pure copper would not hold magnetism even after being exposed to a very strong magnetic field. His studies now indicate that copper will retain its magnetism when alloyed with certain other metals.

Religious faith is also an important factor in Dr. Williams's life. His heavy workload has been made easier because of his sense of spiritual support. He realizes that his odyssey from small town farm boy to program manager, teacher/mentor, and scientific researcher has been a long and difficult one. He knows, too, that it has been a spiritually satisfying journey.

Samuel von Winbush

Born: August 2, 1931, in Henderson, North Carolina

Status: Distinguished Teaching Professor, State University of New York, Old Westbury College, Old Westbury, New York

Education:

Bachelor of Arts degree, Tennessee A & I State University, Nashville, Tennessee, 1953

Master of Science degree, Iowa State University, Ames, Iowa, 1956

Doctor of Philosophy degree, University of Kansas, Lawrence, Kansas, 1960

Research Area: Inorganic Chemistry

Early Years

Samuel's father died when he was very young and his mother, Estelle Winbush, had to work full-time. Samuel and his older half-brother, Edward, were cared for by their maternal grandparents, Clarence and Blanche Eaton Winbush, on their farm near Henderson, North Carolina. The grandparents valued education and religion, and these values were handed down to the two boys.

Samuel was a fast learner. He could walk at eight months and read and understand simple arithmetic by the time he entered first grade. His first grade teacher, Ms. Alice Green, recognized Samuel's aptitudes and his zest for learning and gave him extra assignments to stretch his abilities. He enjoyed his studies and did not mind the long, six-mile walk to school.

Samuel liked to work on the farm with his grandfather Clarence, who also made furniture for the family, smoked his own meats, and distilled his own moonshine whiskey. Samuel also helped his grandmother make medicines for the family from local plants. He went into the woods and fields with her to find the proper roots, leaves, and berries.

When Samuel's grandfather died, the family finances were badly effected, and they had to move to the little village of Bullocksville, North Carolina—named for Samuel's fore-bears. There, Samuel was surrounded by relatives and was much closer to his school.

Just before his ninth birthday, Samuel caught typhoid fever and was unconscious for three days. When he was released from the hospital, he stayed briefly with his mother and her new husband but then went to live with two of his married cousins in Henderson. These women subscribed to two newspapers, bought many magazines, and owned a set of encyclopedias. Young Samuel was delighted with all the reading material and, later in the year, with his first chemistry set. When he was 12, he joined the Boy Scouts and won a merit badge for his knowledge of chemistry. At that time, he also became interested in mathematical puzzles.

During this period, Samuel experienced his first problems with racism. Indeed, he was forced to flee from people who threatened him with violence after he ignored a "Whites only" sign on a public bathroom. Samuel soon recognized the many differences between a school for White children and one for African Americans—located just a few blocks apart. His grandmother Blanche, however, had given Samuel a good sense of self-worth, and he knew race was incidental to a person's real merits. His delivery job at a local drug store also taught him that the differences between people were not always connected to a person's race.

Samuel attended high school at Henderson Institute, a segregated school run by the Presbyterian Church. Because of his rural background, Samuel chose to study vocational education and joined the New Farmers of America organization. Mr. Major Spencer Sanders—who supervised this student organization, taught vocational studies, and coached baseball and football—soon recognized Samuel's ability. He became Samuel's legal guardian and assured Samuel that he would be accepted into college if he continued to excel in school.

Samuel played baseball, football, and basketball—captaining the latter two teams in his senior year. Samuel also learned to play tennis after he helped repair the clay tennis courts at school. In addition, he led student activities, was class president, became editor-in-chief of the yearbook, had the lead role in the senior play, was class valedictorian, and wrote the class history in the form of a narrative poem. In his senior year, he was also chosen to compete in a state-wide history test sponsored by the Daughters of the American Revolution (DAR). He won second prize. Meanwhile, he worked part time as the only Black waiter at a local "Whites only" drive-in.

Higher Education

Samuel von Winbush was offered several two year scholarships when he graduated from Henderson Institute in 1949. However, he took the advice of Mr. Sanders and enrolled in Tennessee A&I State University in Nashville, Mr. Sanders's old school. There was no financial support for him but a work-study program was arranged and a football scholarship was possible. Unfortunately, von Winbush arrived on campus too late to play football and lost the first year of the scholarship.

Von Winbush knew that he must decide between horticulture and chemistry as his major. At first, horticulture seemed a good choice because of his agricultural background. However, after a short time, he decided to major in chemistry and, later, won the prize as the top first-year chemistry student.

In college, von Winbush continued his interest in school sports and organizations. He played football during his second year at college and collected his scholarship. He was sports editor of the student newspaper. He also led his fraternity and various student clubs, was elected to several honor societies, and was listed in *Who's Who* and *American Leaders in Colleges*.

For his senior research project, von Winbush studied the properties of the salts of tin. Salts of this kind are formed when a metal—like tin—is combined with a chemical (usually an acid like hydrochloric acid). Highly reactive and unstable compounds result when tin salts interact with a strong chemical such as a metal hydride.

Von Winbush's faculty advisor, Dr. Clyde C. Dillard, was working on a research grant from the U. S. Navy. Even though von Winbush was still in a very junior position, his research made an important contribution to the success of the project.

In 1953, Samuel von Winbush graduated from college with distinction and was eligible for a direct commission in the U.S. Air Force. However, Dr. Dillard urged von Winbush to begin his graduate studies at Iowa State University in Ames and study with Dillard's friend, Professor R. Shaeffer.

During his first year at Iowa State, von Winbush worked as a research fellow in the chemistry department under the supervision of a young faculty member, Dr. John D. Corbett. Later, he transferred to the Ames Laboratory, a part of the university's Institute for Atomic Research. Preceding his transfer, von Winbush conducted a lengthy review of the research literature on the chemistry of molten metal salts. He became interested in the reactions of pure metals with their own molten salts. For example, the salt of copper and fluorine, copper fluoride, is a solid at room temperature but melts at the very high temperature of 1680 degrees Fahrenheit. By introducing pure copper into molten copper salt, von Winbush demonstrated for the first time that the pure metal actually dissolves in the molten salt rather than just making a mixture. He also showed that when the pure metal dissolves, it reacts with the salt and forms new, unstable molecules. Von Winbush's discovery led to additional research at Iowa State and at other laboratories around the country.

Samuel von Winbush used this research as the basis of his thesis and was awarded his master's degree from Iowa State in 1956. Because of his continued interest in molten metal salt chemistry, he remained at the laboratory at Iowa State for an extra year. Consequently, he did not begin his studies at the University of Kansas in Lawrence until the fall of 1957.

Samuel von Winbush chose the doctoral program at Kansas after hearing a lecture on metal chemistry by one of that school's faculty members, Dr. Jacob Kleinberg. After his arrival at Kansas, von Winbush introduced Dr. Kleinberg and his fellow graduate students to the study of molten metal salt chemistry. Several doctoral degrees, including von Winbush's, resulted from these investigations. Von Winbush's dissertation focused on how nickel forms complicated salt molecules with cyanide called nickel cyanate, a very poisonous and chemically active material.

Career Highlights

Dr. von Winbush received his doctoral degree from the University of Kansas in 1960. He soon accepted a faculty position at his old school, Tennessee State University, where he chaired the chemistry department and served as a thesis advisor.

However, he did not stop attending school. He began to study law at the YMCA Night Law School in Nashville. He believed that a knowledge of law was necessary for anyone who wanted to be active in the field of civil rights.

As the departmental chair at Tennessee State, Dr. von Winbush recruited two recent doc-

toral graduates, Leodis Davis (see p. 64) and Samuel Anderson. The trio worked to revise and modernize the chemistry curriculum so that graduates of Tennessee State would be prepared for any graduate school in the country.

Unfortunately, the president of the university failed to give his support to their plans. This defeat disheartened the three scientists. Dr. Davis transferred to Howard University in Washington, D. C., Dr. Anderson transferred to Norfolk State University in Virginia, and Dr. von Winbush transferred to North Carolina A&T University in Greensboro, North Carolina.

At North Carolina, Dr. von Winbush continued his research on molten metal salt chemistry and was awarded a grant from the Pfeiffer Foundation. At a major research conference in 1963, he met Dr. G. Pedro Smith from the Oak Ridge National Laboratory in Tennessee. Dr. von Winbush learned that the scientists at this facility, funded by the U. S. Department of Energy for nuclear and related research, were very interested in his studies of molten metal salts. After that meeting, he was invited each summer for several years to conduct his research in their well-equipped laboratory.

In 1965, Dr. von Winbush accepted a faculty position at Fisk University in Nashville, Tennessee. The move allowed Dr. von Winbush easier access to the facilities at the Oak Ridge National Laboratory and his fruitful collaboration with Dr. Smith.

In 1969, Dr. von Winbush took a sabbatical leave from Fisk University and became a visiting professor at Wesleyan University in Connecticut. There, his closest faculty colleague was Dr. John Maguire. Before the visit ended, Dr. Maguire had been named to the presidency of a new branch of the State University of New York at Old Westbury on Long

Island. Dr. Maguire asked Dr. von Winbush to serve as a consultant while he put the plans for the new institution together and began to recruit faculty. In 1971, Dr. von Winbush, who appreciated the opportunity to design a new program for the university, accepted the invitation to join the full-time faculty.

At Old Westbury, Dr. von Winbush helped develop the instructional programs in biology, mathematics, chemistry, and physics. He developed team-taught courses, self-paced learning procedures in chemistry, and laboratory-based mathematics. In addition, he chaired the mathematics department for five years and then the department of chemistry and physics for three years. Dr. von Winbush also designed and taught a course on science and racism that was given under the auspices of the department of political science and economics.

In 1977, Dr. von Winbush took a one-year sabbatical leave to conduct research at the Technical University of Denmark in Lyngby, Denmark. In collaboration with Dr. Niels J. Bjenum, his summer projects at Lyngby on molten salt batteries and the chemical analyses of molten salt compounds have continued.

In 1984 and again in 1991, Dr. von Winbush took his sabbaticals at the Argonne National Laboratory near Chicago, Illinois, and worked with Dr. Michael Roche and other scientists. Each summer since 1977, Dr. von Winbush has conducted his research in Denmark or at the Argonne facility. He has worked on the development of new methods for extracting pure metals from manganese nodules—strange lumps of mixed metals found on the oceans' floors. His projects also include research on new forms of storage batteries that use electrodes made of metal salts.

In 1980, Dr. von Winbush was promoted to the rank of distinguished teaching professor—the highest teaching position at Old Westbury College. He has a long record of dedicated service to the college, the local community, the state of New York, his profession, and his country. The collaboration of Dr. von Winbush and Dr. Victor Maroni on their metal extraction project at the Argonne National Lab was recognized as one of 100 best inventions of 1986. In 1989, Dr. von Winbush won teaching awards from the National Organization of Black Chemists and Chemical Engineers and, in 1993, from the Old Westbury Alumni Association.

Dr. von Winbush is now looking forward to his retirement so that he can continue to serve his community and work for social justice, as well as follow another passion of his—writing poetry, fiction, and children's stories.

Geraldine Pittman Woods

Born: January 29, 1921, in West Palm Beach, Florida

Status: Retired, from National Institutes of Health, to Aliso Viejo, California, 1991

Education:

Bachelor of Science degree, Howard University, Washington, D.C., 1942

Master of Science degree, Radcliffe College, Cambridge, Massachusetts, 1943

Doctor of Philosophy degree, Harvard University, Cambridge, Massachusetts, 1945

Research Area: Embryology

Early Years

Geraldine Pittman's family led a comfortable life. Her parents, Susie King Pittman and Oscar Pittman, had no formal education past the eighth grade but were able to establish themselves in farming and the lumber business in central Florida. They also owned restaurants and rental properties in the tourist town of West Palm Beach.

Jerry's first three years of schooling were spent at a private Episcopal school. In the fourth grade, she transferred to Industrial High School, the only public school in West Palm Beach open to African American students. Jerry showed few signs of becoming an outstanding student during her early school years. In fact, there were times when she would fall behind her classmates and her mother would hire tutors to help Jerry catch up.

Even though Jerry did show an early interest in science, she received little encouragement from her teachers and family. In those days, African American women rarely became professional scientists. She led a busy life, participating in church activities, learning to play the piano, and reading everything she could find. Although her young life had few stresses and strains, Jerry's teen-age years were saddened by the death of her father.

Higher Education

As soon as she graduated from high school in 1938, Jerry Pittman was accepted at Talladega College, in Talladega, Alabama, a college established to serve the African American community. Talladega provided an educational environment that was similar to her high school, and Pittman made mediocre progress. However, her days at Talladega ended in 1940 when her mother became seriously ill. The doctors recommended that Mrs. Pittman enter Johns Hopkins Hospital in Baltimore, Maryland, where she could receive the most advanced treatment. In order to be closer to her mother, Jerry Pittman transferred to Howard University in Washington, D.C., just 35 miles from Baltimore. In spite of—or perhaps because of—her concern for her mother's health, Pittman began to work much harder on her studies. Some of her teachers at Howard were so impressed with Pittman's academic ability in science that they made a special effort to find a place for her in the graduate biology program at Harvard University in Cambridge, Massachusetts. In those days, Harvard was exclusively a men's college. However, there were close ties between Harvard and nearby Radcliffe College, a women's school. At the graduate level, women students, who formally enrolled in Radcliffe, took most of their actual course work at Harvard. This arrangement was more efficient than holding duplicate courses in two separate institutions.

After her mother recovered, Jerry Pittman moved to Cambridge and prepared herself for tough competition from top students from all over the United States. She realized the magnitude of the challenge when she walked into her first laboratory session and saw students using apparatus that she had never seen before, but she became completely committed to excel at Harvard. Indeed, Jerry Pittman earned two graduate degrees in just three years and—not surprisingly—was elected to Phi Beta Kappa, the honorary scholastic society.

Pittman's doctoral research was concerned with the early development of nerves in the spinal chord. While still in the early embryo stage, nerve cells are barely distinguishable from other kinds of cells. Then, as the fetus matures, the nerve cells become specialized and begin transmitting messages. Pittman wanted to determine whether this specialization process was governed by the cell's heredity or by its stimulation from other nearby cells. Using chick embryos, Pittman was able to show that both effects took place, and furthermore, the more muscle cells that were present, the more nerve cells that became specialized as muscle activators.

Career Highlights

After receiving her doctorate from Harvard, Dr. Pittman took a job as an instructor at Howard University. After only one semester of teaching, she married Robert Woods, a dentistry student at Meharry Medical School in Tennessee. They commuted back and forth between Washington, D.C., and Nashville, while Robert studied for his degree. As soon as he graduated, they moved to California, where Dr. Robert Woods's friends helped him establish a dental practice. Dr. Geraldine Pittman Woods settled down to raise a family. Then, when all three of her children were teenagers, Dr. Pittman Woods reentered public life as a volunteer for social services, equality of opportunity, and civil rights efforts. At first, she served in local organizations in and around Los Angeles and later moved into statewide activities, such as serving on the personnel board of the California Department of Employment. Soon, her reputation as a tireless and astute worker for minority interests spread to the nation's capital. In 1965, the president's wife, Lady Bird Johnson, invited Dr. Pittman Woods to the White House to help launch Project Head Start. This federal program was established to help children from low-income families gain preschool experience.

Dr. Pittman Woods's activities soon became well known on the national as well as the state level. In 1968, she became chair of the Defense Advisory Commission on Women in the Services and from 1968 to 1972, she was the vice chair of the Community Relations Conference of Southern California. Since then, she has served on a host of governing boards at institutions of higher education, philanthropic organizations, and government bodies. Dr. Pittman Woods is also a life member of the National Council of Negro Women and served on its board of directors from 1969 to 1972.

In 1969, Dr. Pittman Woods became a special consultant to the National Institute of General Medicine, one of the National Institutes of Health. She served in this capacity for almost 20 years. The position merged Dr. Pittman Woods's two main interests, science and public service. More importantly, this position allowed her to address two problems about which she had great concern. First was the seeming inability of scientists from minority institutions of higher education to compete successfully for research grants from various government agencies and philanthropic organizations. Dr. Pittman Woods wanted to determine whether these colleges and universities presented topics in their grant requests that were sufficiently important to the scientific community. She also needed to determine if the laboratories in these minority institutions were adequately equipped to do noteworthy research in biology, chemistry, and physics. If the competition for grant approval was not equal, Dr. Pittman Woods hoped to make it so.

She also wished to improve educational opportunities for minority students in the field of science. Dr. Pittman Woods addressed many difficulties facing young minority members interested in a scientific career, including the debilitating effects of financial problems, the lack of encouragement given to budding scientists by grade school and high school counselors, the difficulty in mastering standardized tests, and the inability of college admissions officers to understand the nature of educational disadvantage. All these factors contribute to the frequency with which students from minority groups become discouraged and leave school.

In order to remedy these conditions, two programs were established within the National Institutes of Health under Dr. Pittman Woods's guidance. The first of these programs, called the Minority Biomedical Research Support or MBRS program, was designed to help grant applicants win their funding. As is usually the case with innovative programs, the implementation needed to be gradual and the politics carefully attended. This was familiar to Dr. Woods, since she had worked carefully with committee staffers and elected members from both branches of Congress. Dr. Woods took great pains to see that important minority members, such as Senator Edward Brooke of Massachusetts, were kept informed of all decisions and problems.

She began to hold seminars and tutorials at minority institutions for those who wanted to prepare applications for federal grants. She became a link between the applicants and the committee members that reviewed grant applications for the National Institutes of Health. By giving the grant applicants an understanding of the requirements and organization of grant requests, the approval rate for funding to minority institutions slowly improved.

As the program progressed, grant applicants became more knowledgeable. Researchers at Xavier University in New Or-

leans, Louisiana, proposed that members of grant review committees and prospective applicants from all over the United States attend an annual symposium held on their campus. These annual meetings would allow the minority scientists to understand the procedures of a grant review. Once the procedures were fully understood, the application documents were sure to be more competitive.

The problem of recruitment and retention of minority science students was also addressed by a new National Institutes of Health program, Minority Access to Research Careers, or MARC. Again, serious effort was put forth by Dr. Pittman Woods to include both the political and scientific domains in her plans. For example, a special meeting of key members of the Federation of American Societies for Experimental Biology (FASEB) was called to explain the program and solicit their endorsement of it. FASEB includes almost every professional biologist in the U.S., and this group's backing of the new program was essential to its acceptance by the scientific community at large.

It was recognized by Dr. Pittman Woods and others that providing scholarships and counseling would not be enough. Drastic changes in attitude and educational opportunities needed to be implemented from grade school through graduate school. One such change was the provision of funds to award fellowships and visiting scholar arrangements to faculty members from minority institutions. This funding would allow the recipients of the awards to work with their colleagues at some of the most prestigious universities in the country. Both students and faculty benefited as the quality of teaching in minority institutions improved. The funding of faculty fellowships was soon followed by the funding of undergraduate and predoctoral scholarships. By 1979, support was provided to 120 students for undergraduate research training. Predoctoral fellowships became available in 1981.

Dr. Pittman Woods's own career as a scientist was brief, but she has been instrumental in directing the actions of the federal government to the research capabilities of minority institutions and the educational needs of minority science students. Starting from a modest base as a consultant to the National Institute of General Medical Science, she involved the whole of the National Institutes of Health in supporting her innovations, a singular accomplishment.

Jane C. Wright

Born: November 20, 1920, in New York City

Status: Retired, Professor Emeritus, New York Medical College, 1987

Education:

Bachelor of Arts degree, Smith College, Northhampton, Massachusetts, 1942

Doctor of Medicine degree, New York Medical College, New York, New York, 1945

Research Area: Chemistry

Early Years

Jane Wright was the daughter of Dr. Louis T. Wright, a famous medical doctor in New York City. He was one of the first African Americans to graduate from Harvard Medical School and the first to be appointed police surgeon in New York City. Dr. Louis Wright was responsible for several important medical treatments and inventions. He pioneered developments in the treatment of gunshot and knife wounds and in the effective medication for a sexually transmitted viral disease. He also invented a neck brace that allowed accident victims to be moved without risking permanent injuries to their spinal cords. Dr. Wright, too, developed an internal splint that permitted multiple breaks in major bones to heal without permanent physical impairment. Finally, Jane's father was an innovator in the use of chemicals for the treatment of cancer, a field in which Jane Wright would later gain fame.

Jane's family lived in the section of Manhattan known as Harlem. In recent years, Harlem has been called a ghetto, but in the 1920s and 1930s, it was an upper-middle class neighborhood. As she was growing up, Jane attended an exclusive private school. The elementary grades were known as the Ethical Culture School, and the high school unit was called Fieldston Upper School.

Even though Jane faced academic competition in this setting, she did very well at her school. Swimming was her favorite sport, and she was elected captain of the swimming team. Her grades were so good that she was awarded a scholarship to Smith College in Northhampton, Massachusetts.

Higher Education

At Smith College, Jane Wright continued her interest in swimming and set sprint marks that held for many years. Her first course of study at Smith was not in medicine but in painting. As a young woman, Wright's ambition was to be a professional artist, even though she had been advised that few artists sell enough to support themselves. At the beginning of her third year in college, Wright had second thoughts and changed her major to premedicine.

Wright's decision to study medicine was not surprising. Neither was the fact that her younger sister, Barbara, became a specialist in industrial medicine. Both had grown up in the company of medical doctors. Therefore, the young women felt comfortable with physicians and understood their interests and concerns.

When Jane Wright graduated from Smith College, the United States was deeply engaged in World War II. The war effort led to major changes in many aspects of American life. Medical training was shortened by one year—from four to three years—because of the shortage of doctors for the armed services. The lost year of training was partially made up by holding classes during the summer months. While the compressed program was grueling, Wright was able to graduate with top honors from New York Medical College in 1945. During medical school, she had been chosen vice president of her class and president of the honor society.

Her internship was taken at Bellevue Hospital in New York City and her residency in internal medicine at Harlem Hospital.

By the time she finished her medical training, the war was over, and Jane felt free to marry. She married David D. Jones, an attorney who became prominent as a founder of antipoverty and job training organizations for young African Americans. Mr. Jones died of heart failure in 1976.

Career Highlights

Dr. Jane Wright's initial plan was to enter private practice in general medicine. However, her father had just established the Cancer Research Foundation at Harlem Hospital, and he invited his daughter to collaborate with him on his research program. The focus of this program was the discovery and testing of chemicals that could be useful in the fight against cancer.

The possibility that chemicals could be used against cancer first came to light in the troubled times of World War II. In 1942, a ship carrying soldiers to Europe was also carrying a quantity of the chemical weapon, nitrogen mustard gas. When the ship was sunk in the Italian port of Bari, some of the gas escaped, and many of the troops were killed by it. The physicians who helped the survivors noticed that the gas reduced the number of white cells in the blood of the victims. In a healthy person, white cells are the first line of defense against bacterial or viral infection. However, there is a condition in which white cells are vastly overproduced in the body. The result of this overproduction of white cells is a type of cancer known as leukemia. The attending doctors theorized that a substance like mustard gas might kill cancerous white blood cells and save the lives of leukemia victims.

Scientists could see an obvious complication with this interesting idea, however. It would be necessary to develop a technique that would destroy the bad cells while preserving the good ones. Indeed, the difficulty of killing only cancer cells plagues all methods of fighting cancer—chemical, radiative, and surgical. There is another problem that must be taken into consideration as well. Chemicals and all forms of radiation can both cure and cause cancer.

Fortunately, cancer cells are generally weaker than normal cells—in part because of their faster growth rate. Many cancer patients loose their hair during treatment because hair cells are among the fastest growing normal cells. Therefore, the healthy hair cells share some of the vulnerabilities of cancer cells.

The two Drs. Wright worked as a team to test a variety of possible cancer treatments until 1952, when Dr. Louis T. Wright died. Dr. Jane Wright became director of the Cancer Research Foundation and continued the work on her own. In 1955, she was given an appointment to the faculty of New York University and was soon promoted to associate professor. Dr. Wright taught classes in surgical research and continued her studies of cancer-fighting drugs at both Harlem Hospital and the New York University Medical Center.

In 1961, under the sponsorship of the African Research Foundation, Dr. Wright and a team of physicians toured Kenya and what is now Tanzania. The group traveled through the African countryside in a mobile medical unit. They went to districts where modern medical services were unknown. While the journey through eastern Africa lasted only three weeks, the experience greatly influenced Dr. Wright's thinking. She became a strong supporter of the African Research Foundation and later became a vice president of the organization.

Meanwhile, the field of anticancer drug development was advancing rapidly. Many more classes of compounds were being tested, and some chemicals within each class showed promise. One such new class of anticancer agents was made up of compounds similar to the antibiotics used against infections. It seemed logical that if medicines could be used to kill disease cells like germs and viruses, similar chemicals might be found that would attack only cancer cells. Dr. Wright thought that a drug called mithramycin—a close relative to the antibiotic, streptomycin—might be helpful. She hoped this drug could be used against a type of brain cancer which is found deeply hidden in the brain and is almost impossible to remove by surgery. In the early 1960s, her team tested the drug with fourteen patients who were otherwise near death. Eight of the fourteen showed some improvements. Three of the eight appeared to have been cured, insofar as any cancer patient is totally cured.

In the last days of President Kennedy's administration, the White House had established a Presidential Commission on Heart Disease, Cancer and Stroke. Dr. Wright was one of the prominent physicians appointed to this commission. Its report led to the establishment of a network of research centers across the country. By coordination through this network, research results from one location were quickly available to the other sites.

In 1967, Dr. Wright returned to her own medical school, New York Medical College. She was still a loyal alumna and was glad to be "home." Dr. Wright was made a full professor of surgery and an associate dean. At that time, this was the highest position reached by an African American woman in a medical school.

In her new position, Dr. Wright's research continued at its established rapid pace. All scientists in cancer research are aware or the difficult problems that arise in treating cancer patients. Not only do different cancers respond differently to the same drug, but also a particular drug might be helpful on a specific cancer in one patient and not in another. Doctors found it difficult to select the treatment that best matched the specifics of the cancer and the unique biology of the patient. Dr. Wright thought the problem might be partially solved by developing a technique to test—in the laboratory—the effect of a given anticancer drug on a patient's cancer cells.

Dr. Wright demonstrated that if a few cancer cells are removed from the patient by surgery, these cells can often be made to multiply in the laboratory. When a colony of these cells has developed, the cancer-fighting drug can be introduced. If the drug does not work on the colony of cancer cells, it will not work inside the body. Therefore, that specific drug should not be used on the patient.

In many cases, the patient was given the anticancer drug while the laboratory tests were going on. Dr. Wright could compare the progress of the patient who was taking the drug internally with the condition of the cancer cell colony in the laboratory. In this way, she could get a much clearer idea of how the anticancer drug worked. For example, if the drug interfered with cancer cell reproduction, Dr. Wright could observe under the microscope that the cell nucleus failed to divide properly.

By now, Dr. Wright had received many honors, awards, and degrees for her work. Even so, she continued to concentrate on her research and the development of new ideas. She began to experiment with techniques for injecting anticancer drugs directly onto the location of the cancer rather than into a more conveniently exposed vein or artery. She also developed ways of tem-

porarily rerouting the arteries that fed the site of the cancer. In this way, the anticancer drug went to that location and nowhere else in the patient's body. By restricting the drug to the cancer site, Dr. Wright reduced the extent of negative side effects from the drug, such as hair loss or other, more serious symptoms.

Dr. Wright was also a pioneer in giving a patient combinations of drugs at the same time. She treated some persistent cancers by using all the medical weapons—surgery, radiation, and chemicals— in one coordinated, all-out assault on the disease.

Dr. Wright, and her father in his lifetime, led the fight against cancer by developing techniques and treatments that have saved or prolonged the lives of countless individuals.

James Howard Wyche

Born: November 14, 1942, in Greenport, New York

Status: Associate Provost, Brown University, Providence, Rhode Island

Education:

Associate of Art and Science degree, State University of New York at Morrisville, 1962

Bachelor of Science degree, Cornell University, Ithaca, New York, 1965

Doctor of Philosophy degree, Johns Hopkins University, Baltimore, Maryland, 1972

Research Area: Cell Biology

Early Years

Greenport, New York, where James Wyche was born and grew up, is located near the northeastern tip of Long Island, across a small bay from the famous Montauck Lighthouse. When James Wyche was born, Greenport was still very rural. Potato and duck farms were more common in the area than industrial plants.

This rural setting was an ideal place for Jim Wyche to develop an interest in nature. He surveyed the woodlands and learned the names of the native plants, insects, and other animals. Jim also observed how the local farmers took advantage of soil fertility, protected their fields from predatory insects and birds, and harvested their crops in the most economical way. These interests were noted by his parents and teachers, especially by his high school chemistry teacher, Roland Sherwood. Mr. Sherwood strongly encouraged James to consider a career in the agricultural sciences.

Higher Education

When James Wyche started college in 1960, his main interests were in human nutrition and the problems of food contamination. He enrolled in the food science program at Morrisville College in upstate New York near Syracuse. Morrisville, a small college in a small town, is one of the many institutions offering two-year certificate programs for people who wish to learn a trade. Tradition-

ally, good students from these schools are readily accepted by another state institution, so that they can earn a full college degree.

Wyche had chosen Morrisville college for several reasons. The town of Morrisville was similar to his home town of Greenport, the tuitions and fees at the college were reasonable, and one of his relatives had graduated from there. Also, the two-year certificate was a valuable credential if Wyche needed to work before he finished a four-year college program.

Wyche's decision was a good one. While at Morrisville, he acquired a solid understanding of the causes of food poisoning and bacterial contamination. In 1965, he graduated from his two-year program and began his studies in bacteriology at Cornell University in Ithaca, New York.

Ithaca, a relatively isolated, medium-sized town, is dominated by two institutions of higher education. In addition to Cornell, with its world-famous faculty, there is Ithaca College, with a fine liberal arts program. The combined enrollment of the two institutions is almost equal to the nonstudent population of the town.

In spite of the reputation for liberal attitudes, neither the university nor the town was particularly welcoming to minority students. Indeed, there were few minority students in any of Cornell's undergraduate programs. Race-related incidents were commonplace during Wyche's two-year stay in Ithaca. Fortunately, two professors, Paul van de Mark and Gloria Joseph, in the bacteriology department of the agricultural school, were very supportive. In fact, the whole department was so focused on their research and teaching that a person's race received little attention. Also, Wyche was pleased that his dormitory room was next to that of a Nobel Prize winner, Dr. Robert Holley. Dr. Holley was living in the dorm temporarily while visiting at Cornell.

Wyche's conversations with Dr. Holley and his other experiences within the bacteriology department helped to reduce his sense of loneliness.

When James Wyche graduated from Cornell in 1965, his good reputation as a biology student led to a job offer from Dr. Milislav Demerec at Brookhaven National Laboratory. In a sense, this was a homecoming for Wyche since Brookhaven is only about 40 miles across Long Island from his boyhood home.

Dr. Demerec later transferred his research activities to the part of Long Island University known as C.W. Post College. This new research facility was in an urban setting next to the New York City borough of Queens. James also transferred to C. W. Post because he wanted to continue his study of genetics as Dr. Demerec's research assistant.

Dr. Demerec attracted many top level scientists to observe or join in his research studies. Among the famous visitors was the French biologist, Andre Lwoff, a Nobel Prize winner for his research on the genetics of single-cell creatures. Another collaborator was Dr. Philip Hartman from Johns Hopkins University in Baltimore, Maryland. Hartman took an interest in Wyche's career plans and suggested he apply for doctoral studies at Johns Hopkins. Wyche followed this friendly advice and was somewhat surprised to receive a letter of acceptance. His year of working with Milislav Demerec had been productive in more than one way.

Johns Hopkins University is modeled after some of the great European universities and has the unusual feature of enrolling more graduate students than undergraduates. Consequently, the main emphasis at Johns Hopkins is on research. James Wyche flourished in this setting. He absorbed the techniques of biological experimentation, as he studied bacterial genetics.

At the beginning of his program at Johns Hopkins, Wyche was the beneficiary of a predoctoral fellowship provided by the National Institutes of Health. During his third year, he supplemented these modest funds by serving as a teaching assistant in microbiology at Morgan State University in north Baltimore. Wyche soon perceived the differences between a research-oriented institution, such as Johns Hopkins or Cornell, and a teaching-oriented institution, such as Morgan State.

During the summer after his work at Morgan State, Wyche was invited to join a research project headed by Bruce Ames from the University of California at Berkeley. The project was to be conducted at the medical school of the University of Naples in Italy, one of the first medical schools in the world. The two Americans were to work at Naples with several Italian scientists. However, the Italian Red Brigade invaded the school that summer and refused to admit native Italian research workers. Probably because of his African heritage, Wyche was allowed to continue with his work. However, the uproar from the miniature revolution made research and study very difficult. Because of this, Wyche was able to spend time away from Naples, visiting other laboratories and making professional friendships throughout central and northern Europe. He was also able to take in the World Cup soccer matches and absorb many other aspects of European culture.

Career Highlights

Dr. James Wyche, like many promising young scientists, was given several opportunities for advanced studies in the form of post-doctoral fellowships. In 1971, even before his degree had been formally awarded, he began the first of two fellowships at the University of California at Berkeley. The two-year appointment was particularly valuable because his research concerned bio-chemistry. This field of study added another resource for his work on bacterial genetics.

The second post-doctoral fellowship began in 1973. To fulfill this position, Dr. Wyche moved down the California coast to La Jolla, the site of the San Diego campus of the University of California. He began a year's work in the biology department under the general supervision of Professor Gordon Sato. At La Jolla, Dr. Wyche, while working with multi-cellular animals, studied the functions of glands and the hormones they produce. Dr. Wyche became fascinated with the processes by which a specialized cell can generate chemicals that affect the body's overall func-tions.

In the following year, Dr. Wyche began his first regular faculty position in the depart-ment of biological sciences and biochemis-try at the main campus of the University of Missouri in Columbia. The Columbia branch, one of four large branches, now has an en-rollment of over 25,000 students. Dr. Wyche taught the usual courses in basic biology and also resumed his research on the production of human hormones. He became particularly interested in how glands control the produc-tion of hormones such as testosterone, the male hormone that some athletes are accused of misusing.

In 1980, Dr. Wyche was promoted to the rank of associate professor. However, the very next year, he saw the opportunity to expand his activities and took a new position with the City University of New York. Dr. Wyche had now come back to New York for a third time. His work sites were at the department of bio-logical sciences of Hunter College and the biochemistry department at the Graduate School and University Center. Both are in the center of Manhattan.

In his new positions, Dr. Wyche was able to act on his interests in encouraging minority

students to seek careers in the sciences and related fields. In 1982, Dr. Wyche became program coordinator for the Minority Bio-medical Research Program at Hunter Col-lege. Then, in 1987, he became director of the program. Dr. Wyche found it very satis-fying to see his own minority students earn their advanced degrees and accept positions at leading institutions of higher education.

Along with administrating this important program for minority students, Dr. Wyche realized that he must continue his own sci-entific activities. His new research concerned the hormone, insulin, and the workings of the pancreas and the pituitary glands. To con-centrate on this research, he took a six-month sabbatical leave in the fall of 1987. He served as a visiting scholar in the pediatrics depart-ment of the Stanford Medical School in Palo Alto, California. At Stanford, Dr. Wyche studied how human growth is encouraged by chemicals having molecular structures simi-lar to insulin, the sugar-regulating hormone produced by pancreatic glands.

When Dr. Wyche returned to the East Coast, he found another opportunity waiting for him. He was invited to join the medical sci-ence faculty at Brown University in Provi-dence, Rhode Island. At Brown, he took on the roles of associate provost for minority affairs and associate dean of biology and medicine. These positions placed Dr. Wyche in charge of a wide variety of programs. Sev-eral of these fit the often misused but descrip-tive term "outreach programs." One of the programs affords the means for faculty and students at the university to reach out to low-income, minority children at an inner-city school in Providence. Both tutoring and mentoring are offered by the students and faculty from Brown University and other colleges in the region.

Another program is aimed at students from financially troubled colleges. Representatives from Brown identify good students with strong interests in academic research and teaching. These young people are counseled and encouraged to consider graduate school. This program, called the Leadership Alliance, was established by a large group of institutions of higher education. The institutions include all the Ivy League schools, Johns Hopkins University, New York University, three of the State University units in New York, and 10 colleges and universities with a tradition of serving minority youth. This same effort is now directed at helping science teachers from minority colleges and universities participate in summer research projects. Through these projects, the teachers can absorb some of the rapid advances in their fields.

The members of the Leadership Alliance are very aware of the rapid growth of educational technology and the growing dependence on expensive laboratory and library tools. There is now an attempt to acquire these necessary tools for financially strapped colleges and universities. All institutions that teach science and technology—whether rich or poor—must have an equal opportunity to benefit from technical advances. In the meantime, the people at Brown are trying to make sure that conditions on their own campus are in line with their ideals. Consequently, they have established internal projects that "reach in" to identify the needs of their own minority students and faculty members.

Although the administration of these important programs poses a serious burden for Dr. Wyche, he manages to continue with his research, which is still directed at understanding the workings of single cells and the way life is controlled by tiny amounts of complicated chemical compounds.

Appendix 1
Chronological List of Scientists

c.1861–1943	George Washington Carver
1867–1923	Charles Henry Turner
1883–1941	Ernest Everett Just
1883–1959	William Augustus Hinton
1893–1961	Frederick M. Jones
1894–1971	Lloyd Augustus Hall
1899–1975	Percy Lavon Julian
1901–1987	Hildrus A. Poindexter
1902	Lloyd E. Alexander
1902	Leonidas Berry
1904–1980	Flemmie P. Kittrell
1904–1950	Charles R. Drew
1909	Warren E. Henry
1911–1992	Walter Lincoln Hawkins
1914	Herman R. Branson
1914	Margaret Morgan Lawrence
1914	Henry C. McBay
1917	James H. M. Henderson
1917	Clarence F. Stephens
1918	Lloyd Noel Ferguson
1919	David Harold Blackwell
1919	Samuel Proctor Massie
1919	Welton I. Taylor
1920	Carroll M. Leevy
1920	Jane C. Wright
1921	Benjamin H. Alexander
1921	Marie Maynard Daly
1921	Geraldine Pittman Woods
1922	James B. Drew
1923	J. Ernest Wilkins, Jr.
1924	Jewell Plummer Cobb
1924	Thomas J. Craft, Sr.
1924	Evelyn Boyd Granville
1925	Emmett W. Chappelle

1925	Irving Wesley Elliott, Jr.
1925	Angela D. Ferguson
1926	Randolph W. Bromery
1926	Carl A. Rouse
1928	John L. Gwaltney
1928	Emmanuel B. Thompson
1929	Meredith C. Gourdine
1929	Don Navarro Harris
1930	Theodore R. Williams, Jr.
1930–1981	Samuel Lee Kountz
1931	Mack Gipson, Jr.
1931	H. Ralph Lewis
1931	J. Tyson Tildon
1931	Samuel von Winbush
1932	Harry L. Morrison
1932	William R. Wiley
1933	Leodis Davis
1933	James King, Jr.
1933	Joan Murrell Owens
1933	Louis Wade Sullivan
1934	Bertram Fraser-Reid
1934	Wade M. Kornegay
1934	Ivory V. Nelson
1934	John B. Slaughter
1935	Linneaus C. Dorman
1936	William M. Jackson
1936	Juanita Simons Scott
1936	Warren M. Washington
1937	William A. Lester, Jr.
1938	Walter E. Massey
1938	Earl D. Mitchell, Jr.
1939	George R. Carruthers
1939	John W. Macklin
1941	Cornelia Denson Gillyard

1941	Wesley L. Harris	**1945**	Renty B. Franklin
1941	Robert W. Harrison III	**1946**	Carolyn Branch Brooks
1942	James Howard Wyche	**1946**	Walter A. Hill
1942	Christine Mann Darden	**1946**	Shirley Ann Jackson
1943	Slayton A. Evans, Jr.	**1947**	Herman Eure
1943	John K. Haynes	**1947**	Sandra Murray
1943	Ronald Elbert Mickens	**1947**	Willie Williams, Jr.
1943	James W. Mitchell	**1949**	Mary Styles Harris
1943	Gerald V. Stokes	**1950**	Freeman A. Hrabowski III
1943	Margaret E. M. Tolbert	**1950–1986**	Ronald Erwin McNair
1944	Joseph C. Dunbar, Jr.	**1951**	Benjamin S. Carson, Sr.
1944	Ambrose Jearld, Jr.	**1951**	Gregory L. Florant
1944	George M. Langford	**1951**	Faye Venetia Harrison
1944	Kennedy J. Reed	**1955**	Joseph S. Francisco
1945	Fitzgerald B. Bramwell	**1955**	A. Oveta Fuller
1945	George Campbell, Jr.	**1956**	Mae C. Jemison

Appendix 2

Scientists Arranged by Research Area

Anthropology

Gwaltney, John L, 131–34
Harrison, Faye Venetia, 148–51

Bacteriology

Poindexter, Hildrus A., 275–80

Biology

Biochemistry. *See* Chemistry
Biophysics. *See* Physics
Cell Biology
Cobb, Jewell Plummer, 49–53
Haynes, John K., 157–61
Langford, George M., 218–21
Murray, Sandra, 264–67
Wyche, James Howard, 353–57
Embryology
Alexander, Lloyd E., 6–9
Woods, Geraldine Pittman, 346–50
Developmental Biology
Craft, Thomas J., Sr., 53–57
Scott, Juanita Simons, 288–92
Turner, Charles Henry, 321–24
Marine Biology
Jearld, Ambrose, Jr., 185–90
Just, Ernest Everett, 201–04
Owens, Joan Murrell, 272–75
Microbiology
Brooks, Carolyn Branch, 27–31
Fuller, A. Oveta, 112–16
Hinton, William Augustus, 171–74
Stokes, Gerald V., 301–04
Taylor, Welton I., 307–11
Wiley, William R., 328–31

Chemistry

Bramwell, Fitzgerald B., 16–19
Francisco, Joseph S., 103–06

Hall, Lloyd Augustus, 134–37
Wright, Jane C., 350–53
Analytical Chemistry
Mitchell, James W., 259–61
Nelson, Ivory V., 267–72
Williams, Theodore R., Jr., 339–42
Biochemistry
Carver, George W., 42–46
Chappelle, Emmett W., 46–49
Daly, Marie Maynard, 57–60
Davis, Leodis, 64–67
Ferguson, Lloyd Noel, 94–99
Harris, Don Navarro, 137–40
Mitchell, Earl D., Jr., 256–59
Tildon, J. Tyson, 314–17
Tolbert, Margaret E. M., 317–20
Wiley, William R., 328–31
Inorganic Chemistry
Winbush, Samuel von, 342–46
Organic Chemistry
Alexander, Benjamin H., 1–6
Dorman, Linneaus C., 67–71
Elliott, Irving Wesley, Jr., 80–85
Evans, Slayton A., Jr., 87–91
Fraser-Reid, Bertram, 109–112
Gillyard, Cornelia Denson, 116–120
Hawkins, Walter Lincoln, 154–57
Julian, Percy Lavon, 197–200
Massie, Samuel Proctor, 240–44
McBay, Henry C., 242–47
Physical Chemistry
Henry, Warren, E., 164–68
Jackson, William M., 181–85
King, James, Jr., 204–08
Macklin, John W., 234–36
Theoretical Chemistry
Lester, William A., Jr., 228–31

Education

Craft, Thomas J., Sr., 53–57

Index